THE ANAMORPHIC I/i

FINDING MY OWN STEP THROUGH
THE (MY)NFIELD OF PHEMINISM AND ART

jan jagodzinski

TOBIOGRAPHICAL CONFESSIONS OF
ROSS-DRESSING AND RE-DRESSING

SCRIPTEASE IN EIGHT TACKY STEPS

Canadian Cataloguing in Publication Data

Jagodzinski, Jan, 1948-
The anamorphic I/i

Includes bibliographical references and index.
ISBN 1-895850-47-9

1. Jagodzinski, Jan, 1948- 2. Sex role. 3. Sex role in art.
4. Sex differences (Psychology) I. Title.
HQ77.J33 1996   305.3   C95-910158-6

Design and Production: Pièce de Résistance Ltée.
Printing: Print Stop Inc.

First Printing: December 1996
Printed in Canada

18228 - 102 Ave., Edmonton, Alberta   CANADA T5S 1S7
Phone (403) 488-1390   Fax (403) 482-7213
e-mail: pdr@compusmart.ab.ca

Duval House Publishing Inc. gratefully acknowledges the support of the
Alberta Foundation for the Arts, the Canada Council
and the Department of Canadian Heritage.

Front Cover: *La Reproduction Interdite I/i i/I*

The illustration on the front cover was designed by the author in 1987 when an earlier 'rough' draft of this book was first completed. The illustration was "grafted" (graft+graph) onto René Magritte's surrealist painting, *La Reproduction Interdite* (Not to be Reproduced, 1937) which was an 'oblique' self-portrait of Edward James, an enthusiastic collector of Surrealism who had invited Magritte to London in 1937 to stay with him. Two books have used this painting as an icon for their contents. Zigmunt Bauman's *Hermeneutics* (with whom the author had the good fortune to study with for a few months at the University of Leeds in the Spring-Summer of 1979 when this book was first released), and more recently Vivian Sobchack has used the same image to illustrate the phenomenological eye of film experience (*The Address of the Eye*). It seems fitting, therefore, to modify Margritte's painting in order to offer the possibility of an anamorphic eye (I/i) of psychoanalysis as developed by Lacan and extended by such theorists as Jacques-Alain Miller and Slavoj Žižek who present both challenges and innovations to the hermeneutic and phenomenological paradigms.

The symbol of the mirror refers to Jacques Lacan's mirror-stage, the metaphorical moment when the narcissistic ideal ego (*Idealich*) is reflected back to the child. However, in this particular case there is no reflective identification. Rather the anticipation of a future perfect moment when the child realizes that to "be" is to be seen by the Other as an ego-Ideal (*Ich-Ideal*), is presented as a moment of paranoia, an uncanny moment of non-reflection—of translucency—when the Real intervenes and the child psychically "sees" a non-specular *objet a* in the mirror as the felt gaze of the Other looking at her "from behind." With this in mind the image has been reproduced physically four times (reproduction as duplication) and reversed for positive-negative effects (investments in the hetero/homo, masculine/feminine divide) as a further play on Magritte's title.

It is no accident that the iconic sign of a young girl, represented by her frilly dress, becomes a central subject for the interrogation of the postmodern self, since, it *should* be argued, that feminism in both its heterosexual and queer developments has proven to be a historical agent of change in postmodern society. The presence of television and technical education manuals replace Magritte's book, *The Adventures of Author Gordon Pym* by Edgar Allan Poe which appeared in the 'original' picture. Poe was his favorite author. They allude to the "enunciated" Voice and Gaze of the social Big Other who speaks to us from a bodiless position in the Name-of-the-Father, the hidden authority that b(l)inds us to a reflection of ourselves in a world other than the one we potentially could become.

jan jagodzinski

*This book is dedicated to my son
Jeremy in the hopes that he may read it one day.
He appears both in the front of this book,
in this dedication, and at its end, in the appendix.*

Contents

THE PRETEXTS OF THE TITLE

GIVE ME A LITTLE SIGN
but make it Intelligible ... if you can? 137

THE MASCULINE DESIRE OF THE IMAGINARY
Are Males Simply Desiring Machines? 165

THE FEMALE GAZE AND ITS VICISSITUDES
Woman as the Copula of Desire 219

CONUNDRUMS OF THE GAZE
Tripping over Medusa's Head 244

> This book is perhaps "too long" to be read from cover to cover, although you can "try" of course. Any project that has been ongoing for such a long period of time grows uncontrollably. It marks, after all, the passage of a subject in process. Who the I was in 1980 is certainly not the I of today. In this sense it should be read with a set of "postmodern" eyes, i.e., by finding a word in the index, a name perhaps, or an interesting sub-title... whatever *catches* you.

Preface
AND ACKNOWLEDGMENTS

PREFACE ONE: "Keep Off the Grass!" *(1990)*

It is always difficult to find a voice in a territory which, sometimes has "keep off" signs. The interpretation of masculinity as immutable, thereby treating all men as the enemy, definitely *erects* boundaries around the feminist landscape. While I/i have personally experienced such discrimination in my search for my place as a male in feminism, it certainly has not been my most frequent experience. Most often female colleagues, whom I/i rightly call feminists, have been patient with an open ear, and those whom I/i call friends have been more than just sounding-boards, offering arguments which sometimes irritated me; sometimes made me feel like some piece of intellectual "mush," but most often made me question my own position. Fortunately such negative experiences have been far and between, and are more telling of my own paranoia in the search to fill out my desire to understand my place *in* feminism. There is, after all, a qualifiable difference between my maleness and questioning the male role I/i have been assigned in my particular location—the University— a male dominant institution which assumes supremacy.

I/i invite the reader to follow my own journey through the labyrinth of "men in feminism" replete with its own signposts, detours and trappings. This is a personal journey, but I/i am certain that there are many other men who have raised the same issues, or have gone through similar incidents. There are no chapters *per se*, for this is not a " book." It is rather fragments, memories which have been interrogated through the polyphony of feminist voices— the networks to be found in feminist books and journals. I/i call the incidences which surround these theoretical discussions- vignettes. There are eight of them, but could well have been four or twenty; it just so happened that eight emerged as I/i looked back over the ten years when I/i was first drawn toward the question of feminism.

There is yet one more thing that needs to be said. As an art educator, it is a sad state of affairs that within academia the possibilities of having the time to develop visual art are painfully short. Scholarship is always perceived to be more important than visual production. Over the past decade, this has personally meant that I/i had to redirect my own energies into an artform that would combine scholarship with the visual. In the appendix is one typification of such an expression. It seems that performance art, which I/i have presented at conferences in lieu of a scholarly paper, has become a vehicle for personal expression. Although the excitement, tension, visual and audible aspects of the text are lost in this form of presentment, it does enable me to push language about—like paint.

At the 29th National Art Education Conference, held in Washington D.C., April 11,1989, a six-member panel was to prepare a five page response to 'men in feminism,' specifically in relation to art and art education. This 'study,' for the lack of a better name, repeats an earlier panel's response to the very same problematic: "Men in Feminism" under the auspices of the Modern Languages Association Conference held in 1987 also in Washington, D.C.— rather fortuitous I would say. At that time it seemed ludicrous to me to present anything worthwhile in five double-spaced pages that could be read in ten minutes without sounding dogmatic and reductionist. Instead my ten-minute spiel revolved around three reflective moments in my personal history. Drawing on bits and pieces of written material over the past ten years. That ten-minute talk has now become a collaged journey that I/i hope the reader might wish to "follow."

Edmonton, Alberta, Canada
April 4, 1990

PREFACE TWO: A Tiresome Task *(1992)*

When I finally received a letter, dated June 10, 1992 from the Social Science Federation of Canada, Aid to Scholarly Publication Programme (SSFC/CFH) that a grant had been awarded for the publication of this "book," if that definition is useful here, I was not overjoyed. Brigitte was confounded as to why I wasn't leaping up and down, tears rolling down my cheeks, the champagne bottles popping—apropos for such an occasion—just didn't happen. My lack of joy came from knowing what I had written was a "frozen" picture, something I painted between 1988-1990 when I tried to question my ten-year relationship with feminism. My conclusions ended in a grand failure and despair. During a panel discussion on the topic of men's privilege, the very same year of its completion, the respondent, a well-respected feminist educator, Jo Anne Pegano, told me that I had exposed my throat. Fortunately she had no intention to cut it, but remarked on its "bibliographical" status. So now, more than two years later, I was being asked to look at this picture once again and re-work it because it was too dense in some places, and in others—perhaps too self-serving, if not egoistic. I don't know? As I write this preface I have not begun to rework the text, to blow off the dust and engage in its conversation again. Rather I wanted to record my feelings and thoughts before that process began.

In this regard, I am especially sensitive to the sexual politics of publishing that my journey has taken. In this area, no matter what one writes there are bound to be strong reactions, both favorable and angry, to the point where someone would do everything in their power to prevent men writing about their relationships to feminism. In a condensed article of my relationship to feminist art sent to *Feminist Review* I was told frankly, in two sentences no less, that the journal did not publish men's writing. In a review of the submitted draft of this project to SSFC/CFH, one reviewer wrote many vehement pages making the point that men have no business writing in this area. I'm afraid my rebuttal was equally as rhetorical. The politics of interpretation appear everywhere on the (my)nefield. So again, the thought of picking up my writing is not very inviting. I am reminded of the many ghostly paintings that haunt any artist. Some I still enjoy looking at, others I want to paint over if I can only get enough energy to do so. This is one of them.

Since my initial writing, the discourse of Men's Studies has been steadily growing. Its discourse, like feminism, is contradictory in its development. My journey may be subsumed under its label, but I hope that readers will find much, much more in this writing than being confined to such a narrow focus.

I certainly do not plan to beat my drum, paint my face, pal it out in the woods with other men, and change my ways by looking up to the new guru –Robert Bly; nor do I have any desire to equate reason and rationality as somehow inherent to masculinity and take responsibility for Enlightenment ills simply because I am a man. More problematic, however, is the belief that biological and social constructions of gender can somehow remain separate, or that venturing into the recesses of poststructuralism will somehow vanquish sex/gender distinctions easily. These questions have emerged in my writing.

In proper protocol then, I wish to acknowledge the support SSFC/CHF:

This book has been published with the help of a grant from the Social Science Federation of Canada, using funds provided by the Social Sciences and Humanities Research Council of Canada

Klagenfurt, Austria
1992, June, 10

PREFACE THREE: Between Tootsie and Mrs. Doubtfire: Is there a Difference? *(1994)*

It has taken a further two years to repaint the picture since receiving notice that renovations could begin. I once thought of including the reviews of the original manuscript and my rebuttal as an appendix to this completed journey, but this would be unfair to the reviewers. The old manuscript functions as an underpainting to the new one. Patches of it are still visible and often identified by the re(mark): "that was then, this is now." I tried to let the old structure stand, speaking to it with four years of footnotes, but that strategy proved useless. I finally decided to begin again, start the journey anew, knowing that some of the undergrowth had been cleared already. It made walking a little easier, but not always. I found that sometimes a tree had fallen, blocking my path to pick up the trail. When that happened I had to figure a way to get through the obstacle. In the end I had reached another clearing.

It is perhaps fortuitous within the contents of this writing at least, that *Mrs. Doubtfire* made its cinematic debut this year (1994). Like Michael Dorsey (Dustin Hoffman) in *Tootsie* (Pollock, 1988), who transforms himself into Dorothy Michaels, Daniel Hillard (Robin Williams) disguises himself as Mrs. Doubtfire, an elderly British matron who applies for the job as a housekeeper for his estranged wife and three children. In a "postfeminist climate" it is time once again to show that a man can be a better woman in drag. This time his

disguise must do triple duty: first, it allows the absent father, who is an immature, irresponsible, out-of-work, voice-over artist who has never grown up,
to reunite with his children, and, in doing so, transform himself into a proper
responsible father; two, Williams's disguise enables viewers to chastise the
mother (played by Sally Field) who is too busy to look after her children
because she is an interior design executive and a workaholic. In contrast to
Williams, she appears humorless, initiates divorce proceedings, and gains cus-
tody of the children because the Law is in sympathy with motherhood as
opposed to fatherhood. Any effort she makes to start life over again with her
dream man is thwarted by the antics of Williams. It's as if her only place
belonged in the home. Williams is somehow absolved of any responsibility
for the family breakup. It is the father who is unjustly accused by the Law
and by feminists of the liberal variety. Lastly, the persona of a British elderly
matron symbolizes discipline and order and strict rules, overlaid with down-
home advise—a cross between a drill sergeant and bed-time story teller. It's
not too soon before all three children are properly trained; they do the house
chores if they are bad; their homework gets done, and all their emotional
problems of growing up become resolved. In the end Mrs. Doubtfire ends up
as the host on a syndicated children's television program where she can give
advice as how to save "dysfunctional families" all across America. The moral
majority would be proud. The family unit is pieced back together in true
postmodern fashion. Fathers are told the message that they need to get back
to the children and find a job; wives are told not to neglect their children
because of their work, and not to start looking for their own sexual pleasures
in other men; children are told that they must work and study hard. In the
end, it is Williams who represents the stability of the family despite the fact
that he is only a visitor on weekends.

Jeremy and I went to see this film together.

Carolyne and I are divorced.

It was easy to partake in the fantasy.

    The "Tootsie trope" runs throughout the book *Men in Feminism*, edited
by Alice Jardine and Paul Smith (1988), as a reminder of a work's failure to
allow its feminist intentions to alter its male-centered mode of signification.
This is a question that may be asked of my own text. What sort of "drag"
have I donned? Have I managed to create a space "between" *Tootsie* and *Mrs.
Doubtfire*, the approximate duration of my own writing? It seems to me, as it
now stands, there is *no* space "between" them. Like Dorothy Michaels, where
the comic motif comes from physical gestures of masculinity, Mrs. Doubtfire

is no exception. Her identity is discovered by his son as s/he pees into the toilet bowl standing up. A near-to-retiring bus driver stares at her legs as s/he sits down while he makes advances; there is the usual ineptness at cooking— her bosom catches fire and s/he has to stamp the fire out with pot lids leaving two large brown spots that resemble the areola of the nipples. Unable to cook s/he orders elaborate take-out meals, and so on. It is Williams's gay brother who makes him over, reinforcing a particular stereotypical association of drag queens as Williams morphs from Phillis Diller to Barbara Streisand to Lisa Manelli. Like her name suggests, picked at random and in the state of chaos, I doubt whether this film will put out the fire that is raging in many households. The only thing that has changed "between" is the technology of appearance. A latex body suit and mask replace the simple make-up kit and wig used by Dorothy Michaels. Drag has entered the space age. It can only become more and more "virtual" in the next decade.

Returning to Klagenfurt, Austria, the face of Franz Klammer, a face known to every Austrian for his heroic downhill racing, stares at me on a billboard. He wears a blonde wig and a low V cut dress, an obvious quote to Marilyn Monroe, selling Hirter beer. What then is *my* drag selling? I hope that it is much more than just beer. I have brought together a number of discourses—feminism, men's studies, queer studies, visual art, art history, popular culture, cultural studies, film theory—to generate a hybrid text that is informed mostly by Lacanian psychoanalytic theory; more so than I had at first imagined. The bibliography has been pushed to postmodern absurdity, so much so that its function is almost hyperbolically "useless" in the sense that these voices cited/sighted/sited form a hypercomplex circuitry of conversations, my voice being an infinitesimal flutter carried along one of its unfathomable trajectories. However, I have personally formed an index to help mark some of the possible journeys a reader may take in its circuitry. My address throughout my narrative remains personal to facilitate doing so.

In the appendix the reader will come across a performance concerning our son Jeremy. Although Carolyne and I are no longer together, we are still together for Jeremy. His presence for me is a constant reminder of life's renewal. At thirteen years old the world is opening up for him, with all the fears I have as an educator as to how easily that world can become closed. It was important for me to dedicate this journey to him. There are other people to thank as well, especially Brigitte Hipfl, my Partnerin whose conversations and argumentations figure throughout this text. We have not always agreed, nor would she want it that way, hence I take full responsibility for all that appears within its covers. Lastly, I would like to thank Jim Parsons and Kathy Sanford, two colleagues who encouraged me to pursue this project and not to give up. Six years later, it is finally over.

Klagenfurt, Austria
June 14, 1994

I wish it were that way, but it seems the project has yet had another set back. The publishing date, i am told, is now scheduled sometime next year, perhaps in Feb., 1995. Since June i have added text about the issues raised. i have also had an opportunity to co-teach a course on cinema with an emphasis on feminism and psychoanalysis with Brigitte Hipfl here in Klagenfurt University. During that course, it was possible to air out some of the ideas contained in this text with her while preparing for classes. It struck me hard one day, during one of our many conversations together, that I/i (which one?) could never fully occupy the same seat as her on the train, nor see the same view as her when we arrive at the train station, and that despite all this writing, it took a moment of realization of the sheer impossibility of trying to grasp this impossible perspective, which made me realize more forcefully than ever before the necessity of doing precisely that: to look impossibly.

Klagenfurt, Austria
Nov 28, 1994

Given the passage of almost another full year, it seems that this project will never see the light of day. Scattered throughout this writing are a few references that are dated to 1995. These are reminders of the never ending task of coming to the question of "Woman" as the *sinthome* of "Man."

Klagenfurt, Austria
July 12, 1995

It seems only appropriate to end this string of prefaces with yet another one. The long journey seems to be finally over... I hope, on Halloween of all days! But I said this in 1994. This is a good example of the so-called *mise en abyme* effect—endless self-reflection and doubling! I do wish to end by mentioning a few people that were not covered by the other "endings." In his own unique was Larry Beauchamp has prodded and encouraged the publication of this work "behind the scenes" so to speak. I appreciated his efforts for it gave me the encouragement not to give up. I would also like to thank Kim Johansen who did the initial layout for the book. She has a wonderful feel for type. Unfortunately Kim was unable to see the project through. Economic priorities and difficulties placed this project on the back end of her busy schedule. Eventually she had to leave it. There is also Jean Poulin to thank for his courage to undertake this project as editor-and-chief of Duval Publishing. As a Canadian publisher it is undoubtedly difficult to manage within a book publishing market where government support has been progressively withdrawn and larger corporate publishers dominate trends, so I understand the economic dynamics, twists of fate, and difficulties that must have delayed this project. I would also like to thank Leslie Vermeer who is simply an amazing copy editor. I was taken aback by her thoroughness, knowledge, and impeccable eye for detail. Lastly, my utmost appreciation goes to Tracy Menzies for her thoroughness and eye for detail.

Edmonton, Canada
October 31, 1996

LIST OF ILLUSTRATIONS

Max Ernst: A Retrospective. New York: The Solomon R. Guggenheim Museum, Publishers, 1975, p.130.

p. 181   fig. 11 René Magritte, *La Condition Humaine* (The Human Condition), 1934, Collection George Meely, London.

Waldberg, Patrick (1965). *Magritte.* Trans. Austryn Wainhouse. Brussels: André de Rache Publisher.

p. 182   fig. 12 René Magritte, *La Cascade* (The Waterfall), 1961.

Gimferrer, Piere (1987). *Magritte,* N.Y. :Rizzoli International Pub., 1987 (#115).

p. 191   fig.13 Vermeer, A Painter in His Studio, 1966, Vienna, Kunsthistorisches Museum.

Goldscheider, Ludwig (1958). Jan Vermeer: The Paintings, Complete Edition. London: Phaidon Press, plate 56.

p. 301   fig. 14 *D'où venons-nous? Que sommes-nous? Où allons-nous?* (Where do we come from? Who are we? Where are we going?), 1897, Museum if Fine Arts , Tompkin Collection, Boston.

Le Pichon, Yann (1987) *Gauguin: Life. Art . Inspiration.* Trans. Mark Paris. Harry N. Abrams, Inc. Pub. 214-215.

p. 307   fig. 15 Paul Gauguin, Tahitian Women with Mango Blossoms, 1899.

Paul Gauguin, *Deux femmes tahitiennes.*

Le Pichou, Yann (1987). *Gauguin: Life. Art . Inspiration.* Trans. Mark Paris. Harry N. Abrams, Inc. Pub. p. 198.

p. 307   fig. 16 Two Tahitian women posing.

Le Pichou, Yann (1987). *Gauguin: Life. Art . Inspiration.* Trans. Mark Paris. Harry N. Abrams, Inc. Pub. p. 199.

p. 337   fig. 17 Gauguin figure as St. Sebastian with suction-cup arrows, *A Catalogue of Accusations and Counter-Actions* (bookwork, 1988).

White, David (1992) " 'The Soul is the Prison of the Body.' " In *Fluid Exchanges: Artists and Critics in the AIDS Crisis.* James Miller, ed. Toronto: University of Toronto, Illustration 30.

p. 501   fig. 18 Carl Lewis, *Achtung, Fertig, Losgestöckelt* (Ready, Set, "Strut"), Kleine Zeitung, Photo: Reuters.

The picture appeared in the *Kleine Zeitung,* May 14, 1994 (an Austrian newspaper) from Reuters.

p. 519   fig. 19. United Colors of Benetton, 1994.

p. 520   fig. 20 Die Ego-Gesellschaft, *Der Spiegel,* Nr. 22/ 30.5.

THE PRETEXTS OF THE TITLE

[T]he real point at which change
must come, exactly ourselves,
the end of "masculinity" –
which, of course, is the
end of "woman" too.

(Heath, 1987:5)

Barthes one day in conversation:
"you study what you desire
or what you fear."

(Heath, 1987: 6)

The Play of Intertextualities:
The Figure of the (My)nefield

This study emerged from a panel entitled "Men in Feminism," presented at the National Art Education Association Conference held in
Washington, D.C. on April 11, 1989. It personally rewrites/ re-rites / re-rights
a similar panel discussion presented in two sessions conducted at the Modern
Language Association meeting also held in Washington, D.C., in December
1984 from which emerged the book, *Men in Feminism* (1987), edited by Jardine
and Smith. Leaving the allusions to "autobiographical confessions" aside for
the moment, the second part of the title refers to Elaine Showalter's felici-
tous essay, "Critical Cross-Dressing: Male Feminists and the Woman of the
Year," included in the above book. This allusion to her essay is purposeful in
that I shall try to carry a similar query, "in the back of my mind," as to whether
a man can ever hope to read/view as/like a woman and be *in* feminism.
Showalter's article, which originally appeared in *Raritan* (Fall, 1983), has received
a wide reading (see Boone, 1989). The sounds of her heckle remain registered
on my unconscious, like radioactive fall-out after an "event," as I initiate my
own journey right/rite/write to its deferred *end*-ing, attempting to reply to
her rhetorical question as to whether it is possible for men to be *in* feminism
at all. I am reminded that the structure of such a narrative can often repeat a
masculine "vision quest," the search for the golden fleece, in which case it is
the quester who is "fleeced" "in his foolish hopes of capture" (Derrida, 1979).

The third part of the title alludes to Annette Kolodny's 1980 essay,
"Dancing Through the Mine Field: Some Observations on the Theory, Practice
and Politics of a Feminist Literary Criticism," which was written during the
same year I began my own involvement with feminist thought and practice.
Kolodny, as do I, begins her reflection on the previous decade of questioning sexual stereotypes in literature, and then proceeds to review and update
the current struggles of women in challenging the established literary canon.
Analogously, my reflection reviews the changing canon of art and art history
as reflected in praxis.

Kolodny's use of the metaphor of the minefield stands for the myriad of patriarchal obstacles buried and hidden from view, which prevent a safe
path from being paved in women's literature. Hence, it is the maverick feminist who must dance around such mines; the dance is that of a "female consciousness turning in upon itself attempting to grasp the deepest conditions
of its own unique difference from the idea of a 'changeless essence'" (p. 11).
And again, "Emma Goldman, a maverick feminist from the late nineteenth
century, once said of the feminist movement: 'If I can't dance I don't want to

be part of your revolution'" (Christie McDonald to Derrida, 1982b:66). The form of this dance involves the issues surrounding feminist sexual politics, but it may well require only other women partners, or is there room for men too?

Replacing dance with "step" then, should be interpreted as connoting my own sense of hesitancy and insecurity of moving onto the dance floor, since there is no "entirely correct" stance of men *in* feminism (Nelson, 1987:164), except perhaps one of castration as Stoltenberg (1984) suggests. Taking on the burden of correctness requires a sense of caution and patience, and here lies the paradox for men *in* feminism: the minefield is *already* our own creation. It *already* holds the dancer hostage over its playing area, and so it must be dismantled, shrunk, written-over, as the mines go off. But, it may well be the case that, like the feminist, I too am an "intruder" in a double sense. First, I "intrude" on her dance (*passe*, Smith, 1987:33; Morris, 1987:174-175), unwittingly enforcing my own kind of violence by interrupting her flow. She becomes an unwilling partner who is now placed in double jeopardy, burdened by my "help" and that of her oppressors. As Nelson painfully and sharply reminds me, "as an intellectual project it [feminism] does not need men" (p.160). "... Feminists have always disagreed with one another; feminism has radically differed from itself since its inception, differed from itself in fact in all of its discursive and political incarnations at different historical moments. It does not need men to [further] insure disagreement and diversity and to prevent a hard legalization of its codes" (p.164). Second, I find out that my intrusion may be naive. It may not be my (my)ne-field after all! I was born into its formation and loath it as much as my unwilling partner. But this doesn't mean I can absolve myself from its constrictions, constitutions and constructions.

I hope the reader will sense that, for the male, the journey is equally unsafe and uncertain. I too, must watch my step. But my journey may be an impossible one. What interests me then, is the stink and stench of the exploding mines set off by my own bungling tactics, sometimes mindlessly leaving ruptures and holes/wholes of difference among us, as I stumble across boundaries - unwittingly transgressing. The metaphor is one of vision but should be that of smell; the traceable odor of footprints badly tracked whose imprints reveal an author who sometimes stepped in shit; not quite the desired scent of perfume he had in mind. But, then again, all writing leaves an uncontrollable excess. However inadequate the attempted tropes might be, they speak to the "ocularcentrism" of Western theoretical discourse as critiqued by Irigaray's (1985a:47-48) re-writing of Lacanian psychoanalytic pronouncements. The sense of sight, the eye, is linked to the constitutional mirrors of the Cartesian ego and, as such, it is an indictment to the repression of feminine difference.

Can such a warrant be defended, I ask?

Border crossings, although purposeful, should always be done in a responsible way; then again smells—sweet and foul—linger and hold no boundaries. Is it possible to develop, in Boone's (1989) sense, "a male voice as a third or odd term in a gendered discourse that consists of (at least) man, woman, and the dominant cultural ideology that we call patriarchy: that is, maleness needn't be assumed to be coeval with patriarchy, with woman symmetrically positioned on the other side of the position" (p.166)? Boone raises my fundamental problem.[1]

Since its inception, feminism has never been a homogeneous grouping. Why should it be expected that men's responses are any less differentiated? Why should we bear the burden of "correctness?" Perhaps, because the burden of change must also rest with men. However, there is no *one* way to do this, for if there was, ~~the~~ (my)nefield would become either a male metaphor for a competitive playing field beset by the homogenizing logic of masculine domination, or its re-formation could lead to a new metonymic field, such as Women's Studies, which constructs a new feminist institutional Law with its own guardians for insuring legitimacy (see, Derrida, 1987b:190). Men's studies is now the "gender-balanced" correlate, polarizing difference yet again. The issue of male or female inclusion/exclusion could be deconstructed through, and in the play of, these (my)nefields as an oblique *side*-step-dance, not so much in syncopation between *just* two sexes and *just* two genders, but an ironic chaotic shuffle where there is a "confusion," or profusion of partners: men side-step-dancing with men, women side-step-dancing with women, men side-step dancing with women, women side-step dancing with men— the ironic distance between them perceived as skewed "masquerade(s)," in Doane's (1982) sense of the term.[2] *This, then would be a "thrift-shop dressing ball."* I am thinking of a tangential anamorphic dance, one which our gaze at this historical juncture as yet cannot see (Bryson,1988b:92). I simply sense that with the development of queer studies, more and more sexual polysemy will show itself as it becomes more and more socially acceptable to live in a world of sexual differences. Compulsory heterosexuality will continue, however slowly, to be challenged in all sectors. Such a position comes close to that of Derrida. In *The Ear of The Other* (1985) he writes:

> The sex of the addresser awaits its determination by or from the other. It is the other who will perhaps decide whom I am -man or woman. Nor is it decided once and for all. It may go one way one time and another way another time.

> What is more, if there is a multitude of sexes (because there are perhaps more than two) which sign differently, then I will have to assume (I- or rather whoever says I - will have to assume) this *polysexuality* (p. 52, my emphasis).

In an earlier context he wrote:

> I would like to believe in ... the multiplicity of sexually marked voices, this mobile of non-identified sexual marks whose choreography can carry, divide, multiply the body of each 'individual,' whether he be classified as 'man' or as 'woman' according to the criteria of usage (1982b:76).

Derrida is willing to risk the indeterminacy of the reader/viewer's sex. Am I? But this is the same Derrida who wrote, "the feminist women are men ... feminism wants castration, even that of woman" (1977:182). In retrospect, the entire book *Men in Feminism* is the (my)nefield, for it covers the conjunctions of contemporary discourses surrounding this issue, none of which offer easy resolve.

Tactics of the First Tacky "Step" Taken: My two (I)(i)'s

It is perhaps apropos and somewhat ironic that the tactics of this essay were extended (in-spire-d) from the final chapters of Paul Smith's (1988) *Discerning the Subject*, the very same author who co-authored the book which members of the art education panel were addressing. In keeping with the above comments my address will then become this anamorphic cross–dress and redress as the title suggests, similar to Smith's position in his later book. Is this a mere coincidence, or is the crossdress/redress dialectic the very position "men *in* feminism" find themselves in ? The cross–dress, which recognizes the alterity of the Other, is matched by an equally resultant redress to let the Other"be." Marx's notion of representation as *Darstellung* is what is hoped for here; trying to imagine how others "see" themselves in order to provide an ethical response in turn. Such a response, however, cannot simply take the form of "love your neighbour as yourself." This gesture denies the possibility of crossdress. She resembles me insofar as I see her in myself. Difference is denied. Nor can it lay the claim of redress of the Other simply because of the position that she already occupies in the social order. Redress is, once again, defined by the symbolic community"I" belong to. Rather the "be" of difference must direct itself to that which is "absolutely particular" about her, her "radical singularity"; that part of her "that we can be sure we can never share"—her *fantasy*. Žižek (1991: 156) identifies such a response as the Lacanian maxim: "do not cede your desire." In other words, "avoid as much as possible any violation of the fantasy space of the other, i.e., respect as much as possible the other's 'particular absolute,'" the way she organizes her universe of meaning in a way absolutely particular to her, since to be conferred the dignity of a person means recognizing that all of us are caught by fantasies which conceal the impasse of our own desires. But there is yet another call to responsibly here. And that is the recognition of the "insistence" of that "singular fantasy" of woman as Other which historically calls out to every single man a reminder of the incalculable debt which he cannot "pay" for his past injustices.

Saying "I" now becomes highly problematic, perhaps impossible to "use" (Martens, 1985). Scattered throughout this essay is the use of both a capital "I" and a lower case "i" (the scare quotes have been dropped). This graphic word-processing devise is used to reflect a tactic and a tension which doubles on itself, reflective of the tension between a humanist phallogocentric language, of which the capital I is representative, and the attempt to redress this (autobiographical) I from yet another, ideally anamorphic sight/cite/site designated by the lowercase–i. It is a lame attempt at utilizing an anamorphic I/i, as the title of the book states. (Such deliberate graphic markings could be extended to the possessives such as m(i), but the impending confusion is enough for now). The phallogocentric, monological, self-conscious I is used to refer to a centered Ego that claims certainty and clarity - even though it deceives itself through repression in the act of objectifying itself through the material of language and word-processing and, in this instance, the "impossible" desire for the certitude of men's relationship to feminism (Heath, 1987:1). The search for "correctness" is forever deferred, the mail/male in this case, will never be delivered. Perhaps this writing is then also a pale attempt at an 'otobiography' in Derrida's (1985) sense?[3] But, the I is probably only posturing, kidding itself without even knowing it.

There is perhaps, yet another way to articulate the "why" of the two I/i's. If the I is the external "preformative" corporeal style, a conscious "drag," if you like (Butler, 1990a:139), then the i tries to effect a change to the performance; the effects of which are not always apparent until after the fact. The blind spots i try to "see" are often missed. i agree with Butler when she says "[t]hat cogito is never fully of the cultural world that it negotiates, no matter the narrowness of the ontological distance that separates that subject from its cultural predicates" (p.143). For her the I is not determined by the rules through which it is generated, rather it remains unified and regulated by a "process of repetition that both conceals itself and enforces its rules precisely through the production of substantiating effects" (p. 145). It is stable only through its repetitions. The i becomes the agent of change to disrupt this repetition. Although it is not my desire to appear clever by using such a graphic trope, at the very least it acts as a reminder to myself that, despite my reflective, seemingly "clear" present inner voice as it writes this narrative, there are other narratives which have already set the stage for its sounds. It is these off-centered, anamorphic voices of which the I needs reminding. Many of these off stage voices are found among the journals that stand in silence on the bookshelves of library cellars. Only the posture, the approach, the tact *without* seduction (Gallop, 1987; Burchill, 1984), may be a moment of possibility in the impossibility. But perhaps i am fooling myself? As Baudrillard, the cynic of postmodernity puts it, all symbolic knowledge is seductive (1990): "... *seduction represents mastery over the symbolic universe, while power represents only mastery of the real universe*" (p. 8, original italic). And if the seducer's "domain approaches that of the feminine and sexuality" (p. 180), he will be accused of yet another maleman´s theft in disguise. Nevertheless, my posture repeats a similar "impossible" stance towards patriarchy by feminists, especially for those who claim radical Otherness - alterity; their position of difference "does not provide an autonomous source of legitimation but is itself constituted through a patriarchal cultural tradition, which women must work within even as they question it" (Felski, 1989:46). A man must become vigilant of that tradition and avoid epistemic violence which is so ubiquitous throughout society. It therefore implicates him in its continual reproduction, as if it were inherent within him, even though as an "individual" he disclaims any involvement.

The "i" has often been referred to as "the subject of enunciation," or speaking subject (Barthes, 1979). It is the speaking subject (*récit*) which is distinguished from the written, painted, sculpted, filmic subject, "the subject of the enounced (*discours*)," or subject of speech (the "I"). As such, "the subject of the enounced" is organized by particular historical and ideological discourses—the essay, the novel, the letter, the genre painting, the history painting, pedestal sculpture. The historical record is left with the discourse of the enounced subject. There is also the subject which perceives the discourse, or the spoken subject, which is probably the most problematic of the three given the difficulty of understanding this subjective constitution in the everydayness of lived life as texts are continuously read and interpreted. Any text becomes polysemous once the spoken subject is taken into account. Kerby (1991) provides a succinct synthesis of these three subject positions:

> The speaking subject is the individual qua [in the capacity
> of being the] site of expression - the language user. The
> subject of speech is the purely signified subject of utter-
> ances, that is, the subject qua [in the capacity of being the]
> position within a signifying network without consideration
> of the flesh-and-blood author of the utterance; in other
> words, the subject projected by, or meant in, the utter-
> ance. Finally, the spoken subject is the audience of the
> utterance or the subject qua [in the capacity of being the]
> listener, or receiver, the individual affected by the utterance
> (p.13).

The interplay of these three subject positions has provided a rich and dense account as to the way meanings are negotiated, resisted, and accepted as dominant or natural. In cinematic theory, Mayne (1993) makes the distinction between the film *viewer* (as the real person or spoken subject), the cinematic or discursive subject and the *spectator* who "is and is not the cinematic subject, and as a subject who is and is not a film viewer" (p.36). Mayne's *spectator* does not entirely correspond to Kerby's spoken subject. It problematizes this subject position by placing its existence somewhere in between the text (as composed of discursive subject positions) and the actual viewer or reader. In other words, "[s]pectatorship occurs at precisely those spaces where [discursive] "subjects" and "viewers" rub against each other" (p.37). This gap between discursive subjects and "real people" is what must be negotiated, but how? Reception aesthetics, reader response theories, discourse analysis, symbolic interaction are just some of the epistemological forms which constitute such an accounting. But have such accounts of textual reading leaned too far over to the discursive subject? On another level, the postmodernist critique of the Enlightenment has laid bare the transcendental historical watchful "Eye" as an organ of sight belonging to Man (see Foucault, 1977; White,1980; Jay,1986,1993 Levin, 1993); a transcendent, metaphysical omniscient overlord which eventually replaced God with the epistemic tools of objective science and a logical positivist philosophy. Ours is a historical present marked by feminist, queer, and postcolonial discourses which have begun to dissimulate that pretense.

Not everything can be accounted for epistemologically within the interplay of these subject positions. The gap of spectatorship is mysterious. The contingent and the incidental escape analysis. There is a "remainder" which is unaccountable and uncontainable. So while the concept of "God" may have been secularized over the past five hundred years, a residual metaphysical "remainder" escapes. In the biological sciences that "remainder" may be identified as "life." Life remains an irreducible concept where epistemology finds its limit. There is also a limit at work amongst the above subjectivities. As soon as one writes the Self, a distancing happens as the inner, monological voice is "translated-represented-interpreted" through the technology of language, or for that matter, any medium of representation. Through the slipperiness of signifiers, through the spaces between them, through the punctuation, through the grammar of the phonetic alphabet, through the words that are synchronically available, or through a similar artistic formal grammar of line, color, texture, size, space, mass, the gap of social construction is always there. Hence an abyss or chasm lies between the speaking self (i) and the enounced self (I). This irreducible distance asserts itself, again and again, when we feel the immediacy of life through our bodies, but can only know that life by naming, arting, writing, poeticizing our pains, pleasures, and symptoms through the technologies available to us. Writing, in this broad sense, will always remain "difficult" and informed by the incidental, our unknown excesses.

Yet life is led without hesitation. There is a continual "throughing" as the subject leaps back and forth across this chasm in good faith, confirming the stability of reality. When we entered the symbolic order of language we began to trust the schemas given to us. We made the leap in good faith and just as writing distances the immediacy of speech, "art-ing" distances the immediacy of perception. Just as composing through musical notes distances the immediacy of hearing, theatrical acting distances the immediacy of the body's feelings. The arts are "subjected" to their respective grammatical technologies. None are able escape the aesthetics of their forms to a pristine space of phenomenological immediacy. Only by positioning oneself paradoxically in-between, over the abyss, facing the groundlessness between the speaking and enounced self does reality again become mysterious. Now our footing may be lost and we can fall into that abyss that Lacan identified as the Real. The (my)nefield has become a bottomless sea of quicksand. Perhaps through a series of such "slips" we undergo change unknown to our selves? Slips are one thing, but complete falls are always possible. This horror lies potentially within us all, for to truly unhinge reality is to go mad and fall into a radical psychotic autism where we are no longer able to make sense of the world around us. Throughout history many cultures, including the West, have taken the art and writing of the mad to be the messages from this abyss, from the Real.

Such a voice may be impossible to attain in "sensible" writing, for surely it must lie somewhere between the grapheme and the zoopheme, between drawing and the alphabet, between the nameless and the named. Barthes'(1986/1970) "writing in the middle voice" comes closest when characterizing what it is the (I)(i) thinks he is doing. There is dialogue between an active (i) and a passive (I) view of the self; the interaction between the "writing self" and the "written self" form this reflexive middle voice. "The one who writes here does not write for himself, but, as by proxy, for a person who is exterior and antecedent (even if they both have the same name)" (Barthes, 1986/1970:43). Hayden White (1992), following Freud, names this middle voice as "obsessionally neurotic," characterized by a "turning around upon the subject's self" (p.184). It is a form of reflexive writing, trying to deconstruct a humanist construction of self. Why is this important?

As an empty shifter (Bienveniste, 1971) the humanist Eye/I is coveted by Man. In this sense "I" am captured by my own "eye" in the mirror of my own reflection when writing/art-ing. But this mirror stage is inconceivable without the presence of another, for example, my Mother, to provide support, "to 'stand in' for the Other," to represent me as Other (Silverman, 1986:142). In the infant years, the (M)other facilitates my seeing myself. Yet this facilitating gaze is almost always under-theorized, as the elisions of Freud testify. There is then, a double blindness to the form of my constituted reflection. "I" see "me;" "I" talk about "me;" "I" hear "myself"; yet, in doing so "I" remain blind and deaf to myself because of the "orthopedic" support given to me by my (M)other. She is never "truly" heard. As a male, I must silence her after she has (hopefully) patiently and caringly orchestrated me holophrastically into the Symbolic order. To become aware of my stare, somehow i must put my own "I" under scrutiny, to stand behind myself, to write in the Other's desire—seemingly an impossibility. As Silverman (1986) so succinctly writes: "The naive subject—the subject trapped within the illusions of Cartesian consciousness—imagines that it is seeing itself see itself, an experience which testifies to the involuted structure of the gaze, if not to the gaze's ultimate exteriority. In fact, the subject sees itself being seen, and that visual transaction is always ideologically organized" (p.143). As a "maleman" (my neologism for sex/gender) the journey (I)(i) am about to deliver is to take notice of this facilitating gaze which feminists have made conscious for me. Somehow, to avoid Medusa's fate,[4] a blind "eye", (i) must intervene before having my head cut off *and*, at the same time, turned to stone—a paradoxical impossibility of the "enunciatory abyss" which separates the two (I)(i)'s (*récit and discours*).

Intervention into this elisionary gap, according to Showalter (1982:201), is the place of women's difference; a "wild zone" of female space for each text is *excessive* and therefore *doubled*. It can be read for its dominant ideological (patriarchal) content or doubled against itself, with the grain and against the grain, producing the double-voice of feminism. Such a conceptualization appears probable, but is it possible to operationalize? What might be the praxiological forms of this re-writing? According to French feminists, it is a place written in "white ink," constituting *écriture féminine*. Is this place then, only occupied by women, a separate sphere? Milk and semen are conceptually at odds, or are they understood as complementaries? For example, the British feminist painter Nancy Spero claims to be developing a "*la peinture féminine*" (Blazwick, et al.,1987:5). Her iconography consists of female figures who announce and delight in their own sexuality. In keeping with the dance motif of this introduction, in Spero's *To Soar II* (1990) female figures run and dance across the walls and spill over onto the ceiling of the gallery, refusing to be "framed." Non-constrained, they take part in the pleasure of their own bodies and in one another through embrace and touch; their unrestrained lesbianism has no use for the pleasure of the male viewer. But in an economics of plenty, where the logic of both/and are in play, the whiteness of both semen and milk produces more supply as the demand increases in strength or frequency. Is this a context-free maternal body?[5]

One variant of writing the body or *écriture féminine* has been attributed, *theoretically* at least, to the pre-Oedipal or pre-symbolic, pre-patriarchal moment of the child-mother relationship by Kristeva (1984). This 'semiotic' pre-linguistic realm might be referred to as the "aesthetic" part of writing - its poetry. It is difficult for me not to interpret Kristeva's argument as anything more than the loss of the aural and the graphic elements of writing historically as modes of communication changed from oral/aural to chirographic culture, then to typographic print cultures (see Lowe, 1982). Today, with electric and now electronic print cultures turning everything into "information," associating the lost oral/aural and graphic dimensions of writing with the feminine seems to suggest that the Symbolic order is male dominant. Yet Kristeva refuses to name herself as a feminist, and the kind of writing she identifies as semiotic has been attributed to men—Lautrémont, Mallarmé, Joyce, Artaud. Needless to say, this has angered many feminists.

So what posture should a maleman take to put his "I" "under erasure" (*sous rature*)[6] as the subject of the *enounce*? Is it even possible to recognize which rhetorical tropes are used to make me "point" in a particular way? Why should i be party to patriarchy which is so often theorized by feminists as a monolithic structure which all men partake by virtue of being men?

Perhaps a patriarchal language does dominates my Eye, although i struggle against it—impossibly. As the joke from Woody Allen's film *Zeilig* reminds me: Zeilig, masquerading as a psychoanalyst, could never accept Freud's theories because he himself believed that penis envy applied to *men*. In a capitalist patriarchy the power of the phallus that was assumed to be theirs is unreachable and, in the end, denied to both men and women. There are many men's groups who believe that they are victims of capitalist patriarchy just like many women. They perceive themselves as oppressed and dominated, "subjected" to a patriarchal system not of their own choosing or making, suffering from corporate and state violence which is capable of drafting them for military action. Competitive sports and an equally competitive work ethic become the only legitimated and internalized venues open to define success. Not living up to these dominant modes set up by a patriarchal capitalist system leaves me(n) emotionally injured. Such a male victim scenario has been accused of reifying patriarchy as the Big Other — that which controls us all; that which is out of our control; that which we (men) can do little about.

From where can a responsible response take place? It seems the only "wild" place men have recently begun to occupy is quite literal: men beating and drumming in nature; men sitting in sweat lodges recovering their lost relationships with their absent fathers and overcoming their domineering mothers; men evoking myths of the "Hairy Man" and "Iron John" (Bly, 1990).[7] Like the "australopithecine" Harry in the film *Harry and the Hendersons*, the male ego seems soft and fuzzy, but completely dumb and out of control, not knowing its own strength, nor what it is capable of doing, nor how it should continue to live in a family setting. It's as if the mid-life "crisis" of the white–male–yuppie–boomer generation has finally come to fore! Perhaps my own exploration is yet another example? I was in my early 40s at the time of this writing.[8] Compared to the wealth of material which deals with fringe personae, my life seems rather boring, less sensationalistic and almost too "normal," meaning too "straight" to be potentially subversive. The "men's movement" offers self-help remedy for what ails us - emotion therapy based on the belief that all men share a deep atavistic masculinity. Bly rejects the model of the "soft male" that evolved in response to feminism - that of a non-domineering, cooperative, supportive and non-aggressive male.[9] Occupying the place of the guru-elder, Bly leans to a belief that there was some romantic time in the past where men knew "who they were." Their current crisis can be overcome by restoring a concern over their sons and daughters; they need to "father" again and restore their authority which comes from a "deep masculinity." Perhaps by writing about one's own heterosexual masculinity is a clever way to reinsert and reinvest an authority that was never displaced in the first place? The rhetoric of "crisis" allows ruling groups to reconsolidate their power by claiming to resolve the very crisis they manufactured in the first place, a common ploy used by governments in power.

Lacan's "Formulae of Sexuation": Woman as the *Sinthome* of Man–or "Woman Does not Exist "

My intent will be to engage in this literature of masculinity when it becomes useful to do so, but not in any systematic way. There are many masculinities, each existing in a number of contexts that are defined by cultural expectations, each shaped by a history and the interests and desires of those who control and define its constructions.[10] My intent is to engage in the literature of feminism, especially (but not exclusively) as it pertains to visual art (including popular culture), and peripherally to art education, by charting instances where the "I" was affected by feminist progressive forces, from a place which is neither "wild" nor easily identifiable, but produced from the excessive writing of an obsessed subject. This place is conditioned by the Thing of my own symptom being a male within patriarchy—Woman (Žižek, 1989a: 71-79). She is my symptom, a sublime object which can never be identified or reached throughout this journey of desire. She is my Thing (*La Femme*), the nonexistent figuration of the *objet a*. According to Lacan, paradoxically "woman does not exist;" she is a "figurement" in the Real. But, what could such an enigmatic phrase possibly mean within the context of my question?

Lacan's formulae of sexuation presents a radical break with a simple biology verses social construction dichotomy regarding sex/gender, as well as any attempts to subsume this dichotomy within social construction itself (cf. Butler, 1990). For Lacan as well as Freud: "'Sexuality' is neither 'sex' nor 'gender'" (Shepherdson, 1994:166). In Lacanian terms male–female do not present a binary logic (i.e., active/passive, cause/effect, sun/moon, public/private etc.) but are different *modalities* to a functional antagonism between these two contraries at the level of logic (Žižek, 1994c:159–160). In Lacanian terms the male/female modality is not an *opposition* at the Imaginary–Symbolic level, i.e., how we see ourselves as an *ideal ego* to the position from which we see ourselves as *ego-ideal*—conforming to a biological cultural norm. This couplet would be characterized by *the role of gender* which can generate multiple possibilities that may offer direct challenges to the established norm. Rather the male/female modality is governed by *the imperative of sex* at the level of representation, i.e., at the level of language as the Symbolic Order which is the level of the signifier itself. For Lacan this means that the male/female modality is a never-ending *antagonism* which happens at the conjunction between the Symbolic and Real—the Real being the unconscious register beyond language, the remainder which is unspoken. Such an antagonism is the result of the limits of linguistic representation itself; the failure of language to achieve any final closure. If there was no failure in the logic of the signifier, i.e., if the sexual relation were a simple matter of combining the Imaginary and the Symbolic so that multiple performative identities could be socially constructed which would fit together, then it would be possible to have perfect relation. Yet there is plenty of empirical evidence that this ideal is never achieved. Sex is, therefore, incommensurable. It is impossible to achieve oneness. Consequently Lacan argues that sex itself presents the *impossibility* between the Symbolic Order and the Real which, paradoxically, make responses to it possible (e.g., the genealogy of family structures, Romantic love, troubadourian love etc.). Sex is, therefore, the deadlock of the Symbolic Order which is presided by the rock of castration—in the Real—which prevents its foreclosure. How then can, "Woman does not exist" be understood given this context?

I turn to Slavoj Žižek (1993b:53-58; 1994a; 1994b:121-126), perhaps Lacan´s most brilliant and accessible interpreter, to try to grasp this *Widerspruch* (literally, a contradictory saying). Žižek begins his account by turning to the discussion which links the opposition masculine/feminine to the opposition beautiful/sublime with Kant. In contrast to the Kantian formulation, Žižek, following Lacan, attempts to demonstrate that *"sexual difference is inscribed in the inherent split of the Sublime into mathematical and dynamical"* (1993b:54, original italic). What he means by this is that the latter experience of the sublime—as the "dynamic sublime"—refers to the telos of nature in both its seeming purposelessness, i.e., in its "enjoyment" which apparently serves no purpose when it reeks chaos and havoc on us (storms, hurricanes, volcanoes), and the teleological observation that there *must* be some purpose to such a destructive impulse. Somehow "nature" is not simply blind, but it "knows." But where "it doesn't know," it *enjoys* (p.49). Lacan reads this contradiction in the dynamic sublime as another instance of the operation of the superego dimension of the Law. This superego dimension as Law is a force of blame which asserts "irrational" pressure on us. As such this guilt is incommensurate with our own agency of responsibility. Nature perceived as a "cruel God" judges us as *a priori* guilty. However, it is precisely this rage of Nature which enables us to marshal the pure or suprasensible ideal of Reason that tries to contain its blind fury. But this leads to the complexities of theorizing the Kantian transcendental categories of pure Reason which, following Copjec's formulation in her final chapter, "Sex and the Euthanasia of Reason" (1994a), have a structural homology to Lacan's "formulae of sexuation." The mathematical and the dynamic antinomies which arise when entertaining objects that are beyond possible experience are specified by the opposition: homogeneity/heterogeneity. Mathematical antinomies arise when pure reason is applied to homogeneous sensible phenomena. They concern the real existence of their object, whose totality, nevertheless, always exceeds our grasp. In contrast, dynamic antinomies are generated by categories of pure reason as they are applied to suprasensible non-phenomena (or noumena); their resultant heterogeneity is generated by entertaining various combinations and possibilities. Mathematical antinomies are defined by the logic of the "non-all" and are defined as *feminine*. Dynamic antinomies of the noumenal field are assigned to the logic of masculine universal. Men and women are therefore split differently and "this difference in splitting accounts for sexual difference" (Žižek, 1994b: 250, ft. 12 cf. Bruce Fink, italic in original).

It should be stated from the outset that the 'masculine' and 'feminine' defined difference is ultimately bound to the paradoxes proper to language. Their "deadlock," or k(not), marks the fundamental impossibility of "neutrality" when symbolizing the real. Since it is impossible to make sense of the sexual relationship at the level of language, Lacan resorted to inscribing sexuality in an analytic formulation, his so-called "formulae of sexuation" (Lacan, 1982). He conceived this sexual difference at the transcendental level wherein the notion of sexual difference is not constituted as a complementary relationship of two opposite poles which supplement each other to form the whole of the human being as in Jungian or Taoist thought (see Žižek, 1991: 17). Rather, the formulations are radically "anthropocentric" in that 'masculine' and 'feminine' are "the two modes of the subject's failure to achieve the full identity of man. 'Man' and 'woman' together do not form a whole, since each of them is already in itself a failed whole" (Žižek, 1994a; 110-111, italic in original). Such paradoxical thinking enables Žižek to write that without this "fundamental deadlock," [or 'knot'] wherein the limit of symbolically representing sexual difference ends only in "impossibility," "we would not have two sexes but only one" (p.112, italic in the original). From these relations of non-reciprocity emerges Lacan´s scandalous claim that "the sexual relationship is impossible" (see Lapsley and Westlake, 1992). [11] Completeness that comes with reciprocity, as in the joining of opposites, is a fundamental fantasy of the imaginary structuring love. Since both sexes are structured by a lack in the Real, this hole can only be made whole through a reciprocally mutual self-deception. Lovers must "look" at each other from the same psychic "place" of desire. If she or he, however, is *not* found in that place, then, as Lacan put it, "You never look at me from the place from which I see you." The fantasy is broken or was never established in the "first place." From this follows that in the actual sex act "man's partner is never a woman in the kernel of her being, but woman qua *a*, reduced to the fantasy-object" (Žižek, 1993b:43). Such thinking produces yet another scandal: if masturbation is an imaginary sexual act where the bodily contact with a partner is only imagined, then the actual sex act becomes a kind of imagined masturbation with a real partner. Masturbation as a "solitary" experience, far from being a separate and distinct act, is intimately intertwined with sexual intercourse as its supplement. Its endless "repetition" seems to confirm the very "failure" of our attempts at completeness; to fill our lack through the desire of sexual fantasy.[12]

Masculine Universal Logic

Žižek attempts to make it understandable that these Lacanian formulae of sexuation are structured like Kantian antinomies; as contraries not contradictions. Such logic, however, takes a while to grasp. Let me begin with his discussion of how the "masculine" dynamic universal logic operates. Lacan's formulation is as follows: all men are submitted to the function of (symbolic) castration which implies the existence of one exception. In other words, a universal produces a particular exception which refers to the Hegelian paradox of a "totality which always comprises a particular element embodying its universal structuring principle" (Žižek, 1994b:45, italic in original). How? And why one exception? The contradiction to Lacan's premise would read: no men are submitted to the function of (symbolic) castration. However, the logic here requires a subtraction from the set, and not an addition to it. The "basic premise is that the leap from the general set of 'all men' into the universal 'man' is possible only through an exception ... " (1994b:123). The exception which separates the general from the universal is a feature which totalizes the general set into becoming universal. Saying this another way: the exception is an element or point that subverts its own universal foundation. It acts as a supplement to the whole, standing apart from the whole, yet necessary for that whole to achieve its closure. This exception imposes a self-limitation of the phallus. It marks a symbolic castration which splits desire between the phallic and the non-phallic (the non-phallic being the exception); between sexual enjoyment and the "domain of ethical goals, of non-sexual 'public' activity" (Žižek, 1994b:108). For Freud, this exception was the primordial father of Totem and Taboo who escapes castration by being the Father-of-Enjoyment: the primal father who possesses all women. His patricide (subtraction) enables the Oedipal father to exist as an agent of incestuous prohibition (as non-sexual "public" activity). In other words, "the figure of the Father-of-Enjoyment is nothing but a neurotic fantasy that overlooks the fact that the father has been dead from the beginning, i.e., that he never was alive, except insofar as he did not know that he was already dead" (Žižek, 1991:24). This neurotic fantasy of the "living dead" primordial father is an insistence that operates in the dynamic sublime informing an ethics of Evil (as total phallic enjoyment without restraint, e.g., a serial killer). Without the dependence on this superego figure, the authority of the Oedipal father as an agent of Symbolic Law or the Big Other which guarantees the restraining of pre-oedipal "polymorphous perversity" would crumble. The perverse father would be set free to roam, rape and kill, like Freddie Kruger and Jason in horror films.

The "masculine" law of an exception has to posit an "origin" or "birth," a point of singularity or starting point which ushers in a new beginning, i.e., the Big Bang theory. This logic of the exception can also be applied to the Christian conceptualization of Jesus Christ as the son of God. His primordial crucifixion (subtraction and sacrifice) and ascent into heaven was absolutely necessary if Church authority was to establish itself as providing the universal ascetic way that "man" should cleanse himself of an "original sin" (total phallic enjoyment), and strive to close the impossible gap between "immoral man" and God (Spirit) (as non-sexual "public" activity). This "masculine" side of totalization-through-exception is further demonstrated throughout Žižek's writings through several other clever examples. The logic of capitalist commodity and labor exchange, for example, must subtract the paradox of universal freedom if the capitalist system is to maintain itself, i.e., the worker is able to sell "freely" his or her own labor on the market, but in doing so the universal claim to freedom is subverted; through this transaction the worker loses that freedom and becomes enslaved by capital (Žižek, 1989:22). Here then, the worker as the exception is the ethical remainder and reminder of the non-sexual 'public' activity of the capitalist. Likewise the universalism of capitalism's claim of honoring the principle of equivalent exchange of commodities must continually answer to the paradox that workers themselves are a commodity since they do not own the means of production.

If the proletariat, for Marx, provided the exceptional "irrational" element to the operation of a rational capitalist order (as a reminder for its conscience, so to speak), the monarch, for Hegel, was the exceptional One, divinely incarnated, to which all men strove to become. The Monarch, as the exception, thus made the rational state possible—God on earth so to speak—by determining law and order. All men were, therefore, castrated. They had to strive to become rational so that the state would itself become a rational totality already incarnated at a "vanishing point" occupied (impossibly) by the monarch. State-istics provided the mathematical aesthetics for such a possibility. The zero (0), as the exception, was the place holder for figures one through nine. The number 10 would then become the basis for digitizing reality through any number of combinations of 1 and 0.

We can see what happens when this masculine logic breaks down in the recent film *The Madness of King George*. If the exception becomes mad, the state is in ruins. The state legislators do everything in their power to restore the King to his "senses." Being 'mad' and being ex-centric, however, are not the same thing. They occupy precisely the opposite ends of the spectrum. King George's madness meant that he had stepped out of his place in the Real (as the exception) and began to act like a normal citizen, rejecting his ascribed status. His ex-centricity, on the other hand, repositioned him as the impossible signifier. As Copjec (1991) points out, President Reagan's impending senility and forgetfulness, his "referential failures" and lies were overlooked by the American public because they loved him despite the media's persistence to trip him up. For the American populace Reagan had some unnameable thing (*objet a*) that made him the exception. Reagan could do no wrong, His forgetfulness was overlooked as being ex-centric. Likewise King George's return to being"himself" meant recovering his ex-centric speech "(What! What!)", and his total disregard for the law since he was once again *the* Law.

A more clever example comes from popular culture. In his discussion of a series of caricatures published in *Mad* as to how a subject relates to the symbolic norm of fashion, Žižek (1994a:110) points out that the lowest rung of society are indifferent to fashion. They are too poor to care, interested only in maintaining a decency of dress. The highest rung, in contrast, are also indifferent to fashion for a different reason: there is no one "above" them which would make a comparison necessary. They are the norm of fashion. For the fashion industry to exist, as a definable and universal symbolic norm, the poor have to paradoxically have no fashion; they are a reflective reversal, the exception to the trend-setting rich. In other words, a (closed) system comes into being, and claims universality for itself, only when it reflects itself in the form of its opposite—when it splits itself as ideal ego and ego-ideal. With the former position (ideal ego), the imaginary identification to fashion by middle and upper middle classes is "constituted" by an image which is likable to themselves, i.e., what they would like to be; while the later (ego-ideal) is a "constitutive" symbolic identification made possible by a place from where they are being observed, and from where they look at themselves as being likable and worthy of love, i.e., to be seen by the Other as one sees oneself in one's own narcissism; to be loved for the ideal one narcissistically takes oneself to be—in this case as being "fashionable" (see Žižek, 1989:105). In this sense, men are wholly submitted to the phallus since it is through the exception that the universal domination of the phallus is maintained.

Feminine Non-universal Logic

If the "masculine" side of the asymmetrical antinomies of symbolization involves the universality of the phallic function founded on an exception, the feminine formulation by Lacan rests on a set that is "not-all," nonuniversal, but "without exception"; the implication of which points "beyond the phallus." Hopefully it will become "clear" that exception/without exception are *not* to be read as contradictions but as contraries, i.e., as, *not* an exception but *no* exception. The "feminine" antinomy is informed by the "mathematical" sublime, i.e., by the sublime feeling that overcomes us when we contemplate the infinity of the universe and infinity itself. The failure of reason in face of this impasse presents the feminine ethics of magnitude, i.e., sustaining the "impossibility" of the idea of "an all," a universal grandeur in which "women would finally be counted" (Copjec, 1994b:11).

The Lacanian formulation of the feminine antinomy reads: not-all women are submitted to phallic castration, which implies that there is no exception.[13] The universal claim that no woman could be exempted from the (symbolic) function of castration emerges based paradoxically on an exception, which again appears confusing. Here there is a *particular negation* which produces a universal, the direct inverse of the masculine antinomy. How can this be? For again this reads like a *Widerspruch*; the conclusion flies in the face of common sense. To begin to unravel this puzzling logic is to first take note that "no woman could be exempted from symbolic castration" is interpreted as a "double negation" rather than as a universal affirmation. If this were a *universal affirmation* it would read as, "*all* women are *not* exempted from symbolic castration." Here a non-Aristotelian logic is at work. This antinomy is governed by an infinite series where there is no phenomenon which is not preceded by yet another phenomenon—*ad infinitum*. Symbolic castration is read as: "to be preceded by another phenomenon in time" (Žižek 1993b:57)—indefinitely deferred. In other words, "there is no woman who could be exempted from symbolic castration" means that each woman *as such* is subjected to symbolic castration. This is the logic of *mise en abyme*—the spiral of infinite regression in representation where an entire image becomes repeated and embedded as part of the primary image like in a hall of mirrors. But, as Copjec (1994b) claims, "to be a girl is to undergo castration *without* the intervention of the father's prohibition" (p.2, my italic) which (at first) appears to be a contradiction to what has been presented here. For Copjec (1994a: 217-227) the woman (in modernity) is also castrated, but by a very different scenario than by the universal phallic male of exception as developed above. She is castrated by the very logic of "no exception" which is "beyond the phallus." What does this mean? As she claims: "She does not enjoy her own body (as Irigaray, among others, have claimed) but that of the Other, the Other body. Her enjoyment is thus *impossible* rather than *prohibited* [as in the male], which is equivalent to saying that her castration takes place without paternal intervention" (p.4). Put another way, her castration is a result *not* of a phallic economy of desire which is a failure to include everything (universalize, make whole, to complete what is incomplete), but a desire that comes from the failure to exclude anything.[14] This can be interpreted as a woman's *inconsistency* of desire that can attain the domain "beyond the phallus" since this inclusion knows no limit. "This impossibility of constructing an all, a whole image of the self, means that the woman is always castrated, cut off from herself, from her *jouissance*" (p.4).

Perhaps a more accessible understanding of woman's castration, as Elisabeth Bronfen clarifies (1992a), refers to the loss of the maternal body, which, like the penis, is a source of ego stability. "Castration refers to all prohibition, all difference that underwrites the illusion of identity, the disharmony and asymmetry of which is bound to re-emerge in subsequent separation" (p.43). In this sense castration defines the genus of our species. It is, in the Hegelian sense, the "immanent determination" of human beings. Cleverly, Žižek applies Hegelian logic to avoid the ontological priority of sexual difference, but the solution, it seems, is far from satisfactory since it uses "masculine" dynamic universal logic, as discussed above, to make its "cut." It is the abstract Universal (woman) that is constituted by way of subtracting from a set of some Particular designed to embody the Universal as such—in this case man. According to him the logic of sexual difference consists in:

> the set of women is a particular, non-totalized, non-universal set; its multitude acquires the dimension of *universality* (that, precisely, of "humankind") as soon as one excludes from it an element which thereby embodies humankind as such: man. The opposition of man and

> woman is thus not symmetrical: *the genus of "man" has one species, woman.* The universality of "humankind" is not (logically) prior to sexual difference, it is posited as such through the inscription of that difference (1994b:44, original italic).

The "difference" that differentiates the genus and its species, is of course the phallus, backgrounded in the above explication. Only by positing woman as the exception; as the element which "is" absence itself (the logic of the non-all, the subject who is non-phallic); as the species who "makes" the genus (the other differentiated species, man), can the Hegelian thesis hold. What makes it phallogocentric is the claim that "woman is a castrated man." Castration remains conceptualized under the master signifier of the phallus. Derrida (1993) calls Lacan on this as well: "Femininity is the Truth (of) castration, is the best figure of castration, because in the logic of the signifier it has always already been castrated; and Femininity 'leaves' something in circulation, ... , something detached from itself in order to have it brought back to itself, because she has 'never had it...' (p.185).

Žižek's Hegelianism tries to save Hegel from himself by avoiding this Aufhebung—a totality whereby woman is absorbed into the male universal. Although the question remains whether or not Lacan was merely describing the effects of phallogocentrism (which Derrida admits might be a possibility), the question also remains whether Derrida's own anti-Hegelianism has escaped this same phallogocentrism. In the "Double Session," if Leslie Wahl Rabine (1990) has it right, Derrida simply restages the same ruse as Žižek in reverse: Woman is a supplement who both lacks (non-phallic) and is excessive (the exception). Here the metaphor of the "hymen" is used to avoid Hegelian "dialectics of totality." A hymen is a tissue that folds over on itself and hence has no center. Derrida uses this metaphor to get at the process of spacing: the blanks, spaces, and silences which make the signifying structures possible, but which, as empty spaces, cannot be signified but remain as traces. The problem here is not unlike how "negative space" serves to inform the figure in art, a long-standing concern of the visual arts. Space signifies only when it is cancelled out through writing (art-ing) itself. Hymen is a figure of feminine logic for Derrida. It has a double or contradictory, undecidable meaning; as both a vaginal membrane and as marriage; as both "*entre*" (between) and "*antre*" (archaic French for cave). Unlike the phallic "cut" of difference, the empty space, the nothing, the cave, the womb, gives birth to the organized structure—to writing, to the universal. Spacing (the unsignifiable) is the exception. It is what lacks: the remainder that a totality must exclude in order to be formed. It seems Derrida arrives at the same place as Lacan (Žižek). Leslie Rabine concludes that Derrida is playing more the ruse of the "bisexual" man, reinscribing in him the feminine by neglecting to recognize the hymen as an institution that ensures hierarchy and men's possession of women, and by excluding the figure of Columbine, the woman "outside" Paul Margueritte's mimodrama Pierrot Murder of his Wife which Derrida deconstructs. Rabine's critique is echoed once again by Roberta Weston (in Oliver, 1995: 71-72) who criticizes Derrida for using a term which has a bloodstained history that marks woman as the property of man, and guarantees him the certitude that she has not been spoilt or possessed by another man. Furthermore, argues Weston, through copyright laws Derrida has marked the woman's hymen as his property, and according to Gayatri Spivak (1983), this "hymeneal fable" has become one of his trademarks!

The above comments perhaps make the first part of the antinomy "Not-all women are submitted to symbolic castration" equally puzzling. It becomes more understandable when it can be apprehended that this particular negation is already a universal; that the part already contains the "whole."[15] "[T]he Universal is already itself particular: it is not "all"—what escapes it (in so far as it is *abstract*, that is to say: in so far as one obtains it through the process of abstracting common features from a set of particular entities) is the Particular itself" (Žižek, 1993b:43, author's italics). The lack of an exception to the castration function "prevents its universal span" because nothing can be excluded. Its logic is governed by a finite series, meaning not all phenomena are preceded by yet another phenomena. Somewhere they stop, yet the phenomenal field is incomplete since no "all" can form when inclusion knows no limit (see Copjec, 1994b:4). Each new addition of "difference" or "radical singularity," destabilizes the finite set and refigurates it. There is "no exception" because there is nothing outside of this field; no "dark continent," no ineffable feminine essence beyond the domain of discursive existence. It is here where the logic of the "woman does not exist" can take on another meaning, for the sense of universal here means that there is a missing fullness, which, as mentioned, is Copjec's claim for feminine desire. In other words the particular universal, "woman," remains incomplete, although she is paradoxically "finite," i.e., particular. An example is helpful here. The feminist axiom, "the personal is the political" exemplifies a "feminine" non-all logic at work (Lacan's *pas tout*). The axiom suggests that there is no position of neutrality which can escape the political implications of feminist critique. There is no metalanguage which would end the debate, for we are always-already implicated and have taken sides whether we consciously know it or not simply by acting in the world. Feminism, in this sense, is the very *limit* for that which cannot be (yet) objectivized, located in our conception of a society. If its demands were met there would be no "feminism." In this sense "feminism does not exist." That is to say, when applying feminine non-all logic, feminism's complete definition does not exist. It cannot be apprehended "as such." Diame Elam (1994) refers to this "impossibility" as a "groundless solidarity" (p.69). *Each particular feminism in this sense is universal*, meaning that each position contains a specific perspective on the entire notion of feminism, which is, itself, absent. By not being totalized and coming into "existence," she escapes male dominance precisely by *not existing*. But is this price too high to pay?

According to Elam (1994) the price would be too high to pay if this weren't the case! "[A] feminism that believes it knows what a woman is and what she can do both forecloses the limitless possibilities of women and misrepresents the various forms that social injustice can take" (p.32). Thus far women have been determined by a phallogocentric order. They don't yet "exist." In this sense the condition of "woman" is like the structure of infinite deferral—the endless reflected mirrors of *mise en abyme* that governs the logic of the non-all. Elam calls this non-all logic of feminine "*ms. en abyme*," as "each new attempt to determine women does not put an end to feminist questioning but only makes us more aware of the infinite possibilities of women" (p.28). "Woman" becomes a "*permanently contested site* [sight/cite] *of meaning*" (Elam, 32, original italic). Elam's notion of "groundlessness" upon which she goes on to develop a feminist "ethical activism" is precisely Lacan's logic of the non-all (which she attributes to Derrida, dismissing Kant). "Woman doesn't exist," explains Žižek (1994b,60: ft. 34), must be understood in the strict sense of Hegel's Logic. "Existence" is not synonymous with "being" but with "ground." Existence is being in so far as it is "grounded," founded on a unique, universal Ground acting as its "sufficient Reason." In this precise sense "Woman doesn't exist": "she does not possess a unique Ground, she cannot be totalized with reference to some encompassing Principle."

As Shepherdson (1994) says "'La Femme' represents herself as '*The* Woman,' the figure who would put an end to the question 'what is a woman' (with emphasis on the *indefinite* article, by seeming to provide an answer for all. Expressed in terms of set theory, the formulas of sexuation distinguish 'women' as an open set (this one and that one and the next... without totality or essence), from 'the one' ('La Femme') who seems to incarnate the totality, to close the set of 'all women' by representing 'Woman' as such" (p.177).

Applying this to deconstruction and feminism, Elam makes the point that ethical judgments are "actually groundless." The search is always for a rule that does not yet exist, but will do justice to a case, e.g., like Spike Lee who gives us the enigmatic imperative: *Do The Right Thing.* Elam provides an example which makes the logic of non-all possibly more understandable. She gives the illustration, "all men are *potential* rapists" (p.108). This is a universal statement, but one which does not have a universal or absolute rule attached to it. However, it underscores the exception. Men are not accused of essentially being rapists (having a Ground in the Hegelian sense), but women must act *as if* this potential existed. Another way to put this: your dog may be chained up, but if it has the potential to bite through its leash and escape, it isn't really chained up. Said yet another way: "it would also be possible, though unfortunately not very likely, for all men to potentially be rapists and at the same time, at a particular moment, for no man to actually be a rapist" (p.108). Bluntly put, in any given moment men rape and dogs escape their leashes.

Copjec and Žižek's re-reading of Lacan's *Encore* makes the claim that in *modernity* there are two independent structural failures to think through the universal and particular simultaneously. They are "undecidable" in the Derridean sense.[16] Rather than linking these two antinomies with the opposition of male and female, they are "grafted" together (Žižek, 1994a:109). Why? A *linking* would be *unlawful* since in the "masculine" antinomy all men are submitted to the function of (symbolic) castration would become *equivalent* to the "feminine" antinomy that qualifies (supplements) it as "no woman could be exempted from the (symbolic) function of castration." Likewise the "feminine" antinomy which states non-all women are submitted to the (symbolic) function of castration would become equivalent to the "masculine" supplement—there is at least one man which is exempted from (symbolic) castration. Linking cancels out the difference which makes the difference. Consequently Žižek can write, "sexuality itself, what we experience as the highest, most intense assertion of our being, is a *bricolage*, a montage of two heterogeneous elements. Herein resides Lacan's 'deconstruction' of sexuality" (1994a:109). From here emerges yet another *Widerspruch*: "there is no sexual relationship" can be read against the background of an "impossible" link, i.e., given that there is a symbolic deadlock of the two antinomies, no union is possible other than the birth of an irreducible gap.

Within this development, cleverly it seems to me, has been the reevaluation of Lacan's seemingly negative statements in *Encore*, Seminar XX where woman is but the other sex—"not one," "black hole," "nothing," through Žižek's (1993b:58ff) reinstatement of a Hegelian logic and re-evaluation of Lacanian meditations on the Cartesian *cogito*. Again the antinomies are put into play to reveal the "ontological scandal" of the two modalities of the *cogito* wherein the unity of *cogito ergo sum* now becomes a sexual difference: the result of a forced choice between *thought* and *being* which reads as: "I am not where I think" (p.59). Žižek explains that the two possible interpretations of this statement that Lacan makes, the choice of "I think" or "I am," holds the key to sexual difference.[17] The first (I think) is a Kantian reading, while the second (I am) is Cartesian. In the case of the masculine "I think," the choice is made for *being* with the consequence that thought is relegated to the Unconscious, as "I am, therefore it (the Unconscious) thinks (ex-sists)." This is the "being" of a person structured by fantasy. The latter choice, the pure "I think," is an inverse procedure. Access to thought requires the loss of being; rather, it is an access to *pure* being which, paradoxically, "doesn't exist" but *insists*. The feminine *cogito* as "I think" must take on all the weight of woman as "not one," and "doesn't exist" by occupying the vanishing point of enunciation that precedes imaginary and symbolic identification of *res cognitas* (I think, therefore I am) which is the masculine position. She is, therefore, relegated to the Real, to the vanishing point where the "I" doesn't exist since it is not part of the symbolic order. She is, in this formulation, pure fantasy of the gaze, of "I think, therefore it (the Id) is." Under this formulation the feminine is given logical *priority* over the masculine and it seems to be a space *other* than the pre-Oedipal since there is already an "I" that thinks. The logic of the non-all, as the incomplete set, the impossibility of wholeness which leads to the "all" (wholeness), is eloquently summed up by Žižek as "the Limit and its Beyond" (1993b:58), wherein the non-all is the limit to what lies beyond it. In other words, the limit opens to the beyond with the addition of a "radical singularity," i.e., a difference that makes a difference. Only then, strictly speaking, is a "decision" possible which is "justifiable." This logical priority of the feminine concerning the "undecidability" ("synchronicity" in Žižek's terms) of the *cogito* must be put in the context of a strategy which is best articulated by Derrida (1987b) in an interview which appeared in *Men in Feminism*:

> Of course, saying that woman is on the side, so to speak, of undecidability and so on, has only the meaning of a strategical phase. In a given situation, which is ours, which is the European phallogocentric structure, the side of woman is the side from which you start to dismantle the structure. So you can put undecidability and all of the other concepts that go with it on the side of femininity, writing and so on. But as soon as you have reached the first stage of deconstruction, then the opposition between women and men stops being pertinent. Then you cannot say that

woman is another name, or a good trope for writing, undecidability and so on. We need to find some way to progress strategically. Starting with deconstruction of phallogocentrism, and using the feminine force, so to speak, in this move and then — and this would be the second stage or level — to give up the opposition between men and women (p.194).

The above discussion of Žižek's and Copjec's reformulations, it seems to me, reads like the oscillation of open (feminine) and closed (masculine) systems that are synchronous events at the level of the Imaginary; the former informed by the Real, the later by the Symbolic Order. It would be wrong, however, to take these developments as ahistorical, universal, and good for all time and all places. Rather, the paradoxes of sexuation belong to the modernism *per se* with the absorption of the subject, i.e., its interiorization to the point where it is its own overseer through the regimes of surveillance, the so called "empire of the gaze"—discussed by Foucault and the rise of a two sex system in the late eighteenth century as adumbrated by Kant. Thomas Laqueur's (1990) history of medical treatises from the Greeks to Freud shows that a "one sex" model construed the sexes as inside versus outside versions of a single genital-reproductive system prior to that time, with woman being the inverted and less-perfect man. Another way to say that the subject "disappeared" is to apply the masculine logic which informed it. Only by positing a neutral, blank, abstract and empty subject as the *exception*, guaranteed by the "democratic state," could the concept of a universal "citizen" emerge. Renata Salecl (1994, Chap. 8, "Why is Woman a Symptom of Rights?") has argued that this absorption and emergence of the split subject as theorized by Lacan gave rise to human rights in the 18th century. A codified discourse on universal human rights came into existence precisely to cover up existent social antagonisms. One might give this development an added comment. In contrast to men, women maintained their "theatricality"; they needn't become invisible since they were "invisible" already, bearing the weight of the spectatorial gaze at the expense of being denied full citizenship, i.e., property rights and the vote. Their bourgeois male counterparts, on the other hand, clad in the "habit noire" of industrialization, presented a sartorial refusal.

It may well be that today we are on the cusp of new reformulations of subjectivity that lead to the incorporation of "blindness" and the re-metaphorizations of "touch."[18] However, being caught up in the machinations of modernism (i.e., through my own "confessions") and postmodernism brings me back to woman as the *sinthome* of man. As a heterosexual the I may well be caught by courtly love without knowing it. Her signifier is said to be closed out by the phallocentric order, and that is why she returns as my *sinthome*, "*as a synthesis between symptom and fantasy,*" existing in the Real, outside the Imaginary and the Symbolic Order. This is how Žižek reads it. "She" remains, as Lacan claimed, an unresolvable "*sinthome*" (1989: 75) for there is no ideal existence for her in the Oedipus resolve. "She" is only "available" as *jouissance*, "a *jouis-sense*, enjoyment-in-sense" beyond the phallus. In other words, woman as man's symptom ex-ists as a non-discursive *insistence*. In such a formulation, woman as *sinthome*—as a *persistence* beyond interpretation and *beyond fantasy*, carries with her the ontological status of being the very support of man; she gives consistency to his being. Without her man is "nothing." To die "of a broken heart" in this sense means that woman as *sinthome* has been unbound; psychic suicide has been committed and the death drive to the total destruction of the symbolic universe awaits. A summative statement reads:

> "Woman is a symptom of man" means that *Man himself exists only through woman qua his symptom*: all his ontological consistency hangs on, is suspended from, is "externalized" in his symptom. In other words, man literally *exists*: his entire being lies "out there," in woman. Woman, on the other hand, does not exist, she insists, which is why she does not come to be only through man. Something in her escapes the relation to Man, the reference to the phallic enjoyment; and, as is well – known, Lacan endeavored to capture this excess by the notion of a "*non-all feminine jouissance*" (1993b:188, author's italic).

Žižek (1993b:6-67) makes the startling argument that self-consciousness itself is the *objet petit a*, an impossible place of occupation by, as a gaze which attempts to perceive the true meaning of the *sinthome*. But that place is the very non-being of the subject, meaning that "gender trouble" will always be with us. The place of this writing should be, therefore, an identification with and a yielding to, woman as my symptom: as "Freud's *wo es war, soll ich werden*. You, the subject must identify yourself with the place where your symptom already was..." (ibid.) Woman, as man's *sinthome* lies beyond fantasy in the sense that fantasy "implies *the choice of thought at the expense of being*; in fantasy I find myself reduced to the evanescent point of thought [pure *cogito*] contemplating the course of events during my absence, my nonbeing—in contrast to symptom, which implies the *choice of being*, since … what emerges in a symptom is precisely the thought which was lost,'repressed,' when we chose being" (1993b:64, original italic).

To reiterate the "impossibility" of men *in* feminism, an obvious male rumination, is to paraphrase Freud's own chauvinism: "women are impossible to bear, a source of external nuisance, but still, they are the best thing we have of their kind; without them, it would be even worse. So, if woman does not exist, man is perhaps simply a women who thinks that she does not exist" (Žižek, 1989a:75). Perhaps, put less pejoratively, "it is compatible to suggest that 'women' don't exist - while maintaining a politics of 'as if they existed'—since the world [of men] behaves as if they unambiguously did" (Riley, 1988:112). In the end, i come to a realization that there is no answer to the perplexing question of men *in* feminism, rather the feminist discourses i paid attention to is embedded in the entire social system—the (my)nefield of sexual rhetorics which have"real" effects, but not of our own choosing. These *sexual rhetorics* play themselves out around a complex dialectic between an illusionary essentialism (the I) and a disillusionary anti-essentialism (the i) for all possible gender constructions within the confines of institutional discourses. The politics of publishing and critique alluded to in my preface already speak to this. Having said this, the hypercomplexity of it all can never be totalized by any One. What I/i have learned from Žižek is that the true meaning of my stain, my *sinthome* can never be discovered, for the I/i cannot truly gaze at myself since it is the product of my very self-awareness. All I/i can do is process myself in illusionment, in mis-recognition.

Standing on the Bridge over the Crack or S(p)(l)ace in the Mirror

So where is this space/place for such writing to be found? If a subject needs to be "stable" in order to be political—what socially constructed masculinity does this "I" represent? From where does it write/rite/right? Is it a "place" or "space" at all? Do spatial metaphors even apply to it? It would be presumptuous for me to know such answers. This journey is not a particularly good exemplar of 'standpoint' theory, although i do describe my social location. i have tried to imagine that this space/place of writing, of which the I is not consciously aware, comes from a location which escapes any description. It can only be pointed to. The word "point" carries with it a double meaning: as location and a direction. In this section i should like to point to this sublime s(p)(l)ace by describing several art-texts which have been pointed at by other critics and writers as instances which are beyond 'that'

fig. 1 Velázquez, *Las Meninas* (1656)

which frames them. i hope that the sheer excessiveness of my "writing points," point to the s(p)(l)ace of the impossibility of knowing my *sinthome*—Woman in any direct way. The difficulty begins with the paradox of trying to "be" where I am not. "Or, as Lacan would put it, there is no I without a stain: 'I am' only insofar as *I am not where I think*, that is to say, only in so far as the picture I am looking at contains a stain which condenses the decentered thought—only insofar as this stain remains a stain, i.e., insofar as I do not recognize myself in it, insofar as I am not there, in it, For this reason, Lacan returns again and again to the notion of anamorphosis: I perceive 'normal' reality only insofar the point at which the 'it thinks' remains a formless stain" (Žižek,

29

1993b:66, my italic). What you are about to read in the following anecdotes remains an anamorphic distortion. If it weren't so, i would claim to be occupying a place where "I am where I think," in other words self-consciousness as self-transparency rather than the irreducible *kernel* or stain that it is. "I am aware of myself only insofar as outside me a place exists where the truth about me is articulated" (p.67). Paradoxically in modernism, the "I am" (feminine *cogito*, subject, thought) has to vanish for the "I think" (masculine cogito, object, being) to emerge, thus producing the illusion of mimesis as exemplified by "realism" and the humanist subject—the self-reflection in the mirror as the self-transparency of, "I am where I think" (what Derrida has referred to as "mimetologism.") For the abolition of the spectatorial self to emerge in modernism meant that the abyss of pure subjectivity (the "I am") had to be voided.[19] In other words, the particularity of "I am" cannot be *counted*.[20] Women are not allowed to assert a *difference* within the language of patriarchy. However, one possible way of making women's "I am" heard is a writing in the future anterior, in a "kind of suspension, in a present that is not at ease with either

fig. 2 Giacometti, *Suspended Ball* (1930-31)

its past or its future" (Elam:1994:42). But the lesson learnt in the previous section concerning the simultaneity of the *cogito* is that it is already split. The two images may be apparently identical, but there is always a surplus that disrupts their specular unity. Visual (or linguistic) mimicry is never perfect because there is no self-contained unified referent to begin with which could be seamlessly reproduced. This difference, which splits seemingly identical reflections, Derrida called the problematic of the "trace," or in Gasché's (1986) formulation, the "taine" of the mirror—as "that" which makes the reflection possible. It is possible to grasp the

30

"absorption" of the subject in modernism and the "gap" in reflection by turning to examples from art.

David Carroll (1987), when discussing Foucault's *Order of Things,* locates this surplus s(p)(l)ace of mirrored reflection as an abyss. In *Las Meniñas,* (fig. 1) Velázquez, claims Carroll, has caught "the border between visibility and invisibility, at a moment when he can still be seen looking out at his model and just before he moves behind his painting in order to paint his model which is hidden from view" (p.62). Between those two glances lies the s(p)(l)ace of the imaginary. A closer examination of the point of view present in this painting reveals that Velázquez was painting a self-portrait of himself painting. Queen Izabella and Philip IV, who appear in the rear view mirror of the painting, make it appear as if they are the spectators Velázquez paints. But in fact, they act as mere stand-ins: Velázquez' ruse was to appease royalty, yet present himself as the true artist creator and spectator. A good example of bourgeois **en-soi** consciousness, i should think. But their position is more than this, for they confirm upon Velázquez the position of subject; placed anamorphically in his field of vision—to the side, so to speak—they witness him painting. He is caught by them in the very moment of *looking* Carroll describes. They *look* at him from the very position he cannot see himself. In other words, they occupy the place of the *gaze* in Lacanian terms: I am *seen,* therefore I am.

The celebrated discussion of Velázquez' *Las Meniñas* by Foucault (1970:3-16) has become the paradigm case to illustrate the elisions of the classicist epistemé; between the subject who looks and the illusionary objective representation being looked at (see Owens, 1982; Searle, 1980; Snyder and Cohen, 1980).[21] i personally like the description Leo Steinberg (1991) inflects when reading this painting. Through his notion of "vital presence" Steinberg gives over to the painting the possibility of it being a mysterious, uncanny object which animates the viewer's eye, captivating and keeping its audience spellbound, like that unattainable figure of "Woman" *gazing* at me. "If the picture were speaking instead of flashing, it would be saying: I see you seeing me—I in you see myself seen—see you seeing yourself being seen—and so on beyond the reaches of grammar. Confronted mirrors we are, polarized selves, reflecting one another's consciousness without end; partaking of an infinity that is not spatial, but psychological—an infinity not cast in the outer world, but in the mind that knows and knows itself known. The mirror within *Las Meninas* is merely its central emblem, a sign for the whole. *Las Meninas* in its entirety is a metaphor, a mirror of consciousness" p.54). What Steinberg is referring to is the *mise en abyme* of the mirror within the picture plane itself. According to Benjamin (1991:13-17) the device of using such mirrors struc-

fig.3 Max Ernst, *A Little Girl Dreams of Taking the Veil* (1930)

tures the possibility of interpretation in advance of the act of interpretation itself. The observer of *Las Meninas* immediately assumes that the king and queen are looking on. However, once it is realized that their reflection can't possibly be the one Velázquez was painting, the observer is sent reeling into a spin, destabilized in his/her inability to grasp the object. The subject becomes "subjected" to a representation that exceeds it. This is a "fall," so to speak, into the labyrinth or abyss of the mirror.

Abels (1990:64-68) refers to the theory of Hermann Ullrich Asemissen's analysis of *Las Meninas*, who claims that Velázquez used a mirror to aid the conceptualization of his painting. Asemissen identifies a painting of the Infanta Margarita painted in 1655 and compares it to Velázquez's Infanta painted in 1659, and claims that her face was painted in reverse in *Las Meninas*. In other words, Velázquez is looking out into a mirror of the painted scene. Abels sums up Asemissen's hypothesis in the following way:

> In a doubled sense, Velázquez shows [us] when he paints
> the reality of the mirror in *Las Meninas*, that this picture is
> an image of the painter and the mirror. He draws the
> observer into the "trap" [s(p)(l)ace] of the mirror. The

observers think they can discover the invisible in the visible of the mirrored picture and not in the visibility of the picture itself. Velázquez plays with the illusion and reality of the mirror. According to the mirror (which is something that is invisible) he is painting the reality of *Las Meninas*. In the mirror, the one which is visible in *Las Meninas*, he paints the non-reality of the king and queen. This doubled invisibility becomes visible—in the mirror (of the king and queen) and as a refection (of *Las Meninas*). Implicit in the self-reference of the reflection is the self-reference of producing the picture, "it is the scene of meaning itself, which is glanced by the entire picture, and it is the image of *Las Meninas* which is being produced in the picture of *Las Meninas*" (pp.66-67).[22]

Taking a similar posture, Krauss's (1988; 1993: 165-167) focus is on Giacometti's surrealist work, *Suspended Ball* (1930-31), fig.2. Her textual reading is an updating of this same elision, but with a difference. In this case she claims that Giacometti has problematized the tension between the enunciated and the enounced positionalities. His is a deconstructed object, an undecidable; an attempt to demonstrate the difference from the modernist rhetoric, like that of Greenberg, who would claim that there is a pure instantaneity of looking—"the abstract condition with no before and no after," "pure transparency," "pure self-knowledge through an optical illusion when vision is connected to its object" (p.52, 53). Here the viewer is positioned in an oscillation, a back-and-forth rhythmic arc resulting in the undecidability of the gender form of an "orb rhythmically sliding over the recumbent form of a wedge" (p.62). This undecidability presents the observer with an understanding that there is a border, which is really an abyss, appearing as a "simultaneity of separation and intactness of figure and ground" (ibid). The difference, however, does not exist *between* the orb and wedge, but exists within them. "Far from constituting the text's unique identity, it is *that* which subverts the very idea of identity" (Johnson, 1980: 220-221, my italic). i point to this art-text to metaphorically capture my own dilemma in this study; my own oscillation between Woman as an object of my desire (as a gaze in the Real), and woman as an empirical historical subject (as my look in the symbolic order, or big Other), both caught within the oppressive structures of "postcapitalist" patriarchy. This oscillation exists throughout my text; i pay attention to psychoanalytic discourse as well as materialist feminist positions, or at least i claim to be trying to do so.

Krauss (1988) provides yet another, perhaps more interesting image from where such "blind" self-reflexive deconstructed moment of desire of Woman may at least be inferred by describing the central image of a Max Ernst collage novel, *A Little Girl Dreams of Taking the Veil* (1930), fig. 3. A little girl is shown caught in the middle of a zootrope while on the inside of the drum segments of a dove in flight are shown. This image is that of a "dreamer as a spectator or witness to the scene of the dream as a stage on which he himself or she herself is acting, so that the dreamer is simultaneously protagonist within and viewer outside the screen of his or her own vision..." (p.59). The zootrope, in this case, acts like a Möbius strip, which in a Lacanian paradigm provides the ever changing interface between the Imaginary and the Symbolic. The little girl stands in the Real of her desire, in the space of "nothingness"; caught by the fascinations of the flickering doves in flight. Such a description is similar to Lacan's "mirror stage." One must infer identity from the advantage created by this doubled or split s(p)(l)ace.[23] Max Ernst used the zootrope to illustrate how it might be that experience from outside of the drum, which appears to be unified, created by projecting a light source through its slots (metaphorical for the Cartesian subject of the Enlightenment that shines his light on the world), be juxtaposed with the experience of the inside, where the same animated image has been broken down into discrete serial components (the rhebus of a dream). But, argues Krauss, this unification of the experience of both inside and outside occurs on a *beat* or *pulse*. It happens when both eyes are closed, so to speak—in a blink. What is being problematized is the gap, the abyss—*an illusionary opaque screen*—which can, intellectually at least, be identified as existing between the oscillations of the inside and outside, between the enunciated "i" and the enounced "I." It is this gap, Ernst's veil, this opaque screen (Silverman, 1992: 147-150) which is denied so that life seems to be led "normally, naturally." This screen, this elision, this opaque veiled curtain that Lacan first problematized during his XI seminar (1979), deconstructing the mastery of the Cartesian Eye, is precisely what modernism was blind to; an impulse which eventually reached an impasse through the mechanization of vision, the processes of bureaucratization which set in motion regimes of surveillance, institutionalization and commercialization after the turn of the century (see Pollock, 1987: 104). In brief, the deconstructed moment always seems to elude the artist when creating, although an artist like Hans Holbein, Lacan's paradigmatic example of the anamorphic look, and other artists like Velázquez, Giacometti, René Magritte (see The Masculine Desire of the Imaginary in this text) tried to do "otherwise," by providing a displaced viewing position from which we might look awry (Žižek, 1991; Krauss,1993).

The contemporary problem of reflection and the s(p)(l)ace of writing desire is not confined to the humanities alone. Floyd Merrell (1985: 38ff.) points to the same problem of "undecidables" in micro-physics. I am reminded of an analogous problematic brought out in the field of quantum physics. Quarks appear to blink on and off, emerging and disappearing from nowhere into somewhere—as though yet another dimension existed which has escaped surveillance. Then there is the paradoxical finding of the Alain-Aspect experiment where two particles that have been split apart in opposite directions change their spin either "up" or "down" according to how one or the other particle has been affected by a magnetic field. A non-causal connection exists between them that happens faster than the speed of light. Bentov's highly readable and entertaining book, *Stalking the Wild Pendulum* (1977), posits a similar possibility, asking the question, what "happens" to an ordinary pendulum when it hesitates and stops at the top of its swing before it begins swinging back? That infinitesimal moment of hesitation seems to step outside the known (seen?) universe. Perhaps, as has been often surmised, this is where the abyss of human unconscious desire hides? The s(p)(l)ace of the Lacanian Real. Perhaps it is a dimension faster than the speed of light which provides the clues to stepping outside ocularcentrism and the en-light-ened tradition: the s(p)(l)ace of fascination. Perhaps space and time here are warped and contorted? Such musings seem distant from the problems of self-reflectivity and feminism. They belong in the realm of science fiction's hyperspace. But do they? Not if the question of my own fascination remains impossible to answer. Harding (1987), Bleier (1984), Keller (1985) and Lloyd (1984) have made a strong case for equating rationality with the Man of the enlightenment and hence denying the recesses of such thought.[24] And although they have not, as yet, offered a sufficient vision for a counter scientific paradigm based on feminist principles, speculations such as these are becoming increasingly important, reviving Gnostic traditions long since leveled by the many forms of phallogocentric religions centered on unitary transcendental signifiers like Zeus, Allah, Yahweh. The response by ecofeminists, it seems to me, has managed to raise such questions, if only to have substituted one transcendental signifier for another - that of the Goddess.[25]

It is these sorts of speculations which make postmodernists like Lyotard claim an undefinable and non-categorical dimension for art. Adorno is referred to again and again as providing an aesthetic theory which sets up the very resistance of art to be easily assimilated and consumed. Krauss's (1988) review of Lyotard's theorizations on this problem, as developed in his book, *Discourse, Figure*, makes the case that Giacometti's *Suspended Ball* might well be an example of a *différend*, a work of art that "unfulfils" desire, which provides a conceptual access to an invisible "matrix" of the unconscious. Matrix (Fr. *matrice*; Latin, *matrix*—meaning womb) has two meanings here: an environment or substance around which something is developed and a mould in which a thing is cast or shaped as in printing type. Since this "matrix," according to Lyotard, cannot be understood as structure, it can only be conceptualized as an anti-structural enabling force which aids in transforming everything into its opposite. The positing of such a matrix, once again, hints at a realm that ties up disparate parts at the level of unconscious fantasy, the "scene" of the fantasy, making such fragments function *en bloc* in conscious form.

David Carroll's *Paraesthetics* (1987) is also an attempt to explicate this inferred dimension through the writing of Lyotard, Foucault and Derrida. It becomes quickly apparent how difficult it is to talk about "that" desire which has no words, and in the end seems like non-sense. To write the relationship of men *in* feminism as a *différend* would be to present a limit-case of an impossible resolution, best done through the arts. Men *in* feminism cannot *figure*, in Lyotard's sense. "They" may only be inferred. It bring me into the realm of Freudian *Unheimlich*, the uncanny and strange space where "what ought to have remained ... secret and hidden" is brought to light. Perhaps "men *in* feminism" is *the* women's joke? "Male philosophers writing as woman, male critics reading as a woman, men on feminism - what is it all about? Clearly it is a *hommage* (the pun is too tempting not to save it), but for what end?" (de Lauretis, 1987a:21). De Lauretis' use of the word "clearly," belies her own rhetorical slip, for nothing is "clear" in men's apparent appropriation of feminist theory. But she does point to an unobtainable desire of Woman as a *sinthome* for a heterosexual man.

And now . . . *Écriture Masculine,*
Écriture Homosexuelle . . . you don't say!

Are men capable of writing with "white ink?" Milk is not our body fluid but our nourishment. Then again, should semen be our substitute? It is a short step to metaphorically equate the penis with the pen as Gilbert and Gubar (1979:6-7) have done. There is a short film, *Life Lessons* (1988), directed by Martin Scorsese which presents Linel Dobie (Nick Nolte) as an aging abstract expressionist living in New York, who must fall in love with his model-assistants in order to have the energy to continue to paint.[26] Jeff Koons' antics have earned him the reputation as "America's premiere bad boy artist," preserving masculine dominance with his unabashed sexism in such works as *Naked* (1988), which reasserts the mysogyny of the Garden of Eden. Then there are the artworks of Matthew Barney, who uses materials that literally refer to male body fluids, an *écriture masculine*, if you will.[27] But to slip into such metonymic displacements of body parts to assign gender difference has its dangers of biological essentialism.[28] Yet, it seems irresponsible to avoid the biological (genetic) discourse, especially when one can read the evidence which can only make one pause for a very long time as to its possibilities (see esp. Midgley, 1988; Konner, 1982, Chap. 6). i suspect that there is an extraordinarily complex relationship between biology and the social construction of gender. And while there is no "essential body" to be found, how the interrelationships between new modes of gendered consciousness made possible through inventive language, the changes in modes of communication, and the shifts in consciousness affect *actual physical changes* is barely understood. The cumulative effects of such a dialectic can only be seen over a broad historical span of time.[29]

The complications between the economies of difference between sex and gender, each being separate but intimately related (Rubin, 1984), are further enhanced when the heterosexual/homosexual binary is evoked. A different economy of the body is in play with homosexual desire. Bredbeck (1992) argues for a *homosexual écriture,* but one which is governed by a *constitutive* mimesis rather than a *specular* one. In other words, Bredbeck posits the possibility of a constitutive body formed by the dialectic of biology and culture i alluded to above. Rather than a writing *from* or *of* the body, he argues for a writing *with* the body. Writing *with* the body is validated by its own materiality. "[W] e are writing with its odors, the effects of the body which can be perceived like smells, but are never reified" (p. 100). He claims that Irigaray and Cixous are still caught by a spectacular or inscribed body despite the claims of their own rhetoric. The distinction Bredbeck makes is that *l'écriture féminine* finds security in the body as a *thing*, while he suggests that power in the body needs to be found as *process.* Again, in keeping with my dance motif, Bredbeck refers to Andrew Holleran's *Dancer from the Dance* as an illustration of what he means by the body's materiality in process. Sullivan, the pseudo-drag campy orchestrator says, "we live in a rude and dangerous time in which there are no values to speak to and one can only cling to concrete things - such as cock" (p. 95, in Bredbeck, 1992:100). i find it difficult to see how Bredbeck is any more successful with this ruse in processing such a written body. He may be referring to the dangerous time of the AIDS epidemic. Many gay artists, who are HIV-positive and face their own mortality, have used their blood in their artistic statements; while others have refused to represent their lovers photographically as dehumanized asexual human beings. Perhaps here lies their specular refusal.

The fundamental relationship men have with their mothers is not something that is universally fixed either. i am not convinced that the Oedipus complex is universal, but itself is a product of recent bourgeois history. Rather i am more sympathetic to anthropologists like Wenda Trevathan (1987) who distinguishes at least five evolutionary shifts in this relationship.[30] Psychoanalysis (both its Freudian and Lacanian variants) have often tried to explain Oedipalization as if it were an ahistorical construct.[31] i am suspicious that as the postmodern age continues to redefine motherhood through various reproductive technologies, psychoanalytic explanations will continue to be rewritten and morphed into something new. As it stands now, a great deal of conceptual mileage becomes possible by applying Oedipalization transculturally and transhistorically because it seems that there are no other comprehensive explanations for desire. The myth of Medusa (witch, hag, bitch, sorceress) becomes a tale of men's inabilities to face their M(others).[32] In the Freudian discourse, the fear of castration leaves us projecting a split image of her. She is either a *femme fatale*, the destroyer of men, the possessor of the evil eye (Siebers, 1983), or a caring virgin—an angel of mercy, there for emotional support. But as the Medusa, she is transformed into a frightening figure with phallic snakes for hair. Should a man directly gaze into her eyes, her look turns him into stone, evaporates his ego, returns his sadistic gaze. It appears that only powerful, dominant women can play the Medusa role. Her reputed chthonic powers provide agency in the tradition of Mae West and Marlene Dietrich, carried to popular heights by Madonna and controversial claims by Camille Paglia (1990). If she is today's executive, she is to be feared for her combative competencies.[33] As the phallic mother, men can only look at Medusa at a distance or see her reflection in a mirror. Paraclesus had to use his shield as a mirror to reflect her gaze and, in turn, dominate her, by reversing her gaze and turning her into stone. Once "decaptivated," her head now becomes an object of fetishization; a displacement of the original anxiety created by the sight of her different body as man's castrated Other. The male searches for that perfect face to displace his castration anxiety. It is a face devoid of aging and frozen in time—caught within the frame of a photograph—like the never-changing face of Garbo (Barthes, 1973:56).

M(asking) Myself

The tension between the two (I)(i)'s is informed by the subjectivity of the face. The graphically marked upright "I," is subject to language and the Symbolic Law, while the lower case "i," appearing ubiquitously throughout writing as just another vowel, "in the order of things," helps to differentiate and defer one signifier from another. It takes on its own graphic meaning when isolated and related to uprightness of the pillar and pedestal of its omniscient Other. The suspended dot that spatially quivers above this, somewhat reduced pedestal, is a reminder of a struggling subject, whose articulation always questions the text it finds itself in—a point that cannot come to rest. It is a subject who wishes to produce yet another "voice" within him, one that he cannot speak as yet. Hopefully not the voice of phonocentrism, a Husserlian monodialogue which speaks only to itself, as critiqued by Derrida (1973:32-47), rather that middle voice that falls between the "I" of the writing and the "i" of speaking; a timbre which, in a *de facto* sense, tries to maintain the propriety and wholeness of the dispersed field of subject positions which play a myriad number of discourses. Will such a voice be written in my journey? (I)(i) wish i were less skeptical.

In the best hyperbolic fashion i am likely to muster the following impossible image emerges: such writing, if found, would play on the border of being both inside and outside of feminism at the same time; a paradoxical and impossible maleman's role which avoids a "dirty" sexual in and out, which may only reveal itself in moments of hallucinatory exhaustion of vertiginous play when both difference and sameness have been recognized. This subject is then no longer graphically placed as an "eye." The two (I)(i)s and the abyss (or opaque screen) that separates them constitute a contorted face where each (I)(i) revolves in its opposite direction—each looking for the other on an asymmetrical playing field. How is it that (I)(i) am scene/seen by others? This is one mask my face might wear. There are others when trying to "figure out" how to put myself in the picture (see esp. Jo Spence, 1988). Another possible mask comes from the image of the spectroscope. Here my two (I)(i)'s see each other—look across each other over the fault line of two disjointed plancs; each eye sees a different picture, but whose superimposition is never exact enough to make up an uncomplicated mimetic picture, but shifts the looking "elsewhere." Can such writing, as double-play, attempt to look in two directions, or two different planes at once in order to examine the gap between complete agency (freedom, à la Sartre) and domination? (overdetermination, à la Althusser) (cf. Smith, 1988:150).[34] Is this gap located not *between* the (I)(i)'s, as was thought, but in the *back* of the head?—as the *taine* of the mirror as Gasché (1986) would say? Is the *new face* to be informed by difference and negativity? Perhaps it is a series of different masks which oscillate at different distances: from afar, moving to the face and through it to the back of my head. Who can answer?

Impossible Positionality

*What I want to look at here is the new kind of
gender tourism, whereby male theorists are able
to take package trips into the world of femininity*
(Moore, 1988:167).

Having discussed the likelihood of not finding an appropriate voice
or place of men *in* feminism, it is somewhat more reassuring to describe the
political sight/site/cite from which the I does write; that of a white, middle
class, heterosexual male of Polish descent, forty something, who has taught
predominantly in university departments which (at the University of Alberta,
Alberta, Canada) are constituted predominantly by white middle to upper-
class professors who teach to a middle to upper-class heterogeneous student
population from various ethnic backgrounds. All in all, a remarkably apt
description of what is said to ail the West—white male privilege. But is *this*
what defines me? Is this my "politics of identification?" (Alcoff, 1988a:432).
Is this who "I" am? Hardly. This allusion to positionality refers to Braidotti's
(1987) observation in *Men in Feminism* of the uncomfortableness of males
being "white, middle-class intellectual[s] at a time in history when minorities and oppressed groups are speaking up for themselves; a hegemony when
the white knowing subject is crumbling" (p. 235). i wonder how she escapes
this accusation, given her university post in Holland? In her categorization
this "I" belongs to the "post-beat, pre-yuppie 28-45-year old men" who have
"been through" the upheavals of the 1960s and have inherited the values of
the neuroses of that period. According to Braidotti, "they" are the "new men"
in the "post-feminist" context of the politically reactionary 1980s. "They" are
the best male friends we've got, and "they" are not really what we had hoped
for" (ibid). Yes, i do admit to being an "ex-hippie." Guilty as charged. As much
as her statement "smarts," as if this "I" was being scolded by his Mother, such
an accusatory finger cannot be entirely dismissed. Given the politics of my
location (see Probyn, 1990), "I" have it pretty good in academia. Despite the
talk of action research between the university and the community, there is a
distance between the university and the everyday reality of working lives
caught in the wheels of capitalism that undeniably exists. Russell Jacoby (1987)
once asked whether intellectuals had all but disappeared from the universities, turning their efforts toward technocratic and bureaucratic thought. i

would like to believe otherwise."I" accept the belief that theory acts as a material force as well. The "I" has to believe this, otherwise this i could not write on.

In her forthright dismissal of men in feminism, Braidotti asks a key question: "What is being exorcised by male thinkers in their act of becoming 'feminized'?" (p. 237). Her answer is rather surprising: envy. The envy a male experiences in his mid-life crisis. "I" hope that i am not one of the "they" Braidotti goes on to condemn, nor that my difference means separation from other differences with males of color, ethnicity, and sexuality. Yet I do fit her "make," and wonder why feminism should be guarded from my contamination. And because of the academic star system that demands its own forms of entertainment—like the guest lecture circuit—envy is front and center in many cases. Gayatri Spivak (cited in Showalter, 1987:118) is skeptical of such men as well. Her admonishment is summed up as: "'they' are unlikely to engage in race and class struggles so 'they' turn to the woman's struggle where 'they' can get a hearing in the (safe) confines of an academic institution."[35] Ouch! In English departments, especially, feminist criticism is then likely to undergo "correction" by male authorities, while men *in* feminism are likely to undergo "correction" by feminists. There is the danger of being reduced (more likely ridiculed?) as playing out a "Tootsie" trope as Marguerite Waller (1987) claims of Stephen Greenblatt's attempt at an ideological analysis of Renaissance studies. Waller accuses Greenblatt for his failure to allow its feminist intentions to alter the male-centered mode of signification. Like Sidney Pollock's film *Tootsie* (1982), Greenblatt's text is unselfconsciously sexist. i wonder if mine is as well?

It seems to me that such guarded positions remain as "erections," still trapped by phallogocentric authority they themselves dismiss; preventing men from actively engaging feminism with the "proper" proposition of the preposition. Butler's (1990) warning note: "The theories of feminist identity that elaborate predicates of color, sexuality, ethnicity, class, and ablebodiness invariably close with an embarrassed "etc." at the end of the list. ... This is a sign of exhaustion as well as of the illimitable process of signification itself. It is the *supplement*, the excess that necessarily accompanies any effort to posit identity once and for all" (p.143). That excess is what cannot be described but happens after the journey. It is left up to the spoken subject, the audience(s). Agency, argues Butler, is not answered through recourse to an "I" that pre-exists signification. There is as much power of admonishment given to women who are in positions of authority as men. The pejorative phase for Margaret Thatcher continues to be "The Iron Lady" who did irreparable damage to the social fabric of England. Does the authority assigned to the political location overshadow the gender distinction? I think so. If the cite/site/sight[36] of a location in a larger system has been historically shaped by masculine competitive values, is the character of that location overdetermined by that discourse despite color, gender, or class? Again, I suspect so. If it were remotely possible, would an Aboriginal woman prime minister of Canada with a similar conservative platform like Thatcher make a difference in changing the political direction of this country? I doubt it. She probably would be more sympathetic to Native rights, but there would be limits to the changes her party platform would allow. Such an outrageous question problematizes any naive essentialist and dichotomous equation between gender and stereotypical masculine and feminine qualities. Men are no more innately competitive or domineering than women who are said to be innately cooperative and compliant.

Perhaps my steps over the (my)nefield should be envisioned as "moments" of an autobiographical confession; a self-conscious narrative which represses as many insights as it claims to reveal. This is the tactic i have chosen knowing fullwell, of course, that such introspection is itself a middle-class preoccupation. These reflections are, in this sense, vivid memories, both painful and pleasurable, "subject" to psychoanalytic readings by others. Spanning more than a decade, they chronicle (not in any particular order) what the I perceives to be key experiences in my relationship with feminist discourse; an I who has already been positioned and overdetermined by a white mythology[37]—framing my very horizon. The following vignettes/anecdotes present distinctive "hinge" transformations of my own praxis as a "subject" in process. Roughly, they begin with a liberalist stance, becoming more acceptive of the radical difference in the profusion of debates between Marxists and social feminists, and most recently i have shifted to poststructuralist and psychoanalytic positions, recognizing that feminism itself, as a heterogeneous movement, disperses the subject over a wide playing field. Queer theory and the men's movement inform this journey as well, for without these conversations, i would not face the question of homophobia that is so ubiquitous throughout society. But that attitude is changing as well.

This last posture, that of poststructuralism and psychoanalysis, has been, for me, the most rewarding and the most frustrating given that this historical moment is embellished by a media society which circulates representation through its numerous signifying technologies. Once the skepticism has been purged that poststructuralism is an apolitical stance, and the availability of the referent may be recalled through the focus on personal experience and the material conditions which define its boundaries, *if only for a moment to "fix" the subject in process*, i have found a 'deconstructive' stance which still honors experience promising.

Autobiographical Confessional Vignettes

> Being an incomplete female,
> the male spends his life attempting
> to complete himself,
> to become female.
>
> *(Valerie Solanas in The Scum Manifesto, 1967:6)*

> Males are simply modified females
> tailored to a particular role in the
> reproductive process.
>
> *(Jeremy Cherfas and John Gribbin, The Redundant Male, 1984:54)*

> Vignette: 1, a short descriptive
> essay or character sketch. 2, an
> illustration or decorative design.
> 3, a photograph or portrait showing
> only the head and shoulders
> with the background gradually
> shaded off.

To "exploit" negativity and difference within the two (I)(i)s requires an auto(bio)graphical confession. All writing is "autobiographical" argues de Man (1979), but an autobiography never tells the truth knowingly. It *lies* since it is impossible for a subject to speak directly to itself. According to de Man, autobiography was defined by the rhetorical trope prosopopoeia: "the fiction of an apostrophe to an absent, deceased, or voiceless entity, which posits the possibility of the latter's reply and confers upon it the power of speech" (p.920). Autobiography may be "specular structure," as he suggests, but such vignettes/anecdotes are also "fragments" where my "I" is placed in a para-doxical position against the very doxa (opinion) which frames the "natural" discourses of the symbolic realm that overdetermine me as a maleman in my location. Both pleasure and pain emerge in the unraveling, deframing, and revelation, or "ideological tearing," of my autobiographical remembrances. Such remembrances are like surgical scalpels that transfigure my *face* in process. They colligate tensions (resistances and rebellions) which are the product of having to adopt any number of subject-positions (m(asks)) throughout this ten-year period. To state a paradox: the "I" is not the same today as then, and yet it is. The taine of my unconscious, like a mystic (magic) writing board, is traced by desires, memories, repressions, and anxieties. My contradictions manifest themselves as (I)(i) articulate my needs and interests in relation to feminism, to questions raised by gay and lesbian theorists, and to my differentiations from other masculine positions. But if "[a]utobiography veils a defacement of the mind of which it is itself the cause" (de Man, 1979:930), how then do i, as an "I," engage the world (Reality) and myself simultaneously? Am (I)(i) condemned to perpetual deferment and impossibility?

Autobiographical confessions obviously allude to a number of previous male writers, especially Montaigne who initiated a humanist centered ego through his reflections on the autobiographical self. There is, of course, Descarte's *Confessions* and St. Augustine's confessions, who, according to Charles Norris Cochrane's reading of St Augustine (Kroker and Cook, 1987:35ff.) is said to have begun the autobiographical discourse of the modern age as far back as the 4th century AD! This is contrary to the usual interpretation which valued self-analysis, *not for its own sake,* but as a way of showing the fallibility of humanity and affirming an unreachable authority of divine knowledge, i.e., secularized as a radical doubt. The Kantian subject could never realize this moral Ideal. It was a dutiful asymptotic process; an ethical act tortured by the possibility that its motivation came for the wrong reasons, from some hidden pathological concern for fame or respect. The ethical status of confessional striving was defined, *by necessity,* as subject to uncertainty and doubt (see Žižek, 1993b:71). It was also this confessional mode of the Church, according to Foucault, which furthered the discourse of science, and confined sexual discourse to intimate, secretive spaces by putting to scrutiny that which was said. This emphasis was most clearly articulated in Protestantism (i.e., Puritanism in England, Pietism in Germany, Calvinism in Holland) which placed such a high value on an individual's struggle to achieve salvation through the recording of one's daily thoughts and actions, i.e., self-scrutiny, self-analysis to reach the perfection of God. From such a foundational discourse, intimacy and self-understanding were articulated by the bourgeoisie. The first order of confession, as a repentance for breaking the law, was superseded by its reinterpretation as a private assertion of freedom. In the search for autonomy, what could be found were the constraints of ideological systems. The problem of overdetermination emerged, resulting in the ambivalences of self-image.

Overdetermination and agency are yet another variation of the two (I)(i)'s. To chart the course between them has been the recent work of Giddens' (1979) notion of 'structuration.' Giddens' structuration theory charts a course between a self-determining ego and an overdetermined structure. "The concept of structuration involves that of the duality of structure, which relates to the fundamentally recursive character of social life, and expresses the mutual dependence of structure and agency" (p. 69). This is certainly one way to proceed. However, it was Barthes' (1986/1970) attempt to write 'an intransitive verb' and his *A Lover's Discourse* (1979) which are the most relevant attempts for me concerning autobiography, especially his notions concerning the loss of self, disruption of comfort, loss of control, and escaping the expected social frame. "The 'I' of the text ... [becomes] both a person and a scene" (Wright, 1984:124). But this "I" is unable to feign the subject as well as Barthes had. Occasionally there are *transgressive crossings* over lawful codes in my life, which try to keep the "I" subjected, but these are few. These transgressions provided Barthes with the release of *jouissance*,[38] but in my case i am not so sure whether the "I" has experienced the ecstasy of *jouissance* like some saint. The two (I)(i)s cannot mimic Barthes' masquerade, but then again the "I" is probably a bad cross-dresser, incapable of Barthes' ability of "making love to one's mother tongue" (Moore, 1988:168), or producing seductive slips of "indifference," according to Schor (1987a).

There is yet another allusion to the confessional which is a direct quotation of feminist autobiographical literature, especially of its middle-class roots.[39] Women's autobiographies are distinct from men's autobiographies, and from the current craze of Hollywood biographies of stars whose narratives tell the story of success, the climb towards privilege and stardom to become objects of envy, e.g., Joan Collins says she is a feminist, too. Rather, the feminist autobiographical focus is on details of domestic and personal life which are typically "fragmented, episodic, and repetitive, lacking the unifying linear structure imposed on life in pursuit of a public career" (Felski, 1989:86). This is said to be due to the lack of control by women over the direction of their lives, resulting from their confinement to the private sphere. i think this is a difficult statement to generalize given the public/private dichotomy has been deconstructed by the electronic invasions into our homes. Nevertheless, Felski argues that such ghettoization is responsible for the predominance of the episodic and journalistic type of structure rather than the synthesizing narrative which is found in men's autobiographies. Analogously, it is i who find myself fragmented when ad-dress-ing my relation to feminism. My narrative turns out to be equally episodic. It may well be because of this felt ambiguity, men must play *in* the question of their impossible relationship to feminism. It is hoped that these vignettes/anecdotes are seen as representations of specific problems and experiences of other men *in* feminism. Yet, they are too thinly developed when compared to feminist autobiographies. Most often they are pretenses to understanding broader social issues.

i am conscious that these vignettes/anecdotes may be "sweet nothings" spoken into a feminist ear. As Megan Morris (1988) says of her own use of anecdotes: "They are oriented futuristically towards the construction of a precise, local, and social discursive context, of which the anecdote then functions as *mise en abyme*" (p.7). Which of my (I)(i)'s is shocked out of smugness and cleverness by Moore's (1988:169) trenchant reminder that "[t]he valorization of feminine pleasure in Barthes' work [*jouissance*] ... fails to recognize that female sexuality is experienced differently, at different times, in different cultures?" Differences are yet to be "faced." i am also reminded by Nancy Miller's (1986b) remarks concerning Barthes' "borrowings" of the text as *hyphology*. The *hyphos*, as the tissue of the spider's web, is chosen over the spider, "and the concept of textuality called the 'writerly' chooses the threads of lace over the lacemaker" (p.271). "Hyphology" as "the discourse of the male weavers rhetorically stages 'woman' without in any way addressing women. This 'masculine recuperation' of the feminine is a variant of the phenomenon Alice Jardine has named *gynesis* – 'the putting into discourse of 'woman' – and Gayatri Spivak has described, somewhat differently as the 'double displacement'" (p.271). Nietzsche's allegorical figure of 'woman' as truth, now twice castrated as truth and non-truth, so that the ladies man can emerge.[40] In Miller's view, woman should not pose as a simulacrum, rather she *is* the spider who weaves her own web (see also Issak,1987).

There is also the last reminder by Bristow (1992) who points out that many autobiographical writings of straight men dealing with their masculinity are often uncritical and guilt ridden; written in a self-indulgent tone that repeats the very forms of egotism on which a more conventional masculinity is predicated.[41] Rarely do they engage the voice of their male "other" —gay writers. i have tried to redress that as well. Lastly, i feel insecure about my confessional mode because of its tackiness. Is this the best way to write/right/rite such a text? Am i like the fool who stepped into shit and hadn't realized it, employing conceptualizations only half-way understood? For that i must suffer any consequences, in the hopes that those who are more knowledgeable can live with my floundering. The scholarship may well be a pretense as well.

Feminism or pheminism - perhaps *Fe(man)*ism?

Throughout this pretext i have used the term "feminism," which obviously refers only to women's movements, but my title states "pheminism." Why? The last part of the title, "pheminism" borrows its de/re-formation from Rossi Braidotti's (1987:233) pejorative comment in *Men in Feminism*. The phallic sub-text is apropos if "men *in* feminism" is to be rightly entertained, for once again it is a reminder that my relationship remains an impossible one. Only certain alliances are possible. Perhaps fe(man)ism may have been the more accurate word, but this strikes me as too much a recoding and reappropriation. Its graphics suggest a man hiding in its insides, exhibiting "womb envy." Perhaps the selection of this title some six years ago was a fortuitous choice? The "ph" has allusions to phantasy. Given the deconstructive movements coming from gay and lesbian theorists and the continued questioning surrounding sexual identity which problematize the margins themselves (here i am thinking of transsexuality), "pheminism" sounds more and more appropriate rather than ironical as the whole playing field begins to shape-shift. "Pheminism" seems hybrid enough to let stand. i may be wrong? But it's done. *And it appears only in the closing paragraphs of the text.*

Scattered throughout this journey are remarks by women critics that men have not deconstructed their (pornographic?) imaginations (Jardine, 1987:61). Perhaps this is a lame start in the micro-politics of her question? What follows then is a montage of intersected explorations. i have tried to concentrate my questions, drawing on discourses in art, art education, cinema and cultural studies. Literary studies, where so much of these debates took place, is missing for a very good reason. The "I" doesn't live there. Films are in abundant supply. A subject in process happens on any number of registers simultaneously. The lived experience is only the starting point. "It is not individuals who have experience, but subjects who are constituted through experience. Experience in this definition then becomes not the origin of our explanation, not the authoritative (because it is seen or felt) evidence that grounds what is known, but rather what we seek to explain" (Scott, 1992:26). Scott's comment helps explain the *pretense* of my anecdotes. Some are minimally described so they can be interrogated theoretically by many other voices that have spoken to the concern raised. Some include bits of my own personal history; some are bits of essays written over the past ten years—never published, and now, when revived, they act like diary entries to understand my own changes; still others call on voices of feminism, gay and lesbian theorists, psychoanalysts who have made theoretical stances particularly clear to me. There are also what appear to be book reviews and historical tracts that were important to me in understanding the positionality of women in the Grand Male Tradition of art, and still other explorations have lead me to no exits. At the end there is an appendix: a performance art-text about my son, yet another register of confession at work.

So ends this pretext, or excuse; my disguised pretense of what the (I)(i) is about to do.

And why scriptease?
You will have to wait until all the articles have fallen off.
Why tacky?
I(i) show poor taste and lack style, and it is impossible not to slip on my own *banana* peel when speaking sex/gender. The current structures of grammar are simply inadequate, especially with *my* English.

[1] This manuscript was effectively finished before Boone and Cadden's edited book *Engendering Men: The Question of Male Feminist Criticism* (1991) was published. I have, however, incorporated their insights into this manuscript against my own response effectively finished in 1990 which grappled with a similar problematic. I wish my response to remain as a marker of my own subject-in-process regarding this question without the added burden of differentiating my response from those authors Boone and Cadden had solicited. They remain an anonymous body of men whom I suspect were raising similar questions at the end of the 80s. Why it took a full five years for this response to be published has been explained somewhat in my introductory preface.

[2] An extensive commentary is required here since the concept of "masquerade" is a key concept in feminist cinematic criticism. Doane has made the conceptualizations surrounding the notion of "masquerade" a central feature of her psychoanalytic musings over the representation of woman in cinema, recently extending it to include the use of the "veil" (1989) in cinema. Next to Laura Mulvey (1975), Doane's seminal essay (1982) stands as a benchmark in psychoanalytic feminist film theory. In that essay Doane explores the elisions Freud made when trying to understand women's difference. She begins her essay by examining the relationship between the deciphering of hieroglyphs and understanding of women alluded to by Freud who chastised his female audience when he read four lines out of context from a poem by Heine about the riddle of the nature of femininity. Hieroglyphs are said to be enigmatic and mysterious if their code is unknown. At the same time they are the most readable of all languages because of their iconicity; their status as a pictorial language where the referent and sign appear less arbitrary and hence "close." Women share this same contradictory status, argues Doane, but this analogy slips because iconicity cannot be maintained but requires some forms of generalizability, some distance in order *not* to be mired in the "concrete;" to be caught, as it were, in the literalness of things. Yet, if women's specificity - as a feminine specificity - is to be identified, it is precisely this closeness, this attachment to the body where the gap between signifier and signified vanishes which needs to be understood. But if the sign and its referent are "one," woman *is* mired in the materiality of her own body. So, while it may be true that "this sex is not one" in Irigaray's sense of dismissing the phallus as her unitary signifier (as it is for men), the woman is "one" with herself, autoerotically and metonymically based on the touching of her own "two lips." This reads as if she does not need a man to fulfill her own desires.

Doane gains conceptual mileage from this proximity/distance dichotomy by assigning the latter to male control of both the look (active spectatorship in its aberrant voyeuristic and fetishistic roles), as well as the cinematic apparatus in its ability to set design and arrange or block the woman into the ideal viewing position for the male spectator. Cinematic distance is once again asserted by presenting the woman as an impossible never attainable desire—as lack despite her full presence on the screen. This dichotomization, extended even further, rehearses by now, well-known distinctions. Because women are caught by their inability to distance themselves from themselves; because they must become objects of desire for men; because they are denied access to fetishization as a form of displacement from themselves, they must either identify with the masculine position, and thereby deny the specificity of their own desires, or attempt to develop a new language which vivifies the sense of touch and care, and a new cinematic apparatus as Mulvey believed (1975). Most often they are caught in an act of cross-dressing. They must oscillate back and forth, adopting a passive or masochistic position when identifying with a woman, and then simultaneously identifying with the active position of the male hero. Women, claims Doane, are the better cross-dressers. Female transvestism is easily worn by women, if you pardon the pun: butch/femme being one possible response of mastery over her image, thereby denying the possibility of attracting the male's gaze of desire by disrupting his fantasy.

Why then, would some women flaunt their femininity by producing its excesses and fall into the narcissism of hyperbolic femininity? This is what Doane means by "masquerade"- a constructed mask. Where a woman's "true" face ends and the mask begins remains an unanswered question; an impossible one to answer if woman continues to be constructed as man's Other. A masquerade already suggests a theft of masculine power in order to successfully compete amongst men if transvestism is to be denied. The masquerade turns out to be a coping or a survival mechanism; a mask for protection as well as manipulation. It becomes a way to gain the very distance that is required in everyday life, and at the same time, a denial of the production of femininity as closeness. It is most often removed at night or perhaps with other women. Without its protection, Doane suggests, hysteria becomes a possibility and might lead to the denial of the 'true self' (whatever that might be) by being everything for the Other; closeness transferred and delivered so completely into another's hands that any hints of refusal of reciprocation lead to total loss of bodily control. Coping mechanisms no longer exist. The surrender has become complete. When the mask is worn, however, it has its obvious dangers, for it both attracts (casts a spell) and must, at the same time, repel. There are then many possible masquerades. If the mask is put on a little too thick it crosses over the established sexual lines into a male "come-on" or into prostitution. This is the wholesale of the entire body as mask which dichotomizes closeness. Prostitutes rarely kiss their Johns or, if they are brothel "workers," they do not meet them in other circumstances as casual dates. Another masquerade is that of the *femme fatale,* like Marlene Dietrich with her obvious exaggerations of femininity.

Williams (1989:214-217) argues that Doane's defense of the masquerade against the overidentification with suffering and victimized woman is mistaken. The masquerade's function enacts an oscillation within sadomasochism, playing off passivity with activity and visa versa. It should be emphasized that Williams addendum is within a sadomasochistic relationship where an agreement between dominator and dominated has been made. The female viewer may be closer to identifying with a suffering female victim, but not condemned in losing herself though a total identification with her, i.e., "too close" in Doane's sense.

Female specificity theorized on spatial proximity is based on Freud's construction of "the subject supposed to know." Another name for this "penis envy." Because of the visibility of the penis there is a temporal gap between seeing and knowing for the boy. The threat of castration is registered as a "later" event for him. Upon seeing the female genitals for the first time he sees nothing, or disavows what he has seen. This primary event is re-read a second time when the threat of castration informs his subjectivity. The delay and the distance between the primary look and the subsequent threat in time enables the boy to invest the knowledge of disavowing what he has seen. In other words, the boy is able to disavow the girl's castration by displacing it with a fetishized object. Girls, on the other hand, lack any distance between seeing and knowing. They immediately know that they are castrated and hence want to have the penis. The woman is unable to fetishize easily since she overidentifies with the image. She can only "desire to desire" in Doane's sense (1987). They can only "fetishize" the penis by envying it.

Feminists have put Freud's "penis envy" to rout, turning the tables around and showing how this very construction is a way Freud disavowed his own fear of castration by claiming that women "lacked" when all along it was he who was lacking; after all, a girl's autoerotic desire could be satisfied through clitoral stimulation. Penis envy masked Freud's real fear of incest that would reveal female sexuality. It turned out that penis envy was itself a fetish while the denial of female fetishism was a way to deny female desire itself. Gamman and Makinen's (1994) study on female fetishism clearly shows this to be otherwise, however they raise the uncomfortable conclusion that postmodernist consumer culture produces a female subject position that is characterized by the very disavowal that is at the heart of fetishism. The woman oscillates in schizophrenic fashion between two subject positions: an expectation to construct herself as an object, as well as experience herself as a subject. In an age of simulacra femininity becomes artifice; the masquerade means that "femininity has no natural reality. ... In post-modern terms this means that gender is the perfect simulacrum — the exact copy of something that never existed in the first place" (p.217). Gamman and Makinen extend this thesis to men as well. "We feel that the concept of masquerade is just as appropriate to discussing masculinity (the average man knows he does not possess the phallus either, only a penis)" (p.217).

Gamman and Makinen's thesis points to a difficulty with Doane's masquerade hypothesis. On the one hand, to justify the masquerade, she acknowledges Freud's analysis that the knowledge of sexual difference is perceptually structured differently for girls than boys, but she then denies it, as if she changed her mind in the last moment: "The entire elaboration of femininity as a closeness, a nearness, as present-to-itself is not the definition of an essence but the delineation of a place culturally assigned to the woman" (p. 87). This quote, which appears on the very last page of her essay, is at odds with essentialist leanings of the French feminists whom she mentions to support her "closeness" hypothesis: Cixous, Irigaray, Kofman and Montrelay. The implication here is that dropping the masquerade is possible once a woman's language with a different cinematic apparatus is developed. But this suggests, to me at least, replacing a masculine bias with that of a feminine essentialist one. Would this be an art form where "closeness" rather than "distance" is valorized? Isn't Gilligan's (1982) "different voice" hypothesis built on this very distinction? Girls are morally superior because they have more "feeling," more "closeness" in Doane's terms? (see also Bick, 1992-1993).

Accepting a Freudian orthodoxy makes the masquerade a theoretical possibility; however Gamman and Makinen's study conclusively shows its theoretical weakness. Why masquerade in the first place, or was there ever a time such a masquerade didn't exist, for both men and women? Essentialism and the reading of the Oedipus myth as a universal invariant allows Paglia (1990) to turn around and claim all sexual encounters are "dangerous," subject to both victimization as well as blissful happiness among the sexes. It is no accident that her study begins with Egypt, a historical moment where the use of malachite green for women's eyes, as well as jewelry and elaborate clothing was empirically evident and in full spectacular sight. Speculation before that time, into the recesses of prehistory, fare no better. A myth has to be rhetorically constructed in order to answer the question of gender and sexual preferences. I have tried to examine the possibility that the transition from the Great Mother to the Great

Goddess may identify the historical moment of Oedipalization (jagodzinski, 1987). Hence, early in this journey I am footnoting the suggestion that the masquerade has to be resignified from its essentialist theorizations to its potential as a structure of artifice where the close/far binary which currently holds it can begin to dissimulate.

3 I cannot pretend that i understood fully Derrida's close reading and discussion of the "flysheet" or exergue signed F.N. and placed between the preface and the text of Nietzsche's *Ecce Homo*. As a demonstration of "otobiography," it touched a number of themes which, at least on the level of desire, echoed my own feelings. Nietzsche wrote the work when he was 43 and apparently in a mid-life crisis; he wrote it to himself, dismissing a possible audience, embodying within himself both the masculine and feminine. For him the masculine part of language was dead and he was trying to address the feminine side but not the trace of woman -"save the mother. ... The mother is the faceless figure of a figurant, an extra. She gives rise to all figures by losing herself in the background of the scene like an anonymous persona. Everything comes back to her, beginning with life; everything addresses and destines itself to her. She survives on the condition of remaining at bottom" (Derrida, 1985:38). So otobiography is an autobiography that exists on the border between living and death. The proper name is doubled: it is dead in the sense that it suppresses the mother's name (she has no proper name), and alive in the sense it speaks a 'mother tongue,' as the trace of the mother, as a life giving force.

4 The allusion is to Cixous's, "The Laugh of Medusa" (1981) and to Owens's (1983) remarkable essay on Barbara Kruger's poststructuralist *oeuvre* at the ICA- "We Won't Play Nature to Your Culture" (1983). Owens asks the question: How is Perseus able to cut off Medusa's head if she has been turned to stone? There seems to be a gap between the two events which is continually sutured. "It [this gap] is the Dark Continent in which Cixous' laughing Medusa and Wittig's *guérillères* reside" (Showalter, 1982:201). Is this so? Should woman reside there?

5 See Elizabeth Ann Dobie's "Interweaving Feminist Frameworks," *Journal of Aesthetics and Art* (1990), for a discussion of Nancy Spero's work. See also Lisa Tickner's discussion of Nancy Spero in "Nancy Spero: Images of Women and *la peinture féminine*" (1987), and her "Feminism, Art History, and Sexual Difference" (1988), for insights on how concepts of difference may be applied to approaches to art history. A full discussion of the relationship between French feminism and the arts appears later in this writing as "The French 'Con'-nection: *écriture féminine* - writing the body," at which time the maternal body is discussed.

6 This concept is explained as crossing a word out so that it remains legible. The creation of such a grapheme is to indicate that the word is inaccurate yet necessary to deconstuct the text. Derrida borrowed this procedure from the late Heidegger who often wrote the word Being thus: Being, suggesting that Being (as opposed to 'being') could never be fully explained. It transcended all signification. Being was the ultimate 'transcendental signified' (see Spivak, 1976: xiv-xv).

7 Other titles of this ilk are John Lees' *The Flying Boy* (1989), written as a example of self-healing following Bly's teachings. Another similar exemplar is Robert Moore and Douglas Gillette's *King Warrior, Magician Lover* (1991). Since the time of writing Sam Keen's *Fire in the Belly: On Being a Man* (1991) has become a best seller on men's healing. When women respond to the "men's movement" it is often assumed that Bly and his tribe represent the core of this movement. See, for example, the edited book by Kay Leigh Hagan, *Women Respond to the Men's Movement* (1992), introduced by Gloria Steinmen. In her introduction Steinmen doesn't agree she is involved in "male bashing." What does she think of Robert Bly? "... though he seems to have started out with some idea that men should explore the full circle of human qualities within themselves ... Bly seems to have returned to the easier sell of warlike language of kings and battles, closeness only to males and measuring adulthood by men's distance from mothers, thus reconstructing patriarchy albeit in a supposedly gentler form" (viii-ix). This is one of the few statements that finds me in agreement with Steinmen who often *is* involved in male bashing. Ironically her name literally reads "stone man" in German.

8 It seems that the middle-class men's movement isn't alone in its exaggerations of the possibilities of change. An analogous development of this might be the rash of writing by a generation of feminists who have reached menopause, now referring to their aging body as occupying the space of the "grotesque" or "unruly women" (cf. Bakhtin) who are immune to the objectifying male gaze. No longer being desirable in a patriarchal discourse, they claim a space from which to critique patriarchy. Here I am specifically thinking of Mary Kelly's *Interim Project* (1991a,b) who deals with the specificity of the middle-aged woman's body; Germain Greer's *The Change: Women, Aging, and the Menopause* (1992), who is in search of her matronly self as the essential old woman, and Wolff's (1990), "Reinstating Corporeality: Feminism and Body Politics," who relates such a body to Kristeva's concept of the 'monstrous-feminine.' See also Joanna Frueh's (1994), "Visible Difference: Women Artists and Aging," who writes: "If the postmenopausal

woman shares with the lesbian and gay man a nonreproductive eroticism, then she, like them, can defy and transgress gender restrictions, compulsory heterosexuality's demand that the female soul-insepa-rable-from-the-body be feminine" (p. 277).

9 This change of masculinity has been favorably defended and supported by none other than a British feminist. See Lynn Segal's *Slow Motion: Changing Masculinities* (1990).

10 Men's Studies is not confined to the essentialism of Bly and his followers, but represents a vast body of literature that explores varieties of masculinities and their relationship to the women's movement. Amongst the most well known recent titles at the time of this writing were the following: Harry Brod, ed, *The Making of Masculinities: The New Men's Studies* (1987); Jeff Hearn's *The Gender of Oppression: Men, Masculinity and the Critique of Marxism*(1987); Arthur Brittan's *Masculinity and Power* (1989); Robert Connell's *Gender and Power: Society, the Person, and Sexual Politics* (1987); Michael Kaufman, ed, *Beyond Patriarchy: Essays by Men on Pleasure, Power, and Change* (1987); Joseph Pleck's *The Myth of Masculinity* (1981); Andy Metcalfe and Martin Humphries, eds, *The Sexuality of Men* (1985); Anthony Easthope's *What a Man's Gotta Do: The Masculine Myth in Popular Culture* (1986); Vic Seidler's *Rediscovering Masculinity: Reason, Language, and Sexuality* (1989b).

11 There is another, more sobering interpretation of this at the level of the symbolic order, i.e., from the very patriarchal system of law we live in. The conjugal rights claim that a man has the right to have sex with his wife, whereas the wife has a certain right over her body. Strictly speaking, when the wife exer-cises her rights "there is no sexual relation" since the law says sex occurs only when the husband is exercising his right. The law interprets that sex is a "commodity" in the woman's possession which should be "given up" on demand.

12 This theme is explored in the film *sex, lies, and videotapes* (Steven Soderbergh, 1990). Given a more generous reading than it has received thus far (see Denizen, 1991: chap. 8), this film raises issues for the postmodern Imaginary; our screened image as to how we put ourselves "in the picture" which is now mediated by the new cinematic apparatus of videotape and Hi-8. The practice of couples (or any man or woman) who cam record themselves making love, and then play back these videos surely begins to short-circuit the structure of the masturbatory fantasies. Graham, the man with the video camera is sexually impotent. He is able to 'get-off' by retrospectively watching the videos, he has made of women mastur-bating in front of him, and listening to their orgasmic discourse that he himself has helped to induce. Ann, a close friend of his, who is also having sexual difficulties, is able to release herself only through one of Graham's "therapeutic" video sessions. In a climate of AIDS and postmodern narcissism, it is as if her desire and his desire can never be satisfied through an "actual" act of sexual intercourse anymore. Sex has become a drive that can only be satisfied through constant repetition made possible by the play-back feature of the video apparatus. Both Graham and Ann remain trapped in their own private, almost "clinical" act of self-narcissism, self-exhibitionism and self-therapy, aided and mediated by the camera that acts as a cite/sight/site of the omniscient symbolic order (the big Other). Ann 'gets off' only by sub-mitting herself to the eye (gaze) of the camera, identifying with the voyeuristic, sadistic gaze of Graham the director. Graham 'gets off' retrospectively by watching the video and imagining himself as the woman ('victim') who is coming. Both comply to a sadomasochistic relationship.

13 Said another way: "The women's logic of the formulas of sexuation has two parts: the first formula says that not all of a woman falls under the phallic function; and the second formula says that there is nothing in woman which is not determined by the phallic function. For women, however, the phallic func-tion does not govern completely" (Salecl, 1994:132).

14 Žižek (1993b: 250, ft. 11) offers the example of human rights as developed by Renata Salecl (1993) as to the differences between masculine and feminine logical antinomies which can help with this discus-sion. Human rights under a masculine logic draws the card of exception when it claims universalization. Human rights are to be enjoyed, by specifying what a "human being" means through discriminations based along sexual preference, color, age, ethnicity and so on. These can take effect under the guise of universalism. The feminine approach to human rights demands an open system where human rights are guaranteed regardless of who one is.

15 The example of a recent Sony commercial is a case in point. The viewer of the television set at home is presented with a view of the Grand Canyon, on the edge of which stands a Sony television. A boy comes over and switches on the television. A picture comes on which is the exact same repeated scene of the Grand Canyon with the family viewing the television, which inside it contains the same scene, and so ad infinitum. In this way each part contains the whole.

16 This means that the context and the pragmatics of the situation will determine which meaning or logic will be used. Thus far it has been a masculine or closed system logic that has maintained hegemony. Further, undecidability here is not meant to be interpreted as indeterminacy. "I say 'undecidability' rather

than 'indeterminacy' because I am interested more in relations of force, in differences of force, in everything that allows, precisely, determinations in given situations to be stabilized through a decision of writing ... " (Derrida:1988:148). I interpret Derrida as arguing for an open system politics along the lines of a "feminine logic."

[17] The move here is similar to the deconstruction of nature/culture binary, or sex/gender binary, i.e., the illusion of culture must rest on the voidance or 'disappearance' of nature; nature is posited retrospectively. Likewise the discursive categories of gender make "sex" possible. Sex is a necessary illusion for gender to exist. A demonstration of how gender "determines" sex, rather than the other way around, can be demonstrated by the horror film *Friday 13th*, pt. 1. For the first half of the film the audience has no clue who the killer is. The killer's perspective is presented through the I-camera. Occasionally we catch glimpses of a hand and a boot. Given that sadistic violence is almost always male, we are fully surprised when the killer turns out to be a woman.

[18] See Martin Jay's *Downcast Eyes* (1993) which traces the denigration of vision in Lacan through Derrida. Jay reads Irigaray and Derrida as providing a turn away from the "mirror" towards its tain or "glace" as in Derrida's *Glas*.

[19] The difficulty with this formulation remains how to interpret the "feminine" here. For Žižek (1994a:103) this "feminine" 'night of the world' is attributed to Hegel. For Luce Irigaray (1985:103) the feminine is "what resists infinite reflection: the mystery (hysteria?) that will always remain modestly behind every mirror, and that will spark the desire to see and to know more about it" (p. 103). Irigaray's feminine is "the dark night of the soul" or "la mystérique," the fusion of mysticism, mystery and hysteria. For Derrida "Woman" was a placeholder for différance, not a positive concept.

[20] Copjec discusses this question of being "counted" as the task for women since the woman occupies the place of zero (the void) in the theorizations of the Cartesian-Kantian *cogito*. As she says of Frege's numbering system, "in order for counting to be possible in the first place, the set of numbers must register one category under which no objects fall. The category is that of the 'non-identical-to-itself'; the number of objects subsumed by it is zero ... Frege initiated his theory by rigorously excluding from consideration the subject who counts; more precisely, Frege began by excluding the empirical subject..." (1993:173). Being "counted," however, does not simply mean becoming another statistical number, rather the force of the count has to do with difference itself, where the injustice done to women can be registered in the language itself.

[21] This form of textural interpretation has now become a paradigm case to re-examine art history as a form of discourse. The best known example is that by Louis Marin (1980). See Owens's (1982) examination of this form of deconstructive reading as applied to criticism of painting.

[22] Personal translation of Abels's text. Abels spells the German word for perception as *Wahr-nehmung* to show its mimetic quality. It literally means to take (that which is to be true). To make this description more understandable, Abels refers to a Berlin painter, Arwed D. Gorella, who painted an exposé of the *Las Meniñas* called "Jenny betrachtet *Las Meniñas*" (1979). A reflection within a reflection within a mirror, the painting is an exposition of the postmodern imagination of the "mise-en-abyne" (see Kearney, 1988). It is a good example of "feminine" logic at work, for here the endless reflecting mirrors confuse what is the object for the subject since the two positions (subject-object) oscillate back and forth. In the far background there is a painting of *Las Meniñas* painted in reverse from the "original," as if the observer were seeing the "original" in a mirror. Standing in front of this copied reversed painting is the Infanta (as Jenny). She appears *outside* the frame of the copied inversed *Las Meniñas* looking on. The viewer of Gorella's painting sees only her back. This then is the "mirror" image Velázquez would have seen while painting *Las Meniñas*. In Gorella's painting the "mirror" Velásquez would have used, where Jenny stands, occupies the second plane from the background occupied by the reversed *Las Meniñas*. The last plane, directly in the foreground, presents the Infanta facing the viewer of Gorella's painting, which is now a reverse image of the Infanta in the second plane of the mirror. The mental gymnastics to imagine this picture comply to the labyrinthine structure of the effects of the *mise-en-abyme* device (to be put into an abyss).

[23] Again my neologism for the split sense of space with place = s(p)(l)ace.

[24] A critique of their position is offered by Salecl (1994: 114-115) who argues that Lacan's re-reading of Descartes along with Kant can still be useful. She reminds feminists who challenge the notion of the *cogito* that in the seventeenth century, when Descartes was writing, there were women who embraced the idea as liberating for it confirmed that "the mind 'had no sex' and that 'anyone can fill the place of the individual subject' because the notion of the subject had no sex" (p.115).

25 For a recent revival of Gnosticism within the contexts of the ecological movement and New Age thinking see Morris Berman's *Coming To our Senses* (1989). For an attempt of applying the concepts of ecofeminism to art and education, see my essay (1987).

26 The film appears as one of three stories in a feature length film entitled New York Stories. Griselda Pollock (1992a) has explored the relationship between the painter and "his" model in "Painting, Feminism, History." In this essay, she notes the difference of working between Helen Frankenthaler and Jackson Pollock, whom, I assume the short film by Scorsese is premised upon. Unfortunately, Pollock does not pursue how this difference plays itself out with the abstracted subject matter. It seems to me that the relationship between the painter and his model has undergone historical changes which need to be noted. For example, i would argue that the Expressionists, like *Der Blaue Riter*, who lived with their models, would have had an entirely different relationship than, say, Henri Matisse when he painted *The Painter and His Model* (1917), whom Pollock uses as a paradigm case of ownership. Artists living with their models is no guarantee, of course, that their objectification (as models) would be mitigated. Yet, the changed relationship would have to be taken into account. John Berger (1972:57), in *Ways of Seeing*, made this claim of Georges La Tour and Rembrant in their depictions of their spouses. Berger claims that these paintings stand out from the other voyeuristic examples of the tradition. However, Berger's claim raises the question that somehow the relationship between the male and female model is inherently natural and good. As Nead (1992:15) so aptly shows, Berger is in effect reversing the naked/nude binary by claiming that LaTour and Rembrandt have transformed the nude into a naked woman by the very virtue that they literally loved them.

27 Laura Cottingham (1994) provides a review of the masculinization of high modernism, discussing American painters like Jeff Koons, Matthew Barney and Richard Prince. Her description of Barney's work is relevant to my own questioning. She writes: "The only female images are those of men in women's clothes, that is, men creating (themselves as) women. His work consistently utilizes various forms of male-coded biological-like materials, such as wax that looks like cum, and tapioca that resembles sperm. These oozy materials collaborate to form various sports-resemblance devices such as bench presses and shoulder pads and other accouterments of football players, weight lifters, and various male athletes. It suggests the body of man who produces, biologically and therefore inevitably, athletic prowess, and this characteristic is, within an art context, the production of value itself" (pp. 145-146).

28 See de Lauretis' (1987b) review of Rubin Suleiman's (editor), *The Female Body in Western Culture* (1986) and Jane Gallop's (1982b) and Heilbrun's (1982) review of Elizabeth Abel's (editor) *Writing and Sexual Difference* (1982) which appeared after the initial essays had been published in *Critical Inquiry* (vol 8. no.2). Both of these edited books have a wide range of articles which problematize the relationship between the body and gender as represented through writing. See also Janet Wolff's discussion "Reinstating Corporeality: Feminism and Body Politics," in her *Feminist Sentences* (1990). A major row concerning feminist essentialism took place between Frank Lentricchia (1987, 1988) and Gilbert and Guber (1988). From reading this exchange i learnt, 1) the power of rhetorical writing that academics are capable of levying, 2) that sexual politics is not for the thin skinned, 3) that i took sides.

29 i have attempted to speculate on such a possibility by reconstructing protocultural changes before the advent of Homo sapiens sapiens (jagodzinski, 1987-1994, unpublished manuscript). See also the writings of Barbara Duden (1991) who makes the claim that the relationship of women's emotional relationship to their bodies and the children they are about to bear has changed over the past century by the intervention of technical medical discourse that, in effect, separates body from mind, treating motherhood as a "classical" emotionless body.

30 "During the past five million years, there have been at least five major transitions in human biology and culture that have resulted in changes in parturition and mother-infant relationship: (1) the origin of bipedalism and associated greater difficulties in parturition; (2) secondary altriciaslity of the neonate associated with encephalization in the genus Homo; (3) the behavioral adaptation of obligate midwifery with further encephalization; (4) postpartum separation and decreased contact between mother and infant following agriculture and sedentism; and (5) technological effects on birth and infant care in the industrial age. Each of these transitions placed different demands on females giving birth to and caring for dependent young" (p.221).

31 There are exceptions like Slavoj Žižek and Joan Copjec who have concentrated on Lacan's late writing where he made a turn to recognizing clinical categories like hysteria, compulsive neurosis, perversion as names for existential-ontological categories produced during modernity. Richard Lichtman (1982) has also placed Freud's theories into a historical perspective. See also Moustafa Safouan's "Is the Oedipus Complex Universal?" (1981).

32 See Pollock (1988: 138-140) for an application to art. For fuller analyses see Owens (1983) and Barbara Walker (1983 and 1985).

33 This myth suggests that there is a "battle of the sexes" which is never ending. This same theme is played out by Susan Faludi's (1991) *Backlash: The Men Strike Back: The Undeclared War Against American Women*. This is a journalistic account of popular films, newspaper articles and magazines that attempt to reposition women back into traditional roles of mothers and housewives. Her study purports that men have reacted strongly to the invasion of women in the workplace. The rise of the new Right has brought about a climate of postfeminism declaring that the various political claims of feminism are all but over. Women's voices have been appeased. See also Jones (1994) for a review of the postfeminist backlash in visual art.

34 This notion of doubling is developed by Naomi Schor (1987a) in her essay, "Dreaming Dissymmetry: Barthes, Foucault, and Sexual Difference," in *Men and Feminism*, an idea which was picked up by Jardine and Smith's "A Conversation," (pp.250-253) in the same text.

35 In 1989 Spivak retracts her accusation in "Displacement and the Discourse of Woman" (1983) and writes "Feminism and Deconstruction, again: Negotiating With Unacknowledged Masculine." In this extraordinary difficult article she supports the complicity of deconstruction with feminism by taking issue with the way Jacqueline Rose in her *Sexuality in the Field of Vision* (1986), had appropriated deconstruction as narrative. Rose accuses Derrida of having suppressed sexual difference in the interest of *différance*. Spivak tries to correct this misconception by reiterating *différance* as a double-bind situation: it is what makes differences possible in the first place. The so-called "graphematic structure" which is said to be the origin of all acts of thought, is endlessly deferred. Spivak reads Derrida's use of "woman" (in *Spurs*) as another name for this double bind situation. Sexual difference is *already* suggested or pre-supposed by *différance*. By this i take it that pure difference in-and-of-itself is impossible once thought enters into it. If i have understood the essay, Spivak tries to save the name of "woman" and deconstruction in this key line which comes at the end of this (arduous?) essay: "Let us divide the name of woman so that we see ourselves as naming, not merely named" (p.220). It seems to be that both essentialism and anti-essentialism are in dialectical play here. See her "French Feminism Revisited" (1992a) for further remarks.

36 Throughout this journey i will use this homology as a reminder of the *process of signification* which pre-exists any location. Cite refers to the discursive formations that impinge on location; sight refers to the spectacular or specular sense of living in a technologically sophisticated electronic world, and finally site is reminder of the specificity of place.

37 Overdetermined here refers to the Althusserian concept where a whole is determined by one of its elements which should be simply a subordinated part in the order of classification but determines the classification itself. i refer here to the phallus. White mythology alludes to Derrida's (1982a:207-272) well-known (and difficult) essay by the same title where he goes on to explore the rule of metaphor in philosophy which turns out to be hardly an unambiguous discourse on Truth once thought. In this essay Derrida argued that the metaphorical and rhetorical expressions in philosophy cannot be cleansed away. The whole of the Western metaphysics was based on the metaphor of light and dark.

38 Like so many other writers borrowing from the French deconstructive tradition, *jouissance* is not to be translated. As Gallop (1984) puts it: "If *jouissance* is celebrated as something that unsettles assumptions, it becomes ineffective when it itself settles into an assumption. If *jouissance* is 'beyond the pleasure principle,' it is not because it is beyond pleasure but because it is beyond principle" (p.112). Does such an experience emerge from the gap *within* the two (I)(i)s?

39 See especially Rita Felski's chapter 3, "On Confession," in her *Beyond Feminist Aesthetics* (1989). Felski raises one of the key issues with autobiographical writing: is it a pursuit of an authentic Self (and hence supports the humanist dream of essences), or is it part of an indispensable aspect of the process of critical self-understanding which constitutes the feminist emancipatory project? In her review of feminist autobiographical forms, she points to the blurring of the distinction between autobiography and fiction. "Feminist confession exemplifies the intersection between the autobiographical imperative to communicate the truth of unique individuality, and the feminist concern with the representative and intersubjective element's of women's experience" (p.93). It is a shift to communal identity made possible through the representative aspects of the author's experience rather than her unique individuality. This allows for the inclusion of fictive representative episodes distilled from the lives of other women. Felski's analysis, while admirable, seems devoid of class and color considerations of the autobiographical genre.

40 i am referring to Derrida here, who remains a controversial figure throughout my journey. He is either dismissed for the way he himself "dis-miss-es" feminism, or is embraced for having rethought the figure of Woman along new ethical lines. Drucilla Cornell, *The Philosophy of the Limit* (1992) offers a theoretically difficult and demanding exposition in defense of Derrida, dedicating this book to him.

41 His paradigm case is Victor Seidler's *Rediscovering Masculinity* (1989b), but also the male writers in Linda Kauffman's reader, *Gender and Theory* (1989). Here he singles out Gerald M. MacLean's "Citing the Subject," as being uncritical of his reflective prose. Bristow also thinks that the essays found in *Men in Feminism* are prolix. They are "hampered by the fact that they produce an introspective discourse, where one essay accretes around another - a symptom of the Modern Language Association panel format from which much of the content sprang" (p. 72).

The Text Scriptease in Eight Tacky Steps

THE FIRST
VIGNETTE

Castration Anxieties

Fourteen years ago, in the autumn of 1980, the I was fortunate to start his university teaching career at Mount Saint Vincent University, in Halifax, Nova Scotia, Canada.[1] The I had at that time, a *cross* appointment between Early Childhood Education and the Department of Elementary Education to teach art education. i say fortunate now, but it felt like a was a very marginal position. Talking to daycare workers, early childhood educators, little children, and having to deal with the early childhood curriculum and teacher education seemed to me to be a very low-status position. The I was hardly filled with any sense of esteem or fulfillment. Any fantasies of the "professorial" role, the I might have had, were quickly shattered when dealing with little children, or visiting with daycare teachers as children slept in their cots during their "quiet time." Such thoughts vividly reveal what the expectations of a Ph.D. in visual arts education were supposed to covet. Certainly not time spent amongst daycare centers talking about redesigning play spaces. The I was supposed to be doing important research.

Added to this was the "Mount's" emphasis on Women's Studies. i believe it established one of the earliest departments in the country, but i am not sure. It was known as a "woman's" university. Stories about its role as a former finishing school still circulated. At that time about 15% of the student body were men. Some of my male colleagues felt threatened by this situation. In my second year of teaching, a close colleague of mine was dismissed on charges of sexual harassment. The affair was ugly. It all seemed so unreal. The I refused to believe that there had been any sexual misconduct on his part. Even to this day the circumstances surrounding my colleague's wrongdoings seem vague. CAUT (Canadian Association of University Teachers) cleared him of all charges. Nevertheless rumors circulated that he could not get along with female colleagues, and that he had established a poor reputation amongst the network of teaching nuns, the Sisters of Charity. Their Mother House rested high on a "mount," overlooking the university. The entire situation seems somewhat ironical as i look back. As a male, to be in disfavor in their network was the flip side of the "old boys club"; their Mother House a reversal of male dominated architecture—the Monastery, the Castle, the Cathedral—all, characteristically perched in a place of dominance. As a teaching order, they had power. Was this then a case of reverse discrimination? Gynocentrism? Had my colleague suffered from mysandry? The I refused to believe this. Some of my other male colleagues felt the exclusion and reacted with disdain to the teaching competency of some nuns, even though many had fulfilled the requirements of their Ph.D.'s at prestigious universities and achieved a high degree of scholarship. Male hysteria could not be denied.

The above commentary seems like a classic tale of a male who has been castrated, or fears the prospect of being castrated at any given time. No longer possessor of the promised phallus, as symbolically represented by his Ph.D., he feels dispossessed and doesn't know why. He is further subjected to the possible domination by a "secret" network of nuns who may well have *crossed* his colleague. Perhaps he too will be persecuted? Is his turn next? Paranoia was in the making. In such a situation, my costume was hardly that of a Dorthy Michaels. "Tootsie's cross-dressing [was] a way of promoting the notion of masculine power while masking it." Like a transvestite, Michaels was the "phallic woman" who derives "pleasure tricking the unsuspected into thinking that he is a woman, and then revealing his maleness..." (Showalter, 1987:123). No, my costume, my masquerade, was that of a "'soft" male. i tried desperately to accommodate myself into the existing networks, to be polite and just listen. With hindsight, i now can have a better understanding as to how the I lived out the contradictions of masculinity in these feminized spaces. Working with little children and women teachers (there was one male) in daycare centers meant that i had to face my own "Mother;" the pre-oedipal love which the heterosexual maleman has to eventually reject. My response turned out to be a masochistic one; a "soft" male by another name; a complex masquerade played to the superego so as to give the appearance of passive submission, but not giving up my agency completely. No wonder the I could not accept my colleague's sexual misdoings. He represented the "father" for me—if not an older brother. Not only as an older, more experienced university teacher, but someone who would not let go of his phallic power. He fought "the system," and the "system" in this case might be likened to the "abject terror" of the "monstrous feminine" of the Mother. CAUT represented the Law. It was his only court of appeal. With their help he had won ... and lost. My "soft" maleman response offered a way of negotiating pleasure by not entirely submitting to the fear of the phallic mother. As has often been pointed out, male masochism reflects oedipal law and subverts it at the same time. The male masochist´s desire for recognition by the preoedipal mother does not entirely escape paternal law (Deleuze, 1971; Silverman, 1988b:55). Upon further reflection, this ruse of mine seems to be a reoccurring masquerade. The I almost always received top marks through grade school, a patriarchal marker of competition, confidence, power and being on top; yet, i would never brag about these accomplishments. i felt genuinely sorry that others did not do so well, so when my fellow classmates would ask, "what did you *get*?" Meaning, what grade did you receive? i always lied, telling my friends that my marks weren't so good. I hid *it* from them: it being metonymic for the displaced phallus as represented by good grades. Secretly though, the ruse of disavowal (what every masochist actually knows to exist but plays the game of denying) brought me pleasure.

The university's art gallery catered to local women artists; it had a women's art registry and regularly tried to promote women's exhibitions. Slowly and with great humility, the I began to become involved with the life-world of children and the people who were committed to their education. These were mostly women. i can only recall one male nursery teacher. Here another reversal of discrimination takes place. Such men are often thought as being potential paedophiles. All this wore on my body more than i wanted to admit. The I began to gain weight and drink beer more excessively. Carolyne stayed home with Jeremy, who at that time was two months old. i recall vividly the president of the university insisting that both Carolyne and Jeremy be present for the official opening of the university year. i was to go home and bring them back with me; a generous gesture which confirmed for me her commitment of caring for her staff. i don´t recall a similar personal invitation ever extended to them again.

Having to teach an introductory art history course, under what was loosely termed the "Fine Arts Department," made things difficult. There were times when i felt schizophrenic—nothing related. All three departments and all three courses had agendas all their own. The I was caught continually adjusting his frame, each and every time changing identities. It's as though my identity crisis as a teacher was like a swinging door. Stepping a foot into the frame of early childhood, the I was dispossessed of power; stepping into the cultural capital of art history, the imaginary signifier of the phallus was miraculously restored to me. The I felt to be dealing with "significant" material. Rather than the "how-to's" of art education, I taught art history course from a sociological perspective. Rather than H.W. Janson's *History of Art* (1962), I chose Arnold Hauser's four volume work, *The Social History of Art* (1951). Here, i thought, was cultural capital from the Left at its best! Hauser contextualized art within a politics making visible his Marxist historical materialism. This proved to be a disaster. Students had neither the desire nor the inclination to wade through the social history of art. I was called in by the dean of humanities. She asked me to justify both the approach and the costs. There must have been complaints on both counts. The I was asked to make it more of a survey course, to cut down the social history, and to use more slides. The stock trade in postage sized celluloids was much more palatable for the class. The tour guide to art history, the same approach which subjected me during my undergraduate days, was under way. At the year's end I had worked my way up to the twentieth century presenting a slide/lecture on women's art both to my class and yet again to a sociology class of a colleague. The CBC radio even did an small interview asking for my views of men and their relationship to the issues surrounding women's art. Although that lecture and the radio interview are now rather vague to me, i do remember receiving a rather nice round of applause after the lecture–perhaps it was out of politeness, or perhaps a maleman had the audacity to deliver such a message. Nevertheless, it was a good feeling, and the I was too naive to question his posture "in" feminism at the time. Was this then, my way of retrieving my lost phallus, fulfilling my lack?

Women's art at this time in the late '70s, early '80s, meant for me yet another dispossessed, disenfranchised group—like any other "minority," a word which today has rapidly lost its currency. Looking at my slide collection, which seemed to travel with me wherever the I went (just in case the social history failed once again!), it was obvious that my main source of inspiration had been Lucy Lippard's *From the Center*. Published in 1976, four years before the I began teaching, it was the definitive American statement at that time. i recall dealing with the names of Judy Chicago, Mary Miss, Louise Bourgeois, and

Mary Stevens' *Big Daddies*.[2] i recall her iconography in particular because they reminded me of Mr. Carrot Heads drawn by three year olds, only now the Mr. Carrot Heads had become a phallic symbol; an army helmet replacing the typical sprig of green sprouting from its head. It was the way the I remembered the images back then.

During the second year of my stay at the Mount, i had a rude awakening. It was suggested to me, filtered down through the gallery hierarchy, that I should not participate in any way in helping with any new women's exhibits. The implication was that any mention of my name may contaminate an all women's production. Hurt, unsure what i had done to offend, i shied away from the gallery and its dealings. It was time to move on.

Today I am reminded of Heath's (1987) own telling remark of "certain exclusion —the point after all is that this is a matter for women, that it is their voices and actions, not ours: no matter how 'sincere,' 'sympathetic' or whatever, we are always also in a male position which brings with it all the implications of domination and appropriation, everything precisely that is being challenged, that has to be altered" (p. 1). Cary Nelson (1987) also reminds me that "feminism remains women's project ... Feminists, however, have every right to protect their own sense of community (and, for that matter, their own peace of mind) by being distinctly, even excessively, suspicious of everything I write" (p.161). At that historical moment, it may well have necessitated that the gallery had to remain exclusive, homogeneous in its ranks in order to make the women's position felt and emergent. The I, as a male, no longer had access to the gallery—metonymically speaking—to women. i felt the sting of exclusion, which awaked in me my own question as to why the I needed to belong in the first place? Was it out of sense of duty to the university? Was the I in it to truly help their cause? i thought so. Maybe it was a way to pad my vita. My admonishment was the same as when Blacks rebuke support from good intentioned Whites. Within a Marxist discourse, i could argue that there was a tint of false consciousness in me; perhaps a repressed and hidden paternalism in my seemingly sincere offer. Being a bit player in the schema of the gallery's administration, i couldn't see how that might have been the case.

Since that time i have continued to try to understand the "gender issue" and the sexual politics that surround it. Admittedly, it is the sexual politics that is often the hard pill to swallow. At that time i was perplexed as to what an appropriate male response was, or whether this issue of exclusion would ever go beyond such divisiveness. Upon reflection, I had accepted a liberalist stance during my time at the Mount. Despite my self-proclaimed socialism, armed freshly with a strong dose of critical hermeneutics,[3] it had been easy to accept that women were "equal but different" in a gallery situation which was promoting and elevating the status of women artists. i have since read Jagger's (1983) excellent critique of the liberalist feminist position: the theoretical impossibility of positing a *rationally* abstract individual who, in the exercise of freedom, was still 'Locked' into property rights, if you will excuse the pun. Despite all possible self-checks, such as those so cleverly argued by Rawls' theory of justice to redress inequality, such a position inevitably led to an insatiable ego whose pursuit for desire was to be found through the acquisition of "primary social goods." Within a deliberately generated post-industrial economy of capitalist scarcity such as ours, these "goods" become translated into a hierarchy of status positions. Separating needs from wants, an impossible task in the first place, fuels the economy and perpetuates such greed. I was a classic example of this social philosophy. I wanted and expected status that went with a freshly anointed Ph.D.[4]

What (white) middle-to-upper class women want in this context is what (white) middle-to-upper class men already have. They want participation on an equal basis in the Symbolic Order. Derrida (1979), reading Nietzsche, called this positional figure of femininity, the first woman, as untruth, "nothing but the operation of a woman who inspires to be like a man" (p.65). Such a position fails to question the absolutes of man and woman as categories in themselves. In this liberalist scenario, *civil liberties* play the key role. White, middle class women have had a long struggle just to prove that they were every bit as rational and reasonable as men so that all civil liberties might apply equally to them, at all institutional levels. The fight for equal pay, daycare, pregnancy leave, just hiring practices, fair treatment of rape victims in court are just a few items of an endless list of inequalities that can be identified since virtually all institutions are insensitive to inequalities suffered by women. At the Mount, graduates of the Early Childhood Program had the lowest status of all the departments; they earned considerably less than grade-school teachers graduating from Elementary Education. They fought hard for recognition and the need for a better and improved provincial daycare system that would honor children. Setbacks were common. In this regard, in the United States it was indeed a tragic set back to have had the Equal Rights Amendment defeated. In her book, *The Power of Christian Woman* (1981), Phyllis Schlafly celebrates the difference between men and women as one of subservience to men. With equal oppositional vengeance, feminist philosophers (i.e. Grimshaw, 1986: 36-74) have had to re-write the Aristotelian misogynistic tradition in order just to get a hearing. "Woman's inferiority had be rationalized by the writers in the Aristotelian tradition as a deficiency in judgment, wit, reason, skill, talent and psychic (and bodily) heat" (Battersby, 1989:8). It is only recently that this tradition has become suspect by men themselves, but *only* as a result of the pioneering work by women.[5]

Since the liberalist feminist position continues to be the one most often equated with feminism, it has received the most media coverage over existent controversies. The elimination of the differences between men and women so that an "androgynous society" might emerge remains naively appealing. The neutral term "person," or the androgyne would replace the extremes of man and woman as gendered subjects with equal characteristics in a "sexless society." The more internal problems that are generated amongst feminists, the more public appeal this position has. This elimination of specific gender roles has led to much in-fighting, both from feminists who wish to preserve difference and yet retain equality, and from women who shy away from being burdened by yet another label. This later group are resentful that they must now wear yet another hat in addition to that of the traditional housewife. As working women they are expected to compete on male terrain in the workforce—thereby giving up part of their autonomy in their traditional space of the home.

As Virginia Woolf noted in *A Room of One's Own* (1929:102), when a writer like Coleridge insisted that the mind of a great artist was *androgynous*, he certainly did not mean that such a mind had any specific sympathy with women. "Nor did he mean that a great creative artist is female" (Battersby, 1989:7). The Romantic androgyne had male genitals with a "feminine" soul. Battersby goes on to point out that the same logic repeats itself in Jung's view of the androgyne. The woman can only inspire the man to greatness. Her role is still one of support; her activity still holds a secondary status.

These problems with androgyny are only a very small part of the controversy. In the radical feminist literature, there was an attempt to wrestle back the neutrality of its meaning and to re-code it as a position of strength. From this perspective, the androgyne constitutes the "Bitch." In the "Bitch Manifesto," Joreen describes the politics of such rebelliousness:

> What is disturbing about a Bitch is that she is androgynous. She incorporates within herself qualities traditionally defined as 'masculine' as well as 'feminine.' A Bitch is blunt, direct, arrogant, at times egoistic. She has no liking for the indirect, subtle, mysterious ways of the 'eternal feminine.' She disdains the vicarious life deemed natural to women because she wants to live a life of her own (Joreen in Alcoff, 1988b:39).

Joreen has stolen the signifier from the heterosexual discourse and redefined its meaning within the confines of lesbianism. Such a "prickly" character presents a resistant posture against the heterosexual patriarchal world-view, a reminder that some backs are never broken despite the many lashes. A "bitch" accusation within a masculine discourse typically represents the decline of femininity and the increase of female aggression. Her concern for her career or her pursuit of goals with competitive determination are interpreted as "power hungry" motivations. The "power bitch" has removed herself from the category of woman by "masculinizing" herself.

Within the confines of a liberalist discourse the androgynous figure is not so easily unhinged. A devastating critique from a psychoanalytic point of view has been persuasively argued by Pacteau (1986). The androgyne, she argues, can only exist in fantasy life as the phallic Mother. Once the overlays of color, class, age, ethnicity, *and* ideology are added to the difficulties of the liberalist discourse, feminism can often become a morass of "contradictions of oppression."[6] But Nancy Miller (1987) sends a reminder to all feminists: "The fight between the girls leaves the Daddies to their old struggles over ownership of the discourse" (p.141). So despite such confusions feminists of a liberalist persuasion *must* continue to act as watchdogs of the ideological state apparatuses (Althusser, 1971)—the school, the church, the family, the political institutions—to insure that the rhetoric of equality is maintained and the line which separates the private from the public domain is pushed back.

Such a division, according to Elshtain (1981), has been established along sexist lines since the Greek polis.[7] It continues to be a key point of contention, especially in such issues as family rape, wife beating, child molestation, and incest where the prevention of women and children from physical and sexual abuse by men almost seems impossible to police. This also seems to be the case with pornography, which lies in a zone somewhere in between the private and the public. The issue is crucial to the current debates between pro-life and pro-choice. If the fetus is claimed to be an "abstract" individual, invoking the very foundation of liberalism, then the state may intervene, confirming full rights upon the fetus. Abortion is prohibited. The woman's body is no longer her own, but belongs to the Law. The issues surrounding illegally induced euthanasia are much the same. The right of premeditated suicide is being denied by the state. A similar argument may be made for frozen sperm. Does a man have a right to stop his sperm from being used in artificial insemination? Our current technologies of sexual reproduction raise such ethical issues, explored recently by Margaret Atwood's dystopia, *A Handmaid's Tale* (1985).

Such issues should not lie outside the realm of art education. Rather, they should provide contemporary cases for representational analysis. It has taken some time, but now there are a sprinkling of teachers who explore AIDS representations within the context of art education. It may be possible to examine the rhetorical use of fetal images through television, video and feature films, e.g., *Look Whose Talking,* by antiabortionists who try to persuade the public as to the merits of their case. Petchesky's (1987) study of antiabortion imagery, especially Dr. Bernard Nathanson's *The Silent Scream*, is an excellent example of this possibility. She provides an analysis of the "politics of style" of late capitalism; how "surface impressions" become "whole messages." Her analysis vivifies how discourses are maneuvered, and how religious authorities are currently being displaced by medical and technical authorities. She forcibly argues that the gory pictures of dead fetuses that are defiantly waved by right-wing women in anti-abortionist demonstrations are taking part vicariously in a "phallic" way of looking by being facilitators for men's fantasies. "Waving these fetus-pictures as icons, literal fetishes, they both propagate and celebrate the image of the fetus as autonomous space-hero and the pregnant woman as 'empty space' (p.281). Dworkin (1983:217) rightly says:

> The liberation of women requires facing the real condition of women in order to change it. 'We're all just people' is a stand that prohibits recognition of the systematic cruelties visited on women because of sex oppression. Feminism as a liberation movement, demands a revolutionary single standard of what humans have a right to, and also demands that the current sexual bifurcation of rights never be let out of sight.

It is unfortunate that Dworkin's own antipornography stance is so one-sided. However she may be right in her assessment of liberalism. Taking up a liberalist feminist stance "in a man's world," and thereby accepting male signifiers, leads to all sorts of psychological maneuvers. Sayers (1986:167-181) notes that historically dressing in man's clothing and changing one's name by writing in a pseudonym, or using sex-neutral abbreviations, or becoming a tomboy, were all accommodative responses which center behavior around male signifiers. Forms of "gender blending" (Devor,1989) raise crucial issues for liberal feminists. Just how far should heterosexual women take on mannish characteristics in order to compete on male turf? In contrast to tomboyism in grade school, gylandrous behavior by boys is quickly policed by boys' clubs in school (Best, 1983). Being called a sissy or a mommy's boy are grounds for exclusion from the machismo code. Often, the understanding of this sexual bifurcation can lead to use "femininity" to gain illusionary power over men, like Greta Garbo or Mae West who, in her half-joking style, said that she had climbed the ladder of success– "wrong by wrong." Erkkila (1985) has argued that Garbo was especially skillful at manipulating male desire for her own ends. If the woman refuses to submit to male fetishization, it can often lead to the refusal of hysteria or damage to the narcissistic sense of self if the boy's game is understood, but cannot be played. A woman not having the 'look' cannot receive the voyeuristic look back. She feels ugly, and in the 80s— fat. But the reverse holds here as well. Boys progressively come to realize that they must display 'hard' bodies if they are to successfully attract women and be popular amongst them. For the middle-class men, excessive addiction to sports (i.e., distance running, Iron Man training) and body building (use of steroids) represent the obverse coin to anorexia and bulimia. As physical strength between the sexes has progressively become less of a determining factor for the work-force through the introduction of push-button technologies, physical strength has been sublimated into the male "look" of the advertising industry—the creation of the "New Man." Professional sports remain as one of the few areas today where biological differences between men and women are still a factor. Should steroids eventually be allowed in Olympic competition, that gap between men and women may begin to close in some sports as well. The signifier of what is considered "natural" currently makes the gap seem wider than it is.

The illusionary fantasy of the look for women was explored by Joan Riviere, Freud's translator during the 1920s. In Joan Riviere's (1986/1929) explanation, woman as *masquerade* (see extended footnote 2, Pretexts to the Title), sets out the psychoanalytic thesis that there is a wish by women for success which comes with being male; to become professional; to be like her successful male colleagues. Yet to avert the anxiety and retribution she fears from men once she attains such status, she puts on a mask of 'womanliness' to displace it." The woman therefore rivals and takes the place of the father, but by flirting and coquetting she placates him through her 'womanliness.' Having castrated him, she then castrates herself, her life consisting alternately of masculine and feminine activities" (Heath, 1986:49). What then is the "feminine" if it's all a masquerade? As Heath notes, Riviere's own queries led her to claim that the price of the masquerade is to deny the attainment of full heterosexuality which coincides with genitality, because the woman continually denies the male fiction of "woman." Yet it must not be forgotten: "[T]o put on femininity with a vengeance suggests the power of taking it off"

(Russo, 1986:224). And in the case of a lesbian identity, why should the male fiction of woman even be a consideration?

What then should the maleman's response be to this positioning? The above discussion has often been used to justify rape cases. The woman's dress, her manner, her posture, her make-up, become an excuse for a heterosexual male´s fantasyful projections. So great is the build up of such desire that there continues to be numerous stabbings and killings by men who have worked themselves up into such a frenzy because certain female stars have refused to recognize their advancements and have outright rejected them. Los Angeles is full of paranoid starlets who fear the retribution of a deranged fan. They must pre-plan all their moves with body guards; their mail/male is screened and read before they can feel secure. Such paranoia is real, but can it be denied that this is a problem of the Hollywood industry itself in the reproduction of a site/cite/sight specific "sexuality"? The industry exemplifies the classical castration scenario. The male rejected, impotent, castrated, seeks revenge. Sex and death are intimately linked in the manufacture of male desire, a "Sadeian identification of murder and sexual possession as an assertion of absolute *jouissance* "(Nochlin, 1988a:10). Such an argument, however, comes dangerously close to claiming an innate "pornographic consciousness," as if the very site/cite/*sight* of a pretty woman caused the rape. The courts can then blame the victim for having in-*sighted* the attack rather than simply exemplifying the right of a woman to enjoy her own narcissism.

In this first vignette i have touched upon a number of issues— pornography, equality, identity, dress, castration—which i shall come back to time and again. With my castration a-side, i would like to examine this liberalist response with its emphasis on individualism and women´s experience as different but equal, as it has been theorized and played out within the discourses of art and art education. This was my position while teaching art history and art education at the Mount. My voice will change to a more academic style.

1 For stylistic purposes the scare quotes which surround the capital I will be dropped from here on in. For the effect of estrangement and distance the definite article "the" will be used where appropriate.

2 Mary Stevens has, of course changed her iconography. Josephine Withers (1987) provides an in-depth view of Stevens's current work.

3 I was fortunate enough to have a small dip at the University of Leeds in 1979 where Janet Wolff, Zigmund Bauman and T.C. Clark were active before Thatcherism set in, forcing some members to leave. My doctoral thesis, "Aesthetic Consciousness and Criticism" (1980), University of Alberta, was influenced by what I managed to take away from them.

4 A far more explicit, well-written account of the problems of liberalist feminism has been brilliantly worked out by Elizabeth Fox-Genovese's *Feminism Without Illusions: A Critique of Individualism* (1991). In her "Afterword" (245-256), Fox-Genovese risks an autobiographical confession which is almost diametrically opposite to my experience. An obviously brilliant and talented student, she held off finishing her dissertation in the fear that she wouldn't know what to do with it once it was completed. With the mentality of a "girl" still within her, she didn't want to grow-up. In contrast, having achieved a Ph.D. the pressure for me was to live up to its title. Not to do so meant a failure in self-achievement and loss of (phallic) power.

5 See Fox-Genovese's review in Chapter 5, "Individualism and Women's History" (1991).

6 An excellent review of the inherent problems of feminism is provided by Ramazanoglu's *Feminism and the Contradictions of Oppression* (1989) and Marianne Hirsch and Evelyn Fox Keller's (eds.) *Conflicts in Feminism* (1990).

7 It should be remarked that this private/public split Elshtain identifies in the Greek polis has radically changed with the emergence of late, post-Fordian capitalism. There is now a profusion of spaces which women occupy. The simple binary opposition of women in the home and men in the factory was a product of bourgeois capitalism. This situation is carefully exposed by Haraway (1990:212-215).

LIBERAL
FEMINIST
ARTISTIC
FORMATIONS

The "High" Response

I do live in a society, and who I am
is determined by the structure of
experience a woman is supposed to
have. My experience is filtered
through a complex interaction
between me and the expectations
that the world has on men.

(Linda Nochlin, "What is Female Imagery," Ms. 3,
No. 11, May, 1975, in Lippard, 1976:80)

Of course, "female imagery" was first used, and should continue to be used, to mean female sexual imagery. I prefer "female sensibility" because it's vaguer, even more impossible to pin down. There is a lot of sexual imagery in women's art-circles, domes, eggs, spheres, boxes, biomorphic shapes, maybe a certain striation or layering.

(Lucy Lippard, "What is Female Imagery," Ms. 3, No. 11, May, 1975, in Lippard, 1976:81)

I think women tend to be more autobiographical in their work then men. ... My work is an open diary. That's what I often miss in men's work — an autobiographical or narrative aspect.

(Joan Snyder, "What is Female Imagery," Ms. 3, No. 11, May, 1975, in Lippard, 1976:86)

Sex is bound to be a factor in women's work precisely because women have been sex objects and are much more aware of their bodies then men.

("Six," Studio International, 187, No. 963, Feb. 1974, in Lippard, 1976:93)

... to deal publicly with intimate
and specifically female experience...body art combined with
feminist consciousness is still
considered more subversive than
neutralized art by women that
ignores the sexual identity of
its maker and its audience.

(Lippard, 1976, p. 123)

Men, however, when not using
themselves, are using women.
Vergine has written about "acute
gynephobia" demonstrated in
much male body art, and sees many
of its manifestations as an "envy of
the uterus as capacity for creation."

(Lippard, *1976,* pg. 133)

    The argument of Lippard's books and North American liberalist feminist discourse in general, as well as their counterparts in Europe (see Ecker, 1985), claim that women's experience is different from that of men, and although personhood is more desirable than this bifurcation suggests, it is their *experience* which has been suppressed. It is further argued that an iconography is in the making which then exemplifies these experiences. In the early phase that iconography was composed of both sexual and erotic imagery, as well as realist and conceptual celebrations of female experience in which birth, motherhood, rape, household imagery, windows, menstruation, auto-biography, family background, and portraits of friends figured prominently. Later, more symbolic or abstract parallels of women's experiences were images of veiling, confinement, enclosure, pressure, barriers, constrictions, as well as growth, unwinding, unfolding, and sensuous surfaces (Lippard,1976:7; Lauter,1984).

It strikes me that a similar stance was taken by feminist lesbian artists at this same time, but the specificity of their identity was overshadowed by gender issues in general (Grover, 1990). Nevertheless, like heterosexual feminists, the focus on the difference of experience remained a central theme but content changed. The problems of coming out, the anger of being excluded from the male dominated artistic main stream, the secrecy and concealment of being lesbian—often represented cryptically and secretively through an iconography of abstracted labias, breasts, vaginas, clits and breasts—and the celebration of the female body which coincided with the call for women's experience in general, were common themes.

The central concern with this approach to lesbian representation, it seems, revolves around the issue of sexuality. At core, the lesbian identity is defined by sex preference. In order to celebrate and exploit this very center requires the exploration of lesbian fantasy and desire, thereby asserting sexuality as the central theme of lesbian identity. However, such a representation is at odds with the larger liberalist (heterosexual) feminist movement which opposes the objectification and sexual exploitation of women in the media and in pornography.[1] As a more confined and limited discourse, in no way did it enter my consciousness in the late '70s, nor would i have been allowed to introduce it in an art history course within the confines of a university whose roots were Catholic based. Above all, i could not have discriminated successfully the differences between the iconography of lesbian feminist artists and straight feminist artists at that time or now unless the differences were explicitly stated for me.

The difficulties with such generalizations regarding women's experience play themselves out in the institution of art. Linda Nochlin's (1973) well-known essay "Why Have There Been No Great Feminist Artists?" raised the question, *implying* that only a particular sort of experience had been valued by the European tradition of art, and thereby excluding women altogether. Yet another interpretation was possible, and this was to identify equally prominent "Mistresses" who were in every way the counterparts to male "Masters."[2] Although the term is pejorative, it is a symptom of the difficulty in finding a comparable sign position that carries a similar connotation for the dominance of skill and accomplishments on a grand scale. Finding Mistresses to match the Masters was, unfortunately, a no-win situation because greatness was already male inscribed; genius meant possessing the phallus, or the very least—striving to possess it.[3] Eleanor Tuft's well-known book, *Our Hidden*

Heritage: Five Centuries of Women Artists, written in 1974, was the representative example for the reformist trend of unearthing women artists. The huge exhibition and scholarly book, *Women Artists 1550-1950* by Linda Nochlin and Ann Sutherland Harris (1976), is often cited as a culminating point of this insurrection.[4] In-depth explorations of single women artists have become common, like Garrard's (1989) in-depth study of Artemisia Gentileschi. In film studies, the search for women directors was the feminist version of *auteur theory*.

To rehearse what has become now a familiar narrative, a heroic art history for women was then and continues to be supportive of "The Great Masters and Masterpieces" view of art history which began with Vasari's biographical summations in the 16th century, and continued paradigmatically on through to Heinrich Wölfflin at the turn of the century. It remained the framework in the 1920s with Bode and Berenson; renewed in the '70s through Janson's *History of Art* and Gombrich's *Story of Art*, and so on down the line. Ralph Smith's current remedy as to what ails art education – *Excellence in Art Education* (1986) – is the latest in line; written to promote and restore this phallogocentric tradition.[5] The art critic Hilton Kramer, the founder of the right-wing journal *New Republic*, E.D. Hirsch, Jr(1987), whose desire is to recover the Great Books tradition to save American culture, and the late Alan Bloom (1987), who proclaimed that American universities were beset by nihilism, represent further patriarchal voices for "the grand restoration."[6]

Today, Nochlin continues her pioneering efforts by examining the relationships of women, art and power (1988). Yet it has been nearly two decades since she first put to question "the great man" myth by showing that art-making was indeed dependent on favorable social and cultural conditions (see Wolff, 1981). This trend continued with such works as Germain Greer's *The Obstacle Race* (1979) and Borzello & Ledwidge's *Women Artists* (1986), as further convictions of a liberalist view.[7] A residual sense of idealism dwells throughout such books: the social is now presented only in terms of obstacles, or "barriers, beliefs, prejudices" (Pollock, 1988:144) placed around an individual's freedom of action. Such obstacles, the result of false consciousness, can be dispelled by an act of will alone. The contradictions of this idealism, swimming in a sea of an overdetermined social set of circumstances, are defined, on the one hand, as the nonrecognition and repression of women's talent by (in Greer's case) a capitalist system that has contempt for "smallness," or, as in Schor's (1987b) reformulation, a neo-classical distaste for "detail." By this Schor means the distaste for the examination of the particularities of everyday life, which is the usual domain of the feminine. On the other hand (again, especially with Greer) there is an admonishment of women who do not aspire to male "norms" of greatness (while Greer apparently has!). This paradox of feminist transformation has been identified by Betty Friedan as *The Second Wave* (1981) of women who are dismayed at the failure of a unified feminist front to curb male power.

In art education these same liberalist arguments are furthered by detailed studies of the autobiographical lives of women art educators: how they came to art (Korzenik, 1985), who they studied with, what their art was like and the lives they led as art educators. Collins and Sandell's *Women, Art, and Education* (1984), provides the paradigm case of early scholarship in this area. The publishing date gives the reader some indication of how conservative and entrenched male dominated art education was (and is), based on masterpieces and an expressive individualistic psychology. Recently, Discipline Based Art Education (DBAE), supported by The Getty Center for Education (in Santa Monica, California), has become the centralizing measure for the promotion of this phallocentric vision. Sexism and the achievement of sex equity are the key values that run throughout *Women, Art, and Education* so that women artists might be given an equal voice. A following publication, *Women Art Educators II*, was likewise a roster of women art educators who were unearthed as a testament that there indeed have been women of equal footing and distinction to match male art educators such as Manuel Barkan and Victor Lowenfeld. Currently, the Women's Caucus, an affiliate of the National Art Education Association, regularly nominates a woman art educator of the year (The Mary Rouse Award) to ensure recognition of the roster's status.[8] And why shouldn't they? The National Art Education Association (NAEA) has honored mostly a roster of men, but this is changing.

Liberalist Follies

As was the case with Post-impressionism, whereby the art gallery system began to solidify the gains made by the Impressionists, one impulse of feminist postmodernism, under a liberalist disguise, can still be easily accommodated within a patriarchal system of "great art." As Pollock writes (1985/1986):

> Feminist concerns with figurative work, overt subject-matter and personalized testimony can be accommodated in this renewed trend towards figuration and expressionism, but subsumed as a secondary category of women's expressionism within the major trope of extreme claims to individualistic creativity in the Grand (Men's) Tradition (p.15).

The main difficulties with this approach have been discussed brilliantly and thoughtfully by Griselda Pollock's *Vision and Difference*, (1988:37 ff.). She questions the claim of a common gender consciousness, a *transhistorically* shared experience that underlies the virtual fact that one is a biological woman. For Sutherland Harris, the woman's point of view assumes "a shared consciousness between women irrespective of differences of class, nationality and historical period." Pollock goes on the dismantle Harris's analysis of Judith Leyster's iconography, pointing out how Leyster had engaged in the historically specific debates surrounding Dutch 17th century art, and had produced an entirely different vision of reality from that of Franz Hals whose style she mimicked. Pollock admonishes Harris for her blindness to the changing history of sexuality, the family and other institutions where the identities of masculinity and femininity were shaped. The result was the linking of women to a separate sphere by virtue of biological sex alone, thereby avoiding the argument that women artists were also social and political subjects involved in contemporary class and ideological struggles.

Recognizing the limitations of this approach, women historians next examined women's perceptual responses as opposed to the male perceptual responses throughout history. This might be identified as being equivalent to what Showalter (1982:185) called *gynocriticism*, and what Cassandra Langer (1988) had called *gynergenic* art criticism.[9] A study in the different iconography was undertaken. Norma Broude and Mary Garrard's *Feminism and Art History*, a collected group of essays produced in 1982, was a dispersion of such concerns. Again, there were careful analyses of women's artists like Artemisia variation on the theme of *Susanna and the Elders*. The male pornographic gaze was explored, recapitulating some of John Berger's early work, but with greater sophistication. Broude dealt with Degas' "misogyny,"[10] while Duncan discussed virility and domination in early 20th century vanguard painting in the same manner as Susan Griffin's argument in *Pornography and Silence* (1982):

women in the medieval period were represented by male artists either as virgins or prostitutes. The male iconography of her body was either that of a whore—the fallen woman like Mary Magdellan represented as a desirable possessable object (as Nochlin's essay concluded in the same volume)—or a virgin. As virgin she was mother, nurturer, and the good wife. Like the Virgin Mary, she was always placed in the back ground, her maternal body a mere prop for the Christ child.[11]

Susan Griffin rests her binary opposition on the analogy that men are to reason–the head and mind–as women are to emotion—the body and nature. Since St. Augustine, men have experienced their sex primarily in their heads (see Foucault and Sennett, 1981). The inability of males to perceive themselves as material (body) and emotional beings has led to what she calls a 'pornographic consciousness.'[12] The objectified woman was a projected image, albeit split, of that part of the masculine self which remained attached to feelings of need, emotionality and dependence. This repressed part of the male psyche insured domination, status and power. In Joelynn Snyder-Ott's (1978) comparison between Renoir's and Cassatt's mother and child pictures, she claims that Renoir's misogynistic tendencies objectified his rendition of his wife nursing their child. In contrast, Cassatt's mother and child were actively involved with each other. All this suggested that visual perception was itself gender biased once form had been placed on the content of life's experiences.[13]

Sevelta Alper's essay, included in Broude & Garrard's collection, was to put the entire approach to question. In her account of the differences between Northern and Italian painting, now developed in her full length book, *The Art of Describing* (1983), Alper's made the observation that Vermeer's use of the *camera obscura* eliminated the spectator from a specific viewpoint. His paintings represented women doing their ordinary duties in the Dutch home. He had not idealized them as had the southern tradition. These women, through their painted letters, revealed their elusiveness. Vermeer's women were a world apart, inviolate, self-contained, but more importantly—self-possessed. Such a vision was the antithesis of the Italian gaze which coveted the woman as object. Alper's concluded her essay with a form of apparatus theory critique: "To want to possess meaning is masculine, to experience presence is feminine. ... It was not the gender of makers, but the *different modes of making that is at issue*" (p.198, my emphasis).

Rozika Parker and Griselda Pollock's *Old Mistresses: Women, Art and Ideology*, written in 1981 from a social feminist point of view, in my opinion, further puts to flight the question of a *distinct* feminine aesthetic. In their first chapter, "Critical stereotypes: the 'essential feminine' or how essential is femininity," the authors chart a strategy which preserves the question of women's art, but does so by examining the way history was written and the way women were recorded and described; positioned by and in it. The relationships between women artists and institutions of art and ideology as they appeared historically in their shifts and changes were examined discursively. "The concept of 'Woman,'" they write, "whose history we have been tracing is not based on biology or psychology, but is rather a structured social category—a set of roles prescribed for women, ideologically sustained and perpetuated by being presented as descriptions of women" (p.113). By this they mean a linguistic signifying discourse which pre-exists as a "series of historically reinforced codes, signs and meanings" which could be manipulated and even transformed, but which could never exist outside of that particular "text." Degas' *oeuvre* remains an "object" formulated at the juncture of numerous discourses which were always under potential contestation by different interpretations.

The term "Old Master," they argue, was equated with a male artist and numerous masculine social roles, like the Bohemian, for example. The notion of genius and greatness was an attribute of the male sex. In contrast the "woman artist" was placed in a different locale, and in the site/sight/cite of femininity. Women were excluded from particular male discourses so that they were unable to represent themselves differently. This was especially true of the academy where women artists were not permitted to study the nude model. From the Renaissance until the mid-nineteenth century the most important art form was history painting—the painting of historical, mythological or religious subjects based on human figures. The male academicians, by keeping women from painting nudes, exercised control over the ideology of art production. "Control over access to the nude was but an extension of the exercise of power over what meanings were constructed by an art based on the human body. Thus women were not only impeded by the exclusion from the nude but were also constrained by the fact that they had no power to determine the language of high art." (p. 115). Men "framed" the representations of "woman" by denying her the power to determine meaning for herself and for culture. "[M]an at work transforming *his* own image the raw material which the model offers to his gaze, matter into form, nature into culture. He controls the brushes and colors and produces the pictorial image" (p.124). For women, the signification of meaning of the visual language was denied.[14]

Parker and Pollack point out that the existence of women artists was fully recognized and continued to grow from the sixteenth century on through to the nineteenth century. Yet, at the moment when women's social emancipation and increasing education should have prompted a greater awareness, a silence fell on the artistic activities of women in the past. After the eighteenth century there was an increase of the female nude. She was painted continually. "All present woman as an object to a male viewer/possessor outside the painting, a meaning sometimes explicitly enforced by the gaze of a subordinate male onlooker in the painting itself" (p.116).

This displacement of women artists has been traced to the new discourse that emerged with the development of the bourgeois family and childhood during the late-eighteenth century. Eventually the cult of the happy mother arose who was to be fulfilled through child-rearing and child-bearing. Femininity, by the nineteenth century, became exclusively domestic and maternal. The bourgeois notions of the artist arose with everything that was anti-domestic—models of free living, sexually energetic pursuits, and becoming social outcasts. Rheumatism became the "art" disease which demanded a change of climate. On this excuse, the *bohème* became a traveler, escaping from country and home, searching for the primitive as paradigmatically represented by Gauguin. The artist and the category of woman could not overlap in this discourse. (When it did, as in the case of Canada's Emily Carr, she fell out of the category and became something else: an asexual figure, neither man nor woman.) Women artists by the Victorian age became stereotypical: men worked in the realm of culture while women remained closer to nature. Men were the true artists, possessing genius, working on serious works of the imagination on a grand scale like monumental sculpture, architecture, and history paintings. On the other hand women had taste, working on minor, delicate, trivial personal pastimes such as the painting of flowers, portraits, miniatures and of course the crafts.

Parker and Pollock have moved the discourse on women and art outside liberalist assumptions, yet without losing sight/site/cite of woman as a socially defined gendered category by a patriarchal structure. Despite the power of their socially informed critique, the dominant art historical narrative could still subsume it. This was distinctly demonstrated by Janet Wolff

(1992) through a personal anecdote. While viewing a television program about Impressionism and Post-Impressionism, Wolff notes, to her surprise, the appearance of Griselda Pollock, who, with Fred Orton, had written a deconstructive critique of those very categories being discussed (Pollock and Orton, 1978). In that segment, Pollock repeated her critique, discussing the way the socio-economic contradictions of the nineteenth century France "could be 'read' in the representation in their works of the city [Seurat, Van Gogh, and Signac] as distant prospect, troubling the edges of the rural landscape or suburban leisure zone" (p. 716). Pollock's deconstruction showed that the very grouping of paintings under the label "post-impressionism" was an ideological construction of art criticism and art history. She then displayed artworks of women, produced at the same time, who had been excluded from "post-impressionism" by the sexual politics of that time. Pollock concluded her presentation pointing to the exoticism of Gauguin and Manet who had made their claims to avant-gardism over the bodies of women. The "host," Michael Wood, summarized this as: "There is no such thing as objective art history. There are only the interpretations of art historians" (ibid).

Here the question of relativism was raised in a form of a contradictory discourse. Saving the totalizing history of modernist art, so that someone like Pollock could be dismissed, required a glossing over the potential of contradiction that her discourse raised. These contradictions were converted into a relativism—just another story, just another interpretation. Such relativism, at first hand, appears as the negative moment of the grand canon of art, for the danger is that knowledge is "only" subjective interpretation. However, relativism must legitimate its own claim to be more than just "one way of looking at thing," by imposing its subjectivity consciously through the authority of Woods, as a meta-narrative. Relativism becomes *the* way of describing *all* ways of looking at things. "Relativism is not so much a break with meta-language as the preservation of meta-language even at the price of relinquishing any content to the transcendent subject it installs. *Cogito* becomes *dubito* but *ergo sum* remains" (Readings, 1991: 67).

The above masculine/ feminine dichotomies which deconstruction puts to question, should not be interpreted strictly along the sex-biological divide. The biological fact of being a male does not necessarily make every male dominant, aggressive, and technologically cold-blooded. Yet, because of the social construction of the humanist discourse in art and art history, and because of the structure of the family it produced, which is rapidly changing of course, these generalizations regarding gender are sufficiently socially reproduced to have a high correlation with heterosexual divisions. The focus on more marginal gender formations–lesbian and gay sensibilities–different senses of masculinity (see Silverman, 1992) and femininity (see Butler, 1990b) has, of course, been the very success of poststructuralist thought in general. They promise the possibilities of different lived realities.

Women and Crafts

If women's sewing, weaving, lacemaking are indeed signifiers of a specific narrational desire, the vehemence with which they are culturally denigrated as lesser arts becomes more comprehensible. It is well known how Freud attempted to contain any threatening aspects of female production or initiative in this area by specifying the activity of weaving as a repetition of an originary desire to *mime the phallus* by braiding together the pubic hair.

(Doane, 1987:110, italic in original)

The "Low" Response

In the feminist liberalist aesthetic discourse there is also a marked affinity between women and the crafts tradition, which easily draws upon cross cultural, folk and indigenous native populations. Since the emergence of the "fine arts" this craft tradition has been rendered inferior and devoid of any conceptual basis. Crafts, therefore, raise a major theme for feminism: what feminist practice would overcome the separation between private—the applied, domestic arts—and the public fine arts? Such a concern echoes the historical avant-garde who were also preoccupied with the separation of art from life. The domestic arts, since the time of *recorded* history, have been defined by men as inferior. Weaponry and metal crafts (copper, iron, gold, silver), traditionally associated with male culture, were placed above the domestic arts such as baking, culinary art, and interior design. It is no accident, for example, that the stone masons were the first "artist-sculptors" to break away from the guilds. The cutting of stone not only had "measure" as part of its practice, but the material and the tools for building public structures carried a prestige that could rival the intimacy of the hearth. Similarly, diaries and letters written by women have never, until very recently, been considered part of what makes up the canon of literature. Quilting, and the fiber arts in general, and by extension the culinary arts, strive for status to be annexed into the great tradition of Art.

Whereas the academic male artist has always been allowed a great deal of time, labour, money and energy for his production, this was rarely the case for women artists who, in Canada and the United States, only began entering fine arts departments in any significant numbers in the '60s. In the 1970s a group of British women began to make art objects small enough to send to each other through the mail to subvert, or at least put to question, privilege. Working small, as opposed to large, was the intended subversion. "Art not Heart" was embroidered on a cushion. "Homemade I'm afraid" was knitted into a panel. Pieces of female anatomy were nestled inside chocolate boxes. Cakes were baked in the shape of babies. The resulting collection was exhibited as *Feministo*. Women networking with each other had broken the bondage of being bound to the house. To the male tradition this exhibition belonged to the order of kitsch and the sentimental world of "baby pictures."

Parker's book, *The Subversive Stitch* (1984), is a re-examination of the link between (liberal) feminism and the radical potential of craft, evoking one of its buried homonyms–kraft. She shows how "femininity" became linked with embroidery and the household, and how the suffragettes, as well as the hippie movement, used embroidery as an oppositional force, personalizing clothing through their "embroidered world." The personal had become political. Parker mentions the work of Catharine Riley, whose embroidery evokes and subtly parodies the emotions associated with needlework—purity and chastity. The Women's Peace movement use of appliqué banners and ribbons to surround Greenham Common air base, England, alludes to Suffrage symbolism through the use of traditional peace motifs and feminist political symbols. "The peace movement women deliberately evoke the meaning of embroidery to emphasize that they are campaigning against the nuclear threat *as women*. Displayed at Greenham, the banners declare the fence a boundary between femininity and masculinity, between life and death, technology and nature" (Parker, 1984, p.211). Most recently, the political use of appliqué banners was powerfully demonstrated in Washington, D.C., as commemorative banners were sewn together to honor and remember those who had died of AIDS. This artistic political action, organized by friends and mothers of those now deceased, was a powerful reminder of government inaction.

The hierarchy between arts and crafts was therefore established along both class and sex lines. As Parker and Pollock (1981) inevitably point out, "what distinguishes art from craft in the hierarchy is not so much different methods, practices and objects but also where the things were made, often in the home, and for whom they were made, often for the family. The fine arts are a public, professional activity. What women make, which is usually defined as 'craft,' could be defined as 'domestic art.'" (p. 70). Indeed, craft doesn't become art unless it is placed in art galleries. Parker and Pollock draw on the example of Navaho blankets and quilts which increase their status once the overlay of formal qualities is bestowed on them.

This appropriation continues today in yet another form, through what Nelson Graburn (1976) has called a "fourth culture": a culture embedded within the first, second or third world which is exploited for its potential "souvenir" value. The Mud "Men" of Papua New Guinea, for example, draw huge crowds of tourists when they dramatize their dance, yet their masks have begun to be more "sardonic" as they learn to play the crowd. In Canada, Inuit artists living in remote regions in the North, e.g., Port Harrison, Povungnituk, Sugluk, Cape Dorcet, have been systematically exploited by the Hudson's Bay Company and the Canadian Handicrafts Guild to manufacture prints and large soapstone carving. These then are billed as true indigenous art forms, sold for huge profits and are said to be a national heritage, Canadian through and through, when, in fact, the Inuit never had any use to sculpt so large in the context of a nomadic existence (Graburn, 1970).

Such a discussion skirts around the somewhat pejorative term "women of color." Black and aboriginal women, who have been denied access to the "high" art of the museum have found their expression through these more 'traditional' art forms which have typically been denied any "theoretical insight," relegated to the heap of "naive art," "folk art" and so on. i need only refer to Alice Walker's (1983) *In Search of Our Mother's Gardens*, to recognize that so much of this expression is simply overlooked, dismissed because it lacks "cultural capital." In an artwork such as Judy Chicago's *Dinner Party* (1973-1978), which might be identified as the quintessential work of art that celebrates liberalist values (each woman's place setting marks an achieved measure of success through individual effort and struggle), a project that clearly transposes the arts and crafts of women into the higher elevations of art through its emphasis on ceramics and embroidery, there is but one black woman represented–Sojourner Truth. "When thirty-six of the thirty-nine places are set with versions of Chicago's famous "vagina" and recognizable slits have been given to such sex bombs as Queen Elizabeth I, Emily Dickinson, and Susan B. Anthony, what is one to think when Truth, the mother of four, receives the only plate inscribed with a face?" (O'Grady, 1994:154).

The divisions raised above are reflected today in our schools. The first division is made between the fine arts and industrial arts, reflective of a similar division which occurred during industrialization. The contradictory role which ceramics plays in each field reaffirms this historical division: one is either a production potter out for 'crass' market sales, or your craft has been elevated to an art form which now means less sales but more exhibitions, some often associated with esoteric Eastern mysticism and meditation where this craft is still honored. Yet there is another division marked along sexist lines *between* and *in* the fine arts themselves. The more public the art is, the more prestigious it becomes, and *more likely* that it is male dominated. In the visual arts, those which are perceived to be "domestic" are usually confined to the classroom—like painting, printmaking, small-scale sculpture. These are distinguished from the public arts of industrial and commercial design, architecture and monumental sculpture, which are rarely engaged at the school level. Music, as composition and conducting, is male dominant (the baton being the displaced phallus); choral singing, back-up sounds, and the playing of instruments in a recital are female dominant. Drama as a public display generally has a male director and script writers, while women form the star system. Classical ballet, with its aesthetic commitment to the weightless body, classical line, the strict limitations of body size and shape for girls and women, has always been dominated by male choreographers. Women remain the prima donnas, whose anorexic bodies are said to, once again, fetishize the male gaze (Kirkland, 1986).

The liberal feminist view most germane to dance is the theory of Bandura (1972). His modeling theory, where an individual tends to reproduce attitudes, acts, and emotions exhibited by an observed model, has becomes the way of explaining how gender roles are learnt. Gender identification for who is passive and assertive; who is the subject and who is the object of pushing, propelling, dipping, lifting, grasping another's body parts; who uses relatively larger or smaller movements in space; who throws the body, clings, or leans and supports; who cries and frowns; who moves on a limb as a unit or in parts; who takes a wide or narrow postural stance, and who uses strong or weak effort, maps the social codes on the body. Intensity, duration, and longevity of the variables that impinge on this socialization could be overcome through an educational curriculum that leads to sexual equity. Role reversals, androgyny, asexual female dances, unisexuality, become ways to change dance forms towards the goals of sexual equity. It is telling that many of the greatest male dancers and choreographers of the twentieth century have been homosexual or bisexual men (Barnes, 1974). The recent death of Rudolf Nureyev of AIDS (in 1993) brought this home to the "general public," again fueling homophobia by equating the disease with homosexuality. Bandura is silent over issues such as class, race, color, ethnicity. The body´s social codes are read decontextually, as if these contingencies took second place to the polarities of gender.

This private/public split in the arts repeats itself in literature where autobiography is usually the genre for the "coming out" story. In literature, Felski (1989:133 ff.) identifies a feminist *Bildungsroman* which charts the conscious self-awakening of women as they gradually enter the public domain. A "process of *separation* as an essential precondition for any path to self-knowledge" (p. 124) becomes necessary. In the contemporary narrative, Felski points out that there is an attempt to escape from the confines of a heterosexual romance plot. "The importance of a symbolic act of separation as a defining feature of [liberalist] feminist fiction suggests that certain notions which were previously unthinkable–women's right to social identity not determined by their sexual and maternal roles, for example–have become embedded within the discursive frameworks of contemporary culture, functioning as an important and influential source of new narratives which attempt to confront and work through in story form some of the contradictions of gender identity uncovered by feminist ideology" (p.126). Neuman (1990) has recently pointed out a similar autobiographical genre where middle-class daughters must rebel against their mothers in order to find their own values.[15]

It should be pointed out that the attack on the public/private binary by liberal feminists searching for equity is largely based on the interests of single, affluent, well-educated women who find the split between the public and the private a barrier to their freedom as individuals. For less privileged women the division of spheres provides a measure for survival. "More often than not, poor women's survival depends upon the possibility of some minimal cooperation with the men of their group. Thus, while elite women may well experience single motherhood as freedom from male domination, disadvantaged women are more likely to experience it as the price of not holding men accountable or of not permitting men to assume their responsibilities as fathers. And while elite women may revel in the availability of pornography as a means of exploring and expanding their own identities, disadvantaged women are more likely to experience it as the dangers proliferating in the street in which they raise their children" (Fox-Genovese: 1993:251).

My interpretation of the liberalist feminist stance in art and art education has informed me, first: that there is a strong recognition by women that the inequality of the sexes is neither a biological given nor a divine mandate, but a cultural construction; and second: that a male perspective, assumed to be "universal," has dominated the institution of art and its history. Feminist scholarship has named names, but, not unlike the trade in stamps, there continues to be a danger that these names become annexed to male names in the great mill of commodity production known as the "fine arts." It is evident that women have been excluded from the Academies and excluded from apprenticeships, but only during specific moments in history when it was in the interest of men to do so. Women in the art world have been, and continue to be, the models, muses, subject matter and suppliers of supper and sex. Patronage and connoisseurship have always been male pursuits. Women artists have been classed as Sunday painters and amateurs; never have they had a high profile. Only by "virtue" of being rich, having artistic fathers, supportive parents, or famous clients, have women managed to gain recognition. Their marginalization and the recognition of the need to rectify art history certainly draws my support; however, embedded within this liberalist tradition came the denial of my support some fifteen years ago. Indeed it is a very conservative position, and one which is, in the final analysis, counter productive. Should we all heed Stacey's admonishment?

> Instead of celebrating the feminine, we need to retain a vital tension between androgynous and female-centered visions. We need to recognize contradiction and to apply a critical perspective that distinguishes between giving value to traditionally female qualities and celebrating the female in a universalistic and essentialist manner (Stacey, 1983: 575)

The above *strong* reading of a liberalist feminist position is one way that the I, as male, might be dismissive of the tremendous effort women—or to be more specific, an elite strata of women—have made to write/right/rite their own history. The "resurrection" (suggesting the finding of an opposing phallus) of an alternate woman's history, what Elsie Boulding (1976) has called the "underside of history," does not merely "add" on or match the male artistic canon, although a strong reading can make it appear so. Rather it poses a threat—which may lead to a threat of *jouissance*.[16] If enough women artists are found who constitute a "different" reality than the one exposed by the male dominant view, both the literary and artistic canons are shaken. But now questions emerge as to who becomes included and excluded in the progressive line of women's greatness. Excellence and reverence for particular artists and their *oeuvre* become a self-serving way to perpetuate the myth of genius and the same danger applies to these Mistresses. "[T]he fact of canonization puts any work beyond questioning of establishing its merit and, instead, invites students to offer only increasingly more ingenious readings and interpretations, the purpose of which is to validate the greatness already imputed by canonization" (Kolodny, 1980:8).

Kolodny's comment is directed to men but it applies equally to women. The fear of the inclusion of women does not necessarily suggest the disappearance of the great Western artistic tradition that our art-slide libraries hold, "but, instead the eclipse of that particular *form* of the text [of art], and that particular *shape* of the canon [great men], which previously reified male readers' [viewers'] sense of power and significance in the world" (p.7) may be shaken. What is introduced into the study of art may continue to solidify the male tradition or begin to reshape it. Paraphrasing Hoy (1978), the continual reinterpretation of the past goes hand in hand with the continual representation of the present, making the future pregnant with new directions and possibilities. It is precisely such reshaping which has called the dominant male artistic canon to question, even though the early beginnings of women's art history was blatantly a "miraculous resurrection."

There is yet another, more profound problem of criticism within the male-dominated grand narrative of art and art education as exemplified by humanist legacy. This involves the question of the paradigmatic role of the critic and art historian who ensure standards and fix a learned or expert interpretation on a work of art, as if to assure paternity over it. Ralph Smith in art education, H.D. Hirsch, Jr. in literature, Allan Bloom in human sciences, and Hilton Kramer in art history, have already been mentioned as a conservative backlash to the pluralization of interpretations. Deconstructive criticism (see Owens, 1982; Burgin; 1986b) has redirected the critics' positionality to one where the interest is in the art "text's" effects, rather than dwelling on their meaning. The discussions between Heidegger and Schapiro over the meaning of Van Gogh's peasant shoes (see Olkowski,1985) has been successfully undermined by Derrida's (1987a: 254ff.) critique of artistic interpretation as a desire for property, which conveys the sense of "power over things." "[T]he Heidegger-Schapiro debate is basically a contest over the proprietorship of the image" (Owens, 1982). To have the "last word" on any discipline is to repeat the folly of appropriation and ensure one's proper name. For this reason, many critics have claimed the 'end of art,' a development which i shall pick up later.[17]

Psychoanalytically Framing the High & Low Arts

The liberal feminist critique of the arts has operated on two registers: a "high" response to the male grand artistic narrative and a "low" response, recovering artistic traditions which have been under the sphere of women. These responses have generated a "hybrid" art form which wedges its existence out of and between these two forms, leveling high art and elevating the crafts. To theorize the complexity of this hybrid form, it is possible to marshal the conceptualizations of Christian Metz's notion of the "imaginary signifier" (1982:59-60) which he applied to cinema. Following Lacan and Freud, Metz points out that both the visual and auditory drives have a stronger, and special, relationship with the absence of the object. They are closely associated with the pursuit of the imaginary and the recovery of the "object" of desire, thus fulfilling the missing lack, at least temporarily until the next object is cathexed.[18] It is the distance of the look and the distance of listening which represents the absence of the object concretely. There is, therefore, a division made between the senses of distance—hearing and looking—and the sense of contact—touch, taste, smell. Whereas orality and anality initiate a "partial fusion" between the object and the "*source* of the drive," by this he means there is pleasure at the level of the source organ (ear, anus, and mouth), vision in contrast keeps a distance between the source (the eye) and the object. "It is no accident," he writes, "that the main socially acceptable arts are based on the senses at a distance, and that those which depend on the senses of contact are often regarded as 'minor arts' (e.g. the culinary arts, the art of perfumes etc.)" (p. 59).

The bifurcation of high and low arts repeats itself here along body organs. Traditionally the voyeuristic male look is associated with high art, while equally a narcissistic female look is associated with touch (hapticity)—the arts of the body. One celebrates content, rationality, analysis; the sensuousness of material is placed in the background; the other foregrounds sensuousness but chases out analysis. A good example of this is the separation between the scopophobic pleasures of the look (claimed to be coded as male) and fashion which is linked to the skin, the body and the tactile senses (Sawchuck, 1987). It's not difficult to see how the idea of "distance" is coded as a masculine bourgeois Kantian aesthetic as developed in Bourdieu's (1984/1979) theory of class "distinction," while "closeness" is coded as feminine and therefore more trivial—mere decoration. This binary has had a long history. The "querelle des Anciens et modernes" is but one historical manifestation of the playing off content over material, mind over body. The issue was fought over which aesthetic element was to dominate painting—the rationality of line or the expressiveness of color.

The same axis repeats itself with purity/impurity, essential/inessential. Historically the coding of impurity, vulgarity, *kitsch*, belong to the realm of popular or mass culture, which has been brilliantly analyzed by Huyssen (1986) as being coded feminine–modernism's Other. Read within the postmodern context, the collapsing of high art with popular culture, beginning with pop art, seems at first glance to provide a possible way out of this gendered binarism. The cross-fertilization between fine arts and popular culture has produced new hybrid genres. Film, television, and the advertising industry are all intimately related, quoting both from the larger fine arts canon and amongst themselves. What has changed little, however is the institutionalized contexts of viewing and the one-way communication based on a specular view. It is conceivable to view Jackson Pollock's output as "all body," one which participates in the Herculean spraying of masculine semen and therefore hapticity. Any painterly work demonstrates such physicality, more or less, but the issue here is that no physical involvement other than looking is involved by the spectator.

The context of the gallery and museum, the way it classically positioned the viewer, was more in line with a male viewing distance. "Don't touch" signs and guards continue their surveillance to make sure the spectator observes such rules. In contrast, fetishized objects, especially those used by "primitive" and indigenous peoples, were meant to be handled, stroked and had use-value. Proximity and closeness to the body did matter. Such was also the case of relics and icons which were meant to be physically touched, or the spectator was to mentally step "into them." Wallis (1983) discusses the iconic crucifix which required just such a positionality. The faithful were required to mentally "back" themselves onto the cross to be in empathy with Christ.

The physical context of viewing art, therefore, remains a concern. The cinema *ideally* sutures the viewer in a place "not too close and not too far away" from the screen, but somewhere in the middle: teeter-tottering in such a way that both viewing extremes are mitigated; allowing for the oscillations of identification of both male and female screen characters. The economics of viewing are clearly evident in a spectacle such as a rock concert or dramatic play where the seating arrangements repeat the classical screen with the viewers set apart from the stage. Sitting in the bleachers the physical distance is so vast that the voyeuristic look can only be accomplished through a pair of binoculars, that optical instrument of the 19th century which permitted spying on others while watching operas and ballet.[19] The use of multiple video cameras to simultaneously show action from different angles and close-ups on monitors placed strategically in the rock concert is one way of providing multiple viewing distances and restoring the look. Fans bring in miniature television sets and listen to their radios during football and hockey events–as if they just can't "see" nor "hear" enough. Both the ear and the eye come into play as heightened, hyperreal modalities, i.e., when one is "upclose and personal" achieving the full effect of voyeuristic and narcissistic identification. This "closeness" has little to do with the sense of "touch" or "smell." The claims that cyberspace is yet another male dream, the apotheosis of specularity, has been well established (Ross, 1992; Conley;1993; Hayles, 1993).[20]

To come back to hybrid works, feminist art works, for example, which require textual readings, or which demand participant observations by being physically activated, or which have strong fibrous smells, or which include recordings, seem to put into question the masculinity/femininity binarism. Not only is the spectator's body motivated, but the intellect is taxed as well. The eye and the hand are not confined to the text but are extended as an effect through the body. And if we come back to Bourdieu (1984) once again, it may be that these hybrid works do collapse high and mass art together, art becoming just one more cultural taste like food, fashion, sport. Thinking this way moves us away from the high-mindedness of psychoanalytic theory towards the material body. Perhaps, as has been suggested, the body in pain and the body in pleasure, i.e., the material body which lives within the extremes of laughing and crying (Plessner, 1973) which is the primordial body that is 'moved' by the arts, can be theorized otherwise?[21]

1 According to the recent writings by lesbian artists, both explicit and implicit sexual imagery defines their identify in the '90s. Harmony Hammond (1994) provides a historical analysis of such imagery, including her own which was influenced by Eva Hesse and Louise Bourgeois—two artists who were engaged in the representation of explicit body parts during the late '70s. Cassandra L. Langer (1994) is explicit in defining a lesbian identity as gyn-affection which is different from mainstream art historical feminism and from gay men. Her polemic against the misreading of the lesbian artist Romaine Brooks, by the feminist art critic Whitney Chadwick, boldly asserts her own sexual politics. Her essay embodies the kinds of ambiguities and contradictions that can be expected of a discourse which does battle with heterosexuality. Most notable, for me, was the contradictory remarks concerning the threat of a lesbian discourse for men. At first she approvingly quotes Jungian analyst Karen Lofthus Carrigton who "argues that relationships between women are 'particularly threatening as an archetypal image to man and the patriarch' because men feel rejected by such intimacy between women" (p. 309). Six pages later the reader is informed that "[p]sychologically we know that lesbian themes have always been an invigorating spectacle for heterosexual men and are the second most popular fantasy listed in Masters and Johnson for both sexes" (p.315). Using a both/and logic, it may be possible to salvage the contradiction. However, the material existence of lesbianism is itself defined by contradiction, overlaid as it were, by heterosexuality, gay politics and patriarchy; making it particularly difficult to define an iconography which isn't just confined to libidinal energies, and which tries to clear space for the lesbian self by concentrating on the issue of identity.

2 In another context Nancy Armstrong (1987) argues that the novel in the eighteenth century was read by middle-class women as a courtesy book. It provided a blue print as to how women were to behave in the domestic sphere. Armstrong's work is a corrective: rather it writes in the missing history to Ian Watt's *The Rise of the Novel* (1957) which presented the realist novel paradigmatically through the novels of Richardson, Fielding and Defoe's *Robinson Crusoe* as the independent bourgeois male subject of individualism (see Landry and MacLean, 1993:86 ff.).

3 A thorough examination of this question has been recently undertaken by Battersby (1989). Her thesis, brilliantly and concisely argued, claims that genius required feminine traits. Genius was a delicate matter which required nurturing. "A man with genius was *like a woman* ... but was *not a woman*" (p.8). Consequently only supermales had such "feminine" qualities. Women remained excluded from the ranks of genius. The distinction between ordinary females and males remained. Men were rationally superior to women. Battersby then goes on to question Parker and Pollock's (1981) claim that masculinity was equated with genius while femininity was synonymous with 'woman.' Rather, it was the rhetoric that praised femininity in males which created men of genius.

4 It can be noted at this time that Joanna Frueh's (1988) perceives a slightly different sequence than the one which i follow. She sees three "critical" stages in feminist literary and art criticism: the first was a resurrection of lost or ignored women artists and works. In the second stage critics developed a women's tradition—a "female sensibility" or "female imagination" that either countered or related to the male literary tradition. The third stage is a re-vision and a re-examination of both men's and women's art along gender lines, mostly by French feminists.

5 For a harsh critique see my "A Para-critical/sitical/sightical Reading Ralph Smith's *Excellence in Art Education," The Journal of Social Theory,* No. 11, (June 1991): 90-137

6 All this has been referred to as the new "cultural wars" (see Hunter, 1991). For the critique in education see Giroux (1988).

7 This paradigm is far from outliving its rhetorical currency. Mira Schor, more than two decades later (1994), argues that the genealogy of women artists is continually subverted by patrilineage. Women's art exhibitions are subsumed by a patrilineal system that attributes their artistic influences to other men. The same thing is repeated on book covers where well known male authors, who carry the necessary cultural capital, are called on to promote sales. In the "culture industry" the names of six Bs are of particular importance: Baudelaire, Benjamin, Brecht, Beckett, Barthes, and Baudrillard. Sprinkle in Jacques Derrida, Sigmund Freud, Michel Foucault and Jacques Lacan, and the complement is complete. Schor calls for a matrilineal heritage of women artists whom women have failed to acknowledge. i believe this is changing. With an established counter women's art history, the liberalist discourse can now call on its own cultural elite from numerous feminist discourses: Irigaray, Steinman, de Lauretis, Haraway, Cixous, Kristeva, as well as begin to quote the '70s feminist iconography in proper postmodern fashion to maintain a separatist canon based on the fine arts tradition and a homogeneous women's experience. Arlene Raven (1994) lists the key points of that history, still bearing an "archaic smile" despite the current backlash that is in progress.

8 The journal *Feminist Studies* regularly features the iconography of a current female artist.

9 It is instructive to read Langer's earlier essay, "Against the Grain: A Working Gynergenic Art Criticism", first published in 1982, against her more recent 1994 essay, "Transgressing Le Droit du Seigneur: The Lesbian Feminist Defining Herself in Art History." In the former essay gynergenic criticism is subsumed under women's gender politics, especially along the radical feminist lines, with only hints that she might be speaking from the political space of lesbian politics. It is quite clear what gynergenic criticism means for her now.

10 Broude's essay on Degas' "misogyny" first appeared in the *Art Bulletin* in 1977. Since then the theme has been taken up and reworked by Bernheimer (1987) and Armstrong (1988) who have stressed Degas' voyeurism.

11 See Kristeva's essay "Motherhood According to Givanni Bellini," in *Desire in Language* (1980), for a variation.

12 Historically masculine and feminine binary oppositions are 'vivified' in paradoxes for rhetorical advancement. For example, Athena was the Athenian goddess of war, but she was also compassionate and benevolent. Her qualities were abstracted for allegorical purposes to mask masculine domination. The woman's body is often appropriated by males to salute high idealism, as in Delecroix's painting of *Liberty at the Barricades* which represented the ideals of the French Republic. Incidentally, this image was poached by Linda Nochlin and appeared on the front cover of her recent book, *Women, Art, and Power and Other Essays* (1988), reinscribing "liberty" for feminist gains. Women's bodies were often appropriated allegorically for general ideals of Motherhood or Justice. The founding fathers of Rome even deny being born of her body; after all, Romus and Remus were suckled by a she-wolf. Even rape of the Sabine women was justified so that Rome might be populated. Titian's image, *Rape of the Sabine Women*, was poached for the cover of Brodribb's book, *Nothing Mat(t)ers* (1992), making such practice a strategy to recode historical meanings embedded in these famous masterpieces.

13 Renoir is alleged to have said "that he painted his paintings with his prick" (Gilbert and Gubar, 1979: 6). There is also a strong passage by Kandinsky written in 1913 which metaphorically sees painting as a rape: "Thus I learned to battle with the canvas, to come to know it as a being resisting my wish (dream), and to bend it forcibly to this wish. At first it stands there like a pure chaste virgin . . . And then comes the willful brush which first here, then there, gradually conquers it with all the energy peculiar to it, like a European colonist" (in Nead,1992:56). Perhaps the apotheosis of the male "using" his female model as a brush was Yves Klein who literally printed their paint-covered bodies by juxtapositioning and pressing them over paper as he pleased. He called this concept, *femme pinceau* (female paintbrush), and the resultant prints, *anthropométries*, which connotes measurement (see Nead, 1992:72-73). The same issue has been raised concerning the relationship between Stieglitzer and Georgia O'Keeffe (Chave, 1990). Was it misogynistic? And what of Beauvoir and Sartre? (Moi,1994)

14 Pollock has updated this general thesis in the contexts of postmodernity. See Pollock (1992a). See an excellent chapter by Whitney Chadwick's "Women Artists and the Politics of Representation" (1988), which covers the ground of women's participation in the history of art thoroughly.

15 Shirley Neuman's "Your Past...Your Future? Autobiography and Mothers' Bodies," Monday, January 29, 1990. Presentation at the University of Alberta, Edmond Kemper Rorodus Lectures.

16 Again, i turn to Gallop's (1984) insightful paper where she notes the relationships between the pleasure of transgression and threat. The threat rests with the male's possibility of having his cultural accomplishments diminished and his ego lessened.

17 A great deal more may be said about the "end of art history" thesis which is prevalent in postmodernist literature. i shall come back to this later in my journey. For now i refer the reader to several books which have explored this issue further: Hans Belting's *The End of Art History?* (1987); Arthur C. Danto's *The Philosophical Disenfranchisement of Art*, especially Chapter V, The End of Art (1986); David Carrier's *Artwriting* (1987); Norman Bryson's (ed.) *Calligram: Essays in New Art History from France* (1988a); A.L. Rees and Frances Borzello's (ed.)*The New Art History* (1988).

18 Freud's term was *Besetzung* meaning an "investment" (*besetzen*-occupied), often an unconscious stake or "investment" in the identification with a certain subject position or object.

19 It is Griselda Pollock who poaches this vision, as the cover of her book *Vision and Difference* (1988) presents us with a nineteenth century middle-class woman looking through her opera glasses.

20 Andrew Ross's "Cyberpunk in Boystown," in *Strange Weather* (1991), offers a gendered reading of the rash of cyberpunk literary fiction and film referring them to "urban fantasies of white male folklore" (p.145). These "cyberpunk cowboys," according to Ross, belong to the western genre. Hayles, in "The Seductions of Cyberspace,"(1993) writes: "In its collaborative aspects, virtual reality emphasizes con-

nectivity, sensitivity to others' choices, open-ended creativity, free-wheeling exploration. It can, of course, be co-opted into masculinist ethics of competition and aggression" (p. 184). For the fantasy of cyberspace from a women's position see Marge Piercy's *He, She and It* (1991) and Jenny Wolmark's, *Aliens and Others* (1993). Scott Bukatman's *Terminal Identity* (1993) offers a critique of cyberspace by feminists in his last chapter. For having made the line, " . . . I would rather be a cyborg than a goddess," famous, see Donna Haraway's well known essay, "A Manifesto for Cyborgs: Science, Technology, and Socialist Feminism of the 1980s" (1990:181). Haraway argues for the feminist possibilities of cyberspace since the cyborg can escape the Oedipal myth—at least in fantasy. See also Constance Penley's " Feminism, Psychoanalysis, and the Study of Popular Culture" (1992) for an exploration of women's fanzines which rewrite the Star Trek series. Spock and Captain Kirk become transformed into men who love each other. Penley argues that such characters are developed since no men can be found in a patriarchal society that could live up to such women's fantasies. These themes are further developed in Penley et al. (1991) *Technoculture.*

21 The recent theorizations in this direction come from Steven Shaviro's *The Cinematic Body* (1993) and Elaine Scarry's *The Body in Pain: The Making and the Unmaking of the World* (1985).

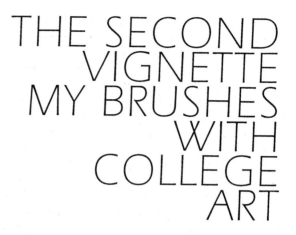

THE SECOND VIGNETTE MY BRUSHES WITH COLLEGE ART

The Question of Essentialism

The Voyeur Drops "in"

My first College Art Association (CAA) conference was in 1985, in San Francisco. The I had been so used to National Art Education Association (NAEA) conferences that this conference took me by surprise. There seemed to be more emphasis on criticism and what that meant for the arts. Women were a definite *presence*. There, for the first time, I heard both Mary Kelly and Rosiland Krauss speak about art and art criticism from their respective positions. Kelly, at that time, related her psychoanalytic rewriting of Lacan and her reliance on her own phenomenological experiences (see her project called *Interim* as described by Pollock, 1987:188-199; Kelly, 1991a,b). Krauss essentially forwarded some of the tenets she brilliantly wrote about in her book, *The Originality of the Avant Garde and Other Essays* (1985). She related the circumstances surrounding the journal *October*, which belonged to the same genre as journals like *BLOCK* (see Bird, *et al*, 1966) (England), *ZG*, and *Art*

& Text (Australia). All four were are devoted to poststructuralist issues. Debate was brisk and lively and the I was sent away reeling.

In 1986 the I attended the Women's Caucus of the CAA in New York, which always meets a week before the "official" conference begins. Here, for the very first time, the I was exposed to an incredible variety of "feminisms." Some women were into performance art; others were simply recovering women artists (pun intended); yet others were simply applying normative criticism to works of art; and for some, autobiography was crucial to their work. It was during one of their panel presentations that a marked discussion took place between the discussant and the rest of the panel members. Incomprehensible French names were tossed about. i wrote what I could phonetically, in the dark, and left confused. In 1987 the I again attended the Women's Caucus meeting in Boston. This time I was at least a little more prepared. Curiously, as an art educator i felt marginalized both at the CAA and in the Women's Caucus. Not being on the roster, i was there illegally and invisibly—for I never did register—i remained a nobody; simply sniffing the climate, i suppose? Those trips always left me in despair, a feeling that art education, with its entirely modernist agenda, would never tolerate what was going on here. It hasn't moved much since the time of this writing–1989.

The above experiences with CAA were decisive turns for me into other explorations. In 1985 i had begun speculating on the protocultural evolution of art. (A manuscript was subsequently completed in summer 1989, but despair had set in: i couldn't find a publisher). That trail had led me to a strand of feminist essentialism linked to mother goddess worship and ecofeminism. At that time i wrote an essay relating green politics and the ecofeminist movements and related these to women artists who were essentialist in their ideological stance.[1] Perhaps one of the strongest growing currents of feminist iconography was and continues to be the link to mother goddess worship brought about primarily through the investigations by women anthropologists such as Merlin Stone (1976) (*Paradise Papers, When God was A Woman*), Barbara Walker (1983) (*The Woman's Encyclopedia of Myths and Secrets*), and feminist historians beginning with Helen Diner (1965) (*Mothers and Amazons*), French's study *Beyond Power* (1985), and recently, an extremely well-argued book, perhaps the definitive statement about the rise of patriarchy to (that) date: Gerda Lerner's *The Creation of Patriarchy* (1986). Once again, it was Lippard's uncanny ability to collate these currents in her book, *Overlays* (1983), which provided the link between women, art and nature. Earlier these relationships had been developed by Joelynn Snyder-Ott in her *Women and Creativity* (1978). "Because I am an artist and my training is in the visual intuitive processes, I experienced strong visual messages as well as intuitive feeling about Stonehenge," she claimed. For Snyder-Ott, the similarity of her own body with fruit that carries seeds; with flowers that resemble the layers of the labia, like unfolding petals; and with the insides of vegetables, was symbolic of a woman's body; not for erotic reasons, but for their beauty. Orenstein (1988) provides a summative statement of the Great Goddess Archetype in art by contemporary women, while Göttner-Abendroth (1982) offered speculations of what might have been a matriarchal aesthetic. One might also add Lauter's work, *Women as Mythmakers* (1984) which also documents an emerging iconography in poetry (Susan Griffin, Margaret Atwood) and visual arts (Mary Beth Edelson, Ellen Lanyon, Danziger, Mary Frank). The woman's body was metaphorically equated with nature.

This line of feminist development argued that women's closer link to "nature" provided for a different vision. Because women were mothers, bore children, menstruated, socialized their children, a different posture towards life emerged. For Lauter (1984), her investigations of the "goddess" figurines and their relationship to animal, mineral and plant life, form three identifiable strands for an emerging and enabling myth of transformation. Georgia O'Keeffe is often cited as an early predecessor of this development. Ortner's influential essay, "Is Female to Male as Nature Is to Culture?" (1974) and Eleanor Munro's (*Originals: American Women Artists*, 1974, qtd. in Lauter, 1984) provocative statement, "nature is to the female artist as the female body has been to the male artist", form the early ground of these artistic developments. Finally added to this development is the suggestion that women's closer link to "nature" is directly aligned with the organic or yin qualities. This implies the right side of the brain and intuitive nature of being a woman is contrasted with the industrial logic and reason exhibited by men. Women are more likely to feel more than men, have a direct link with Goddess figures, and of course be involved with fertility rights.

In the field of literature, Felski (1989:142ff.) once again maps out the implications of this position in what she refers to as the "novel of awakening." In these narratives "the journey is inward, rather than outward [here she is referring to more social activist political novels], in search of a hidden female self. Self-discovery is not portrayed as a historical process, but takes the form of an abrupt and visionary apprehension of underlying unity which leads to an overcoming of ironic and altered self-consciousness. The conceptualization of female identity as an essence to be recovered rather than a goal to be worked toward is reflected in a literary structure which foregrounds the symbolic and lyrical dimension of the text rather than the chronological development of narrative" (p.142). This form, as Felski rightly points out, is imbued with Romantic notions of a paradise lost; a nostalgic search for a lost subjectivity which is authentic and subversive to modernistic values of technology, instrumentalism and rationalism. Nature, as the true sphere of spiritual regeneration, as opposed to urban culture, becomes an idealized conception—a utopian view of harmony and non-alienated existence.

Jean Grimshaw (1986:135-138) argues that within such feminist thinking there has been a dichotomization between an "over-socialized" view of the human being where women are said to be totally victimized, conditioned and indoctrinated, and the biological view of women as free, pure, and authentic, who can emerge if only patriarchal indoctrination is smashed or rejected by reestablishing contact "with an essential femaleness that is buried under the layers of conditioning" (p.135). Felski identifies such a strand of feminist *Bildungsroman* which relies on a sense of women's community for essential womanhood. "The transference of allegiance from a heterosexual relationship to one of intimacy between women overcomes the negative value which women have been conditioned to place on their own sex; the recognition of the other woman serves a symbolic function as an affirmation of self, of gendered identity" (p.138). Thus the feeling of envy amongst women, as competition for men, is mitigated. This provides an exploration of subjectivity amongst group solidarity inspiring activism and resistance rather than passivity and complacency.

Essentialist Religiosity

As i reflected back on these brushes with an essentialist feminist position of Goddess worship, it began to occur to me how being raised a Catholic had made this development particularily appealing to me. Its transcendentalism was seductive. This thought came to me while reading Wendy Martin's (1984) analysis of Andrienne Rich's prophetic vision, and then hearing another voice from my past: Rosemary Ruether.[2] I first met her Voice at Mount Saint Vincent in 1980 when she presented several lectures. At that time i never really comprehended her critique. What i could understand was her attempt to strengthen woman characters throughout the Bible. Now, eight years later, it was possible to "re-visit" her at the University of Alberta when she presented her lecture at St. Stephen's College. That was in 1988. During her talk, i raised the question about the tone of her talk—whether the possibility existed that her position might be interpreted as being misandrous. The I was quickly dismissed. In a partisan crowd she asked for someone with a more positive question! It was i who had projected misandry onto her and she, of course, was *not* misandrous! Case closed. Next question, please.

i think i am now able to finger my uncomfortableness with her writing. There is little, if any, social critique throughout her entire *oeuvre*. But there is a clear and decisive account (cf. Griffin, 1982), of Woman split apart as a Virgin Mary or Mary Magdalen by the Church Fathers. There is also a comprehensive examination of Maritology as a male fetish by the priesthood. (Ruether does not *couch* it in these terms; psychoanalysis is not a discourse she draws upon, but see Michael Carroll (1986) who does.) The fetish of Maritology is akin to an equally secular fetish of the screen siren: cast as Virgin or whore to be possessed by male desire. It is worthwhile to reiterate the antics of the pop singer Madonna who deconstructs both these projections. Not only does she appear in *Playboy* nude, *seemingly* playing into male hands by being an accomplice of her own objectifications, but, as Owens (1983:75) so cleverly remarks about a similar accusation made concerning Cindy Sherman's centerfolds: "while Sherman may pose as a pin-up, she still cannot be pinned down." So true of Madonna who went on to reverse dress codes, wearing male fetishes on the outside—slips and bras—and doing outrageous videos; her song, *Like a Prayer*, is an irreverent statement on the Church and the repressed lust of its priests. Madonna occupies the cultural space of the "streetwise," "New Young Woman," who could parody the classic pornographic peep show by "*looking back*" (Shelagh Young, 1989:184). i shall come back to Madonna throughout my journey, praising her as much as being confused by her irreverent antics.

Ruether is part of a long list of first-wave feminist nuns who desire to reform patriarchal World religions *within the confines of the institution* along feminist lines: a Thomist revision is offered by Mary Daly (1978); Fiorenza (1985) offers a Protestant critique; Phyllis Trible (1978) rewrites Biblical theology; and Goldenberg (1979, 1982) questions Judaism. Islam and Confucianism have their respective representatives as well. This is merely the leading edge literature that has now become available ten years later, whose radicalness has pushed open the doors for women priests and churches for gays and lesbians. In every religion there is an attempt to question representation and change the images of women as represented in their sacred books and teachings, i.e., Bible and the Koran. Salman Rushie's infamous *Satanic Verses* emerged out of this climate. Interesting historical analysis of the changing image of the crucified body of Christ has also been undertaken in relation to periods in history where gender relationships had undergone conflict and change. Eve is now deconstructed by introducing us to Lilith—Eve's opposite; a powerful figure who is conspicuously absent before Adam "invents" Eve from his rib. Lilith is represented as the woman on the "outside," trying to breach the walls of the garden (Goldenberg, 1982:105). She is the primordial mother, denying her castration. Similarly, Queen Vashti is vindicated in Judaism as an assertive woman who did not give into the wishes of the king's commandment as did Queen Esther (p. 90). Such stories point back to Sophocles's *Antigone* who disobeys the order of Creon while her sister Ismene is obedient to his every wish.

What is most troubling with these positions discussed above is the implication that there is an essentialist nature of woman; a "biological" essence that is then manifested in the iconography or better yet, the style of art. Ortner (1974) for example, holds that women tend to experience feelings of people as concrete rather than abstract, subjectively and interpersonally rather than objectively. Both Dinnerstein (1976) and Nancy Chodrow's (1978) psycho-analytic theories have been used to argue that there is a distinctive female personality which is created by the structure of the family. In a similar fashion, Carol Gilligan (1982) has claimed a distinctive feminine morality. The assumption that women's experience is *directly available* in the artworks produced by women, and that autobiographical statements which rely heavily on the phenomenology of subjective experience as providing for more "authentic" experiences, needs to be (and has been) seriously questioned. In the Anglo-American context feminist criticism, feminist history, and artistic production have assumed that both the artwork and the media it is rendered in reflect a pre-existent reality, rather than being signifying systems which inscribe ideology and are constitutive of that reality; or that the artwork reflects an essential truth (for those who have built their theories on the hermeneutic tradition of Hans–Georg Gadamer *et al.*), in this case the essential truth of the essential woman.

Of all the positionalities of feminism, "cultural feminism," as coined by Alice Echols (in Alcoff, 1988a), is perhaps the most threatening to males. It is an uncompromising stance: female nature or essence exists and it should be celebrated; in doing so, undervalued female attributes are elevated. The enemy is masculinity itself and male biology. Mary Daly's concept of *Gyn/Ecology* as life-loving female energy and Adrienne Rich's "female consciousness" of the body valorize this essence. Showalter (1982) ends her review of feminist criticism by claiming a "women's culture" which turns out to be as evasive an entity as any commitment to biologism, or to an innate woman's psyche, or to a unique language (*écriture féminine*). This essentialist position has often been criticized for adopting a homogeneous, unproblematized, and ahistorical conception of women, especially by women of color who view the situation in much more complex terms. Cultural feminist anthropologists have been especially critical of such a position. They argue for the social construction of reality in materialist terms.[3]

Feminist essentialists attribute to women's art qualities that express a feminine essence. They interpret a feminine aesthetic by claiming that there is a central "core," imagery derived from the form of female genitals and from female bodily experience. Special pleading for women's art to be assessed by different values ensures that women's art is confined within a gender-defined category, and at the same time, that the general criterion for appreciating art remains the one employed when discussing work by men. Men's art remains the suprasexual norm.

Given this strong critique of essentialism, i think it is instructive in this regard to make mention of Teresa de Lauretis's essay, "Upping the Anti [(sic)] in Feminist Theory," (1990) which is a paradigmatic example of how major players who are able to shape feminist discourse recognize the folly of the field and self-reflexively redirect the flow of the conversational playing field. In that essay de Lauretis rhetorically unhinges the meaning of essentialism from the way i and the critics i mention have basically discussed it— as a difference inherent in "women's nature" which has affinities with nature, as a "real essence" underlying the phenomena of woman—to "a difference in the feminist conception of woman, women, and the world." de Lauretis slips the discourse of feminism over the question of "woman" *per se*. Essential difference is given a new spin; it now becomes the *essential* difference between feminist and a non-feminist understanding of the subject and its relations to institutions. "That difference is essential" (p.255). A further slippage over the question of "real essentialism" takes place when de Lauretis dismisses the possible differences amongst cultural, radical, liberal, socialist and poststructuralist feminists by gathering them all up into a category where it is said that they *all* "agree that women are made, not born, that gender is not an innate feature (as sex may be) but a sociocultural construction."(p.257). This is ingeniously false. She then installs a "nominal essence" (existing in name only, not real or actual) over "real essence." It is now possible to rescue women's movements which might have openly declared essential "real" difference with a redefinition of essentialism: "It is a totality of qualities, properties, and attributes that such feminists define, envisage, or enact for themselves (and some in fact attempt to live out in "separatist" communities), and possibly also wish for other women" (p.257). Such rhetoric is quite brilliant for she is able to both rescue and at the same time preserve the two meanings of essentialism (real and nominal) without condemning either one. By letting the implication that sex is "innate" slip by, de Lauretis can recuperate lesbianism as the possible existence of a "real" essentialism, which is strengthened further within her parenthetical comment concerning "separatist" communities—a word further marked by the scare quotation marks. Within feminism, "real" essentialism as "separatist and radical" essentialism can now be recuperated as a question of degree rather than kind. Everyone can once again be happy campers. To risk a generalization, the question of "essentialism," in whatever form it is signified, is more likely to be argued by lesbian feminists because of their same-sex preference.

Spiritual Materialism

Yet despite all of the above reservations, what drew me to these writings was my catholic (in the sense of an interest in the universal) background, especially the blurring that had occurred between subjectivity, spirituality and myth (even though it was a Romantic subjectivity that was "backward" looking, almost nostalgic.) A book such as Spretnak's *The Politics of Women's Spirituality* (1982) raises again the heterogeneity of positions which exist in and amongst essentialists themselves or better still 'cultural feminists'. It raises the question of transcendence and whether such transcendence is reserved only for men as Genevieve Lloyd (1989) has argued. Taken together, this position did not cut away a commitment to social and political change. The movement of boundaries between what was "forward-looking" and progressively and politically emancipative, and what was "backward looking," as the search for a nostalgic past, a paradise lost—that place of myth, spirituality and the transformation of subjective consciousness—has begun to shift. Forwardness and backwardness, past/future were again binary relationships which could be deconstructed so as to place time in flux. Words like implosion, de-evolution, negentropy rolled easily off my lips. From 1985-1988 i was drawn to a new emerging spiritualism and ecological consciousness which was quite evident with Native feminist communities (Allen, 1986) and Black communities who were reclaiming a collective, ancestral spiritual tradition. i was particularly drawn to Balbus's (1982) last chapter in his book, *Marxism and Domination* (1982). In that chapter he demonstrated the interconnections between feminism, ecology and participatory democracy as the "active participation of all is the condition for the maximum development of each, 'being' the political counterpart of the one that informs the feminist movement" (p.358). Just as women were objects in the subject/object dichotomization of rationality and scopophobic perception, analogously representative democracy transformed the voting subject into an object of political process over which she or he has littlecontrol; collective decision making and personal development remained apart. Balbus called for a new "participatory" democracy (which we are unlikely to realize for some time yet).

Feminists from a variety of persuasions have developed non-instru-mental and non-hierarchical forms which are compatible with ecological movements and participatory democracy. Balbus mentions the early con-scious-raising groups which, confined to a small scale, allowed everyone to participate. He goes on to mention women's collectives and the development of alternative life-styles, particularly in service industries such as legal and medical clinics, restaurants, bookstores, and presses. The ecological movement holds a close affinity to those ecofeminists who are attempting to redress the current biological paradigm. Perhaps because women have been traditionally more preoccupied with and conscious of the fate of the future generations through their children, ecology and peace are cherished values. i seem to be a long way from the concerns of art and art education, but this is hardly the case. Closing the gap between art and society requires an entirely new rela-tionship. There are values of repair and mending, recycling which can be directly incorporated into new art process. These could be explored by gen-erating a new "ecosophy" (jagodzinski, 1992a).

What had been so appealing in this position, for me, was the Romanticized view of linking ~~the~~ Woman's Body to the Earth in a histori-cal moment which has proven ripe for an ecological discourse to emerge. To heighten repressed feminine characteristics of compassion, care, and love for all creatures held a broad appeal. Such an appeal, coupled to the political rhetoric of Adrienne Rich's poetry and writings, made made it possible to envision a state where women loved women, thereby lessening differences amongst them. Here the "negative" Oedipal moment of homoerotic love between Mother and daughter was translated as "woman's culture," "woman's space," "women's community." Such a naming of the world de-pathologized lesbianism, which historically had been subsumed under the discourse of homosexuality, and created a new space from which to re-mythologize women's tradition from being moored up in a whole/hole or cave. Lesbianism now became a political discourse, its space logically created in alterity by distin-guishing itself from the violence of masculinity. Women who did not join this newly formed island of cultural activity were said to be "Painted Birds" and "roboticized women" (Daly, 1978). The first wave of discursive formation around lesbianism moved from the strictly genital, to the diffuse holistic anatomy of women allowing for differences to coalesce under the dome of "women's culture." In Adrienne Rich's (1980) well-known formulation, there is a "lesbian continuum" which covers "a wide range—through each woman's life and throughout history—of woman-identified experience" (p.659). "All women are lesbians."

Since then the infamous "sex wars" amongst lesbians have taken place (which i shall address later on in my journey). My idyllic world of ecofeminism has drifted so far from the main shore that it has lost sight/site/cite of at least entertaining the need to accommodate some forms of technology within its body. *We* are, after all, already cyborgs; technology informs our very existence. Eco-feminism is Romantically adrift. It has devolved into questionable goddess worship (Biehl, 1991; Shiva, 1988). The critique by Andrew Ross of New Age science (1992) has sobered me up as well. Yet the thirst for some form of "spirituality" remains. There is a residual metaphysical *presence* i do not wish to throw away and simply follow Haraway's cyborgian future; yet i feel that the compromise must meet at twin borders: between humans and machines in one direction, and between humans and animals in the other, in some form of "spiritual materialism." The closest i come to having a hint of what that may mean on one side of the divide comes from Michael Taussig's (1993) study of mimesis and alterity, which is a sustained re-reading of some of Walter Benjamin's thoughts on optics. Taussig makes a strong case for an *optical unconscious* which is informed by a *tactile* eye that speaks to this *presence* or "aura" in Benjamin's formuation. Although there is a danger of falling into "authenticity," Taussig's study of the Cuna Indian healers (chap. 8 and 9) brings out the workings of this "spiritual materialism" as a *maternal touch* practised by powerful earthly maternal hermaphroditic men who chant "their curing stories of voyages into the body and womb of the great mother..." (p.42).

As far as the issue of essentialist religiosity, i came across an intriguing essay by Jennifer Ash, "The Discursive Construction of Christ's Body in the Later Middle Ages: Resistance and Autonomy" (1990). Ash, a Medievalist, offers a fascinating account of the relationship which existed between the dying crucified body of Christ (as represented through various statues of the crucifixion) and the body of the medieval worshippers, especially women. Ash combines semiotics, French feminist theory (Kristeva) and Lacan to offer an insightful account of the erotic hysterical relationship that ensued. As a penitential practice, Christianity in the later Middle Ages practised forms of mimicry whereby the body of the worshipper would literally experience the pain and suffering of the crucified body of Christ. Ash argues that women, more than men, participated in this hysterical practice of body identification with an-Other. Hysteria functioned for them as a stratagem, a psychical resistance to the Symbolic Law and Order of patriarchy. Asceticism, too, was part of Christianity which meant heroic fasting, self-flagellation, long periods of prayer, psalm reciting, and wearing hair shirts. Ash mentions that this asceticism was pushed by women hysterics to an extreme, like some of today's "high" performance art, e.g., "Mary of Oignies hacked off pieces of her own flesh while immersed in a vision of the Crucifixion" (p.94). However, fasting and food deprivation were the more usual expressions of such asceticism , which brought nuns to the point of getting out of control and ending the ritual sometimes in death.

Ash argues that these women were anorexic hysterics, like the anorexics of today who stage a refusal and rebellion against the Symbolic Order which had locked them into passivity. Hysteria was a way to locate a different "self" In their ecstasy, in their excess, which was *ex*-static, these nuns tried to meet with the Divine and by-pass the priests and thereby, be beyond control of their Other. This strategic "holiness" (cf. Kristeva) transported them beyond, as pleasure took them out of themselves. "Her excess, unsymbolisable, unspeakable, is her 'jouissance': excess beyond the phallus" (p.97). The anorexic "suffers from maternal corporeality, the plenitude of the pre-Symbolic body"(ibid.). Ash makes the following summary:

> The medieval woman mystic, the 'holy anorexic,' through her intense devotion to an excessive identification with Christ's crucified body, attempts to relocate, reconstruct, her Symbolic body (and being). But this is also her attempt to recreate the wholeness, the completeness of the mother-child relation in the Imaginary state of being. That is, mystical union with the Divine can function as fusion with the maternal body. Christ's body, the human body of the Divine, has become the body of the phallic mother (p.97).

Given this picture, the "host" eaten during mass generated intense eucharistic fervor and "was a basic constituent element in the feminine mysticism of the late Middle Ages" (ibid.). In this sense the body of Christ (as host) functioned as the woman's object of desire, "a body discursively (re)constructed as both lover and mother" (p.98). This outraged a male clergy who were excluded from this relation between the mystic woman and the Divine. It is said that the French feminists are now the new postmodern hysterics, and it is to their hysterical voices i now turn.

1 A small part of these early explorations eventually appeared two years later as a chapter, "Towards an Ecological Aesthetic: Notes on a 'Green' Frame of Mind," in Congdon & Blandy's (eds.) *Art in a Democracy* (1987). At that time i was attempting to link this movement of essentialism with the issue of ecology. i have not entirely abandoned this possibility but have come to realize its limitations.

2 The feminist critique of women in various religions opens up a vast literature. I have found Reuther the most consistent in opening up the question in a Roman Catholic context. However, I would argue that the Roman Catholic faith has dragged its heels behind Protestantism in defining the subject. The current Pope John the 22nd introduced the question of subjectivity through his doctoral thesis, an achievement Martin Luther had achieved some 300 years earlier.

3 See Henrietta L. Moore's *Feminism and Anthropology* (1988) for a comprehensive analysis of this problem. Her arguments against essentialism are to show that the contribution feminist anthropology makes is precisely the analysis of cultural constructions of gender and the bases of the sexual divisions of labor (including capitalism). Difference, rather than homogeneity, is celebrated.

THE FRENCH "CON"-NECTION

Écriture féminine-writing the Body

[I]t is not simply that to a
non-feminist male academic one
feminism looks very much like
another. Sometimes one feminism
is very much like another, and their
name might well be "French
feminist theory," signified by the
Holy Trinity—or is it a limited
company?—of Hélène Cixous,
Luce Irigaray, and Julia Kristeva: the
law according to French feminism
(FF).

(Landry and MacLean, 1993:54)

For readers of French the pun in my title has yet another connotation than meaning "around" or "about."

Eventually some of those incomprehensible names that the I had heard at the 1986 Women's Caucus of the CAA began to appear in the literature; rather, they had been there all along and i merely had found their "trace". It did not take long to determine the "pedigree" of French Feminists. I say this with sarcasm only in the sense that the same names began to appear over and over again in key feminist *and* literary journals: Kristeva, Cixous, Irigaray, whose texts were indebted, even by way of rejection, to the two "Jacques": Jacques Lacan and Jacques Derrida. Lacan's reinterpretation of Freud along semiotic lines is well known, while Jacques Derrida, whose name is virtually synonymous with deconstruction, has had a tremendous impact on American literary criticism.[1] The shadow of both "figures" cannot be entirely dismissed and that, in itself, has raised the ire of American feminists who found their texts, at first, difficult and incomprehensible. Who hasn't?

French feminists, drawing upon these theories, were seen as forming a certain posture which was coined *écriture féminine*. Perhaps this interpretation of French feminists was only due to the American reception of their work? (Jardine, 1985). An entire industry of criticism has emerged over the *oeuvre* of Kristeva, Irigaray, and Cixous, with Monique Wittig holding her place as sister "outsider," at least amongst some circles.[2] Obviously, some of the early spade work had already been done through the excavations by Simone de Beauvoir and, i am certain, should one have had the privy to the broader network of French feminists, as Jardine had, many other "minor" players would have emerged as offering other feminist stances. Beauvoir's socialism cannot be likened to Irigaray's and Cixous's essentialist leanings. Jones (1981:255) clearly states that *Questions féministes*, a journal founded in 1977 with Simone de Beauvoir as titular editor, refers to these feminists as *néo-féminité*. French materialist feminists like Christine Delphy and Colette Guillaumin feared the reinstatement of a long existing binary: *féminité* becoming a celebration of women's difference which defined men as rational while women were caring and empathetic. To differentiate their stance, the editors of *Questions féministes* outlined three stages of feminist consciousness which roughly corresponded with three stances of women's relationship to language: "femininity" accepts women's exclusion from the world of social discourse. Women are systematically excluded from public discourse—silenced; "feminitude," where difference is valorized as a creation of a separate women's language characterized by a specialized vocabulary and syntax, i.e., witches' hexing, hysteria and madness; and lastly, "feminism" as the appropriation of all forms of discourses so as not to be alienated from them (Editors of *Questions féministes*, 1980).

Earlier still, *des femmes* publishing house had been founded in 1974 to specifically publish *écriture féminine* for the group Psychanalyse et Politique (*Psych et Po*) to whom Cixous belonged. According to Shiach (1991:28) things got nasty between these publishing houses. There were violent attacks on the *des femmes* book store. Personal conflicts flared at conferences. *Psych et Po* registered the acronym 'MFL' (Women's Liberation Movement) which now included Luce Irigaray. Past anthologies by Marks and de Courtivron (1981) present a glimpse of that untranslated silence. Through English translations, names such as Duras, LeClerc and Felman[3] have been added to the list of important theorists. With the publication of *The Future of Difference* (1980) by Eisenstein & Jardine, as well as Allen & Iris Marion Young's *The Thinking Muse: Feminism and Modern French Philosophy* (1989) it seems that French feminism had turned full circle: the love-hate cycle had came to a completion. More and more dissatisfaction has emerged (in some sectors).[4]

As the I tried to comprehend these (often incomprehensible) French theories, the trace kept getting stronger and stronger. Very soon i realized that it required an understanding of Lacan and semiology, Derrida and deconstruction,[5] before i was able to have an inkling as to what was going on. It seemed to be a simultaneous process, reading psychoanalysis and deconstruction and then coming back to the writing of the better-known French feminists. In 1986, under the auspices of the Women's Caucus at the 27th National Art Education Association, Boston, Mass. meeting, the I presented a paper entitled: "Is there a Distinct Feminist Aesthetic?" Hardly an original title, but i thought so at the time. Since then i have now found no less than two other citations with the very same question in their title: Penelope and Wolfe's (1978) "Towards an Feminist Aesthetic", and Bovenschen's (1985), "Is There a Feminine Aesthetic?" This paper, at the time, was an attempt to show the differences *in art* between American feminists, and their European poststructuralist "sisters" who had put the representation of woman to question by treating it as a signed value in an economy of exchange. Looking back, it was rather a brash attempt to claim, *as a male*, that the American feminists had it wrong while the European post-structuralists somehow had it right. Yet there was no direct challenge to this thesis by those in attendance; a surprising number came considering it was an 8 am. session. That was eight years ago, and the theoretical winds have changed! What was unclear to me at the time were the differences between post-structuralist feminists who began to generate difference within the representation of a homogeneous understanding of "woman," and French feminists who were preserving difference along more essentialist, that is bodily, lines but still used deconstruction to differentiate themselves from a phallocentric view. The I was tripped up by both words: "difference" and "deconstruction" which seemed to appear in every essay i read.

Having misread the uses of "difference" and "deconstruction" at that time did not prevent me from finding a way to accommodate myself as a maleman within, what i also hadn't realized at the time, was an exclusive feminine writing. i read only what suited my needs. In my interpretation there was *no* distinctive female/women's consciousness or separatist experience of reality which legitimated a distinct feminist aesthetic; however there was an *écriture féminine* which men could write as well, because it tried to disrupt or transgress the phallocentric symbolic order. In other words, i thought men could be feminists by fiat of doing this kind of writing. (The performance about my son's experience of being disciplined, which is reproduced in the appendix, was an example of what i thought such a writing would be like.) In what way language was *anaclitic* became a concern for me.[6] Such a stance was *not necessarily* a characteristic of female psychology and hence it opened the space for male participation as well. This, i found out later, leaned more towards Kristeva is theories of the semiotic rather than Cixous or Irigaray. The latter two theorists specify women's desire by referring to a feminine language that is censored or repressed. It is a "non-unitary" language specifically written for the woman's body, sex and imagination. Both theorists used deconstruction differently: Cixous turned to Derrida to displace found binaries, while Irigaray deconstructed Freudian-Lacanian psychoanalysis by writing an alternative account of feminine desire. No wonder i was confused. i had read Moi's *Sexual/Textual Politics* (1985), but misread her as well. i could readily understand her attack on Anglo-American feminism for presenting a non-contradictory perception, a too homogeneous a view of the world, and for promoting a humanist subject which masked differences amongst women. But when it came to French feminisms, her support for the critical stances of Cixous and Irigaray and her strong support for Kristeva seemed justified. i was especially drawn to Kristeva because she had placed so much emphasis on the innovations of the avant-garde. i could relate to her emphasis on the arts. Irigaray and Cixous seemed distant for me. i "read" Alice Jardine's *Gynesis: Configurations of Woman and Modernity* (1985), and then there was her visit to my campus which offered me only more misreadings and confusions. French feminism, postructuralism, and postmodernism all seemed to swim together again as they had when the I attended College Art Association conferences. Jardine seemed to be on the forefront of theory, and theory had always been seductive to me(n). Some clarifications were needed.

What then is *écriture féminine*?

In my "Pretext" chapter i have already referred to *écriture féminine*, including its masculine and homosexual variations. Obviously my performance (see appendix) wouldn't stand up to this label as "body writing." Here i would like to continue that conversation which started there. *Écriture féminine* is densely summarized by Heath (1982:chap.8, in Rodowick:1988) by four basic assumptions: 1. *The woman is by nature a writer* because her excessive *jouissance*, always in excess at the expense of the phallus and the signifier, is itself a limit-experience and an experience of *écriture*. ... 2. *The woman's experience of écriture is profound because she is close to the body, less divided from it in the symbolic, and closer to the 'source' of writing. ...* 3. *The woman's position with respect to language falls outside the law, the logic of patriarchy, and the order of the symbolic. ...* 4. *Écriture féminine has no metalanguage,* in fact, *it is antitheoretical* (pp. 247-249, original italic). It all sounds so enigmatic.

Ann Rosalind Jones (1981), Carolyn Burke (1981), and Hélène Vivienne Wenzel (1981) are considered "readable" translators of Irigaray, Cixous, Kristeva and Monique Wittig. i shall draw on their lucidity. The point of agreement amongst these feminists is in their form of resistance: *jouissance* —as the direct reexperience of the physical pleasures of infancy and of sexuality, "repressed but obliterated by the Law of the Father" (Jones, p. 248). Both Cixous and Irigaray argue that women have been prevented from their own sexual desires, remaining sexual objects for men as prostitutes, virgins, wives and mothers. Finding a new language will give then a place from which to deconstruct phallogocentric concepts. Wittig's experimental writing (*textes féminines*) desires that this language emerge amongst women, rather than being derived from men. *Jouissance* is theorized by Kristeva as "semiotic discourse," a pre-Oedipal "language" of bodily drives: the gestures, rhythms that are poetically heard in writers such as Artaud, Mallarmé and Joyce. "These men, rather than giving up their blissful infantile fusion with their mothers, their orality, and anality, reexperience such jouissance subconsciously and set them into play by constructing texts against the rules and regularities of conventional language" (Jones, p.249). The semiotic is an incestuous challenge to the symbolic order for it is a return to the pre-verbal holophrastic stage where the identification is with the mother, and not the father. Women can also speak and write as "hysterics" since they are marginalized by masculine culture and their drives are related to anality and childbirth.

Kristeva has claimed she in *not* a feminist. Her specification of woman is closer to Derrida: it is "that" which is unrepresentable, outside discourse. "By 'woman' I mean that which cannot be represented, what is not said, what remains above and beyond nomenclatures and ideologies. There are certain 'men' who are familiar with this phenomenon" (Kristeva in Jones, p.249). *Gynesis* is Jardine's term for the same phenomenon. It is precisely this dissimulation of "woman" that has angered many feminists about Kristeva's work.

In contrast to Kristeva, Irigaray calls for a specificity, but one based on the woman's body, the diffuse sexuality of Irigaray's infamous "two lips" of the vulva. This diffused sexuality is taken consciously as being hysterical. "That is undoubtedly the reason she is called temperamental, incomprehensible, perturbed, capricious ... Contradictory words seem a little crazy to the logic of reason, and inaudible for him who listens with ready-made grids, a code prepared in advance" (Jones, p.250). To her supporters, Irigaray utilizes a "both/and logic," a case of postcultural thinking (Bannet, 1992, 1993: chap.6). Cixous is also of the same mind as Irigaray. Women's unconscious is different from men's; women's psychosexual specificity speaks an id-liberated female discourse. Both Irigaray and Cixous call for the expression of women's sexuality, and that sexuality "begins with their bodies, with their genital and libidinal difference from men. ... to write from the body is to recreate the world" (Jones, p.252). It seems possible to conclude that *écriture féminine* is a linguistic equivalent of visual vaginal iconography.

The Hetero/Homo Matrix of *Écriture Féminine*

Below i want to examine the writings of these four feminists as they pertain to the arts, as best as i am able to. The thesis i have come to maintain is that Kristeva is to Irigaray as Wittig is to Cixous: Kristeva/Irigaray-Wittig/Cixous. Kristeva and Wittig represent the two ends of the continuum of the hetero/homo divide; Irigaray and Cixous are intertwined in between. Their writings are comparable. Kristeva and Irigaray represent the written body in maternal heterosexual terms, a positive Oedipalization; while Wittig and Cixous are representative of the lesbian response, negative Oedipalization. Amongst them they form the hetero/homosexual matrix of a feminism that does battle with phallogocentrism, yet still retains the essentiality of the feminine in some form. In this sense they *do* form a "sisterhood" with its usual squabbles and fights.

The similarities and differences between Kristeva and Irigaray have been identified brilliantly by Grosz (1989: chap. 4). They may be summarily stated as the difference between sexual differentiation opposed to sexual difference. Kristeva, who never called herself a feminist to begin with, is closest to Derrida in calling for a dissolution of all sexual differences. Her aim is to "uncover women's (repressed) masculinity and men's (disavowed) femininity through the acknowledgment of a repressed semiotic" (Grosz:100), the foundational maternal bedrock for both male and female identities. In this regard, i read Kristeva as the most Oedipalized of the four, to the point where, as Judith Butler argues (1990a:84), it becomes necessary to become a mother and give birth in order to enter into the Symbolic properly. "By giving birth, the woman enters into contact with her mother; ... She thus actualizes the homosexual facet of motherhood, through which a woman is simultaneously closer to her instinctual memory, more open to her psychosis, and consequently, more negatory of the social, symbolic bond" (Kristeva, 1980:239, in Butler: 84).

Irigaray, who is seeking a notion of women's *"sexual autonomy and specificity"* (Grosz, ibid.) is one step removed, attempting to pull away from her Father (Lacan) rather than, as Jane Gallop (1982a) says it best, becoming a "dutiful daughter." Irigaray disavows that she has been castrated, even though she has. i say this because of the following two reasons: First, it is her mocking, parodic, mimicked, intertextual style which addresses the two Jacques, and a host of other male philosophers—Plato, Aristotle, Levinas, Heidegger, Nietzsche, Freud—so that she might displace phallocentrism, and find her own specificity which she then generalizes as Everywoman. She is constantly trying to define herself against that tradition. Second, it is her rethinking of the mother-daughter relationship. In contrast to Kristeva, Irigaray argues that the maternal function should be prevented from strangling a woman's existence. "[Irigaray] shows that being a woman is always excessive to maternity. The woman in all mothers, a woman not reduced to the preservation and care of others, must be conceived if women are to assert their particularity" (Grosz: 120). Motherhood must be reconceptualized on political grounds.

The Wittig/Cixous lesbian relationship can be read as butch/femme, Wittig's Amazon to Cixous's Dora. Wittig's butch is quite strident. Men do not figure in her Amazonian society. Wittig has definitely refused castration. She *is* the phallic mother, pejoratively put, a "ball crusher." Cixous is more ambivalent. She views the categorical division of "man" and "woman" as a natural biological result. "Liberation from phallocentrism would not negate these differences, but would place them into an equal relationship by reestablishing bisexuality" (Crowder, 1983:137). Cixous's bisexuality is not androgyny; rather, it is her claim that women are more bi-sexual than men. She condemns "lesbians" who deny their femininity and want to be men and praises "feminine homosexuality" which is associated with "non-power" (p. 138). Cixous is the castrated hysterical woman who has denied her castration and relocated it in another body part. This could well be the "laugh" of the voice which plays such an important role in her writing. Crowder takes notice of how often Freud's Dora enters her writing. "For Cixous the hysteric is the archetype of woman in all her strength who turns against patriarchy and its own prohibitions" (p.140).

Luce Irigaray: The Undutiful Daughter

It is one thing to attempt to read the translated works of these very complex and sophisticated women writers (Kristeva and Cixous have their roots in semiotics, Derridean deconstructivist and poststructuralist thought, while Irigaray has virtually rewritten and spat out her mentor Lacan, as she, herself had been spat out from Lacan's *École freudienne*) but it becomes even more difficult to make their work accessible by demonstrating its applicability to the arts,[7] or in comprehending the enormous range of interpretations by feminists themselves who are at odds as to how they are to be read. Who has the "right" Irigaray? If Lacan's concept of the Imaginary is ignored, writes Whitford (1988:109), then Irigaray can be read as an essentialist (e.g. Sayers, 1982:131; 1986: 42-48). Or, perhaps Irigaray has misread or misunderstood Lacan's Imaginary as Mitchell and Rose (1982:54-56; Rose,1986:136-140) and Ragland-Sullivan (1986:273-80) seem to think? In trying to "write" a female libido, Irigaray has often been accused of essentialism. In contrast Paul Smith (1988:143), along with Gallop (1983), view Irigaray's essentialism as a metaphorical attempt to present a *concentric logic*, a "somantic scenography" of femininity as opposed to Freud and Lacan's phallic 'ones,' in order to break the specular logic of patriarchy.

Recently, Fuss (1989:55-72) has given an almost 'summative' statement of Irigaray's tactics as an attempt to replace Lacan's metaphoric phallus with her metonymic signifier of the two lips, which are "both at once." For Fuss, Irigaray's playfulness of being "both at once," as an essentialist and not an essentialist, is a tactful ruse to put to question the entire Aristotelian tradition. Fuss explains that the Western philosophical tradition has denied "woman" an essence. "Woman is the ground of essence, its precondition in man, without herself having any access to it; she is the ground of subjecthood, but not herself a subject" (p.71). In Irigaray's struggle to do away with Lacan's phallocentrism, argues Fuss, she has laid claim for an essence denied in Western philosophical discourse. What enables Lacan to claim "the woman does not exist" is supported by this tradition. As Fuss cleverly argues, Lacan's distinction "between *being* and *having* the phallus" is what distinguishes the genders. The child in the pre-Oedipal phase is already a phallus for the mother, a fetish that gives the Mother meaning and legitimacy in the social order, but the boy goes on *having* the phallus while the girl remains *being* the phallus. In brief, this repeats the Aristotelian logic that the women is *Essence* but does not possess *Essence*. She is only matter which does not matter. Only the man matters in fulfilling his *telos*, his destiny.

Following Derrida's detours, Irigaray's deconstruction of this Western metaphysical tradition is to flip the binaries: fluidity/ solidity, metonymy/ metaphor, form /matter, developing and displacing these binaries with a new undecidable—the two lips, constantly "in touch," as in *femme parler*. Like Derrida's "account that replaces phallogocentrism with a 'hymeneal' fable" which involves both sexes and sexual difference, Irigaray dispenses with the male sex and "valorizes female sexual sufficiency, in a fable that may be described as 'vulval' or 'vaginal' (Carolyn Burke, 1981:294-295). Despite such rhetoric i wonder how Fuss would answer Jones's (1981) skepticism: "What is the meaning of "two lips" to heterosexual women who want men to recognize their clitoral pleasure—or to African or Middle Eastern women who, as a result of pharaonic clitoridectomies, have neither lips nor clitoris through which to *jouir*? (p.257). Jones reminds us that *féminité* "flattens out the lived differences among women [and] is more likely to blind us to our varied and immediate needs and to the specific struggles we must coordinate in order to meet them" (ibid.).

Just how to read Irigaray points to the larger question of postmodernism. The distinction between primary texts and secondary texts has broken down,[8] and the *oeuvre* of Irigaray is no exception. The variety of readings tell us more about the critics than about her text. Each is a subject position that would interpret a different Irigaray. The complications of color and class, race, age, religious convictions and sexual preferences, *within the context of lived reality in a given historical moment*, provide an overwhelming array of possibilities. Consider Suzanne Moore's (1989) biting comment: "To escape the ultimate sin of objectification ... Irigaray retreats into the world of transcendent organic bliss where subject melts into object and where differences dissolves, arguing that touch is the 'true' feminine sense. In a culture where the power of visual images assumes ever greater importance in our lives, this seems to me to be taking the position of the child who shuts her eyes believing that no one can see her any more. Touch may be peculiarly female sense but then so might smell for that matter—and where would that leave us?" (p.57).

If one was to make a *strong* reading of Irigaray as presenting the irreducibility of the different sexes, then Irigaray's attempt is to deconstruct the phallocentrism of the one (male) symbolic order with yet another. To do this she does not focus on the biological or natural body, but on the body as it is produced and lived meaningfully through its entwinement in various systems of representations. It is the body's meaning, not its nature. This same "double gesture" is applied to politics which she perceives at both the local and global levels. The larger question of the universal oppression of "woman" is exposed through the local specificity and complexity of the situation where a woman finds herself. But such a generous interpretation is barely audible in her texts.

Her representational systems try to inscribe the female body positively rather than as having a lack, or being a complement to man. Her claim is that images of women, up to now, are projected, inverted images of men. They are images of women as men's counterpart or double, not as women. She is particularly indignant with Lacan's *Encore, Seminar XX* wherein he takes up what Freud avoided—*Was will das Weib? What does the woman want?* specifically discussing the pleasures of women. In *Così Fan Tutti* (1985b), written in 1975, two years after Lacan gave this seminar (1972/73), Irigaray presents the reader with a remarkably ironic scornful 'laugh' at Lacan's claim to explain women's pleasure. Her style is instructive for its parodic resistant display. Unless she is taken seriously, her ruse loses much of its power to sting. In Irigaray's words for Lacan's own, the truth of "*the feminine occurs only within models and laws devised by male subjects*" (p. 86). Mocking Lacan's claim that Bernini's statue in Rome exemplifies St. Theresa's *jouissance*,[9] Irigaray writes: "Just go look at Bernini's statue in Rome, you'll see right away that St. Theresa is coming, there's no doubt about it. 'In Rome?' 'So far away.' To look? At a statue? Of a saint? Sculpted by a man? What pleasure are we talking about? Whose pleasure? For where the pleasure of the Teresa in question is concerned, her own writings are perhaps more telling. But how can one 'read' them when one is a 'man'? The production of ejaculations of all sorts, often prematurely emitted, makes him miss, in the desire for identification with the lady, what her own pleasure might be all about. And ... his?" (pp. 90-91). This is paradigmatically Irigaray's hysterical laugh.

In his celebrated article "Difference," Heath (1978) examines the same seminar, exploring the myriad of nuances involved when phallocentrism is given privilege. If i have read him correctly, Heath is more forgiving of Lacan, almost reading the self-assurance of the Bernini statue on the cover of Seminar XX as a recognition that by not discussing the *imaginary* of the *evidence* of the statue, the observer is always placed in a masculine position;

the elision of difference has already occurred. What does he mean by that? Heath points to passages where Lacan is claiming that "the woman is caught up in phallic jouissance but not-all, there is 'something more,' 'a supplementary jouissance'"(SXX, pp. 68-69, in Heath, 1978:60). That 'something more' is what remains at issue. But that space is a remainder left over from the symbolic. It has no voice, no language, no position of its own. The pleasure beyond the phallus appears vacant. If it goes beyond specularity, as Irigaray claims, what then is the masturbating woman 'seeing' with her eyes closed? (see Burgin,1984:33). Who dares to answer this in the fear that there may be many fantasies? Lacan spent over a year examining the issues of sexual difference, and although his phallogocentrism is not to be defended, it may well represent the status of desire within the confines of a patriarchal family structure. i am still haunted by his statement: 'the phallus is a fraud' which, to me, is every bit as theatrical as 'woman does not exist.' This vivifies Lacan's own refusal to be pinned down in a subject position, dancing around as much as those who wish to pin him down. Perhaps in late capitalism the family structure has changed and the usefulness of his analysis lessened. It is perhaps the ambiguity of the current historical transition which requires Irigaray to open up the question of sexuality through her parodic style of Lacan's and Derrida's writings.

Irigaray has not specifically written about the arts that i am aware of, but so much remains untranslated, and i am not an Irigaray scholar. Battersby (1995) for example, recognizes Irigaray's potential contribution to a feminine Imaginary which takes the mother/daughter relations as primary, and which doesn't theorize identity in terms directed against Otherness. The speculum does indeed jam the mirror stage. This said, however, Battersby also notes that "Irigaray's own comments on painting are deeply flawed" (p.128), and her "treatment of art as mere propaganda cannot be excused" (p.131). Battersby is unable to push Irigaray's feminine Imaginary any further, and ends up in adopting a position which falls back to a "resistant gaze"where, for instance, women artists like Kay Sage and Ithell Colquhoun in the 1940s were able to adopt, and at the same time undo the surrealist 'male' perspective of de Chirico. Most applications of Irigaray have been made to avant-garde film. Holmlund (1989) examines Irigaray for the possibility of her lesbian insights and tries to apply her Freudian deconstructions to the mainstream film, Fatal Attraction. On the former account, it is not surprising that Holmlund finds contradictions with Irigaray's lesbian revisions of Freud, and being lesbian, it is not surprising Holmund reads Alex Forrest (Glen Close) as Irigaray's lesbian-cum-independent woman who is a threat to hom(m)osexual exchange and phallogocentrism. But her reading seems forced and the application thin.

Grosz's (1989, chap. 4 and 5) review is more readable than most, freely admitting that Irigaray's style is not prone to a systematic analysis. Yet it seems to me that the implications of her work are extremely pertinent to the arts with her questioning of ocularlogism. The privileging of sight by psychoanalysis when fixing gendered categories (castration); the rule of sight in the empiricism of ocular scientific speculation (microscopes, telescopes), and the male gaze, not only in the objectifying look of sexual desire, but in more devious unassumed everyday glances such as the *creation* of the "news" when we, the audience, are all objects of the gaze, and *potential* subjects to the voice and vision of the "anchor man," despite our proclaimed resistances to be otherwise. Perhaps Noam Chomsky is right: the panoptic Eye is hidden once again. It has moved beyond the confines of the earth and now rotates in any number of orbits, both spying and broadcasting programs to any location where there is a receiver.

Julia Kristeva: The Dutiful Mother

What has been said about Irigaray can be said for Julia Kristeva as well. On the one hand she might be sympathetically read as a defender of marginality (Moi, 1985; Smith, 1988: Chap.8), or as someone who has reconfirmed maternal desires, opening the door to the charge that women's symbolization and feminine desire (as developed in her theorizations on the pre-Oedipal dimension she calls semiotics) are again mysterious, chaotic, plural, and spontaneous (Oliver, 1993). This plays into the hands of the usual symbolization of woman in Western society despite her claims that motherhood, as she theorizes it (Kristeva, 1986b), is different from the Christian perspective.[10]

What interests me here is her position concerning the arts and what this says for male artists.[11] One of Kristeva's central conceptualizations has been the dialectical tension between what she calls the semiotic and the symbolic. Simply put, the semiotic is the blind cite/sight/site of the pre-Oedipal phase she calls the *chora*. But here the "cite" is the holophrastic, echolaliac, glossalaliac, mimetic musical voice of the mother whose rhythms, timbre, pitch, intensity is only felt on an affective level, while 'sight' is not spectacular as yet, but more to do with the mother's face. As such, *chora* is the space, the *envelope* of the maternal and feminine, while the symbolic is the sight/cite/site of Lacan's Name of the Father—the systems of language, law and exchange and representational practices which may be non-verbal and verbal. The Symbolic is therefore the Oedipal phase of unity. It is Kristeva's central belief that in the passage from the pre-Oedipal to the Oedipal stages, the child is gender positioned as an agent—an "I," (as in my use, *the* I) by sacrificing, or renouncing pre-oedipal sexual drives, and all processes of the *chora*, which, in the first instance, were directed toward the mother's body.

The maternal and the feminine aspects of the pre-Oedipal phase are thus the grounds or conditions of representation. They are themselves unrepresented or inadequately represented. Symbolic and artistic functioning is only possible through the *repression* of the feminine, but this semiotic realm is never far away. It is possible to tap this source in episodic moments she calls "madness, holiness and poetry." Such art defies the unity under the primacy of the phallus, and hence it becomes an index of social instability. The semiotic must be continually repressed so that the energies may be directed to acceptable social outlets and cover its desire. When it erupts, the impending transformations and subversions of artistic norms and canons anticipate upheavals in the symbolic order.

The dialectic between the semiotic pre-Oedipal drive and the Symbolic phallic Order may be identified in literature and art. Her claim is that the symbolic order must repress the feminine pleasure of the infant's sexual drive to be "heard." The feminine and the maternal is renounced. To analyze art and text in order to shake loose this apparent unity of the Symbolic at the expense of the semiotic becomes the task of the critic—the feminine and the maternal mark the unspoken and unspeakable conditions of representation. The "figure" of Woman here is the maternal body. The speaking, writing, or artistic subject is split—decentered—between the conscious/unconscious, maternal/paternal, semiotic/symbolic. (This is similar to Derrida's notion of otobiography. See Pretext to the Title, footnote 3.) In revolutionary practices the paternal Symbolic boundaries are constantly spilling over into dreams and 'hysterical symptoms.' Hunter (1985) has hypothesized that the 'hysterical' speech of a woman exhibits this semiotic which Kristeva infers. The hysterical woman refuses to take part in phallic discourse. Having no positionality in it, her speech appears enigmatic and incomprehensible—mad. If this is so, it may well be possible to identify "hysteric" artforms which participate in this same refusal throughout "hystery."

Scattered throughout her writings on the arts is an attempt to provide a theory and practice for uncovering the subject's position in the operation of the text as the interaction between the semiotic and the symbolic. Certain avant-garde artists are said to disrupt and subvert the apparent unity of the Symbolic Order. It is the maternal semiotic excess which, through privileged moments, threatens to transgress the limits of intelligibility, sociality and identity.[12] In "Giotto's Joy" and "Motherhood According to Giovanni

Bellini," two essays which appear in *Desire in Language* (1980), Kristeva discusses her understanding of the impact of the *choric* play of rhythm, color, tonality and silence. In some sense i feel that her stance is a rehearsal of the quarrel between the Ancients and the Moderns of 18th French Academy. Somehow it is these pure *chromatic* differences, "differences of light, energetic charge, and systematic value" (p. 219) as semiotic elements which are the repressed conditions of the symbolic. (In this "quarrel" colors were said to be more chaotic, more amorphous than the orders of linearity that champion reason and enlightened thought.) Art is then a politically harmless outlet for these impulses which might normally be threatening. Color is said to "rupture meaning."[13] "Matisse spells it out in full: it is through color—painting's 'fundamental device' ... that revolutions in the plastic arts come about...The chromatic apparatus, like rhythm in language, thus involves a shattering of meaning and its subject into a scale of differences..." (p. 221). The semiotic, feminine residue is found in art through rhythm, intonation, vocal pleasure, the phonic qualities in speech, or in the movement of brushstrokes, the play of color and light in painting or rhythm and tone in music. This corporeal and maternal zone must be repressed and remain outside the rule-governed Symbolic Order.

For Kristeva, then, it is the feminine, resistant, corporeal, subversive, unspeakable and unknowable which is the impulse to rupture and *jouissance*. In a succinct passage she writes,

> Art—this semiotization of the symbolic— ... represents the flow of *jouissance* into language. Whereas sacrifice assigns *jouissance* its productive limit in the social and symbolic order, art specifies the means—the only means—that *jouissance* harbors for infiltrating that order. In cracking the socio-symbolic order, splitting it open, changing vocabulary, syntax, the word itself and releasing from beneath them the drives borne by vocalic or kinetic differences, *jouissance* works its way into the social. In contrast to sacrifice, what poetry shows is that language lends itself to the penetration of the socio-symbolic by *jouissance*, and that the thetic does not necessary imply theological sacrifice (1984:80).

But again this *jouissance* is related to motherhood (Moi, 1985: 168).

It is a position outside, on its own with no voice and no language. It is only a murmur, a remainder. Kristeva's passage reminds me of the missing body, the materiality of language itself, as it became historically more and more "rational." Calligraphy (from time immemorial until the turn of the nineteenth century) still had the felt physical presence of the body. It lay somewhere between visual art, the grain of the voice, and conceptualization itself. The "look" of the letters and their sounds, which were read out loud, were as important as what was said. The feel of the writing instrument, stylus, or brush; the sounds made on the surface while writing; the ritual of preparation for writing—all these aesthetic layers became stripped away as writing became more and more rational; mere information to be silently read, finally reaches a point where all the I hears is the tapping sounds of his computer keyboard. The recovered body here can be metaphorically understood as the mother's body, and if it is, then i am back to Derrida's figure of "Woman" as a textual figure. It might be added that Lyotard presents a similar argument in his *Discours, figure* (1971). "Figure" is his term for the loss of materiality in language. In effect, Kristeva's pre-symbolic is the *affective* state as presented by the maternal body.

Elizabeth Grosz (1989) has lucidly explained the dangers Kristeva identifies that come with this erupting and potentially menacing *jouissance*. The energies liberated by the semiotic, we are told, "entail grave political risks, including engendering totalitarianism or fascism on the one hand; and political co-option or recuperation back into mainstream capitalism on the other" (p.56). The later is more of a harmless safety release which doesn't change things dramatically, but the former can possibility lead to terror. By this i assume what is meant is the whole appropriation of the concept of the "motherland" and the violence that goes along with men defending the "motherland" from the infiltration of foreigners as the abjected Other, as exemplified by fascism and the terror of the Holocaust. Here, "the semiotic is tied even more firmly to a symbolic organization brutal in its control of *jouissance*" (ibid.). In this instance the symbolic has lost its hold over the semiotic. How authoritarian men "read" their mother's body; how they are then able to mobilize that affective state and translate it into a mass psychology; and to what use they put these energies, is a question Kristeva tries to answer through a psychoanalytic explanation of the risks of challenging the Law-of-the-Father. Either way, it is the repressed or sublimated maternal body's function in the symbolic which is at question.

There are then two psychical extremes risked by avant-garde artists who dance and balance themselves between the semiotic and the symbolic: fetishism and psychosis, which often manifest themselves in an artist's life.

"Where avant-garde artistic practices *symbolize* the thetic [Kristeva's word for the threshold between the semiotic and the symbolic, correlated as the two moments of unification of the subject—the mirror stage and castration threat] fetishism *semiotizes* it" (p.57); meaning that identity is less assured by the fetishism of the poet than it is by the artistic signification in the symbolic. i take this to mean some art works, especially performative works, throw gender identity into question. However, this is a risk an artist takes for if fetishism is both a *disavowal* and an *acknowledgment* of maternal castration, then it is easy to see how art could easily be co-opted or recuperated into the symbolic order. It strikes me that this is precisely what Laura Mulvey (1975) had in mind concerning the fetishization of movie stars. The Symbolists would have been an artistic group who raised "woman" to the level of the cult object. i immediately think of Gustav Klimt, Muche, Gustave Moreau, Redon, as well as the Pre-Raphaelites like Dante Gabriel Rossetti and Edward Burne-Jones.[14] Perhaps they present the fetishization of the maternal body as Kristeva theorizes it, their fetishization of an ideal Woman represented through a distinct ornamental and patterned style.

If maternal castration is denied, "*foreclose[d]* or *repudiate[d]*" (p.58), then the law-of-the-father (castration) is not registered. It strikes me here that certain lesbian and gay performances would be a disruption of the maternal *chora* itself. "[W]here the fetish *displaces* the maternal phallus, the psychotic *hallucinates* it ... The psychotic has no stable boundaries or borders, and finds his identity confused with that of the m(other)" (Ibid.). But hallucination is *not a total refusal*. Total refusal brings the danger of being the mother and this is where Butler's (1990a:82-91) critique of Kristeva's work becomes focused. Kristeva's psychoanalytic explanation of the psychotic is privileged on the "structuralist assumption that heterosexuality is coextensive with the founding of the Symbolic ... [S]he fails to allow that homosexuality is capable of the same nonpsychotic social expression" (p.84). Kristeva is unable to shake the paternal law; poetry and maternity are privileged practices. A coherent selfhood requires heterosexuality otherwise a woman suffers a psychotic unraveling of identity. Ultimately Kristeva's theories treat "female homosexuality as a culturally unintelligible practice, inherently psychotic: on the other hand, it mandates maternity as a compulsory defense against libidinal chaos" (p.86). Lesbian becomes "Other" to culture. On a broader cross-cultural basis Butler makes a case that the repressed maternal body is not only a biological destiny, but also posits a universal—or univocal signifier—rather than the subversive multiplicity of drives that it is supposed to represent. Univocal paternal law is replaced by an equally univocal maternal law. Butler ends her critique with a very good question: if the semiotic as the pre-paternal cannot be held up as being prior to signification; if it is not an originary female economy of pleasure and meaning, then can this semiotic economy be understood at all "as a production of a prior discourse?" (p.91). The question is not answered, but i wonder if pointing to this non-discursive realm can ever be answered? The kinds of "poetic revolutions" that are possible risk the kinds of political realities that go with them. How the avant-garde works with the "already ready" to push the limits of the symbolic always requires a historical assessment on socio-economic grounds, and always runs the risk that it has gone too far, or not far enough.

Kristeva's conclusions about a "maternal language" of the semiotic has been severely criticized (Silverman, 1988a: Chap. 4) for denying the power of the Mother's Voice in intervening into the Symbolic Order because woman has no access to Symbolic Language except in this repressed position. Kristeva has valorized male avant-garde artists (Joyce, Céline, Artaud, Mallarmé, Lautréamont, Bakhtin) who were able to release this transgressive feminine. It could be argued that they embody the very qualities of the feminine male of the Romanticism, the genius who breaks out of the Symbolic Order and adds to it; the very "fragile" effeminate male that Battersby (1989) had critiqued so well. Kristeva has been criticized for implying that only men are able to break with the social contract, for the feminine has no voice. Only the male can break with parental authority. Hence Bellini, as painter, is able to go beyond the normal Christian vision of the cult of Motherhood as "tenderness, love, and seat of conversation" (Kristeva, 1980: 237). "The faces of [Bellini's] Madonnas are turned away, intent on something else that draws their gaze to the side, up above, or nowhere in particular, but never centers it on the baby" (p. 247). "At the intersection of the sign and rhythm, of representation and light, of the semiotic and the symbolic, the artist speaks from the place where *she is not*, where *she knows not*. He delineates what, in her, is a body rejoicing" (my italic, p.242). The problem lies in Kristeva's inability to show why disruption of the artistic discourse effects changes in the political and social structure, and why she continually valorizes men.

Kristeva's corrections to the above potential criticisms were developed in her *Powers of Horror* (1982). The once idyllic pre-Oedipal stage which was potentially disruptive of the Symbolic Order, is rectified by abjection–the expulsion of that which is unclean and disorderly so that the body "clean and proper" may emerge. Kristeva develops three categories of the abject: food, waste, and signs of sexual difference (i.e., especially menstruation). As abjected "objects," it might be possible to call them undecidables for they neither belong entirely as part of the body nor are they distinctly away from it. Tears, wax, faeces, urine, vomit, food, later help to specify certain erotogenic zones—

the anus, mouth, genitals, eyes, ears. Abjection functions both on the socio-cultural and on the individual level. On the social level, rituals, ceremonies, and the arts enact different strategies against the "other." Religion is said to displace abjection by an ideal of God; literature, poetry and the arts are attempts at sublimating the abject—a way of dealing with the excrement of our mind.

In lengthy and penetrating analysis of *Powers of Horror*, MacCannell (1986) analyzes the role that art plays in sin and abjection. If i understand her correctly, it was the genius of Christianity, according to Kristeva, which established this new category of sin. Sin displaced evil into the subject. Such an interiorization of abject was also the requisite of the Beautiful. In brief, Kristeva's thesis as interpreted by Juliet MacCannell appears as: "The various means of purifying the abject—the various catharsis—make up the history of religions, and end up with that catharsis par *excellent* called art, both on the far and near side of religion. Seen from the standpoint, the artistic experience, which is rooted in the abject it utters and by the same token purifies, appears as the essential component of religiosity. That is perhaps why it is destined to survive the collapse of the historical forms of religion" (p.17). Literature, arts and poetry might be envisioned as a way to sublimate the abject.

What Kristeva's theorizations did for me, as a maleman, was provide space for my participation in such a disruption, but then again Kristeva has *denied* that she is a feminist. For Kristeva "woman does not exist" (1981:34). Although feminists have equally applied her theoretical insights, i took this to heart in my *Is There a Distinct Feminist Aesthetic* paper.

Hélène Cixous: The Hysterical Daughter

As the reviews of Irigaray and Kristeva have shown, their radical formulations posit the body of woman as the enunciatory source of *écriture*. It could well be characterized as a feminine phenomenology. "What's it *like* to be a woman?" with each feminist defining woman differently. The most frequent critique made of this position is to raise the problem as to just how can a feminine discourse lie outside the symbolic order of language? How can it present an alternative form of representation standing against the signifier of lack? Brown and Adams (1979), in particular, have presented a blistering critique in this regard. The danger always remains that woman is figured once again under a patriarchal stereotype as being irrational, disordered, hysterical, mad or, on the otherhand, caring and motherly. The single most devastating critique of écriture féminine comes from materialist feminists who part company with the assumed universality of the feminine. The dissent of the feminist journal *Questions Féministes* is particularly succinct:

> It is at times said that women's language is closer to the body, to sexual pleasure, to direct sensations and so on, which means that the body could express itself directly without special mediation and that, moreover, this closeness to the body and to nature would be subversive. In our opinion there is no such thing as a direct relation to the body. To advocate a direct relation to the body is therefore not subversive because it is equivalent to denying the reality and the strength of social mediations, the very same ones that oppress us in our bodies. At most, one would advocate a different socialization of the body, but without searching for a true and eternal nature, for this search takes us away from the most effective struggle against the socio-historical contexts in which human beings are and will always be trapped (Marks and de Couritivron, 1981:219; in Cameron, 1992:180).

It is interesting in this regard to present commentary on the hetero/homo matrix of *écriture de corps* with Hélène Cixous since she moves from the political body writing of Everywoman in the '70s (1976-1982), but complicates such a blanket reading of her with an ambiguous bisexuality; and then in 1983 moves to the political practice of theater where the specificity of women's differences become more and more important. What follows is taken from the commentaries by Crowder (1983), Richman (1980) and Moray Shiach's (1991) in-depth study of Cixous's *oeuvre*. i have paid attention once again to artistic visual appropriations of Cixous when mentioned.

Impressively, throughout her writings and theater productions, Cixous has never lost her political commitment which was shaped by the colonial rule of French Algeria where she, like Derrida, was born of Jewish descent. (Perhaps this is why she has an affinity with Derridean deconstruction?) Throughout her writings Cixous has continually attempted to deconstruct hierarchies, through allusions, intertextual referencing and metaphorization. Her early work was historically intertextual, deconstructing and rewriting Greek myths (i immediately think of Christa Wolf's *Cassandra* here) and examining Egyptian mysticism. In particular, she focused on the figure of Electra, reading her as an ambiguous figure. In *Oresteia* Electra's undecidabilty between the masculine and the feminine is finally resolved through the eradication of her voice. *Le Nom d'Oedipe: Chant du Corps Interdit*, written in 1978, is a working through the dramas of Sophocles. The question of woman during the historical transition from matrilineality to patriarchy informs these writings. Cixous's interest, like Kristeva and Irigaray, is in the material texture of the language understood in relation to the body. "[M]yth and dreams are used in her text as a way of exploring the archaic and the repressed, and as ways of unsettling the illusion of subjective autonomy and conscious control" (Shiach: 70). Shiach reviews many, if not most, of Cixous's novels and concludes that many are "concerned with the social implications of sustaining an oppositional subjective and ethical economy" (p.101). Myth continues to play a central role throughout most of her writings.

Despite her detractors, Shiach argues that Cixous rejects both Freud and Lacan and moves into a bisexual position which is "open to all subjects who can escape the subjective and social effects of the dominant structures of desire" (p.16). She favors texts of Genet and Kleist, Joyce, and Shakespeare who are excessive in their characterizations and undermine fixed categories of sexual identity. "It is Genet's homosexuality that enables him to practice 'feminine writing'" (Crowder:140). Misreading Cixous as an essentialist, claims Shiach, was due in part to the vicious attacks that came from *Questions Féministes*. Divided loyalties meant black/white readings. The forces of *jouissance* were called upon through political writings that were bisexual in their disruptive potential, although i am hard pressed to read, "The Laugh of the Medusa," other than as an "Amazonian" gesture, which is to say, i have probably misread it. Crowder (1983:133) reads "Medusa" as a body fragmented in pieces: the breast, the abdomen, the mouth, the vagina, the head, despite the professed unity. "White ink," menstrual blood, "fluid," "formless," "fluid," are her root metaphors, hardly exemplary of an ambiguous "bisexuality." Yet Richman (p.67) claims that Cixous's metaphor of "sortie" or exit is precisely used to escape this essentialism and dichotomization, and the denial of sexual difference through the figure of the hermaphrodite where the masculine and the feminine are canceled out, neutralized. Cixous is searching for a (heterosexual?) bisexual desire where it is precisely the *destablization* of both terms which comes into erotic play. This is not unlike the lesbian-femme's desire where the "masculine" in a butch identity is quite a "different" masculinity figured on the female body than when figured on the male body. However Cixous outright rejects lesbians who appropriate the "man-within" to the point of inverting phallic power (Cixous, *Rethinking Differences*, 74-75, qtd. in Crowder, p.135). It is not clear what kind of "destabilization" she favors; what kind of "boy" her girl should be. What is telling, however, is her support for female

homosexuality which values the feminine and non-power, thereby supporting a lesbian continuum.

Shiach defends the "Laugh of the Medusa" as Cixous's way of "trying to explore what feminine writing '*will do*' "(p.17, Cixous,1981:39). Her
description of sexual pleasure (*jouissance*) is neither masculine nor feminine.
Siach's interpretation of this undecidability is based on Cixous's desire for the
masculine to augment the multiplicity of pleasure in the female libido. A
"flight," as well as the "theft" (*voler* has this double meaning) of the masculine libido informs her *jouissance*, which i take to mean that the "newly born
woman" can poach masculine signifiers in order to free herself. But, then
again, it is not articulated what kind of "boy" this girl should be. *Jouissance*
returns her to the body, but not to a natural one but to a cultural one, for
masculine repression prevents this breaking away into full flight. Despite
Shiach's defense, Gallop (1982b), Stanton (1989) and Moi (1985) have offered
extensive critiques of Cixous's biological essentialism. The ambiguity produced here, i would conclude, is telling of Cixous's hysteria and her valorization of Dora as the "newly born woman" that appears throughout her
writings. As Adams (1991) has demonstrated, "[h]ysterical identification is
characterized, it turns out, by oscillation" (p.5) between the masculine and
feminine positions.

According to Richman (1980: 63-65) Cixous interprets *feminine
economy* as a 'gift' (cf. Marcel Mauss) in the special sense of not mere exchange
(c.f. Lévi-Strauss), which would be a masculine gesture (as in the exchange
of women); but rather as a relation of giving through speech, whereby moral
and social implications are exchanged. The gift is in the giving of the self more
fully. In this sense of communication and conversation, Cixous "mobilizes a
materialist account of social relations which constitutes a critique of 'mass
society" (Shiach: 21). The specificity of feminine writing is described as a spatial metaphor: woman already functioning "within" a man's discourse can
explode this space. Such writing can happen within the cracks between, that
is, in uncertain spaces. Her desire is to "liberate the New Woman from the
Old. ...The gesture that characterizes the relation of women to the cultural
is one of flying and stealing [*voler*]" (p.23).

According to Shiach, Cixous makes a theoretical turn in 1983 when
she explores the figure of Tancredi, as represented by Torquato Tasso in *Jerusalem
Delivered*, and by Rosini in the opera *Tancredi*. This turn amounts to an insistence that the nature of "femininity" could not be determined but only
glimpsed at across a range of texts. By 1986 Cixous became frustrated with
language, making her consider the transgressive potential of painting as a form
of representation. In "*Le Dernier Tableau ou le Portrait de Dieu* " [The Final

Painting or the Portrait of God] she explores the way painting might challenge the clichés of language. Examining post-Impressionists like Monet and Van Gogh, Cixous develops the concept of "quasacles" (quasi-miracle-instants) which becomes her neologism for capturing the intensity of the moment through the force of colors and textures. (This seems hardly insightful; it sounds like another term for an aesthetic experience.) Cixous wants to find a form of writing which captures this intensity and instantaneousness. To this end she paradigmatically views Monet's paintings of Rouen Cathedral as a record of time which might provide her with a basis for an invigorated writing. "Painting [as she sees it] then becomes a struggle against change and time, an attempt to capture the temporal within the instantaneous" (Shiach:35).

Cixous now begins to think dualistically, combining conceptually painting with writing, i.e., the instantaneous plenitude of painting with the temporal intersubjectivity of writing, and the speed of painting with the slowness and deferral of writing. Cixous seems to be searching, as well, for that lost materiality of language—an embodied aesthetic—which language lost as it became more and more informational and abstract. She finds this possibility in the aesthetics of painting and tries to transfer its plenitude and speed into writing. For example, the "speed" of painting forces the artist to push past the cliché. But artistic speed requires the need for repetition—the "plenitude" of representation as paradigmatically demonstrated by the twenty-seven views of Rouen Cathedral. The habitual meaning of a thing begins to disappear as the painter works through its many varieties. Like the waterlilies of Monet, one of Cixous's favorite examples, the painter repeats a motif in many forms pointing to the infinity of representation, which is itself impossible. But, in this act of impossibility, the new is achieved. Cixous seems to be saying that extreme constructionism loses its object. You can paint a subject to "death." You must know when to stop; some mystery has to remain. One might say her search has been for a painterly writing of the body.

In mid 1980s Cixous turned to the theater and collaborated with *Théâtre du Soleil* to continue her exploration of "the inside, the underneath, the taste and the texture" (Shiach:p.36). This seems a logical extension of her painterly writing for it offers even more bodily "presence." Theater is important because it offers a space "where the poetic can still survive within the forms of a public an accessible ritual" (Shiach:p.106). The temporal forms, remarks Shiach, allow her to explore this temporal dimension and open up the possibility of multiple differences. The audience is locked into the bodily experience of time. Voice and music can be explored, plus the intensity (from painting) provides for the vividness of the here and now. Cixous opposes the artifice (*simulacrum*) of the mass media against the "weight of the present moment." Her theatrical intentions were to move away from spectacularity of the stage and to stress the bodily presence of actors. Theater was meant to bring the body back to writing. At first, this sounds like a nostalgic solution to the technologization of postmodernism, a going back into the past, to tradition. But on second reflection, Cixous may well have turned to such thinkers as Emmanuel Levinas who stressed the ethical encounter of the face-to-face interaction. It may be favorably said that recovering dialogue within the theatrical performative context restores that ethical, moral and social commitment as "gift." The musical voice addresses the call of the other within a specified context and with a specified feminist intent, without giving up an essential "woman."

Shiach concludes the study aptly: "Writing in theater ... has allowed her to explore different relations of otherness. ... These developments have led Cixous's work away from the intense focus in feminine subjectivity and its relations to the female body that were so important to her work in the 1970s. Instead, she is now committed to understanding women's struggle as part of a broader political and ethical movement: to realize the subjective and collective dimensions of feminine economy, to preserve cultural diversity in the face of homogenization and to resist the deadly cynicism of subjective and social domination" (p. 136).

Monique Wittig: I'm not your Daughter!

The disruption of psychoanalysis for its heterosexual bias has been made by queer theorists rethinking lesbian positions as represented by the French "materialist" feminist Monique Wittig (also a member of *Questions féministes*).[15] This is not to deny the insights of psychoanalysis; rather it is to recognize its limitations, and begin to rewrite missing aspects of "negative Oedipalization" that never appeared within the pages of mainstream psychoanalysis; thereby making current psychoanalytic structures even more complicated to the point of their possible transformation. Notable lesbian theorists like Fuss (1989: chap.3) and Butler's (1990a: 111-128) perceptive, but scathing, critique, draw on Wittig's ground-breaking work as take-off points for their own projects to deconstruct psychoanalysis. Part of that work is to blow the whistle on the way "sex" and "gender" are conceptualized in a heterosexual order.[16] These terms are more often than not collapsed, or the former is considered natural while the latter a cultural construction. Sex is fixed while gender is changeable. Often the more neutral and disarming term "gender" is substituted for "sexual difference" as an analytical category for feminist theory. The role of the unconscious in the formation of subjectivity and sexuality is displaced by a theory of a socially divided and contradictory subject, especially as theorized by Dorothy Dinnerstein and Nancy Chodorow. Wittig deconstructs the sex/gender binary by calling attention to sex as a term defined for the purposes of sexual reproductivity. Without that necessity there would be no reason to sex bodies into male and female categories. Unmooring sex from gender no longer places sex as the limit case of gender. A gendered body is not restricted by the apparent duality of sex; the sexed body likewise is not restricted by its gender.

Such cross-thinking is not unlike looking at yourself mirror and imagining that the image can be reversed and turned up-side down. Fuss (1991) utilizes a "disfigured binary,"–"inside/out"– with a paradoxically complicated "knot" on the cover of her book (with the same title) to convey the difficulty at hand. Such logic (both/and, both at once), which exceeds simple binaries, is extremely difficult to imagine, for it often requires the addition of a fourth, fifth and sometimes a sixth dimension. It may be likened to the hypercomplexities of hyperspace that have emerged with computer graphics where the illusions that produce three dimensionality (the West's common or "natural" sense of what is "real") are themselves deconstructed to produce an ever-changing, rotating figure which the mind cannot easily (if ever) grasp. The length of this sentence is purposely written with this in mind, for what is proposed by the disruptions of this "third sex" is to throw sex/gender into such a rotating flux. i read Butler's (1990a) reference to gender as pointing to such a possibility: "Consider the further consequence that if gender is something that one becomes—but can never be—then gender is itself a kind of becoming or activity, and that gender ought not to be conceived as a noun or a substantial thing or a static cultural marker, but rather as an incessant and repeated action of some sort" (p. 122). Contemporary sex/gender politics requires theorizing the rotation of the hetero/homo matrix looking through a kaleidoscope anamorphically. If this is pushed to the limit we end up with the trajectories of "bodies without organs" and the "precession of simulacra, "BwO's and schizo-bodies," as Curnick (1993) calls them. This concept, developed by Deleuze and Guattari (1983), is an abstraction of the body's annihilation. It is a being at degree zero which doesn't stop at finding a "self," as psychoanalysis would have it, i.e., some "depth" core at the center of the psyche; rather the self as an "organic organization" is what is being dismantled. The organs are malleable sites/cites/sights for re-embodiment for the "new flesh," orifices and electronic parts. The fantasy of the BwO, so prevalent in cyberspace literature, is already a reality as a nomadic electronic body-double that exists in the information circuits of banks, insurance companies, loan offices, government tax departments, and so on, argues the Critical Art Ensemble collective who tries to subvert and resist the "nomadic power" of this cyber-elite (1994). Many artists are now engaged in the pursuit of BwO's (see, Schade, 1994) where "*terminal flesh* is [being] played out on the *surface* of the body" (Bukatman, 1993:328, original italic).

Wittig might be perceived as a precursor of sorts for this development. Her strongest interruption is to state that the lesbian is not a "woman" (Wittig,1980). There is no space for a lesbian in the binary structure fixed by the heterosexual bond of sex that presupposes woman in opposition to man. The lesbian refuses to participate in the categories of this heterosexual matrix. Within this matrix, sex always refers to women, not to men. In other words, to become a "woman" in a heterosexual society requires bearing children. Rather than an internal critique of this discourse, Wittig attempts to formulate a new grammar, one which in particular avoids pronominal differentiations which would reinstate man/woman binary. Unlike English translations of Derrida, which require an understanding of punning and word play to convey the radicalness of his syntax, Wittig does not use puns, neologisms and word play. What she does do is use latent structures already found within grammar to create her new language. Her form is "very lucid, controlled, and correct in grammar and vocabulary." Nevertheless, lesbian writing "restructures the meaning of words and of literary forms because it is written from a social position in which masculinist thought has been nullified" (Crowder, 1983:127).

Wittig's lesbian writing, compared to *écriture féminine*, writes the body concretely, stripping it free of metaphor and imagery. Like lesbian painting and sculpture, the vulva as the nonreproductive organ (as opposed to the womb) is prominently featured in her novel *Les Guérillères* where the entire body is defetishized of its feminine mystifications. Writing is acting like a "war machine." "The *j/e* of the *Lesbian Body* is supposed to establish the lesbian, not as a split subject, but as the sovereign subject who can wage war linguistically against a "world" that has constituted a semantic and syntactic assault against the lesbian" (Butler, 1990a:120). The "guérillères" value the physical functions of strength and agility. They are passionate as well as violent; they use their "sex" (expose their breasts in order to lure in the male army so as to annihilate them). "Wittig's language is replete with colors, textures, odors, movement, and song" (Crowder: 120). Although Wittig would never use the term, these are 'virile' women who have refused to be castrated. In *The Lesbian Body* Wittig literally and violently dismembers the body, describing it part by part, eroticizing every abjected part as equally desirable as the most selective of parts, i.e., the vulva and the breasts. This could very well be read as a form of literary s/m ritual. It is left up to the reader when to stop this literary beating for no metaphors appear in this text. Violence informs her text throughout, represented as a slash through all first person and possessive pronouns (j/e, m/a, m/on, m/es). The Amazon, as the outlaw lesbian, becomes part of the tradition of an autonomous female culture. The family is abolished. Desire and love are experienced amongst companions, as well as amongst mothers and daughters. Few men appear in her writing. *Jouissance* "is not mystical and private, but concrete and shared in a cultural bonding" (Crowder: 125).[17]

Wittig inspires political action by rewriting the myths of men which keep women in ignorance and oppression, e.g., Eve becomes a Medusa-Euydice in *Les Guérillères* where she is guided by her counselor snake from the hell of ignorance. She recodes words by reversing the values placed on them: "woman," "wife," "mother," are pejoratives, while "amazon," "dyke," and "witch," are expressed with approval. Stories of sabbat witches, Amazons and heroic women help solidify and unite lesbians with one another as a plural "we" (*elles*) in a tradition and culture of strength and autonomy. Her writing acknowledges the historical silence and the lacunae as the absences of this discourse. Characterized by symbols and similes, and avoiding metaphors, Wittig is searching for concrete signifiers that are literal in their effects—close to the body as if they had a direct relation to reality—the plenitude of a phenomenological description. i would say that Wittig is trying to recover the figure of the ancient goddess who bears her own offspring without the need of a man; the figure of the mother before patriarchy; before castration.[18] "Lesbian writing" is "[n]ot a new creation, but the recovery of an original mode of discourse lost when women identified themselves with motherhood [the recognition of a father], this language would act immediately upon the cultural environment to restore the lost harmony" (Crowder,129). In effect, Wittig is offering us the other side of ecofeminism. Crete's paradise is now replaced by the Sappic isles of the *Guérillères*. The rule of the benevolent castrated peace-loving mother is now replaced by the Mother who denies her castration. The witch, the Amazon, the hag, the crone all meet in Mary Daly's "Intergalactic Wickedary of the *French* Language."[19]

Ultimately, in Butler's mind at least, Wittig's essentialist position remains untenable because of its separatist stance which reinscribes a binary. Politically, as heterosexual one always remains the enemy. For a lesbian identity Butler favors a subversive and parodic redeployment of power based on performance rather than the "impossible fantasy of its full-scale transcendence" (p.124). For Fuss (1989:46) gay men drop out of focus entirely in Wittig's *oeuvre* and begin to function as an oppressed other—a subversive category that threatens her essentialist lesbianism.

Irigaray, Kristeva, Cixous and Wittig's "writing the body" in the early '80s presents the last barrier before the postmodern dissolve of "woman" took place. All four searched to recover the "materiality" of language. Kristeva's "poetic language," Cixous's "painterly writing," Irigaray's "two lips," and Wittig's "lesbian writing" characterize a "feminine phenomenology" where the presence or plenitude of the signifier was thought to be possible. Language figured the body essentially. Paradoxically, i would argue, *they all adumbrated* the postmodern dissolve of 'woman' and took part in it. "Writing the body" meant disseminating it at the same time as claiming its unity. Each part was a whole: Irigaray's two lips, Wittig's body parts in *Le Corps Lesbian*, Kristeva's semiotic, and Cixous's "white ink," and the severed body parts in *"The Laugh of the Medusa."* But the "parts" wouldn't hold together. Once re-ensembled they became "organs without bodies," as Braidotti (1989) puts it, ready for the 'brave new world' of reproductive technologies, sex changes, blurring of sexual differences, to enter the short-circuit of informational technologies.

1 The most readable account of deconstruction and its translation into the American context is Leitch's *Deconstructive Criticism: An Advanced Introduction* (1983).

2 French women writing poetry from this position are reviewed by Jane McLelland (1983).

3 Margarite Duras (see Willis, 1987) and Shoshana Felman (1977,1987) hold a special place in French feminist thought. Felman, by far, has made a major contribution by examining the juncture between literature and psychoanalysis, literature as the structure of the unconscious and the unconscious, in its 'literariness,' for its slippages of meaning. Duras, on the other hand, writes the limits and boundaries of the body of the writer, reader, and the text.

4 Domna Stanton, who was positive in her assessment of the French feminists in her earlier easy (1980) became critical of that very tradition nine years later (Stanton, 1989). Recently, Duchen (1987) has offered yet another generation of French feminists, attempting to redress the over-emphasis on psychoanalytic reading. Second, and now third generation French feminists remain divided as ever (Jardine, 1989).

5 i recommend Kaja Silverman's excellent study, *The Subject of Semiotics* (1983), as a readable text to grasp an understanding of the subject in Lacanian thought. Silverman makes an application of his insights to feminism throughout numerous cinematic examples. Also Weedon's *Feminist Practice & Poststructuralist Theory* (1987) for a broad overview of Lacan and Derrida to feminism. Derrida, like Lacan seems incomprehensible at first. i found Jonathan Culler's *On Deconstruction* (1982), and Madan Sarap's *An Introductory Guide to Poststructuralism and Postmodernism* (1988), as two excellent starter texts. It is impossible to "keep up" with the pretense of claiming currency with the industry that surrounds figures like Derrida and Lacanian spin-offs. It requires more time and patience than i sometimes have. Derrida's chronicler, Christopher Norris is helpful for his lucid and thoughtful commentary. i admire greatly Žižek's application of Lacan to popular culture as is evident throughout my text.

6 This bothersome word is explained as "attachment" by Laplanche and Pontalis (1973:30). "Its main function...is the establishment of a link and an opposition between sexual instincts and self-preservative ones" (p.31). The problem of writing on the body in general is raised here. What is the relationship between discursive and non-discursive elements of language? The gap between the body and psyche is not absolute. If an image, i.e., a symbolization of the body, is fundamental to its construction then its "figurative" embodiment becomes crucial.

7 For an accessible overview of psychoanalytic applications to literary criticism there is no finer study than that of Elizabeth Wright (1984). In chapter seven where she examines the Lacanian interpretations, she makes note that little application has been made to the visual arts, providing several examples by Lacan himself. In the area of deconstruction, the same can be said of Catherine Belsey's (1980) *Critical Practice* and her review essay 'Constructing the Subject: Deconstructing the Text' (1985).

8 There is Althusser's distinction between the younger and older Marx, Derrida has concentrated on the 'late' Heidegger, while in the Eastern bloc an entire generation of scholars has rewritten Marx and Lenin.

9 Heath (1978) has also examined this particular seminar. The passage comes from *SXX* p.70 (in Heath,

p.50): "...just as with St. Teresa—you only have to go and look at the Bernini statue in Rome to understand immediately she's coming, no doubt about it. And what is she enjoying, coming from? It's clear that the essential testimony of the mystics is that of saying they experience it but know nothing about it. These mystical ejaculations are neither idle gossip nor mere verbiage, in fact they're the best thing you can read—note, right at the bottom of the page. Add to them Jacques Lacan's *Ecrits*, a work of the same order. Given which, naturally, you'll all going to be convinced I believe in God. I believe in the jouissance of the woman in so far as it is *en plus*, something more, on condition you block out that more until I've thoroughly explained it."

10 There is no shortage of critique on Kristeva's notion of the pre-oedipal semiotic. See the following: Stanton, 1989; Silverman, 1988a, Chap. 4; Coward, 1984; 22-27, Felski,1989:56 ff). For a more sympathetic reading of the pre-Oedipal see Moi (1985: 165).

11 The most readable examination of the avant-garde and its transgressive potential is found in Grosz (1989:55-60).

12 These remarks were drawn from a presentation by Elizabeth Grosz on "French Feminism and Representation", given in 1988 at the University of Alberta. See also an earlier article (1987) where she discusses the work of Irigaray.

13 Bové (1984), in his sympathetic reading of Kristeva politics of desire, points out that such rhetoric is scattered throughout *Desire in Language*: "Similarly in the passage quoted above (p.5) 'carnivalesque discourses *breaks through* the *laws* of a language *censored* by grammar and semantics and, at the same time, is a social and political protest.' The variations of this rhetoric are endless: 'opening up' (p.26, 33), 'bursting' or 'clashing' movement (p.225), 'shattering' of a surface (pp. 23,261), 'transgression' (pp. 65,70). The 'shattering' of a surface, for instance, is often the form taken by the subject's negating energies in Kristeva's analysis of both Bakhtin's dialogism... and of Jakobson's innovations in linguistics and commentary on the Russian Futurists, Mayakovsky, and Khlebnikov: ...*a code* (mores, social contract) *must be shattered* in order to give to the free play of negativity, need, desire, pleasure, and jouissance, before being put together again, although temporarily and with full knowledge of what is involved" (p.23, my italic) (Bové, 1984:p.222). This is hardly a "feminine" stance but speaks of overcoming a violent action in order to overcome a resistant barrier. Kristeva does address the dangers of *jouissance* which can lead to terror.

14 Philippe Jullian's *Dreamers of Decadence* (1975) is as good as anyone writing on the decadent side of the *fin de siècle*. Chapter 2 is on the "New Beauty."

15 Wittig's materialism rests on the grounds that "woman" is a political rather than a biological class. According to Wittig, only lesbian societies can (an have) abolish "sewage," (after "slavery")—the oppression of women.

16 To flag this development, i have used the neologism "maleman" where appropriate to identify that both sex and gender can be sent into flux.

17 Crowder refers to Rosenfeld's analysis of the linguistic techniques Wittig's "lesbian writing" employs: "the use of the present tense to abolish time distinctions; the passive voice; a concrete vocabulary; repetition; multiplication of the female subject; the transformation of intransitive into transitive verbs; and the elimination of grammatical forms pre-empted by the masculine gender" (p.130).

18 The literature is vast here. Barbara Walker's, *The Woman's Encyclopedia of Myths and Secrets* (1983) is a compendium of the various historical forms of goddess worship. If Gaea is considered the oldest of the goddess it is possible to write/rite/right her as a lesbian—an Amazon—since it can be hypothesized that the male did not "figure" (is not recognized) at this time. In Merlin Stone's *Paradise Papers* (1976) she traces the rites/writes/rights of Spring performed by the goddess to insure the growth of the cereal crops. At first the rites are performed alone. In the mythological historical record, the goddess then takes a son—the flesh of her own body which she magically produces; then a brother appears, followed by a husband. Eventually both the priest and priestess are equally in charge of the ceremony. This semiological chain charts the changes of power from the early Neolithic to the Chalcolithic period when the transition to patriarchy has become complete. The priest organizes the ceremony which has become secularized. Metallurgy now rises to significance. i interpret Wittig's "lesbian writing" as an attempt to recover the ur-woman, the non-castrated Mother. It is in direct contrast to a similar recovery of the castrated Mother of Riane Eisler's *The Chalice & the Blade* (1988) who posits the Neolithic period, i.e., Crete as a romantic time of nurturing and peaceful co-existence among the sexes. Wittig's Amazons are political warriors. They recognize the need for violence. i would point to the writings of Janet Biehl (1991) who questions the whole ecofeminist movement based on feminists like Eisler. Wittig offers the flip side of this development. It is now witches and Amazons who lead women to the promised land. In this regard Christine Fauré's essay is appropriately titled: "The Twilight of the Goddesses, or The Intellectual Crisis of French Feminism" (1981).

19 The pun is on Mary Daly and Jane Caputi's dictionary, *Websters' First New Intergalactic Wickedary of the English Language* (1987).

GIVE ME
A LITTLE
SIGN

but make it intelligible ... if you can?

We [*m/f*] include two of our
male authors in this section. This
decision is consistent with our
antiessentialist position. For it is not
a question of a man's thinking or a
woman's thinking, but of thinking
the category of women *otherwise*
than both women and men had
thought before.

(Adams, 1990:44)

The last vignette and the issue of *écriture féminine* raise the question of essentialism, which, as was demonstrated, can be extended to ecofeminist movements and those feminists who still believe that religious institutions can be transformed through internal critique. Fuss (1989) in *Essentially Speaking* writes,

> Essentialism is *classically* defined as a belief in true essence—that which is most irreducible, unchanging, and therefore constitutive of a given person or thing. ... Constructionism... insists that essence itself [is] a historical construction (p.2, my italic).

"Classically" is the operative word here, for it is possible to reinstate the binary of essentiality/construction once more. For a constructivist to say that there is something "essential" in the essentialist position is already to sneak in a form of essentialism within the very boundaries of the constructivist paradigm itself. Such an argument is not new. It is often used to deconstruct the impossibility of any dichotomous position. To say you want a value-free objective science is already to state a value; to say you are saying things clearly is already using a metaphor. Such paradoxes can always be found. With swift and deft deconstructive moves, Fuss's project is precisely to expose how constructionism depends on essentialism. "To insist that essentialism is always and everywhere reactionary is, for the constructionist, to buy into essentialism in the very act of making the charge; *it is to act as if essentialism has an essence*" (Fuss, 1989: 21. italic in orig.). It seems more accurate to say that feminist essentialists posit a reality which is ultimately impenetrable and irreducible, which resists full linguistic construction. But is that void or abyss ultimately feminine or maternal? The answer is more one of strategy, putting that political discourse into motion, than ascertaining the truth of such a proposition. Cut off from ethics and politics theory can just as easily fall into an academic game, and unfortunately it often does.

All the French feminists discussed previously used deconstruction in various ways, i.e., as an internal critique of Lacan (Irigaray); as a way of rupturing the symbolic (Kristeva); as a way to overturn hierarchies (Cixous); and as a force to undo heterosexuality (Wittig); yet all preserved difference, never losing the cite/site/sight of essential womanhood. Difference understood as a *divided* subject kept its ground. Were they, like Nietzsche's accusatory second woman, simply inverting the hierarchy–replacing femininity with masculinity? This is certainly one possible interpretation. The way difference came to be used in feminist debates forms the contemporary landscape of post-modern feminism. Camps are as divided as ever, for as i shall argue, even "essentialism" can be recoded as one form of difference amongst many.[1]

A descriptive vignette, this time coming from Janet Wolff (1992), places the issue in context within an artistic framework.

> The feminist art historian, Griselda Pollock, published an article in 1977 entitled "What's wrong with images of women?" This piece has been reprinted several times. ... Ironically, in each case a mistake in the printing of the title has undermined the argument of the article. The phase "images of women" was intended to be inside quotation marks, and their omission in publication produced a very different question—one, indeed, which Pollock was concerned in the article to prove illegitimate. The title as printed asks "What's wrong with the *actual* images of women in circulation?" But Pollock is asking the question "What's wrong with the very *notion* of "images of women?"
>
> It was (and in some circles still is) common for feminist art historians and literary critics to reread texts in order to expose and dismantle stereotypes and dominant forms of representation of women in patriarchal culture; reading lists in women's studies courses are full of these texts, which do address the question of what is wrong with images of women—that is, with the ways in which women are represented. But this type of critique is premised on the assumption that on the one hand we have "women," and on the other hand we have (distorted, partial, inaccurate) "images" of them. Poststructuralist theories have demolished this opposition, and Griselda Pollock is objecting to the very notion that there can *be* in this uncomplicated way, "images of women." Representation is central to the constitution of the category "woman." It is for this reason that feminist work in the past ten years or so has been preoccupied with the cultural formation of gendered identities. What is wrong with "images of women" is that the notion obscures the

> constitutive role *of* images ("women" do not somehow pre-
> exist representation) and that culture is this still perceived
> in terms of earlier reflective theories of art (p. 711).

Wolff's story, which i have quoted at length, is instructive for several reasons. First, it makes clear that mis-reading goes on despite the best intentions of the author or artist (after all, the content of Pollock's piece should make it clear that the title was in error). Second, Wolff's italic of the words "actual," "notion," "be," points to how the "metaphysics of presence" operates in language to "fix" language as representation. Third, it points to the contestation of various images of what "constitutes" the representation of "women" (see Betterton, 1987a). As Wolff further remarks, the work of Lynda Nead (1989) on nineteenth-century painting in England has shown that the constructions of femininity and domesticity in the Victorian period actively produced the ideology and the social relations that went with the image of the "fallen woman."

As theorized by the British feminist Elizabeth Cowie (1978), treating woman as textual sign, whose representation varied from text to text, from situation to situation, dispersed any naive belief there was a continuous field of experience shared by all women. The image of Everywoman could no longer be easily maintained for such a position naturalized sexual differences and further universalized culturally constructed and historically specific definitions of femininity and masculinity. The French feminist *écriture* began to fall out of favor. *Ten years* after Cowie's ground-breaking essay, an American feminist, Denise Riley (1988), could sound the same sentiment, albeit from a more socio-historical descriptive argument: "'[W]oman' is historically, discursively constructed, and always relatively to other categories which themselves change; 'woman' is a volatile collection in which female persons can be very differently positioned, so that the apparent continuity of the subject of 'woman' isn't to be relied on; 'woman' is both synchronically and diachronically erratic as a collectivity, while for the individual, 'being a woman' is also inconstant, and can't provide an ontological foundation" (pp. 1-2). Riley, who is often quoted as sounding the constructivist clamor for the discursive subject "woman," differs significantly from Cowie and the *m/f* collective to whom Cowie belongs/belonged. Their differences hinge on the concept of the subject. For Cowie, following psychoanalytic discourse, the subject is fundamentally *split*, alienated from the self. For Riley, the subject is decentered, or non-unitary, produced through the intersections of competing social discourses and practices which position an individual subject in complex heterogeneous ways; often impossible to "pin" down in certainty for the subject is always in process. i shall try to clarify and discuss this difference below.

If i were to go back to my "Pretexts of the Title," where three subject positions (as summarized by Kerby) were given, it is possible to place the poststructuralist positions of the subject, like that of Riley, into gender terms. First, the subject of speech, i.e., the subject of the discourse like characters in literature, actors and actresses in film, or the self-reflective author in discourse as represented by the "I," can be equated with the "technologies of gender" (de Lauretis, 1987a), or more accurately "sex/gender technologies." These are sex/gender definitions which are available in the discourses themselves. In my discussion of Ruether's religious discourse, the virgin, the whore, and Maritology (mother) were the only subject positions available for women, although all three could be rejected. Ruether's own discourse excluded oppressed subject positions of women outside the religious sphere, although she did include Lilith as the non-castrated woman which may provide space for lesbian positions within the Bible. Second, the speaking individual, i.e., the sex/gender of the author of the text, (in my case as represented by an impossible "i" since the subject of speech and the speaking subject are often collapsed together in an autobiography through the pronoun "I") can be likened to the gender position the speaking subject takes. Here the controversy that fuels my own journey is highlighted, i.e., "Can a 'man' read like a 'woman?' However, whatever sex/gender positions are taken slip easily into the third subject position: the spoken subject as a sex/gender identification taken by actual subjects; you, the reader. What emotional commitments are involved in taking up one subject position and not another? My *changing* sex/gender position has been formed by the vignettes that i write and theorize about. These three discursive subject positions may be summarized as interrelated sex/gender definitions, positionings and identifications which, taken together in their complexity, inform the poststucturalist decentered subject.[2]

What then is the difference between this conception of the subject and Cowie's? Under the influence of Derrida's neologism *différance*, difference and deferment opened the system up and unmoored "Woman" as a universal and transhistorical, cross-cultural fiction. It dispersed "her" across texts as poststructuralist theories of language introduced the rhetoric of diversity and polyvocality. Derrida was entirely supportive of a position of femininity which was "affirmative," contradictory, and Dionysian. "Woman" as *gynesis* (Jardine, 1985) was a metaphor of textuality or "style" for the unveiling of truth. It was this 'third woman' in the Nietzsche's discourse (see Berg, 1982) who refused to be assigned a stable position for feminism. Sexual difference was to be displaced from the feminist rhetoric, for the third woman did not recognize any *absolute* difference between men and women. Such a "figure" lived on the borderlines of masculinity and femininity. "She" had to be both active and passive, refusing to be assimilated into the masculine mode, yet participating in its activity.

> Beyond the double negation of the first two [woman as truth and untruth], woman is recognized and affirmed as an affirmative power, a dissumulatress, an artist, a dionysiac. And no longer is it man who affirms her. She affirms herself, and herself, in man. Castration, here again, does not take place. And anti-feminism, which condemned woman only so long as she answered to man from the two reactive positions, is in its turn overthrown (Derrida, 1979:97).

In this sense she was bisexual, existing in the impossible space *between* positive and negative Oedipal resolutions. Derrida's description of Woman as the metaphor of truth's *dissimulation*,[3] could easily fit Cixous's writings. Yet, whereas with Cixous there may have been a residual essentiality, making her writings at times ambiguous as to where she herself stood in these debates, anti-essentialist and anti-humanist theories often cleared away that ground which had funded essentialism itself. It seemed as if one could just as easily tip the scale too far towards yet another idealization: Derrida's "Woman" as the textual (discursive) figure of *gynesis*, or, as in Baudrillard's writings, "seductive power" which operated on the level of cultural symbolization. "Woman" became dissimulated to the point where she might disappear entirely. What ought to be done in the "name" of woman if the differences between women were often greater than the differences between women and men?

First, it should be pointed out that the British journal *m/f*, under the editorship of Parveen Adams and Elizabeth Cowie, helped explore the terms of this debate. Founded in 1978 and closing its covers in 1986, Adams and Cowie edited a review of their work four years later. *The Woman in Question* offered a summary account of the debates and issues that had taken place over the past nine years. In the introduction to the *m/f* project Joan Copjec (1990) makes two exceedingly important points regarding their contribution which remain divisive issues in today's "postfeminist" climate and for questions concerning the subject. First she makes the point that the anti-essentialist stance of *m/f* had never lost sight/site/cite of psychoanalysis (the divided subject), but strove to incorporate it along with social critique. "The analysis of the

142

inscription of the woman in different social practices must be supplemented by a psychoanalysis of the construction of the female subject. ... It is the critical relation between the psychic and the social that is the ultimate concern of this feminist project" (p. 12). The second significant point Copjec makes refers to the whole question of fantasy. "By doubling its investigation in this way [social with the psychological] *m/f* effectively argues that the subject position inscribed by a discourse is not the same as the position of the subject who is engaged by that discourse, no more than the 'I' of the statement is the same as the 'I' who speaks it" (ibid.). For the visual arts this aspect is crucial because of the pleasure of the image; "pleasure not [only] of what I come to know—signification—but of what I come to desire, that is the scenario [the *mise-en-scène*] of desire that I come to participate in as I watch a film, view an image, or read a text. This is a desire not for something, but for desire itself. What is signified is thus the position of desire for the spectator" (Cowie,1990:115).[4]

The importance of these two points cannot be underestimated in relation to the poststructuralist question of the subject. It raises the relationship of discursive and non-discursive factors in *every* text: the absence within the presence, the transgressive within the law, the disavowal within the avowal, the non-essential within the essential, the misreadings in every reading and, of course, the unconscious in every conscious act. Regions of the unspeakable and the unutterable lead to the greatest amount of speculation and, in my mind at least, also identify the impossibility of an entirely materialist, i.e., constructivist or discursive, theory of the subject. Again, applying paradoxical logic, every materialist theory is informed by an idealism that forms its origins since some first principal must be posited. Some degree of metaphysics must seep in; the question is more one of "how much?" This experience of an irreducible remainder, what i take to be sublime, is always bound up with the issues of the limits of representation. The sublime *is* the postmodern aesthetic, as any number of writers have argued.[5] The strength of this becomes a recognition of radical alterity; a recognition of "othering" —the projection of foreign others in relation to the self; of seeing the Other in oneself. "However unfeasible and inefficient it may sound, I see no way to avoid insisting that there has to be a simultaneous other focus: not merely who am I? but who is the other woman? How am I naming her? How does she name me?" (Spivak:1981, p. 179).

Remaining strictly with a constructed or discursive subject, as Riley does, with a *multiple* subject as opposed to a *divided* subject, can lead to a sociologization of identity based only on positivity. Reality becomes entirely permeable to history. Fantasy structures, which enable the gap between the speaking subject and the spoken subject to be theorized, are missing. The question of desire can be avoided. How to deal with the textual "remainder" is a question mark. How the text "speaks back" will always remain problematic, so much so that this prompted Stockton (1992) to argue persuasively that post-structuralist feminists (especially Jane Gallop) have returned to a similar position held by Victorian feminists: their belief in a spiritual materialism in the name of God! Stockton points to a very subtle distinction between the way Barthes *poeticizes* the body compared with Gallop, who misreads him. To poeticize for Gallop "refers to the use we make of language's metaphorical properties—its discursive figures. Barthes's *poetize* means nearly the opposite. ... We poetize when we (think we) point to a reality that exists outside our discursive figures. Truly, then, this distinction collapses, since we can only poetize by poeticizing in a mystical vein" (p.125-126). For Barthes, every materialist (constructivist) must poetize, i.e., must make the non-discursive reality mystical. Gallop repeats Riley's view of the subject in this instance. She sociologizes the subject. This dilemma presents the "difficulty of writing," and the difficulty of representation in general. This "difficulty" is part of the human(e) condition of being a *split* subject. Copjec is suggesting that this fantasy space, this Thing, Lacan's Real, will *necessarily* require psychoanalytic examination, preferably of the post-Lacanian variety. Without this non-discursive factor, what Žižek (1989a) calls the *sinthome*, there can be no way of making sense of the formations of desire that inhabit the social imaginary as Castoriadis posits it (1984), nor with the fundamental sexuation of the body. Hence, Žižek's (1993b: 265, ft.9) response to Butler's (1990a) title "Gender Trouble," was the following. Noting that every prescriptive performative formation she suggests is an endeavor to patch up the trauma of this original split, he writes: "*Because gender as such is a response to a fundamental "trouble"* : "normal sexual difference constitutes itself in an attempt to avoid an impasse" (original italic). Or, in Copec's formulation: "*sex serves no other function than to limit reason, to remove the subject from the realm of possible experience of pure understanding*" (1994c:21, italic in original).

On the other side of difference, then, is to precisely do what feminists with a psychoanalytic bent fear: throw out psychoanalysis and carry on with the differences that exist amongst women grounded in various social locations. This becomes a postmodern, materialist poststructuralism based on (usually Foucaultian) discourses alone. The mantra of race, color, religion, ethnicity etc. can be effectively be explored to identify the oppression of various subject positions. Further, a reception aesthetics becomes more and more acceptable as attention is paid to what meaning interpretants are bringing into the text. This development opens up the whole field of "reader response theories" which eliminate the unconscious altogether, usually displacing it with a psychological theory of the imagination.[6] It is important, therefore, to further clarify the distinction between the subject in psychoanalysis as distinct from the constructed subjectivity of historicism understood as a discursive formation, especially by cultural studies.

Can You Fuck With Sex? The Antinomies of the Transgendered Body

The distinction between the split subject of psychoanalysis ($) and the Foucaudian subject of discursivity has been usefully and carefully articulated by Shepherdson (1994). He makes the crucial point that 'sexual differentiation', unlike gender, is *not* subject to human law and its institutionalization. Like 'death,' it is not subject to human intervention and cannot be situated at the same level as 'social roles' that concern 'gender' constructions. "This difference between *contingent*, historically constituted forms of life, and the *inevitable* dimension of sexually marked embodiment, is what we have indicated by distinguishing between *the role of gender* and *the imperative of sex*" (p. 161, original italics).

The historicist *construction of subjectivity* (i.e., role) and the psychoanalytic *constitution of the subject* (i.e., imperative) is clarified by Shepherdson by referencing both Freud and Lacan's attempts to go beyond the oppositions between biology and history, nature and culture, essentialism and historicism. Freud argued that the sexual 'drive' (*Trieb* and not *Instinkt*) was *constitutively denatured*, meaning that the drive was *subject to representation*, i.e., language which he spoke of in terms of 'displacement,' 'condensation,' 'substitution' and so on. Lacan furthered these speculations in terms of his 'formulae of sexuation' (see Pretexts to Title). Against a realist notion of language which collapses *what is seen* and *what is known* as a 'concept' or 'idea'—as something 'seen' which the classical term *eidos* indicates—Lacan deconstructed this immediate reality into the Imaginary and the Symbolic, and, like Freud, furthered a distinction between the *organism* and the *body* by introducing the complications of the Real. On one level "the 'body' is *constitutively* denatured, [or] 'organ-ized' ... by the image and the word" (Shepherdson: 170). In this sense the *constitution of the body* in psychoanalysis recognizes that human sexual roles are inevitably historical. But that is not all. The intrusion of a primordial absence into language—as a void or nothingness that is 'beyond' language (the Real)—what Lacan took up with the concept of 'object *a*', is the *first substitution* around which the 'body' is structured, closing the 'body's' difference

145

between the inside and the outside as being both perpetually unstable, and yet relatively secure. This means (for Lacan) that 'gender trouble' will always exist as a permanent condition between the sexes because there is no guarantee that bio-sexual difference (as held firm by collapsing the distinction between the Imaginary-Symbolic couplet where absence/presence of a body part "rules") will align itself with the symbolic cultural-sexual difference (as theorized by the discursive subject which offers a multiplicity of gendered roles, and where binary distinctions rule, e.g., active/passive, public/private, etc.), nor with the Real logical-sexual difference as defined by the failure of the signifier, i.e., signifier/Other, male/female, man/woman, masculine/feminine. As developed in Lacan's 'formulae of sexuation,' the logic of sexual differentiation occurs at the level between the Symbolic and the Real, whereas in cultural studies 'the construction of the subject' collapses the Imaginary and the Symbolic where the symbolic is assigned double duty, designating both images and words and thereby foreclosing (barring) sexual difference.

Can the discursive subject of poststructuralism be reconciled with the constitutive subject of psychoanalysis? This question underpins the debate concerning the disruptive force the deconstruction of essentialism has wrought in feminist debates. If the Real of embodiment drops out of the debate then it appears that the *subject's embodiment* collapses into the *subject's role*, and anatomy, through surgical intervention, becomes malleable—subject to 'reconstruction.' Sexual difference, is once more, foreclosed. Shepherdson evokes the clinical work of the Lacanian psychoanalyst Catherine Millot (1990b) on transsexuality to demonstrate the ethical concerns the medical profession overlooks when it avoids the question of constitutive subjectivity, and disregards the distinction between the patient's *demand* and *desire*. If the medical profession acts as an omnipotent Other, when there is no limit placed as to what surgery is capable of doing, or when questions are avoided to *listen* to what is behind the patient's demand, then they act as if they were 'outside the law,' a position of omnipotent *jouissance*. They complete the demand of the patient without seeking to know "his" or "her" desire which is precisely what the patient's demand seeks to evade. In this sense, the demand the patient seems to make 'freely' and without coercion in fact comes from the medical profession. A percentage of transsexuals *do not* identify with 'the other sex' as lacking; that is, as entailing the ambiguity and uncertainty that such an operation will bring. Rather, they are *horsexe*, 'outside' this distinction, nearly psychotic, believing that the 'other sex' is *not lacking*. Such a phallic identification eliminates sexual difference as lack. In their fantasy of 'otherness' sex/gender trouble will disappear since symbolic ambiguity, i.e., the failure of the signifier that accompanies difference, is eliminated. The perfected body is fantasized as being outside of the historical ex-istence which it currently suffer. Their identification is 'outside sex,' with '*La Femme*' or The Father; a narcissistic image wherein the phallus becomes 'incarnated' (Shepherdson:177). For the *horsexe* male transsexual, identification with '*La Femme*' forecloses the position of 'a woman,' since now what it means to be a 'woman' has been totalized. In contradistinction, those transsexuals who desire an operation are— properly speaking—men trapped in women's bodies (male femaler), or a women 'born' in man's body wants to be get rid of it (female maler). The transsexual has not yet *constituted* a 'body' that can be mobilized in relation to society in order for 'him or her' to act as a subject (Rees, 1996; Ekins, 1996). Such a position is radically different from bi-sexualism where the oscillation between the heterosexual and gay and lesbian divide can take place by 'passing' in either camp (see Garber, 1995). Transgenders are not *necessarily* bi-sexual, however as "outlaws" to the hetero/homo divide they *necessarily* must struggle for a sense of identity which comes with such "gender confusion."

It is at this point that the issues and politics which surround "transgenderism" (Ekins and King, 1996) become complex and contestory. During the '90s a transgendered community has emerged that has pulled itself away from gay and lesbian enclaves that once gave them shelter (much like the radical lesbian split from the earlier feminist movement) raising a new set of theoretical differences progressively termed *queer theory* (see Whittel, 1996). No longer satisfied with being pejoratively called the "third sex," those who choose partial technological sex changes and those who cross-live without the mediation of medical intervention have attempted to form communities and enclaves of their own (Perkins, 1996; Buhrich, 1996). As gendered "outlaws" they attempt to disrupt the hetero/homo binary by way of a "gender fuck." The best known practitioner of such a position is Kate Bornstein who, in *Gender Outlaw* (1994), claims that if gender is partitioned often enough it will dissipate the hetero/homo divide creating a hybrid "third space," a space outside of the current bifurcated gender differences. For her, transgendered positions already signify a possible coalition of the "trangressively gendered" (p. 134-135). This *could* include not only pre-operative and post-operative transsexuals, but also transvestites, drag queens, cross-dressers, bisexuals, gays and lesbians, and also straights who exhibit transgressed gender-roles. Sandy Stone (1991) in her article, "The *Empire* Strikes Back" argues that transgender transsexualism needs to identify itself in difference to the established binary, oppositional mode of gender identification by recognizing the array of identities which transsexual autobiographies present. Passing should no longer be the road to affirmation. A transsexual needs to take up a sexed subject position in difference to heterosexual and homosexual positions.

Such a stance, not surprisingly, has drawn criticism from the entire spectrum of sexed identities. The "empire" Stone refers to is the one identified pejoratively as *The Transsexual Empire* (1980) by Janice Raymond's hard hitting book which argues that it is especially male femalers who reinforce the sex stereotyping system of patriarchy by presenting themselves as pastiches of women men would like to see. The medical establishment reinforces these patriarchal defined stereotypes by attempting to cure them of their 'incipient' transsexual leanings. Despite her male transsexual retractors who argue that they too are involved in feminism and are sensitive to women's oppression (e.g., Riddell, 1996) no amount of passing will change Raymond's fundamental accusation. Raymond, a committed lesbian activist, identifies 'woman-identified women' as the strategy against patriarchy. Consequently, in her 1994 Introduction to a new edition of *Transsexual Empire*, when reviewing Leslie Feinberg's *Stone Butch Blues*, she spells out why transgendered lesbians who undergo surgery and hormonal treatment to become more like men end up in "gender-neutral *otherness*," ..."*from being woman-identified to being other-identified*" (Raymond, 1996:220, original italics). Their disavowal of womanhood has them lost to participate in feminism. Raymond sees k.d. lang as the exemplary lesbian when she is in control of the situation, pointing out that her photo spread with Cindy Crawford in the August. 1993 issue of *Vanity Fair*, is a classic example of how that strength can be usurped and reappropriated under heterosexual dominance.

Raymond charges transgenderism of "*style* rather than a *politics* of resistance, in which an expressive individualism has taken the place of collective political challenges to power" (p.222, original italics). Again the echoes of Foucault's 'technologies of the self' can be heard. Bornstein is presenting the proliferation of postmodern gender identities as a form of expressive individualism based on liberal humanist assumptions of self-determination. But such gendered roles are not masks that can be put on and off at will. Butler made this point quite explicit in her *Bodies that Matter* (1993). There is a danger that Bornstein's position is read in this way so that it falls into androgyny where each sex borrows a little from the other. That, however, is not where she is coming from. Rather, Bornstein's ruse is to do away with gender by *paradoxically* proliferating gender. This is a *mise en abyme* logic of the non-all. Her strategy is consonant with Judith Butler. Whereas for Bornstein everything is gender—sex simply refers to the social relations of "fucking" (1994:116)—for Butler sex is an "effect" of gender arrangements. Sex cannot be thought of as prior to gender if gender is what organ-izes sex in the first place. In both cases the body (as the anatomical or physiological sexual difference) "drops out." She accepts the premise that gender or sex is socially constructed, urging us to understand such construction as involving the materialization of determinate types of bodies through the repetition of gender norms, i.e., as materialized matter (body) made stable over time through discursive power. Tested against Lacan's "formulae of sexuation" (as articulated by Shepherdson earlier) such a position necessarily falls back to the *antinomy* of masculine/feminine positions.

Bernice Hausman (1995), working within a Foucauldian paradigm, brings an interesting perspective into these theoretical difficulties by convincingly pointing out that "gender" as a discursive term was the result of plastic surgery and edocrinological research by John Money in 1955. Gender, as a concept, prior to that time did not exist, rather sex roles and sex orientation were the assigned words for sexual difference. A gender terminology emerged to deal with the emerging research on intersexuality. In her reading of transsexuality using Barthe's semiotic model of mythology, the first-order of signification—the body as a signifier for sex—was eventually replaced by the mythological second order of signification—gender—which then became naturalized. "Gender achieved a simulated physicality when it was taken to be a signifier *for* the body and its sex" (p.188). Hausman provides a historical explanation for Butler's ahistorical deconstruction of the sex/gender binary. However, this is not all. Hausman tries to call back the "body"—its material rather than its materiality—by raising the possibility of attacking the category "sex" by privileging the semiotic critique of the discourses of medicine and science (following Laqueur's (1990) historical analysis of the change from a one sex to a two sex model of the body). Hausman wants to perform a *mise en abyme* effect on "sex" by proliferating the scientific narratives that offer alternative scenarios. However, she does not do so in this book, but simply gestures and hints towards the work of the molecular biologist Anne Fausto-Sterling's (1985; 1993) concept of the five sexes. So, what is this "real material body" she hopes to examine if not the body caught once again by Lacan's Real? As she admits, "The body participates in a physiological semiotics that operates outside of the languages in which it is described" (p.189), and once again in the closing paragraphs of her book, "Theorizing the body means taking it seriously as a material structure that exceeds the power of language to inscribe its functions" (p.200). The medical discourses that "sex" the body are in competition with one another much like ecological discourses of different political orientations. Sex like Nature is "beyond" language.

Lacan with Baudrillard: Simulations of Sex or Simulating Sex—What's the Difference?

Hausman's thesis opens up yet another possibility of seeing the intersection between Lacan's Real and Baudrillard's "process of the simulacra" where the "real" has disappeared. The manufacture of female genitalia that fool the eye of even expert gynecologists, and technologies and endocrinology which can produce simulated genital and secondary organs that appear authentic raise the question of the nature/culture binary. Such bodily *trompe l'oeil* effects operate at a first-order level of signification based on a two sexed system which now appears "natural." However the transsexual body can be constructed by inverting the primary characteristics of the sexed body itself, e.g., through breast implants, surgically inserted female genitalia, and phalloplasty (less successful) along with hormonal treatments. This constitutes a first order deconstruction of the "real" by introducing the ideal of Lacan's Real, i.e., the possibility of becoming (simulating) the sex one is not as the "real Thing." At the second order of signification, a "core gender identity" based on the way a transsexual feels—his or her gendered behaviors—present a discordant picture to this already deconstructed "natural" base. The idea of gendered identity overrides the "natural" sexed body making this a "self-erasing system" that disrupts 'normal' sexual differences. A "core gendered identity" sets in motion the surgical change to the "natural" sexed body by the knife and hormonal treatments to meet this imagined gendered image. These two discordant orders of signification, which now appear to act homologously as the inside (identity) and the outside (body), are like the metaphor of the Möbius strip in Lacan's system: an Imaginary sexed body and a Symbolic gendered identity, both of which are outstripped by the Real. In the Real transsexuals continue to fantasize the "real Thing" (for at least six months anyway to qualify for surgery). Sex in this case, is a *simulacrum*. It 'does not exist.' Such a position is not removed from Butler's view of the body in *Bodies that Matter* where her pun "bodies matter" speaks to the amenability of human matter (the body) to intelligible form (discourse) which is the source of its dynamism. *If* transgenderism highlights the body/sex and gender divide, I would conclude that it is possible to "fuck with sex and gender" but not with the Real which plunges the transsexual back to the cultural fantasy of a stable identity that is marked by the antinomies of the masculine and feminine. If, however, the Lacanian Real characterizes matter as being immutable, and hence uncritical (as Butler suggests), then the Real itself has to be rethought in dynamic terms, but then this takes us to the limits of this particular train of thought (see Cheah, 1996).

The above discussion falls decisively on the side of sexual difference when the figure of the horsexe transsexual is considered. A book such as *The Essential Difference* (1994), edited by Schor and Weed, presents an array of responses written in the late '80s and early '90s from the journal *differences*, which stage various ruses of compromise to come to a settlement between essentialism (the split subject) and anti-essentialism (the discursive subject). In my mind, the most inventive and persuasive essay was by Diana Fuss (1994), a Lacanian who tries to reconcile the two notions of the subject by pointing to 'hybrid' forms of anti-essentialist feminism and essentialist deconstruction. The former is represented, not surprisingly, by Monique Wittig, who keeps the set 'woman' open by avoiding the idea of a 'class of women' who share the same biological experience. Wittig would be presenting one solution to the feminine side of Lacan's formulae of sexuation wherein the essence of woman is without totality. The problem, as noted previously, is whether Wittig presents a totalizing gesture of The Lesbian. The latter form (essentialist deconstruction) is maintained by Luce Irigaray, also a 'Lacanian' if only in the antagonist sense of the term, who "bases her feminism on the bodily metaphor of the 'two lips' in order to construct and *deconstruct* 'woman' at the same time; for Irigaray, the very possibility of radical deconstruction is based on the simultaneous displacement and *redeployment* of essentialism—a "thinking through the body" (Fuss:101).

The question remains open, i believe, whether Irigaray can stage this ruse successfully at the level of the other (primary identification of sexual difference) and the level of secondary identification (the Other). According to Shepherdson (1994:170) the two contradictory misreadings of Irigaray, and French psychoanalytic feminism in general, as either a 'biological essentialist' or 'reducing everything to language,' is a result of the collapse of the psychoanalytic subject with the subject of cultural studies, and hence the disregard that the Real plays in her work which, admittedly, remain a concern. Schor (1994) believes Irigaray can successfully maintain feminine specificity though her evocation of *fluid* as functioning in the Real. It may be said that Irigaray also offers a solution to the deadlock of Lacan's anti-dialectical sexual differential logic through her stress on open system science (i.e., non-One); not only as a science of fluids, but the recognition of Prigoggine's 'dissipative structures' and the like. The question whether 'feminine fluidity' is primordial to the *constitution* of feminine embodiment remains a moot point. Derrida is not far away to "appropriate" fluidity himself when addressing the question of the "beyond" (Lacan's Real), and in answer to Lacan's own formulation that "woman" is beyond the phallus. The "beyond" for Derrida is *au-delà* (in Bannet, 1993:62), a step into an unbounded medium of water (*eau*), which is an 'infinite metaphor' or a 'metaphor of the infinite' leading to an extraordinary number of directions. Water leads us to the sea (*mer*), and to mother (*mère*) and to the generative merging and submerging liquids and fluids (galactic, seminal, parturient waters).

> By assonance *au/eau* becomes the 0—the nothing from which everything comes and to which everything returns, the 0 of the Wholly Other, that is nothing like what we know and the zero of self-effacement. As a pictogram, the letter O is also the round hole in the ego (*moi*), in the word (*mot*) and in the thing (*chose*), the hole of death (*mort*), in the opening of the gift (*don*). And as a *pas*-sage to all these Os, the step (*pas*) also requires a certain pas-sitvity" (Bannet, 1993:62).

Derrida, like Irigaray is espousing a feminine logic in answer to Lacan's 'logic of sex.' Is this then another coveting gesture on Derrida's part, as Scholes (1994) seems to think his work in *Spurs* was? One thing seems 'certain': the feminists of difference identify difference "not as difference from a pre-given norm but as *pure difference, difference itself, difference with no identity*. This kind of difference implies the autonomy of the terms between which the difference may be drawn and thus their radical incommensurability. "Difference viewed as distinction implies the pre-evaluation of one of the terms from which the difference is drawn; *pure difference* refuses to privilege either term" (Grosz, 1994a:91, my emphasis). What Grosz posits as "pure difference" is none other than the 'failure of the signifier' as Lacan had defined it. Masculine logic, defined by an exception which closes the system (the archaic Father), and feminine logic, defined by the exception that keeps the system open ('La Femme' - the phallic Woman) co-exist as "pure difference" presided over by castration so as to constitute the 'body.' The desire to attain the exception remains impossible in both cases. Like the hare chasing the tortoise, one of Zeno's paradoxes, the object of desire is never attained. The hare is either to fast or too slow. If the hare is caught, sexual difference is foreclosed, i.e., one becomes psychotic and 'outside the Law' for now the *objet petit a* has been materialized and 'devoured.' The question can be restaged by asking whether the phallus can be "queered" (Bergoffen, 1996) through a reconciliation between the Imaginary and Symbolic registers. Conventional Lacanian dogma gives the Symbolic order priority, aligning it with the Name of the Father and saving the child from the tyranny of the mother. For Irigaray this effectively silences the mother and takes voice away from women since the Imaginary is coded as feminine. Irigaray insists on the importance of recognizing sexual difference whereas Lacan, borrowing from Hegel's idealism tried to do away with difference by claiming that both sexes are equally affected by the phallic signifier, thereby presenting a universal subject. However, if such a masculine logic can be coordinated with the open system logic of the non-all (which his 'formulae of sexuation' seem to insist) where the *mise en abyme* effect opens the door to a universally accessible subject through the Imaginary register, then a reconciliation of sorts can be achieved.

Fuss (1994) believed that within Lacanian theory itself there was another possible reconciliation between essentialism and anti-essentialism by pointing to the importance that "place" plays in both theories of the subject. Lacan's revision of Descartes's *cogito*: "I think therefore I am," to an *anti-cogito* positionality: "I think where I am not, therefore I am where I do not think," is where Fuss locates a sense of "place" (who is speaking can only be answered by shifting the ground to 'where' I am speaking from). This sense of place comfortably overlaps with an anti-essentialist notion of a subject-position, i.e., from where one is not standing when engaged in a discourse. Whether such a ruse can be maintained is doubtful simply because "place" functions differently in the Lacanian paradigm. It is more ambivalent, transitional and "flickering." When de Lauretis refers to a "subject that is not divided in, but rather at odds with, language" (in Fuss: 109), or Mary Gentile argues for woman's 'tentative' subjectivity which is a result of an ambivalent positioning as a castrated object in the Symbolic order, this sounds more like answering to the feminine logic of an open system rather than a denial of the subject divided by language. Fuss's own solution to the impossible reconciliation is rather clever: she defers the possibility of essentialism by calling for a politics of coalition: an *affinity* rather than *identity* between women. In this way a 'class of women' would emerge from the passage from a coalition to a class chosen on the grounds of political choice rather than nature. Such a position is consonant with Kate Bornstein's attempt at a coalition of transgendered "queers."

Whether this discussion thus far has come to a reconciliation between the subject of discourse and the constituted subject of psychoanalysis remains questionable. It seems that the split subject remains crucial if fantasy and desire are to remain enabling concepts, and if sexual difference remains as a question of desire, and attempts are made to develop a specificity of women's desire that escapes the phallic signifier. MacCannell's (1994) attempt at showing glimpses of such a possibility through her examination of the hysteric's discourse as presented by Offred in Margaret Atwood's *Handmaiden's Tail* demonstrates, more than proves, how difficult it is to theorize a feminine superego if the bedrock of castration that defines sexual difference is accepted. Irigaray, for instance, *does not* provide what female sexuality is, that would deny impossibility and the Real. Rather her essential deconstruction, by working with feminine logic, exposes the paradoxes and consequences when only a masculine logic is left to preside over castration.

Doing away with the repression hypothesis entirely opens up channels to a narcissistic-self (Foucault's 'care of the self'), which has had liberating effects for queer subjectivity. Foucault tried to do away with the split subject of psychoanalysis. Like Butler (1990) who has followed his lead, sexual difference (i.e., sex), as represented by various morphologies of the body, is a product or effect of a socio-discursive regime of sexuality (Foucault, 1980a, p.155). Power is historicized and internalized within society. There is no Real for Foucault, no external constitutive imperative of castration. For the lesbian theorist Grosz (1994,a,b,c, 1995), such a model is more liberating than a psychoanalytic model that seems stuck with the dominion of the phallus, the structure of an external power as theorized by the phantasm of the father of total enjoyment, the denial of the mother's body and the impossibility of women being self-defining and autonomous subjects. Grosz accepts Foucault's call for 'different economy of bodies and pleasures,' and a reorganization of libidinal structures that would escape 'heterocentric regimes of sexuality.' As already argued, queer pleasures can be subversive performative attempts which open up possibilities of becoming. For Grosz (like Butler) "sexuality in and *for all of us* [a universal claim] is fundamentally provisional, tenuous, mobile, even volatile, igniting in unpredictable contexts with often unsettling effects: its power, attraction and danger the fundamental fluidity and transformability or liquidity of sexuality and its enactment in sexed bodies" (1994b:152, my emphasis). For Grosz, this statement holds the promise of subversion given that "[h]omophobia is an attempt to separate being from doing, existence from action" (p.151). In other words, if the gay or lesbian body's *actions* are disavowed by the heterosexual majority, specifically their sexual activities, then the 'Big Other' as the heterosexual society can treat and recuperate 'queers' as being the same as long as a public/private border (the closet) can be maintained. From this follows that: "In separating what a body is from what a body can do, an essence of sorts is produced, a consolidated nucleus of habits and expectations takes over from experiments and innovations; bodies are sedimented into fixed and repetitive relations, and it is only beyond modes of repetition that any subversion is considered possible ... (p.152, my emphasis). For Grosz (esp. 1994c, 1995) the sexually differentiated body cannot be chained down. Somewhere, at sometime, it can escape its yoke of Oedipalization which indicates a primordial bisexuality. Her logic is feminine and anti-dialectical, but do those who escape (the closet--the public/private split), escape castration? or must they continually challenge the phallus, offer yet another performative embodiment of repetition to maintain their resistance?

Do gay and lesbian subject positions, then, escape Lacan's 'formulae of sexuation?' As Catherine Millet has shown, the transsexual does not as yet have a morphological embodiment that partakes in society. They suffer the ambivalency of simulated sex. However, gay and lesbian 'bodies' already do. What their body is, in distinction of what it can do, is 'already ready'—relatively secured. They are embodied 'negatively' (if i may be permitted to use this word). Their subject positions do not lie 'outside' of society, although they are rendered to a state of being heterosexual's Other. Both Grosz and Butler seem to be addressing the malleability of *gender roles* rather than the embodiment's of sex *per se*, although they would want it 'otherwise.' Butler (1990) even adds gender to Foucault's sex/sexuality dualism (the first term standing for sexual difference, while the latter term refers to sexual impulses, i.e., wishes, desires, pleasure, behaviors, practices, hopes). This, as Grosz points out (1994b, p.139), seems to be an overlay on a pre-established foundation of sex, and therefore at odds with Butler's own 'totalizing' constructivist theory. Further, both Grosz and Butler point to hesitations in Foucault's own theory which address sexual activities which escape the internalizations of power. The road to embodiment implied by pedestrian, innocent, disinvested sexual pleasures between infants, let's say, already suggest a denaturing of the drive. And lastly, do not gay and lesbian relationships reenact the impossibility of the signifier, i.e., the impossibility of union. Do not butch/femme, the masculine gay contra to the feminine gay, once more replay the failure of the Symbolic order of language? Are there no questions to be raised about the inequality that arises in these relationships as well?

There is no quarrel between psychoanalysis and the notion of gender performability and its potentially disruptive power which may be at odds with the heterosexual norm. Rather its discourse *insists* on the need for a sexual embodiment which cannot escape the problematics of desire, i.e., a subject who lacks. This is not to fall back into an essentialism, nor a biologism, or reinstall an opposition between 'nature and culture.' Its theoretical challenge lies in the *impossibility* of sexual reconciliation, of eliminating "pure difference" which is paradoxical and antinomous. In this sense psychoanalysis is not ahistorical, nor universal, for there is a recognition that the various societal manifestations—solutions to sexual difference must be judged on 'real' material grounds which, in a phallogocentric order, have proven historically to disadvantage women, gays and lesbians, and transgenders not to mention racist and imperialist domination that present more complex overlays.

The question often comes to the accusatory proposition which claims that psychoanalysis is ahistorical and still caught by a "family romance" that has had its day. Conservative psychoanalytic theory is often accused for its cover up of child abuse, which seems justified given that Freud's emphasis had been to rehabilitate the maladjusted into the bourgeois order. There is a sustained critique by Somer Brodribb (1992) who has no use for any male theorist participating in feminism whatsoever. She is especially harsh with Lacan. Derrida fares no better. Coward's (1983), review of the use of psychoanalysis to inform Marxism concludes that "[n]either [Lacan nor Freud] paid attention to the emergent criticism of unilinear theories of the family. This blindness reveals the place occupied by a universal history of the family in both theories" (p.257, my italic). The danger is always turning psychoanalysis into a form of fundamentalism. This problem occurs with Rose (1983) who claims that the force of psychoanalysis is "that it gives an account of patriarchal culture as a transhistorical and cross-cultural force. It therefore conforms to the feminist demand for a theory which can explain women's subordination across specific cultures and different historical moments" (p.9). According to Landry and MacLean (1993:173-174) Rose continues this claim in her *Sexuality in a Field of Vision* (1986) raising a response by Spivak (1989a; see ft. n. 22, Pretext of the Title).

Perhaps, then, it's time to move on? Yet feminists like Rachel Bowlby (1989) think otherwise. For her, the gendered implications of "repudiation" still have force. Also Elizabeth Abel (1990) tries to hybridize Lacanian psychoanalytic discourse with object relations theory (cf. Chodorow) within issues of class and race which are undeveloped concepts in both discourses. By reading Hortense J. Spiller's "Mama's Baby, Papa's Maybe: An American Grammar Book," "a psychoanalytically informed mediation on the devastations wrought by slavery on African-American kinship and gender structures, and Carolyn Kay Steedman's *Landscape for a Good Woman: A Story of Two Lives*," Abel persuasively shows the strengths of psychoanalysis in the way both authors answer to "gender trouble" informed by issues of race and class. "Spillers and Steedman share ... a preference for delineating situations and figures at the boundary and reticence about representing the subjectivity of persons entirely dominated by oppression" (p.199). Abel concludes with, "It is too early for feminists to foreclose on psychoanalysis" (ibid.). The question remains whether psychoanalysis used judiciously within social critique can still be a useful strategy? i shall examine this issue in the next vignette by questioning my understanding of the "gaze" which is such an important appropriation of Lacan into the visual arts. In the remainder of this reflexion, i wish to took at the issue of antiessentialism and poststructuralism with regards to art.

Art in the Wake of Poststructuralism

The power of a psychoanalytic deconstructive reading was strongly brought home to me by Shoshana Felman's (1977) reading of Henry James's *The Turn of the Screw*. Foremost, in my mind at least, was her radical assertion of "misreading." All texts were said to elicit a question which anyone reading "answers." There are many interpretations possible given that all texts are ambiguous and hence cannot be read "literally." Arriving at this point and going no further leaves the process of interpretation at the level of the multiple or decentered subject. Felman, however, does not want to lose sight of the unconscious and fall into this pluralism.[7] She demonstrates how each reading is "true" in that it "answers" the ambiguity that the text asks, but it is false in that it excludes other possible interpretations—the remainder or residue. In this sense the truth of a particular reading is no truer than the positions it excludes. Every false reading is "true" in that as an oppositional reading it asserts the contradictions that are found in the text *in the very act of denying that they exist*. In this sense such readings are true to the extent that they are false. Through such paradoxical logic Felman can conclude that any "authentic reading" is then both true and false. What Felman does then, following Lacan, is to give "something" over to the text side of things. The way any text "speaks" to the unconscious of the reader in creating the fantasy it answers. The same way Velázquez' *Las Meninas* catches the viewer within the endless mirrors of the unconscious. She recognizes the working of unconscious desire as the rule of the signifier, whose circulation throughout a text never arrives at its destination as to that which it signifies as each reading participates in answering the reader's own desires.

Felman's critical deconstructive method presents an anomaly. The split subject is most often supplanted by the multiple subject. The potential radicalness of its stance has been lost to a pluralism of a pastiche postmodernism that recovers styles and continues to recycle the grand tradition of art in new disguises. Even the Getty Center for Education in the Arts, a conservative institution, is said to be engaged in *post*-modern art history by way of its revival of the old master dialogue–a historical repetition like Postimpressionism which came after bourgeois Impressionism. Under Getty's auspices, multiculturalism has become a new way to restore art's lost "aura" in an age of "electronic reproduction." Art education, with its preoccupation with back to the basics, trying to regroup and recenter American education on the nostalgia of Getty's Discipline Based Art Education (DBAE), draws on the tenets of modernism.[8] Art is broken down into history, studio, aesthetic, and art criticism. It is best described as the artistic marketing logic of late capitalism. As Christa Bürger (1986:105-106) points out, the new museum culture is now the "total work of art," a total environment from which to continue the "cultivation of the aesthetic-hedonistic attitude necessary for the functioning of consumer society." A classical example of this attitude is the new Canadian National Art Gallery in Ottawa. The "disappearance of art and the aestheticization of reality," as "two sides of an inexorable historical process," takes on new meaning. The gallery's huge windows which open up to the environment, reverse the spectacle. "It transforms the outer world into an aesthetic world, won back into the perspective of the Museum" (p. 105). Many art journals pander to a pluralistic nihilism of an anything goes attitude as long as it's art has or will be "eventually" promoted into the Book of Art.

This is certainly one of Danto's (1986) conclusions. For him "the end of art" has been reached because art has arrived at a point in history where, according to Hegelian aesthetics, it has become "clear" to itself. "[K]nowledge is its own object, hence subject and object are one" (p. 113). For Danto, this is the state of art today. The art of the recent past needs more and more theory for its existence as art. The very theory insures the object it seeks to understand, "so that in understanding its object it has to understand itself" (p.111). In the art of late capitalism, the objects approach zero as their theory approaches infinity, so that virtually all there is at the end *is* theory. Art has become an idea no longer based on the history of art but on what can be justified. Amazingly Danto gives the example of the feminist *Bildungsroman* as a paradigm example of such a process. In his reasoning, the novel of self-education climaxes in the self's recognition of the self. The question the heroine raises for the reader and for herself, "is at once who is she and what it is to be a woman" (p.110). Danto goes on to claim that this model again follows Hegel's *Phenomenology of Spirit*. The "end of history" has been reached when *Geist* knows itself. Art, as one stage in this processes, ends when it is known what art is and what it means. Stripped of idealist overtones, the feminist *Bildungsroman* becomes a form of Absolute Knowledge! And this absolute knowledge, i would add, is now recoded as the hyperreal of Baudrillardian simulacra, total artifice; thus exemplifying the constructed consummerable subject.

Danto must have greatly benefited from the publication of an earlier book, *Ende der Kunst—Zukunft der Kunst* (1984) [*The End of Art—The Future of Art*] which featured a number of prominent artists, historians and philosophers (Gadamer, Sloterdijk, Fußman) who adumbrated the same thesis in the German-speaking world. The call for the "end of art" for Hegel was due to its secularization, its deflation of *Geist*, its inability to ponder over utopian solutions and provide moral questions. For Danto art had become "disenfranchised." But art wasn't "disenfranchised," nor was it at its "end"; rather the secularization between high art and popular culture brought a new conversation as to what its function and role should be. The "end" hypothesis referred to its modernist roots. In this sense the Hegelian project had been completed if the critical subject was posited. However, for those artists, critics, and historians who were more interested in theorizing the "split" subject and the vicissitudes of poststructuralism, art was far from "dead."

In the English-speaking world, this was paradigmatically made explicit through the leadership of the British journal *Screen*; its intellectual fervent lasting through the '70s and early '80s (see Barry & Flitterman-Lewis, 1988). In the mid '80s and early '90s it has continued to maintain its intellectual vigor; however it began to be criticized for its over-emphasis on theory, élitism and lack of empirically grounded studies. Reception aesthetics, especially in its ethnographic varieties, took a big bite out of its Lacanian emphasis. This was true of *Screen Education* as well.[9] While all this was developing in Britain, there was little spill-over into North American art education circles who were more willing to borrow the more conservative variety of Continental philosophy-phenomenological hermeneutics. In England the names of Mary Kelly and Victor Burgin have been well known as exponents of Lacanian and Derridean postures. In America, Barbara Kruger and Sherrie Levine, Hans Haacke, Cindy Sherman and Susan Holzer have explored similar tenets. These are perhaps the best representative examples of the intersections of sexuality, meaning, and language of this generation. But now a new generation of women artists working within textural problems of representation have emerged (see Cottingham, 1989 for a partial list); virtually all of whom explore media that has characteristically not been co-opted by males: video, photography, performance, installation. "Women's performance art has particular disruptive potential because it poses an actual woman as a speaking subject, throwing that position into process, into doubt, opposing the traditional conception of the single, unified (male) subject" (Forte, 1988:220). Lisa Steel's *Birthday Suit: Scars and Defects* (1974) is a video production where a woman stands naked in front of a still camera and proceeds to identify defects on her body and how such "flaws" were acquired through illness and accidents which map out the artist's personal history. Woman as spectacle has been inverted to woman as subject. Carole Schneemann's *Interior Scroll* (1975) was performed nude in front of a mostly-female audience. Standing with ritualistic paint on her face and body she pulled out a "rope like text" from her vagina. The text dealt with her rejection as a film maker in an all-male world.

The list of such examples can be potentially endless. The issues of lesbian sex, nudity, birth control, rape, sexual harassment, "slashing" are the subjects of feminist video art in a recent survey of Canadian feminist video tapes called *Rebel Girls* that was held at the National Gallery in Ottawa, Feb. 14- May 21, 1989 (Conley, 1989). Performance is perhaps one of the most developed areas where the narrative structure is examined from psychoanalytic and textual examinations. Judith Barry's (1980) review of women's performance art in Northern California in the '80s, and Jeania Forte (1988) and Judith Butler's (1988) update of feminist performance almost a decade later shows that, as a genre, it continues to be a powerful medium for making statements about personal life. Yet recently it seems more and more feminist writers see the limitations of this perspective (Alcoff, 1988a:415 ff.; Felski, 1989:156 ff.) on the grounds that the public it reaches is limited. A much more serious accusation concerning such work is that it eventually is subject to mainstream assimilation, losing all its critical thrust and political insights. Both are Catch-22 propositions. Early performance art was able to deconstruct the binary opposition between good/bad acting. Only those who had talent and dramatic training could hope to find a place in theater. Performance art put this to question. The Voice, trained or not, was important. It seemed to have a roughness and authenticity that did away with the veneer of a "stick free" Teflon style. Butler points out that there is a current trend towards slick productions; the ability to act, sing, and dance are becoming more in vogue. Above all, it becomes more and more difficult *not* to be co-opted into the mainstream (e.g. Laurie Anderson) or to find a public who can still be shocked. The price of "professionalization" has been, paradoxically, the loss of Voice and complete autonomy for the control of representation. The question of class interests and color never emerged in questions concerning this genre. Was it restricted to middle-class white feminists? Nevertheless, for me, since 1985 poststructuralism and performance became important sources to think through sex/gender issues; i think, because i secretly wanted to believe, especially with Kristeva's work, that ~~the~~ woman, and ~~the~~ man did not exist. This Lacanian ruse was, *at that time*, emotionally satisfying for me.

Kelly is to the Phallic Child as Jo Spence is to Her own Shit

French poststructuralist theories shook the very grounds of representation. First, and foremost, the issue of clarity in language became a key issue: "We can never say what we mean and mean what we say!" (Hoy, 1986a). It might be noted parenthetically then, in Mary Kelly's (1983) well known and celebrated piece of Lacanian analysis, *The Post-Partum Document*, which charts her relationship as a mother to her son Kelly in his formative years, purposely avoided any *photographic* representation as part of her documentation. Rather "transitionary" objects were used instead—dirty diapers, insects and collected flowers, early scribbles and drawing, and Kelly's proto-writing. Gamman and Makinen (1994:189-195) have challenged the thesis that *PPD* represents the process of the maternal fetishisation of the child. The nappies, hand-casts, gifts, drawings and writing, they suggest, are not the psychological fetishisation of disavowing the separation and loss of the child-as-phallus. Women have access to psychological fetishisation in the same libidinal way as men. Making a distinction between anthropological, commodity and sexual fetishism, they argue that Kelly's transitional objects belong to the first category: as anthropological or "religious" fetishisms whereby relics, statues, occult objects derive power from a deity. Kelly therefore, can be said to be "deifying" her son through these objects, which should be interpreted as equivalent practice within the context of post-industrial Western culture as that of non-industrial societies. Further, they argue, there is no sexual arousal documented in relation to these objects. The concept of motherhood has subsumed sexuality within the absorption of the child-as-phallus theory. To make their point sting a little, they hypothesize what an art work would look like if a male artist documented "1. the progress of his child," and "2. the movements of his dick over the same period" (p.193). In this formulation, they suggest that the penis/phallus is conflated since it refers to the evaluation of the child (progress), as well as documenting the child's libidinal desire (movement of his dick). In contrast, the child-as-phallus refers only to progress. If the same male artist were to document "3. objects that signified the presence of the child," and "objects that aroused his dick to erection" (p.194) then that would be an example of sexual rather than anthropological fetishism. The model of female castration that Kelly adopts, therefore, denies woman as a sexual subject.

Gamman and Makinen's is not the only deconstruction possible of this work. There are others. When the book on the *PPD* was published, in 1983, a picture appeared (inadvertently?) with Mary Kelly and her son on the inside cover photographed by the father, Ray Barrie during a recording session in 1975 (fig. 1). The picture of her son nestled between her legs seemed to confirm the very claim Lacan had made, and which Mary Kelly had documented: having a child becomes a fetish fulfilling the woman's lack in being able represent the phallus. It reinscribed Kelly back into the very discourse she tried to deconstruct.[10]

The *PPD* stands monumentally in poststructuralism in the 1970s as the *Dinner Party* stood in "cultural" feminist discourse during the same decade.

(By so stating, i wonder if i am not simply repeating the Grand Narrative in feminist art works. And, if so, there are a myriad of books which mention these two lengthy projects—in terms of time and energy—who do likewise.) In contrast, and alluding to this very photo of Kelly and her son, Jo Spence (1988), a well-known political photographer, included a photograph of herself sitting on a bed pan on the inside cover of her book (fig. 2). "My God ... I've got an Imaginary lack!" is written in the balloon drawn from her mouth. On the bottom of the photograph, in italic type it says: "From a photo therapy session on the end of my anal phase." Since castration is said to appear in the Imaginary, in fantasy, again the question of "*seeing*" is at issue here: of the child's relation to *having* or *being* the phallus. Jo Spence *literally* and *figuratively* shits on this idea! "Freud had theorized the gaze as a phallic activity linked to the anal desire for sadistic mastery of the object. Freud's argument links the act of seeing to anal activity, which he sees as expressing a desire for mastery or for the exercise of power over one's (libidinal) objects, a desire that underlies later (phallic or Oedipal) fantasies about phallic (masculine) power. Thus the gaze enacts the voyeur's desire for sadistic power, in which the object of the gaze is cast as passive, masochistic, feminine victim" (see Moi, 1985, pg. 134, note 8).

This is crucial to the theorizing of Irigaray where she equates Freud's "specular" philosophy with mastery and dominance in "looking." Oedipus demonstrates the fear of blindness as the fear of castration. If the desire for scopophilia is not satisfied (and the little girl has nothing to be seen), then there is a threat to male sexuality. Jo Spence's photograph also alludes to the work of Irigaray's The Speculum of the Other Woman (1985a) which, as has been discussed, is a critique of the Imaginary of Western philosophical and psychoanalytic discourse "aiming to show that the conceptualization of sexual difference in this discourse is governed by an imaginary that is anal, that is to say which interprets sexual difference as though there were only one sex, and that sex were male (women are defective men)" (see Whitford, 1988:121). In other words, Jo Spence deals with her own "shit." Her photographic sessions are about therapy and healing, "crapping" patriarchy out of her system. Her photographic text is her autobiography of reflexive resistances. Rather than avoiding the visual discourse, she uses it, manipulates it and shits it out. Jo Spence died in 1992 after a long bout with cancer leaving behind her a method to perform an "art of transgression" (1995). She was a photographer/educator who in her words was "available for divorces, funerals, illness, social injustice, scenes of domestic violence, explorations of sexuality and any joyful events." In other words, Spence dealt with the postmodern sublime seeing the "otherside" of beauty. She exemplified what the business

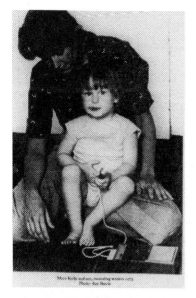

fig. 4 Mary Kelly and Son   fig. 5 Jo Spence's Anal Phase

of art education should be about in this postmodern age. With these remarks on the feminist appropriation and deconstruction of Lacanian psychoanalytic discourse to art and literature, i turn to the usefulness and the difficulty of psychoanalysis when applied to the masculine gaze in the next vignette.

1 This was already demonstrated by de Lauretis (1990). See *The Essential Difference*. Naomi Schor and Elizabeth Weed, eds,(1994).

2 The idea for this comes from a discussion by Ang and Hermes (1991). It has been modified by remembering the necessity of the gender/sex couplet.

3 i think it is necessary to point out how often "dissimulation" is used to convey the notion of dispersion and dissemblage, almost like a reference to the background radiation from the Big Bang. Its force is felt working outside the visible and knowable. The problem is, of course, this can easily be read as the slippage of new forms of spirituality. See Stockton, 1992 for this interesting accusation.

4 Cowie provides a ground breaking article on fantasy in her "Fantasia" article which appeared in *m/f* 9, 1984 (repr. 1990).

5 Theorists of the sublime include familiar names like Jameson, Lyotard, and Hebdige. A departure could be made here to map out the debates surrounding the feminine as opposed to the masculine sublime, but i have done this in another place (see jagodzinski, 1993). Arguing for the possibility of a feminine sublime, as against the Kant's masculine sublime (admirably defended by Crowther, 1993) see Weiskel (1976) and Yaeger's (1989). See the comments in the "pretexts to the title" on Lacan's sexuation hypothesis as developed by Copjec (especially 1994a,c).

6 To list the more prominent supporters, each of whom has their own particular take: Wolfgang Iser, Stanley Fish, Roman Ingarden, Rosenblatt, Holland, etc. Janet Staiger offers a succinct review of reception studies in part one (pp.1-98) of her book *Interpreting Films* (1992). See also Culler (1982) for an earlier review.

7 Recall the example previously developed where Griselda Pollock's radical critique of Impressionism was recuperated as just another interpretation of the historical record, and thus the force of her arguments were mitigated. In another context consider Ellsworth's (1986) descriptive reception of the way lesbian feminists read the film *Personal Best* differently from mainstream feminists: some imagined what would happen to the characters in a lesbian future, rejecting large sections of the film that led to a heterosexual orientation as to the film's meaning; others elevated the lesbian, Tory, to a central narrative focus and identified with her as the main character, and still others interpreted the fierce competition, bawdiness and loyalty between women as erotic moments of lesbian love. *Personal Best* is being read within the context of lesbian fantasies, the structure of which Ellsworth has not explored, rather her claim was to demonstrate that multiple resistant reading of the film are possible. Felman would want to describe the *mise-en-scène* of that fantasy.

8 A sustained and radical critique of The Getty Center for Education in the Arts and the Discipline Based Art Education it disseminates through curricula material, conferences, and teacher training can be found amongst the pages of the *Journal of Social Theory in Art Education* founded in 1979 with the expressed intent to offer critical social commentary on visual art curricula which are presented in formalist, context free terms (see jagodzinski, 1993 and 1995).

9 Manuel Alvarado, Edward Buscombe and Richard Collins in their "Introduction" (1993) provide a history of *Screen Education* in relation to its parent journal *Screen,* and the cultural studies program brought out by the Centre for Contemporary Cultural Studies at Birmingham University where Stuart Hall, James Donald, Angela McRobbie and Richard Johnson were its main proponents.

10 (I)(i) have purposely put my son on each of the two covers that form this book; in the dedication and in the picture that appears at the end of the performance in the appendix. Is this then my aporia? It may be read this way—of course—as a father passing on the "tradition" to his son, a patriarchal gesture, but that "tradition" includes my desire that he question his own masculinity.

164

THE MASCULINE DESIRE OF THE IMAGINARY

Are Males Simply Desiring Machines?

But the artist's point of view is
necessarily manipulating... :all art is
derived from the hand, after the
eye.

(Mary Ann Caws, 1985:267)

Are men simply desiring machines? The next three sections explore
the question of the gaze, as opposed to the look, which has been such a vital
part of poststructuralist issues of representation and Lacanian applications to
the visual arts, especially the cinema. This first section explores the male gaze
in particular which has been a major point of contention in feminist cinematic
theory. Lacan's Imaginary (capitalized here, imaginary with no caps usually
refers to its common usage as a conscious mental image) is for me, of central

importance when linking Lacan with the arts. The Imaginary is the order of perception and hallucination, "fantasy-full but never fanciful" (Wing, 1986:164). It mediates between Lacan's Real and the symbolic order, acting as the screen upon which we define ourselves and are defined by the Other. The story told by Pliny about the nature of Western painting is developed by Lacan in his lecture, "What is a Picture" (1979:111-112), or the XI seminar, to demonstrate the generation of desire in the gaze. Both Norman Bryson (1983:1-12), Elizabeth Wright (1984:119) and Ernst Gombrich (1977:173) utilize the same story to show how Western art has pursued the illusion of Truth which has tried to capture the essential copy of Nature. In this sense the question of representation might well be considered the issue of postmodernism and poststructuralism. Silverman (1992), in particular, has made a brilliant application of Lacan's formulations in this seminar to forms of masculinity that are at odds with the dominant Enlightenment masculine model of looking, i.e., ocularism. This section ends trying to comprehend and elaborate her very impressive thesis, and then taking the horror genre as yet another instance where the relationship between the look and the gaze can be understood.

It seems that one day Zeuxis and Parrhasius were having a painting contest as to who could best paint nature in all its verisimilitude. Zeuxis went away and painted grapes which were so lifelike that birds came and began to peck at them. Overjoyed, he thought that he had won the "mimetic" prize. Parrhasius, on the other hand, had painted a picture of a curtain. When Zeuxis came over to see what Parrhasius had done, he wanted to see what Parrhasius had painted behind the curtain. When he tried to pull it away, he realized that he been fooled. But, it was not the quality of the curtain (The Latin *linteum* is translated as 'veil') which fooled Zeuxis. Neither the birds nor man need an exact representation to be "drawn in." Such gestalts could vary widely in quality and yet serve their purpose. Birds merely require a crude stimulus to be attracted, and Zeuxis was not deceived so much by the representation of the veil (curtain) itself, as by his gaze which had lured him "into searching for the fantasy by the fascination of presence beyond absence" (Wright, 1984:119). *His gaze had been seduced.*

It was Zeuxis, and not Parrhasius, who was curious to see what his competition had painted. In the search to find out what was behind the veil of representation, Zeuxis became an object of a joke. In that very moment of his "surprise" of being fooled, he was startled by the gaze of the symbolic order (the big Other, i.e., western view of representation) that made the contest meaningful in the first place. What he failed to recognize was that behind the veil was yet another veil, in this case only the canvas. The *trompe l'oeil* effects of the *mise-en-abyme* were at play here. Zeuxis thought he had won because he believed that there was a "reality" that could be perfectly captured through the illusionary effects of *trompe l'oeil* (deceiving the eye). In this regard Parrhasius did *not* deceive Zeuxis; what he did do was to shatter his very illusion. This was achieved only when Zeuxis had *traversed* his fantasy: the time of thinking that he had won the contest to the time when he realized that he was the butt of a joke. He came to realize how Parrhasius, through his "deception," had kept to the rules of the contest yet at the same time presented an exception that the very contest seemed to exclude.

It was this very "deception" Zeuxis himself had invented which was his downfall. It is as though Parrhasius was like a detective or a psychoanalyst, someone "who knew too much." He knew how to take Zeuxis's desire into account, and he knew how meaning had been constructed by the competition. His painted curtain was like an absent supplementary signifier that both constituted the game and lay outside the game itself. What drove Zeuxis to remove the veil was what Lacan called *object petit a*, the object that caused his desire and at the same time, paradoxically and retrospectively, did not exist! Zeuxis experienced that his desire was part of the mimetic game from the very beginning. His was a failed gaze, a misrecognition, which became reduced to a look. From such a tale many feminists have written about imagination's desire for that ideal closure—the hidden picture which fulfills fantasy, the "final" signifer so to speak to fulfil the perpetual "lack" which lays beyond our grasp, but paradoxically doesn't exist. In this regard "the enigma of woman" conceals that there is nothing to conceal. There is "nothing" behind the mask, behind the veil but yet another displaced signifier, yet another veil *ad infinitum—ms. en abyme* (Elam, 1994).

Le Viol/Le Voile : In Search of Magritte's Desire

The effects of the gaze are developed by Wright (1984:118) through her examination of René Magritte's picture *Le Viol* (The Rape) fig. 6. Here, she says, the subject of the picture is apparently a face styled by hair in "what was then a consciously fashionable manner." On closer inspection, however, the viewer sees that this is an illusion: the eyes become nipples; the nose is a navel, and the mouth becomes the woman's pubic hair. If the hair is removed, the naked torso is made plainly visible, suggesting yet another level of reading of *Le Viol* which Wright overlooks. The viewer, by removing the hair through an intentional act of the imagination, rehearses the removal of hair from painting of classical nudes, exposing once again the scopophobic unconscious Imagination. Hair, after all, is a sign of virility. Its removal adds to the passive quality and objectification of flesh. At the same time it eroticizes looking and feeling. The *trompe d'oeil* effect, however, is to mitigate such a possibility. The viewer is caught.

> The picture is a metaphor for any gaze, signifying desire and an invasion of the other's desire ('The Rape'). The face, framed for culture by the hair, becomes fully sexual, a metaphor for desire being operative in everything. The face not being hidden is indicative of the public (not the pubic) personality, here unmasked, unveiled as the private(s). The (symbolic) eye (the painter's) has disturbed the (narcissistic) gaze of the viewer by turning the illusionary eye in the picture into a nipple via a visual pun which removes the blind-

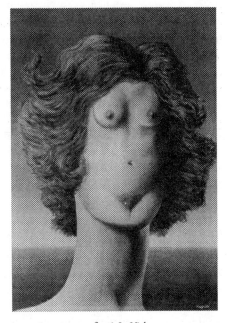

fig. 6 *Le Viol*

> fold and makes the viewer see the ubiquity of the libidinous. He is caught out of his own looking; his eyes see themselves seeing themselves (p. 118).

Wright's succinct exposition presents a further question. Her reading of the (potential) disruptive powers of *Le Viol* are not found exclusively in the text, but in the subject position she takes when reading it; in Wright's case, that of a woman who recognizes the objectification of women as objects by men. Yet, a heterosexual male may go no further than the scopophobic view that the work suggests: lured/leered into the picture he takes sadistic pleasure in the very fragmentation of the woman's body, labeling the work "clever," and amusing. Or has such a possibility already been drained away from him by his initial misrecognition? It seems so. What Magritte demonstrates in *Le Viol* is the inability of the male's *look* to capture the female object with his *gaze*. Rather than being the controlling voyeur he, like Zeuxis, has been humiliated—caught "looking," overwhelmed by the sexuality of the female he wanted to master with his gaze in the first place. As Lacan claimed in his XI seminar, the "gaze" and the "look" were not the same thing, although

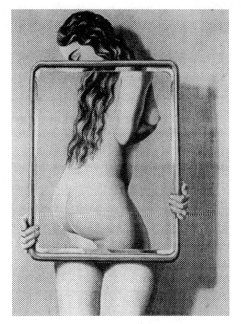

fig. 7 *Les Liaisons dangereuses*

the look aspired ceaselessly to become the gaze. Like the phallus, the gaze belonged to the Real, while the look, like the penis, belonged to the symbolic order. The title turns out to be a pun, demonstrating its very "impossibility."

169

Caws (1985), like Wright, sees the potential disruptive possibilities of Magritte. She draws upon Krauss's analysis of surrealist photography for its transgressive potentials, as the "denial of presence."[1] "Within surrealist photography, doubling also functions as the signifier of signification. It is this semiological, rather than stylistic, condition that unites the vast array of the movement's photographic production. ... In this way the photographic medium is exploited to produce a paradox: the paradox of reality constituted as sign— or presence transformed into absence, into representation, into spacing, into writing" (Krauss and Livingstone,1985:31). Caws explains how this same "doubling" of vision is possible so that the singularity, the unifying experience of looking, is ruptured, destroyed. The viewer is caught looking at his /her own looking. "The denial of presence is exactly the problem with such [surrealist] photography, as we see ourselves seeing ourselves in it" (p.267). Magritte's painting *Les Liaisons dangereuses* (1936), fig. 7 serves as her example of the denial of presence. Paraphrasing Caws' description: Here a woman is shown down to her ankles with her head bent down in profile. She is holding a mirror exactly in the middle of her body. Portrayed in the mirror is a *side-view* of her nude. It is reversed in the center of the image, parts of her hair in the mirror do not match her hair outside it, nor does the lower part of her body match her thighs that are outside the mirror. "The deformation can be read as central to the self, for the woman divided is also watching herself— without seeing us see her from behind" (p.272). The narcissistic glance in the mirror is reversed. Caws adds: "*Woman reading woman*, ... she fails to locate her image in the mirror image, an image reversible as it is inescapable.... Deprived of *natural frontal beauty*, seen only askance and from the side, completely under the domination of the male painter, the model simply exhibits the shame of the self and the difficulty of self-reading" (p. 274, my italic).

Caws' interpretation of "Dangerous Meetings" as the loss of presence of the self is a disparaging one. It borders on the very "dangerous" belief in a humanistic subject which Magritte wanted to avoid, i.e., as if the model could "read" herself (as "natural frontal beauty") in a mirror provided that she had been painted "right." Another way to read *Les Liaisons dangereuses* is to take the pun of the title seriously: the self should not be confused with the mirror image of the self, as Zeuxis did–otherwise, "sour grapes" are in order. In other words, desire of the self should not be confused with the object that proposes itself to satisfy the desire, i.e., the mirrored image. A "dangerous meeting" happens when this is forgotten. That is why Magritte paints a side-view of the nude in the mirror. It is an anamorphic projection, a mirror within a mirror, or *mis en abyme*, which sets up the acknowledgment of the "split subject;" the subject who "is" only insofar it is *not where it thinks it is.*[2]

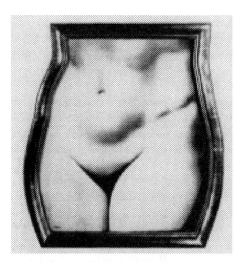

fig. 8 Représentation

A more obvious example Caws mentions is Magritte's *Représentation* (fig. 8) which is dramatic for the simplicity of its form and the complications of its reading. The painting is that of a mirror, rather a painting seen as a mirror, "or a mirrored form painted as a painted form" (p.279). The frame of the painted mirror follows the contours of a female body part cut from the lower stomach to her thighs. This is also its content. The heavy frame around the torso may be read metonymically as the way she is seen. "What is representing here, and what is represented? the reader is bound to ask. Is it the self-reflexivity of the form looking at itself as framed, by itself, as a mirror? Does the title indicate that to represent is to mirror, that to frame is to wed the outline to form, that to look at ourselves framed up is already to represent ourselves?" (p. 279). Again, this painting is an illustrative case of an undecidable; its meaning forever differs and is deferred, an example of a *mise en abyme* and "feminine logic" (see pretext to the title).

An entirely different reading of the same work *Le Viol* is given by Gubar (1987:721-724), whose antipornographic stance is well known. Magritte's "body parts" are indicative of the historical degradation of women which pornography has wrought. After presenting the contradictory readings of *Le Viol*, including the radical disruptive possibilities of Magritte's surrealist rhetoric developed above, she settles for a more conservative reading: Magritte's imagery is a vindictive mockery over the loss of his mother in a suicidal drowning while he was still an adolescent. In other words, it is sadistic. Such a reading plays into Griffin's (1982) "pornographic consciousness."The rejection of his mother leads to rejecting the feminine part of himself. Gubar returns to the "scene/seen" of the crime playing, by now, a familiar card.The ambiguity surrounding the interpretations of surrealist art and Magritte in particular (is it art? is it pornography?), comes down to *Le Viol* as a projection of Medusa; the ambiguity involved in the male's pleasure and horror of women's genitals as a direct result of a castration anxiety. Magritte's *Le Viol* is a decapitation of his lost phallic Mother, who, having drowned, remained omnipotent, and now needs a proper burial so that Magritte may reduce the threat to his own vulnerability! Given that *Le Viol* suggests a male face (according to Gubar) and given that there are many paintings of absent men pictured in empty suits, or with missing heads throughout Magritte's *oeuvre*, Gubar suggests that Magritte has also been castrated. *Le Viol* now becomes an inverted portrait!: "the man without the mother sees the mother as himself" (p.733). If that is not enough, *Le Viol* becomes a fearful portrait. "By re-creating in his own image the woman who created him, by repossessing through fantasy the woman who had to be relinquished, by punishing the woman whose separateness was itself experienced as a punishment, and by eroticizing the woman whose eroticism was taboo, the pornographer converts his greatest trauma into his greatest thrill, a fact that explains why the perusal of pulp magazines and the communal showings of stag films function like *rites de passage* for so many adolescent boys" (p.737).

We have gone from *Le Viol* being an art of rupture to a pornographic, sadistic art of domination. Startling! Historically situated, Gubar along with Gilbert, claim that the surrealist image reflects the masculine anxiety of the Great War and the breakdown of heroic individualism. Poor Magritte, once a hero, his images of corporeal absence are now balanced by his disgust of the female subject. Deconstructed, he has joined the ranks of "pornoartgraphy," that "third" term which avoids assimilation in the previous opposition: art/pornography–a realm between art and pornography where all artists are buried who searched for revenge on their Mothers! Things don't look any better for him with the publication of *Surrealism and Women* (1991), edited by Caws, along with Rudolf W. Kuenzli and Gwen Raaberg. In her introduction Gwen Raaberg informs her readers: "The Surrealists conceived of woman as man's mediator with nature and the unconscious, *femme-enfant*, muse, source and object of man's desire, embodiment of *amour fou*, and emblem of revolution" (p.2). More devastating for me is Rudolf Kuenzli's essay which features Surrealists around a painting by René Magritte published in *La Révolution surréaliste* (1929) (fig. 9). Sixteen figures, all with their eyes closed, surround a nude placed against a solid black background, who appears to have her head turned aside in a gesture of modesty, and a hand covering her breasts. Above her head is written the caption: *je ne vois pas la* (and below we read) *cachée dans la forêt* [I don't see it ... concealed in the forest]. How to answer this seemingly obvious image of masculine desire? "Why belabor the obvious point that Surrealism, in celebrating the masculine unconscious, brings forth representations of the least-censored misogyny?" writes Kuenzli (p.21). He has no use for Krauss's defense; his text is an angered polemic against her "collusion with the male gaze" (p.24).

fig. 9 Cover of *La Révolution surréaliste* (1929)

Defending Magritte

Will this be just another gesture of a "boy" coming into the fight, like Frank Lentricchia's dispute with Gubar and Gilbert's essentialist feminism within the prestigious pages of *Critical Inquiry*? (Lentricchia, 1987, 1988; Gilbert and Gubar, 1988) Where do these contradictory readings leave the viewer? Can Magritte be accused of a "pornographic conscious," never getting over his Mother? Gubar thinks so. Or, does his oeuvre provide the possibility of a disruptive reading? Wright and Caws share such a conviction. In the first case, it should be noted that Gubar believes that a certain *universal woman* can "fix" the meaning of Magritte's images as "pornoartgraphic" because, following Chodorow (and Dinnerstein) whom she mentions approvingly, all men are mothered, and so they must struggle to differentiate themselves in such a way as to remain dominant. Hence, this relationship can provide her with a generalizablity as applied to pornography. This, in-and-of itself, is problematic for it relies on Chodorow's emphasis on *regression* to a pre-Oedipal moment of being nursed, which is a reductive account of male fantasy. Here pre-Oedipal regression is, for Magritte, ultimately negative, enacting a revenge fantasy on women. Chodorow's unconscious identification are sociological categories, a more or less conscious role-modeling theory. A Lacanian description of fantasy allows for a multiple (and often contradictory) subject positions. There are multiple possibilities of identification that do not seem to just originate in the time and space of pre-Oedipalization. Secondly, Gubar (along with Gilbert) believes she can fix the reading in another way; i.e., through the historical claims of a changing consciousness at the *fin de siècle* when there was a redefinition of sexuality and autonomy as exemplified by the suffragette movement. Accordingly, the surrealists mark a fundamental male anxiety in their "disgust with the female subject" (p.739). Similarly, it is said, the recent rash of pornography is a reaction to the Women's Liberation Movement of the '70s. All this is quite surprising if one of Magritte's intentions was to put reality into flux through his non-representational view of language, reflecting another crisis—that of science, as Husserl's *Crisis of European Sciences* (1970) demonstrated while Ferdinand de Saussure developed a direction in opposition to Husserlian phenomenology. The very fact that Gubar must come up with a new category "pornoartography" speaks for itself.[3] How then do we deal with the body parts which women artists (cunts, cocks, pricks, vulvas)[4] themselves have sculpted and painted? In Gubar's terms would the inverse hold true? Is such feminist "pornoartgraphy" aimed to overcome *their* phallic fathers, a historical reaction against male authoritarianism? Is their revenge then, equally sadistic?

In defense of Magritte i might begin with Magritte's title, *Le Viol* which translates as violation or desecration. It is well known that Magritte's linguistic theories problematized the naming of things through his puns and play of the signifier. Reversing just two letter and adding an "e" we arrive at "*Le Voile*" or veil, and we are back to Parrhasius's "curtain." In this sense both Gubar and Caws are like Zeuxis, reading their own desires as to what's behind the veil when there is nothing there except another veil (the canvas). There is another interesting aspect of this title. In German, Magritte's *Le Viol* translates as *Vergewaltigung*—literally a misuse of power. Freud took advantage of the German language to present these parapraxes (errors and slips in speech) of everyday life. In German the prefix "ver" performs an anamorphic function, a displacement to the side, calling up the unconscious. So *verrückt* (mad, insane) means making a jerking motion to the side, *Versprechen* (a slip of the tongue) means an intervention into speech coming suddenly from somewhere in the unfathomable unconscious; das *Vergessen* (forgetting) means a repression of something well known in the unconscious; *das Verlesen* (misreading) means repressing other readings in the unconscious, and so on. *Vergewaltigung* means a violence coming from the unconscious; the desire to remove the veil of the woman and forcibly possess the Thing she hides without her permission. Magritte is providing us with an anamorphic view, a "looking awry" as Žižek (1991) would put it, of this form of masculine desire. As mentioned earlier, the title refers to the male's *failure* of possession.

To go back to Magritte's painting, which Kuenzli provides no commentary about the same punning possibilities are in evidence. The two phrases: *Je ne vois pas la*, [I don't see it]...cachée dans la forêt [hidden in the forest] separated by a nude figure in an obvious state of modesty, surrounded by men with their eyes closed immediately takes us back to the scene/seen of castration. *Forêt* is a metaphor for pubic hair, "bush" in English. But this is not a castrated woman, although the painting can easily be read paradigmatically as fetishistic, especially if the nude is interpreted as a "virgin"—a virgin forest never touched. But this is too simplistic. The play is on the indefinite article "la" which is marked as feminine. If the surrealists are remembering their childhood experiences of castration, their disavowal is a particularly curious one for the "la" suggests a *retrieval* of the phallic mother. Inflected in the French it becomes a "question" of doubt, not disavowal. "I don't see it?" Again the phallic mother is affirmed. She holds her hands over her breast, not her pubic area, assigning her more masculine qualities. There is yet another possible reading. By itself, "*Je ne vois pas la*" connotes, "*I don't see the place*," while "cachée" can also mean "secret." This now connotes, "I don't see the place (the nonseeing place is further connoted by the black background)—a copula is necessary here to join the two phrases which is represented by the nude figure— *the secrets in the forest.*" This is yet another reinstallment of the phallic mother. All these punned readings refuse the masculine and sadistic reading. They side with the feminine and are antipatriachal in this sense.

The surrealistic and dadaist use of parody and punning and self-conscious appropriation of Freud is vividly demonstrated by Susan Suleiman's (1990:150-162) reading of Duchamp's defaced "assisted readymade" *Mona Lisa, L.H.O.O.Q* (1919) and Max Ernst's *The Blessed Virgin Chastising the Infant Jesus before Three Witnesses* (1926. fig. 10). Her discussion is instructive for my defense, and Gubar's accusation of Magritte, because of their self-conscious strategies to stage an act of *refusal* (if not entirely to escape the law of the father), like Magritte staged himself. Duchamp penciled in a Dali-like mustache and a small goatee to the mass-produced color reproduction of Leonardo's portrait. This facial hair is stylized by curlicues and appears as two separate V's (the inverted V of the mustache on top, and the regular V of the goatee on the bottom). In the bottom left and right corners were the inscriptions "Paris" and "Marcel Duchamp" respectively. On a strip of white paper beneath the reproduction, Duchamp hand-lettered the inscription in capital letters: L.H.O.O.Q. Like Magritte's punning playfulness, when the title is pronounced aloud, "Elle a chaud au cul," "She's got hot pants," more pejoratively today, "She's got a hot ass," plays with Leonardo's alleged sexuality and Duchamp's own feminine ego, Rrose Sélavy, which itself is a pun on sexual identity. The name pronounced aloud, "Éros, c'est la vie," is a pun on erotic life.

Suleiman draws upon the Oedipal drama being enacted here. The bilingual pun on "LOOK," she says, like the words DADA itself, "suggest the antics of a little boy wanting to be seen performing by (usually) his mother. ... the son counting on the complicity of his mother, declares his rebellion against the name—and the law—of the father" (p.152). She then makes this reading of the mustache and beard:

> [I]t becomes obvious that the two V's, minus their appendages, are mirror images of each other—and are also fairly standard iconographic representations of a woman's pubic hair. It would appear that by a humorous 'displacement upward,' Duchamp has produced not, or not only, the Mona Lisa as a sexpot ('elle a chaud au cul'), nor the Mona Lisa as a young man, but the Mona Lisa as a phallic mother (pubis plus 'appendages')—indeed, a phallic mother doubly marked, redundantly phallic. We are no longer in Oedipus but its fetishistic perversion: Sexual difference no sooner recognized than denied" (pp.152-153).

In this reading, as Krauss would have it, Duchamp's comic *mise-en-scène* of fetishism is transgressive. Duchamp's gesture refuses to accept the castration of his mother. But there is another reading which Suleiman undertakes to analyze, and this is queer reading. What if the caption, "she is hot in the ass" (Suleiman's translation) refers not to Leonardo's *Mona Lisa,* but to the defaced Mona Lisa with a phallus? What happens to the son's desire, especially if that son is a cross-dresser, i.e., Rrose Sélavy, a woman with a phallus? The work can now be read as homosexual desire: "the fantasy of being sexually possessed by the father?"

The case of Max Ernst is equally complicated. Ernst's painting, *The Blessed Virgin Chastising the Infant Jesus before Three Witnesses* (fig.10) is an intertextual reworking of the well known painting by Parmigianino's *Madonna with the Long Neck*. Drawing on the interpretation of Margot Norris (1985), Suleiman recognizes it as a critique of Christian myth, an example of the dis-

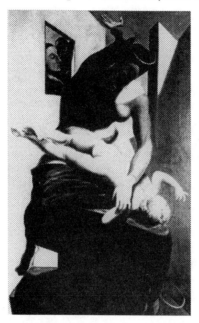

fig. 10 The Blessed Virgin Chastising the
Infant Jesus Before Three Witnesses

ruptive, transgressive potential of parody. "By deranging the traditional iconography of Nativity and Crucifixion scenes, Ernst demystifies the Christian salvation myth by stripping away the religious signification of the actions and representing them in their de-signified secular form" (Norris,p,150). Norris's reading stresses the antipatriarchal aspects of this work accomplished by Surrealist parody. She lists the many inversions Ernst makes around two points of reference in Christ's life: the Adoration of the Magi and the Agony of Christ, which allow certain Freudian elements to emerge from the religious myth. One of those Freudian references becomes Suleiman's focus. She reads Ernst's painting through Freud's 1919 text, "A Child Is Being Beaten." Why this is significant for this discussion will become apparent when i shall examine re-readings of this essay by Silverman (1988b), Rodowick (1991), and Parveen Adams (1991).

"Max Ernst's and Marcel Duchamp's sexual habits and preferences, whether straight or perverse, are not the issue. The issue is how a certain *figure of perversion* functions in their work, and possibly in male Dada/Surrealist practices and parodic intertextuality in general" (p. 157). As we shall see, Suleiman's conclusions support Gubar, but once more at least two contradictory readings are possible. Like Gubar, Suleiman draws on Max Ernst's life experiences to make her case by reading it as a classical example of the "beating" fantasy. Suleiman accepts Freud's supposition that the beating fantasy is exactly the same for men and women. In the boy's case, the repressed fantasy of being beaten by the father is interpreted to mean: "*I am loved by my father.*" This *unconscious* fantasy for the boy becomes transformed as a *conscious* fantasy to mean: "*I am being beaten by my mother.*" For Freud this is an evasion of homosexuality (of being sexually loved by his father) by displacing it onto his mother; thereby engendering a feminine attitude that no longer has a homosexual object-choice. The male masochist retains his heterosexuality. The male masochist covets the woman who is beating him with masculine characteristics, and attributes dominance to the phallic mother, thereby both retaining and disavowing love for the father. In the girl's case, "a child is being beaten" is interpreted by an authority figure—a replacement for the father—while she and other children look on.

This reading is then applied to Ernst's painting. The child (Jesus) being beaten (by the Virgin Mary) is clearly a woman with masculine attributes: large, muscular and authoritative. Three figures look on: Paul Eluard, André Breton and Ernst himself, but *only* Ernst looks directly at the scene/seen. He participates in the beating. Suleiman interprets this as Ernst taking the subject position of the female conscious fantasy as Freud describes it. Doing so leads her to the same place as Gubar does with Magritte, i.e., being ruled by his mother, for Ernst now adopts a "feminine attitude" in his male fantasy. According to Freud, adopting a "feminine" attitude (masochist position) requires that he (Ernst) be the child who is being beaten. Suleiman goes to some lengths to associate the child being beaten in the painting with a portrait taken by his father of him as little Jesus. Paradoxically then, can Ernst split himself as both sadist (onlooker) and beaten (castrated) child (masochist)? He seems to have done it visually. Suleiman makes no comment on this but concludes with Ernst masking his homosexual fantasy of being loved by his father by displacing it onto his mother (The Virgin Mary). In classical Freudian fashion then, Ernst identifies with his mother, with the feminine in order to suppress his homosexuality, and repress "I am being beaten by my father."

178

But there is another possible interpretation presented by Silverman's reading of male masochism as influenced by the writings of Deleuze. "In inviting the mother to beat/or dominate him [the male masochist] transfers power and authority from the father to her, remakes the symbolic order, and 'ruins' his own paternal legacy" (1988b:57). In this reading, complicity with the mother directs the son's perversion against the law of the father. Although patriarchy is not "entirely" overcome by any means, there is an exclusion of the father. This is what i take (some) Surrealist men to be doing, especially Magritte and Ernst. Like Silverman, both David Rodowick and Parveen Adams re-read Freud's Oedipal triangles for the ambiguities of subject positions that can take place in fantasy. Ernst provides evidence of such ambiguity by splitting himself as both sadist and masochist within his painting. Both David Rodowick and Parveen Adams develop the masochistic subject positions overlooked by Freud's "A Child Is Being Beaten." There is something missing from "masochistic scenario of the *modern* period" Adams writes (p.6, my emphasis). During this historical period (*fin de siècle*) of gender instability the masochistic position may well have been missed by Freud. "Something about masochism eludes Freud" (Adams,p.20).

Adams states in the very beginning of her essay: "I will argue that it is *not possible* to determine sexual position through identification" (p.4, my emphasis), and then begins to unravel the constant oscillations which takes place in the dreams between the binaries.[5] Dora, she says, must take both the active and the passive positions at once. The subject, argues Adams, is not structured in terms of Freud's pairs but in hysterical oscillation. If this both/and logic is applied to the readings of Gubar, Suleiman, Krauss and Caws, it would seem that each is taking her reading on one side of the fence or the other. Adams concludes: "What the masochist is doing is quite contrary to Freud, is to defy castration and disavow sexual difference. And this of course is a complete travesty of the Law the Oedipus complex is supposed to institute. It is important to note that the masochist's disavowal does not make him psychotic; his perversion is a stable position grounded in his refusal of the symbolic father and in his contact with the phallic mother. The masochist can subvert the Law because he too knows the paradox of conscience that Freud had recognized, the paradox that the more strictly the Law is adhered to, the greater the guilt" (p.21).

i submit that the Surrealists were conscious of this paradox, and Magritte's pun, "Je ne vois pas la ... cachée dans la forêt," was a recognition of this masochistic contract with Woman among the Surrealist men. Kuenzli (1991) states: "They preferred to celebrate female hysteria as attitudes passionelles, as *l'amour fou*, in the last issue of *La Révolution surréaliste*" (p.19). Rather than the sadism they are accused of, i would claim that they were upholding a version of Romantic love. The woman was an unattainable Ideal, like Breton's Nadia who was a visionary and could answer for him his questions. She was "cold" in this regard, a "creature" whose "crazy love" could never be entirely fulfilled; she was the unobtainable Thing, the Surrealists symptom; a contract with her had to be made; her cold phallic power had to be disavowed and fetishized; i would say seduced. These men were seducers who lived in fear that they might not perform up to her expectations. This helps to explain such works as Dali's *The Great Masturbator*, an image of erotic desire and feared impotence. But i'm sure this is only part of the story. The recent re-examination of Surrealists' alleged revolutionary interest and revision of sexuality, especially by Breton, has been brilliantly deconstructed by the gay art historian Richard Easton (1992). Nevertheless i would like to think Magritte was definitely an exception in this regard, and therefore i should like to get back to him.

Magritte's Deconstructive Moves

In his examination of Magritte's tropes, Jean Clair (1979) is not fixated on just Magritte's nudes, like Gubar; rather, from a broader perspective Clair provides the reader with a sense of Magritte's "problematic." Unquestionably, Magritte set out to deconstruct the perspectival system. "Without abandoning this system, but using it in reverse rather than according to custom, he thereby becomes involved in displacing things from their expected sites [sights/cites], assigning a dimension different from that provided by the ordered spacing of the perspective grid. The representation is consequently in every case either overloaded or impoverished to the point where it becomes incomprehensible to any eye with a possible claim to mirror things" (p. 93). i believe this to be a fair statement of his problematic. Anamorphosis and scenography were used to disturb the rational order of perspective. A "tropologia" (p.96) of excessive and perverse rhetoric was developed to make perspective order "strange." Clair provides historical traces to authors and texts Magritte had referred to and borrowed from to form his tropes and surprising effects. Marquetry (inlays) and the space of intarsia were particularly useful devises which allowed him to translate Freudian ideas graphically.[6] The similarities and contiguities which existed between various painted objects were left to the viewer's interpretation. Fragmentation was purposely used for allegorical readings. The female torso was a prop straight out of the classical academy which was often used allegorically to put to question the "measurable" universe.[7] His use of flat figures, and the absent ephemeral portraits of himself can be read as contradicting "crystallographic structure." Objects in classical painting do not really conceal one another, yet "[i]n Magritte's painting, one is never certain of the nature of that which remains hidden" (p.103). "We all know how stubbornly Magritte has always denied the attribution of figures to given symbols in his paintings. And they are not produced by a mysterious dream work, in the Freudian sense of the word, insofar as they seem—and in this they are antithetical to other surrealist art— not to conform to 'an inner mode'" (p. 107). Davis's alternative reading to that of Gubar is to state that the game is played out within the boundaries of the perspectival code as in Magritte's *The Human Condition* (1933), fig. 11, where a painting of a landscape stands in place of a window, or again in *La Cascade*, fig. 12, painted almost thirty years later (1961).

fig. 11 *La Condition Humaine*

Here a landscape painting resting on an easel is painted nestled within the very landscape that is represented in the painting. Leaves and branches are painted over some parts of the frame. The viewer is left peplexed by the paradox of the titles, *La Cascade* (The Waterfall) and *La Condition Humaine* (The Human Condition). In both cases (figures 11 and 12) there is no easy distinction between inside and outside, no "break." The representation of "reality" is put into question by the effects of oil paint. Derrida (1987a) was to provide a deconstructive demonstration of Magritte's clever *mise en abyme*, arguing against the work of art (the *ergon*) by showing that it was always already polluted by its framing contexts (the *parergon*). There was no pure aesthetic discourse which could avoid intermingling with those it tried to eclude— economic, ethical, cognitive. What was inside and outside a picture was undecidable. No frame was capable of holding its representation.

fig 12 *La Cascade*

Gazing Traditionally

Significantly then, castrated or not, the surrealist René Magritte, by deconstructing the signifying code of the *trompe-l'oeil*, exposed hidden fantasy in what was taken to be the *mise-en-scène* of realism, and positioned spectators in such a way that they were forced to stare at themselves. The mileage begotten from this concept is immense for feminists working in photography and film, the very technologies which have extended the *trompe-l'oeil* effects. There is now a wealth of literature on the subject of the scopophobic gaze and its problematics.[8] i would like to engage in this literature now, going over what every student who enters "film studies" must eventually become familiar with. As my junior-high art students used to say, "But we've done this before!" Please bear with me if this turns out to be familiar territory.

The milestone article, so often cited, was Laura Mulvey's "Visual Pleasure and Narrative Cinema" (1975). Mulvey essentially laid the groundwork for the male gaze as a fetishization of woman's lack. Mulvey articulated the way the unconscious of patriarchal society structures the classical film-narrative to represent woman as a castrated Other. Her theoretical base relied heavily on the work of both Freud and Lacan in privileging the dominance of sight in the Oedipal conflict and the fear of castration. (i.e., Irigaray's specularology). It should be remembered that for Lacan desire is in every-thing we see, for while the observer takes the objects of looking for granted, there is the desire of the gaze inscribed on the unconscious. This splitting of the ego means that there will always be a mis-seeing. "Unconscious and re-pression, desire and lack - this dialectical opposition is present in every visual recognition" (Wright, 1984:116).

Lacan, therefore identifies a 'scopic drive' for this desire in looking. The scopophobic instinct is the pleasure in looking at another person as an erotic object. It is a search for a fantasy that will represent for him/her the lost phallus. It is the phallus during the mirror stage of recognition which is fixed as the *difference* between genders (see Pollock, 1988:138-140). Before this time of recognition, prior to language acquisition of the Symbolic Order, the woman is perceived as an all-powerful phallic mother. When her lack is discovered (i.e., that she is castrated), then there is a fall from grace—she now becomes a symbol of castration. The anxiety of castration is one of disavowal. The boy knows, but he represses this knowledge. There is always the anxiety of being confronted with this threat. Fetishism becomes a way of coping with this forbidden knowledge. It is the displacement of anxiety which is created by the sight of a different body onto another object. Shoes, legs, fur, velvet, underclothes are items associated with the moments before the discovery of the Mother's lack. These are the male's way of compensating for the differ-ence based on the privileging of his difference (i.e., the phallus), not hers.

"The mirror phase occurs at a time when children's physical ambi-tions outstrip their motor capacity, with the result that their recognition of themselves is joyous in that they imagine the mirror image to be more com-plete, more perfect than they experience in their own body" (Mulvey, 1989:17). i often wondered whether the male fantasy of being the fastest "gun" in the West, or being the fastest "man" on earth (Superman), wasn't embedded in Mulvey's insight about trying to outdo your reflection. Male masculinity always tries to outdo the mirror through projecting such idealizations into the cult of the superhero who has extraordinary dexterity. Professional sport-ing events thrive on such a fantasy. This important passage from Mulvey (1975: 12) seems to encapsulate the above discussion:

> As the spectator identifies with the main male protagonist,
> he projects his look on to that of his like, his screen surro-
> gate, so that the power of the male protagonist as he con-
> trols events coincides with the active power of the erotic
> look, both giving a satisfying sense of omnipotence. A male

> movie star's glamorous characteristics are thus not those of
> the erotic object of his gaze, but those of the more per-
> fect, more complete, more powerful ideal ego conceived
> in the original moment of recognition in front of the mir-
> ror.

The anxiety associated with the identification of this ideal masculine ego can often lead to emotional reticence and silence (Neale, 1983:7).
This is a symbolic castration since language threatens a narcissistic ideal ego
that stands alone, one which requires no-body, no need for communication.
Heroes say very little.

The lesson of masculine desire often rehearsed through Mulvey's
original thesis has provided an explication of just how male fantasies are constructed through the (classical) film form, and just how women are embedded in the Symbolic Order of language so that they play into the pleasurable
look of the male spectator-voyeur. In a traditional exhibitionist role, women
are simultaneously actively looked at and passively displayed. As cinematic
stars, their entire bodies are reshaped into a fetish which acts as a substitute
term for the phallus–the lack of the maternal body. This voyeuristic look is
especially made evident by a probing camera lens which produces a technology of sadistic pleasure. Her body is examined as if by a male gynecolo-
gist:[9] the camera looking up her skirt to assure the male audience the difference. Because the starlet's masochism and exhibitionism makes her the ideal
passive counterpart to the active sadistic voyeurism, heterosexual eroticism is
maintained. Hence Mulvey's theory of masculine pleasure positions the *heterosexual* male gaze as either voyeuristic or fetishistic. To paraphrase John Ellis'
(1982:47-48) explanation of such positionality, voyeurism depends upon a
distance between the act of seeing and the object seen. This typifies the sur-
veying, scientistic, objective, roving eye which assures sadistic dominance and
power in its demand to know, to be curious, and to understand the Other. In
contrast, the fetishistic look tries to abolish the gap between spectator and
image. A "subjective fallacy," is commited. The screen character is captivated
by the viewer. In the spectacular display of the body, the viewer makes no
demands to know, to inquire any further. The viewer is smitten by flesh, costume, and the masquerade. Mulvey's thesis works both ends of the object-
subject distinction. In both cases the female is seen as passive, and therefore
prone to masochism by allowing herself to be manipulated. The male is the
active subject, prone to sadism and violence.

Pollock (1988) applies Lacanian and classic Freudian theory of fetishism and castration to help explain the binary representations of the *femme fatale* (vamp) and the idealized beautiful face for the male consumer, especially in the portraits of Rossetti and the Pre-Raphaelite painters. During the phallic stage, which is that point when the body is able to satisfy the need for comfort and provide gratuitous pleasure, there is a fear of damage—i.e., castration, representing a threat to the body's narcissistic possibilities signified by this organ of gratuitous pleasure. This is not localized as a specific loss of an organ; rather it is the fear of damage to the wholeness of the body and to the sense of the self which is being formed through the Other, i.e., to feel complete through the Mother. To "see" the visual difference in the body of the female, i.e., as one of the absence of the primary signifier, opens up the possibility of damage to the boy's body as well since he interprets that damage has already done to the maternal body, which, up to that moment before was a guarantee against such disaster. In Freudian theory, the discovery of anatomical difference is traumatizing. Such knowledge may be disavowed; the boy knows but pretends not to know. The little boy lives in constant danger of being threatened by this knowledge. "Generated at this intersection of knowledges and still sliding meaning are twin images of what will later be fixed as woman (as difference). One is the compensatory fantasy of the pre-Oedipal mother, still all-powerful phallic; the other as the fantasy of woman not only as damaged, but as damage itself, castrated *and* the symbol of castration" (Pollock, 1988:139). Thus the representation of the woman is split as vamp or an idealized beautiful woman.[10]

"In those familial structures organized by the sexual division of labor, a female caretaker is usually the primary source of life and love. Over this foundation is laid a split image of that dominating figure, one part powerful but forever threatening, the *femme fatale*; the other powerful but forever lost, the perpetually desired phallic mother of infancy" (Pollock, 1988:139). Cinema plays off this split image for the male gaze—like the recent *Fatal Attraction*, where Dan Gallagher's (Michael Douglas) wife Beth Gallagher (Anne Archer) is the protective mother who stays at home with her children and looks after her husband, whereas Alex Forrest (Glen Close) plays the *femme fatale* (see Holmlund, 1989). Or take a more recent example in the film *She-Devil*. Here the split is exaggerated and inverted. Meryl Streep is the vamp whose seductive qualities are played for laughs. She comes across as seemingly good, while Roseanne Barr, the *good* wife of the delinquent husband, has turned devil, complete with a Medusa-like stare and the power to hex. In *Fatal Attraction*, the wife is stereotypic and uninteresting, defender of the hearth, while in *She-Devil*, it is the husband, easily seduced and weak, who remains in the background. The variations seem endless. *Dynasty* is yet another example. Alexis

Carrington (Joan Collins) is the vamp, the bitch, the "spider woman," the evil seductress. Her sexual powers, disruptive of male patriarchy, aligned with her economic independence, make her a match for any man. Krystle, Blake's wife, plays the virgin Mother, the good wife to her husband and children (see Belinda Budge, 1989).

Although Lacan's theories have been criticized vehemently and relentlessly for their phallocentric bias, most notably by Jane Gallop[11] (1982a, 1985) and, of course by "French feminists," his defenders continue to argue that Lacan's theories go a long way in explaining the pornographic, scopophobic "look" that (in)forms the majority of men's fantasy life today. His phallocentrism is, therefore, both his weakness and his strength. The ambivalent position is displaced throughout his text as when he slips up from using the phallus, not symbolically but as a body organ—the penis (Gallop, 1981). By providing feminists with an analysis of the male Imaginary, it points to the necessity of displacing the dominant representation of both the MAN and the WOMAN. Problems lie in how that is to happen, and what then woman's representation is to be. In Irigaray's accounting, since the female subject is not permitted in masculine discourse, that discourse cannot specify femininity. As argued in Wittig's anti-essentialist polemic, Lacan's transcendental phallus is to be replaced by another transcendental signifier, "the lesbian body." But the lesbian does not exist either (Fuss, 1989: 42-43). Yet both theorists have generated important insights. Wittig, by demonstrating the exclusions of the 'straight mind,' while Lacan demonstrating the power of the 'scopic' look.

Masculine Desire Modified

Mulvey's dualistic positionality of the heterosexual male gaze has been expanded, both through her own re-thinking of her original problematic (1981) and yet again by Steve Neale's (1983) analysis of the way masculine eroticism is displaced in male genres (the western, adventure films, gangster and war movies, and the usual police buddy films) by de-sexualizing the male body through mutilation, shootings, woundings, and stabbing, typified by ritualized fight scenes and gun battles so that homosexual voyeurism is denied. Such an "economy of sadism" is now played off between the homosexual gaze and the male hero. Sadomasochistic spectacles like battle scenes, shoot-outs, fight scenes, duels, are linked to the repression of eroticism.[12] Voyeuristic looking is engaged when the hero and villain duel it out, both by spectators as well as amongst the male characters themselves. Such looks are not marked by erotic desire, but through fear, hatred or aggression. Fetishistic viewing is therefore permitted; yet when the rookie upstart looks up to an accomplished male "fighter" (policeman, knight, gunslinger), homoerotism always leaks in and remains a potential undercurrent for the homosexual gaze. In such moments this homosexual gaze is socially sanctioned like the slap on the bum amongst players during a sporting event. Often, leading men are handsome and muscle bound, the body presented as one huge phallus, again obliquely providing male to male identification (see Richard Dyer, 1982). Only in the dance genre is the male's body permitted to be on direct spec-ular erotic display; however a fine line is often maintained between dance and athleticism.[13]

Mulvey's rethought thesis was to show the distinction between male leads who held an image of narcissistic authority against the Law, on the one hand, and on the other, male leads who accepted the image of social author-ity. The former position might be euphemistically thought of as a time when "men were men," unmarried, celebrating their freedom, and omnipotence. Lone rangers. Lone heroes. Undercover Agents. Lone but not a-lone. They have themselves and the knowledge that they are "Simply the Best," as Tina Turner's song puts it. In this sense women pose a threat, as does society and the Law. As Outsiders they love and then leave. They are never caught by love. The male identifies in sympathy if they are shot or suffer a splendid, heroic death. In contrast, those within the jurisdiction of the law have already accepted their Oedipalization.

Norman Bryson's[14] current work on sexual difference as it mani-fests itself in French Revolutionary painting is very important to the ques-tion of "men in feminism," particularly how it relates to psychoanalytic dis-course. His remarks concerning the relationship between power and gender, especially as to their relationship to the social and historical construction of masculinity, are particularly crucial to extending the valuable work by film feminists. Bryson develops what Silverman (1983) has called the negative Oedipal relationship between father and son, mother and daughter. In both cases, it is the homoerotic love for the similar sex which must be displaced elsewhere. Bryson deals specifically with the problem of masculinity. The son loves his father but is unable to possess the phallus for fear of castration and retribution. There is a lack which exists in the gap between the son's desire to own the phallus and the impossibility of fulfilling such a desire. Therefore, it is this homoerotic remainder, this excess which is censored by the incest taboo. The son must never know the father's strength, which is always on the outside, projected upon other males. His son may wrestle with him, but, if this homoerotic "cover" is to be maintained, the rough-housing should never end in physical violence. The result of all this is the inauthentic phallic power which the son must forever displace until he owns the phallus himself. Such a masquerade is played out in the social order in the projects of the ideal male *imago*. The son must recognize this ideal in society, yet must disavow it. He is compelled to continually strive to possess it. As Bryson points out through his lecture series, it is the classical male sculptures which are the projections of this heroic ideal, the male *imago*. Curiously, Bryson notes, in Greek sculpture, the sweat of Herculean musculature is proportionate to the genital region. The larger the muscles, the smaller the penis. Phallic virility is displaced into the register of the entire body—the inflated muscles, exposed veins and the removal of bodily hair. The genital area appears hidden, usually by the customary fig-leaf. Apparently, in muscle magazines, often the genital area of the swim-suit are airbrushed. The penis, then, as body part remains hidden, illusionary, part of the phallic mystique.

Collectively, the sex orchestration of the masculine *imago* is dispersed throughout the social order. The politics of a male looking at another male is one of *rank*. Penis size is sublimated to a positioning of power. It appears that the hierarchy of the political order bites into the male psyche through a gradation of rule. In the academic discourse, it is the male who possess the code, the last word on a discipline, who is then considered its Master. Males are ranked in terms of inferiority; their publishing record for example. Rank fills the desire to complete the masculine ideal *imago*; to be the "top gun," the best of the best. Medals worn on the chest and stars on the shoulders are a record of that continual desire to reach the top. Trophies are no different. If Bryson is right in his summations of the negative male Oedipal libidinal displacements, our popular culture is full of superheroes to be emulated. These superheroes wear special spectacular costumes and have Herculean bodies. There is no sartorial refusal here.[15]

Straining to reach the masculine *imago* has its hazards for, as Neale (1982) points out, there is also the disappointment of reaching a third stage of the Oedipal process when masculinity is questioned. In the first stage, dependent on his Mother, the male strives to fit himself to her desires, while in the second stage, the recognition of sexual difference reveals the phallic mother as lacking the phallus. This then leads to the third stage where Neale, quoting Colin McCabe (1978:108) says:

> But simultaneously, in a logically distinct moment, he recognizes that the mother's desires are organized in terms of the father who is understood as a rival phallus. If the mother is now understood to be fundamentally lacking in her being

(thus her love for the child and the father), the father is understood as full presence. As the father is without lack (he is the phallus incarnate), he functions as the cause of his own desire, The element of hate enters when the child realizes, in a third stage, that the father is also articulated within an organization of desire that he does not control. The father is not the full presence that he promised to be; he, too, is lacking in his being.

Such a third stage makes the questioning of patriarchy a possibility, yet it is the second stage which confirms masculinity. Neal goes on to analyze *Chariots of Fire* as confirming the second stage, while a film like *Raging Bull* (see Pam Cook, 1982), which traces the "rise and fall" of Jake La Motta, ex–middleweight champion of the world, places masculinity in its third stage—in crisis. It seems to me that Puig's excellent book, *Kiss of the Spider Woman* (and the subsequent film), is yet another deconstruction of masculinity, positioning the spectator in this last stage. Molina, the homosexual protagonist finds strength of character attributed to machismo, while Valentine, his jailmate, a heterosexual leftist "macho" male, brings out his own repressed homoeroticism as his feeling for Molina grow. The "kiss" between them presents the spectator with the fantasy that both heterosexual and homosexual love might meet in some impossible place; impossible for it becomes a "kiss of death" for them both in the end. This is much too short a commentary on such a brilliant deconstructivist text, yet it provides one of the very few exemplars where male masculinity is contested, which, to my mind, displaces *both* the heterosexual and homosexual gaze to a position where the male viewer must question his own sexuality as the text looks back at him from the abyss (the opaque screen) of the "kiss." i shall return to these issues when discussing the postmodern "hysterical" masculine body toward the end of my journey.

Vermeer meets Silverman on a Fassbinder Set with Lacan Looking On

By far the most interesting and daring attempt to provide insights about male masculine desire has been Kaja Silverman's recent book, *Male Subjectivity at the Margins* (1992). Despite my pretentious remarks in the beginning of this text to examine my two (I)(i)s, it is a woman, and not a man—to put the matter "tac(k)tlessly"—who has given both heterosexual and homosexual men "something" to think about, much like it was Eve Kosofsky Sedgwick (1985) who provided an understanding of the "homosocial pact between men." Both Silverman and Sedgwick have managed to place themselves outside the field of vision, looking at "us" awry—anamorphically—so as to disturb "us" from the peep-holes of "our" own choosing. Silverman's text is rich so i mean only to concentrate on Chapter 3 where she brings Fassbinder and Lacan together in order to sort out the gaze from the look, and offer an example of another form of masculine subjectivity, a maleman who accepts lack.

Fassbinder's "radical refusal to *affirm*, his repudiation of positivity in any shape or form," writes Silverman, "his refusal to provide affirmative representations of women, blacks, gays, or the left, ... place[s] at risk ... identity itself, which is no longer able to secure an 'interior' foothold" (p. 126). What Silverman means by this is my ability to "see myself being seen" (Lacan's 'I am seen, therefore I am'), as experienced by the subject of consciousness, is deconstructed by Fassbinder. This phenomenon, "see myself being seen," is illustrated by Vermeer's *A Painter in his Studio* (fig. 13) which also appears on the front cover of Norman Bryson's book *Vision and Painting* (1983). Vermeer paints himself painting a picture with his back to the viewers, as a spectacle to be seen. Unlike Velázquez who looks out at us in *Las Meninas*, Vermeer has put himself "into the picture," so to speak, by imaginatively stepping out of the canvas and looking (imagining) himself painting. Two things need to be said here. First, Vermeer paints an *ideal* picture of himself; it is how he imagines himself to be in front of a *camera obscura*. Second, it can be imagined that this was exactly what Vermeer was doing—taking a "picture" of himself with a camera, albeit a "painted photograph" at this moment in history. The same could be done today by setting the auto timer of a camera and putting oneself in the picture. There is certainly less control in terms of the mechanical aspects of framing and so forth; yet, just about anyone can position themselves in front of the lens and pose as they please.

Silverman wants to identify that "stepping out" as Vermeer positioning himself at a point which Lacan had designated as the "gaze." By going to the other side of the canvas, Vermeer has taken on the operation of the gaze by "seeing" himself being seen, even when there are "no pairs of eyes" on him. In other words, his movement over to the other side of the canvas is to participate as an object of his own look.[16] This is *not* a part of the Renaissance perspectival system; rather, it is the place occupied on the other side of the usual geometrical point of looking. Vermeer made great use of the *camera obscura*; consequently, it seems fair to say that he placed himself behind the pin-hole of the camera, in silence, without the sound of the modernist "click"

fig. 13 Vermeer, *The Artist in His Studio*

(See Alpers, 1983). Vermeer, then, occupies the place of the object that would be illuminated by geometrical perspective of Dürer or Alberti. Another way of saying this is to go back to *Las Meniñas* and imagine that Velázquez has found a very clever way to split himself into two, as both the object and the subject of his gaze, yet appeasing royalty. Velázquez, like Vermeer, has put himself in the picture in a very cunning way.[17] The point that needs to be made here, and this is where the difficulties of language come in, is that it is *not* that Vermeer has positioned himself as the gaze; rather he stands in relation *to* the gaze "as its effects within itself" (p. 128). The gaze occupies the second vanishing point outside the canvas, an impossible place to occupy. Vermeer could not paint himself from that position because he would "disappear"—literally, too far away from the canvas to paint. The logic of the technology he is using limits his body position, i.e., distance being controlled by the reach of his hand, the size of the canvas, the brushes used. Since he is imagining himself painting, he need not step very far away from his canvas to see how he is "shaping up."[18]

The gaze, as the outside vanishing point, therefore doesn't exist in any one place. Its "point" is aporial. It just *is*-a given. Its totality can never be grasped; it is transcendental and hence it is a sublime concept (see preface). Likewise, the vanishing point from which the "look" from the canvas comes also stands in relation to an all-mastering transcendental geometrical point that casts its surveillance on the objects outside. The "pure" gaze and the "pure"

191

look are the end points of the perspectival system, what was described as the optical theories of *lumen* and *lux* respectively (Jay, 1993). What happens in between them is where life is lived. As you move more and more towards the gaze side of the canvas, the artist moves more and more towards abstraction and mathematization of pure numbers, Stephen Hawking presenting its most sublime formulation to date.[19] The metaphor of being "blinded" by the light comes to mind, the *lumen* of St. Augustine's *City of Gold*. In other words, it is difficult not to think of the gaze as historical manifestations of Being, God, Absolute Spirit, Big Bang, Yahweh, the Sun and so on, "white mythology" as Derrida called it. In Žižek's (1993b) terms this is the pure empty *cogito* of fantasy (see pretext). Moving the other way from this impossible idealism, towards an equally impossible materialism, prompts my rhetorical question as to how much metaphysics should be allowed into theorizing? Man, believing he is occupying the inside geometrical point, invents the panopticon—the Masterly look of "ocularism." Often it is said that this is a "masterly dominating gaze," meaning that *the look has mistaken itself for the transcendental gaze* as in Magritte's *Le Viol*. Man replaces God with technological instrumental science, with its impulse to find the "hard" facts of matter itself. Here, the feminist critique claims that matter is a metaphor for *mater* (L.), the Mother's body that must be dominated and exploited (Somer, 1992).

Lacan describes an abyss between the subject looking and Reality as it truly is, a conceptualization so well captured by Magritte's painting *La Lunette D'approche* (1963). A half-opened window presents the simultaneity of "reality" as the observer sees it through the windowpane as blue sky and white clouds, and the Reality beyond the windowpane, as represented by the black nothingness in the narrow opening where the windowpane has been slightly opened. "[T]he frame of the windowpane is the fantasy-frame [the Imaginary] which constitutes reality, whereas through the crack we get an insight into the "impossible" Real, the Thing-in-itself" (see Žižek, 1993b:103-104). The frame is like an opaque screen; the looker can only dimly see through it as the images on what is seen/scene fall on its precipices. Perception is not like Dürer's *lucido*—a plate of clear glass that can be gridded and the object faithfully copied; rather, argues Silverman, the abyss is the screen through which culture and history intervene: the language we use and the discursive practices that come with the instruments of our seeing[20] —in short, all those cultural interventions which deny us ever "literally" and "materially" possessing the knowledge of reality. The abyss, the screen, the opaque curtain, the veil, are like a stain that colors our world from knowing reality "really," or knowing materiality in reality, or, in Lacan's terms—knowing the Real, always capitalized to indicate that "reality *does* exist," but we can never know it as it is. In a Heideggerian sense, Being is denied to us. Yet that Being, that Reality can summon us—can call on us—can catch our look seemingly by passing over the abyss, (or directly through the screen), perhaps faster than the speed of light *might be a way to theorize this*—unseen until it hits us to get our attention, i.e., recall the "surprise" registered on the face of Zeuxis when he realized he had been fooled. Something happens below the level of consciousness—in the unconscious. It shifts the frame of our looking. Such seemingly hallucinatory moments disturb the conjunctions of our Imaginary (as the screen) with the Symbolic and awaken us to the Real.[21] In the past that beckoning by the gaze could be interpreted as a summons by God, or it might be called by any other metaphysical concept—"a calling" perhaps. In the context of cosmology it is the "after effect" of the Big Bang; the universal radiation that seemingly has the same measurement in every direction. In short, the gaze cannot be apprehended in its entirety. It is a sublime concept; in its very subtleness it is enabling when we catch glimpses of it.[22] There is a disturbance in our psyche, as if something came at us "out of nowhere," and we recognize its presence on the precipice of the abyss. This precipice of the abyss can be thought of as a screen or stain, or the "transitional space" of culture, as D. W. Winnicott (1974) would have it; a mysterious fog composed of the interplay of the Imaginary and the Symbolic Order (metaphorically Lacan's Möbius strip that continually twists and turns me in my relation to the Real).

The more interesting question is how Vermeer comes to embody the relationship between the look (*lux*) and the gaze (*lumen*) as the two aporial points of this binary system of outside/inside. It may be said that the slash (/) between them, is the frame, the precipice of an abyss, Derrida's parergon (1987a), or in Lacan's terminology which Silverman uses—the image-screen. A clarification should be made at this point. Silverman uses the word "screen" for this "slash"—this "cut" that i refer to. i am happier with the term "frame" for my own use here—more accurately, "a moving, shape-shifting, morphing frame" is more apt to this historical period of electronic postmodernism. Frame, by itself, has a static ring to it; screen, while better, connotes a planar surface which is meant to have moving images written upon it. Even my personal trope of (my)nfield works here, as might Freud's "magical writing pad," and Lacan's own image-screen as another formulation. Lacan has used stain as well, which seems contradictory when he describes it as being "opaque." Then there is the Derridean list of metaphors, like hymen which seems to function like a "membrane." Frame and membrane, as words that exist in the vernacular; they carry the sense of this "slash" to me. The "slash" (rather than "bar" of no entry) has the advantage of considering an initial alienation from language of the split subject, i.e., the "hymen" is ruptured at some moment of genital maturation. Men have been in possession of the inscription tools that have written woman as lacking in the Freudian sense of a specular logic. Women are "missing" something that men have. Castration as an anatomical referent to the penis is violent. It means metaphorically bestowing on the woman her disabilities compared to a man. Lacan shifts the ground in saying that no One possesses the phallus as gaze. He "extends castration to the male as well as the female" (Silverman, p155). In effect, what is needed is not only just one word for frame, but many. Here, i will stay mostly with a morphing frame.

It is in the "frame" of the picture, pejoratively put —"how one is framed," or, in Silverman's terms (1994), how one is "screened," that the transitional space of culture also enters "into the picture," and Vermeer's identity becomes constituted. The morphing frame is historically and socially moving, formed by the technologies of how we represent ourselves to ourselves. Donald Lowe (1982) has described these shifts from the oral-aural, chirographic, and typographic to the current electric-cum-electronic frames of postmodernity which have dramatically incorporated and surpassed the typographical frames of print. Silverman argues much the same: the logic of the camera apparatuses in all their guises, which form the western systems of representation, create a certain standardization or "mimicry" as we become framed by these technologies into *idealized binaries*. It might be hypothesized that this "framing" or "screening" happens at the "ideal level" in our electronic world, epitomized by virtual reality and the reduction of everything to a designed *simulacrum*, i.e., the impulse towards perfection in body and mind of an individualized narcissism. On another level, however, Silverman evokes a second notion of mimicry from Lacan which is much more resistant and manipulative. Here she refers to the ability of being able to play with masks, disguises, masquerades, that "exaggerate and/or denaturalize the image/screen" (p.149). If i go back to Velázquez for a moment, Velázquez knows the framing power of royalty—the way he is "screened" or "framed" by them. They represent the power of the transcendent gaze; they have this power of the *noblesse oblige* which comes from God. They possess the gaze in the guise of their spectacular look. All the props of clothing, ceremony, manners (i.e., Bourdieu's *habitas*) point to the power as their gaze. But they cannot totally possess this gaze. So Velázquez has to play with that frame. He has to include them "in the picture" and himself as well. Goya played with similar artistic "stunts" by representing royalty in a less than an idealized way, often making their portraits look ridiculous. In the basement of the Prado in Madrid were found many drawings of animal heads, especially asses, which had been superimposed on the portraits of Spanish royalty, especially King Charles IV and his wife Maria

Luisa. Such resistant moves, and there are many of them, are forms of protection; a way to distance the "subjected" subject (the I) and the "self" (i), as the literature in cultural studies has begun to unravel through the writings of Fiske's (1989,a,b) utilization of Michel de Certeau's (1984) conceptualizations of tactics.

The frame is therefore the mediated *relationship* between the gaze and the look, historically conditioned through the discursive apparatuses of representation (oral-aural, chirographic, typographical, electronic) which define what is seemingly "natural." The gaze might also be interpreted as the Big Other (Žižek 1991) in that it is a ubiquitous sense of power that we cannot totalize. Its bigger than us and no one person can control or own it—like the Lacanian phallus; although there are historical figures who are invested with its "presence" for purposes of both good and evil, i.e., if there is a Hitler, then there is a Christ. These figures seem enigmatic and mystical since they seem to rise "out of nowhere," as if they have become attuned to how the gaze, as "the presence of others as such," has defined them. They have, somehow, amassed this presence to themselves so when they are "experienced" by others, they appear as being larger than life—even "holy," in the earlier sense of its meaning of accumulating an "aura." It becomes possible to continue this line of arguement, which can dangerously lead to a Biblical reenactment of the grand narrative, or to the Great Man theory of History, or perhaps even to some bizarre conclusion that Michael Jackson, who is out to "save" the children of the world through the auspices of Pepsi Cola, is the re-figuration of the "early" Jesus! However, if the gaze rests on the side of objects and the Real, then some figures do seem "larger than life"; it seems that some people, "as objects" in the Real, do "strike us," and can be experienced in a powerful way through our Imaginary within our lived symbolic order. How else to explain the mass hysteria that followed the Beatles? They possessed the power of the gaze for many people.

If i continue this track of thinking, the power of this gaze changes historically, taking on different forms and differentiations. It is possible to identify instances of its materialization by identifying the possessors of the look who frame the world through means of the logic of the communicational apparatuses. In other words, the *frame*—as the conflated relationship of the gaze (ubiquitous power)—and the look (as an identifiable human being) has "real effects"; it is a real material and psychic force of a specific institutional sight/site/cite. It sculpts and contorts the body. So, historically one might say priestesses, priests, royalty, the bourgeois, colonialists, the current technocrats, are instances of the gazed appropriations of a transcendent position which comes at us through looks. They control the logic of discourse (or frames) in order to subject us into mimicking a particular way of being, of disciplining our bodies. It should be noted, as does Silverman, the appropriation of this gaze-look relationship, as i have been formulating it, can be spectacularly visible and central—as in the case of royalty; or it can be non-visible as in the case of the bourgeoisie who displaced spectacular visibility onto the site/sight/cite of women as they, the captains of industry, dawned the *habit noire* of the business suit.(Today, in a postmodern world, men are trying to reinstate their neglected spectacularity by the formation of the New Man of the advertising industry and his spectacular image on MTV.)

These frames are then the ideological apparatuses that write our bodies. The contestations over power, in my view, must happen at a number of levels. At the cosmological level, the gaze is the contested form of power. Replacing a male God with a Goddess *does* change the relationship between the Imagination and the Symbolic Order in terms of the frames that would structure culture, albeit in an inverted form. Identifying a whole other level of heroines who have drawn their strength from other sources than male, is a form of resistance, de-framing and de-doxifying. Contesting power at the level of the look—not the Big Other, but the Other—provides other forms of resistance, i.e., masquerades, masks, parodies. In other words, both *Woman* (as a figure that challenges the Big Other or Big Bang—the all ubiquitous Gaze) is needed as well as *woman* (contested at the level of the look, as lack, as heterosexual, as white, as educated, as....). This double de-framing of the screen, from the ontological ahistorical and the ontic or historical position, would form a much-need critical art education. The agency of resistance, framing rather than being framed, has been discussed throughout Žižek's writings as an anamorphic look: a metacomment that displaces the idealized binary of the frame. The most prevalent vernacular practice of this is by political cartoonists who are able to capture the blind side of politicians and issues, and shift the frame. Obviously the political cartoon is "not enough," but with enough frames being jostled by the interface of the Imaginary with the Symbolic on many levels, change does come.

It may be that these frames organize identity much the way Laclau and Mouffe (1985) have theorized the "nodal point," which brings together scattered signs into some sort of gestalt. If the self can only be defined in relation to others to confirm it, then it exists as an entity in sameness and difference formed in culture. Others are introjected, and that requires an ability to "step out" of yourself to see who you are; however that stepping out is never alone, by the individual self: you drag with you the absent others that have helped form that identity, i.e., your mother, the father's voice, etc.—royalty in Velázquez' case. The gaze, then, is really "absent" in this regard. It exists outside your own looking. Vermeer, as his own object, standing *with* and *amongst* the gaze of others, is now imagining himself painting during the time that he was actually painting himself. The labyrinthine corridors of this last sentence provide a sense of the trace of images that must somehow oscillate back and forth, and around, to finally settle down, as it were, at a given time, to provide a sense of identity, which remains stable only for a given period until another significant figure is introjected. Identity is then once more sent into flux through the rebounding, reshuffling, or redintegration of images (phantasms) as the new phantasm is accommodated. It is that moment when an object "looks back at you"; catches your eye—your look; transports you over to it. You are *summoned* by its gaze as it sees you, but you don't see it. This is your perceptual blind spot. By summoned, i want to say that this is a "happen-stance" event, and that the object can be a person as well. It happens only in a moment, in a blink of an eye, in the glitter of a "presence" that "peeps" back at you. (Earlier, i referred to this phenomenon as "spiritual materialism." Perhaps this what has been called a "calling".)

So in the Lacanian paradigm my look can never close the gap and see the Real. No matter how much the I extends *his* mechanical eye and searches for the sub-atomic particles that are the substance of the "real," as the new physics tells us, the quarks blink in and out of "reality"—like Bentov's (1977) pendulum. Some particles are never "seen": their traces can not be found after a cyclotronic explosion. Perhaps such quirks and quarks can only *touch* us in other ways of knowing that the Enlightenment paradigm can not imagine, and that touching is most sensitive only in the *dark*, with our eyes closed. Such theorizations are probably in the direction of deconstructing Lacan, whose gaze is a point of light. Perhaps on another occasion the I must go back to Irigaray and discover her "touch" (?) in the hopes that she is not simply presenting an inversion—which the I believed to be the case. But after this long important discussion, it is time to go back to Silverman and her extraordinary analysis of Fassbinder in relation to this Lacanian paradigm.

"What happens with Fassbinder's cinema is that both the gaze and the images which promote identity remain irreducibly exterior, stubbornly removed from the subject who depends upon them for its experience of 'self' (p. 127)—a sort of fragmented Vermeer, if you can imagine; not able to affirm his identity painting himself. There is no one to confirm Vermeer as to who he is. No one to look back. Vermeer teeter-totters as a "nobody" who wants to be a "somebody," but can't. Vermeer desperately looks to be seen by others, like an exhibitionist who seeks a perfect confirmation of his desire in the imagined desire of the other, but fails. No one cares to look. The gaze, which is dispersed through the absent others, is wanting and wanted, but there is no one to "click" his picture.[23]

Silverman points out that in Fassbinder's cinema no character, male or female, "is ever represented as possessing the gaze" (p.129); or, to continue with my trope, occupying Vermeer's place as an object outside the canvas. Vermeer is, however, allowed to have a "look"; in other words, Vermeer is allowed to be in the canvas *only painting*, but not seeing himself painting. The look props up the gaze in this sense: it supports it. The look and the gaze are not the same. Whereas metaphorically the gaze exists in exteriority as the absent others that confirm Vermeer *and includes* Vermeer's projected Imaginary of himself amongst their presence (in their absence)—the look is internal— it is Vermeer at his own geometrical viewing point, only painting his canvas within his picture. What can happen, however, is Vermeer can think that his look is all-powerful, and covet the gaze so to speak, to "aspire to the transcendental status" as a voyeur. The voyeur finds all his desire in his own looking, afraid to accept the Symbolic Order's dictum that it is not found there. The male voyeur thinks he possesses the gaze. You have now arrived at Mulvey's door step. The voyeur, however, can be disturbed, "caught looking" at the keyhole (that geometrical point), and made guilty. So whereas the gaze remains outside desire, the look participates fully in it. Silverman bringing Mulvey and Lacan together says "[if] the gaze always exceeds the look, the look might be said to exceed the gaze—to carry a libidinal supplement which relegates it, in turn, to scopic subordination" (p.130).

A lot has been made out of this "peephole effect." On first reading, it seems that the perceptual apparatus that is being applied here is rather common; the "tunnel-vision" experienced by anyone who is looking through the surveillance optics of a microscope, telescope, binoculars, that surround the eye with a characteristic tunnel which cuts off peripheral vision. Scopic perception can be easily startled because of the intensity of the focus, and because perception is funneled to one point. A similar effect is given over to placing *one* eye into the viewing position of a camera. Peripheral vision is cut down significantly, but not entirely eliminated. The old portrait cameras, where a photographer would be covered with a black shroud, represent one end of the scale where peripheral vision would be eliminated. The waist viewfinder of large-format cameras represent the other end of the spectrum. Both eyes are open as you look down to manipulate the framing of your object. Depending on the degree of concentration and focus (how fascinated are you with what you see), and the amount of peripheral vision available, you can be disturbed in a variety of ways: tapped on the shoulder unexpectedly if you under a shroud; catch someone's glance peripherally who is looking at you; or you might be startled when all of a sudden, that which you are spying spies back at you; it's got your "number" so to speak; or even something may dart up to or by the lens of your artificial eye (an experience one has scuba diving where a mask also blocks out peripheral vision). But Lacan talks of a disturbance "unseen." You get this creepy feeling that someone is watching you and you don't know where it is coming from. So where *is* it coming from? One possible answer is from objects that look at you from where you don't see them. You are "caught by them." So if the woman looks back at the voyeur at the peep-hole, it's as though she possesses the gaze of the object as a subject. It's not the "look" of the woman staring back; it seems as though there is a harnessing of the gaze as proposed earlier.[24]

Given the way i have tried to write my own account of the XI seminar with Silverman, Vermeer, Velázquez as my props, it seems that Silverman's account of Fassbinder, a gay man and an excessive individual who died from those very excesses of drugs and alcohol, presents a cinema where there has been a refusal of the phallus and of the gaze. One might say his focus was on nobodies. Fassbinder's males acknowledge their lack rather than denying it. As Silverman says, "Fassbinder's cinema might almost be said to model itself on Holbein's *The Ambassadors*, with its anamorphosic death's head—to seek to induce in the viewer a recognition of him or herself as 'annihilated in the form ... of castration'" (p.154). It should be recalled that Holbein's painting that Lacan discusses in this seminar, is a metacommentary "on the disappearance of the viewing subject at the perspectival vanishing point. "It [anamorphic skull] reflects our own nothingness, in the figure of the death's head" (Lacan, in Silverman, 147). Insofar as Fassbinder's cinema speaks to this, Silverman goes as far to equate the "look" of his male characters with "lack." "His films oblige look to acknowledge itself not only as carrier of libido, but as a signifier of castration. They refuse to cover over the void which is at the core of subjectivity, a void which gives rise not only to anxiety, but to desire" (p.130). Fassbinder always points at a character's mirror reflection rather than the character him or herself; shots are compulsively through windows—as if the characters reexperience their mirror stage; his focus is always upon figures who are erotically, economically, and/or racially marginal. He obsessively de-phallicizes and at times de-idealizes the male body as limp, mutilated, amputated, tortured and crucified. In some sense Fassbinder's cinema is a remark on both human frailty and strength. It acknowledges lack as both a necessity and a deficiency, as both a strength and a weakness, for only in the failure to know can we know.

The Perverted Gaze of the Possessed Eye/I

In popular culture, it is perhaps the genre of the occult film *(occultus,* L. that which is hidden, past participle of *occulere,* " to conceal") that the summoning of the gaze is given its most obvious and purest expression as *possession.* The possessed being is the gaze personified and it turns out to be a purely Evil Thing. But why Evil and not Good? In a painting like Breugel's *Garden of Earthly Delights,* evil was fully exposed and visible, but dispersed and diversified over any number of deeds and acts. With modernism, however, the possibility of *ethical radical evil,* or "diabolical evil," emerged, which was to rethink the entire relationship between them. Žižek (1993b:95-101) develops the thesis that this "ethical radical evil" could not fully be articulated by Kant. It seemed to contradict Kant's reasoned argument that there was an *a priori* character for the propensity of Evil, but that the experience of moral Law, i.e., feeling morally responsible for my evil, was proof positive that there was a counterforce present that tended towards the Good. But *ethical radical evil* meant that the person did not repent for the evil act, but was willing to choose suicide; the act had been done on the grounds of Evil *as a principle.* This was what made it "ethical." (A popular version of this would be D-FENDS (Michael Douglas) in the film *Falling Down,* who at the film's end realizes what he has done but does not repent. Rather he makes a gesture to pull a gun knowing full well he will be shot and killed. The image, for the audience, of a pathological killer all of a sudden takes on a new meaning. D-FENDS' evil "makes place" for the good.) Something existed in humans which gave preference to a pathological leaning over a tendency to follow the moral Law. To be "human," then, was to *"always-already have chosen Evil"* (p.98). Žižek concludes from his discussion that Evil ontologically precedes Good in order to make Good possible. The "original" choice is not between Good and Evil, but between submitting to this pathology or choosing ethical radical evil, i.e., terminating your life willingly. For Žižek this explains Kierkegaard's epithet: Evil is Good itself "in the mode of becoming" to a "mode of being." In other words, the left glove is really the right glove; all you need to do is pull it inside out.

In a possession film the horror of the Thing, of radical Evil, of the trauma of life itself, is personified as a possessed devil, e.g., twelve-year-old Reagan in *The Exorcist,* (William Friedkin, 1973) who has supernatural powers and supernatural strength; or she is a "witch" like Carrie *(Carrie,* Brian de Palma, 1976) who has telekinetic powers and can make things move (or "swerve"); while vampires and werewolves can "shape shift," not only into bats and wolves, but now, thanks to computerized digital technology, they can *morph* "virtually" into any object they wish. Zombies, on the other hand, belong to the lowest rung of those possessed. They represent the complete lack of will, mere body "soldiers" capable only of "blind" destruction. They have no *eye*, being either mummified, bandaged, or stare blankly into space. The gaze of the possessed is "literalized," as a materialized abstraction through their eyes: cat's eyes, animal eyes, and "special effect" contact lenses are the most common. The voice is "disembodied." It speaks from the depths, not attributable to any subject, the voice of the Thing itself. The body makes sounds that seem alien to it. The possession is literalized as well. It is passed on by invading the body, i.e., biting the exposed neck (the vampire mode), attaching itself onto or into a body part or cocooning the entire body (the alien invasion mode), drinking ancient fluids or inhaling sacred vapors (witchcraft mode), sticking pins into dolls (voodoo mode) and even vomiting into the mouths of others (devil mode).

As Clover (1992) so ably *demon*strates, it should come as no surprise that the woman, ever since Eve in the Garden, acts as the "portal" for the devil to emerge. The vagina, the black hole of male fantasy, is often explicitly the supernatural port of entry, either literally or through impregnation by the Thing itself. "The world *vulva* itself related to *valve*—gate or entry to the body—and so it regularly serves for all manner of spirits, but the unclean one above all, in occult horror" (Clover, 1992:76). The woman's body is, therefore, the *site* of abjection in these occult films; holes, orifices are penetrated, invaded and colonized. But why? One way of answering this is to argue that the devil is personified as a woman in order for the patriarchal male to face his perverse radically evil nature. In this case what seems to be happening, as Clover argues, is the exchange of "Evil becoming Good" is operating on women's bodies in order for the "new man" to emerge while the "old" *macho* male is buried. The left glove (male) becomes the right glove (female) through the feint of "one-sex" experience (cf. Thomas Laqueur): "women are but men turned outside in" (p.111). Clover makes the point that the occult horror, as a male narrative, presents the split of two competing systems of explanation where White Science (in all its metaphorical associations) does battle with Black Magic (again with all its metaphorical associations) as the feminized Other. The narrative ends with the male protagonist accepting the reality of the irrational as that which is unexplainable, unobservable, and unquantifiable. It is this *interiority*, as all that which is hidden from sight (the occult), that becomes attributable to him as *his* feminine mirror. This is what "opens" him up, and makes him a kinder and gentler human being. In contrast, the women protagonists are physically degraded by the possession, always "opened up" a few more degrees than the male to excessive monstrous proportions in order to make his feminization appear plausible. By comparison, their transformation is towards evil and simple restoration. It is the male protagonist who undergoes a spiritual rebirth by becoming feminized; a clear case where the phrase "men *in* feminism" fits both literally and figuratively in its theft of the women's "insides." In Clover's view, then, there has been little movement from literally burning women as witches in the middle ages to the screened version of "burning" them in an occult movie today.

There is yet another way of reading the occult narrative: from the standpoint of a masculine sublime view of nature—as the uncontrollable feminine (see pretext to the title). The sublime chaos of nature that cannot be regulated, which has no law, and enjoys its destruction with blindness, i.e., as in hurricanes, volcanoes, tornadoes, floods, and other "natural" disasters, is thus evil personified in nature as pure and utter obscene enjoyment. This perverse side of nature is feminized in patriarchy as that which requires battle. This is the archaic Mother, or the maternal superego, whose rage needs to be stopped. In the struggle against such impossible odds, the male feels both triumphant and yet humbled by the experience. In occult films the chaos of nature is literalized by "cold draughts," gusts of wind, and blinding lights. Often it is made present as The Thing, or The Fog, the plague in Oedipus's Thebes, or Hitchcock's film *The Birds*. Here the "new man" is given some reprieve within a Lacanian reading when the family disorder of the '70s and mid '80s, the time many of these occult films were produced, left an absent father with no paternal function to instill the law. The deficiency of the paternal ego-ideal "makes the law 'regress' toward a ferocious maternal superego, affecting sexual enjoyment—the decisive trait of the libidinal structure of 'pathological narcissism'" (see Žižek, 1991:99). For Žižek the "new man" is a "pathological narcissist" (p.103) ruled by the "maternal superego." The so called "old" or macho male was the heteronomous "organizational (bureaucratic) man" who had supplanted the "autonomous" individual of the Protestant ethic. The assumption is made that the quality of care by the mother during this time was inadequate. She was a "possessive" mother. The child's aggression towards his mother was fantasized as one of being devoured or s(mothered) (i.e., *vagina dentata*). These occult films mask the family conflict during this time. They are mere pretexts for what was amiss in the symbolic order itself. This is true for the girl's story as well. Carrie has to deal with her dominating mother. In *The Fury* (Brian de Palma, 1978) the adolescent girl Gillian, who becomes possessed, is angry at her divorced mother. In virtually all cases it is the mother (as the maternal superego) who understands the supernatural. These narratives end, as Clover indicates, with a restoration of the family through marriage because the male has undergone a transformation. This would be one explanation for the narcissism of the "new man" and the sheer number of occult films produced and consumed during this time.

It is perhaps the figure of a woman transformed into a devil, a whole further step from her role as the *femme fatal*, which strikes out at the male psyche, invoking its worst nightmares."[T]he demon is a liar but always mixes lies with truth," says Father Karras in *The Exorcist* (Clover, p.92). Asshole, opening, portal—orifices in general have to do with the anal phase, and where there is Satan, Sade is sure to follow for the devil is the perfect pervert. The "pervert's ultimate fantasy," writes Žižek (1993b), "is to be a perfect servant of his other's (partner's) fantasies, to offer himself as an instrument of the other's Will-to-Enjoy" (p.71). The *Faustian* pact is made to have everything you ever desired; in other words, to become like the devil yourself. The devil (Malifeitor) is free from doubt. He knows perfectly well what he is doing and what the Other wants from him. In this sense he escapes being a subject insofar as there is no uncertainty, no anxiety in what the Other thinks he is. The Other knows he is the devil who can "open up" the kernel of the male fantasy and tempt, that is seduce, his host into becoming perverse as well-ceding to one's desires. "The entire difference between the pervert [i.e., the devil] and the analyst hinges in a certain invisible limit, on a certain 'nothing' that separates them..." (p.72), says Žižek. The devil confirms or *tempts* the host's fantasies while the analyst *at*tempts to bring the analysand to transference so as to gain a distance away from them. The devil is a devourer of souls, the very kernel of men's fantasies. He is the all-seeing "Supreme Evil Being." He haunts Father Karras's fear of being a homosexual. Karras commits an act of "ethical radical evil" by committing suicide when the devil enters him, thereby acknowledging his own pathology. The opposite solution to an evil ethics of desire is offered in *Witchboard* (Kevin S. Tenney, 1987). Malifeitor haunts Jim's narcissism, his alcoholism, his lack of feeling for anyone. Jim has to shatter the Ouija board, and thereby no longer yields to his enjoyment (*jouissance*); he has to make compromises with others. The devil, as pervert, therefore, finds pleasure not in pursuing his own activity, but in the pleasure of his victims yielding to their fantasy (through the call of a Ouija board, for instance), and the enjoyment in seeing them "open up."

One way to explain the fear of the devil and why he has to be dressed in drag, is to "summon up" Lacan's anal phase. It is my contention that these "pathologically narcissistic" men and women in occult films are caught up in the anal phase; passing into the "phallic" stage ends the narrative. The anal stage is defined "by the adaptation of the subject's desire to the demand of the Other. ... [T]he subject (child) can only satisfy his need on condition that he thereby complies with the Other's demand. ... [P]leasure is 'barred,' prohibited, in its immediacy, ... [I]t is permitted only in the function of complying to the Other's demand" (Žižek, p.72). The anal phase is therefore marked by an obssesive, compulsive attitude; by masochism and being "open" to the other's demand. This is precisely what the devil demands and temps. But the male protagonist, who like the small child, eventually refuses to shit in the proper place and eat up all his food. To defeat the devil for the boy, now to be read as the maternal superego in these occult films, is to enter the phallic phase which means disengaging from the enslavement to the *demand* of the Other. In brief, overcoming an identification with the mother.

For the girl's story, the possession by the devil is reversed. The devil is the paternal superego, the father of enjoyment who incestuously rapes his daughter and impregnates her through the possession. Here the girl's fantasy of perversion is lived out in horror once she yields to her own incestuous desires: the *father alone loves me*. The devil acquires his initial status as an "object-instrument" of her *jouissance*, i.e., her wish-fulfillment to have a child with her father, her rebellion against her mother and authority in general. By then it is too late. She is caught. But is she? Freud's general account reads that the fantasy of being beaten by the father as a punishment for such an incestuous fantasy is repressed and acts as a substitute for the forbidden genital relation. The original incestuous fantasy also undergoes regression into an anal-sadistic libidinal economy which still satisfies sexual love. Enter the devil to undo all these repressions. Her possession is her punishment for having yielded, ceded to her desire made possible by his cunning and seductive ways. In the occult narrative this has either already taken place, or happens quickly enough at the start. The devil, as the father of enjoyment in the girl's case, is her *sinthome*. His is a constant demand, a temptation she must forever face. In an occult film her body is placed in the uncanny space of "between the two deaths" as she undergoes the Sadean torture of having yielded masochistically to this demand. However, there is pleasure in her pain, for the girl is also subverting the Law. A pact with the devil has been made through the time of her perverted possession up until the time she is released (the narrative's end). She submits to the contract with the phallic father and refuses the symbolic mother, knowing that the game is over when the devil will be exorcised from her body by the Law of the father (the male protagonist). In other words, this is the story of the "new woman" as much as the occult is the story of the "new man." Read this way, her possession is a form of resistance; romantic of course, with the devil playing the cold, distant unlovable Thing while her vomit is that of a bulimic. No wonder her narrative "is an ABA story [B is the possession] of restoration in which she emerges unaware what has transpired" (Clover, p.98). It is the pattern of a bulimic. Rather than the refusal to shit in the proper place, she vomits up the mother's nurishment, rejecting the s(mother) of the breast: her oral stage to his anal one. It also helps to explain occult practices of many teenage girls and the fantasy of being witches. The pact with the devil is a way to cope with the "no" of the father and the perverse order of society which *demands* her to be perfect and slim. The syllogistic structure, or "dual focus" (p.70) of the occult narrative that Clover mentions, bears out the above analysis. The woman's story, as it is montaged with the man's story, is analogous to the "anal" stage montage or "parallel montage" which alternates two interconnected courses of action shown coexisting *horizontally* with a tension between them (see Žižek, 1991:89). A "phallic" or *vertical* moment happens at the narrative's end when the girl accepts the new "reformed" man who has now entered "manhood" to her liking (and often her mother's liking). The *demand* is over and the torture stops.

The Male Gaze: Alive and Well, But Living in Horror

In summary, then, it was once thought that the cinematic gaze belonged entirely to the male, with men simply lustful desiring "machines." This assumption was summarized by E. Ann Kaplan (1983) in the following way: "within the film text itself, men gaze at women, who become objects of the gaze; the spectator, in turn, is made to identify with this male gaze, and to objectify the woman on the screen; and the camera's original 'gaze' comes into play in the very act of filming" (p.15). The above discussion has tried to put that view to doubt, or at the very least complicated its core hypothesis. However, no feminist would deny that we no longer live in a phallogocentric order where male gaze has been mitigated to such an extent that its effects are not felt on their bodies. i would like to further the complications of the male gaze by commenting on the very interesting hypothesis developed by Carol Clover (1987,1992) in her study of slasher films from the '70s to the mid '80s. As developed in the above section, the occult horror is a response to the "trouble" going on in the Oedipal household. What makes her hypothesis so interesting in the context of the discussion here is that "the typical patrons of these films are the sons [and daughters] of marriages contracted in the sixties or even early seventies," a time characterized by "the women's movement, the entry of women into the workplace, and the rise of divorce and woman-headed families" which "would yield *massive gender confusion* in the next generation" (p.62, my italic). This "gender confusion" echoes the same "gender confusion" during the turn of the century, and the hypothesis Clover puts forward repeats some of the issues already raised with the Surrealist movement and the controversy surrounding their sadism. In other words, the slasher genre might be another sight/cite/site for the male gaze in disguise, hiding behind the cloak of feminist liberalism since it appears that a new "female victim-hero" has appeared on the scene/seen.

Clover raises the question why is there such a large male audience, most of whom are adolescent males, who identify with this female victim-hero, or the "final girl" in these slasher horrors? The Final Girl is the last one left standing at the narrative's end after having defeated, killed, or sent the killer back to "hell," but only after the killer has left a long trail of bodies and she has done a long arduous battle with him.[25] As she argues, it is doubtful that the male audience identifies with the "good" male characters. They are usually boyfriends or schoolmates of the girls who are marginal, underdeveloped characters that are dispatched with quickly. The would-be rescuers, i.e., policemen, fathers, sheriffs, are usually presented as incompetent or incapable of stopping the killer. Often they are dispatched quickly as well. The killer himself is often unseen or barely glimpsed in the beginning of the narrative. When he does make an appearance, he is ugly, fat, masked, deformed, or dressed as a woman, or sometimes *is* a woman (e.g., *Friday 13th, pt. 1*). The killer is himself eventually killed or dispatched as well from the narrative to live again in another sequel. It is the Final Girl who lives to tell the tale. All this conclusively suggests that identification rests on the Final Girl; the diegesis rarely varies.

Clover's thesis is that slasher films play out a male fantasy despite the appearance that the hero is a young woman. Despite this, she has little to say about the way girls in the audience experience these slasher films. Rather, she proceeds to argue that these films specifically engage in forms of "cross dressing" and games of gender-identity in order to make possible the disavowal of the fantasy, "a boy is being beaten by his father" (p.51-52). To recall, this is the fantasy that boys suppress and interpret as, "I am loved by my father." However, to avoid the homosexual implications of male love, heterosexual boys displace this entire fantasy as, "*I am being beaten by my mother.*" Sadomasochistic incest fantasies and castration anxieties, the taboo subjects of male adolescence, are explored in relative safety through the femaleness of the victim. The Final Girl is always "boyish." She is set apart from her more "feminine" friends. She is sexually reluctant, can look death in the face, is resourceful, intelligent, clever, while her name signals her "masculine attributes": Marti, Terri, Laurie, Stretch, Will, Joey, Max, or as a surname like Ripley in *Aliens*. Such gender displacements, claims Clover, are obvious in these films where the Final Girl is really a girl in boy's drag, a "congenial double for the adolescent male," while the killer is really a woman in men's drag—the phallic mother. On rare occassions, like *Friday the 13th.*, the killer is the mother. The killers are not only, upon occasion, dressed in drag as transvestites and transsexuals,(e.g., Norman Bates in *Psycho* was an earlier forerunner), but are virginal and sexually inert. Their masculinity is severely hampered. Rape, as Clover points out, is not normally part of the stalker genre. The defeat of the killer for the male audience might now be interpreted as the castration of the phallic mother.

Through her paradigmatic example, the film *Peeping Tom* (Michael Powell, 1960),[26] Clover attempts to vindicate her Final Girl hypothesis psychoanalytically, by developing the very "blind spot" in Mulvey's theory: the masochistic potential of fetishistic scopophilia. Clover identifies two gazes which both belong to the psychotic killer Mark, the protagonist of the story, and by extension, coexist in the cinematic spectator of horror films. The first is the sadistic phallic gaze, or the predatory "assaultive gaze" through the lens of Mark's movie camera, which, in this case, literally kills. The second is the "reactive gaze" which takes place after the event; that is, when Mark and the audience are gazing at these same images as they are being projected on a movie screen, i.e., these images alternate from being projected by Mark on a screen in his home-studio to covering the entire screen in an actual movie house. What distinguishes the difference between the "assaultive" and "reactive" gaze is only the presence or absence of the cine-camera cross-hairs on the image. Metaphorically, one might say that the cross-hairs form the "cut" of castration as marking the specific difference which divides the cinematic apparatus into masculine sadistic work of the film director on one side, and the masochistic feminine stake of the spectator on the other. This then is the sadomasochistic pact of horror according to Clover. Mark places himself in the role of a masochist, as a spectator of the very terror he himself films in order to be assaulted by it. Why? Having suffered a childhood where his father, a prominent scientist who was studying the effects of fear, terrorized and induced fear in him through constant surveillance, i.e., by training a camera on him day and night; waking him up at night with a flashlight; making him view his mother's corpse, and so on. Clover reasons that Mark experienced a perverse pleasure in the sight of pain that he had inflicted on others because he could then identify with their suffering. The pervert, it should be recalled, wants to be the object that insures the *jouissance* of the other. Such masochistic enjoyment of the horrified gaze of his victims was a surrogate for his own terrified face in the past which he could never see. "Inside every Peeping Tom is a peeped-at child, trying incessantly to master his pain by re-viewing it in the person of another," she writes (p.175-176). Clover's defence then might be stated in the following way: Mark is split into masculine and feminine halves which, theoretically, can never be joined or overcome. Every filmed-killing and retroactive looking merely begets another round of the same, a repetition. On the one hand, Mark is a sadistic voyeur, and on the other hand, a castrated male. The only way to stop his rampage is for him to eventually die, which he does by committing suicide with the use of his own "magical camera." The voice-over of a frightened boy saying, "Goodnight Daddy—hold my hand" is heard as the screen turns to black. The logic would have it that Mark disavows his father's sadism ("I am being beaten by my father"), but the price is his own victimization. "[T]the pleasure of looking at others in fear and pain has its origins in one's own past-but-not-finished fear and pain" (p.230).

Like the Surrealists, who were wrongly accused for their sadism by Gubar et al, the horror genre, Clover would argue, has suffered from much the same misunderstandings. *Peeping Tom* is a "literal" metastatement on the cinematic pact of sadomasochism that the audience makes with the director of horror: to be "scared to death," i.e., the fear of castration. The fear-mirror that is attached to Mark's camera which records the face of the terrified victims as they die, acts as a *mise en abyme* devise. There is more reflected in it than the face of horror. It makes explicit the alignment of the audience with screen victims in general, and it sets up in advance the eventual fate of the protagonist who sees his or her own fate in those who have been killed in the line ahead of him or her. It also heightens the effect of imagining oneself to be the "next victim." In the case of *Peeping Tom*, the protagonist Mark, doubling both as killer and victim, knows full well what awaits him at the end each time he "gazes" into the fear-mirror. For a brief moment then, this *mise en abyme* devise short-circuits the diegesis and addresses the spectator directly in the second person as "you"—in acknowledging the bargain of facing your own terror.

To sum up, just like Magritte's *Le Viol*, and Ernst's *The Blessed Virgin Chastising the Infant Jesus Before Three Witnesses*, the horror genre reenacts, time and time again, *the failure of the male look to possess the gaze.* Recall, the aim of the pervert is to make the look and the gaze coincide (Adams, 1994). The male members of the audience experience this defeat in every slasher and rape-revenge horror they see. Their look fails to capture the gaze. They experience the pain/pleasure of a rape fantasy, or the defeat of a psychopathic killer by identifying with the woman victim-hero, thereby disavowing their own capacity to commit such acts of atrocity; yet, at the same time, recognize that they too might be capable of such acts of horror. By inviting the mother (ersatz the male killer in feminine drag) to beat or dominate them (ersatz the girl in boy's drag, the revengeful woman), they can then fantasize themselves in a "feminine masochistic" position, thereby repressing the father's beating fantasy as well as the homosexual implications of his love that comes with that repression. The satisfaction of the pleasure in the pain usually comes during the "late" middle of the narrative (p.222) when the tension is at its greatest, and the audience body is most engaged in the contradictions of what needs to be resolved: that the killer be laid to rest so that "it" (perhaps) may live again for yet another episode.

The horror film genre, just like the occult horror genre with its victim female-hero, in this regard, can be interpreted as instilling the "name of the father," (his "no") during a time when the conventional patriarchal family was breaking down and sons were in the flux of gender identification from '70s to the mid '80s. Single-parent families with the father absent and the mother raising the children meant a time of gender uncertainty, not unlike the uncertainty already mentioned during the *fin de siècle*. The question of incest and sexual abuse continues to remain highly visible on the postmodern sexual landscape as the family continues to change and feminisms continue to assert their claims. For the Name-of-the-Father to function it is not necessary that an actual father be present, but that the mother's relation to the symbolic Father limits the maternal desire. The anxieties of the possible rule of the maternal superego have already been discussed. According to Lacanian psychoanalysis the moral order is established "because we recoil before the violence and obscenity of the superego's incitement to *jouissance*, to boundless and aggressive enjoyment" (Copjec, 1989:78). It is the "father of enjoyment," the primordial father of Freud's *Totem and Taboo* who has to be "ritually" killed if the moral law, through the Oedipal father, is to establish itself at the level of the ego-ideal. However, this cruel and obscene father functions at the level of the superego which is *not* internalized as law. It does not regulate desire, rather it is enslaved to enjoyment and addiction. Perversion. The struggle is, therefore, between the father of enjoyment and the Oedipal father who bounds desire to the law; he puts a limit to it. The former is entirely perverse and sadistic, but paradoxically, the latter exercises his power on the grounds of this very sadism, i.e., he must deny the male child the very enjoyment of the primordial father. Perverse enjoyment must be foreclosed if the symbolic law is to be instilled in his son. The son has to be "beaten" and "loved" at the same time. He has to choose the side of desire and symbolic castration. In the Lacanian paradigm this means the choice of *objet petit a*; that is, the lack of the signifier for this enjoyment which remains forever deferred.

To understand the significance for the choice of *object petit a*, is to understand the difference between the choice of neurosis from psychosis; a key to understanding the horror genre and instilling the Name of the Father.

A slight detour is required here to explain the difference. A summary statement by Salecl (1994) is extremely useful for its succinctness:

> Every screen of reality includes a constitutive 'stain,' the trace of what had to be precluded from the field of reality in order that this field can acquire its consistency. This stain appears in the guise of a void Lacan names *object petit a*. It is the point that I, the subject, cannot see. It eludes me insofar as it is the point from which the screen itself 'returns the gaze', watches me; i.e., the point where the gaze itself is inscribed into the field of reality. The invisibility, the preclusion of this stain is what allows the rest of the field to make sense. In psychosis, however, *object a* is precisely *not precluded*. It materializes itself, it receives full bodily presence and becomes visible — for example, in the form of a pursuer who 'sees and knows everything' in paranoia (p. 106).

In my pretext section on Lacan's "Formulae of Sexuation," the masculine logic of the exception to the universal was explained. *Objet petit a* is that exception. It has *no signifier* and hence belongs to the Lacanian Real—beyond language—and hence has been variously called a void, a hole that makes a whole, a stain, a blot, a "piece of the Real," or "bit of reality." The logic of its effects, as far as i am able to understand them, acts like a Derridean supplement to the whole. A supplementary logic paradoxically posits a part that is both outside the system and inside it at the same time; yet it is this part that supplements the system, making it whole (universal, total). It stabilizes reality but does so at the level of the Imaginary. Without the supplement the system would not exist. The *objet petit a* acts like a supplement. The Lacanian version of this reads: "The field of reality rests upon the extraction of the object *a*, which nevertheless *frames it*" (my italic). This is graphically demonstrated by Jacques-Alain Miller (in Žižek, 1991:94). i present his explanation because of its accessibility in three figures, the last of which replicates Miller's own diagram.

Fig. 1 is simple a square which represents a field of vision, a screen. This is the level of the symbolic order, "normal" reality.

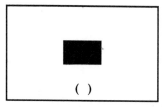

( )

Fig. 2 has now an inner box appearing it in which has been shaded. This represents the "stain" in our screen of vision. Underneath it is an open set of parenthesis indicating that this stain belongs to the Real. It is a signifier that cannot be named. In this sense "it does not exist."

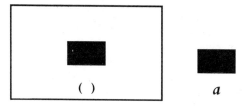

( )   *a*

Fig. 3 is then fig. 2 with the objet a removed outside the field of vision. It is from this point that the object gazes at me, which I cannot see. Fig. 2 should now be interpreted as having a gaping hole in it — an abyss. This is not a "negative space" in the traditional sense of perspective since it is "groundless" or "bottomless." Imagine the space around this hole or abyss as a "frame." It is here also that the effects of the *mise en abyme* show themselves. If the shaded hole or abyss is covered over by a mirror it paradoxically telescopes the viewer further away from the object of the look; as in Mark's case, the concave terror-mirror could never quite capture the "face" he was looking for, although he planned each murder to be his last. The "light" was somehow always wrong. On another level this abyss may be covered by an anamorphic projection which tries to capture the gaze of the object *a* that is outside the picture from an oblique perspective. Such was my suggestion for the mirror of the king and queen in Velázquez's *Las Meniñas*, and Lacan's constant reference to the anamorphic death skull of Holbein's *Ambassadors*. "Around it [illusion] one finds a sensitive spot, a lesion, a locus of pain, a point of reversal of the whole of history, insofar as it is the history of art and insofar as we are implicated in it; that point concerns the notion that the illusion of space is different from the creation of emptiness. It is this that the appearance of anamorphoses at the end of the sixteenth and the beginning of the seventeenth centuries represents. ... that is to transform it [illusionary space], to a certain extent, a work of art always involves encircling the Thing" (Lacan, 1992:140-141). The anamorphic projection might be interpreted as a devise that *deflects* the total brightness of the gaze which would blind the subject. It can temporarily insert a "wedge" between the look and the gaze, as when the camera pans to a glowing EXIT sign in the climatic sequence of *Texas Chain Saw Massacre II*, as Stretch (the Final Girl) is trying to find her way out of the underground labyrinth; or the sign nailed to the tree in the beginning of *The Silence of the Lambs*: HURT, AGONY, PAIN — LOVE IT. Both examples, as Clover says, act like a "naked disclosure of the cinematic signifier" (p.201). They momentarily shield the horror as your look changes perspective, becomes self-reflexive, placing you back in the theater, and the object of the gaze is suspended, or "drops."

The above diagrams belong to the world of neurosis, where the *objet a* is the object cause of desire, meaning that the subject is formed when it encounters the lack in the Other. The child comes to realize that the mother or the father is not all-knowing and not all-powerful. The *objet a* fills out that lack. In choosing desire the *objet petit a* is the very fantasmatic kernel of being, the "stuff of the I" or the blind spot of the eye. A psychotic response happens when there is no lack to be found in the Other, consequently there is no *objet petit a* and no fullness of being. Mark's father is an all-seeing and all-knowing Eye (Gaze/I) who prevents Mark's subjectivity from emerging. Mark's mother is absent. There was no place for him to hide which would help him conceal the gaze in his vision through the *objet a*. His impotence was a reaction to the surveillance techniques of his father. Enjoyment was impossible for him since there were no spaces (no gaps or holes in the Other) that weren't under control. It was through the killings that Mark hoped to escape the all-powerful gaze. His search was for that moment in the face of terror when the gaze, *as objet a*, would materialize in his victim. As Salecl explains, "The *objet a*, the paradoxical object/lack, is considered by the psychotic to be really present" (p.108). Through a murderous act the psychotic "tries to 'kill' the *objet a* in the Other (another person) in a desperate attempt at normalization." She or he hopes to remove the *objet a* as it has been materialized in the victim "by stabbing or otherwise blinding the victim's eyes." To recall a remark by Clover:

212

"Much of the art of horror lies in catching the spectatorial eye unaware — penetrating it before it has the chance to close its lid" (p.203). As a sublime object that is embodied in the victim, the psychotic killer tries to engulf it literally by eating parts of the victims. In *The Silence of the Lambs*, Hannibal Lecter's cannibalism could be said to *literally* represent his attempts at eating a "little bit of the real." He is, in Žižek's (1993b:48) account, an eater of souls as well, given that he asks for the kernel of Clarice Sterling's being: the crying of the lambs.

Horror films, especially the slasher genre, therefore, re-stage the primal story: the mythical killing of the father of enjoyment by his sons through a sadomasochistic scenario. The girls in the audience can partake in this very same fantasy as well since it is the Final Girl who stops the father of perversion. The psychopathic killer in these horror films is the father of enjoyment, the perverse and obscene psychotic killer (Freddie Kruger, Jason, Michael of *Halloween*, Leatherface, Terminator). He is the rapist or child abuser. The boy in the audience accepts his death, chooses the side of desire and is castrated. In this scenario, it is the Final Girl, or the revengeful woman, who stands in for the son with whom the boy identifies. Her fantasy is also satisfied as each of her rapists dies through her own sadistic act. Are these perverse *neurotic* fantasies, acts of sublimated violence, to be seen as a necessity grounding of moral law?[27] In horror, the figure of the psychotic killer "has been dead from the beginning," writes Žižek (1991:24), part of the "living dead." In choosing his own castration, by being frightened "to death," the boy accepts the fantasy of the primordial father as the possessor of lost enjoyment as embodied in the *objet petit a*. The oscillation back and forth across the "camera lens" so to speak, between the sadistic, voyeuristic masculine view and the masochistic, castrated feminine view, re-enacts the continual oscillation between *drive*[28] and *desire*; between the insistence of the father of enjoyment, his *demand* and the necessity of his ritual killing. In horror, this *drive* is the Thing, the killer, the pure evil which exists "between two deaths," neither alive nor dead, but which insists on a certain symbolic debt. To give evil its "proper burial" then, requires the choice of desire. In the end it could be said that the male gaze is alive and well, but perpetually living in horror.

1 Krauss has argued that Surrealist photographs "fetishize reality" by doing away with the "naturalness" of photographic objects through such techniques as solarization, rayography, negative printing, multiple exposures, photomontage, collage, and doubling. Fetishism is that perversion which substitutes a fabricated object for a natural one that is perceived to be missing. This is precisely what Surrealist photographs do, offering a challenge to "straight" photography. In her "Corpus Delicti," in *L'Amour Fou: Photography and Surrealism* (1985) published with Jane Livingston, Krauss develops the notion of Bataille's *informe* as a transgressive gesture of formlessness—throwing gender categories into flight, like Giacometti's Suspended Ball discussed in the "Pretexts to the Title."

2 This has already been developed in the "pretexts to the title." See the very interesting reading of

Choderlos des Laclos's novel, *Les Liaisons Dangereuses* (and the movie with the same title) by Alenka Zupančič (1994) who makes a brilliant application of Lacanian ethical theory to the vicissitudes of love as being "radically evil" (diabolical) in the 18th century. This novel may well have served as a template for Magritte's painting.

3 To be fair to Gubar, there is a body of literature which presents the case for surrealism's misogyny which "just happened" to come during this time of crisis. The comparison with today's pornographic growth industry is just too uncanny to be dismissed; hence i concur with her on this assessment. Kuenzli (1991:19) points out that the actual demands of French women for social emancipation in 1924 were dismissed as bourgeois by Surrealist men.

4 These terms come from Maryse Holder (1988) in her examination of the explicit genital imagery of the early '70s by Louise Bourgeois, Marge Helenchild, Shelly Lowell, Ann Sharp, Juanita McNeely and so on.

5 Earlier questioning over the multiple masculine and feminine positions which lead to the definition of spectatorship was developed by Doane (1984) and Hansen (1986). See also Judith Mayne (1993:86-91).

6 *The Bold Sleeper* (1927) is a representative example of this. A painting is cut into two planes. On top is a person sleeping, below is a wax tablet in which various objects have been pressed into a wax tablet.

7 *Delusions of Grandeur* was painted in 1962 . Magritte had not abandoned the female torso for again it appears with no head or legs, stacked up in a sculptural in form. Davis offers no less that three readings of the torso figure: an excessive taste for luxury, excessive size that has gone mad, and "the unreasonable nature of wanting to measure and attribute dimension to things" (p.104). The thesis of a feminine logic holds here.

8 Without a doubt the most prolific and powerful writings in this area in America are by Tania Modleski, Kaja Silverman, Constance Penley, Judith Mayne, Mary Ann Doane, Patricia Mellencamp, and Teresa de Lauretis whose definitive statement begins with *Alice Doesn't* (1984); her title repeats the very last sentence of her book. Her opening essay, "The Technology of Gender", in her book with the same title (1987) extends her initial arguments. Silverman, after an in-depth discussion of *The Subject of Semiotics* (1983), has gone on to examine the voice in cinema (1988a) and male subjectivity (1992). Constance Penley (1988, 1989) has continued to extend and develop cinematic fantasy. To the list of American film feminists pursuing similar examinations are E. Ann Kaplan (1983) whose lead article "Is the gaze male?" extends Mulvey's insight in 1975. In Britain, where psychoanalytic theorizing prevails with the journal *Screen*, Cowie and Adams have already been mentioned, as has Jacqueline Rose. Annette Kuhn (1982, 1985) work also helpful in understanding Mulvey's original insights. There are, of course, other prominent names that constitute the Anglo-American feminist cinematic discourse who have not been given the same profiles in print, but who are equally as competent and incisive

9 Such sadistic voyeurism has been recently exemplified by David Cronenberg's *Dead Ringers*, a story about two identical twins, who as gynecologists invent terrifying and hideous instruments for examining their patients.

10 There is a problem here which will be discussed further below. Walkerdine (1986:184-188) points out that Pollock's analysis and critique of Rosetti paintings of Elizabeth Siddall (his model and mistress) are themselves subject to critique. Pollock (1988:91-114) claims that Rosetti's idealization of Siddall's face in order to create a stereotypical category for masculine beauty, distances her representation from a living historical being. It is, therefore, objectifying. Walkerdine argues that such an analysis in effect dismisses the idealized fantasy image of Siddall and denies one part of her lived historicity. There is no "fixed" historical identity called Siddall. She has many faces. The idealized face, Walkerdine claims, belongs to the whole system of wardship and patronage whereby poor women "became 'kept' women and in which their objectification consisted in the utilization of their bodies to keep them, as it were, from the streets" (p.184). Rosetti's protectionist fantasy was manifest in such portraits.

214

11 On Gallop, see Munster (1986) and Toril Moi's (1988) reflections on Gallop's book, *Reading Lacan*. Moi, whose political leanings are in the direction of socialist feminism, presents the critique that the concrete, historical, and political analysis is missing in Gallop's text. It is a text on feminine stylistics not feminist politics.

12 i was struck how a recent cyberspace movie that I had seen with my son made Neale's point particularly vivid and still contemporary. *No Escape*, directed by Martin Campbell (1994) about the future world of prison reform, features Ray Liotta as the wrongly accused hero who rarely talks; he prefers to stand alone and fight his own battles. Male bodies are blown up everywhere; there is not a single female character in the entire narrative, and, to spoil the fun of those who have yet (or want to) "see" this film, it turns out that the one homosexual character in the film is the informant—the bad "g(a)y." Racism is appeased by under-representing the number of black bodies that have been imprisoned; a Black is head of security, and is told that he will become the new leader of the "Insiders Community" in the future.

13 i shall expand on this issue when discussing the contemporary "hysterical male" towards the end of my journey. The number of commercial movies dealing explicitly with homosexual relationships appears to be growing rapidly.

14 Bryson delivered the Henry Kreisel Lectures on Literature and the Visual Arts a series entitled, "Painting Text and Sexual Difference," at the University of Alberta, Edmonton Canada on Jan. 12, 15, 16, 1990 where he discussed his recent work: 1) Women, The French Revolution and Jacques-Louis David, 2) Géricault and Masculinity, 3) Stendhal and David.

15 See Kaja Silverman's "Fragments of a Fashionable Discourse" (1986) which is a study of men's sartorial dress informed by history and psychoanalysis.

16 If this is becoming too confusing, helpful diagrams, which perhaps should be reproduced here, can be found in Seminar XI, as well as in Silverman's chapter 3 (1992;p145). Theoretically Vermeer could "stand" outside his own canvas at a point where he would "disappear;" this point theoretically being the vanishing point of his own look from the canvas. In this system, when there are two intersecting isosceles triangles, their points touching each other's bases, two vanishing points are available; one being the geometrical point of his own eye as it looks out from the canvas, and the other is a vanishing point which is on the other side, looking in. Lacan calls this second vanishing point the gaze. It would be impossible for Vermeer to project himself (i.e., split himself apart imaginatively) to occupy this second vanishing point. He would evaporate and be unable to put himself in the picture. To be "put in the picture," an image has to be formed at some place between these two vanishing points that exist on the inside and the outside. The gaze occupies the impossible position on the outside, while the look occupies the impossible position on the inside. Between them there is the formation of a screen-image.

17 This discussion can be found in Pretexts to the Title. The suggestion by Asemissen is that he used a mirror.

18 This is familiar territory to any practicing artist (cinematic or studio) who must know the limitations of what the recording instruments that mediate between the body and "written" art-text. The interesting aside here is that artists have played with the distance of the technology of self-representation like phoning in instructions to hired help as how to paint their self-portraits. Imagine instructions given to a police artist by any citizen whereby the person giving instructions has chosen a pair of eyes, a nose, hair etc. from a composite book of pre-drawn facial parts. The physical distance of body presence has been overcome, but the screen-image of what you think you look like exists. There is a threshold as to when the actual physical body of the artist is still a felt "presence" and when that trace of the touch is gone. In many formalist works, the physical body is no longer present. Linguistic theory is substituted for the body, promoting such theorists like Danto (1986) to declare "the end of art."

19 This conceptualization is in accord with Hawking's own physical disabilities and his need to use technology to function "in the world." It is here that Hawking is utilizing a "not-all" feminine logic in Lacan's sense. By introducing "imaginary time" Hawking vanishes the difference between time and space. Time now becomes finite but has no limit (see Žižek, 1991:47). Bentov (1977) has played with the various conceptualizations of the universe that are possible using "imaginary time" once Big Bang is recognized as being one variant. In a Lacanian application he comes up with a doughnut shaped universe where the whole/hole in the middle is the void and what surrounds it is the illusion of reality.

20 There is a lot of literature about the way particular instruments both limit and delimit of what can be seen or not seen. The well-known example here is Heisenberg's uncertainty principle: when an atom is illuminated by light, its path can no longer be charted since the light itself causes it to swerve— but then again, this allows its mass to be measured. On the other hand, the atom's position can be identified when it is not illuminated, but its mass can't be measured. This is to say, there is no way to "simultaneously" find out the two variables: mass and position. They remain two mutually exclusive isolated readings with an irreducible distance between them since the effect is inherent to the technological apparatus being used. The same may be said of the gaze and the look. When the look claims to have "captured" the gaze (metaphorically having its light deflected through some masquerade), the look's social location can be identified but not its "true" power or magnitude (metaphorically its mass). On the other hand, when the look is exposed to the impossibility of capturing the gaze, its power is exposed for what it is, but then its position is "swerved."

21 Several speculations are possible here. This illumination or light, radically de-anthropomorphized by Lacan, might be interspersed as "aura" after the spiritual materialism attributed by Walter Benjamin; a sacredness is conferred on the object which dates to time immemorial in terms of visions, religious sights, relics, religious experiences. Another speculation is that this energy which Kirlian photography or auroscopy shots have identified as the electric fields surrounding objects, is somehow "released" when such objects catch our Imaginary in the Symbolic.

22 If you accept this analogy it can be argued that this perpetuates the phallocentric order of Lacan. One can easily substitute phallus as dissipated semen—the "glimmering" spermatozoa are the after-effect of the Great Ejaculation, They are everywhere as unconstituted, incomplete forms which are to be completed through an act of the imagination. The phallus, therefore, requires the prop of the penis. In Silverman's argument, the phallus is to the gaze as the penis is to the look.

23 Silverman's way of saying that sound of an imaginary camera constitutes the subject.

24 The disturbance of "shame" Silverman mentions and attributes to a Lacanian sentence, "a gaze surprises [the subject] in the function of voyeur, disturbs him, overwhelms him and reduces him to shame "(Silverman, 130: Lacan, 84), could not possibly succeed if the voyeur didn't already feel that what he was doing was somehow "wrong." Surely, not every man is bothered by his masterful gaze. Desire, as i understand her, has an implied touch of the puritanical. This point was clarified by Silverman (1994) in the following way: First of all, "shame" is attributed to Sartre and not Lacan in that shame here does not mean something shameful. For Sartre it references a Christian paradigm where shame is felt when you have reduced someone to an objet and you know it. In Sartre's account, the one who looks at the woman is the Master who is in command of the gaze—an absolute Subject, while the woman becomes an absolute object, recapitulating a Hegelian Master-Slave dialectic. For Lacan, the Master is not real since no one can control the gaze. The gaze is not a subject for Lacan; he therefore does not explore the possibilities of the Hegelian Master-Slave, and woman is subject because she is not a separate entity, but a subject who lacks, needing the other for confirmation. Since the completion of this book Silverman has furthered the discussion introduced in this chapter. See her *The Threshold of the Visible World* (1996).

25 The killers are almost exclusively male. Here Lacan's concept of " between two deaths" as represented by the oxymoron, "the living dead," comes into play so often in horror movies. As Žižek (1991:21-29) explains, the "living dead" are like "drive(s) without desire." They return again and again to haunt the living because "they were not properly buried." In other words, they *insist* from the place of the Real because of some injustice that has been done to them, that has, as yet, not been rectified. In *Friday the 13th. pt. 1,* the audience finds out from the revengeful mother that her son Jason was not properly supervised by the camp supervisors; consequently he drowned. But did he? Jason comes back, again and again, in the following episodes to address this initial "unconditional demand" of not being properly cared for.

26 This film has received wide comment in the past thirty years as a horror metafilm which exposes the psychodynamics of specularity and fear. The story, in brief, is about a professional cinematographer, named Mark Lewis, who moonlights as a photographer for pornographic magazines. Mark is a psychopathic killer of the models, prostitutes and actresses he photographs, but how these killings take place remains a mystery throughout the narrative until its end. The audience is permitted to voyeuristically participate in these killings by looking through a cross-haired lens, as in a first-person camera, of a close-up of the victim's face as Mark is about to photograph his model. This is followed by her face registering bewilderment as bright lights flash into her eyes, and then terror as something near the camera, which the audience doesn't see, kills her. It turns out that this "magic camera" is equipped with a hidden extendible spike in its tripod, while the movie camera itself has a concave mirror attached to it. The movie camera registers the horror of the victims seeing their own death as the spike pierces into their throat. Mark then views these recorded deaths (See especially Adams, 1994;1996).

27 The difference can be illustrated by the film *Henry: The Portrait of a Serial Killer* (John McNaughton, 1989) which is a psychotic fantasy. Clover also doesn't place this film in the horror genre (p.229). Like Mark, Henry is a law unto himself. Having had no father and a prostitute for a mother who made Henry watch as she did her Johns, a subjective self could not develop. The hate for his phallic mother manifested itself every time a woman approached him. He would nonchalantly kill them since they posed a threat to his very being. Each woman he killed was a way to still the gaze of his mother. The picture ends with Henry still on the loose, no ritualistic killing of the father of enjoyment has taken place. It should be noted that serial killers have no fear of being caught since it is through killing that they think they are escaping from the all-powerful gaze of the symbolic order. In contrast, mass murders want to be caught and be recognized by the symbolic gaze.

28 A drive is an unconditional demand devoid of desire (Žižek, 1991:21-23).

THE FEMALE GAZE AND ITS VICISSITUDES

Woman as the Copula of Desire

Before providing an overview of some of the ways the female gaze has been theorized since Mulvey's ground-breaking paper, it is important to grasp an understanding of how the figure of Woman circulates through language in Lacanian gaze theory. This is a complicated issue so what follows, i hope, is not a convoluted morass of sentences, but my own simplistic clarifications as to what it's about as best as i am able to undersatand. In the fort/da game that Freud plays with his grandson, the call to language and the theorizations that surround the ur-signifier (the originating signifier) of language are entertained by Lacan. The difference between the Freudian and Lacanian account of this game turns around the way each understands the object of representation that the fort/da couplet calls forth. Lacan's account is a deconstruction of Freud's in the following manner: when Freud's grandson, little Ernst, throws the cotton reel away from his crib and says "fort" (gone away), and then reels it back into the crib and says—"da" (here), completing the binary circuit of gone/here (implying it's come back), the account is read differently. "Fort," in and of itself, is a "non-sense" word. It forms the grounding, base or originating signifier which takes on sense only when its dialectical complement appears, i.e., something reappears that has been lost, or gone away—in this case the cotton reel. This nonsense signifier belongs to the unconscious, and is made conscious when the reel returns on two different registers, now functioning on both the unconscious and the conscious levels when the cicuit is completed. The question is now raised as to how that sense of understanding comes about when objects complete the circuit. For Freud, presence/absence, which is the binary established by the fort/da circuit, is completed by the objects themselves i.e., the absent Mother who comes back to the child, like the cotton reel that comes back into the crib. Language stands "for" these objects. What is signified by the ur-sign of absence/presence is an object. For Lacan what is signified is registered only as difference—the differentiation of sounds, of phonemes between the "o" and the "a." i think of this almost as an exclamatory "oh!" (something has happened) and "aah" (it's come back, desire has been fulfilled). For Lacan, then, language is a signifying system. Language is formed through negation, as that which is "lost" (i.e., the cotton reel, mother). It stands "in" not "for" these "lost objects," and signifies the desire for them. The presence/absence couplet puts the child into language—into the Symbolic Order which is immediately intertwined with the Imaginary as the demand for the return of the cotton reel (or Mother) which becomes a fantasy wish, a desire. The absence, or lack, as represented by the ur-nonsense signifier is filled in by the signifiers of language. Reality can only be known through the relations of difference amongst other signifiers. The process of coming into language produces an alienation effect; we are always in search of "lost" objects to feel complete. In this formulation, the word is a death or murder of an object. As soon as reality is "captured" by a symbolic network of signifiers, the objects become more present in the word and its concept than in the immediate physical reality. Immediate reality seems to escape our grasp. The word already gets "in the way." Even when we turn to the physical presence of the cotton reel its appearance is already marked by a lack. We only know what it means by the word which already marks its absence. Here the dangers of phenomenology and the metaphysics of presence present themselves when we take the signifier for its meaning. Such a direction is best avoided, for the signifier defers, supplants, and demotes the imagined presence it sets out to name—the process of différance.

But there is yet another danger to be avoided here as well, and that is the demotion of the feminine itself through its association with "death" and "murder" of the object. This is what Bronfen (1992b) argues in her critique of Freud's reading of the *fort/da* game. Given Freud's claim that femininity and death were the most consistent enigmatic tropes in western culture, the anxiety surrounding death and the failure to repress its desire, Bronfen argues, was conflated with the aesthetization of feminine death. The female corpse acted as a displaced signifier for this masculine fear and lack of repression. Within the context of her thesis, the death of Freud's sister Sophie Freud-Halberstadt/the mother of Freud's grandson Ernst/during the writing of his *Beyond the Pleasure Principle* where the *fort/da* story first appeared, takes on a special significance. Bronfen argues that the absence/presence of the reel, which Freud likened to the absence/presence of the lost maternal body, was like the *image of the female corpse*. The female corpse was both an absence and a presence in that it lacked materiality (the "real" woman was dead—absent) and yet at the same time the woman was strangely present—as an image in the materiality of the corpse. Death and the feminine "haunt" language in Freud's formulation.

Reeling "in" the cotton reel is only the beginning of these lost objects which don't have "strings" attached to them. Metaphorically, the "string" is a "track" or a "trace" of the object's "coming" and "going" which language tries to latch onto through its signifying "chain" to keep the signifier and the signified close together. The "string" or "trace" is like a film track—a record of the "remains" of the experience of the disappeared body through a "language" which attempts to represent the comings and goings of objects across a moment of time. But these objects can never be completely "found"; they can never be fully represented as they "are" — as being present. They become "little objects" of unattainable desire (*objet petite a*) that belong in Lacanian realm of the Real. They are non-discursive elements which are unrepresentable. The search for their full completion can only stop at death. In this sense, Lacan says that language is ruled by the signifier whose signified can never be ultimately tied down to a correspondent "realistic" meaning. We are condemned to never being able to say something—exactly, clearly, purely, precisely. This brings about the startling claim that we are, in a sense, always lying! There is always something that escapes our grasp since no one person can control language completely and totally.

The presence or absence of the penis, a "biological object" in Freud's case, as the linchpin of psychoanalytic theory around which sex/gender differences are established, is rethought by Lacan as the relations of *having* and *being*. The material penis "vanishes" into the register of the Real. It is lodged there as an unobtainable phallus, a transcendental and privileged signifier that determines other elements in the system. It becomes, in Derrida's (1975) formulation, a metaphysical construct, the creative logos itself, the 'purveyor of truth.' Such a discussion becomes complicated by the slippage of signifiers caused by the conflation of the penis with the phallus. The penis/phallus conflation happens on the register of the Imaginary. The phallus belongs to the Real (outside of language, in the psychic non-discursive realm) while the penis belongs to the Symbolic Order, in this case as a biological signifier. In this sense their difference in meaning is between words which "exist" (in the Symbolic Order, i.e., penis) and "ex-ist" or insist (in the Real, as phallus). The phallus "ex-ists" in language only as an "insistence." It cannot be described by language. Castration is *both* "literal," (at the level of perception) *and* psychic (at the level of the Real). The tension between its existence and insistence is played out on the Imaginary register *both* as an object of the *look* (penis) *and* as an impossible object of the *gaze*, the desire for the phallus that belongs in the Real. The castration complex for the boy is an "insistence" of the Law of the Father. It is a processes that "persists," and not simply a "one-time event," but a psychic structure that is "there" in the unconscious structuring a phallogocentric order. If it is not obeyed the boy becomes an outlaw and all that this term covers both psychically and socially as discussed in the previous vignette.

In the Symbolic Order the woman *is* the phallus for the man (being), while man has the phallus (having). The Imaginary register mediates this structure of desire since the equation of phallus and penis is an illusionary one. This formulation has continuously angered feminists because the phallus, which belongs in the register of the Real, and the penis (which belongs in the register of the Symbolic order), continually conflate, Lacan himself even saying so in his "Subversion of the Subject and Dialectic of Desire in the Freudian Unconscious" (in *Écrits*, 1977:292-325). Lacan tries to escape from this accusation by claiming it is a signifier (like the gaze) which can only be defined with reference to an entire field or network of other signifiers and signifieds. No one has privileged access to the possession of the phallus, like no one has exclusive possession of the gaze, nor the complete grasp of language. It exists only as a mediation of the other and the Symbolic Order through the screens of culture. Both men and women are "castrated." In this sense Ellie Ragland-Sullivan (1987:24) argues that castration refers to all forms of prohibition for both masculinity and femininity. It is a primordial lack of separation governed not only by the father's phallus but also the child's relation to the maternal body. Her body, like the penis, is a source of ego stability which provides symbiotic fulfillment for the child, but she also effects a separation between the child and herself which threatens to damage the image of the self as a stable entity obtained during the mirror stage.

The relations to the phallus are therefore regulated by the two forms modifying the verb–to be: being and having. The child must master the move away from being the phallus of the mother's desire—her phallus—(the legitimate role she is given in society by having children)—to having it. If the child is a boy he must *have it*; if the child is a girl, she must *be it* for someone else. To have the phallus you have to enter the Symbolic Order acquiring a place in the masculine/feminine order. However, one cannot have nor be the phallus in one-self. It is not an attribute, or a property, of a subject; only through an other's desire for the penis (a signifier in the Symbolic Order) can a man have his possession of his phallus confirmed; and only through another desiring her body can a woman feel as she is the phallus. This entails the symbolic equivalence of the man's penis and the woman's whole body; they are both objects of the other's desire.

The phallus, as a transcendental signifier in the Real, is a term that designates the possibility of the union of the two sexes, the copula of copulation. (In the English language it is that part which connects the subject and the predicate; the copula makes possible what is to be affirmed or denied about the subject, e.g., Jan went home —*went home* is the predicate of Jan). What is affirmed or denied about the subject is the predicate made possible *by the means of the copula* (e.g., in "all men are mortal"—"mortal" is the predicate made possible by the verb "to be"). In the Lacanian paradigm the *phallus as the copula* affirms and denies what is possible for women. This copulation—the act of intercourse—is imbedded throughout the language we use. If i now say, "sugar *is* sweet," the copula "is" predicates sweetness of the sugar: "is" makes sweetness present as a predicate of sugar but we know it is a constructed presence by the absence that supports it (like the *fort/da* game). That absence is found in the "taste" (analogously the "string" attached to the reel) which exists only as a trace that can be found in the intertextualities of similarities and differences amongst the signifiers within culture. It is conceivable, for example, that sugar does not taste "sweet" in some cultures where there is no refined sugar. In countries where sugar cane is eaten, the predicates for sugar may be different. Now if we imagine that woman is _____.
Whatever predicates might be put there, in the Lacanian paradigm, they are ruled by the copula of the phallus. Like sugar, her definition is predetermined and "fixed." Like the predicate "sweet," which is difficult to dislodge from sugar in Western culture, the lack of an imaginary or detachable *penis* predetermines the predicates that can fill the blank as to her definition. She is the object of the subject who lacks. The phallus fills this lack—organic lack as well as ontological lack, the lack in desire itself. The phallus does "double-duty" as a sign of sexual difference (penis) and the signifier of the object of the other's desire in the imaginary as the unobtainable object existing in the Real.

The penis takes on the function of the phallus only because that organ can signify (in fact, in order to produce) the exclusion of women. The penis is displaced from being a real organ, to becoming an imaginary (detachable, present, or absent) object, possessed by some, desired by others. After oedipalization it functions as a symbolic term in the Real (an object of union and /or exchange) between the sexes. It becomes a master signifier—a signifier of signifiers. Pro-Lacanian theorists like Juliet Mitchel and Ellie Ragland-Sullivan claim that psychoanalysis merely describes rather than participates in the social subordination of women. It is an anchoring term which 'saves' the subject from psychosis by granting it a social position outside the incestual web of desire in a nuclear family. However, this very psychosis has been challenged by lesbian women which i will take up later. In this sense Lacan remains a phallocentric thinker.

The Varieties of the Female Gaze

In this section i would like to review some of the discussions that have shattered Mulvey's conceptualization of the gaze. The first part of the discussion is dated to an earlier period of writing, but still valuable in its review of the issues concerning the "female gaze." The later part of the essay brings the discussion up to the mid '90s. i begin by recounting Janet Walker's (1985) identification of three major uses of psychoanalysis in feminist film theory. The first, as discussed earlier, is to investigate the oppression of women in classical narrative cinema which centers around the male gaze. In this case woman is absent; femininity is engulfed by masculine desire and hence difference is stressed. Woman remains the non-male Other. The second is to problematize the notion of femininity. Here the melodrama with a woman as its central character is examined instead of heroic male films. Identity once again becomes an issue for there may be both lesbian and heterosexual contradictions which emerge throughout the narrative, often with no conflict resolution. The work of Doane (1987) has been influential here.

The last appropriation of psychoanalytic theory for feminist theory leads into yet another corridor of the labyrinthian gaze. Walker mentions, ever so briefly, the psychoanalytic analysis of female psychic development, where there is an attempt to extend the general category of woman's sexual identity. Both her sexual pleasure and her general existence is analyzed so that the interplay of both body and psyche are made specific. Again, the melodrama (weepies) and the *film noir* constitute the genre where this is best exemplified (Doane, 1981, 1987). To recall Mulvey, the female gaze must either identify itself with the active male hero, and hence become "transvestite," producing a hermaphroditic sexual body, or it takes a narcissistic identification with the female figure as spectacle.[1] In 1982, Mary Ann Doane continued to argue that the female spectator, in Mulvey's system, must become a transvestite: "the woman who identifies with a female character must adopt a passive or masochistic position, while identification with the active hero necessarily entails an acceptance ... a certain 'masculinization' of spectatorship" (p. 80). If such transvestitism is denied, then she can don the masquerade of femininity.[2] What performative forms this takes is dependent on what type of game she intends to play against the dominant spectacle of a heterosexual society. The masquerade becomes a realignment of femininity in order to achieve the distance between an imagined self and one which is already constructed at the conjunctions of patriarchy. She becomes her own "phallus," says Montrelay (1978), "the woman will disguise herself with this lack, throwing into relief the dimension of castration as *trompe-l'oeil*" (p. 92). By not playing the man's game, but playing her own game, flaunting the Law, she is seen as an "evil flirt," a woman to be reckoned with.

Doane proceeded to develop one such masquerade, the "woman with glasses" which now seems historically dated some ten years after. "The woman who wears glasses constitutes one of the most intense visual clichés of the cinema. The image is a heavily marked condensation of motifs concerned with repressed sexuality, knowledge, visibility and vision, intellectuality, and desire. The woman with glasses signifies simultaneously intellectuality and undesirability; but the moment she removes her glasses... she is transformed into spectacle, the very picture of desire" (p.82-83). By wearing glasses, Doane argues, the woman is appropriating her own looking and analyzing, becoming a threat to the whole system of representation. Thus Doane concludes: if the cultural *place* assigned to femininity in cinema is in "closeness, a nearness, as present-to-itself," then the masquerade becomes one way of gaining critical distance.

To further her examine the female gaze Doane analyzes specifically "women's film" of the '40s. In her study *Desire to Desire* (1987), Doane demonstrates that women's films of the '40s are able to *produce* feminine subjectivity. As Elsaesser (1988) puts it: "At once rewriting the woman's body (destroying it as image, rearticulating it as a site of symptoms and illnesses) and reformulating sexual desire as masochistic fantasy in scenarios of persecution, suffering and self-sacrifice, the woman's film does not repress woman, but supports, in often contradictory ways, an overdetermined production of the feminine" (p. 111). Despite the "highly unstable and often unpleasurable subject positions [created by women's melodramatic film], the spectator is captivated, fascinated and bound to the representations" (p.112). Doane explains this as the ability of melodramas "to satisfy the desire to see the woman's desire. By dramatizing the difficulties of her having access to her own desire, the genre adds its own sadism to the masochistic 'scenarios of waiting, giving, sacrificing and mourning' "(Doane, 1987:180 in Elsaesser, p. 114).

Despite Doane's analysis, there is still the problem of why women watched this cinematic genre in the '40s with such enthusiasm. Where is pleasure found in such masochism? Why do these films still hold an audience today? Why do i (as a maleman) cry when i watch them? Do they merely reconfirm the 'woman as victim' scenario? Such questions raises the contradictory subject positions available even for the melodrama. For instance, Miriam Hansen's (1986:15) analysis of Rudolf Valentino's appeal to female spectators shows an oscillation—an interchangeability of active and passive categories—between the look and the object of the look. Further caution needs to be raised. As Kaplan (1983:24) argues, the Oedipal conflict as Lacan explained it, is *not* an ontological structure; rather its relevance may only be to the state of industrial social organization characteristic of the twentieth century. Further, it denies a "female gaze." "... in locating herself in fantasy in the erotic, the woman places herself as either passive recipient of male desire, or, at one remove, positions herself as watching a woman who is a passive recipient of male desires and sexual actions" (p.24). This latter case certainly seems to be the case with melodramas. However, Linda Williams (1984) argued that even in a quintessential maternal melodrama such as *Stella Dallas* (1937, King Vidor) there were multiple and conflicting points of view that act to prevent identification with a single character. Stella presents a heroic attempt to live out the contradictions of being both a woman and a mother in patriarchy. Williams went on to suggest that perhaps the female spectator of the melodrama "tends to identify with contradiction itself" (p.17). And, as Copjec (1994b:11-12) concurs, Stella testifies to the "impossibility" that her castration brings. Her ethical gesture is of "magnitude rather than [male] might. ... the ideal of an all in which women would finally be counted" (p.11).

Perhaps more problematic has been the attempt to theorize female spectatorship and women's films by calling on the "object relations" theory of Nancy Chodorow (1978), which is a basic re-reading of Freudian theory as to how mothering is reproduced, and Carol Gilligan's (1982) "different voice" hypothesis that claims a "caring" moral attitude for women. Jackie Byars (1988, 1991) is a strong voice for this development. She hypothesizes "resistant women's voices" in the Hollywood melodramas of the 1950s, but her attempt to do so by "re-reading psychoanalysis" through an analysis of cinematic enunciation in the films *Picnic* (1956, Joshua Logan) and *All That*

Heaven Allows (1955, Douglas Sirk) (1988, 1991: 171-209) is unconvincing. The question of women's "resistance," as a "different voice" in these two (exceptional) films does not come through. Rather it seems to confirm that the female voice, which is allowed to speak in these two melodramas, requires "compensatory emotional function" of the sensitive, romantic hero to "fulfill [women's] needs unmet in daily life" (1988:121). What Byars does show however, is that various filmic strategies that attempt to manipulate the spectator's gaze into gender identification are never homogeneous but change according to genre. Representations of gender and its rhetoric vary. Penley (1992) has criticized this turn to the "sociologized psyche" of Chodorow as a "reduced account of female viewing, reading, or consuming because of her emphasis on *regression* as a specifically feminine mode of identification" (p.479). Jacqueline Rose (1982) has criticized Chodorow for relying on Robert Stoller's concept of "gender imprinting" which establishes an unambiguous and unquestioned gender identity. [T]he acquisition of sexual identity and its difficulty— is sidestepped in the account" p.37). Chodorow questions "sexual roles, but only within the limits of an assumed sexual identity" (ibid.) The question of "resistance" and a "female voice" is problematic since romance novels and melodramas "'work' to the extent that they successfully induce the reader imaginatively to regress, through identification with the heroine, to a pre-Oedipal moment of being nurtured and absolutely taken care of, a privilege typically denied adult women in this culture because they have the sole responsibility for nurturing" (ibid.). For Penley, this turn to pre-Oedipal regression has the danger of essentializing female subjectivity by limiting it to the pre-Oedipal wherein a positive valence is given to nurturing, thereby establishing a moral difference between women and men. Byars seems to be aware of such a danger (1991:144-145) but dismisses its implications. (This criticism rehearses the problematic of essentiality that i had raised previously.)

Byars claimed that exceptional melodramatic films did exist which were the exception to the rule. Similarly, Norman Bryson's (1990) analysis dealt with the emergence of the bourgeois family structure during the French Revolution. Where he could he pointed to artists who appeared as anomalies to the dominant position of the male viewer; some where the viewer was assumed to be a woman or a homosexual gazing at a highly sensuous male body, almost androgynous in its rendition. Obviously the spectatorial gaze can take many positions, not only the dominant heterosexual male, which itself was essentialized by Mulvey. With the changing family structures of late capitalism, mothers are now seen as working and children have any number of parental combinations, including gay and lesbian couples in rare instances where it is permissible. Surely this has an impact on the changing relationship of desire? But how? It remains an unanswered question, even though it is recognized to be a central issue.[3] Perhaps such multiple spectatorial positions that have come to fore in the past decade is an indicator of these familial changes? The issues surrounding both soft and hard core pornography, and the wider viewing public made possible by the new technologies of television and video (and most recently computer porn), has complicated Mulvey's original insight which posited a unified cinematic masculine model, for surely the issues of accessibility and audience constructions have problematized the subject positions available?

Teresa de Lauretis, in *Technologies of Gender* (1987), argued for a decentered subject. "[G]ender is nothing but variable configuration of sexual-discursive positionalities" (p.7). But how those various gendered-sexual positions are cathexed (*Besetzet*), occupied, invested with an emotional commitment for satisfaction, reward, and pleasure, remains a speculative guessing game; yet it is here where agency is found as the *negotiation* between the psychic subject positions of the text and the actual empirical spectator (Gledhill,1988). "To assert that the social representation of gender affects its subjective construction and that, vice versa, the subjective representation of gender—or self-representation—affects its social construction, leaves open a possibility of agency and self-determination at the subjective and even individual level of micropolitical and everyday practices which Althusser himself would clearly disclaim" (p. 9). The relationship between ideology and desire has to be accounted for ... somehow. de Lauretis ends her essay by repeating, as other theorists have, that feminism remains in a contradictory position. It is a back and forth movement across the boundaries of difference. What she means by this "is a movement from the space represented by/in a representation, by/in a discourse, by/in a sex-gender system, to the space not represented yet implied (unseen) in them" (p.26). Such problems raise the issue discussed earlier: the difference between the discursive representation of woman in a text and a historical subject called woman, for the gaze of the feminist film critic will be different than that of a female viewer. The problem is further exasperated between a split subject (of psychoanalysis) and a decentered one (of sociology). How is the gap between text and viewer to be theorized? The tension that the feminist gaze must negotiate, then, is between the representation of woman in cinema (the discursive subject as Woman) and woman outside the *cinema* as "real" historical subjects (as woman) (Mayne, 1993:73). It seems that the interaction between the subject of speech (the discursive subject of a text) and an actual historical viewer, which would provide an understanding of the *spectatorial* subject who is both a *subject* and *subjected* by discourses, is best theorized within the confines of a specific location wherein specific texts have meaning in people's lives.[4] It appears that this specificity has taken place in television studies as discussed below; however, Jackie Stacey (1994) has made an attempt to theorize the specificity of the "historical female spectator" of Hollywood melodrama both during the war and then after in postwar Britain.

In her review of female spectatorship in cinema, Stacey (1994:19-48) points out that theorists such as Elizabeth Cowie (1978,1990) have moved the debate from fixed subject positions to positing multiple positions of cross-gender identification available to both sexes. Fantasy is interpreted as a structure—as the *mise-en-scéne* of desire—the inner world of idealized scenarios and wish-fulfillments rather than mere content. Despite such innovations, Stacey maintains that the formation of their social identities remains unsolved since a "politics of location is missing" (p.34). According to her, the particular social and historical discourses and representational practices outside, as well as inside, the cinema must be accounted for. Such an approach would go beyond the textual determinism she claims that psychoanalytic theories are caught in. The way out of this impasse is to turn to the conceptualization of audiences as active participants in meaning as developed in cultural studies, especially through ethnographic studies. This provides an accounting of female agency through an interactive model of text/audience/context provided that the spectator is a "historical subject" understood in such a way that the cultural location of the text-audience encounter is understood. Stacey then goes to apply such a methodology to the Hollywood films of the '40s and '50s shown in Britain. Stacey's study might be read as a critique and a supplement to Doane's study (1987) of the same period, but placed in the specific context of Britain. What enables Stacey to make "good" her claim of a "historical viewing subject" is her reconstructed simulacrum of "what it was like" for a woman to identify with Hollywood stars during this wartime and post-wartime Britain through the recollection of memories and reminiscences gathered from letters sent to an advertisement. She then correlated these empirical results to the socio-political economy at that time. Escapism, identification and consumption formed her three central discourses of spectatorship which emerged from this material. Escapism included not only the fictional narrative viewed on the screen, but the whole aesthetic experience of the cinema interiors "which have been culturally ascribed to femininity: perfumed air, the plush texture of the curtains and seats, the glistening chandeliers all contribute to what could be seen as a feminized environment for consumption" (p.97). These glamorous interiors of British cinemas provided the cultural space for the consumption of Hollywood's glamorous femininity. The fulfillment of utopian fantasies of luxury and glamour were in stark contrast to the hardships of wartime and post-wartime Britain. American culture offered the femininity of Hollywood stars and consumerism which were unavailable to women in wartime Britain due to the rations.

Stacey explores the question of identification of female spectators with Hollywood's ideal stars through the contradictions of identity and difference, recognition and separateness. These identifications are conscious categories identified through memories, and hence Stacey's challenge to psychoanalytic theories of identification "is limited by such a focus" (p.137). She begins by making a distinction between fantasies and practices of spectatorship. The range between imaginary identification within the cinema to actual practices of identification outside the cinema are systematically developed. The former, which take place in the spectator's imagination, are divided into two categories. There is identification through 'devotion,' 'adoration,' and 'worship'. These are an "intense, often homoerotic bond between idol and worshipper" (p.145). The self here is denied. And there is identification through 'transcendence,' 'aspiration and inspiration' which involves the loss of self in the fantasy world of the star ideal. The self merges with this ideal. The latter form of identification might be characterized as the "wanna-be" phenomenon: actual activities where women spectators begin to dress and act like the stars in everyday life. Stacey identifies them as 'pretending,' 'resembling,' 'imitating,' 'copying.' In the last case a new feminine identity is produced, "one which combines an aspect of the star with their own appearance" (p.170). Here the identity of the spectator takes over; the star is marginalized.

As Stacey claims, these forms of identification are also forms of consumption. Hollywood's stars were consumed for the production and reproduction of particular formations of female subjectivity during this wartime and post-wartime Britain. The 'feminization of consumption' is given a twist by Stacey who argues for consumer agency: although female spectators were "successfully constructed as consumers by Hollywood cinema *and* that they also used commodities connected with stars in ways that do not conform to the needs of the market ..." (p.189). Strategies of resistance included naming the products and hair styles after the star's name, displaying a 'trademark,' but especially establishing new feminine identities that contrasted their roles as wives and mothers at this time. In other words, the use of American femininity as represented by the Hollywood stars was used to rebel against restrictive British norms. Forms of self-assertion were butted against expectations of self-sacrifice. Stacey is remindful that these very forms were also 'white' fantasies. Such 'white' female fantasies have been recently explored by Vicky Lebeau's *Lost Angels* (1995) who re-reads Freudian theories of femininity by examining three youth films of the 1980s—*Ferris Bueller's Day-Off, Rumble Fish* and *River's Edge*. Significantly, Lebeau develops the multiple locations 'woman's desire' takes as it circulates in the Oedipal networks of the filmic structures.

Visual Technologies and the Female Gaze

The issue of the gaze is further complicated, then, by the type of visual technology and the particular representational discursive practices that come along with it. The portrait camera (still camera) may be a more privileged apparatus to the formations of identity than, say the video or movie camera, although this may be changing with the flood of home cam recorders that are becoming available, changing the way people are looking at themselves, given that the playback on television is almost immediate e.g., *Sex, lies, and videotape*. How much this self-surveillance further shapes the way they (We, (I)(i), you) look and act has not been adequately theorized. Nevertheless, historically, since the *camera obscura*—the photograph remains outside of movement, frozen in temporality—like the perfect moment of a pose, where our desire to be immortalized exists. This desire to capture the "perfect" ideal moment is part of the Enlightenment project, already formulated in the seventeenth century with Lessing's discussion of the *Laokoon* where the moment of dramatic action had to be captured in a frozen moment of expression, splitting temporality in two as past and future. The idealized moment is the apotheotic moment of presence—forever young, ageless, colorless, androgynous—like the iconic and emblematic figure of Michael Jackson of postmodernism today.

In contrast to the study of cinema, John Ellis (1983) points out that the gaze of the cinema may not be applicable to viewing television which is a much more interruptive medium, allowing for familial interactions. Television is more about the look, the glance and the sound. Walkerdine's (1986) analysis of a working class family (the Coles) watching *Rocky II* is instructive in this respect. It is an example of where psychoanalysis addresses a specific social configuration. Unlike Mulvey's notion of two types of visual pleasure at the two poles of objectivity and subjectivity, an active objectifying look (i.e., voyeuristic or fetishistic look) or an identification with the screen image (narcissism), Walkerdine finds a class-specific coding of identifications. The Rocky series presents the fantasy of the fighing working class male who overcomes "the forces of humiliating oppression which mutilate and break the body in *manual labour*" (p.173, my italic). This is a *class-specific masculinity*, where brawn compensates for brains. The key signifier in the film—fighting as a coded form of masculinity—is presented as the only way of overcoming possible humiliation and cowardice. The spectacle of winning, the body triumphant creates that fantasy. "Physical violence is presented as the only way open to those whose lot is manual and not intellectual labour, and another aspect of this classed masculinity is the wardship of a woman who does not have to work (like a man) but whose domain is domestic" (p.173). Walkerdine develops the role of fighting as a central signifiers in the Cole family but its interpretative meaning is class specific. "Fighting is a key term in a discourse of powerlessness, a constant struggle not to sink, to get rights, not to be pushed out. It is quite unlike the pathological object of a liberal anti-sexist discourse which understand fighting as 'simply' macho violence and would substitute covert regulation and reasoning in language as less sexist" (p.182). This is an extremely important point Walkerdine is making. Fighting is not an oppressive ideology in the micropolitics of the working-class family. The signifier as incorporated in lived-life provides a fantasy of hope, an escape from oppression, and a resistance to domination. She is suggesting that this is not "false consciousness" or an "oppressive ideology" nor is she denying the pain of that lived reality; she is, however identifying the material and psychical reality. This is a long way from seeing the audience of popular entertainment as voyeuristic, scopophilic or trapped within a given subjectivity without defining the specificity of class, race, gender. Significantly, Walkerdine recognizes her own voyeuristic invasion into the Cole family and the imbalance of power a researcher from an institution brings with her. She tries to psychoanalyze herself so that she might have a better understanding of the mother-daughter relationship that she was observing. Walkerdine has continued to develop this form of psychoanalytic and post-structuralist theory which has the great merit of maintaining the split subject. In her recent study (with June Melody, 1993) of the Portas, a working class family designated by social welfare services as pathological, unhealthy and abusive, Walkerdine voyeuristically (and acknowledgingly) examines the way the film *Annie* participates in the fantasy life of one of their four children, six year old Eliana. Given the family dynamics of an abusive husband and an alcoholic mother, along with an oppressive situation of poverty and illness, Walkerdine is able to place the film *Annie* and its fantasies in the dreams and nightmares that make up the narrative of the life of Eliana and her family. "It is my contention that Eliana finds solace in a narrative of a little orphan girl, who escapes from her drunken mother-substitute to find true happiness with a wealthy man and thereby ensures that she also obtains a good and beautiful stepmother. Such a narrative provides for her a pleasurable, comforting reading of her situation, both in terms of its poverty and oppression and in terms of the way in which her relations with her father and mother can be told through that story. In other words, her deep pre-Oedipal feelings about her mother can be turned into dislike for a woman who it seems must deserve the beatings she is getting, and who comes between her and the deeply admired father, the father who abuses his wife" (p.82). Walkerdine contends that films like *Annie* belong to a Shirley Temple genre which present narratives of a mythical working-class girl whose function it was to induce love in the rich so that they would promote charity. These films offer an escape fantasy for the working class into the life of the bourgeois class. The film *Annie* "offers a way of picking up and talking about issues that are very painful and difficult for the family, and also presents a way of understanding and working with those issues" (ibid.). The Portas desire such an escape but are unable to do so. Like Abel's (1990) analysis of Spillers and Steedman's psychoanalytic appropriations mentioned earlier (in the section, Give Me a Little Sign), Walkerdine's studies combine psychoanalysis with social critique; each supplements and supplants the other.

With a similar specificity, but without a psychoanalytic dynamic, Janice Radway's (1983) ethnographic examination of the readership of white middle-class women was able to demonstrate how the plots of such novels address particular problems and desires that are characteristic of their lives. Her reader-response ethnography goes beyond the usual simplifications that women who read romances simply perpetuate and reinforce patriarchal attitudes; rather the complexities surrounding the *psychological* and not psychoanalytic desires to "digest" such novels were uncovered. Escape or relaxation from their surroundings, routines, pressures, and tensions of being wives and mothers, to a world which was complete and emotionally gratifying, was overwhelmingly the major goal for reading the romance. Reading was an act of resistance which provided much-needed time and space for themselves. More importantly, the romance plot satisfied psychological needs that emerged living in a patriarchal arrangement where, as wives, they stayed home and looked after the children while the husband worked; a situation which has changed drastically over the past ten years since Radway's study. The tensions brought about by that arrangement, the feelings of "house wife blues," were psychologically answered through romance plots which constructed a fantasy idealized world as to how things should be between a man and a woman; especially if he showed his love for her and if she, as heroine, satisfied him emotionally through her intelligence and charm. Romance novels provided hope, pleasure and contentment that such an arrangement was indeed yet possible. Monogamy remained a prized value. The man was "spectacularly masculine, but at the same time [was] capable of remarkable empathy and tenderness" (p.64). If he abused the heroine or was brusque with her, explanations were given to the reader (unbeknown to the heroine) which justified their own husbands' outbursts of bad temper. In each case the heroine "tamed the beast within him," so to speak, so that the couple gradually, by exploring each "other's foibles" and feelings, discovered that they were in love. The success of this plot ensured immense popularity, as the film *When Harry Met Sally* testifies.[5]

"Romantic escape is a temporary but literal denial of the demands these women recognize as an integral part of their roles as nurturing wives and mothers" (p.66). Radway does not excuse this behavior, but points out that the volumes which such novels are consumed (up to 10 per week) are an indicator of the failure of patriarchal marital arrangements. They are read to subdue the "dissatisfaction and disaffection" these middle class white women feel. Caught in a contradiction "[t]hey long for emotional attention and tender care; on the other hand, they wish to rehearse the discovery that a man's distance can be explained and excused as his way of expressing love" (p.68). They wish to keep this myth alive. Unlike Wakerdine, who attempts to provide a psychoanalytic reading within the context of the social, Radway only hints at this possibility, but recognizes the need for it given that the effects of romance plots "help to dismiss or justify their husbands' affective distance" (p.67). Analogous to the fight genre discussed by Walkerdine, a particular sort of romance plot offers a form of resistance but does not change the social conditions.

Both Radway and Walkerdine recognize that site/sight/cite specific research, oriented either psychoanalytically or ethnographically, is able to help comprehend the construction of desire between class, gender, and the need to consume a particular art genre; but whereas Walkerdine develops fantasy along the lines of Freudian and Lacanian scholars Laplanche and Pontalis (1968), Radway in her full-length study *Reading the Romance* (1984) turned to Chodorow to explain how the romance novels "work." Identification with the heroine was explained by the imaginary regression of the reader to the pre-Oedipal moment of being nurtured which was being denied them since they had the sole responsibility of nurturing. Such a position essentializes and reduces female subjectivity to a daughter-mother relationship. i have already presented the problems with such a position.

Walkerdine and Radway represents a generation of feminists who have gone beyond Mulvey's original insights, bringing into feminism questions and conceptualizations emerging from the new field of "cultural studies." *The Female Gaze* (Lorraine Gamman and Margaret Marsment, 1989) is a recent collection of such an attempt, each author problematizing the female gaze as it locates its "object" like the New Man created by the advertisement industry of late capital.[6] What strikes me about these essays is the wonderful playfulness between popular imagery drawn from the cinema, television and advertising interspersed with the *full* range of psychoanalytic feminist scholarship. In Suzanne Moore's (1989) discussion of the female gaze, for example, there is a thought-provoking discussion as to why "[p]referred reading may not always be preferred..."(p.52), reiterating the complex process of identification. These essays point to the multiplicity of subject positions now available to women, problematizing the gaze which had traditionally been theorized as masculine.

Elizabeth Ellsworth's "Illicit Pleasures: Feminist Spectators and *Personal Best*" (1986), examines how lesbian feminist reviewers of a commercial film about a friendship between women athletes, redefined who was the film's protagonist or "object of desire." Heterosexual romance segments were ignored. Lesbian viewers rewrote the ending for themselves by speculating on the future relationship of the characters. "Lesbian feminists, academic feminists, liberal feminists, radical feminists, feminists of color, all formed competing interpretive strategies around these issues [media representation of women's bodies, the status of women in sports and lesbianism]. Those communities' responses to cultural practices aside from cinematic representation informed the terms in which reviewers associated these issues with *Personal Best*" (p. 48). As Ellsworth points out, *Personal Best*, reviewed both by socialist and liberalist feminist publications, expressed pleasure in the undermining of stereotypes, "the achievement of women in male-dominated fields and the representation of women athletes as beautiful, graceful and strong." Socialist feminists found pleasure in "exposing the working of patriarchal discourses and constructing a discourse in opposition to it" (p.53).[7] Ellsworth's findings are consistent with reception theories especially as represented by Tony Bennett (1983) who insists upon the social position of the readers and is sensitive to their class and gender positioning. The lesbian gaze (Staccy, 1989), the Black gaze (Roach and Felix, 1989), and women gazing at the New Man of advertising present the problems of difference which are a long way from being fully theorized, but necessitate an understanding that the text itself will be manipulated for pleasure and rejection alike.

i end this section with a reference to Efrat Tseëlon and Susan B. Kaiser's "A Dialogue with Feminist Film Theory: Multiple Readings of the Gaze" (1992) which reviews the developments of the female gaze and touches on many of the issues presented thus far. In their last section, "alternative approaches," Tseëlon and Kaiser sketch out two broad approaches the feminist gaze can take: alienation of texts and the negotiation of them, both of which are "subsumed loosely ... under postmodernist and symbolic-interactionist frameworks" (p.127). They make the point that both these approaches that are based on non-representational views of language, i.e., the signifier and the signified are uncoupled, but that the former (symbolic interactionism) negotiates, contests and contextualizes the binary positions of the dominant culture, while the later (postmodern perspective) draws on postructuralism and abandons the usual primary opposition.

Tseëlon and Kaiser put their gaze categorizations to a test by reading two films, *Stakeout* and *Monsieur Hire* from a psychoanalytic, symbolic-interactionist and postmodern perspective; however these readings are brief and hastily done (perhaps due to space constraints). They conclude that all three perspectives (symbolic interactionism, poststructuralism, and postmodernism) often overlap when applications of their abstract concepts were concretized. It was especially difficult to distinguish between *negotiated* binary meaning of the symbolic interactionist position and *abandoned* binary positions of postmodernism which made binaries even more ambiguous. They further concluded that textual analysis often became a heuristic process with the abstract differences between all three positions overlapping. If symbolic interactionists claimed that meaning was always variable and subject to revision, and that categories always emerged from the interpretative process, then this was close to poststructuralist positions which declared an end to fixed binaries and celebrated decenterdness and indeterminacy. They concluded that by applying all three approaches assured more flexibility and insights for liberating subversive meanings along side dominant ones. Tseëlon and Kaiser's conclusions are not very satisfactory. The feminist gaze requires a commitment to social change. For this reason it is important to raise the spectre that haunts it.

After the *Fort/Da* Game:
The Danger of a 'Simulacred' Perverted Gaze

"A few pages after the initial analysis of the *fort/da* game," Copjec (1993) says, "Freud adds that his grandson later developed a variant of the game. In this later version the child himself functioned as the cotton reel; hiding beneath the mirror for a time, he would suddenly jump up to see the emergence of his mirror reflection"(p.182). The difference in the two versions, explains Copjec, is significant. In the first game, the child chooses to be a subject. Doubt and anxiety are introduced into language because there is uncertainty about the other. Hans was not always sure that his mother would come back, nor that the reel would return. There was always a relief that came with the "da!" Hans chooses desire in the sense he doesn't know what the m(other) wants from him. What is in him is "more than himself" so that he then becomes an object of desire for his m(other). Uncertainty defines the subject. Hans does not know what he is for the m(other). There is a felt lack on his part for the status of the m(other), who, like the reel, always oscillates in her coming and going. Such a choice is necessary for a love bond to establish itself; an attachment for the object is confirmed in the repetition because of *loss*. The demand to have the mother or the reel back is repeated endlessly as a desire in the hope, but not the certainty, of capturing that which was lost or has escaped (as "fort").

In the second game a perversion happens. The subject reconfirms himself over and over again. The academic version of this game is called "multiply or perish." A radical self-objectification takes place since Hans seems to know what he is for the Other. In otherwords, *he loses his status as a subject.* He posits himself as the object-instrument (the reel) of the Other's *jouissance* (pure enjoyment)—himself. There is no loss. [R]epetition is driven not by desire but by satisfaction" (p.182). The choice between games is "between desire and drive," a familiar construction that has already been developed in the horror movies (see last two sections in The Masculine Desire of the Imaginary). This shift towards drive, argues Copjec, was already described by Lacan as a general historical transition where the old modern order of desire, ruled by the oedipal father, is giving way to a new order ruled by the drive where there is no longer the "recourse to protections against *jouissance* that the oedipal father once offered. These protections have been eroded by our society's fetishization of being [drive], that is of *jouissance*" (p.182). Another name for this is "pathological narcissism." The private space of *jouissance* has now become a public demand. The private no longer becomes hidden but exposed, furthered by the media, especially television, which have exposed all the adult secrets and "eroded" childhood, a thesis maintained by Meyrowitz (1986). This transition may well be the one which Juliet Flower MacCannell (1991, see ft. 3) has identified as the "regime of the brother."

The contradictions which oscillate between the two games, between desire and drive, in today's society can be identified by what Gamman and Makinen (1994) have named "the fourth fetish:" bulimia. This eating disorder, i believe, can be interpreted as a perverse fantasy where there is a constant oscillation between not being a subject (bingeing) and its recovery (purging). The first is ruled by the structure of the drive, the second ruled by the structure of desire through a sadomasochistic pact with the self. Whereas anorexia, and its obverse, obesity, has been interpreted as a " 'flight from femininity' which unconsciously denies female sexuality and may involve a flight from 'the male gaze' " (Gamman and Makinen, p. 123), the bulimic is *inversely* caught between the swing gates of living out the old "femininity" and trying to escape into the new, for the bulimic still embraces some of the traditional assumptions concerning femininity. It is the *compromised* disorder of "the new woman" whose horror has been fantasized in the popular media as devil possession.[8] The bingeing might be compared to a hyperbolization of game 2; the binger tries to amass the object in herself, a "little piece of the real" so that it is never lost; a reversion to the mother's breast. Her food fetish is the literalization of her desire to *deny* or disavow that she is merely a fantasy object for men. As Gamman and Makinen argue (p.135), food can act as an 'orthodox' sexual fetish where the food *takes the place* of a sex partner. Such narcissistic display is, however, a "radical ethical act" for it brings her to the brink of an unreserved acceptance of the death drive as she puts herself in the position of what Lacan called the "second death." She is ready for self-annihilation through the binge rather than cede to the desire of the Big Other (Symbolic Order) who *demands* that she be slim and perfect. There is no doubt of her sadism, the self-torture in over-eating. However, when she realizes she is a helpless victim of the forces that she cannot control, she begins to feel uncertainty. By vomiting she becomes an object for her self, and thereby becomes a subject (game 1) once more. It is the purge through vomiting which brings her pleasure in her pain (*jouissance*). To be a "subject" in the Lacanian sense is to experience oneself as an object, a "helpless victim" (game 1), the point where the bulimics gaze confronts the "nothingness" of her narcissistic pretension.

The flip side of this, of course, is the pathological narcissistic "new" woman, the daughter who has abandoned her mother's "old femininity" and stays satisfied with game 2; the so called "post-feminist woman," or is it "girl"? who has escaped bulimia, anorexia, and obesity. Or has she? In a review article on postfeminism in both American and Germany (*Der Spiegel*, 1994) "Emmas Töchter" (the daughter of the emancipated woman) is described as strong, clever, egotistical, sensitive, self-confident, and very feminine; good girls on the outside, but bad on the inside: "Lolitas who kick like Bruce Lee." (Boys are said to be just the opposite: bad on the outside, good in the inside.) A picture features a girl standing with her hand on her hips. On one side of her arm is written "witch," on the other, "slut." They have their own magazines, i.e., *Sassy* in the US, *Planet Pussy* in Germany; their own style of dress— "girliewear;" their own music —"Girlsm;" their own stars (i.e., Madonna) and a comic, *Tank Girl*, which is now being filmed. Magazines and books promote their slogans like: "Be a beast," "Good girls go to heaven, bad girls go everywhere," and "Get fit, get rich, get laid" (Madonna). Post-feminist girls call themselves "girlies" or "babes." They are further identified as a generation

238

between 15-25 years old who demand equal wages for the same work; believe that they have the same life chances to get ahead, and have accepted the achievements of feminism as a precondition for their own lifestyle. Such an ideal ego is presented by 23-year-old cover girl model, Nadja Auermann, who comes across as a dangerous "big-city" Amazon: "the bombshell next door," a complete contrast to the supermodel Claudia Schiffer who is described by one 27-yr.-old interviewee as someone "who looks as if she has been built by a man out of a child's construction kit" (p.116). Yet it is also Hollywood's "Jazz Babes" who provide the "right stuff" for these girls, having made their careers from their "baby images:" Barbara Stanwyck, Joan Crawford, Jean Harlow, but also Holly Golightly of *Breakfast at Tiffany's*, Winona Ryder and Uma Thurman.

"Not to be treated like a piece of shit," is the best advice she learnt from her mother, says Girlie-model Kate Moss. If the paternal superego is breaking down and the maternal superego is taking over, it may well be that the symbolic law of the father is being replaced by rules of knowing how to succeed (Žižek, 1991:102-103). The "girlie" lifestyle embraces the Madonna ego-ideal where it becomes important to know the rules of the game and how to manipulate people and assume roles. As another interview said, "Madonna is able to have fun [*jouissance*], sex, million dollars, and besides this her own mind, and besides this a shaven ass ..."(p.115). Her "girlie" followers radically conform to her lifestyle, yet paradoxically experience themselves as outlaws and rebels. "What's love got to do with it?" sings Tina Turner. Precisely nothing. For the pathological narcissist there is no transcendental attachment, only a descriptive shopping list of characteristics that fulfill a pre-ordained "body." The more "bodies" it consumes, the more satisfied it is. Prostitution, in all its forms, now begins to take on the appearance of a "normal" acceptable activity. As Doane (1991) has argued, the figure of the prostitute collapses the boundaries between sex and work, private and public. She has become a potent figure linked with devouring and demonic imagery, of seduction and cruelty.[9] The "maternal" superego "does not prohibit enjoyment but, on the contrary, *imposes it* and punishes 'social failure' in a far more cruel and severe way, through an unbearable and self-destructive anxiety" (Žižek, p.103, my emphasis) which brings me back to the pathologies of eating disorders.

Garmman & Makinen's (1994, chap. 2 and 5) survey of the increased acceptance of perverse sex and the eating disorders in this culture of slenderness suggests that the "girlie" lifestyle is not so free as it is made out to be. In their last chapter they suggest that postmodernism is a culture of fetishism (and i would add narcissism)(cf. Christopher Lash). "Unlike displacement or sublimation, fetishism does not involve *repression of the desire* experienced" (p.214, my italic). The girlie lifestyle is a perfect match for commodity and sexual fetishism *where the drive for pleasure supplants desire*. The fragmentary, decentered subject makes the perfect capitalist subject who can expand the range of his/her *jouissance* to an ever increasing array of new "mirrored games." Unlike the bulimic, anorexic, and obese woman, the perversity of this post-feminist gaze is marked by the "girlie" subject's attempt to escape her own split by occupying the gaze of the big Other (Symbolic Order) which assumes the form of a "supreme evil being." Being "bad" is what unites masculinity and femininity in a one-sex model (cf. Thomas Laqueur). The "girlie" is a boy inside out. The clearest example of being "bad" is found amongst the fascist youth culture of the neo-nazi right in Germany, Britain, France, and the USA; the bands names reflect the violence that accompanies the sadomasochistic pact with this "order": *Brutale Haie, Endstufe, Freikorps, Werewolf, Sturmgesang, No Remorse, Elite Terror* (Grüninger, *et al.*,1994). The bulimic, then, might be considered the very symptom of this development: a subject who is unable to decide which mask s/he should wear. The "male" bulimic seems to be the very inverse. He is often the long-distance runner, the marathoner or the fitness fanatic; a fetishistic addiction to exercise which allows him to "have his beer and drink it too." Is not the spit and the sweat that comes out during exercise a form of vomit? abjected fluid? Is the narcissism and devotion to his own body, which can substitute for a sex partner in a world where AIDS and the loss of commitment to others are a matter of course, the new rules to live by? If Baudrillard is right, and we do live in a hyperreal world of *simulacrum*, then it may be said that the gaze has become perverse: we are caught in an elaborate house of mirrors, in Neil Postman's (1986) terms "amusing ourselves to [the edge of] death."

1 To recall, in 1981 Mulvey had revised her thesis, now suggesting that the woman could indeed oscillate between spectatorial positions but only if she donned "transvestite clothes" (p.79).

2 Doane's concept of the masquerade is footnoted at length in Pretexts of the Title, footnote 2.

3 Here i point to the Lacanian anthology edited by Teresa Brennan's *Between Feminism and Psychoanalysis* (1989). Brennan, in her Introduction claims that the changed parenting patterns have consequences for the symbolic, but no essays address her remarks. Juliet Flower MacCannell's *The Regime of the Brother: After the Patriarchy* (1991) is an attempt to theorize this post-Enlightenment, post-patriarchal period by developing the thesis that the previous patriarchy based on God, Father, King has been replaced by a brotherly "generalized ego" which is narcissistic, an *It* which feigns sexuality. The brother does not desire but fully enjoys himself. His longing is always being satisfied. "Sexuality" now becomes a substitute for the parental relation, a fundamental narcissistic structure wherein one "couples" with a fantasmatic projection of oneself made possible more and more by the electronic means of reproduction, such as cyberspace. In this "regime of the brother," the former Oedipal "symbolic sexual difference," wherein gender is constructed as an opposition to serve reproductive ends, no longer holds. Women potentially can come into their own because the paternal/parental pattern has been diminished making the relation of sister to brother the central event. However, MacCannell argues, the sister is once again denied her identity and desire.

4 In the "Pretexts to the Title" there is a discussion between Mayne's use of spectator and Kerby's use of the spoken subject. The spectator is the spoken subject. The spoken subject is formed from the inter-

action between an actual historical person and a specific text. In this sense the spectator (or modified spoken subject) is not the discursive subject, not the actual subject, but a subject position formed in between them both. This may be confusing in the sense that i have been also using the speaking subject which, most often refers to the author, writer, artist. The speaking subject and the discursive subject can be collapsed as in a self-portrait or an autobiography or a written letter. Here the "I" conflates both subject positions. To reiterate my graphic play, "i " (as a speaking voice) have tried to split of from my discursive "I" throughout this text, however unsuccessfully.

5 A clever insightful reading of *When Sally Met Harry* as an example of postmodern "yuppie" love can be found in Denizen (1991). Denizen is very good at placing this narrative within the broader oppressive issues of capitalist patriarchy.

6 The concept of the New Man is the complement of the New Woman of advertisement industry. This is developed later in the section on Male Hysteria.

7 i shall return to these developments in queer studies later. See also footnote 7 in, Give Me a Little Sign.

8 See the section, The Perverted Gaze of the Possessed Eye/I

9 Liz Borden's film *Working Girls* is an example of this very collapse. Although the inside/outside distinction between the bordello and each of the private lives of the prostitute is maintained, the film brilliantly shows their exploitation by the very capitalist system they think they are subverting.

CONUNDRUMS OF THE GAZE

What we must do ... is on the contrary to isolate the *sinthome* from the context by virtue of which it exerts its power of fascination, to force us to see it in its utter stupidity, as a meaningless fragment of the Real. In other words, we must (as Lacan put it in Seminar XI) "change the precious gift into a piece of shit"; we must make it possible to experience the mesmerizing voice as a disgusting piece of sticky excrement.

(Žižek 1989, p. 11)

Tripping over Medusa's Head

With the previous analyses in mind, it makes me wonder whether the current fashion of psychoanalytic criticism, especially of painting, is still applicable given that the *spectator is often not problematized*. i ask this question now because, in my reading, the "I" was continually "tripping over Medusa's head"; so much so that i began to take notice of her more and more, without shield in hand. The "I" began this search with my own appropriation of the Medusa myth. It soon became apparent that many critics referred to this myth to justify their own interpretations. It seemed uncanny (*Umheimlich*) in the way they were are able to weave this myth into their explanations with relative ease to help explain (away?) male anxieties. i have already mentioned Owen's (1983) brilliant application of the myth in relation to Barbara Kruger's work. His claim is that Kruger's visual texts reverse the gaze onto the male. She is the Medusa decapitating male stares.[1]

Tobin Siebers' (1983) study of the "mirror of Medusa" traces the myth as the intersection of an archaic belief in the evil-eye and the narcissism of Western civilization. Such a myth provides a chiasma, a conjunction which spans the gulf between "primitive" and modern societies. For that very reason alone, i am suspicious that this may be why such a myth is able to hold so much currency in explaining away two desperate "bodies" of experience; the primitive and the modern. It strikes me that so many dualities are analogously represented: illiterate/literate, the imaginary/ symbolic, the pre-Oedipal/ Oedipal, Classical/ Modern, upon which the allegory of the Medusa myth is then able to explain the male fear of castration whenever the Symbolic Order— the Law—is shaken. The sight/cite/site of the woman's body, as a *femme fatale* (Doane, 1991), the castrating Mother, becomes an excuse for projecting male anxieties. The myth becomes particularly effective, therefore, in its explanatory powers during the transitionary times of upheaval. The recent examples of critical readings: Gericault's *Raft of the Medusa* as interpreted by Norman Bryson (in 1984, see also 1981, 1991et al.); Griselda Pollock's (1988) Medusa myth as played out in Rosetti's painting *Lilith*; Bram Dijkstra's (1986) study of Symbolist representation of nudes; Hertz's exploration of the myth in the literature of the French revolution of 1848; Louis Marin's (1980) reading of Carravagio's *Testa di Medusa* as contrasted to Poussin's allegorical style, and lastly Bois' recent (1988) psychoanalytic reading of Picasso's *Les Demoiselles d'Avignon*, which play's off transitional oppositions: "realist" *énociation* to the historical *énoncé*, discourse as opposed to history, the omniscient absent author against the screaming ego. Before this claim can be substantiated, it is necessary to "regress" into the myth of the Medusa.

First, the magical, mythical, "primitive" side of the myth is easily related to the pre-Oedipalization of the child and the idea of an omniscient observer. A timelessness exists in such a state. The child in the pre-Oedipal stage has no idea that it is being looked after, observed, and enabled by its Mother, a powerful Being who "controls" its very needs and wants. It feels omniscient as if nobody, except itself, is present in its primary narcissism. But it is this phallic, enabling mother which will later be fetishized once difference has been discovered. As the ego is "formulated," and the child passes through Oedipalization, narcissism—as a gregarious desire for total self(ish)-fulfillment—is not possible without the recognition of the M(other). Pathological narcissism occurs, therefore, if the M(other) is totally disregarded; a megalomaniac ego emerges and infantile omnipotence is retained through to adulthood. This may well be what is happening in our culture of "youth"; the perverse gaze of the "simulacrated self's" *drive* for a BwO. The more "normal" course of events requires that the image of the child's body, which is incomplete and unstable in knowing what it is, be perceived from the outside to be complete, coherent and self-sufficient.

As a precondition to subjectivity and ego development, this requires that the Mother become recognized. The discovery of sexual difference as the absence of the penis, i.e., when the boy sees his Mother's genital area, becomes traumatic and threatening. She has been castrated; she is capable of castration; she is a threat. From this initial trauma the woman is split into two images: at the pre-Oedipal level of fantasy she remains an ambivalent figure of bisexuality—benevolent, beautiful, caring, but at the same time capable of great cruelty. If the male cannot come to terms and "free" himself from her, she remains someone to be feared– Medusa herself. To fetishize the mother's body then, to give her a phallus, has been the way a heterosexual boy copes with identification and threat. Through a fetish he is able to maintain an identity with her, i.e., she is like me, and at the same time disavow the knowledge that she isn't. This is something the heterosexual boy knew before but needed confirmation, one way or another. Medusa's head can becomes his fetish object as a beautiful face, or her castrating look can become the shine off her nose, which was Freud's example (Ellis, 1980/1992: 162). The mother, in turn fetishizes the phallus. She knows that the boy has it but disavows it to maintain the paradox of having him close and distant at the same time.

As is well known, the form of Oedipal struggle the boy and girl go through is structured differently. For the boy, the struggle to differentiate himself away from his M(other) is more intense. The Medusa myth can now be read as an allegory of that struggle: to be caught, to be "fascinated" (bribed, coddled) by the Mother, is to live in pre-Oedipal bliss and therefore in the fear of becoming like her. This phallic mother of infancy must be abandoned, for she is not *always* so benevolent, but makes demands of her son. Perseus's mirror, as the shield, might be described as a metaphor for this process of eventual differentiation, since the mirror does not *just* reflect back Medusa's gaze; rather it is a transformative reflection: the transformation is one of eventual death. Her identity is presented as difference in the shield's mirror, and hence prototypically her reflection is a mask. It's as if she sees her terrifying power for the very first time and recognizes that she must let her son go on his own course, and put up with his "pushing back" once he enters into language and begins to "talk back" to his Mother.[2] Yet the terror she possesses over her son as the *femme fatale* is always lurking in the background. Whenever this Eden-like unity is threatened, especially during times of upheaval of the Symbolic order, a political threat is in the making to disturb the "natural" order of things; her castrating glance is lurking in the shadows. As *femme fatale* she poses a threat to male gratification. Such an explanation would account for the Medusa myth achieving more and more prominence as feminist ideology begins to penetrate bourgeois institutions.

To avoid this castrating look, to repress her evil, she is often idealized, fetishized for the male gaze. The mirror now becomes the embodiment of her narcissism; a beauty who is able to caress herself in the mirror, or hold it up to admire herself. In this case, it is her entire body which is fetishized. Yet, the displacement of male anxiety created by the sight of difference can be displaced by any object sensuously associated to moments before the discovery—such as shoes, legs, underclothes—while the head of Medusa takes the place of female genitals, as in the face of "Garbo" (Barthes, 1973). *But the fetish need not be an object.* The phallus that is "granted" can equally be something felt, heard or smelled. Ellis (1992) argued that the female orgasm itself had become the fetish object in certain forms of pornography.

With this myth in hand all sorts of hypothesis now become possible. i can postulate that the Medusa myth allegories the transition from matriarchy to patriarchy, which is then repeated as the Oedipalization myth, dragging us back to the Greeks every time it is evoked (see Fromm, 1951). This reading is strengthened by Siebers' discussion of Athena's role in the Medusa myth, as guiding Perseus's hand in the slaying. "The queen of the city and the queen of hell share a history of rivalry, which is dramatically stressed by the fact that the birth of Athena presents the mirror image of Medusa's death. After either Hephaestus or Prometheus opens Zeus's head with an ax, Athena, fully armed, springs from the wound. Medusa dies from the sword blow of Perseus, and from her head spring Pegasus and Chrysaor. These two scenes, by virtue of their similarity, again present the violent competition between goddess and monster ...Athena must overcome Medusa to establish her own identity" (p. 14). Siebers goes on to show that Athena and Medusa are never quite separated. Athena appears with snakes around her waist or snakes coiled in her helmet. Again, it becomes possible to comprehend the duality of woman by the male as either a monster or a benevolent beauty. Siebers points to a "transitional" Gorgonian phase between her evil and beauty. Here she is presented in a "both and logic." The Symbolists were fond of presenting Lilith and Lamia as beautiful mother and daughter with a snake wound around their waists (Dijkstra, 1986: 306–310). Such depictions of evil "serpentine feminine bestiality," were linked to late nineteenth-century feminists, the "viragos" or wild women. Lamia "was thought to have been a bisexual, masculinized, cradle-robbing creature, and therefore to the men of the turn of the century perfectly representative of the New Woman who, in their eyes, was seeking to arrogate to herself male privileges, refused the duties of motherhood, and was intent on destroying the heavenly harmony of feminine subordination in the family" (p. 309). This is beginning to sound a lot like the "girlie" culture of today! As may be recalled, according to Kristeva, this would be a fetishistic artistic response to the disruptive forces of the semiotic.

This has now become a familiar story. Every time male Symbolic Law is threatened, the Medusa myth becomes the uncanny scapegoat, for the male is fearful of loosing his many privileges associated with the phallus. She is to be seen for what she is—a common whore, a prostitute. Neil Hertz's (1983) discussion of Medusa myth, as it plays itself out in the textual and visual representations during the political climate of the French Revolution of 1848, is instructive in developing such a thesis. During the French Revolution of 1848 he writes, "All three writers [Edmund Burke, Victor Hugo, Tocqueville] have produced intensely charged passages that are about a confrontation with a woman, a confrontation in each finds an emblem of what revolutionary violence is all about" (p.40). Each and everytime the beautiful woman becomes a whore representing the forces of upheaval and change. It appears that the Medusa myth becomes particularly strong during transitional phases. The forces of history, allegory, and the Law on one side, as the objective pole associated with distance and omniscience, are juxtaposed to fetishistic association—the compression of time, discourse, and subjectivity. Postmodernism is obviously such a historical moment.

The Disputes of Representation:
Gauguin, Salle, Picasso...and so on, and so on ...

Despite these theoretical gymnastics in history and criticism, the issues of representation and the role of psychoanalysis are far from being resolved. In a panel discussion at the 78th Annual Conference of the College Art Association, held in New York (1990), entitled "Denaturalizing the Nude," the literary critic Peter Brooks argued that Gauguin's nude studies in Tahiti served to put to question the entire European tradition of nude studies, representing the women's body in such a way that the male gaze was mitigated and made problematic. Gauguin's nudes, some like *Te arii vahine* and *Spirit of the Dead Watching* (1892), were a direct comment on Manet's *Olympia* and *Dejeuner Sur L'Herb.* They acted like a Derridean 'supplement' to the entire tradition, hence putting that tradition to question. But such a reading was in direct contrast to to the thesis developed by Solomon-Godeau which had appeared in *Art in America* a year earlier (1989).

Solomon-Godeau argued that Gauguin's modernist primitivism was a form of *mythic speech.* His life was a paradigm case of "primitivism as a white, Western and preponderantly male quest for an elusive object whose very condition of desirability resides in some form of distance and difference, whether temporal or geographical" (p.120). And that object was an earthly paradise, a place of plenitude where compliant female bodies presented themselves everywhere. Gauguin's heroic journey out, to find himself, was part of the mythic sense of being avant-garde, original, self-creative, and heroic. Further, Solomon-Godeau claimed, this vision was abetted by racial and sexual fantasies. His sojourn as a "savage" into Brittany, as his "initial encounter with cultural Otherness" into a "more archaic, atavistic and organic society," was more accurately a mystification of Brittany as a folkloric paradise. Brittany was a center of an international artist's colony (the *Pont Aven* circle) and tourism; its peculiar visually distinctive aspects, especially women's clothing, were a sign of its *modernity.* The textual representation of Breton as being primitive was part of a broader discourse created by colonialization where a natural primitivism had emerged through the encounter with tribal arts, *Japonisme,* and *cloisonnisme.*

The significance of Gauguin's religious and mystical iconography, as exemplified through the representation of numerous Calvaries and self-crucifications, marked a crisis of representation brought on by the crisis of capitalism during the *fin de siècle.* The flight out from urbanity presented Breton as the Other of Paris—feudal, rural, spiritual and static. As Solomon-Godeau argued, the absence of men presents a "purely feminized geography," an unchanging rural world, an atavism where women, adolescence girls and children's perception are said to be closer to nature and the spiritual. Gauguin's nudes from this period are said to participate in this quest for the primitive. "The savage woman" was to exemplify the natural link between Eros and Mother Nature—the constellation of imagery around "Eve/ Mother/ Nature/ Primitive." His depiction of Maori culture and women continued this mythic primitivism. The figure of the *vahine,* represented either monstrously (as in cannibalism and tattooing), or idealized as a noble savage, became a "metonymy for the tropic paradise tout court" (p.124). "Going native" was a façade. Gauguin never learnt the Polynesian language; the customs he wrote about were plagiarism drawn from previous accounts; his very survival depended on *vahines* he so idealized; and his life was but a continuous rape of images and "pillaging the savages of Oceania" (p. 128).

Such a scathing indictment of Gauguin raised many questions as to the ethics and politics of any textual reading. Feminist member's of the audience, notably Griselda Pollock objected to Peter Brooks' reading on the grounds that it was *still* a male's appropriation of the woman's body. Needless to say, artists in the audience reacted with some trepidation. Just what sort of representation of a woman's nude body was permitted to avoid such accusatory wrath? Such discussion brings up serious consequences for artists like David Salle (Eleanor Heartney,1988) and Eric Fischl, whose representations of the female nude body are quasi-pornographic. These male artists would be chastised for such representation regardless of how good their rhetoric may be. Salle insists that 'his' female nudes are "the body in extremes—often seen from strange points of view and spatial organization. It has more to do with the abstract choreography and angles of vision than with pornographic narrative" (in Heartney, p. 123). Such a statement is reminiscent of the painter Pearls, with his careful positioning of female nudes, again supposedly only for formalistic concerns.[3] Are such paintings to be denied their fetishistic status? Do they indeed subvert the fetish of the iconic nude in Western art?

Heartney, a female critic and certainly not a feminist, vindicates Salle's work as not being pornographic. There is no world of voyeuristic ocular looking, she says, "even the spread-legged female one." Salle is able to present the viewer with an anti-narrative to the representation of the nude in Western art. Similarly, Cindy Sherman, who has equally presented a photographed "fiction" of herself in "sluttish" poses, is excused on the grounds that her art puts the male gaze to question, while Fischl's voyeuristic poses are dismissed on the grounds that he has embedded his sexual references in a more "acceptable" social field: the depiction of intimate family scenes and adolescent sexual awakening. It appears that the game of whether Salle or Fischl's art is pornographic or not is a game of rhetoric; how might a statement like the following pass, if not in the context of an art journal for the promotion of "high" art by a critic?

> In Salle's universe, the exploration of the body as the 'location of the human inquiry' leads back to established dualities between soul and body, man and woman, first and third worlds (Heartney, p. 123).

Salle is here to save the world in the name of art and "cash in" while doing so, presenting viewers, paradoxically, with a nihilistic world. How else to make sense of the following statement: "The bodies Salle represents are more like artificially preserved species than participants in the flow of life. If they are vessels of anything it is only their own emptiness" (p.124). Further: "The viewer is frequently invited, indeed coaxed, to see bodies as things in Salle's paintings—cropped, often headless beings, seemingly unrelated to the rest of the world except by their passive offerings flesh" (p.124). It becomes more and more difficult to justify Salle's female nudes, despite his grisalle renderings of them. "Rarely, if ever, does a woman in Salle's painting get the *full color* treatment" (p.126, my italic). So true!

Can Salle be "rescured" like Magritte? Has he also made a sadomasicistic pact with his mother? This is difficult to tell. What continues to be disturbing for many feminists is the way women's bodies have become the territory over which modernism and postmodernism is written and fought over. A recent example of this practice is Yves-Alain Bois' (1988) psychoanalytic reading of Picasso's "Les Demoiselles d'Avignon." The fetishization over this particular work is made evident by the immense exhibit at the *Musée Picasso*, Paris, documenting the entire process of its painting. Bois makes the claim that Picasso's composition lends itself to Medusa's ruse. The five figures "share neither a common space nor common action, do not communicate or interact, but relate singly, directly, to the spectator" (p.136). Invoking Louis Marin's analysis of the Caravaggio's *Medusa* in the Uffizi, which marks a passage from "historical *énoncé* to a "realist" *énonciation*," or, put in other terms, marks the passage from Poussin's allegoricism—the presentment of a story as an impersonal statement of fact—to implicating the spectator as in Courbet's realism. Picasso is said to have repeated in this major work a similar movement from the "narrative" to the "iconic." This "apotropaic brutality" or "savagery" of the castration anxiety (again there is a return to the so-called Medusa effect which was said to have "petrified" Matisse, Braque, Derain when they first saw it, much like Poussin had been "petrified" by Caravaggio) is then said to be linked to the "apotropaic savagery" of African art. Bois ends up by commenting on Picasso's deconstruction of classical pictorial tradition by disregarding "unity of theme (allegory), of geometry (proportions), of style (Iberian—African) or of medium (flat planar surface)" (p. 172). This being so, these transgressions were made in a brothel, at the expense of women's bodies and at the cultural borrowings (or is it now to be called rape?) of African images by a man who feared syphilis and was known for his sexual prowess (or was it appetite?).

Are Salle's nudes of women a recent "postmodernist" deconstruction of Picasso's modernist *énonciation*? Is he quoting Picasso? Or has the "woman" become *once again* the sight/cite/cite for apotropaic "savagery?" This time, is it Salle's cynicism and nihilism being played out over her pornographic body, repeating Picasso's bordello? Allusions to a similar "rape" of the black culture seem to be present by a painting such as Salle's *Blacks Fall Down*, a diptych which "juxtaposes the stark image of a prone nude black woman viewed from behind to the bold-faced caption in the other panel" (Storr, 1988:24). Are these works taunting Lacanian "Symbolic signifiers" as Yves-Alain Bois claims that Picasso's *Mademoiselles d'Avignon* had? "If we have the courage to kill the father (tradition, law) symbolically, this is what we will get, this thing so monumentally terrifying in both its freedom and its constraint?" (p. 138). As with the horror genre examined previously, the "killing" is best done over the woman's body, and in the "safety" of the House of Art.

It is difficult to accept such arguments such as those made by Storr, Heartney, and Bois in Salle and Picasso's defense unless they are once again to be read as sadomasochistic pacts men make during a time of their sex/gender uncertainty. It is instructive to raise the historicity of sexual difference that revolve around the playing off iconicity against narration, *énoncé* against *énonciation*, "realism" against "classicism," whenever the Medusa ruse is evoked to raise the concerns of male anxiety over the "shaking" of the Symbolic Law. Both Gaugin and Picasso painted during historical times of upheaval, as does Salle today. The discussion between Gallagher, Hertz and Fineman (1983) is instructive in this case because they historicize and raise the ideological question as to why the Medusa myth is continuously invoked. (There is now even a filmic spoof on Madonna as Medusa). There is, in my mind, a qualitative difference between these applications of Freudian and Lacanian readings to those discussed earlier like Walkerdine and Abel's exemplars: Spillers and Steedman. The sense i have is such readings are prone to formulaic applications of the Medusa myth without *enough* concern with addressing specific socio-historical configurations of the symbolic order.

Fucking Marilyn Over... and Over ... after 1962: The Necrophilic Practices of Psychiatry

If Elvis is not dead, neither is Marilyn Monroe, for she is now caught within the machinations of post-Freudians who re-write her body to both expose, and at the same time to hide, the complicity and phallocentricism of their discourse. Even as she is dead, she is not allowed to die—but continues to be "fucked over" by men. On Monday, 30 of May, 1994, the I attended a lecture given by Peter J. Swales, a historian of psychoanalysis and a practicing psychoanalyst himself, entitled "Freud's Last Patient: Marilyn Monroe," at the University of Klagenfurt, Austria. Earlier, with Klaus Kamolz, he had published a three-part series in the Austrian magazine *Profil* (1992) (which is roughly equivalent to the German *Spiegel,* America's *Time,* and Canada's *Newsweek*). The lecture, which lasted three full hours, fetishistically and voyeuristically covered Marilyn's life. Virtually each book of her library was catalogued; letters were obtained; people interviewed; every minute step of her comings and going were charted, even the times she might have prostituted herself on the "casting couch."

Swales' thesis maintained that Marilyn was a "very smart woman." She read books like Joyce's *Ulysses* for instance. Carl Sand was a favorite poet of hers. She even wrote poetry, "not bad poetry at that," according to a poet friend of Swales. She studied acting, self-improvement and wanted to be a mother. Swales' purpose in amassing all this evidence was to show how the psychiatric community had failed Marilyn: their negligence; their inability to stop her from taking drugs; their mishandling of her will, and their complicity in her death. During the talk two "asides" were made. The first was a mention of her "tortured soul, " while the other was the reference to her "mentally-ill" mother whom Marilyn feared she might become. i claim no psychiatric competence with accreditation, but it seems utterly unbelievable to me how a psychoanalyst like Swales made no mention of how patriarchy had positioned Monroe for a fall. i don't think you need fourteen years of Freudian training to note the following, which would be more of a Lacanian exposition.

First, it seems obvious that throughout her entire life Marilyn tried to live out her life as a male fantasy, and position herself in the light of the male gaze. She had no defenses that would allow her to play the game without falling into depressive contradictions between her own desires (as Norma Gene), and the construction of the male fantasy (Marilyn Monroe). Whereas someone like Mae West could play with masculine desire and render it flaccid through her sarcastic tongue, Marilyn couldn't. Throughout her life she married men who were heroic figures, like Miller and DiMaggio, or either married men who would help her in Hollywood to become a star, or she would prostitute herself to get bit roles. Abe Lincoln was her hero. She carried a portrait of him whenever she resettled. Marilyn tried to read literature which was given to her in order to "improve" her mind. It was no different with the art. Her interest in art was fueled to be as smart as Miller. Ironically, a copy of Michaelangelo's *The Creation of Adam* hung in her home. Her self-improvement courses, acting classes, and her "love for Freud," was done in the hopes that both her acting and her well-being would improve so that she could be loved by her fantasy men. The result was the failure of idealization, of striving to be in a place impossible for her to occupy.

Dyer (1986) in his essay "Monroe and Sexuality" examined how sexuality circulated in the '50s. He notes that Monroe could never be sexually fulfilled. Not only was she beaten and abused by DiMaggio, she was unable to reconcile and distance herself from an object of male desire that she had to occupy. She was a spoken subject. The only place left for her was to become a mother—to possess the phallus so that she might find another identity. She became pregnant, but was unable to carry her child, perhaps because of a number of previous abortions—fucked around in yet another way by the illicit abortion trade. Her escape from one coast to another—to New York where she tried to find a "new identity," never worked. She could not intervene in the male screen that had shaped her. The "new" Marilyn was only another version of the old Marilyn. This is where the Freudian discourse caught her; fucked her over again and again—in New York and then in Los Angeles as she began therapy. Lastly, the very idea of having a "mentally ill mother," however that may have been interpreted by her, meant that Marilyn was unable to get "back" to that pre-Oedipal moment and draw the maternal support she needed; rather, she turned to men for the most support, with disastrous consequences. Placed in a state mental hospital, she was afraid that she might become "like" her mother. If Chodorow and Irigaray are right about the necessary attachment of the daughter with her mother, here we have a case where the castration from the mother's body has been so complete that the trace of this attachment is just too far away to make any difference.

As McCann (1991), who has studied the biographies of Monroe, writes, "The books on Marilyn Monroe [and there are many] do not contain 'the real Marilyn,' signed, sealed, delivered, and yours. The human being that was Marilyn Monroe cannot be reconstructed by piecing together the black and white marks in the text, but what *can* be reanimated is the cultural praxis at work in each interpretation, each word-picture. One may not find out 'all

about Marilyn,' but the metabiography can provide (at least) a proper appre-
ciations of her fictions" (p. 334). Whatever may be the consequences of my
psycho-babble above, which might equal the frenzy of Swales' performance,
it seems unlikely that Madonna would be fucked around in this same way.
For whatever i might say about Madonna throughout my text, it cannot be
denied she knows how to play with the camera apparatuses of male fantasy.
As Warren Beatty remarked, she would not do anything without a camera eye
witness (e.g., *Truth or Dare*). That Dick didn't have a chance. If the look and
the gaze have become collapsed through the discourses of the logic of the
camera, Madonna knows the discourse and exploits it for her own gain.
Whereas Marilyn might have feared becoming crazy like her mother, Madonna
exposes the craziness of her parents and diffuses it by taking her own talking
cure. So, to end this short diatribe on Marilyn and her indefensibility, she was
"too" close to the fetishistic positioning, to use Doane's sense of the masquerade. i read Swales' lecture entitled, "Marilyn: Freud's Last Patient" ironically. After her death the feminist movement got going, eventually fucking
Freud over, e.g., Kate Millett's *Sexual Politics,* (1969) and Juliet Mitchell's
Psychoanalysis and Feminism (1974). In this sense, Marilyn *was* his last patient,
for Madonna would never subject herself to such a fuck.

The Proleptic Installations of the Exotic Gaze

i think it is useful to draw attention to Catherine Lutz and Joan
Collins' typology of seven colonizing gazes which emerged from their reading of photographs that comprise the discourse of the *National Geographic*
(1993). It will provide a marked contrast to the section that follows, which
rethinks the gaze as a *sinthome,* the limit condition of psychoanalysis. Some
of their analysis overlaps with such film makers and critical ethnographers as
Trinh T. Minh-ha (1989 a,b) and recent deconstructions of anthropological
narratives initiated by Clifford and Marcus (1986) and Clifford (1988). The
journal *Visual Anthropology Review* (V.A.R.) has been influential in its questioning the Western eye of the anthropologist's camera (see anthology by
Taylor, 1994). The strength of their work is the all too often forgotten emphasis on race and ethnicity when thinking about the gaze. "When people outside the Western world are photographed [as well as deviants, criminals] the
importance of the look is accentuated" (p.188). As Gaines (1988) demonstrates, an overriding issue for theorizing the gaze is the question of the privilege of looking that operates within a racial system embedded in a socio-historical and local set of coordinates, i.e., Black men looking at white women

and visa versa, the white privilege of looking openly vs. those who steal glances and look illicitly. However Lutz and Collins are quick to state that there is "no simple rendering of the spectator of the magazine, including the spectator's gender" (p.190). Their interpretation of Lacan's concept of the gaze to the way the "native" is photographically presented is instructive for the possible readings that it provides. Surprisingly, this appropriation of Lacan is *not* part of their topology of gazes. (It will later become evident as to why not.) His theory is recognized as a significant approach which they apply to the following thesis: the photograph of the native-other pacifies the Western gaze by reducing the strangeness of the Other through photographic and editing choices. These procedures familiarize and "naturalize" the looking to make it more comfortable and pleasurable. In other words, the native-other becomes an "it" within the Western I/Eye which serves the purposes of imperialist tourism. Western desire is being appeased by exoticizing the native-other, a charge that is heard so often. This insight provides an opportunity to take their psychoanalytic reading a step further.

Wright (1984) offers a clue of what might be the significance of exotic desire for Westerners when she identifies one of Lacan's remarks concerning love. In the German, love (*Verliebt*) conveys the notion of a displaced looking from the side. Where then is the look of love to be found? When in love, the "I" solicits a look; but what is often found profoundly unsatisfying and always missing is that— *"You never look at me from the place from which I see you."* The lover (i'm going to stay with the masculine pronoun here) narcissistically projects a desire that magically completes his own; that looks at him from the place he wishes her to be. "What do you *see* in that person?" is a question often asked. Should she be "absent," the fantasy is broken for he finds that, *"she never looks at him from the place he sees her."* When both look into each other's eyes and fill the *place* of desire, love flourishes. This *place* is where he has placed her in the field of scopic vision, and she him. If he is discovered *not* to be there, the spell is broken as well. The 'reality' does not correspond to his wish, for her desires have to be reckoned with as well. Lacan adds: *"What I look at is never what I wish to see."*

The Western exotic gaze looks and expects that place to be filled with an admiring look back, an invitation to come over and live "there" for a while; "there" refers to the *mise-en-scène* of the fantasy, and that place "there" must already bear the expectations of the Western eye. It must be *proleptic*. If that wish isn't filled, disappointment, anxiety, fear, and hate are all possible racist responses, especially if the look is turned back. "Native" read against the background of a racial body by a Westerner is not the same "native" read amongst themselves. The "native-other" is unable to answer back easily. It is often too dangerous to stare back. One resistant "hybridized" (Bhabha, 1985:97) response has been to perform their once sacred rituals ironically, with ornamental excess for the tourist's eye, like the Mudmen of Papua New Guinea whose ceremonial masks began to take on a wry expression. i am tempted to say that they began to look (a)wry through their masks at the tourists, a point i shall return to. Native mimicry of imperialism is one possible moment of civil disobedience. But these exotic rituals, "faked" or "real," are often read within the same colonizing fantasy structure; a way to re-capture the "aura" of the sacred that has left the West with its technological rationalizations.[4] "Exotic dress alone often stands for an entire alien life-style, locale, or mindset. ...The highlighting of native dress contributes not only to a view of others as different, but also to their framing as picturesque and erotic, beautiful and sexually alluring" (p.92, 93).

The exotic body must be constructed in that space which is not too threatening, not so different that it is abjected—yet familiar enough to Western habits of mind that it provides a titillating and exciting difference: strangely beautiful or beautifully strange. The spectacular aestheticization of the Other, in typical fetishistic fashion, both discredits the significance of the foreign at the same time it embraces it. If the language is so incommensurate that it could not possibly be comprehended, then the distance is too far; it sounds too cacophonic. "In its search for the photogenic in the far corners of the world, the magazine [National Geographic] consistently beautifies and dignifies (at the same time that it exoticizes and objectifies) people and places that are not ordinarily perceived as beautiful in Western culture" (p.274). The place of exotic desire has to be paradoxically neither too close nor too far away. This construction is one of Zeno's paradoxes—"Achilles and the tortoise." It identifies the habitual Western tourist who is caught by a repetitive drive to discover the *exotic,* the object-cause of the travel, which can never be attained. The exotic seems to be perpetually elusive. Each trip is just somehow never "exotic" enough, never quite meeting the expectations of "authenticity;" a new trip must be immediately planned or thought about. Despite the frenetic activity of traveling, the habituated tourist doesn't seem to get anywhere. The exotic is then the *objet petit a* of desire which remains both present and yet never to be found (see Žižek, 1991:3-6).

This is not, however, a one-way street. The look back by the native-other has to be disarming, invitational and interested enough to make contact. It must also connote a difference in status. This is achieved in *National Geographic* photographs by the predominance of smiling faces that look into the camera; most often these are head shots, quoting portraiture passed on from Western art tradition. This frontal view, according to Tagg (1988), is a socially inferior code since its use dates back to the photographic documentation of deviants and homosexuals at the turn of the century. The civilized classes turned their heads away from the camera, like the advertising photographs of men today.[5] The word "profile" still maintains this meaning of importance. It is quite obvious that finding exotic "hot" spots today is increasingly difficult, given the threat to tourists in many third world countries. An important study would be to examine the current interest in interracial models by the fashion and modeling industr —"cross-colors" i believe is the pejorative name for those who fit into this in-between space of exotic identities.

Catherine Lutz and Joan Collins provide a typology of seven colonizing gazes. These might thought to be the screens that Silverman had referred to in her work on "marginal masculinities." They include: 1) *the photographer's gaze* where the gaze of the photographer and the viewer overlap; 2) *the magazine gaze* which is the institutional decision-making process as to what is and isn't included in the magazine; 3) *the magazine reader's gazes* refers to the viewer's idiosyncratic responses to imaginary world(s) that the magazine's photos hold for them, read in various contexts; 4) *the non-western subject's gaze* refers to how and where the Other looks: "she or he can confront the camera, look at something or someone within the picture frame, look into the distance, or not look at anything at all" (p.197); 5) *a direct Western gaze* refers to the changed matrix of gazes when the Westerner is inserted in with the natives; the predominance of Western pictorial representation grew less and less as decolonization took place and their presence took on an unwelcomed, sometimes embarrassing sight/cite/site; 6) *the refracted gaze of the other: to see themselves as Others see them* identifies pictures where the native-other is shown with a camera, a mirror or its equivalent. As tools of self-reflection and surveillance, the mirror, the camera and the tape recorder can be used to present the native-other as lacking in self-awareness, and therefore ignorant, childlike, lacking a sense of history and cognitively immature compared to the West which prizes reflexivity, i.e., like this self-reflexive journey! This comment somewhat ironically leads to the last gaze: 7) *the academic spectator* refers to the identity politics in photographic reading. Lutz and Collins admit to their white, middle class, female, academic positions which bring with them certain techniques of photographic analysis. There are often at odds with the pleasures that these photos bring. The contradictions between pleasure and analysis remain; after all, why spend all that time and energy examining *National Geographic* if they didn't enjoy its discourse?

Gentrified Tourism: *I like you ...*
I mean, I like your money!

> On a recent trip to Crete for a summer vaca-
> tion the I had the perfect opportunity to *play*
> the tourist. Greece is well known for its hospi-
> tality; a former escape for Hippies. It caters to
> tourism and it lives with the garbage this
> brings. Having learned a few Greek words, I
> came up to the till to pay for my meal.
> Mustering the few sentences i knew, the I
> politely thanked the owner. He looked at me
> and laughed. "I like you"... he then hesitated,
> looking at me from the side and said... "I mean,
> I like your money!"

Catherine Lutz and Joan Collins' study is a remarkable synthesis for understanding the colonizing discourses that run through the particularities of a hegemonic organ like the *National Geographic*. It offers a wealth of socio-historical understanding of how the Other's representation is colonialized and contained; however, one other important aspect of their work is missing— and that is the issue of exotic desire itself, which they themselves are complicit in. The "exotic gaze" is their *sinthome*, that which their study tried to grasp, but couldn't. This question remains at the non-discursive level, at the level of fantasy. i have tried to point to this lacuna by developing some possibilities of how exotic desire might be theorized, but the question as to how the Other *looks back*; how the Other is able to ward off the tourist's post-colonial gaze is also a lacuna in the Lutz and Collins study, i.e., the question that the Mudmen of Papua New Guinea pose for their study. The excruciatingly difficult writing style of Homi Bhabha (like a second Lacan) is certainly helpful here, but often his sentence structures are just too convoluted to make any sense, which is my problem and not his. However, as a teacher i am particularly disappointed in his intolerance to questions from the audience.[6] That aside, i shall return to his insights shortly.

In another context, Bill Nichols has tried to grapple with the construction of the ethnographic documentary in his *Representing Reality: Issues and Concepts in Documentary* (1991). i want to make a transition to the next section by raising the question of "excess," that non-discursive sublime realm of the *sinthome* which is "missing" from Lutz and Collins's study of the inter-cultural gaze. "Fiction films are burdened by excess," writes Nichols (p.141). "Some things exceed the centripetal force of narrative."What things? "[E]xcess is the random and inexplicable, that which remains ungovernable within a textual regime presided over by narrative" (ibid.). What remains ungovern-able? "It is better to say that in narrative films excess is what does not fit into a given analytic scheme; it is the noise that remains when we agree upon lim-its for what will pass as information" (ibid.). "It can be conceived as that which exists outside the law" (p.142). The exotic is somehow "excessive" for Lutz and Collins (as Woman is "excessive" in my text). Without a dominant West the exotic would not exist as a site/cite/sight of resistance, qualification, con-testation, and revolt against the very system from which it gains its identity. "The exotic resists all attempts to naturalize it with words attending to appear-ance, function, value, or meaning. The words are familiar and the explanation reasonable but an excess remains. The exotic remains different, beyond famil-iarity" (p.144). To theorize excess within the gaze: this is what seems to be "missing." i want to suggest that this "excess" in the exotic gaze is precisely what the postcolonial gaze cannot entirely control. It is precisely *that* which allows the possibility for the dependent Other to negotiate and maintain iden-tity, or to resist and *look back* in defiance, *unnerving* the dominant gaze. Excess is the very *embodiment* of their subjectivity (the *moi*) carried by their *look*. i draw on the work of Michael Taussig's (1993) notion of mimesis and alter-ity, Kaja Silverman's (1993) distinction between the camera/gaze and the "*moi*" of the look, Vivian Sobchack's (1992) reference to the phenomenological embodiment of film, and Homi Bhabha's (1994 a,b) concept of hybridity to work out this claim.

To begin: Taussig draws on the suggestive insights of Walter Benjamin to argue that Benjamin's concept of "aura" was all about *optical touching*. Sensuous knowledge as *presence* is physiological and established during the pre-Oedipal period, before language, when the child's "gaze is directed towards objects which the hand tries to grasp but fails to reach" (p.35). This gesticu-lating hand in the form of a tactile eye plunges the child into a place where the object world and the visual copy merge—*into the mimetic sensuous connec-tion with things.* This embodiment of vision is worked out by Sobchack's phe-nomenology of film experience, since film offers such a place of convergence from what was once the oral/aural art of the storyteller. "I see, therefore I am embodied," refers to a particular social lived-body or "being-in-the-world." All this seems familiar enough up to now. However, a swerve can now be made. What interests Taussig is the role that mimesis plays as optical tactility in relationship with alterity (the Other), particularly from the descriptions of "first contact." Charles Darwin's writings on the first contact between the Fuegians (inhabitants of Tierra del Fuego) and the sailors of the *Beagle* serve as one paradigm example to explore this relationship. Mimesis in mimicry, he concludes, becomes "as a 'space between,' a space permeated by the colonial tension where it is difficult to say who was the imitator and who is imitated, which is the copy and which is the original" (p.78). The Fuegians were "born mimics," according to Darwin. In this sense mimesis plays the trick of dancing between the very same and the very different. As Lacan (1979:108) claimed, mimicry was a form of camouflage; a form of resemblance that defended a sense of presence by displaying it only in part—metonymically. "It [mimesis] registers both sameness and difference, of being like, and of being Other" (Taussig, p.129). This game of maintaining sameness through alterity fits perfectly with the description of fetishism. It is a form of disavowal which is *agonistic* but not *antagonistic*. To parody a person is, on the one hand, to pay a compliment of sameness, yet paradoxically, there may also be a moment of laughter or mockery. Mimesis as a fetishism is also a form of sympathetic magic, says Taussig: "the power of the copy to influence what it is a copy" (p.250). Taussig's other paradigmatic example, the Cuna (inhabitants of the San Blas Islands of Panama), were so good at the game of mimesis (in mimicry) that they were able to " 'stay the same' in a world of forceful change" (p.129). Lest one think that this form of "anthropological fetishism" is *passé*, Gamman & Makinen (1994:18-27) refer to the phenomenon of "fandom" where the same form of behavior goes on with fans mimicking their stars as a form of reverence and identification, i.e. an "aura" is bestowed on their *idols*. But this is not the direction of my inquiry. Here "authenticity" of identity overlaps with "aura." A *mockery* of the exaggerated performance is more the issue.

With this in mind, i now move briefly to Bhabha's two essays, "On Mimicry and Man," (chap. 4), and "Signs Taken For Wonders " (chap. 6) where he develops the concepts of mimicry and hybridity. Both concepts overlap Taussig's formulations. Says Bhabha, the "colonial mimicry is the desire for a reformed, recognizable Other, *as a subject of a difference that is almost the same, but not quite.* Which is to say that the discourse of mimicry is constructed around an *ambivalence*; in order to be effective, mimicry must continually produce its slippage, its excess, its difference" (p.86, italic in the original). In other words, the dominant gaze of the postcolonialist wants sameness with a slight bit of difference, i.e., this is the structure of the "exotic gaze" that the *National Geographic* magazine desires. It wants a "simian Black" or a "white Indian" (see Taussig, p.162). "*Almost the same but not white* : the visibility of mimicry is always produced at the site[sight | site] of interdiction" (p.89). This is the "excess" of the *National Geographic's* discourse; what is unspoken, concealed and read between its photographs: "not quite/ not white" (p.92). It's what the Mudmen "know" as they put their "wry" masks on and perform for the crowd. Mimicry represents an *ironic* compromise to this postcolonial gaze. Like Taussig, Bhabha also identifies such mimesis in mimicry as an area "in between," but it is an area "between mimicry and mockery." It is from here that "excess or slippage produced by the *ambivalence* of mimicry (almost the same, *but not quite*)," (p. 86, italic in the original) can rupture, displace and render the gaze of the *National Geographic* as a "partial" presence. Like the example of Magritte's *Le Viol* (The Rape), the hired photographer who works for the magazine is "caught looking." Mimicry now emerges "as the subject of the scopic drive and the object of colonial surveillance" (p. 89). Mimicry is therefore both resemblance and menace. "The *menace* of mimicry is its double vision which in disclosing the ambivalence of colonial discourse also disrupts its authority" (p.88).

What this means to the "national geographic tourist" is that he or she faces the very *object a* that formed his or her fantasy of exoticism, and it comes at them *anamorphically,* as a form of terror, a threat that makes them uncomfortable and ashamed. So while the Other turns the "national geographic tourist" into a "partial presence," the tourist caught looking is made more *present* to him or herself. With this "otherness" exposed, and the tourist-photographer's desire laid bare, his or her *jouissance* becomes deflated as a critical distance appears between these "two" contradictory selves. To avoid the shame this brings, the tourist disappears once again behind his "hide" (skin). Because such "mimicry *repeats* rather than *re-presents*" (p.88. original italic), it wears away the tourist's gaze. "For the fetish mimes the forms of authority at the point which it deauthorizes them" (p. 91). Bhabha makes the further point that such mimicry is metonymic. It is the part, the differential feature of the *ambivalence* which enables the dissimulation of the gaze (see Gamman and Makinen, p. 44-46).

The other formulation Bhabha develops is hybridity which is "more than the mimetic but less than the symbolic." Hybridity here is the *reversal* of disavowal. It is where "the trace of what is disavowed [as in mimicry] is not *repressed* but *repeated* as something *different* — a mutation, a hybrid" (p.111, my italic). What Bhabha is developing here is to identify that which escapes classification, essentialism and tradition necessary for the colonial gaze to secure its domination. This is a movement from symbol (category of classification) to sign. "Excess" (because of the repetition) becomes a feature—a sign that makes the hybrid (the bastard) not fit the pre-set categorization prepared for him or her. "If discriminatory effects enable the authorities to keep an eye on them, the proliferating difference evades that eye, escapes that surveillance" (p.112). This excessive feature is again metonymically present, making easy categorization impossible, thereby also diminishing the presence and power of the authoritative gaze. Whereas in mimicry, the disavowal happens prior to the perception of difference, Bhabha makes the point that hybridity happens "*after the intervention of difference*" (p. 115, original italic). What this means is that the distortion or displacement (*Entstellung*) produced by hybridity occurs after the categorizations by the colonial gaze have taken place. "It is the power of this strange metonymy of presence to so disturb the systematic (and systemic) construction of discriminatory knowledges that the cultural, once recognized as the medium of authority, becomes virtually unrecognizable. ...The display of hybridity—its peculiar 'replication'—terrorizes authority with the *ruse* of recognition, its mimicry, its mockery" (p. 115, original italic). Hybridity belongs to the photographic discards that *National Geographic* avoids should its categorical discourse become threatened.

The above discussion now brings me to Kaja Silverman (1993;1996) and the question of *optical tactility* associated with "excess." Taussig and Bhabha's discussion dealt at the level of "contact" where the face-to-face ethics demonstrate the way the "look" of the colonized can resist the gaze of the colonizer. *National Geographic* takes that threat away to create the fantasy of tourism through a hyperbolic aesthetic investment on its subjects through photographs, much like Spielberg's film, *Schindler's List* (1993), is a hyperbolic aesthetic investment of the atrocities of WW2. Despite its subject matter, death is presented in all its sublime beauty. An audience feels no "shame" when it walks out of the theater. Like the *National Geographic*, Jewish "excess" has been contained. There has been no "witnessing." i mention this film as a direct contrast to the thesis Silverman develops through her close reading of Harun Farocki's 1988 film, *Bilder der Welt und Inschrift des Krieges* (The View of the World and the Inscription of War) which is a deconstruction of Enlightenment vision. Silverman makes the argument that the camera and the gaze are synonymous and instrumental in projecting a *screen image* on its subjects. The camera/gaze functions to "memorialize " and to "mortify." Separated from the uncertainty of the "look," the social apparatus of the recorded camera/gaze "kills" its subject. Its efficiency records, militarily inscribes and freezes its subject for examination and surveillance. Despite its gaze, Silverman illustrates from Farocki's film how these screens of surveillance both manipulate and may be manipulated. The photographing of Algerian women by a conscript French soldier (Marc Garanger) in 1960, for the purposes of issuing identity cards, is an example of colonial manipulation. These women, when photographed, are asked to remove their veil, which acts as a kind of mask, making these women publicly invisible. Their visibility now replaces one screen with another. Silverman's second example is a picture of a young beautiful Jewish woman smiling at her photographer at Auschwitz. Argues Silverman, the woman's attempt is to use the screen of "femininity" to override the screen of racial difference. Perhaps a vain gesture, but a gesture nevertheless to influence her fate. Silverman ends her essay by making the claim that the "look" has the capacity to "see" things that the mechanized camera/gaze cannot— and that is *memory* or *recollection*. The look is able to "witness," which is what the camera apparatus can never do. "It apprehends the other less as a clearly delineated object than as a complex and constantly shifting conglomeration of images which at all points implicate the self" (p.46).

The look is therefore an "imprint," or "memory trace," a phenomenological embodiment (Sobchack's (1992), like "the corporeal and psychic 'reality' of being female and Algerian in a French colony in 1960, or female and Jewish in Germany in the early 1940s" (p.52). Without this look, resistance to the gaze would not be impossible, for such a "look" carries with it its *optical tactility* of the "eye witness," perhaps the very "aura" itself.[7] Whether the German photographer in Auschwitz or whether Marc Garanger (as Mark the "Peeping Tom") in Algeria were ever "shamed" of what they were doing by these "looks" back: the "smile" of desperation of the Jewish woman or the sheer "horror" recorded on the face of the Algerian women as her veil was removed, no one will ever know. i suspect "otherwise," for i do know how my I/eye in Crete was displaced from its moorings by a proprietor who had just too much tourism in his past to keep his masquerade of hospitality contained. Rather he "looked" back at me and displaced my gaze which the I thought I never carried: I like you... I mean (*I don't like you*), I like your money.

Optical Tactility: The "Nervous" Gaze

The appropriation of psychoanalysis for the analysis of sex/gender constructions can be fruitful, insightful, startling in its revelatory powers, as well as formulaic and repetitive in its possibilities. It is quite obvious that throughout my journey the figure of Slavoj Žižek plays a prominent part to make that understanding more thought-provoking. His applications of Lacanian analysis to popular culture are remarkable in their lucidity and clever in their argumentation. But here i would also like to point to Craig Saper's "A Nervous Theory: The Troubling Gaze of Psychoanalysis in Media Studies" (1991), as someone who has also recognized the radical potential of Lacan's late writings.[8] He begins his essay with the sentence, "The gaze is in trouble," and then spends the rest of the time not only reviewing the various shifts that have gone on beyond Mulvey's position, as well as the various problems that have been encountered, but attempts to rescue the gaze as still a potentially disruptive concept, referring to it as a "nervous theory." i wish to highlight a few points that he makes and develop an anecdote that keeps me believing that psychoanalytic theory is still a worthwhile pursuit for my question.

To cut to the chase, Saper, like Žižek, wants to treat the gaze *as a trope*, a figure that sets what is "missing" in motion. If Lacan's paradoxical logic is ignored, then the eye (the look) becomes confused with the gaze. For example, Lutz and Collins' study of the *National Geographic's* discourse is confined to the conscious level of the look. So here is Saper trying to describe this shift of the gaze as a "paradox into perception:"

> Rather than an instrument of a patriarchal law or Symbolic order, the gaze interrupts and sways the law like a *clinamen* [inclination, bias], a crucial component of Epicurean atomic theory, which creates a lack of balance and makes the atoms swerve, setting the world in motion. That paradoxical construction is difficult for practical criticism to understand. The gaze is part of a Symbolic structure and opens onto a hole in that structure (p.36).

It should not be forgotten that it was Marx who wrote his doctorate on the Epicurean materialism where atoms had their own "will," swayed "by chance," whereas Democritian atoms "took their orders," moved by "necessity." In this formulation i take Saper raising the possibility of optical tactility.

Here is a collage of phrases Saper uses to provide you a sense of that which is impossible to write:

> This *objet a* "decorates or encloses a void." ... The void is Real. ... "a place where knowing and desiring come together in an encounter or impasse" ... [*objet a*] are "objects we cannot bear to see that force knowledge of discontinuity and fragmentation while marking an impasse or loss. ... *objet a* as the return of the repressed, neither image nor word, is the enigmatic mark (or missing intention) of loss (p.42-43).

> The *objet a* marks a missed encounter; it does not illustrate
> or describe an abyss or any other positive phenomenon...
> but it re-presents literal discontinuity or lack in a structure
> (p.44)

Saper, i believe, is referring to that physical blind spot at the point where the optic nerve opens up onto the retina (Crary, 1990,p.75). In cybernetic language, it is *that* which opens the system up. Without theorizing this impossible knot/not, entropy rather than negentropy would inform the system, causing it a thermal death. *The Thing* is Lacan's theorization for this opening—void—hole. Put more poetically, Leonard Cohen in Anthem (*The Future* album) sings, "there is a crack in everything, that's how the light gets in."

Saper's "nervous theory" is close to, if not the same as Žižek's theorizations of the *sinthome*, The Thing—"the final limit of the psychoanalytic process" (Žižek, 1991,p.137). Žižek's (1989b) formulations of the *sinthome* come from the writings of the "late" Lacan, the Lacan of *Ethics of Psychoanalysis* where he made the turn from the signifier to the object; the voice and the gaze were precisely *objet petit a* that Saper has referred to. As Žižek develops these concepts, the "gaze" and the "voice" are transferable concepts to Derridean deconstruction: the gaze can be likened to "presence" (as theory attempting to grasp the "thing itself") while voice may be equated to "speech" or phonocentrism.[9] Deconstruction converts the gaze into the "look," or point of view by showing the limits as to what can be seen from what cannot be seen within a system. Again, to recall the early discussions of Velázquez' *Las Meniñas* and Giacomettit's *Suspended Ball*, there is "that" which escapes total capture by the gaze. With the voice, Derrida demonstrates how it is informed by the trace of writing; after all the words i speak belong to a written language. In this sense my two (I)(i)'s are completely implicated in one another; there is no gap between them, except a stylistic one. Writing needs speech as much as speech needs writing. But this is where Lacan parts company with Derrida, for in his formulations the gaze and the voice are almost in exact reverse. i quote Žižek's succinct passage at length which is often repeated throughout his books:

> First of all, they [the gaze and the voice] are not on the
> side of the subject [as with Derrida] but on the side of the
> object. The gaze marks the point in the object (the picture)
> from which the viewing subject is *already gazed at*: it is
> the object which is gazing at me. Thus, far from guaran-

teeing the self-presence of the subject and her/his vision, the gaze functions as a spot or stain in/on the picture, disturbing its transparent visibility and introducing an irreducible split in my relation to it. I can never see the picture at the point from which it is gazing at me: the view and the gaze are constitutively dissymmetrical. The gaze as object is a blemish that prevents me from looking at the picture from a safe, 'objective' distance, framing it as something which is at the disposal of my grasping view [as a point of view]. It is, we might say, the point at which the very frame (of my view) is already inscribed in the 'content' of the picture. And the same goes, of course, for the voice as object. That voice, the voice, for example, of the superego, addressing me without being attached to any particular bearer, floating freely in some horrifying interspace, functions again as a stain or blemish, whose inert presence interferes like a foreign body and prevents me from achieving self-identity (1989b, p.8).

What can all this possibly mean? In the horror genre section of the masculine gaze i tried to clarify the *objet a* by referring to Jacques-Alain Miller's figures. Coming back to Saper is a way to attend to the potential of the *sinthome*, and to the "nervous gaze" it calls on as a form of *optical tactility*. Saper (p.45-46) points to Lacan's formulation of *tuché* (by chance), a review of which will help clarify Žižek's remarks. What needs to be kept in mind is that the *tuché* "can rise from inanimate objects." This means that inanimate images, which are intentionless, like paintings, films, and dreams can, "by chance," arrest the flow of seeing or speaking. In short, you can be "struck" by them. Here we have a possible version of "spiritual materialism" that i spoke about earlier.[10] A form of intentionality is given over to inanimate things. "In short, we do not by chance encounter the inanimate; it, as Lacan says, "knocks" us by chance. It is an incidental cause of our existence in reality. It marks a limit; it points at you. And it opens a hole in the Symbolic ordering of the world" (p.46).

Žižek's particular turn of phrase helps what's at issue here: "The gaze marks the point in the object (in the picture) from which the subject viewing it is already gazed at, i.e., it is the object that is gazing at me" (also in 1991, p.125). The point being made here is that objects fascinate us; we are caught by them, as it were, unconsciously. We can get "butterflies in our stomach." "The Real affect occurs when vision is cut from the subject. Looking is usually connected to the body or an intention. When *vision is cut from the subject*, either the artist or the spectator, it creates anxiety" (p.48, italic in original). These are *not* objects of conscious speculation which we try to master with the eye; they are moments when we are "caught looking" by the object staring back at us, like Magritte's *Le Viol*. These must be incidental moments, not intentional and open for prior intellectual deliberation. They are like a "summons" from the Real. "[T]he by-chance event is never completely subsumed under a Symbolic law ..." (p.46). I am reminded of the film *Looker* which, for all its voyeurism and silly plot, has a redeeming feature, and that is the invention of a special "ray gun" that emits negative light which stuns the victim to a point of frozen seduction and persuasiveness. Could this ray gun be a synecdoche for the gaze that looks back? During these moments victims are "blinded"; they discern something about what they cannot see. The gaze the self encounters is, in Lacan's words "not a seen gaze, but a gaze imagined by me in the field of the Other" (1979,p.84). It is that imagined gaze by the Other that can be so threatening, so "troubling," that makes us nervous, like my moment on the isle of Crete.

This reminds me of Robert Sheldrake's theories in speculative biology where he imagines the possibility of morphogenetic transhistorical connections for each species. Something must exist "outside" of the genes themselves for nowhere can it be explained where the image to orchestrate the genetic blueprint of a species comes from. The genes seem to know where they are going, by themselves. Again, the question: how much metaphysics—non-discursivity—should be allowed to enter deliberations of social reality? Žižek points to the example of the sinking of the Titanic as an example of the Lacanian Thing; it is a sublime object, the "material leftover" which still exerts a fascination for us. It looks back (1989a,pp.69-71). After this "by-chance" event, the historical understanding of our relationship to technology changed. Lyotard's conceptualization of "the event" is quite consistent in this regard. Postmodern is not a historical period for him; rather it is when history becomes changed by the incidental *event*. The invention and explosion of the atom bomb, as well as the tragic explosion of the spacecraft *U.S.S. Challenger* are such "events." But these are large scale; the point is that these events go on in the micro-scale as well ... on Crete, for instance!

Towards the end of his essay Saper provides me with a *raison d'etre* for art. "[A]rt does not merely picture the trauma of the Real or the lack which our knowledge moves. It attempts to re-present the gaze—our look returned...cutting into a present absence. It appears as our struggle with limits and constraints and arises from the symbolization of lack" (p.50). Perhaps no other theorist has taken these words to heart as Slavoj Žižek. At first reading, his readings of the Real in popular culture are stunning and breath-taking; skillfully applying Lacanian insights with ease in a manner few of us could ever hope to accomplish. i had the "by-chance" occasion to listen and meet him in Klagenfurt, Austria in June of 1993. What was so unusual were the circumstances under which all this occurred. No one came! Here was (what i thought and still do) a brilliant scholar with no audience! The irony should be apparent. Lectures had been set up for other members of the Ljublijana psychoanalytic circle. i heard the equally provocative readings by Renata Salecl and Miran Božović. When it was his turn to close the lecture series, no one showed. i think both Žižek and Božović took pity on me and gave me working copies of their (now published) papers: Miran Božović's "The Bond of Love: Lacan and Spinoza" (now in *New Formations*, 23 Summer, 1994) and Žižek's "From Courtly Love to *The Crying Game*" (1993a). i relate this story at the end because it points to me how chance does direct desire. i was struck, stunned and seduced by their readings about courtly love, criminals and the law, and a psychoanalytic application to the Bosnia-Hercegovia war (Salecl, 1993).[11]

1 An equally impressive study of Kruger which employs psychoanalysis is Mignon Nixon's "You Thrive on Mistaken Identity" (1992). Her work is a pleasure to read in its bending of Lacanian insights to expose yet other level of Kruger's work. It vivifies that such criticism is as socially responsible as Kruger is in manipulating the gaze..

2 This is brilliantly demonstrated in Mary Kelly's *PPD* (1983); especially sec. IV where she records her give and take struggles with her son on pieces of his blanket.

3 For the relationship between the artist and 'his' models see footnote 13, in "Pretexts to the Title."

4 i am using the word "aura" as first utilized by Walter Benjamin (1973/1935) as that human mode of belonging to the world which involves a recognition of our affinity and reciprocity with things. Art educators have now "found" this aura in the multicultural studies that fill the pages of the new Discipline Based Art Education Curriculae of the Getty Center for Education in the Arts, a neo-racist agenda for justifying fine arts. (See jagodinski, 1997, in press).

5 The social history of photography is admirably examined by John Tagg's *The Burden of Representation: Essays on Photographies and Histories* (1988). In his introduction Tagg links up Barthes' *Camera Lucida* with Foucault's technologies of surveillance to illustrate how deviance and homosexuality came to be controlled through the documentary photograph. Tagg's work in post-Althusserian questions of ideology has the great strength of being historically specific, to the degree that might be an achievable intention.

6 After his "Postcolonial Authority and Postmodern Guilt" paper presented at the University of Illinois conference, "Cultural Studies Now and in the Future," and subsequently published in Lawrence Grossberg et al. *Cultural Studies* (1992), the discussion that followed was recorded and transcribed. The exchanges show little tolerance on his behalf for those who earnestly tried to understand his talk. On a visit to the University of Alberta, the four papers he delivered were equally incomprehensible, not only to me, but for many others in the audience. The same intolerance and dismissal repeated itself; strange behavior for someone involved in intercultural studies. This could be interpreted as a performance; giving it back to the academics who gave it to the native-others. Unfortunately, it doesn't further communication, but perhaps his is a necessary stance? There is no escape; he has to be read for his thoughtful discourse, if not *listened* to!

7 Here the possibility of theorizing the "difference" that science fiction trades on between humans and machines can be explored, for it is precisely the "memory trace" or "psychic reality" which distinguishes

the two: the border between being "alive" or "dead." Once again the cyborg becomes another one of those mysterious creatures living between what Lacan called the "two deaths." In a special issue of *Genders: Cyberpunk: Technologies of Cultural Identity*, edited by Thomas Foster (1993), this question is explored within the context of what this means given the embodiment of woman. Claudia Springer's "Muscular Circuitry: The Invincible Armored Cyborg in Cinema" (1993) provides an excellent overview to this question.

8 Perhaps Noël Carroll's *Mystifying Movies: Fads and Fallacies in Contemporary Film Theory* (1988) is equally against psychoanalysis and the gaze as Saper is for it. (See also Carroll, 1990.)

9 Derrida's well-known deconstruction of speech/ writing binary (in Derrida, 1973).

10 Murray Bookchin's book *Ecology of Freedom* (1982) presents the same view at the end of his book.

11 A brilliant application of Balibar's theory with Lacanian psychoanalysis to explain the racism of Serbian, Croatian and Muslim interrelations can be found in "Phantasmen des Krieges: Patriarchat und Mutterland - Heimat und Rassismus," *Lettre International*, (1993) by Renata Salecl who teaches at the University of Ljublijana, Slovania in the Department of Law and Justice. See also her *Spoils of Freedom* (1994).

THE THIRD VIGNETTE

The Unhappy Marriage of Marxism & Feminism

Though a number of critics have talked about a period of cohabitation, or marriage, between Marxism and feminism, these metaphors are themselves an effect of the sex-gender system.... It would appear, then, that it is no longer expedient to invoke the figure of marriage, or even divorce to characterize the association between Marxism and feminism,

especially when and where Marxism is reflexively understood as "masculine" Other of feminism.

(Miklitsch, 1991:120)

The title of this vignette is now ironically inflected.[1] In 1980 i had finished my doctorate thesis at the University of Alberta in art criticism and art history in the Faculty of Education influenced by the perspective of a phenomenological Marxism, i.e., a Marxism inflected with subjectivism. The Czech marxist philosopher Karl Kosik and the Frankfurt School of critical thought were of central concern for me; *Telos* and the questions it raised centered me. i realize now, with hindsight, that my thesis was gender-blind. Teaching for two years (1980-82) at Mount Saint Vincent had laid the foundations for my first encounter with feminist thought, but the question as to what the difference between feminine and feminism was had not been resolved. As discussed earlier, feminist politics,the feminine, and French feminism seemed to swim together. I returned one year later to the University of Alberta in Edmonton to teach art education. On March 12,1983, Carolyne and I traveled with my colleague, friend and teacher, Harry Garfinkle to attend a conference celebrating 100 years of Marxism in Winnipeg, Manitoba. Harry had been involved in the former CCF (Canadian Communist Federation) in Saskatchewan and had a superb knowledge of Canadian politics.[2] Once more i was confronted with the issue of feminism. During the conference, which had virtually all the factions of Marxism one could ever imagine—Trotskyites argued with Maoists; Althusserians (Gordon Therborn had come before his tragic suicide) argued with "critical theorists"; the right-leaning social democrats argued with their more radical left-leaning party members. Ralph Miliband was there; Ernest Mandel gave a talk from the position of the 5th International; Stanley Aronowitz made mention of (the then current?) crisis in historical materialism—but all these positions were shattered as, throughout the four day conference, more and more women's voices could be heard. Their concerns came to a head when in a keynote address, they demanded their own microphone to address the main speakers. It became quite obvious to me that any form of Marxism, from the most traditional to the foremost current critical stances, were not meeting their needs. i recall, in particular, a panel where Zillah Eisenstein spoke—a name unknown to me. At that time i could not grasp the meaning of her critique. As always, one only truly "wakes up" from a dream when it begins to unravel itself.

The next three years—to about 1986, i spent unraveling that dream (along with my consistent attendance at College Art Association). The problem was the question of human nature. i always excepted (and continue to do so, but with great modification) the Marxian anthropological premise that the line between nature and culture does not exist. Through co-operative productive praxis, human(e) beings continuously re-created their physiological and psychological constitution. Human nature was a historically changing phenomenon so neither of our natures were universally fixed, neither the man's nor the woman's. Influenced by the anthropological work of Harry Garfinkle (1981) i had drafted a manuscript that traced the protocultural developments of aesthetics (jagodzinski, 1986-1994), arguing that the deep, deep structure of human "nature" was subject to change. i couldn't square my materialism with feminist materialism.[3] As Jagger (1983) succinctly put it: "A historical and dialectical conception of human biology, sees human nature and the forms of human social organization as determined not by our biology alone, but rather by a complex interplay between our forms of social organization, including our type of technological development, between our biological constitution and the physical environment that we inhabit" (p. 110).

Yet, it had been *radical* feminists, claiming an essential difference, which again jostled my mind from its slumber; the same repeat performance which had happened during the College Art Association when the Women's Caucus formed their own pre-conference format. It was radical feminists who had spoken up at the Marxist "celebration." The key to women's oppression was men's power over women, a power which could not be overcome unless there was a general transformation of society. A *verticality* of women's oppression across lines of class, color, race was posited, pointing once again to an essential difference at the bottom of it all. Social feminists claimed that unless the economic inequalities and class oppressions of capitalist society were addressed, no change for women would happen. They had politicized sexuality and exposed men's everyday behavior as physical domination and control over women. Yet, not all women claimed to be "oppressed" by this ubiquitous sense of patriarchy. The situation seemed to repeat the same problem of the fourth International which failed to unite the workers across national lines. When WW1 broke out, nationalism overcame any loyalties to a broader vision of a less-repressive world run by workers. Feminist Marxists and Marxist feminists were divided amongst themselves as to the new vision. Eisenstein (her name literally translated as "iron stone" seems metaphorically apt for her position!) argued that women formed a "sexual class" divided only by way of their class and racial differences. Women, because they perform "socially necessary labor," cut through all economic classes; "they require that economic class differentiations within sexual class be recognized" (1984:149). But how were they to form a revolutionary subject, a class "for themselves," as Eisenstein would want it, when not all women were conscientized as to their plight? Eisenstein's Marxist feminist project was precisely to do this—make women conscious of their oppression by making alliances with liberal, radical and social feminists rather than with Marxists *per se*.

As the I understood vaguely some of the debates between women socialists who wished to either revise Marxism or recenter it, the critique of capitalism was perceived to be just one more variant of patriarchy—a patriarchal capitalism or capitalist patriarchy. It was necessary to build a dialectical analysis of it as a political system which oppresses women, not only economically, but through the patriarchal arrangements of family, motherhood and the sexual division of labour, so well examined by the now well-known and often quoted social British feminists like Annette Kuhn and Michèle Barrett. Barrett's *Women's Oppression Today: The Marxist Feminist Encounter* (1980/1988) was considered a key text in this literature. The 'politics of reproduction,' as O'Brien (1981) was to call it, rather than economic production, constituted the base of society. Here was a direct challenge to Man the Creator of Culture. Marxist analysis had never examined the inequality which existed between men and women on the level of procreation. The woman's position was taken as a relationship to the economic system; women had been primarily subsumed under the male wage labor force, or as producers of surplus value through housework which benefited capitalism. With the feminist critique of Marxism, economy was relegated to part of the superstructure. Within these critiques, particularly in Firestone's (1979) formulation of them in *The Dialectic of Sex*, the primary division of society, *at base*, was no longer along class lines; rather it was re-theorized along the psychosexual division between men and women. The sexual-reproductive organization of society around the biological family—male/female/infant—generated the entire superstructure (economics, judicial, political) of a given historical period. Freud was de-biologized; penis envy now become an envy for the social power held by the male. Yet, the problem with such a reformulation left history with no sense of movement. How have women changed their condition if oppression in all its forms was derived from the male/female division? (Sheila Rowbotham, 1981:365). For me, it left patriarchy as an ahistorical term. i shall return to these thoughts after a slight detour.

Its Splendor No Longer Glitters

In Leeds, England, in 1979, while still preparing for my doctoral dissertation, the I had the good fortune of having been, however briefly, influenced by the art sociologist Janet Wolff and the art historian Tim Clark at the University of Leeds. At that time, both Wolff and Clark had not yet incorporated a gendered discourse (Lacan) into their own critical theorizations in any major way, but both had a strong socialist orientation towards aesthetics and art history. (Clark is still occasionally reminded for his gender blindness in his analysis of Manet's *Olympia*, e.g., Pollock, 1988:51.) Clark had to fill the shoes, more like the seat, of the former chair of art history—Arnold Hauser, whose writings in the social history of art were a bench mark for leftist cultural politics. Wolff was engaged in the sociology of art. What happened to me, however, was a reorientation to what the meaning of art was within this politicized social context. This was something i took away with me back to Canada. i began to perceive art as a social practice and production and began to ask what were the conditions of that practice. i began to treat art as a form of representation and consumption rather than an isolated object whose meaning lay behind the work, a substitute image for something that wasn't there. A broader sense of art as cultural practice emerged in my own discourse. These practices were signifying systems, practices of representation, sites/sights/cites not for the production of beautiful things evoking beautiful feelings, but codes in rhetorical textural/pictorial forms—distinct from social existence. Michèle Barrett's early essay, "Feminism and the Definition of Cultural Politics" (1982) outlined this material aesthetic perspective rather well. Her arguments adumbrate many of the tenets of cultural studies that have emerged since. She began her argument by claiming that feminism had virtually transformed and reassessed artistic and imaginary expression. Drawing on Raymond Williams, she put forward a view which interpreted literature as an issue of "signification." Meaning as a "system of signs" was constructed, represented, consumed and produced, but this depended on who was reading or receiving the text. In Barrett's view, there was no fixed or inherent meaning; rather, following Raymond Williams, specific formal qualities helped to determine "dominant or preferred, reading" (p.42) within precise sociohistorical contexts. A rape scene watched by feminist viewers in a play had an entirely different meaning for "men from the rugby club who rushed in from the bar (laughing) when they heard what was going on" (p.39). In her "Max Raphael and the Question of Aesthetics" (1987b) article, she solidified this position: "no text can be inherently progressive or reactionary—it becomes so in the act of consumption" (p.85). In her view artistic intent and references to an artist's life were no guarantees that an artwork was progressive, since all such cultural products were marked by inner contradictions. Woman's art was not necessarily feminist since it may not be aligned with political interests. "[F]eminist art could be seen as a category within a tradition of women's art but I fail to see how it could be generated outside it" (p.47).

Barrett also made an important distinction between cultural production in general from the specific production of "art" within the broader framework of an historical materialist critique of ideology; a development which was later expanded by Griselda Pollock. She wrote, "[I]deas about art are profoundly influenced by, and entangled with, a particular historical conception of art which affects feminist as well as other types of thinking (p.47). In capitalism, there was a marked division between "work" and "art." The latter was valued as being creative because there was some control over the product, while the former was devalued as merely the display of manual skill. Such a division was a road block for a more democratic leveling of aesthetic value and pleasure. Barrett's suggestions here have been taken up with vengeance as the division between popular culture and high art have been deconstructed.

Another democratic leveling was her call for the elimination between the producer and consumer of art, again an important distinction advanced currently by Paul Willis's (1990 a,b) notion of "common culture" and the writings of popular cultural theorists like John Fiske and Michel de Certeau. "[I]f we can identify levels of aesthetic skill in the construction of works of art, and the expression of critical and fictional representation of the world, it becomes clear that the reading of the work will inevitably depend upon the corresponding consciousness and knowledge of the audience" (p.52). Barrett called for a cultural milieu whereby feminist visions could be both creatively consumed and imaginatively produced. Women's genres (soaps, romances) were not to be dismissed outright but actively interrogated for the pleasure they brought. Felski (1989), writing seven years later, made a similar point with regards to literature:

> [I]t is impossible to speak of 'masculine' and 'feminine' in any meaningful sense in the formal analysis of text; the political value of literary texts from the standpoint of feminism can be determined only by an investigation of their social functions and effects in relation to the interests of women in particular historical context, and not by attempting to deduce an abstract literary theory of 'masculine' or 'feminine,' 'subversive' and 'reactionary' forms in isolation

> from the social conditions of their production and recep-
> tion (p.2).

Like Barrett, gender analysis and gender politics were two separate, but not mutually exclusive, issues for Felski.

The experience in Leeds opened new doors, however. Art education as practiced in North America at that time was defined by a formalism, a positivist research ideology and an idealist aesthetic.[4] As i write/rite/right this, i can still recall the feelings of despair i had as gallery art all of a sudden became a rather boring space for me, as did classical studio courses. i began to realize that this tradition was not only phallogocentric but mostly a middle to upper class pursuit run on the principles of capitalism by a dominant white culture which dictated the discourse of art and art education.[5] It also hit hard at this time, that as an immigrant of Polish descent, and in my parents' desire that i should make the "grade" in Canada, culture with a capital C required study and internalization, which the I did diligently. Looking back with new eyes, i could now only engage that tradition through critique. The naïve gaze was gone—beauty somehow stripped away—simply not in the proper 'aesthetic' posture, critics would say. It was about this time that i stopped shopping for antiques. The seeming "truck-load" of artifacts brought over from England began to lose all meaning and "charm." This sounds like Benjamin's accusing finger pointing at me; telling me that the 'aura' had somehow vanished from these works. It had.

The writings of Lucy Lippard, especially *Get The Message? A Decade of Art for Social Change* (1984), became increasingly more important to me, as did the journal *Heresies*, copies of which i back-ordered. Lippard's early work (late 1970s, see 1984:88-105) reflected the tensions between social feminism and Marxism. Lippard pointed out that the art establishment in its current infrastructure was, by and large, a middle to upper class pursuit with an art market geared to generate capital. Artists should therefore envision themselves as workers rather than "professionals" since they did not control the products of their labour. Art's contradictory basis became most visible in art schools and universities where it played a contradictory position between both upper and lower classes. On the one hand, abstract art was inaccessible to public comprehension; it was there not merely to entertain. Yet on other hand, it had to communicate. The paranoia which the art market suffered with the loss of content was quickly re-established through the celebration of figurative painting and magic realism (Burgin, 1986b). The power of the artist's signature was restored (although it was never really lost); but further contradictions manifested themselves, for example, in the style of dress! As Lippard suggests, middle-class sons had to dress 'down,' to 'look' poor in order to feel superior to the rich. Middle-class women artists, on the other hand, had to dress 'down' in order to don the uniform of working class men. To end this personal crisis i was having with art and art education as i took the feminist critique to heart (in all its conflicting forms), at about this time a group of us founded the *Social Theory Caucus in Art Education* which eventually became an affiliate of the National Art Education Association in 1982. Our mandate, along with the publication of an annual journal (*The Journal of Social Theory in Art Education*), was to raise critical social issues as they related to art education.

Materialist Feminist Collaborations

To return to the main road once more, which meets at the conjunction between Marxism and feminist materialism, is to wonder how the two are to be reconciled. "What is the future of Marxism-feminism?" (1991: 120) asks Robert Miklitsch. Miklitsch goes back to the texts of Marx and Engles to examine the "woman question" in classical Marxism and comes up with the verdict that Marx's humanism was indeed predicated on the unexamined notion of sexual differences. He concludes that rather than reflexively re-troping the relation between Marxism and feminism, collaboration could take place "within and between" their respective discourses; but this requires attention to the limits of both classical Marxism and radical feminism. If classical Marxism put into play prostitution as a rhetorical metaphor of exploitation without paying enough attention to woman's subjective position in capitalism, then radical feminism's notion of patriarchy was "too monocausal and ahistorical to account for the diversity, complexity, and specificity of women's oppression" (p.135). (This was the position that the I had experienced at the "celebration.") Both require revision. Miklitsch proposes that the hybrid term post-marxism be taken seriously to "comprise a renewed, critical attention to the construction of (re-)production, the representation of those sociosexual relations of economy and consciousness, production and 'sex-affective' reproduction, which the concept of sex-gender attempts, in part, to name" (p. 136). Drawing from Cocks' *The Oppositional Imagination* (1989), Miklitsch agrees that masculine power in late patriarchy operates on dual thematics: "the thematic of species reproduction" ('patriarchal right') and "the thematic of sexuality" ('phallic right'). These dual concerns are best understood through the logic of late capitalism. He believes that the concerns of feminism have converged with the concerns of Marxism in their turn from economy to hegemony as best illustrated through Cultural Studies.

Someone like the Cambridge Marxist economist David Harvey (1989) has never lost his belief in the necessity of ideology critique, so as to be swallowed up by postmodern theories that do away with "the social" as a historically produced category. Nor has Morton Wenger (1993-94) who concludes his overview of postmodernism with: "There is no question that postmodernism is Idealist and anti-materialist and that it is explicitly anti-communist in its history and its theory" (p.76). The strength of Marxist analysis for both authors is still viable. But, as Wenger sarcastically notes, if "contemporary Marxists cannot link NAFTA [North American Free Trade Agreement] and Oprah, Khomeini and cocaine, neo-nazism and architectural neo-classicism more convincingly than do the postmodern Idealists, then who needs such 'Marxism' anyway?" (ibid.). David Harvey is such a theorist who is able to do precisely that. His analysis of the postmodern condition, written as early as 1989, stands as a testament that Marxist analysis can still provide a solid understanding of post-fordist 'flexible' capitalism. Harvey doesn't confine himself *just* to the economic base, although that perspective is present as well, but he engages himself with the cultural artifacts of postmodernity: architecture, art, literature and film. Much of his book is in the area of cultural critique, examining the roots of modernism, postmodern art and even analyzing Wim Wenders' film *Wings of Desire* in context of postmodern society which he had just described. This shift to "post-marxist" analysis of everyday life is to place more emphasis on the non-economic and subjective aspects of human activity as a crucial way to understand the production and reproduction of everyday life. Such praxis, following the influential work of Raymond Williams, has been referred to as "cultural materialism" which recognizes that the production of discourses—signs, representations, the very signifying systems of ideology—are themselves material activities with material effects that may have a bearing on the economic structures as well. Not only economic structures, but each sphere of cultural production can be treated as a "base." All artists and writers are engaged in a politics of discourse. But, it must be admitted, not acknowledging the powerful influence of the economic structures, "in the last instance," makes for a less than satisfying critique.

The synthesis of *Materialist Feminisms* (1993) by Donna Landry and Gerald MacLean is equally impressive for its scope and insights of the Anglo-American scene. They speak to the kind of discursive cross-fertilization Miklitsch called for, and they incorporate the critique of postmodernity that Harvey's study so admirably did by maintaining a global perspective on capitalist expansion. As in the previous vignette, both reject the concept of an ahistorical category of "Woman," and look towards the de-fetishization of "experience" by recognizing the necessity of a logic of difference wherein the incommensu-

rable is not only tolerated but enables those differences to speak. A materialist feminism does not focus on gender alone. Feminists working with Marxist
and socialist paradigms have posed the problem of "dual-system" theories:
should class precede gender or visa versa in the determination of social life?
What happens then, they ask, when a third or subsequent terms are added—
race, color, age, ableism, ethnicity, sexuality—to complicate the situation? "A
feminist politics, projected exclusively in terms of women's equality cannot
recognize, much less challenge, those current existing socio-political structures and institutional settings which divide women by class, race, sexuality,
and ethnicity, and in which a simple concept of women's equality with men
may seem rather beside the point" (p.12). Conference dynamics have changed
since 1983!

Landry and MacLean's solution to this dilemma is to take the political claims of deconstruction seriously without losing sight/cite/site of class
struggle and gender ideology within specific historical-political sites. After a
historical review of the varieties of feminist materialisms, the mid-section
offers some direct applications. The specificity of the novel form for women,
following the lead of Rita Felski's development of a "feminist counter-pub-
lic sphere," is advocated. Felski reads how feminist fictions differ by country
and social differences. Canadian feminist fiction often pits the opposition
between nature and culture so as to examine gender differences and national
identity. In contrast, West German feminists are often opposed to political
movements and are influenced by a tradition of German idealism. Landry and
MacLean praise the feminist detective genre and the political writings of
African American women writers, i.e., Octavia Butler and Gloria Naylor;
women of color, i.e., Bessie Head and Mariama Bâ; and postcolonial writers
like Hanif Kueishi for offering a historical materialism through the fiction-
alization of women's lives in specific historical and cultural contexts. They
conclude with a materialist feminism which is not only globally sensitive to
class contradictions within gender ideology and gendered social practices, but
one which also gives material weighting to social and literary analysis that
calls itself materialist, i.e., the ideological analysis of race, sexuality, imperialism and colonialism, and anthropocentrism.

i have found reading through Rosemary Hennessy's *Materialist
Feminism and the Politics of Discourse* (1993) as yet another recent attempt preserve the insights of an ideology critique. Like Harvey, Landry and MacLean,
the strength of Hennessy's work is her passion to continue to problematize
the *global perspective* of women. She continuously comes back to the social
problems that plague thousands of poor women who are disproportionally
women of color. Women of color, lesbians, working-class, and "third-world"

women who find themselves outside the feminist liberal mainstream, are all subsumed under materialist feminism. Issues of race, class, color and sexuality are forwarded. Hennessy engages critically with those feminists who remain ahistorical and essentialist in their thinking, i.e., French feminists. *Feminist standpoint theory* is particularly well-developed and pushed beyond its current, more conservative, understanding towards its radical possibilities. "Standpoint refers to a 'position' in society which is shaped by and in turn helps shape ways of knowing, structures of power, and resource distribution" (p.67).[6] She argues that standpoint theory is unable to explain the material relations between the discursive (feminist critique) and the non-discursive (women's lives). Postmodern marxist ideology critique offers a way out of this. Here she refers to a marxist hermeneutics theory of 'symptomatic reading' which politicizes the Freudian concept of 'symptom.'

> It [symptomatic reading] applies Freud's theory of the dream-work (as the process of translation from an unconscious to a conscious logic) to a materialist understanding of representation as ideology. Hegemonic ideology performs the work of displacement, condensation, and substitution in the discursive articulation of meaning. In the process, the political unconscious—the historical forces mystified by the naturalizing impulse of the social imaginary—are obscured. However, as in the dream-work, they are not concealed for good. They make their reappearance in the form of 'symptoms,' lapses in the coherence of the hegemonic culture, indexes of the insistence of another logic in everyday life (p.93).

What Hennessy has specifically in mind are the advances of post-Althusserian theories which can further the Gramscian concept of hegemony. A good portion of her book is spent providing the limitations of Laclau and Mouffe's (1985) formulations, arguing that, despite their innovative appropriations of semiotics, they are unable to demonstrate how discourse is limited by the more permanent institutional structures of capitalism. Foucault is critiqued as well for his aestheticism, his forwarding ethics as opposed to politics, and his blindness to imperialism which Spivak's now well-quoted essay,

"Can the Subaltern Speak"(1988), points out. Consequently, Hennessy turns to the theoretical advancements of discourse theory proposed by Michel Pecheaux's *Language, Semantics and Ideology* (1975). Pecheaux's concept of *inter-discourse* helps to explain the textuality of hegemony: how subjects are produced and sustained through common sense. Interdiscourse consists of two features: "the *preconstructed* and *articulation*" (p.77). *Preconstruction* simply means what is "always already there" conveying the common sense knowledge; while *articulation* "is both the means by which the subject is constituted in the dominant discourse and the discursive mechanism that determines the domination of the dominant form" (ibid.). Interdiscourse is not a unified speaking out; rather, it is a complex movement of distinct terms which are between, with and against each other. Through *transverse discourse* (which establishes the relation of the part to whole) and *intradiscourse* (a set of co-references that secure the discourse of the subject in terms of what is said now in relation to what had gone on previously, and then after) Pecheaux is able to explain ideology in a lived context by making connections between this *intradiscourse level* and that which is *preconstructed*.

Pecheaux's discourse analysis is obviously complex, but it is especially useful for explaining how ideology shapes women's lives. Hennessy applies Pecheaux's insights to the discourse of the New Woman (see chapter 4), especially attending to what is *preconstructed* because it is such a crucial regulator of ideology. She tries to *historicize* this emergent ideology in the late '80s and early '90s by examining a pair of texts that appeared in the *New York Times Magazine*, a set of essays on feminist historiography, and a series of critical readings of Freud's *Dora*. Through these discourses Hennessy applies a materialist analysis as to how white, middle-class feminism re-establishes itself within the context of postmodernism, more specifically "postfeminism." Her arguments are based on how the symbolic order of patriarchal capitalism is maintained through a *strategy of transference* which forms the *preconstructed*. "This transference allows the social order to be reproduced through times of social upheaval by being attached to 'new' ideas, signs, objects, or activities that pass through the cultural censor of reformed public values. Thus, when a set of values becomes forbidden in the hegemonic culture it can continue its hold upon the social imaginary by merely acquiring a 'new' life in disguise. In this way structures of oppression and domination survive under the mantle of new-ness because they are embedded in the preconstructed categories onto which 'new' subjectivities are articulated" (p.104). Hennessy is trying to articulate how the logic of capitalism is being renewed in its postmodernist phase under the signifier of "new-ness," i.e., the moral majority's campaign for the New Traditionalism which sends the woman back into the home and family (as in the ads found in the *New York Times Magazine*); the development of a New Women's History which revamps liberalist individualism; and the recovery of a Eurocentric Freud through recent re-readings of *Dora*. The social imaginary is thereby contained and managed with the least amount of disruption. As i shall argue in a later context, the dispersal of signs that rigidly defined the homo/hetero divide through the fashion industry offer yet another example of the "strategy of capitalist transference."

Hennessy is optimistic that counterhegemonic discourses, also appealing to the "new," can still be forces of disruption. These counterhegemonic theories of the subject-in-language re-narrate cultures particularly as "the social construction of women as a multiply-differentiated and historically-specific subject positions" (p.137). Again, it is Pecheaux's concept of "dis-identification" (p.96) which steers a path between compliant identities (or "good subjects") who consent to hegemony, and "bad subjects" who rebel against it, which Hennessy hangs her hopes on. Dis-identification "consists of *working on* the subject form. Dis-identification is critique, enacted in the disruption and re-arrangement of the pre-constructed categories on which the formation of the subject depends" (ibid.) Founded on ideology critique, a dis-identification occurs when the *interdiscourse* of a culture is called into question and, the *preconstructed system* "across which subjectivities are constructed" is historicized. There are many "experiences" at view here. To avoid the problems of identity politics, which may prove divisive, such a position is taken as a counterhegemonic collective subject. There is no one group claimed as a dis-identifying subject of critique.

Where is such a collective subject of counter-hegemony to emerge? Hennessy sees this dis-identifying collective subject of critique shifting the concerns of authority from the *grounds* of knowledge, as women's lives or experience, to the *effects* of knowledge, "as the invested ways of making sense in the world" (p.97). Feminist specificity is not lost if the object of inquiry remains how the feminine subject is reproduced through the complex ensemble of social relations. Such a critique begins with the devaluation of "woman" under all patriarchal relations and can align itself with other marginalized subjects. Is this at all possible, or realistic? Such a stance goes against the current identity politics of post-colonial, African-American, and queer politics. The sub-altern enter into discourses of individual identity that differ significantly from western bourgeois individualism. For most of the world, identity has been denied to them. Spivak (1988b) calls for a strategic, essentialized, sub-altern consciousness. The well-known writings and films by Trinh T. Minh-ha, *Woman, Native, Other: Writing Postcoloniality and Feminism* (1989) and *When The Moon Waxes Red: Representation, Gender and Cultural Politics* (1991), forwards a consciously specific identity politics of the "native" woman. Her films deconstruct anthropological ethnographic filmic discourses like those of the *National Geographic* which exoticize the native by turning the ethnographic discourse on itself through her poetry and conscious camera work. For example, in *Reassemblage*, 1992, a "documentary" film which focused on an African tribe whose name is never mentioned, only women are shown at work and in display. Men remain purposely invisible throughout the documentary. There is no translation of informant voices; only the critical commentary of her voice-over is heard, which problematizes the camera's framing.[7] Rey Chow's collected essays, *Writing Diaspora: Tactics of Invention in Contemporary Cultural Studies* (1993) is similarly an attempt to rewrite the Chinese diaspora within the context of postmodernism.

Both Chow and Trinh try to avoid talking from a position of an essentialized Third Woman, an accusation often levied at Chandra Mohanty (1988); but the question remains how successful are they in doing so? In Trinh T. Minh-ha's films, the question of how the Other is being appropriated for the purposes of Western dissemination, no matter how critical her discourse might be, should not go unanswered. The aboriginal is still being fetishized for the purposes of theory. Perhaps not all her projects partake in this so blatantly. Her poetry which shows sensitivity to the native-other makes it evident that the ethical considerations are always problematic in this kind of self-examination. In contrast, Spivak's (1988b, 1988a, Chapter 12) work with the Subaltern Studies group, who are 'literally' rewriting (in the sense it appears non-theoretical) the history of colonial India from the perspective of peasant consciousness and insurgency, offers an entirely different formation of identity and agency. Deconstruction remains a force in such rewriting. These issues of identity politics with regards to art require a sustained meditation. The politics of difference within marxist feminism or feminist marxism that emerged in the mid '80s have become contentious. The next two vignettes raise this as a question for me.

1 This title refers to Heidi Hartmann's (1981) lead essay in an edited book that bears the same name. Hartmann's attempt to reconcile these differences is considered to be one of the earliest contributions to this debate. Cockburn (1986:85) recently has changed the tone of that proposal to one of 'cohabitation.' Hamilton (1979:104) offers a more contemporary metaphor as a "decent period of shacking up perhaps under the same roof but with separate bedrooms." Miklitsch (1991) suggests a new era of post-marxism/feminism that recognizes the "necessity of collaboration between the two even as it acknowledges the impossibility of a simple, uncritical resolution of their discursive differences" (p.121). This is also the intention of the playful title by Leslie Rabine in her critique of Derrida, "The Unhappy Hymen Between Feminism and Deconstruction" (1990).

2 For me, Harry Garfinkle belongs to a small coterie of scholars who have been more concerned with helping graduate students than publishing themselves to achieve recognition despite their obvious abilities and comprehensive knowledge. Not only Socrates, but Ferdinand de Saussure and George Mead belong in such company. Harry Garfinkle is now professor emeritus and actively involved in Green pol-

itics. He currently is the Western leader of the Canadian Green Party, actively organizing and writing its platform.

3 The manuscript, which i have tried in vain to publish, has a strong feminist orientation. In my subsequent revisions i attempted to place Woman as gynesis in motion since there is a point where the "historical" woman is impossible to "find." It is this issue which caused my initial difficulty with the new marxist feminist materialism that i began to read. Where i could i did write/rite/right in the historical figure of woman as feminist anthropologists developed that missing record. Nevertheless, no anthropologist will ever know for certain whether a matriarchy existed before a patriarchy, and the arguments that surround that issue must be treated rhetorically and politically.

4 The certainty of this characterization comes from my M.Ed. degree (1977) which was a content analysis of the National Art Education Association (USA) key journals, *Studies* and *Studies in Art Education* from 1950 to 1977.

5 See my (1989/1990) A Wolf in Sheep's Clothing/ A Sheep in Wolf's Clothing.

6 Standpoint theory is associated most closely with the theoretical writings of Nancy Hartsock (1983, 1989-1990a,b), Katie King (1990) and especially Donna Haraway's "Situated Knowledges" (1988/1991).

7 See the section, The Proleptic Installations of the Exotic Gaze, and Catherine Lutz and Jane L. Collins' study on *Reading National Geographic* (1993) which is a sustained deconstruction of its discourse showing precisely how the preconstructed photographed images play into the exoticization of the advertising industry.

THE FOURTH VIGNETTE

Radical Alterity and Identity Politics

My Backyard

Currently in Canada the language problem remains acute. A number of Ontario municipalities, (27 by last count, in 1989, including Sault St. Marie, Napanee, Thunderbay, Niagara) have passed in their city councils an English-only policy. They can no longer afford programs which cater to a French minority, and they are tired of being dictated to by a "minority." The Northwest Territories debate the possibilities of dropping French and making aboriginal languages and English the new "bilingualism." A national coalition has been established which wants virtually the same thing, a Canada with English as the official language. The politics of bilingualism are being played out by the various political parties in a desperate attempt to unify (or is it re-unify) Canada. English-speaking Canada is upset with Quebec's desire to have a 'special status' clause within its new Constitution, the so-called Meech Lake agreement (which has since failed). Quebec, in a desperate attempt not to lose its language, has passed a law that all commercial signs be in the French language, upsetting the English community, and putting into question whether bilingualism will ever be possible in that province. The Canadian political scene has been so divisive that in 1993, after the national elections, the ruling Conservative Party were virtually wiped out (reduced to two seats), and ironically Lucien Bouchard, the leader for an independent *Bloc Québecois* found himself as the official leader of the opposition facing the victor, Prime Minister Jean Chretien of the Liberal Party in the House of Commons–a strong federalist! Native self-government does not figure in this scene/seen.

As a Canadian, the "I" lives in a multi-pluralist society. Our rhetoric has always been that of a "vertical mosaic" rather than a "melting pot." One would think that there would be greater tolerance to the differences amongst the various ethnic populations that constitute the 26 million plus people living in Canada, the entire population of California! i am raising this vignette because, as a university professor, i should be sensitive to the racial/ethnic mix in my classroom. i myself am of Polish heritage. Some public schools in Edmonton, which is where I live and teach, "boast" up to an incredible 56 different ethnicities. Yet, the predominance of white middle to upper class students which make up my university classes makes me color blind and ethically inept when i teach art education. i speak "kitchen" French, German, Polish, some Russian and Ukrainian, yet i feel totally inept. Speaking the language, while it does open some doors, does not translate into intercultural sensitivity. There are numerous ethnographic studies of the curriculum which point to the teacher's inadvertent dismissal of ethnic differences. Given the contemporary problematizations of reader-response theories, educational practice has not come to terms with the differences of interpretation. At the University of Alberta less than one percent of the Education faculty are native students. The foreign student body, usually less than ten percent, are mainly South Koreans, Chinese, Japanese and Africans—generally Tanzanians and Nigerians. Debates about "differences" are not a question of *between* these groups, but the differences *in* their sameness. Such a deconstructive ruse problematizes both ethnicity and race.

It appears to me, just like Canada has bifurcated its politics into English and French to satisfy its constitution, thereby glossing over the differences of other minorities, especially its aboriginal peoples, the literature of American feminism seems to be caught up in an analogous fix. i am referring to the divisions between white America and African-American Blacks—with American Natives, Latin Americans, Chicanos, Chinese, Southeast Asians and various other ethnicities making up the remainder. Their oppression is now ranked against African-American Blacks forming yet another binary, making the whole question of race and ethnicity a considerable problem. Said's[1] (1978) well-known deconstructivist study of Orientalism and current anti-colonial discourses have slowly and relentlessly questioned and broken down the centralization of European cultural hegemony. Such fracturing has dramatically repeated itself in the Eastern European bloc countries, where a country no less powerful than Russia continues to economically struggle, caught up in a web of identity politics, having to revise its own constitution which has always assured its one party state. In Hungary, for example, in 1989 as many as 100 parties have formed numerous coalitions. As maginalized groups are being heard globally, the issue of differences come into play again and again; the Grand Narrative of Art is (potentially) shaken.

The issues are as complex as the problem. Racism always shows its ugly head as there is likely to be more and more neo-fascist groups coming to the fore as nations undergo internal changes. Identifiable groups such as the Russian Baltic States have already formed their own governments. The war in former Yugoslavia continues to smolder as Serbs, Croats and Moslems try to settle territory disputes. In the province of Alberta where I currently reside, there has been a wrath of racism. A major campaign was launched to prevent Sikhs from wearing their turbans in the Royal Canadian Mounted Police by two seemingly innocuous elder sisters. Pins have been sold which show a small white, middle class man surrounded by a stereotypical barefoot Blackman, a Sikh, and an Oriental in a straw hat. The pin reads "Who is the Minority?"

In the past, Canada's rhetoric of "ethnicity" has served it well, providing for the maintenance of a historical plurality. Many Canadians drew on their ethnicity first, and then called themselves Canadian (e.g., Polish-Canadian, German–Canadian). However, with the continued influx of Other peoples into the country, the white, English speaking, Royalist, aging strata feel threatened. There is a renewed sense of nationalism creating the paradoxical conclusion that there is no center to a Canadian identity. To be Canadian and a nationalist is to recognize the myriad of ethnicities—reflecting a decentered and fragmenting nationalism, which is uncomfortable for those who wish to fix the signifier as what it means to be Canadian. Like the postmodern fiction novels, boundaries continually shift and break down. The signifier /Canadian/ remains "slippery." (Because naming is such a problem i have turned against accepted grammatical convention and capitalized the *adjectives* of color throughout my narrative: both "Black" and "White" discourses receive equal capitalization, as do all the other "colors.")

Slippery Signifiers of Race: The Case of /Black/

Similarly, it becomes extremely important to recognize that the signifier /black/, for example, varies tremendously from country to country, as does being /white/,/red/,/yellow/,/brown/, and so on. Some colors fall outside this neat typography, which further clouds the issue; typology itself becomes a way to totalize, categorize and manage the racial picture. Whereas ethnicity may dilute the rich signifier /race/ in the American context, it becomes all the more powerful signifier in the Canadian context. The American context, with its history of imperialism and colonialism, constructs the meaning of Blackness as Other. In Canada, with a very small population of Blacks, and as a country that had been colonized and held onto British allegiance until recently, "Blackness" holds an entire different signification. It is the treatment of Native people by past governments which proves to be Canada's nemesis. Yet, the issue cannot be so easily glossed over by confining the signifier /black/ within neat national borders. Canada's own Ben Johnson story is a painful reminder that such borders are fluid. The myth of the Black man is globally constructed like that of Said's Orientalism. As Rutherford (1988) remarks the Black man has always been the White's Other, the projection of what he himself represses. White men have always treated him as Body. Nowhere is this more apparent than in spectator sports, like boxing, basketball, football and track and field events. The Black man is more primitive, less cultured, more sexually active, more animal-like, prone to violence and rape.

In Fuss's (1989) excellent examination of the controversies surrounding the signifier /race/, through her examination of three prominent African-American theorists, Anthony Appiah, Henry Louis Gates, Jr., and Houston A. Baker, Jr., there is an attempt to outline what is at stake between those theorists who wish to deconstruct "race," and those who wish to maintain a Black identity. The ruse can be easily played. Color, no matter which one is picked, can be deconstructed. To divide white into non-white is already to presuppose non-white is *not* a color. The racist is always color-blind. Gates' (Gates, 1986) strategy is to treat the sign /black/ as arbitrary, examining its use in discursive production in literary texts. He argues that in 'applying' the readings of Black texts, the critic transforms them, providing new insights. These are obviously Derridean moves. Gates also argues that African-American writers utilize a repertoire of additional tropes to those of the West: "'marking,' 'loud-talking,' 'specifying,' 'testifying,' 'calling out,' (of one's name), 'sounding,' 'rapping,' and 'playing the dozens'" (in Fuss, 1989: 84). In one of Gates' key essays, "The Blackness of Blackness: A Critique of the Sign and the Signifying Monkey," Fuss observes that Gates is utilizing a Black mythological archetypal signifier. The 'Signifying Monkey' is a trickster which he himself often plays.

His critics have accused him of conservativism. By deconstructing "race" his opponents claim Gates is abdicating, negating and destroying Black identity. There is a fear that African-American texts will loose their authenticity and become detached from their cultural roots. As Fuss argues, this is a failure of his critics to realize that "race" itself is a historical construct, including the claim by scientists that 'race' as a concept does not exist e.g., *Discover*, 1994. On the contrary, Gates and Baker's "blues criticism" revitalize and re-historicize the sign /black/, keeping the critique alive. Gates plays off intertextual signifiers, like in his essay, "Criticism in the Jungle," which alludes to Showalter and Hartman's use of 'wilderness' in their influential essays.[2] Baker holds onto the concept of race but provides it with a 'blues sound;' politicizing it by knowing that it is a biological fiction and a historical formation.

Race in everyday life, however, still comes down to a "speculogical glance" and a "auralogical ear"; how you look, the color of skin, the curliness of hair, the thickness of lips, the slant of the eyes, the quality of your accent in relation to 'standard' English, can (over)determine your social location.[3] The lesson to be learnt by Gates's ruse of what has been called "myth-critique," is succinctly articulated by Foster (1985). Quoting Baudrillard he says:

> In fact, the two practices of myth-critique 'are generated in the spirit of one of the two terms that compromise [the sign]: that is, either in the name of the signified (or referent: same thing), which it is then necessary to liberate from the stranglehold of the code (of the signifier) —or in the name of the signifier, which must be liberated from the signified (p.173).

Given this economy of the sign the first practice becomes "the move to *reclaim* the appropriated sign for its social group, [which] may succumb to an idealism of the referent, of truth, meaning, use value (as if these things, once abstracted, can be readily restored), and the second practice, the move to *remythify* or reinscribe the mass-cultural sign, may be compromised by a 'fetishism of the signifier'"(Foster, 1985:175).

Gates recognizes that there is never a "going back"; rather there is only continual translation of what /black/ means, a continual re-mythologizing by playing off both current and past signifying chains of "Black-ness" and re-cite/sight/site/ing these in different contexts. Yet, the issues of identity are crucial here. Amongst Blacks there are differences in national origin, in religion, language and so on that are frequently glossed over by the Black label. Mercer and Julien (1988) speak about the struggles of The Gay Black Group of African, Asian, and Caribbean descent. "An integral part of [their] process was the use of the word 'black' not as a biological description but as an inclusive term of political identification and solidarity forged through common struggles against racism" (p. 98). The space created by this group allowed them to feel a sense of identification and empowerment since the white gay groups had no interest in issues of race, while the Black radical politics had no space for raising issues of gender or sexuality.

The same issue of Black identity has been examined in a *Screen* (1988) special. In Stuart Hall's (1987) assertion, films are not necessarily good because Black people make them. "They are not necessarily *right-on* by virtue of the fact that they deal with the black experience." "Once you enter the politics of the end of the essential black subject you are plunged headlong into the maelstrom of continuously contingent, unguaranteed, political argument and debate: a critical politics, a politics of criticism. You can no longer conduct black politics through the strategy of a simple set of reversals, putting in place of the bad old essential white subject, the new essentially good black subject" (quoted in Julien and Mercer, 1988:5). This begs the question: Is there an essential White position? a question to which the Canadian context must be particularly sensitive.

Complicating these issues is the American feminist Alice Walker, who not only writes about the art of her mother's garden, but has received international acclaim for her *The Color Purple*, a novel that not only focused on Black women, but exploded the image of Black people as "one homogeneous, lumpen, classless mass" (Andrea Stuart,1989:62). What is to be made of Black representation when the same book becomes a commercial film success by being directed and produced by a highly influential and successful *White* entrepreneur–Steven Spielberg? And what happens when all the male figures in the movie are represented as drunken, sadistic, and womanizing? This controversy has been explored by Jacqueline Bobo (1988). Reviews brought mixed responses. Barbara Smith felt that sexual distortions and sexual violence in the Black community were matters that needed to be confronted and changed. Michelle Wallace made the point that Spielberg represents them as "minstrels, more than a little ridiculous; we dance and sing without continuity, as if on the end of a string" (p.92). But generally Black women were able to identify with the characters, while Black men felt it was a distorted representation of their behavior. When Alice Walker wrote her text, in 1982, this was a historical moment when Black feminist writers produced a renaissance in writing about their experience of Black women in the '70s and '80s; their personal lives and collective histories of Black women were "articulated" by a Black women's writing community. Filmed in 1985, *The Color Purple* was produced at the height of this articulation; the same time that Black women scholars began to challenge Black poststructuralist writes like Gates and Baker.[4] Barbara Christian's well-quoted essay, "The Race for Theory" (1987) appeared around this time, defending the need to retain a "racial" sense of Black; especially since Black women had found their voice and Black men want to take it away from them.

In Britain, Roach and Felix's (1989) interviews with a Black feminist writer—Joan Riley, a Black actress—Judith Jacobs, and a Black West Indies singer—Judy Boucher, found a broad spectrum of Black representation. Riley wrote about incest in Black families; her central characters were cleaning women. In contrast Jacobs wanted to present a 'positive' image of Black women on T.V.; she was continually searching and playing professional parts to raise Black pride and self-esteem. For Boucher there was no direct link between the popularity of her songs and her being Black. She was just another person who was content in raising her children in a non-sexist way. These three strategies, while all different, live the contradictions of being a Black in Britain, and at the same time, influencing the larger picture of Black reality through popular culture. i do not think this range of perspectives is isolated to Britain. i think of The *Jeffersons* and the popularity of *The Cosby Show* as representing Blacks as successful entrepreneurs, living out idealized middle-class family situations. Are then such shows beneficial to the self-esteem of Blacks in America? Is it a legitimate tactic, as Judith Jacobs suggests? Or is it just another White middle-class way of relieving guilt and averting viewers eyes from the real plight of Blacks in America? This has been subject to two conflicting readings—as both a breakthrough and a sellout (Julien and Mercer, 1988:9). A Black comic like Eddie Murphy, who is popular with both White and Black audiences alike, presents an equally difficult assessment. His is a pastiche of the stereotype of a "street-credible, but ideologically unthreatening, macho loudmouth" (ibid.). Again, is Murphy working one of the few cultural spaces given to a Black comic? Paradoxically as both a sellout and a breakthrough for Black identity?

These difficulties of "negotiating Black differences" have recently been examined by Michael Awkward (1995) who, through autobiographical address, questions his role as a Black man "in" Black feminism. Controversial Black figures like Mike Tyson, Spike Lee, and Michael Jackson are also examined for the racial and gender complexities they set in motion. Michael Jackson's transmutations are read as possible anti-essentialist (constructivist) performative interventions into both race and gender. Awkward reads Jackson as self, consciously imitative and mimetic; simulation is a central feature of his art. In other words, Jackson is a racial hybred who refuses to be reduced to "a [single] color"(p.190). But, paradoxically, he can never escape essentialist historical learnings that re-center him as a /black/ signifier. He is, in his own words, "a *slave* to the rhythm" (p. 190, emphasis added).

The Aporial Limit of Imperialism: Thinking About the First Nations

Gates, Appiah, Baker, mentioned above, present yet another strategy at the level of literary criticism to remind "us" that literary criticism is predominantly white, and male dominated.[5] In the province of Alberta, the Metis community has been successful in changing the historical account in school text books from the Louis 'Rebellion' to read as the Louis 'Resistance,' a classical case of revisionist history and the change of value in the play of signifiers. This would be an example of the *remythication* of a sign. They refused any stories or images which present their culture in less than an idealized way. By defining their own "essence," their own reformed image of themselves, are they doing an injustice to students who read about them? Sweeping under the carpet, as it were, the difficulties of past assimilation, the problems of drunkenness, and the pain of living as a marginal member, neither as a status Indian nor a fully fledged White? Or are they indeed practicing a form of "tactical subjectivity"? (Sandoval, 1991). Fuss (1989:31) points to Gayatri Spivak's (1988b: 197-221) turn to subjectivity while discussing the Subaltern Studies Group, an historical collective who wishes to expose and undermine the elitism of approaches to South Asian Culture. Although they are subject to the critique of the impossibility of recovering an authentic subaltern (peasant) consciousness, Spivak approves of their use of a positivist essentialism as an important strategy to gain political ends. In other words, a humanist essentialist position may become politically interventionist, even disruptive, if such essentialism is used by the dispossessed themselves. In a similar sense the Metis and the current *coalition* of Canadian Natives, through their claim to an essential pan-Native vision of Nature as centered in their creation myths and through their self-naming as First Nations, provide an effective way to thwart the efforts of the national government in hastily settling land claims, and protect forests from the continual devastation by the forest industry.

Ultimately, in Spivak's argument, the subaltern "cannot speak." Why? If they could, they would no longer be marginalized, occupying the place of the subaltern. This means there will always be a voiceless strata—the aporial limit within imperialism. In this sense, postcolonial criticism works towards the eradication of the subaltern. One cannot say that the Metis and First Nation coalitions are subaltern, for they do have a voice. Yet "epistemic violence" (Spivak, 1988a) continues to happen. The imperial imposition of codes and practices upon the colonized is especially malicious when the history of how the Canadian government has defined who is and who isn't a treaty "Indian" is told. The narrative of imperialism, installing itself proleptically as law, is made visible by tracing the signifying chain of the definitions that have taken place over time, and comparing them to the indigenous sign-systems already in circulation. No wonder the First Nation peoples want their own form of government. Spivak's (1988b:279-280) distinction between two different meanings that Marx used for representation, which has been so useful for postcolonial critical discourses, is helpful here. The political sense of representation (*Vertretung*) requires that the First Nations have Canadian government representation by *The Department of Indian and Northern Affairs*, which turns out to be a paternalistic proxy of power. Another meaning of representation is the imaginative, aesthetic, performative sense of restaging (*Darstellung*). It is this sense of representation that the *portrayal* of the constituents requires vision. Without that form of representation in the control of aboriginal leaders, it can be said that they have no voice either.

It must be added, as Fuss (1989: 95) does drawing on Nancy Miller's (1986a) analysis, the female subject does not have structurally the same relation to identity as males. They are not "burdened by too much Self, Ego, Cogito" (Miller, 1986a:106 in Fuss, 1989:95). Perhaps, Fuss goes on to say, the fragmented condition of the subaltern needs to be overcome through identity. The Native population seems to be doing just that. Matriarchal women, who have traditionally been the centering shamans of their tribes, are calling their children home. i perceive a renewed spirituality in their move and the I recognizes that this train of thought draws me dangerously close to "Mother goddess" worship, but standing in the location of Native peoples, this myth increasingly provides powerful political signification in our ecologically taxed world.

The Machinations of the Pluri-cultural Gaze

As the above discussion has shown, the difficulties of ethnicity and how they are represented have become highly problematic. And the problematics surrounding the differences of the female gaze, as already discussed, becomes even more complex when the many conflicting identities within an 'imagined community' of a nation are taken into account. Such complexities have been recently examined in a recent 'next to the last issue' of *Screen* (1988) where the journal itself has been accused of functioning "as a kind of corporate 'name of the father,' a 'theoretical super-ego' or even a 'phallic mother' ... in the '70s" (Julien and Mercer, 1988:7). Jane Gaines (1988), in particular, demonstrates the enthocentrism of psychoanalytic discourse by analyzing the film *Mahogany*. Here, she says, race is depoliticized by transporting the star, Diana Ross, from her Chicago South-side neighborhood to Rome where she becomes a model. The conjunctions of gender, class and race oppression are continually denied; the name *Mahogany* presents Diana Ross as "either all woman tinted black or mostly black and scarcely woman" (p.19). She has lost her community identity and has become commodified. Further, Gaines points out, there are racial categories traditional psychoanalytic theories does not recognize. The look by the Black male gaze (Brian) is continually denied throughout the film. She is held captive to the White male character of her photographer, Sean.

By reading the film as a Black feminist, Jane Gaines is able to draw on this particular psychoanalytic structure as relating to the signification of 'rape' in the context of Black history. "[T]he black woman [was] sexually violated by the white man, but the fact of her rape [was] repressed and displaced on the virginal white woman, and thus used symbolically as the justification for the actual castration of the black man" (p.24). Against this background, Brian is denied his gaze of *Mahogany*. His is a symbolic castration which at one time may have resulted in an actual castration or lynching. The 'right to look' has now racial implications and miscegenation to consider. (Josephine Baker's reception in Paris, France would become yet another, more complex variation of these issues raised by Jane Gaines.)

Manthia Diawara (1988) makes a similar point concerning Black spectatorship. Rather than pleasure, he points out how Blacks resist in their reading of such recent popular films as *The Color Purple*, the *Rocky* series, *A Soldier's Story*, and *Forty-Eight Hours* where, in each case, a Black man is punished or highlights the white main actor. Like *Mahogany*, the Black man is deterritorialized; a textual deracination takes places by removing him from his community. Perminder Dhillon-Kashyap (1988) registers a similar complaint concerning Asian representation (i.e., people defined as living in or originating from the Indian sub-continent, now Bangladesh, India, Pakistan, Sri-Lanka) in British cinema. In such films as *Gandhi, A Passage to India, Jewel in the Crown,* colonial history is presented from the view of White central characters. Stereotypes of the 'darkie,' or 'alien' are created and used to justify colonialism while making a "pretense of questioning the morality of impe- rialism" (p. 122). The Asian perspective becomes another form of Said's ori- entalism. The Asian community is presented as a "polarized opposite to the West's own image: *traditional societies* are ridden with *religious belief* and *social custom* while western society is seen to provide its women *education, access to financial resources and extensive civil and political rights*" (Avtar Brah in Dhillon- Kashyap, 1988: 122, original italic). Even *My Beautiful Laundrette* is seen as a predominately white male fantasy. These issues are indeed complex, for the struggles are over the doubled sense of representation as *Vertrenung* and *Darstellung*—both for representing and imagining the Other. If bell hooks (1990) reads *Sammy and Rosie Get Laid* as a racist movie, Spivak (1989b) reads Rosie as the paradigmatic 'unreadable' complex figure of white radicalism, "the white ideological subject-position of reactive welfare-state socialism" who "loves all the right people [lesbians, blacks]" (p.81), and is in an interra- cial marriage which accommodates her lesbian relationships. Such issues of media representation of the racial Other have been comprehensively discussed by Ella Shohat and Robert Stam (1994). They review an 'ethics of resistance' by diasporic artists who reclaim archaic sources for their art, including the canivalesque, the anthropophagic (cannibalism), disembodiment and syn- cretism (or hybridity) in order to disrupt Eurocentric bias and imperialist domination.

More Complications: The Ranking of Oppression!

This painfully brief and inadequate discussion of ethnicity and race highlights once again why the Grand Narrative of European Art history is slowly waning. Is there a distinct Black aesthetic? Is there a distinct Polish- Canadian aesthetic? is there a distinct _____ aesthetic? repeats once more whether there is a distinct feminine or feminist aesthetic? How, for example, does any theorist, male or female alike, handicapped by White skin, deal with Bonnie Thorton Dill's (1983) indictment that feminist Black women have historically formulated their identity and political allegiance, not in terms of class and gender, *but in primarily terms of race* and who do not see Black men as patriarchal antagonists but complicitly sharing in their mutual racial oppression. Patriarchy, it is said, was historically introduced into the African-American community by modelling the white bourgeois household after their release from slavery. Sisterhood, as Dill notes, is a monolithic concept which translates as the inevitable feminist concerns of White middle-class women. In its stead, Dill suggests a working towards a recognition of the differences between all women of color. Flax (1990a), too, in examining differences amongst feminists states: "Black women's sexuality has been represented as primitive, powerful, 'free' from cultural constraints and morality, as contrasted to the delicate, repressed hysteria of middle-class white women. This representation, in turn, has been utilized to justify and deny the continuing sexual abuse of black women and the absence of tenderness and respect in relations with them" (p.175).

Black feminists wish to hold to a humanist essentiality, while yet other voices, like Hazel Carby (1987) wish to de-essentialize the Black experience. The polyphony of ethnic identifications, which have no essential criterion for identity, has evolved through negation. Sandoval (Haraway, 1990:197) notes that the 'privileged' oppressed authorial categories called 'women and Blacks,' stand at the top of this negative location. "The category of 'woman' negated all nonwhite women; 'black' negated all non-black people, as well as all black women. But there was also no 'she,' no singularity, but a sea of differences among U.S. women who have affirmed their historical identity as U.S. women of color" (pp.197-198). One can well imagine the further negative class locations of the incredibly diverse ethnic groups in Canada. For Sandoval coalitions become possible in this polyphony. In Lourde's "biomythography" of a Black gay woman, de Lauretis says (1988:164) Lourde's image of the house of difference points to a conception of community not pluralistic but at once global and local—"global in its inclusiveness and macropolitical strategies, and local in its specific, micro-political practices" (p.164).

These differences come down to local micropolitics. Deconstruction can be a powerful tool to dispense with any forms of either essentialism or constructivism based on class, color, gender and age locations. Fuss's (1989) examination of this issue is exemplary. Often essentialism and biologism can be effectively used as disruptive concepts in yet other subject positions. In a recent article by Lowery Stokes Sims, "Aspects of Performance in the Work of Black American Women Artists" (1988), she identifies and specifies both Black males and female artists who have purposely chosen the medium of performance (a non-commodity form), as political action in order to deal with political, economic, and social issues of the "community." Performance art, in conjunction with video, serves as a bridge between the seclusion of the studio and gallery to the "real" world, the street. It also reclaims for these

African-Americans a connection with the traditional African nuances of his or her task, whereby the art object was created to be used as part of a grand performance piece; "a ritual that addressed the needs of an entire community, rather than serving as some kind of trophy for a privileged, elite, art-consuming class" (p. 208). Sims, like Gates, identifies "acting out" as an identifiable trope which Black women can use to rupture white stereotypes. "The suitability of 'acting out' as an extensive strategy for a class of individuals who have few accepted or sanctioned means of self expression—and women of color in this society are particularly stymied in this regard—also comes into consideration here" (p. 208). Shifa Goldman's "Portraying Ourselves: Contemporary Chicana Artists" (1988), supports Lucy Lippard's concept of a "advocate" critic, a critic who endorses and supports "minority" voices which have been marginalized, but who does not relinquish the right and responsibility to be critical within that advocacy. "Our role is to assert, and reassert, that the art of women and of peoples of the Third World (women and men) are crucial elements in the construction of the history of art" (p.189). Like the lumping of all Black nationalities as "Black," Goldman argues that the label Spanish American and Hispanic once more glosses important distinctions and differences between Mexicano and Mexican Americans. The diversity exists amongst the Chicano themselves; not all are brown, Catholic, speak Spanish, or have Spanish surnames. Artistic quoting from local traditions can cause difficulties within the Chicano communities, i.e., the revival of the Pauchuco style of the 1940s has been at the expense of the Pachuca—the female embodiment of cool, hip, and distinctive dress and behavior during World War II.[6] It seems that the (my)nefield of multi-plural identity politics is yet another overlay to contend with.

Identity politics for the question of art, feminism, and art education are extraordinary difficult to sort out. Much of what i have written in this vignette was formulated in 1988-90. The reflective essay which follows emerged from a recent conference experience at the International Society of Art Education Through Art held in Montréal, Quebec in 1993. Where possible i have continued to use the personal address of i/you (the reader). It is an attempt to read critically essentialist and non-essentialist identity politics in light of the above review and Hennessy's call for de-identification, which emerged for me under the concept of Bhabha's "hybridity," and Landry and MacLean's call to take the claims of deconstruction seriously within specific historico-political sites/sights/cites.

1 Said's thesis has been extremely influential in deconstructing European colonialism. A pioneer in this area Said articulated how Europe was able to identify itself as civilized by setting itself off from the "infidels." East/West, Orient/ Occident, define each other in a Master-slave dialectic. This is also a gendered discourse since the East takes on feminized traits, while the West retains its transcendent masculine qualities.

2 Showalter's " Feminist Criticism in the Wilderness"(1982) and Hartman's *Criticism in the Wilderness* (1980).

3 Fuss cites the work of Michael Omi and Howard Winant's *Racial Formation in the United States* (1986) as an exemplar study which analyzes how racial attitudes are formed.

4 The controversy was with Joyce A. Joyce's (1987a,b) attack on Baker and Gates in the *New Literary History*.

5 The same accusations are made concerning white feminism's blindness to race and class (Amos and Pratibha, 1984).

6 One such attempt to show the variety of social and political oppositions in a micropolitical context is Douglas Kahn and Diane Neumaier's editorship of *Cultures in Contention* (1985). Here the London's dockyards are explored, and an oppositional cable network is presented. A whole variety of Third World oppositional art forms are documented, e.g. , the effects of popular theater in Kenya, women's song as form of resistance in Uruguay, film in Nicaragua, and Jamaican women's theater. Other articles include free radio in Japan, Chicana muralists Los Angeles. Lesbian artists were interviewed, and so on.

THE
POLITICS
OF
IDENTITY

Art in An Age of Identity Crisis: Between Essentialism and Constructivism

fig. 14 *D'où venons-nous? Que sommes-nous? Où allons-nous?*

Six years since its last conference in Hamburg, Germany (1987), and with the unfortunate political unrest in the Philippines which cancelled its plans for its 1990 meeting, the 28th World Congress of the International Society for the Education Through Art (INSEA) finally met once again in

301

Montréal, Canada in August of 1993. The weeklong conference quoted as its theme the title of one of Gauguin's acclaimed artworks: *Where do we come from? What are we? Where are we going?* (fig. 14). (These three questions, i assume, were identified by the conference organizers in order to bring the membership's attention to an historical climate where issues of identity have become a global concern.) After a lapse of six years, these questions further held the promise of centering a globel sense of educational community sometime in the future as evoked by the rhetorical use of the empty signifier "we."

Displayed prominently in the lobby of the conference center was a *faithful* copy, both in scale and content, of Gauguin's achievement. References to Gauguin, or this particular painting, were made numerous times in the program catalogue by various presenters - mostly all positive.[1] Leading the parade of praise for Gauguin was the current president of INSEA, Anna Mae Barbosa of the *Museu de Arte Contemporanea de Sao Paulo*, Brazil. In her address to the Congress, *"From Gauguin to Latin America: Who we are?"* she wrote the following as a description of her presentation:

> Gauguin's early experience in Latin America can be seen as one of the reasons for his flexibility to see different lands, different people in their own way, not as colonizer or invader. As a white European, he interpreted those so called "primitive with respect for their environment and their myths." Those myths are represented by him as expression of their beliefs and aspirations, not as exoticism. Certainly his contact with Latin America and his Peruvian heritage made him flexible and sensitive enough to look to the "other" (Catalogue, p.55).

Barbosa defended Gauguin's character even further during her address by an aside to the fact that he had left his wife and children and travelled abroad, an act for which he should *not* have been condemned; for today, argued Barbosa, he would not be judged so severely. Her reasoning was that divorce and separation had become so common as to have become an accepted social value. Barbosa's defense of Gauguin as an exemplary artist who was sensitive to the Other was further buttressed by quotes from his own journal writing as testimony of his sincerity. (i now repeat an incident that the I wrote four years ago, which appeared earlier in my text under the heading "The Disputes of Representation." It is re-presented again within the context of a new understanding.)

In 1990 the I attended the 78th Annual Conference of the College Art Association (CAA) held in New York. In a panel called "Denaturalizing

302

the Nude," the literary critic Peter Brooks argued that Gauguin's nude studies in Tahiti served to put into question the entire European tradition of nude studies, representing the women's body in such a way that the male gaze was mitigated and made problematic. Gauguin's nudes, like *Te arii vahine* (The Noble Woman, 1896), *Manao tupapau* (The Spirit of the Dead Watches,1892), and *Nevermore*, were direct comments on Manet's *Olympia* and *Dejeuner Sur L'Herb*. Brooks argued that Gauguin was wrestling with the problem of painting the nude 'naturally' - fully erotic, without the connotations of shame, scandal, and exposure - which was problematic at this time, for the artificiality of the neoclassical style displayed the nude as a prostitute: the spectator's glance matched the glance of the paying customer (cf. John Berger, 1972). Manet's *Olympia* had not solved this problem. Eve's nakedness was to replace Venus's nudity. His paintings acted like a Derridean 'supplement' to the entire tradition, hence putting that tradition into question and disrupting its assumptions on sexuality. Such a reading was in direct contrast to the art critic Abigail Solomon-Godeau whose article, "Going Native," had appeared in *Art in America* a full year earlier. Was Brooks' interpretation, then, an example of one-upmanship? i suspect so.

Solomon-Godeau (1989) argued that Gauguin's modernist primitivism was a form of *mythic speech*. His life, a paradigm case for "primitivism as a white, Western and preponderantly male quest for an elusive object whose very condition of desirability reside[d] in some form of distance and difference, whether temporal or geographical" (p. 120). (The "elusive object" referred to by Solomon-Godeau was an earthly paradise, a place of plenitude where compliant female bodies presented themselves everywhere.) Gauguin's heroic journey, to find himself, was part of the mythic sense of being avant-garde, original self-creative, and heroic. Further, Solomon-Godeau claimed, this vision was abetted by racial and sexual fantasies. His sojourn as a "savage" into Britanny, as his "initial encounter with cultural Otherness" into a "more archaic, atavistic and organic society," was more accurately a mystification of Britanny as a folkloric paradise. Britanny was a center of an international artist's colony (the *Pont Aven* circle) and tourism; its peculiar and visually distinct aspects, especially women's clothing, were a sign of its *modernity*. The textual representation of Breton as being primitive was part of a broader discourse created by colonialism where a natural primitivism had emerged through the encounter with tribal arts, *Japonisme*, and *cloisonnéisme*.

Like Symbolism, the significance of Gauguin's religious and mystical iconography, as exemplified through the representation of numerous Calvaries and self-crucifixions, mark a crisis of representation brought on by the crisis of capitalism during the *fin de siècle*. The flight out from urbanity presented Breton as the Other of Paris - feudal, rural, spiritual and static. As Solomon-Godeau further argues, the absence of men presented a "purely feminized geography," an unchanging rural world, an atavism where women, adolescent girls and children's perception was said to be closer to nature and the spiritual. Gauguin's nudes from this period are said to participate in this quest for the primitive. "The savage woman" was to exemplify the nature link between Eros and Mother Nature - the constellation of imagery around "Eve/ Mother/ Nature/ Primitive." His depiction of Maori culture and women continued this mythic primitivism. The figure of the *vahine*, represented either monstrously (as in cannibalism and tattooing), or idealized as a noble savage, became a "metonymy for the tropic paradise tout court" (p.124). "Going native" was a facade. Gauguin never learnt the Polynesian language, the customs he wrote about were plagiarisms drawn from previous accounts, his very survival depended on *vahines* he so idealized, and his life was but a continuous rape of images and "pillaging the savages of Oceania" (p. 128).

Such a scathing indictment of Gauguin raises many questions as to the ethics and politics of any textual reading. Feminist members of the audience, notably Griselda Pollock,[2] objected to Peter Brooks' reading on the grounds that his reading was *still* caught by a male's appropriation of the woman's body. Needless to say, other artists in the audience reacted with some trepidation. Just what sort of representation of the female nude body was to be permitted by men to avoid such accusatory wrath? From within the confines of a patriarchal view, Gauguin's representations of Tahitian women represent an advance; from a feminist perspective, Gauguin had not gone far enough.[3] From the perspective of a colonialist, Gauguin represents a heroic search for himself; from the perspective of a postcolonial position, he is an exploiter and an invader. Each interpretation of Gauguin implicates the viewer/reader under a different set of ethical and political imperatives. What was it in Gauguin's own blindness which could not make him see past the exotic Other? Turning this question to more familiar territory one could equally ask: why was it that Jewish intellectuals could see through the contradictions and the barbarity of German National Socialism while high-minded German intellectuals like Heidegger and the Belgian intellectual Paul de Man were complicitous, aiding and abetting a racist regime? (see Carroll, 1990). The politics of identity and difference are at play here.

Since that time, Brooks has published his account within a collection of essays that examines the representation of the woman's body in modernism. "Gauguin's Tahitian Body" appears as chapter six in his larger work, *Body Work: Objects of Desire in Modern Narrative* (1993). Reading this essay three years later, it is obvious Brooks had not entirely changed his mind. Brooks maps out the metaphorical discourses that had shaped Gauguin's desire: the *Exposition Universelle* of 1899 which presented an exhibition of the French colonies; the fantasies associated with exotic travel; the search for the body of a beautiful woman and the care-free life; the search for the noble savage. Gauguin's "authentic" journal voice begins to sound very unauthentic as he mimes colonial travel discourse sounding like a "Club Med travel brochure" (p. 164). In short, Brooks rehearses many of the insights that Solomon-Godeau had identified earlier, yet he concedes very little to her, claiming that her discussion holds a "general truth" but requires a "more nuanced discussion" since she "distorts the original discursive framework of the European encounter with Tahiti" (p.179). Gauguin, according to Brooks, was engaged with the problem of Enlightenment philosophy and ethnology, actively seeking to invent a version of Tahiti earlier than the one he found in the 1890s in order to provide a commentary on the civilization which had produced Eve. Further, Gauguin had denounced colonialist appropriation after his initial participation in it. In Brooks' account, Gauguin once again emerges as a hero. "Solomon-Godeau's argument does not do justice to the disruptive, interrogative force of Tahitian sexuality in Western discourse, and to the figuration of that force in Gauguin's Tahitian painting" (p.180). The rest of his chapter is a defence of this thesis.

i am back once again to an earlier discussion. From a *historiographic* and modernist point of view, within the confines of a male phallocentric discourse, Gauguin's "naked nudes" provide an "advance" on the representation of the female nude. Although Gauguin pre-dates the rise of the avant-garde, he is interpreted as their precursor. The notion of the avant-garde, within the context of critical postmodernism, has had a thorough critique (see Docherty, 1993:15-18). (In the context of this discussion, most notably the need for the avant-garde to define itself by "shocking" its audience from the solace of its comfortable forms of identity by always presenting a radicalized Other.) This whole practice, Docherty notes, must be in "the time of the other." The avant-garde project is characterized by the forces of elitism, historicism, and individualism. "The avant-garde is elitist because the artist is the hero who has seen the future in advance of everyone else, and whose task is to risk her or his own greater powers on behalf of the tardy common masses. The avant-garde is historicist because its artists are necessarily out of step with the masses around them [they have to catch up if progress is to take place]; ... finally, and most explicitly, ... the ideology of avant-garde has to be individualist, for its whole practice is based on the 'expression *du Moi*' " (p. 17-18.). This 'expression of Self' distinguishes the avant-garde Self from its Others, and thereby produces its Other. Such a ruse today has itself become a tradition: fine artists separate themselves as "individuals" in distinction from the "masses" and the mass culture that they consume.

Does Gauguin escape such ideology, so that he might be reinscribed as an exemplar of intercultural learning; as someone who enriched his sense of difference without falling into elitism, individualism and historicism? This and the question of phallocentrism are the hinge pins around which the politics of interpretation are played out. Gauguin's invented Tahiti in his autobiographical account *Noa Noa*, was a critique of Judeo-Christian mythology. But read from the hindsights of today's feminist and postcolonial analysis, Gauguin had not managed to escape very far from the discourses that captivated him. As Linda Nochlin (1988) vividly illustrates, there was "no high art in the nineteenth century based upon women's erotic needs, wishes, or fantasies" (p.138). All such erotic art was meant for the male gaze, both homosexual and heterosexual. The very painting Brooks praises as Gauguin's greatest achievement in disrupting the lascivious gaze of male spectators, *Deux femmes tahitiennes* (1899), (pp.193-194) is the *very same work* chosen by Nochlin to illustrate the opposite thesis: merely another example of illustrating the prime topic of erotic imagery in the 19th century painting: "the comparison of the desirable body with ripe fruit" (p.139). For Brooks, the title reads - *Two Tahitian Women* - while Nochlin rewrites the title as *Tahitian Women with Mango Blossoms* (the signifier /bosum/ is not far away). Each uses a different title to put forward their arguments (fig. 15). The artificiality of their pose is made blatantly obvious by the exotic gaze of the camera; the faces of the two Tahitian women express a certain somberness and sadness (fig. 16) (Le Pichon, 1987:199, illus. no. 376). Lynda Nead's recent book, *The Female Nude: Art, Obscenity and Sexuality* (1992), however, brilliantly deconstructs the nude/naked binary that informs this Western phallocentric practice of representing the nude in art. No amount of apologetics for advances in a male artist's nude representation by Brooks can deny the force of her critique. Yet Brooks points to momentary passages in Gauguin's autobiography of a male trying to question his own constructed masculinity, wanting to explore a 'polymorphous body' (p.183) but unable to do so, in the end falling back to asserting sexual differences. It should not be forgotten that "imagining" oneself as an artist, the psychology of the "enacted biography," was enormously popular at this time. Biography and journalism enabled the artistic persona to emerge. "Fact and fiction, history and biography, psychology and journalism, merged and overlapped in the mapping of an artistic 'type,' and hence in the provision of raw material for new identities" (Tickner, 1992:6). Gauguin appears Janus-faced. Which face the interpreter reads has severe consequences as to how the modernist canon is judged. More disturbingly, these two faces are comfortably attached to the same body; each face can no more exist without the other than can the two sides of a coin. Which one shows itself is often dependent on the conditions Gauguin finds himself in, making a final verdict on him seem *impossible*. Hal Foster (1993) has tried to identify this ambivalence by giving Gauguin a Freudian interpretation. "This conflict occurs because the primitivist seeks to both be *opened up to difference* (to be made ecstatic, literally taken out of the self sexually, socially, racially) *and* to be *fixed in opposition* to the other (to be established again, secured as a sovereign self) ... (p.85, original emphasis).

fig. 15 Tahitian Women with Mango Blossoms *Deux femmes tahitiennes*

fig.16 Two Tahitian woman posing

i have introduced this section with the controversies surrounding Gauguin as an example of the political play of identity and difference. Who then has the "right," "true," or "authentic" Gauguin—Barbosa, Solomon-Godeau, Brooks—who? This question is somewhat misleading, for it is the rhetorical effects of putting the figure of Paul Gauguin into play which form the important issues for artistic praxis and conference problematics. It is the different effects that the name of Gauguin *as a signifier* is asked to do that is the issue, for he is now an "invented" figure. Should Gauguin continue to be defined as an artist who did indeed bridge the two worlds between the colonizer and the colonized, or should the multiple discourses at play during his historical time be recognized as that which caught his artistic imagination within the metaphorics of colonial exoticism? If you choose the latter, should

307

INSEA have chosen to put the figure of Gauguin into play the way they did, or should provisions have been made to accommodate against-the-grain readings which identified his authentic biographical voice as a form of "fiction-making"? Rather than working with a model of possible consensus, INSEA's committee members might have promoted the examination of the contradictions of alternate interpretations, highlighting the incommensurabilities of multiple differences. In this essay i shall continue to pursue such dilemmas of difference and identity, first by describing the current global condition where identity politics have become such a major issue, and then go on to develop the various uses of difference weighing the costs and benefits of these approaches in the context of cultural practice, specifically introducing examples of artistic practice to highlight these issues whenever appropriate.

The New Globalism

Three quotations from the recently established transnational journal *Diaspora*, which appeared on its covers, highlight the play of identity in a postmodern world. The first quotation comes from Hamid Naficy, at UCLA, who writes about the poetics and practices of Iranians in exile.

> Fragmentation and deterritorialization force us to experience time differently ... We experience the present as a loss or, as Baudrillard would have it, as a phenomenon that has no origin or reality, a "hyperreality." .... For the exiles who have immigrated from the Third World countries, life in the United States, especially in the quintessentially postmodern city of Los Angeles, is doubly unreal, and it is because of this double loss of origin and reality that nostalgia becomes a major cultural and representation practice amongst the exiles ... Nostalgia for one's homeland has a fundamentally interpsychic source expressed in the hope of an eternal desire for return, a return that is structurally unrealizable (cover, *Diaspora*, Vol. 1, No. 3, (Winter, 1991).

The second quotation comes from the anthropologist Roger Rouse who practises a radically different postmodern ethnography when working with Mexican migrants into the United States. Rouse charts how their ethnicity is actively and socially produced from the opportunities and constraints that they face living in a border town, and talks about the ways they appropriate, accommodate, or resist the forms of power and domination, opportunity and constraint that they encounter. He writes:

> We live in a ... world of crisscrossed economies, intersecting systems of meaning, and fragmented identities. Suddenly, the comforting modern imagery of nation states and national languages, of coherent communities and consistent subjectivities, of dominant centers and distant margins no longer seem adequate ... [We] have all moved irrevocably into a new kind of social space (cover, *Diaspora*, Vol. 1, No.1, (Spring,1991).

And the last quotation comes from Salman Rushdie who needs no introduction as a paradigmatic writer of postcolonial literature.

> If I am to speak for Indian writers in England, I would say this: The migrations happened. "We are, We are here." And we are not willing to be excluded from any part of our heritage, which includes ... the right of any member of this post-diaspora community to draw on its roots for its art, just as the world's community of displaced writers has always done (cover, *Diaspora*, Vol. 1, No.2, (Fall, 1991).

From these three quotes it can be readily seen that living in a postcolonial, postmodern world offers new challenges to questions of identity and difference. We live in a historical moment where there seems to be two opposing and contradictory trends occurring simultaneously, which i shall develop sequentially. First, that is to say, on the one hand, more and more people of different backgrounds share an overlapping culture, influenced by the global homogenization of the electronic media, especially television and (Hollywood) film, and the influence of North American popular music all over the world, disintegrating folk cultures and redefining cultural identities. (In my trip into Poland during the summer of 1993, the number of satellite dishes were visible everywhere - not only in major cities but also in small villages - making readily available television programs from the U.S., Germany, Italy, France, and England. Apparently this phenomena is repeated in virtually every Eastern European country, except in the poorer countries such as Romania and Albania. What this means to the changing Eastern European identity is only now taking shape as recognized by the theme for the *First European Film and Television Conference* scheduled for 1994, appropriately entitled *Turbulent Europe: Conflict, Identity and Culture*.) My observation of this homogenizing phenomena applies equally to popular music. Musical tape casettes are cheaply reproduced in Poland and virtually every recent pop group can be purchased there. The same phenomenon is repeated in Ljubljana, the capital of Slovania. At the level of popular culture, at least, multinational capitalism continues to homogenize the globe. In contrast, fine art does not have the same appeal as the popular arts of television and rock music. The 1993 Biennial Graphic Exhibition which the I attended on a Saturday, in Ljubljana (represented an international array of artists), was spread massively over three museums, but the attendance could be counted on one hand.

You have then a situation which Barber (1992) refers to as a McWorld of video, film, and television which attempts to homogenize cultural experience through satellite technology. The hegemony of both central Europe and the United States is reproduced globally since they control the communications media. Television and film media present lifestyles and news that would otherwise never be seen in many countries. Joshua Meyrowitz (1986), in his book *No Sense of Place*, argues that this electronic media - especially television - has blurred the dividing line between public and private, severing the traditional link between physical and social place. The result has been a diffusion of group identities. Meyrowitz speaks of a '*placeless* culture' (p.125). Groups whose place was formerly shaped by physical isolation are no longer segregated from larger social groupings, e.g., American Indians on reservations, or aboriginal groups living in the Amazon forests like the Tukano Indians who have become media stars through their protests against the Brazilian government's destruction of the rain forests, and from their visit by the pop star Sting. Therefore, Meyrowitz argues, aspects of group identity that were dependent on physical place, and the experiences available to them, have been permanently altered by the electronic media. In these cases, cultural identity is shaped by the media as a *symbolic* rather than a physical place. People can now escape from their traditional place-defined groups. The 'situational geography' of social life becomes altered (p.57). Geographic identity or identity of place is continuously changing.

The notion of belonging to a West-East European community is yet another aspect of the homogenizing effects that are taking place. How this works i felt that same summer of 1993 when travelling through the Czech

Republic with my son. As Canadians, we required a visa, a whopping 45 U.S. dollars, just to travel through the country. Travelling companions we met from Austria, Poland and even Great Britain belonged to the European Community and required no such visa. Fitzgerald (1992) mentions that the Samoan islanders immigrating to New Zealand, no longer identify themselves as Samoans from a specific island in Samoa but lump themselves as 'Pacific Islanders.' Such "morphing" identities make the identification of a corresponding artistic culture difficult.

This global homogenization of culture, however, is best understood economically. In a brilliant display of historically grounded political and economical insights, Masao Miyoshi (1993) develops his thesis that transnational corporations (TNCs) have continued this 'cultural' colonialism. This "is not an age of *post*colonialism," argues Miyoshi, "but of intensified colonialism, even though it is under an unfamiliar guise" (p.750). Miyoshi traces the loss of faith by the populace in nation-states; the failure of the state as a political authority to provide adequate public health, control currency, provide general education and guide the national economy. It is not the nation as a whole which benefits from these services; rather, only certain privileged classes receive the majority of state support. With the rise of multinational corporations (MNCs) in the late 1960s to the mid-1970s, and then with the advent of transnational corporations, the entire landscape of culture has changed.[4] Manufactured products are advertised and distributed globally, being identified only with their brand names and not with the countries of origin. In order to talk to one another, the transnational class of professionals who live and travel globally are expected to avoid cultural eccentricities and speak English, "the lingua franca of the TNC era."

> National history and culture are not to intrude or not to be asserted oppositionally or even dialectically. They are merely variants of one 'universal' - as in a giant theme park or shopping mall. Culture will be kept to museums, and the museums, exhibitions, and theatrical performances will be swiftly appropriated by tourism and other forms of commercialism. No matter how subversive at the beginning, variants will be appropriated aggressively by branches of consumerism, such as entertainment and tourism, as were rap music, graffiti art, or even classical music and high arts. Cable TV and MTV dominate the world absolutely. Entertainment and tourism are huge transnational industries by themselves (p. 747).

Like Barber, Miyoshi has no use for economic, environmental and cultural devastation that TNCs wreak in their host countries. "While they homogenize regions, they remain aliens and outsiders in each place, faithful only to the exclusive clubs of which they are members" (p. 749). In this context, most disturbingly, multiculturalism becomes an important strategy for TNC managers, who can now pay lip service and display sensitivity to the myriad of migrant workers who are on their payroll.[5] However, "[n]either nativism nor pluralism are in their thoughts, only *survival*" (p.748, my italics). David Rieff (1993) essentially agrees with Barber and Miyoshi, demonstrating the close link between multiculturalism and MNCs. He shows how the market economy has embraced multiculturalism for its own ends. (As it shall be argued later, art education makes the very same gesture.) Reading the feature articles in *Commentary, Barron*, and *Fortune*, Rieff points out how MNCs are eager to let in women, blacks, gays and any other marginalized group as paying customers. Multiculturalism has given capitalism its second wind.

Second, in contrast to this homogenizing trend, that is to say, on the other hand, there is a strong tendency for many groups today to insist that they are, at the very least, *symbolically* distinct. Most often the argument is premised on being linguistically and culturally distinct, and in some extreme cases biologically distinct and pure. These groups form what Barber characterizes pejoratively as a Jihad, a diversity of common cultures each trying to maintain their own sense of unique identity. War, for the Jihad, is *not* an instrument of policy, but an emblem of identity, an expression of community as an "end" in itself, like the colors of LA gangs. Jihads may be characterized as cultures, not countries; parts not wholes; sects not religions; rebellious factions and dissenting minorities at war not just with globalism, but with the *traditional* nation states they find themselves in. They form a mirrored reflection of the decline of the viability of nationalism as a politically unifying force. Their list seems endless. They include the Kurds, Basques, Puerto Ricans, Ossetians, East Timoreans, Québecois, the Catholics of Northern Ireland, Abkhasians, Japanese Kurile Islanders, the Zulus of Inkathat, Catalonians, Tamils, and the Palestinians. These are people without countries inhabiting nations that they do not perceive as their own. David Binder and Barbara Crossette (1993) count forty-eight ethnic wars currently in the world. Stories carrying the Jihadic side of identification can be found daily in any newspaper. On my flight to the INSEA conference on Wednesday, August the 11th, the Toronto *Globe & Mail* ran as cover stories the plight of Russians living in Estonia who are denied citizenship on the grounds they have no Estonian ethnicity. This situation is the same throughout all the Baltic states. White South African women were protesting against the first Black Miss South Africa on the grounds she was not "pretty" enough. Ernst Zundel, a neo-Nazi Torontonian, had been given permission to broadcast Holocaust revisionism via his radio program named rhetorically, "The Voice of Freedom." There was even a story how cowboy poets were trying to protect the purity of their craft from the invasion by "city slickers." This sampling is indicative of the numerous "nodal points" (Laclau and Mouffe, 1985) that solidify their Jihadic consciousness around "floating signifiers" that temporarily form and secure the kernel of meaning of their identities.[6]

Given this situation, i therefore take the characterization formed by the ampersand between the local and global - local&global - to be indicative of the postmodern world. Both the multiple and contradictory centrifugal, that is the decentering forces of the Jihad, and the centripetal, that is the centering forces of the McWorld, are held in dialectical tension by what has been characterized as a "dissipative structure" where the process of both homogenization and fragmentation are at work simultaneously. Whether it is the McWorld of homogenized communication or the Jihad world of identity difference, neither process, argues Barber, leads to democratic ends but to new forms of neo-racism. The worst part of this is to recognize that the use of difference by a minority or a marginalized group to assure its identity leads to fascism and Serbian ethnic cleansing, Islamic fundamentalism and Muslim and Hindu antagonism in India. In this context nationalism and strong cultural identities can be interpreted as hold-overs from Enlightenment rationality, the formation of modern nation states and its resultant colonialism and imperialism. Yet it may be equally argued that as globalization intensifies, such neo-ethnicism becomes appealing because it offers simple solutions in such a complex situation, a point argued by Miyoshi (1993). Perhaps, he argues, "the inadequacy of the nation-state is now fully realized, and the provincial strongmen [in Czechoslovakia, Yugoslavia, India, Myanmar] are all trying to grab a piece of the real estate for keeps before all is incorporated and appropriated by transnational corporations" (p.744).[7]

The Uses of Difference: Essentialist Tactics

i would like now to clarify and develop the *uses of difference* that have played such a vital role in the discourses on race, gender and ethnicity that characterize the dissipative structure of the ampersand—global&local. It is in the interests of oppressed, marginal groups to appropriate difference for themselves for strategic socioeconomic and political purposes. Most often the pur-poseful use of "difference" by marginalized, feminist and subaltern groups is to counter a now outdated racist and sexist discourse premised on nature and biology which used "difference" for exclusion and separation. It was premised on the deviation and a deficiency from a norm. Difference was and often still is, therefore, categorical and exclusionary - a difference of *kind*. In its weak form, biological and natural differences were applied primarily to gender dif-ferentiation: women, especially white women, were given a separate but not equal sphere. Their difference replaced natural inferiority with a rhetoric of containment, i.e, they were more nurturing, loving, caring, and mothering so they should remain in the home and out of public life. The realm of public life was sold to them as not being worthy of women due to its harshness (Rothenberg, 1990). The strongest reading of biological and natural "differ-ences" is readily observable as physical differences in appearance, interpreted most often as moral deficiencies leading to genocide (e.g., Holocaust, the Cambodian "Killing Fields" of the Khmer Rouge), and to the castration and sterilization of "mentally retarded" men and women.

To challenge this exclusionary use of "difference," marginalized groups argued "difference" was a matter of *degree*, not kind. The normative use of difference now becomes one of description. "Separate but equal" and "different but equal" becomes the familiar *liberal model* for gender and racial equality. Cultural pluralism and the celebration of cultural diversity has been the familiar rhetoric of a Canadian cultural mosaic and a multicultural edu-cation which attempts to maintain this *impossible* plurality. The focus on lib-eral pluralistic notions of culture replaced *race* with *ethnicity*, making race a social category, and thereby leveling the centralizing effects of race itself. According to Sollors (1986:25) "ethnicity is a relatively new term coined by W. Lloyd Warner in 1941." Ethnicity became fashionable in the '60s and in vogue by the '70s. However, this state of affairs has proven to be particularly problematic.

By replacing race with ethnicity the *essentialism* of race, which pro-vided a centralizing principle for socioeconomic organization and cohesion, inadvertently denied the history of racism. In the U.S. this meant White respon-sibility for the present and past oppression and exploitation of both Blacks and Aboriginal peoples could be smoothed over or avoided. (In a related but different sense, selective forgetting applies equality to national ethnic identi-ties. By not recognizing Québec as a distinct society, the history of the inequal-ity of French and English relationships in Canada could be downplayed and eventually forgotten.) In the U.S., by identifying themselves as "Black" and now "African-Americans," race was reasserted as the primary social-political-economic category of social organization. It was constructed as an ideology and essentialized (Henry Louis Gates, Jr., 1987). Further, it was and still is in the interest of well-known African-American intellectuals to act as the representative voice of a Black marginalized minority.[8] By offering a "counter-discourse" and a "counter-memory," deconstructing the historical memory that has been formed by the dominant White hegemony, Black and Aboriginal leaders formulate and center a stronger identity by affirming a "Black" and "Red" cultural aesthetic. Afrocentricsm and Pan-Indianism present alternative educational historical narratives identifying a whole different set of cultural heroes. The history of slavery and aboriginal genocide is therefore kept current. Chela Sandoval has called this a "tactical subjectivity" (1991:4). The same use of radical difference may be said of all such cultural conflicts where a cultural essentialism is maintained, be it racial or ethnic or gendered, in order to keep the injustices *aktuell,* as part of the cultural memory of identification. The same reasoning applies to the separatist movement in Québec. In order to preserve a definitive French Canadian culture, it becomes necessary to generate a distinctive Canadian history which tells their side of the story; local sitcoms on television must be produced that are reflective of the trials and tribulations of French Canadian life styles; the French language has to preserved, i.e., a provincial law (Bill 101) makes it illegal to advertise in English; plus traditional folk culture and festivals are circulated as points of identifiable cultural reference.

This use of *essentialist difference* and the claims to a "distinct society" are, of course, the antithesis to the U.S. 'melting-pot' ideology. As Joan Copjec (1991) remarks in an often-quoted passage:

> America's sense of its own 'radical innocence' has its most profound origins in [the] belief that there is a basic humanity unaltered by the diversity of the citizens who share in it. *Democracy* is the universal quantifier by which America - the 'melting pot,' 'the nation of immigrants' - constitutes itself as a nation. If all our citizens can be said to be Americans, this is not because we share any positive characteristics, but rather because we have all been given the right to shed these characteristics, to present ourselves as disembodied before the law. I divest myself of positive identity, therefore I am a citizen (p. 30 my italic).

Sollors (1986:89-90) offers an amusing anecdote regarding this melting-pot metaphor which he claims is an ethnic extension of the religious drama of redemption and rebirth, portraying ethnicity in the imagery of melting in contrast to the stubborn hardness of boundaries. In the Ford Motor Company's English School Melting-pot ceremony in 1916, foreign-born employees would undergo a ritualistic rebirth especially designed by their employers. During the graduation exercise, they were led down into a symbolic 'melting pot,' emerging fully dressed in American clothes and carrying the American flag. The melting-pot ideology has been typically a neoconservative project of "hegemonic universalism" (Winant, 1990:130) where both the denial as well as the overcoming of racial difference (understood as ethnicity) is to assure the workings of *laissez-faire* capitalism. As Winant argues, the implications of hegemonic universalism defend the political and cultural canons of Western culture. The late Allan Bloom's *The Closing of the American Mind* (1987) and Ed Hirsch Jr.'s *Cultural Literacy: What Every American Needs To Know* (1987) present paradigmatic arguments as to why the Eurocentric canon should stay in place. Both authors argue that the decentering tendencies of both secondary and higher education have been brought about as each ethnic and racial group insists on its own version of cultural knowledge that should be transmitted to students in the name of tolerance and understanding, in order to balance the present historical record of intercultural relations. These demands of investment into the cultural capitalism of schooling have, according to the authors, produced an illiterate school and university populace who have no common core of cultural beliefs. The result has been a failure of the educational institution to provide the necessary leadership of centering knowledge and preserving the canon of core beliefs as represented in Western literature, art, philosophy, history. In contrast to these neoconservative views are university programs which promote African-American or racial-minority studies; deliberate attempts to further decentralize the hegemony of the Western canon.

Gains and Losses of Essentialist Tactics

This embracing and maintaining a separate "equality of difference" through forms of gender, ethnic and racial essentialism have made both gains and losses against the perceived hegemony, be they patriarchal, racial or ethnic. Looking at the gains made by Black identity politics of the '60s and '70s, Stuart Hall argued in 1988 that the "relations of representation have been challenged by first, an *access* to the rights to representation by black artists and black cultural workers themselves and second, through the *contestation* of the marginality, the stereotypical quality and the fetishized nature of images of blacks by the counter-position of a 'positive' black imagery" (p.28).

The benefits of *access and contestation* gained from this position have direct benefits for education. There are now school curriculums in virtually every *democratic* country in the world where it becomes possible for children of minorities to receive an education partly if not totally in their own language; the official curriculum is supplemented with their own history and traditions *if* there is enough economic support and resources for doing so. *Access and contestation* of representation was vividly demonstrated by the Métis Society in the province of Alberta in 1988, who insisted that their representation in the new social studies texts books for junior-high be devoid of the psychological problems they may have had in adjusting to Canadian society. They insisted that the Louis Riel *Rebellion* be changed to the Louis Riel *Resistance* in order to have their side of Canadian history told in a positive light. Without such a change the curriculum material could not be released. The result provided a form of historical revisionism which was contradictory in its effects: on the one hand students became aware of the misrepresentation of Riel as a political enemy, and instead recognized his achievement as a leader striving for equality and justice. On the other hand, the difficulties of intercultural conflict were masked. The historical overcompensation of memory merely reversed the blame.

Radical feminists claiming access and contestation based on essential difference (here i am thinking of ecofeminists, Goddess worship theologies, Firestone's *The Dialectic of Sex* (1971), Gilligan's "different voice" hypothesis, 1982) have led to the claims of a *moral superiority* in the very spheres that were coded as being the patriarchal inferior other: the so-called affective spheres of caring and nurturing to name one; non-rational affective forms of knowledge such as gossip and witchcraft to name another. The ruse of *moral superiority* has been often used by indigenous and aboriginal groups in their claims to having a more symbiotic relationship with the land and nature than Whites who exploit it for profit and material gain.

i would argue that the downside of claiming *essential difference* for radical feminists, ethnic and racial groups far outweighs its benefits. Outlining some of these contradictions presents us with further dilemmas for cultural identity, intercultural learning and artistic practice. The problem of essentializing gender, ethnicity, or race is that a culture (or a sex) is presented as a monolithic, self-contained and sexually stabilized entity. Being a member requires displaying the homogenizing characteristics of the cultural formation. Only members of the in-group, usually cultural intellectuals, those often furthest removed from the inherited traditions, are entrusted with the rights of representation. Fitzgerald (1992) has argued that it is in the most vocal champions of cultural revivals are the educated elites amongst such minorities; a group has to be well-off before they have more political clout to say anything. For example, often only Black film makers and artists are allowed to make statements about Black experience. By virtue of belonging to this racial group they are always "right-on" and "politically correct." This leads to what has been called artworks of "cheering fictions" (Hanif Kureishi, 1985, quoted in Hall, 1988), or more pejoratively, "Aren't Negroes Wonderful School" (in Fitzgerald, 1992:119). The writer, musician, actor or visual artist becomes a public relations officer—a hired liar. The artworks are automatically considered "critique-free."[9]

In the case of radical feminism, their ruse has virtually backfired, for in a context where wealthy, White males set the standard, race and gender paradigms which assert "separate" or "different" but "equal" status always have difficulty maintaining what they claim to be "different" and even "superior" *from*. They are often reinscribed, that is, recoded as "inferior." The claims by radical feminists and radical lesbians for their "matriarchal values" such as non-violence, nurturing, caring and mothering capabilities reinforce the separate sphere made available to them in the nineteenth century; while liberal feminists' claims of being equal to men in all spheres conflates in an androgynous position where difference runs on a continuum of human possibilities. This androgynous paradigm, since it relies on a concept of person, makes both race and gender differences invisible. Women are then reinscribed to do double, triple duty as mothers, executives, and home makers.

In the case of aboriginal peoples, their claims to the superiority of their relationship to Nature has been cleverly used to relieve White guilt from their responsibility in creating an ecological disaster, elevating them as "noble savages" who provide the West with a solution to its ills in any number of recent Hollywood movies: *Dances With Wolves, Thunderheart, Mosquito Coast, Emerald Forest, The Medicine Man, The Last of His Tribe, Clear Cut, Black Robe*. In these films, and in others like them, New Age spiritualism, combined with Aboriginal mysticism, is offered as an allegory for the West's redemption so that a new Garden of Eden might emerge.

The purposeful essentialization by the Other also leads to the polarization and alienation by those who do not perceive themselves as being in places of dominance or oppression; who are sympathetic to marginal causes but who find no space within the oppressed groups to accommodate their hybridity. This point is particularly important if intercultural learning is to take place; if any sort of bridge-making is at all possible between genders, ethnicities and races. The exclusion of men from feminist circles is one such consequence; the exclusion of Whites from participating in the Black emancipatory movements in the U.S., Britain, South Africa or the Caribbean, is another. Consolidating an alternative, vibrate, active, and proud Black culture centered on race has left White identity in a social vacuum, stereotypically and singularly perceived as being oppressive. Such a state of affairs has been ripe for inciting racism by White Supremacist groups who can say now, with outright conviction, that "White culture" is under siege - immigrants and "illegal aliens" are taking jobs away from White Canadians; in the meantime the state supports their rights to promote their ethnic self-identity. "For the far right, it is now whites who are victims of racial inequality" (Winant, 1990: 127). The state has become the new target of hate for it has betrayed its "people." Many young people, as the Toronto "race riots" of 1992 indicate, are easily persuaded by this traditional fascist argument. Bob Suzuki (1991, in Giroux,1993:23), teaching multicultural education to a group of high school students in Philadelphia, writes in the journal of *Liberal Education* how little his white ethnic students were knowledgeable about their family backgrounds compared to African-American students who had long narratives to tell. Many White students felt that they had no "culture." For Black youth, "ethnicity" seemed to be something which applied to them, which they could transform or adopt as they pleased. There was a feeling of energy, exuberance and creativity growing out of this sense of self and exploration of potential. In this sense, "ethnicity" belonged to Black kids in a way it didn't belong to White kids.

Diana Jeater (1992), a White British academician, talks about the problems of her White identity in the British context. Jeater studied African politics at university; she wrote her doctorate about the construction of moral discourse in White settler-occupied Zimbabwe, and now teaches a course on Black history. She lives in Brixton, her lover is Black, as well as the woman she stays with; she can cook *sadza* or curry at the drop of a hat but she hasn't a clue how to make Yorkshire pudding or cook roast beef. She occasionally reads the "Voice" and listens to Choice FM (Black British radio station). Despite her protests, such a lifestyle has earned her the status of being called an "honorary black." Her actions are often interpreted as "arrogant" and typically White - an attempt to silence and deny the experience of Black people who have suffered from the patronage of White people "wanting to be black." In her analysis of the situation of Whites in Black studies in England she concluded that there were only three subject positions available to Whites who were sympathetic to the Black cause.

We could embrace a cultural conception of 'whiteness' as bestowing a limited and conservative 'Englishness'; we could be guilty liberals; or we could accept that our marginalization from mainstream 'whiteness' made us in some sense 'honorary blacks' (p.118).

The identity politics in the late 1970s and the 1980s achieved many useful things but it drove a wedge between people whose identities were presumed to be in opposition: male/female, Jewish/Palestine; Black/White. i believe that this same argument applies to the exclusion of men by the radical side of feminist movement, turning many women (and men) away from its cause. Men's studies has begun to show the array of masculine identities that exist, not all of which can be branded as oppressive and patriarchal.

Postmodern Racism

The claiming of essential difference is fraught with a further danger, perhaps the most pernicious one as yet. In the strong sense, it leads to apartheid, where separate and different spheres are used for purposes of containment and exclusion, as in issues of bussing in the U.S., i.e., the parent's right to send their child to the school of their choice, and to withdraw a child from school because the curriculum was not reflecting the culture which they wanted taught. In 1987, the Yorkshire town of Dewesbury, Scotland became the focus of national attention when White parents withdrew their children from a local school with predominantly Asian pupils, on the grounds that "English" culture was no longer taught in the curriculum. In Vienna, private schools are rapidly opening up to teach Austrian culture as east Europeans flood in from the decentering effects felt from Russia, Yugoslavia and Czechoslovakia. Many parents feel that too much time is being spent in school catering to the children of refugees and immigrants, thereby depriving their own children of their language and heritage.

In the weak sense, the "different but equal" status has produced what Etienne Balibar (1991) has called a neo-racism or "differentialist racism" in the postcolonial, postmodern period where "decolonialization" is taking place.[10] Others have identified this as a "symbolic racism," or the "new racism," and even the ironical term "civilized racism." There are many shades to this development; all of them use the democratic parading of cultural pluralism as a means to preserve dominant hegemony and national identity while at the same time appearing tolerant, inquisitive, helpful and respectful of the Other.[11]

In contrast to the old racial biologism which was presented in a direct, raw and brutally physical fashion, neo-racism requires the "reflective" theorizations of an anthropological culturalism for justification of "difference" and "otherness." In a postmodern era, writes Balibar, "There is in fact no racism without theory (or theories)" (p.18). This "meta-racism," as developed by academics, constructs a scientific theory which immediately explains and justifies the racism of the masses, linking up their "visible" collective violence to a set of "hidden causes," thereby fulfilling an intense desire for an interpretative explanation as to *what* individuals are experiencing in this postmodern decentralization, and who they *are* in the social world. This new "differentiated racism," is for Balibar a "racism without race"; that is to say, racial tensions exist only as the incompatible differences between cultures, lifestyles, sexual preferences, traditions and so forth. The necessity of maintaining these differences now parades as a "democratic" solution. Such a theoretical position "naturalizes" cultural differences in order to contain individuals or groups in an *a priori* cultural genealogy. They become essential, fixed entities separated by a margin of "cultural distance." In this way cultural differences are maintained by erecting borders. The older notion of superiority of race is replaced by a multicultural theory which gives various groups status on the grounds that there is an essential culture to which they belong, which can be observed and learned from at a distance as long as the barrier, the boundary, or distance is maintained. The Other can be admired and exoticized for its difference, but at the same time this very difference and particularity is maintained in order to maintain inequality. The category of *immigration* now replaces the old racist word for the biologically determined race. No sense of cultural change or hybridity for the Other is allowed or permitted. From a similar perspective Stephen Greenblatt (see Doerry, 1994) has argued that when the Other gets too close and begins to assimilate, then difference has to be reasserted in order to maintain distance. It is precisely that point in history when Jews become the National Socialist Party's Other, or when the Spanish conquer the Aztecs for reasons which include their human ritualistic sacrifice resembling too closely the symbolic sharing of Christ's body during the Christian mass.

Multicultural educational curricula (especially as it is developed in art education and social studies), popular media and anthropology partake in this new form of neo-racism by claiming to be more progressive and universalistic in their attempt to understand the Other by getting at an emic or particularist view. A culture's informants or "interlocutors" and their artifacts (music, art, dance, myths and so on) provide the "authentic data" on which to premise the documentary or news report. In doing so, by implication, such action presents the Other as less progressive and more "primitive" because such inquisitive action on the part of the dominant culture is promoting, bestowing and conferring a sense of cultural individualism on the Other.[12] "[T]he cultures supposed implicitly superior are those which appreciate and promote 'individual' enterprise, social and political individualism, as against those which inhibit these things" (Balibar, 1991:25). Homi Bhabha (1990) reconfirms this enterprise in yet another way:

> In fact the sign of the 'cultured' [culture in the sense of *Kultur*] or the 'civilized' attitude [here i would flag the word *Bildung* which makes a distinction between academic and popular knowledge, and between technical and folkloric knowledge] is the ability to appreciate cultures in a kind of *musée imaginaire*; as though one should be able to collect and appreciate them. Western connoisseurship is the capacity to understand and locate cultures in a universal time-frame that acknowledges their various historical and social contexts only eventually to transcend them and render them transparent (p. 208).

Meta-racism claims that it is natural for groups of difference to live together in a multicultural society provided the borders are not crossed. Doing so would be committing the intellectual death of humanity, perhaps even endangering the very mechanisms that ensure biological survival. Cultural pluralism (anthropological culturalism) is thus turned in on itself, for academic meta-racism argues that it is "natural" for human groups to preserve their traditions and their identity. Cultural hierarchy functions as a double logic: it is both denounced and reconstituted at the same time through the practical application of the doctrine. As Bhabha puts it, there is "a *creation* of cultural diversity and a *containment* of cultural difference" (ibid.). Culture now functions like nature. Should this necessary and "natural" distance be abolished, then interethnic conflicts and violence are sure to arise. Racism is therefore explained, and a solution towards its prevention is also given. Such a liberalist theory thus appears *anti-racist* at first sight, but actually is yet another weaker form of apartheid; a more benevolent face of modernist (humanist) *barbarism* which can host the argument justifying White supremacist activities (such as ethnic cleansing) on the grounds that such groups are simply preserving their own "White culture" by maintaining distance and reinstating a "tolerance threshold" so that racist conduct is *prevented*. Armed with this neo-racist theory, the Klan can claim to be "truly" anti-racist and "truly" humanist, discarding their hoods and boldly running for senatorial office as happened in the state of Louisiana with David Duke's National Association for the Advancement of White People and Grand Dragon Charles Lee who ran for the governor of Texas. They now claim to represent the disenfranchised Whites.

Neo-racism forcefully shows how the humanistic project of the Enlightenment can be effectively used for fascistic ends. Zygmunt Bauman, in his *Modernity and the Holocaust* (1989), has usefully shown how the Holocaust represents the barbaric side of its rationalism, developing Walter Benjamin's (1973:258) often-quoted statement: "There is no document of civilization which is not at the same time a document of barbarism." The Holocaust, rather than being "an aberration, more than a deviation to an otherwise straight path of progress," was yet another face of modernist society (p. 7). The principles of its barbarism exhibited the horrors of its rationality. Structurally, the gas chambers were driven by the same presiding principles that were taken for granted as the positive aspects of modernity: the principles of rational efficiency. The structure of thought which facilitated the possibility of the Holocaust were inscribed in the philosophical structure of the Enlightenment itself. The drive for the Third Reich or for Serbian "cleansing" or for the French National Front of Le Pen or, in Austria's case the FPÖ (Freiheitliche Partei Österreichs) Party of Jörg Haider, is the drive towards a rational society converted into a drive towards rationalism itself, a rationalism that can be used for fascist as well as emancipatory ends. As Bauman put it commenting on Lanzmann's film *Shoah*, it is difficult to discriminate the 'rationality of evil' from the 'evil of rationality' (p.202). In another context, Derrida makes the point that "the history of apartheid (its 'discourse' and its 'reality,' the totality of its text) would have been impossible, unthinkable without the European concept and the European history of the state, without the European discourse on race—its scientific pseudo-concept and its religious roots, its modernity and its archaisms—without Judeo-Christian ideology and so forth" (in Venn, 1992: 44-45).

Another form of neo-racism is perpetuated by ethnographical museums, museum education and the inherited history of art that you teach and promote in our North American schools. This aspect of meta-racism in ethnographic museums has been forcefully exposed through the writings of James Clifford (1988).[13] The brunt of his argument, and others who have followed his lead, has been to expose the interest of western anthropological discourses and western museum educators to essentialize and exoticize other cultures as if they were frozen in time, displayed under glass as the West's Other. By documenting a "disappearing world" through the collection of artifacts, the ethnographical museum has managed to gain respectability, status, grants, and a sense of moral righteousness; adding to their collections on the grounds that the producers are disappearing – only their artifacts remain to show the once thriving culture. "Ethnicity in the museum," Handler (1989:19) argues, "reproduces an ideology of culture which homogenizes and domesticates rather than enhances cultural diversity. ...All such groups are [represented as] being more or less identical (doing the same thing) in such self-conscious claims for uniqueness based on so called authentic culture. ...Due to this media homogenization and support, ethnics are becoming more alike even while many such groups continue to identify as 'different' in certain expressive domains of their lives."

The cultural theorist Lawrence Grossberg (1992) provides an interesting confirmatory anecdote:

I attended a conference in Ottawa which focused on the new Canadian National Museum of Civilization: participants were given a tour of the facilities, hosted by the designer/ curator and the architect. The papers were all predictably critical of the capitalist, imperialist, Eurocentric, ethnocentric, racist, sexist biases, not only of the particular displays, but of the design philosophy of the museum as well. They demanded that, in one way or another, the entire project be dismantled or turned over to "the people" on behalf of whom the various critics were all sure they could speak. Admittedly, the museum is perhaps most impressive as a suggestion of what would have happened if Marshall McLuhan and Walt Disney had ever gotten together: every technological gadget and marketing technique are deployed in its archetectonic spaces. And undoubtedly, the critics were right; it is easy enough for those who are trained to find evidence of the structured inequalities in our society - classism, nationalism, imperialism, racism, sexism, homophobia, Eurocentrism - coded into the practices of the museum. But then, wouldn't it be more surprising if the Canadian government had produced a museum that did not somehow incorporate inflections of these various relations? (p. 89-90).

With the rhetoric of an essentialized but equal cultural identity, comes the issues surrounding "cultural property." To validate ethnic identity in the face of cultural erosion, the cultural artifacts of "art" have been used to prove the existence of a group in a concrete way, as well as provide evidence for its sense of worthiness. Many Indian artifacts are now returned from museums to tribes or groups that once possessed them.[14] Besides seeking material goods, ethnic groups are clearly seeking recognition, respect and self-esteem. Their claims for material goods and resources (land claims) are often intimately related to the process of gaining recognition and respect, since Western capitalist culture equates the two. The upsurge of this "revival" ethnicity is largely related to the perceived socioeconomic gains it allows individuals whose identities have been submerged or whose status has been denigrated in the past (i.e., the large cash settlements for aboriginal lands). In this case, identity functions as a political assertion of pride in what the minority regards as its rightful heritage, in spite of any considerations of cultural authenticity. Geographic identity–a strong sense of land and place–remains the dominant metaphor for the definition of the aboriginal self in North America despite the dissipating power of dislocation by the media.

In major international ethnographical exhibits in a postcolonial context, argues Annie Coombes (1992),[15] where contact and exchange between dominant culture and aboriginals is supposed to exhibit an intercultural understanding, rarely if ever are the socioeconomic interests and conflicts exposed. For example, the Tukano Indians of the Amazon made a protest against the "Hidden People of the Amazon" Exhibition in 1985 at the Museum of Mankind, London on the grounds that the exhibit avoided to document the resistances that Tukano Indians undertook with the Brazilian government against the devastation of the Amazon Forest. A recent example, closer to home, is yet another instance of hidden conflict. It involved the Glenbow Art gallery in Calgary, Alberta where an exhibition, "The Spirit Sings: Artistic Traditions of Canada's First Peoples," was curated to coincide with the Winter Olympics in January 1988. This exhibit became the center of controversy which further illustrates just how the presentation of the absence of any self-determination by Indians occurs.

> The Lubricon Lake Cree organized a demonstration and boycott of the Olympic Games in order to draw attention to their forty-year-old land claim. The exhibition itself gradually became the focus of the boycott since its very existence was only assured as the result of a substantial grant from the Shell Oil Canada Ltd. - who also happened to be drilling in precisely the area of the land claim. Bernard Ominayak, Chief of the Lubricon spoke: The irony of using a display of North American Indian artifacts to attract people to the Winter

> Olympics is being organized by interests who are still actively seek-
> ing to destroy Indian people, seems obvious' (p. 47).

Ominayak made it quite clear that there are complex interests at
stake in the representation of culture contact in western museums. This goes
beyond the contextualizations which present the mythic and ritualistic significance of the objects, and beyond the reassessment of the validity of these
practices for the canons of western art establishment, for it exposes the way
these cultural displays are framed by a global politics. The results of such
activism on the part of Aboriginal peoples has forced the closing of some
exhibitions and in some cases feature films.

Like the discourse of the ethnographic museum, the visual art canon
of modernism, which you so vigorously promote in your classrooms, has been
equally exposed for its incorporation of the "primitive" as its Other by
Torgovnick (1990). i think just one quote from her book, *Gone Primitive:
Savage Intellectuals, Modern Lives,* is sufficient to give the kind of dilemmas art
educators face when introducing works of Modern art in their, all too often,
formalist fashion.

> Continuing and expanding an older tradition of including blacks as
> signs of sensuality, paintings of the modern movement like Manet's
> *Olympia* and Picasso's *Les demoiselles d'Avignon* had used blacks and
> African masks in connection with debased sexuality, especially the depic-
> tion of prostitution and brothel life. Is it an accident that these two
> paintings - linking nonwhites, women, and sex for sale - have become
> the icons of modern art? (p. 99)

Had Gauguin then, indeed solved the problem? Torgovnick thinks
not. As she notes, the famous exhibition - Manet and the Post-Impressionists
- organized by Roger Fry in 1910, featured one of Gauguin's paintings from
his Tahitian phase. In contrast to the modernism of Matisse and Picasso,
Gauguin's " 'realistic' works were the only ones the public really liked"! (p.85).

Pastiche Multiculturalism

Softer versions of neo-racism appear in multicultural education which has modelled itself on the "pastiche" and "quote" style of the conservative end of postmodernism. Here many art educators come dangerously close to embracing this perspective by finding clever ways to reinstate and recirculate the signs of the Western artistic canon by having children reinterpret 'famous' works of art from their own perspectives. Such practice requires the activation of art historical works through performance. Such tasks as having children identify famous works of art by matching the jig-saw puzzle pieces they have faithfully blown up and copied is a further illustration of such practice. i would argue Annie Smith's *Getting into Art History* (1993) is an example of such an approach. The "new" and "improved" face of the Getty Center for Education supported Discipline Based Art Education (DBAE) is *the* prime example of multicultural pastiche style. The profitability and benevolence of this curriculum approach matches beautifully with the appropriation of multiculturalism by MNCs and TNCs mentioned earlier.[16] In this context, i would argue that the dominant culture practises a cultural pluralism by catering to an "ethnic pastiche" of symbolic borrowings from other cultures to display a sense of tolerance and benevolent cosmopolitanism as the centering notions of nationalism become more and more difficult to sustain. Like the Eurocentric canon of art history, especially architectural history which becomes self-referentially used again and again in conservative postmodern discourse to invigorate and sustain a 'decline of the West' syndrome, a "multiculturalist pastiche" is most evident (and at its tamest) in its unabashed celebration of exotic food and clothing to add spice to culinary delight and flare to clothing. As an example, i offer a descriptive advertisement of *the Polos Cafe* which appeared in an Edmonton newspaper:

> The theme of the Polos Cafe is West meets East, or more to the point, West collides with East. The menu calls the cooking Orie-Ital cuisine - that's Oriental cooking with Italian flavor. There are many ways to eat here: the tapas approach (nibble on appetizers); or consider the pizza (no. 1 is tofu Italian); or enjoy a more traditional evening of salad (Caesar Oriental) and entree (chicken with honey ginger sauce). Polos also offers something called "the kebab symphony," which is merely a selection of 'babs' ranging from the alluring beef with ginger apricot dip to the alarming calamari with spiced Hoisin sauce (*Edmonton Journal*, 1993, Sept.4, G1).

What can one say? *Bon appétit!*

Black ethnicity, especially as marketed by basketball stars like Michael Jordon and Magic Johnson, Black rap musicians and the marketing firms of Cross Colors and Mondetta labels, promote a superficial, that is 'surface ethnicity' where any specific connection between "race" and "ethnicity" is lost (e.g., it is perfectly possible to be Black and French) (see Dyson, 1993). Ethnicity in its postmodern conservative form now becomes "superficial" and "surface," marked by clothes, speech patterns, and music. Such ethnicity belongs to the homogenizing trend of transnational corporations mentioned earlier. White kids, who have no identifiable ethnicity to draw from, can now purchase it as a commodity form. With no strong community roots, a consumerable and surface youth identity becomes a way to center a sense of place. This is a very different sense from a shared politics of ethnic difference outlined earlier.

The exoticism, fetishization and selling of cultural identities rides on a parallel wave with urban gentrification and the fashion industry of late capitalism. Fine ethnic food restaurants can be found in virtually every major city in the world.[17] As for the fashion industry, an anecdote is suitable here. On an overseas flight the I watched the AIR CANADA "news film." (i use the word cautiously since it is one gigantic advertising "scam.") Nevertheless, i found out that fashion was going "primitive" during the spring-summer of '92. Here are a number of phrases the I wrote down that capture the language of appropriated alterity for exoticization, fetishization and consumption: "let the native spirit run," "jungle fever that is raising the temperature," and "fashion takes a trip to paradise." Regarding the print patterns themselves: "tribal gazelles and ethnic shields," "the Congo line of African beauties," and (i save the best for last), "Go primitive, it's the most civilized way to go!" Gauguin's distant trace is still there!

Anti-essentialism and Hybridity

In the last part of this section i would like to briefly outline the stance of anti-essentialism, that is post-structuralist approaches to cultural identity. In the late 80s identity politics came to a point where there was a realization that the differences *within* ethnic groupings, genders and races were often greater than the differences *between* other ethnicities, genders and races (see Barrett, 1987a; Gordon, 1992). Binaries began to be deconstructed. Issues of class, color, gender, age, ableism, ethnicity, location, began to take more and more significance. Among feminist circles this meant the realization that the representation of "woman" was a "sign" structured in-and-through differences. White, middle-class, academic women, who had first given shape to feminist discourse, had to concede to issues of class, color, education as mediating factors of power as women of color protested their hegemony. The hegemony of Blacks as the dominant oppressed minority also came to be questioned by other marginalized groups of color in both the U.S. and Britain. In Canada, as is well known, a similar questioning took place, especially by Aboriginal peoples when French Qúebec wanted "distinct society" status during the Canadian Constitutional debates of 1992. Their change of name to call themselves, "First Nations" actually inverted the hierarchy by claiming: "We were here first!"

The differences *within* being greater than the differences *between* is interestingly illustrated by the anthropologist Michael Smith (1992) at University of California, Davis. Smith illustrates one of the emerging dilemmas of an anti-essentialist stance: who now gives voice to authentic marginal sensibilities when issues of ethnicity, race, class, and culture are conflated and often encountered by conflicts over group identity? This is vividly illustrated in the recent controversy which took place between Black film maker Spike Lee and Black poet Amiri Baraka (LeRoy Jones) over the right to interpret the meaning and legacy of Malcolm X. This film was shot during the furor started by Baraka; "[T]he black nationalist poet and playwright attacked Lee's credibility at a political rally in Harlem, proclaiming: 'We will not let Malcolm X's life be thrashed to make middle-class Negroes sleep easier.' Baraka exhorted his crowd to write to Lee, warning him " 'not to mess up Malcolm's life' " (p. 515).

Spike Lee's reply, while granting the right of " 'anyone and everyone' " to interpret the story of Malcolm X in their own way, was equally abusive; challenging Baraka's own claim to be the sole authentic spokesman for X's legacy. His response was published in *Newsweek* wherein he used the discourse on class, like Baraka, to settle the presumed racial conflict. " 'In fact,' proclaimed Lee, 'when Malcolm was alive, Amiri Baraka was down in Greenwich Village running around with Allen Ginsberg and living that 'Jungle Fever' beatnik-bohemain life style ...' " (ibid.). In response to being called a bourgeois liberal, Lee retorted, calling Baraka a " 'limousine radical,' " stating that " 'after the ... rally to protest the film, Baraka, the Black Marxist Revolutionary, jumped into a black limo and sped off down Lenox Avenue, past the lumpen proletariat in Harlem. And he calls me a 'middle class Negro!'" (ibid.).

As Smith underlines, the rhetorical exchange conflated race, class and culture. "Not only do both would-be voice givers imply that the essence of black racial experience is rooted in underclass status, they also suggest that black intellectuals who can lay claim to slightly more proximity to the lumpen proletarian experience have a greater entitlement to speak for 'black people' than those above them in the hierarchy of social classes." Further, "[b]oth of these would-be marginal voices fail to acknowledge the diversity of the experience of being black in America or the class and gender differences that are part of that experience. The controversy does reveal, nevertheless, some of the complexity of the seemingly straight-forward postmodern project of giving voice to marginal sensibilities and constructing a political space in which racial and ethnic 'others' can name themselves" (pp. 515-516). In another context, Sollors (1986) makes the point: "[A]n Afro-American and the grandson of a Polish immigrant [living in the U.S.] will be able to take more for granted between themselves than the former could with a Nigerian or the latter with a Warsaw worker" (p.14).

The awakening to an anti-essentialist positionally has meant treating ethnicity and gender as *signs*; cultural and gender identities are *constructed* in difference from within a particular place, out of a particular history, out of particular experience, and out of a particular culture. Such construction is not *merely* a textual matter confined to the imaginings of fantasy and the rhetoric of words. The cultural theorist Stuart Hall, in his early publications of an anti-essentialist Black experience in 1988, made it quite clear that textual constructions produce *real*, that is material, effects. As he writes,

> My own view is that events, relations, structures do have conditions of existence and real effects, outside the sphere of the discursive; but that is only within the discursive, and subject to its specific conditions, limits and modalities, do they have or can they be constructed within meaning (p. 27).

This process of 'emerging ethnicity' has been called *ethnogenesis* (Roosens, 1989): the development and public presentation of a self-conscious ethnic group even, as it has been argued, when such a culture simply exists as a Baudrillardian *simulacrum* (a copy of a copy). For example, the 'counterfeit culture' or 'unauthentic' culture of the Hurons of Qúebec who no longer know their own language but who deliberately construct a stereotypical neo-Huron *counterculture,* is a way to achieve a phenotypical Indian identity. Theirs was a staged culture, ethnically militant in their determination to reclaim their territorial rights :

> When I compared the characteristics of this neo-Huron culture with
> the culture depicted in the historic records, most of the modern
> traits, virtually everything were 'counterfeit' : the folklore articles, the
> hair style, the moccasins, the 'Indian' parade costumes, the canoes,
> the pottery, the language, the music. There is one thing, however,
> that all these constructed cultural characteristics have in common:
> they represent attempts to introduce a perceptible difference between
> Hurons and the surrounding Canadians in a way that suggests some
> Indian stereotype (Roosens, 1989: 47).

Historically the Hurons were decimated by disease through contact with the French, and slaughtered by the League of the Iroquois (especially the Mohawks), who were their traditional enemy. Eventually they were left with a tiny reservation area, the size of a small village. Given this historical memory, can their "faked" reconstructed culture be looked down upon given the fact that they have no legal claims to other lands, only the argument that they feel cheated, and that this land was stolen from them? Didn't Gauguin reconstruct his own Tahiti as well so that he might make ethical claims to living a different relationship with Tahitian autochthons ?

Much too often Indian elders have forgotten their cultural heritage, but there can never be any simple "return" or "recovery" of their ancestral past which is not re-experienced through the category of the present; there is no simple reproduction of traditional forms which are not transformed by the technologies and identities of the present. The cultural erosion felt by the "second generation" is, as Roosens (1989:137) claims, a "true cultural mutation" which cannot return to a traditional culture that it never had in the first place. This especially hit home for me during a film and cultural festival celebrating Native ethnicity last year in Edmonton, Alberta, called *Dream Makers*. There, for the first time, the I experienced the music of Indian rock and the Hip Hop of the First Nations Society, as well as hearing traditional native music blended with popular country music. Such forms seem to identify the decolonized "third space" of hybridity that cultural theorists such as Homi Bahbha (1987, 1988, 1990) and Stuart Hall (1988, 1990) called for at the end of the '80s where "difference" was to be used strategically, yet incorporating other influences.[18] Stuart Hall (1990) put it in the following way:

> The diaspora experience as I intend it here is defined, not
> by essence or purity, but by the recognition of a necessary
> heterogeneity and diversity: by a conception of "identity"

which lives with and through, not despite, difference: by *hybridity*. Diaspora identities are those which are constantly producing and reproducing themselves anew, through transformation and difference (p.235).

In a similar tone, Homi Bhabha (1988) called for the construction of a "Third Space":

It is significant that the productive capacities of this Third Space have a colonial or post-colonial provenance. For a willingness to descend into that alien territory ... may reveal that the theoretical recognition of the split-space of enunciation may open the way to conceptualizing an international culture, based not on the exoticism or multi-culturalism of the diversity of cultures, but on the inscription and articulation of culture's hybridity (p.32).

This anti-essentialist stance therefore deconstructs the binarism between what are "authentic" and "unauthentic" cultural identities. This may be said of a new generation of Inuit youth living in Frobisher Bay who have never experienced the mush of a dog sled or learnt the skill of throwing a harpoon. Skidoos, rifles and television satellite dishes have transformed their culture to such an extent that the rich myths only influence the older generation of soap stone carvers and lithographic print makers. What is produced as a distinct Inuit art today is also a *simulacrum* of the past in the name of a cultural identity. These i believe are examples of cultural "translation" which Bhabha (1990) addresses: the activity of displacement within the linguistic sign.

Developing that notion, translation is also a way of imitating, but in a mischievous displacing sense - imitating an original in such a way that the priority of the original is not reinforced but by the very fact that it can be simulated, copied, transferred, transformed, made into a simulacrum and so on: the 'original' is never finished or complete in itself. The 'originary' is always open to translation so that it can never be said to have a totalized prior moment of being or meaning - an essence (p. 210).

Bhabha seems to be advocating a form of textual poaching so brilliantly analyzed by de Certeau (1984), a rewriting of the established canon of the Other, much like Salman Rushdie's ideas of an altered narrative structure make it quite clear that the techniques of his novel, *Midnight's Children*, reproduce traditional techniques of the Indian oral tradition: the techniques of circling back from the present into the past, building a tale within a tale, persistently delaying climaxes. Such features are reinscribed over the Western linear sense of progressive time. There is now a whole body of postcolonial literature which tries to create this hybrid third space (see Ashcroft et al., 1989). You should remind yourself, however, that the established canon which is being "translated" is *not* simply a body of texts *per se*, but rather a set of reading, listening, viewing practices which reside in a nation's institutional structures of reproduction and dissemination: in its literary, music and art educational curricula and in its communication networks. A specific form of "critical thinking," as embedded in the aesthetics of disinterestedness and distance, which ground Eurocentric notions of connoisseurship and distanced objectivity, are difficult to challenge. "Translation" requires the the mutability and diversity of other cultural forms to perform its displacement. Geyer (1993) calls them skills of transcoding. Following the seminal work of Niranjana's *Siting Translation: History, Post-structuralism, and the Colonial Context* (1992), Geyer describes these acts as "based on modes of inquiry that encompass, on one level, strategies of coping with the fear of otherness while honoring difference. Such strategies are familiar from a variety of therapeutic activities such as antirape or antiracist education. They can be made prominent features of the curriculum and form a scholarly and educational site for bringing together a great variety of disciplines in common projects, such as intercultural reading or explorations in symbolic exchange" (p.531).

In Canada the concept of the mosaic has been an important cultural determinant which has gone beyond the nationalist stance of the 'melting-pot' of the U.S.A. One would suppose that the space of hybridity is ours to claim as an exemplar for the global community. Unfortunately the internal perception of the mosaic has not generated a hybrid literature to replace the nationalistic approach. Canada has tended to remain monolithic, to differentiate itself from Britain and the U.S.A. It has retreated away from the dynamics of difference into a neo-Universalist stance.[19] Many Canadians live with a hyphen within their identity, but this often leads to cultural schizophrenia rather than the decolonized space of hybridity. An autobiographical reflection by a Korean-Canadian which appeared in Toronto's *The Globe and Mail's* Facts & Arguments column last year is a good example of this.

After sixteen years, Sun-Kyung Yi (1992) writes about how the hyphen in Korean-Canadian often snapped in two, obliging her to choose to act either as a Korean or a Canadian, depending where she was and whom she was with. She was called Angela at school and Sun-Kyung at home - this split name calling is experienced by many immigrants. At school she ate bologna sandwiches in the lunch room so that she would not be different. At home it was kimchee and rice for dinner. She waved hellos and goodbyes to her teachers; at home she bowed to her parents' friends visiting the house. The two separate hyphenated worlds could not be maintained without questioning both sides. "Many have tried to convince me that I am a Canadian, like all other immigrants into the country, but those same people ask me which country I came from with great curiosity, following it with questions about the type of food I ate and the language I spoke. It's difficult to feel a sense of belonging and acceptance when you are regarded as 'one of them.' 'Those Koreans, they work hard ...You must be fantastic in math and science.' '(No).' 'Do your parents own a corner store? '(No.)' " (p.U1).

She talks about her working for a small Korean company in Toronto. Her parents were ecstatic that at long last their daughter finally found her roots and an opportunity to speak her native tongue and absorb the culture. It turned out that Canadianized Koreans were not tolerated. She looked like a Korean, therefore she had to talk, act, and think like one too. Being accepted meant a total surrender to ancient codes of behavior rooted in Confucian thought. The Canadian part of her had to be left "outside." Unmarried, she was bombarded with every single available bachelor in the company and in the community. She was expected to accept her inferior position as a woman and behave accordingly. She could not practice her feminist views - Little Korea was for men who filled all the senior positions. She was supposed to act like a lady and smile. She was scorned for her lack of ability to speak Korean better, scorned for her lack in cooking skills. Finally she had to leave because she just wasn't "Korean enough." "But now I remain slightly distant from both cultures, accepted fully by neither." She concludes with: "The hyphenated Canadian personifies the ideal of multiculturalism, but unless the host culture and the immigrant cultures can find ways to merge their distinct identities, sharing the best of both, this cultural schizophrenia will continue" (ibid.).

For arts education, the lesson to be learned from this is not whether the culture is "authentic" or "unauthentic"; rather it is the way its representation of difference is used within specific situations for socioeconomic and political gains and in new formations of identity which might find forms of hybridity which escape the worst of both words. This is very different from the homogenizing effects of consumerist "ethnic pastiche" of conservative postmodernism. Representation is therefore foremost a *formative*, not only an expressive place in the constitution of social and political life.

This hybrid space of difference (by the way, the word comes from *hybris*, which means violence, excess, extremeness, outrageousness) is being developed today through the process of ethnogenesis by a youthful generation of artists who use and poach difference working within a logic of both/and —the local&global. It is most evident by the cut'n' mix style produced from the combinations and borrowings from other ethnicities, yet it is a hybrid style which does not loose a distinctiveness that is specifically Aboriginal or African-American. During the same *Dream Speakers* festival the I met a young native film director and producer who told me that there was a lively exchange of cam-recorded videos amongst various West Coast American Native tribes so that they could learn to know each other better and appreciate their differences. It seems that the generation often identified pejoratively as the "baby busters" are the ones creating these new spaces. i am reminded of Hungary, for example, where anyone older than 30 is suspect of being a member of the former communist party, and therefore devoid of generating new political possibilities and potentialities for the country. This more creative, and i would say progressive, form of difference, however, co-exists with all the other forms of difference i have outlined: essentialist, homogenizing, racist and neo-racist alike. It requires intercultural nurturing.

All this then draws me back to Gauguin, INSEA and Anna Mae Barbosa's talk. If hybridity and the formation of a 'third space' provides a theoretical justification for dealing with the incommensurabilities between cultures, it seems there is justification in identifying Gauguin as someone whose self-chosen *difference* turned against and stood in contrast to the inherited discourses of colonialism and nude painting in his day. "The labor of creating and maintaining the conditions for choosing and fashioning one's identity requires more than a faithful rendering of what is. It takes the assertion of artifice, the *expression* of difference and its simultaneous translation in order to redeem it. It takes, as it were, culture in the original sense of cultivation" (Geyer, 1993:531). Barbosa gives Gauguin company by demonstrating that Tarsilio do Amaral also had been influenced by Gauguin, Léger and other European modernists. She "exercised similar flexibility to the 'other' as a part of herself analyzing the Black heritage in Brazil despite being White and descendent of a family who owned African slaves" (Catalogue, p.55). Both Paul Gauguin and Tarsilio do Amaral demonstrate a non-sovereign self, a decentering or fragmentation of identity which is a "recognition of the importance of the alienation of the self in the construction of forms of solidarity" (Bhabha, 1990:213). As Jane Flax (1993) gleans from her therapeutic practice, such individuals exhibit an increased "tolerance for differences, ambiguity and ambivalence" (p.39). Both artists changed their identity, constructing a new social imaginary through a re-telling of the past. However, their negotiation could never *entirely* escape the discourses that shaped them. If Gauguin was caught by a phallocentrism, surely Tarsilio do Amaral was caught by the discourses of feminization. Yet both proceeded to rework and rethink their identity through the Other thereby maintaining a spirit of alterity.

This Third Space of hybridity is as much informed by sexual difference as by racial difference, and it is to the credit of Barbosa to have developed Tarsilio do Amaral's story in this regard for a "third attitude" of hybridity has also been projected by Kristeva (1979/1986a: 209). Kristeva argues now that a third generation of feminists have come into their own, learning and rewriting their own experiences from the experiences of the previous two generations. It is now possible to deconstruct the man/woman dichotomy. In this regard, i believe the films of Marguerite Duras present yet another compliment to Gauguin of a White female colonizer living in French colonial Indochina who, by recounting her childhood memories, has opened up a hybrid space (see Holmlund, 1991).[20] If art education was given such a mandate to develop the hybrid space of intercultural learning it would indeed become a powerful tool to educate against the vicissitudes of neo-fascism, neo-racism and a humanist tradition which continues to perpetuate, in Spivak's (1992b) turn of phrase, an "epistemic violence."[21]

fig. 17 Andy Fabo's quote on Gauguin in
A Catalogue of Accusations & Counter-Actions, 1988
Gauguin figure as St. Sebastian with Suction-cup Arrows

1 The possible exception might have been Richard Yoeman's presentation (session 43), "Child Art and Modernism, " whose description reads: "Gauguin's quest for an art of spiritual purity initiated an appetite for the 'primitive' in early modern art. This new 'primitivism' encompassed child art along with the arts of Africa, the South Sea Islands and folk art, and it can be argued that early modernism took possession of child art, elevating it, making it a significant branch of the Modernist movement" (Catalogue, p. 64). Others like Annie Smith (session 64) saw an opportunity to examine it as a historical text open to interpretation. Still others interpreted Gauguin's 'spiritual' return to 'Nature' as the direction needed today (i.e., P. B. Lall, session 10).

2 See her recent remarkable essay "Painting, Feminism, History" (1992a) where she clarifies the relationship of the artist and 'his' model.

3 The recent work of Lynda Nead (1992) is a brilliant deconstruction of the phallocentricism associated with the nude in Western art. She deconstructs the binarism of nude/naked as developed by Sir Kenneth Clark and then goes about examining how feminists have sought different representations.

4 Miyoshi makes a distinction between MNCs and TNCs. MNCs still have loyalty to a nation and its headquarters are centered there. In contrast TCNs have no loyalties to any nation. They are decentered, constructing a new networking space that has its claws in many host countries. They form their own corporate selves.

5 Davis, in the *City of Quartz* (1990), writes about Los Angeles's Festival which is funded by Pacific Rim capital writes: "Since Los Angeles is the only city in the world whose ethnic diversity approaches or exceeds New York's, (eighty-six different languages were recently counted amongst its school children), multiculturalism seems an obvious emblem for its new globe-trotting pretensions. Yet (so far) this is still largely an import strategy, focused on an emerging network of transactions between elite cultural institutions, and designed to pluralize the tastes of Los Angeles's upscale arts consumers" (p. 80-81).

6 Following the psychoanalytic work of Jacques Lacan, they argue that the structures of meaning are constituted through "nodal points" (*point de caption*) in which the signifiers and signifieds are temporarily sewn together. These overdetermined points operate to fix the multitude of "floating signifiers" which circulate in the ideological field. This process seems to provide a suitable description of the postmodern Jihadic consciousness as adopted from Barber.

7 This dystopia of transnational corporation takeover has become the "stuff" of cyberpunk science fiction film and literature: William Gibson, Bruce Sterling, John Shirley, and Rudy Rucker are writers loosely grouped under the name of "cyberpunk." Films such as *Bladerunner, Free Jack, Demolition Man, Logan's Run, The Running Man, The Terminator, Brazil, Millennium,* and *Fortress* are just some examples of the filmic genre. See Andrew Ross (1991) who characterizes this entire development as a male fantasy of the space western.

8 In this regard i take Jesse Jackson's Rainbow Coalition to be an exception. As Winant (1990) claims, the second Jackson presidential campaign moved the ground from race to class and attempted to institute a "radical democratic project," that is, to articulate a class agenda in racially conscious terms. Winant writes "*in the postmodern political framework of the contemporary United States, hegemony is determined by the articulation of race and class*" (p. 137). However, the weakness with this project was that so much depended on Jackson himself, deifying him as a leader.

9 The issues surrounding being 'politically correct' apply equally to emancipatory methods of education which claim to help Others to critical self-reflect in order to overcome their "false consciousness" and thereby come to a "true" ideological understanding of their position. In this sense emancipatory education, as preached especially by Henry Giroux (1993) and Peter McLaren (1993) are the obverse face of this ethnic correctness. Both authors have moved into the postmodern, postcolonial debates attempting to salvage their embarrassment from such criticism by quoting everyone in sight/cite/site in order to have the "last word" in this developing discourse. Guru-like status replaces their prior elitism, assuring that their dominance is maintained through the presses.

10 Balibar interprets 'decolonializations' as "the reversal of population movements between the old colonies and the old metropolises, and the division of humanity within a single political space" (p.21).

11 A brilliant application of Balibar's theory with Lacanian psychoanalysis to explain the racism of Serbian, Croatian and Muslim interrelations can be found in "Phantasmen des Krieges: Patriarchat und Mutterland - Heimat und Rassismus," *Lettre International*, Heft 21 (1993):8-11, by Renata Salecl who teaches at the University of Ljubliana, Slovania in the Department of Law and Justice.

12 Since the seminal work of Said (1978), where the critical importance of textural representation in the work of appropriation demonstrated the colonizer/colonized relationship, the whole issue has raised the way ethnographical educational research appropriates the Other. This question was first raised by the now well-known conference at the School of American Research, Sante Fe, New Mexico, published as *Writing Culture* (Clifford and Marcus, 1986; see especially Opie, 1992 for an informed review of the issues in the context of feminist research). Art educators globally reproduce such appropriations of the Other particularly within the context of 'helping' teachers to *empower* native and aboriginal cultures with whom they work with. Following Spivak (1990:94) i would argue that this has become postmodern, postcolonial art education's way of recovering art's lost "aura." This "aura of alterity" provides another way of restoring "spirituality" to art which is said to have lost in an electronic age. The project of emancipatory education (i.e, Henry Giroux and Paulo Freire series *Critical Studies in Education*, published by Bergin and Garvey Press), which always had a tone of being politically correct within the discourse of a neo-marxist liberationist theology, can now be put to service in such ethnographical appropriation.

13 Especially chapter 9, "Histories of the Tribal and the Modern," and chapter 10, "On Collecting Art and Culture," in his *The Predicament of Culture: Twentieth-Century Ethnography, Literature, and Art* (1988).

14 Fitzgerald (1992) mentions the preserved head of a Maori warrior which was returned to New Zealand. In Canada and in the U.S. newspapers have printed stories about young Native men on 'vision quests' to museums to reclaim sacred artifacts that once belonged to various tribes.

338

15 Coombies examined 5 such exhibitions: Museum of Mankind's *Lost Magic Kingdoms and Six Paper Moons for Nahuat l*,1986 in London; Museum voor Volkenkunde's *Kunst uit een Andere Wereld* (1988) in Rotterdam; Beaubourg's *Les Magiciens de la Terre* (1989) in Paris, and the Museum for Contemporary Art's *Africa Explores* (1991) in New York.

16 See Parks (1989) for his conservative defence as to why the Getty Center for Education sponsored DBAE curriculum fits so well into 'postmodernism' as he defines it. Parks supports what i would call a corporate pastiche multiculturalism.

17 The rise of these 'ethnic' restaurants has been a coterminous with the rise of gentrification (Zukin, 1991).

18 A similar space has been philosophized by William Desmond (1987). He coins such a view "metaxalogical," a space that goes beyond dialectics of a Hegelian *Aufhebung,* grounding a *positive plurality* where "each of whose members is rich in its distinctive identity, and whose mediation is not only self-mediation but also *inter*mediation" (pp.7-8). (See also Shohet and Stam, 1994.)

19 This perception *is* changing. Michael Ondaatje, born in Colombo, Sri Lanka and now living in Canada, has achieved an international reputation with his recent book, *The English Patient* (1992) which was awarded the prestigious Booker Prize that same year.

20 See the special issue *Quarterly Review of Film and Video*, edited by Naficy and Teshome (1991) on the "Discourse of the Other: Postcoloniality, Positionality, and Subjectivity."

21 In proper postmodern fashion, this essay ends within the confines of a footnote, for such a mandate for "art education" has already been successfully carried out through an examination of the discourses surrounding AIDS. How the AIDS 'victim' has been constructed in the media, health campaigns, literature and how alternative representations might rewrite these dominate views have been discussed at length by Douglas Crimp (1988, 1992), Boffin and Gupta (1990), Patton (1991) and Treichler and Cartwright, 1992). There is now an edited book by James Miller (1992) which is a compendium of alternative artistic representations of the AIDS body. In the same book David White discusses the art of Andy Fabo, a Canadian artist born in Calgary who is a member of ACT UP. White describes Fabo's own 'translations' of Picasso's *Demoiselles d'Avignon* and interestingly enough, Fabo's dialogues with Gauguin. "In *A Catalogue of Accusations & Counter-Actions* (1988), the central figure from Gauguin's *D'où venons-nous? Que sommes-nous? Où allons-nous?* recurs at intervals throughout the book, and at one point the St. Sebastian pose [Fig. 17] is mocked by the substitution of suction-cupped toy arrows for the original weapons of his martyrdom. Since Gauguin and Picasso are 'notorious heterosexuals', Fabo's intentions cannot be interpreted exclusively as allusions to gay history" (pp.71-72). If, as Peter Brooks says, Gauguin was unable to deal with the 'polymorphous body,' Fabo, who identifies himself as gay, could. An art education which makes identity politics possible is also an art education that few will embark on in our secondary schools or universities. Will this gap ever be closed?

THE
FIFTH
VIGNETTE

Splitting Ourselves Apart:
The Contradictions of the
Pornographic Body

I do not see how ... there is any
possibility of using the image of a
naked woman ... other than in an
absolute sexist and politically
repressive patriarchal way in
this conjuncture.

To use the body of the woman, her
image or person is not impossible
but problematic for feminism.

Experience of the body even at the simplest level is mediated by a presentation of the body, the body-image.

The positing of the body *is* a condition of discursive practices.[1]

Lisa Lyon has been 'framed.' By contouring her own body she turns its surfaces into a kind of carapace, a metaphorical suit of armour. But what may start out to be a parody of ideals of masculinity and a claim to a progressive image of femininity is easily reappropriated. Rather than transgressing sexual categories, Lyon simply re-fixes the boundaries of femininity.[2]

In the next four reflexions i shall try to make sense of pornography and its relation to feminism and (me)n in pheminism. A text such as this cannot avoid this issue. i hope i have covered the whole gamut of issues that surround art's other. i have tried to make sense of gay and lesbian pornography since that debate has been so crucial for feminist politics. i start by reviewing some of the debates earlier in my text, and then raise the question of the representation of the female body which has been so contentious in feminist debates—to recall the exchange that took place between Peter Brooks and his critics. These sections will provide an opportunity to re-visit earlier discussions such as the masculine gaze and the masculine imagination. My title refers not only to the divisiveness that pornography has brought to feminism, but to the many "splittings" that go on in general.

The mind/body split characteristic of humanist and liberalist theory had positioned women to pursue yet another tactic to assure equality in the arts: a sustained response to elevate the arts of the body, i.e., the crafts and the minor arts which have had their "place" relegated to the home and the private domain as the characteristic sight/site/cite of woman, to the level of fine art, typically associated with mind, cognition and the public domain. Typical examples of such transformative strategic displacements would include matching the art of illuminated and illustrated manuscripts in the monasteries with an equally rich art of embroidery found in nunneries (i.e., *opus Anglicanum*) (see Dorothy Miner, 1974); interior and home designs were placed on equal footing with architecture; and Callen's (1979) study of women's arts and crafts movement in England from 1870-1914 (which included ceramics, embroidery, needlework, lacemaking, jewelry and metalwork, woodcarving and furniture, interior design, hand printing, bookbinding, illustration and women's design education) demonstrated that these crafts elevated the role of middle-class women in achieving an economic independence and autonomous cultural identity. The arts and crafts movement, like the teaching profession, provided an opportunity and venue for women to enter the public domain.

Today the breakdown of the barriers between fine art and crafts, between professionals and amateurs, has succeeded to the extent that fibre arts and pottery are now seen as legitimate hybrid forms (i.e., weaved sculptures, the fibre arts of wall-hanging, cloth dyeing, fibre installations, and ceramic displays), and to the extent that local women's art registries—documenting artists at all levels of ability—have been established throughout numerous galleries. Yet the residual of the mind/body division remains within the women's movement itself. It inadvertently separates, along class and color lines, those who believe that Women's Studies departments in American and Canadian universities are distinct and removed from feminism fought in the trenches.[3] While there is no question of overlap, each has a different agenda to carry out given its societal location. Bridging the gap between the academy and the private lives of women through action research projects is more difficult than was first imagined, given the inequality of cultural capital which exists between the two societal sectors. The former perceive themselves as dealing with a distinct women's intellectual history—women's history, women's education, women's accomplishments in the arts and sciences. Academic feminists search for a distinct women's psychology and a 'distinct way of knowing,' challenging epistemological androcentric views. In the early theories of Gilligan (1982), Nel Nodding (1984) and Mary Field Belensky et al. (1986), women's difference was directed at bodily experiences, perhaps inadvertently reinscribing the traditional markers of femininity—caring, personal knowledge, and recovering the lived-body through phenomenological approaches to knowledge. Women's acclaimed superiority in moral and ethical virtues in these areas provided a strong rhetorical force to change research orientations in social sectors where women were dominant. It is not surprising, therefore, that graduates from health and welfare programs, nursing, elementary and early childhood education, were influenced by this direction. If medicine had its positivistic side, nurses provided its subjectivistic obverse. In contrast, feminists of the trenches concerned themselves with the improvement of material conditions in the workplace and in the home. Company day cares, abortion, women's health, sexual harassment in the workplace, child abuse, wife battering and rape were key issues. More militant, their bodies became more and more visible in the news, attempting to fire up the public to emotionally support them in their cause. On the whole academic feminists retained their intellectual rational pose, somewhat removed from those unruly women who gave feminism such a the "bad" name of male bashing. This brief sketch repeats "roughly" the differences usually found between liberal and materialist feminists discussed earlier.

According to Jardine (1989:85,n.38) there are now four generations of academic feminists in the United States that are split generationally: Ph.D.s before 1968, those who got them between 1968-1978, then another generation with degrees from 1978-88, and finally, the newest generation, their decade projected to 1998. This last generation is less likely to have been politicized through women's groups, or activist organizations around women's issues, more likely to concern themselves with designer theory and scholarly approaches for the academic marketplace. (The I is not exempt form this charge either.) When various academic feminisms take on political issues, political differences and professional rivalries often emerge. Competition for academic status and material awards like research grants that make one mobile is endemic. Various presses and journals are often at odds with one another, i.e., *Feminist Review* versus *m/f, m/f* versus such women's presses as *Virago, The Women's Press, Women of Color Press.* "Commodified labor in academic life is what takes place thousands of feet above the clouds in airplanes, shuttling between apartments and conference hotels, commuting in order to have a personal life, living on credit. Such a scene of writing lends new meaning to Marx's description of the private labors of individuals who have no sense of their fellow workers except at the point of exchange—airports, conferences, MLA conventions. ...When lovers and friends are also professional colleagues, the professional and the personal are conflated; one's professional life *is* one's personal life and visa versa" (Landry and MacLean, 1993:56). This description truly hits home. What academic—male or female—has not experienced some version of this?

This divide repeats itself in the arts community. Art produced by women in the academy and shown in galleries can often be dis-"armed"— "Venus de Milo-ized"—relegated to the ghetto by incorporating it into the larger male structure of the museum, art gallery, or literary department. Women's art can become just another label for categorizing the growing diversity of "isms" since the 1960s. In contrast, "feminist art" which implicates a critical political posture to patriarchy, whose sites/sights/cites are often in the "real" social world, have an uneasy relationship with the artistic institution. Some feminists have felt that this institutional attachment was an impossible one to further change. Other tactics were required. The paradigmatic example of this would be *The Guerilla (Gorilla) Girls*, whose artistic antics live up to their name. Donning gorilla masks, their art action projects are done in disguise and often as raids, slapping placards over patriarchal messages to subvert and poach their meaning. In brief, then, one feminist group *can* act like Ismene, the dutiful daughter; the other is *more* like Antigone, who defies the laws of Creon.

Such divisiveness makes artistic responses to critical questions concerning the entire patriarchal structure of the university controllable and contradictory both at the same time. It produces what Cornel West (1990) has termed as an oxymoronic double bind of the leftist academic, one that is "simultaneously progressive *and* co-opted" (p.20). The academic feminist is forced to bite the (patriarchal) hand that feeds her and, at the same time, caress the wounds she's made so that her position is not lost. It strikes me that this is the compromise women's departments make. They need to dance their way between militant feminism, on the one hand, and the more conservative positions of 'a distinct way of knowing,' on the other. This often produces an iconography that is difficult to sustain, as the quotes introducing this section indicate. For example, one of the most controversial tactics used by feminist artists was their use of vulva images, e.g., Louis Bourgeois, Judy Chicago, promoting a gynocentric vision. Committed feminists attempted to reverse the prevalent scopophobic view which treated a woman's body as a mere object. The graphic use of female genitals was said to strike fear into men's hearts.[4]

> At a deeper and unconscious level, the image of the female nude signifies male fear of sexual difference. In European art the signal omission from the depiction of the female body is exactly the sign of her femaleness, her difference. Female genitals are almost never exposed. The positive assertion of female genitals in so-called vaginal imagery

> represents, for many feminists, a rejection of male views of
> woman's body and an assertion of the female sexuality. It
> attracts the idea of women's genitals as mysterious, hidden
> and threatening (Pollock, 1988:126-127).

So the rhetoric goes. But the reception of such images suffers from the contradictory sight/site/cite of its display. They often backfire in their intent. Male critics either are repulsed by the excessive vulva images, as in the works of Judy Chicago which are claimed by them not to be art, or, in the case of painting and sculptures of frontal nude displays, often reinforce the established pornographic images that are now visible in the inside covers of any adult magazine at any newsstand. But this insistence that the female nude can be a disruptive force still persists today, two decades after such imagery was first introduced. Amelia Jones (1994) apparently has found a position *outside* most of the conceptualizations that collapse sexual preferences with gender, and thereby body art can question patriarchy, again, if not entirely escape it. In a defense of women's body art, especially the infamous advertisement of Lynda Benglis who posed in *Artforum* (November, 1974) with her bikini removed, naked, wearing only sunglasses, holding in her crotch a huge dildo, Jones informs her readers that Benglis and Robert Morris were lovers at that time, and then writes:

> I both identify with the project they [women who present
> ambivalent gendered bodies like that constructed by Benglis]
> represent and desire the highly sexed bodies themselves.
> I want to see these bodies as neither simply male (with
> penis) or female (the anatomically sexed Benglis) nor sim-
> ply hetero—or homosexual objects of the viewer's (simply
> 'masculine') gaze (p.36).

Just where is Jones "coming from"? It seems to me, one possibility is from the position of transvestism (tv) which offers distinct radical possibilities. Yet Benglis's extra-long dildo definitely quotes the pornographic discourse and her pose reconfirms that knowledge. She even paid for the advertisement herself. This is no tv disruption, but a parodic pun on pornography. But that's my reading. Yet, if Benglis's photo is a point of departure for Jones's fantasy, i must ask again, "where *is* she coming from"? If her own ontological subject position is split apart, as i assume it is, what are the markers of her sexual desire? For there can be no neutral space. It is quite obvious from a lesbian feminist standpoint, the male gaze is not even a consideration. There appears to be less of a contradiction with the explicit display of female genitalia and a dildo-body for sexual pleasure. i assume that Benglis's photo offers the possibility of a lesbian fantasy, but Jones makes no mention of taking this stance. If i have dismissed tv as the other possible disruptive possibility, then i am left puzzled over what Jones envisions as a radical patriarchal intervention.

Lisa Tickner (1978), recognizing this problematical history of the nude in western art, saw the challenge to its re-representation through "de-eroticizing and de-colonizing" of the woman's body, challenging its taboos, celebrating its rhythms and pains of fertility and childbirth from the political space of four strategies. The first strategy was to use a male motif that reversed the nude genre and transcended it by painting highly individualized male friends, androgynously blurring the male/female dichotomy. Such painting (e.g., Sylvia Sleigh's portrait of *Philip Golub Reclining*, 1972), i should think, would receive favorable viewing by a gay gaze as well. Sleigh, received complaints by (heterosexual?) men claiming discrimination, reconfirming for her that this genre was already "staked out as male turf." The recognition of a masculine side by feminist artists was a way to overcome the passivity of a women's body. Tickner's articulation of the second strategy, probably the most problematic in my opinion, was the use of vaginal iconography as already discussed. But the last two strategies fare no better. The strategy of "transformations and processes" are body performances of resistance which question the masquerade women are subjected to, i.e., the documentations of weight loss (the critical performative stance taken here is that women must sculpt their bodies to fit classical lines through diets and exercise), the themes of aging, decay and menstruation. Perhaps the extreme example of this strategy today must be that of Orlan, a 44-year-old performance artist and professor at the Fine Arts School in Dijon, France who undergoes beauty operations (five so far in her quest for *The Ultimate Masterpiece: The Reincarnation of St. Orlan*) in front of a live audience. Her idea of the performance is not so much about getting younger or becoming more beautiful (so she says), but to be totally transformed into a new person—complete with a new name and passport. Such "authentic speech" suffers a credibility gap given that she chose five historical beauties—Venus (chin), Diana (eyes), Europa (eyes), Psyche (nose) and the Mona Lisa (forehead), on which to base her transformation. More often than not, i would argue, such performances as Orlan's feed a patriarchal appetite for sensationalism rather than critique.

i think this is also the case with the last strategy Tickner identifies: parodying the self as an object as in the performances of Annie Sprinkle, i.e.,

Post-Porn Modernist where she inserts a speculum into her vagina so that her audience can have a "good" look, and take photographs if desired. For Sprinkle, an "ex" porno film star, prostitute, porn photographer and porn magazine editor, turned artist, "porn and art aren't that different, ... it's all creative .. it is just a different attitude and different people. It is all being creative and to me it does not matter if it is good or bad, the rest of it, it's all just judgments" (interview with Ann Douglas, 1993:23). For Sprinkle the difference between porn and art is one of degree, not kind. "[W]e have a joke, that the difference between art and erotica is the lighting." Because she is supported by the art world, Sprinkle is legitimated as a performance artist despite her pornographic content. Douglas's description of her performance might be summed up as a parody of the confessional mode of *scientia sexualis*, a show-and-tell of her life as a sexual performer with all its transitions—an anti-porn porn. But, in the end, Douglas remains skeptical that Sprinkle's explicit sexual performances escape very far from the exploitation of both sexes.

In contrast, Linda Williams (1993) has little qualm finding agency in Sprinkle's sexual performances. Marshaling Butler's (1990a) theories of identification, Sprinkle enacts "subversive repetitions" within the discourse of the "whore" she finds herself in. If identity is a process of repetition, according to Butler, then Sprinkle can "act otherwise," and still "be herself" through such practices as six-minute orgasms, bosom ballets, and female money shots (the signs of female ejaculation whether parodic urination or sincere). There is no *other* scene of agency than that of the whore, argues Williams. It's not that Sprinkle is ob/scene, as Linda Nead (1992) would have it; she is rather on/scene. Sprinkle finds her own desire in the whore discourse by taking her performance seriously, extending pleasure to 'objects' often not regarded as acceptable objects of desire like dwarfs, burn victims, transsexuals, persons with AIDS, and amputees. Her pornographic films provide educative pleasure for women, as well as recalling the traditional Greek notion of pornography where "whores" were considered "shameless" because they spoke of sex. Sprinkle struts and markets her "shameless goods." Williams, however, is cautious in her conclusions, maintaining that the subversive potential of Annie Sprinkle's strategies do not lie outside the realm of the sexual. Given Williams's position, one wonders at the antics of Madonna. Although applauded as a feminist by the controversial Paglia (1992:3-13), Madonna's nudity and bisexuality both play well and pay well within the history of the nude that feminist artists of the '70s tried to subvert. Madonna has even extended the nude discourse to include the paedophiliac gaze by appearing as "little girl nude" in *Vanity Fair* (October,1992:204-214.) as a promotion scheme for her new book, *Sex*, which i shall return to later.

Perhaps the best discussion to date of body art and its subversive possibilities is Lynda Nead's *The Female Nude: Art, Obscenity and Sexuality* (1992). Her deconstruction of the naked/nude binary along Derridean lines is insightful and helpful to further the debate. Very early in her work, Nead makes short order of Kenneth Clark's *Nude* (1957) study, wherein this classical binary is fully articulated. Clark's argument is a repetition of the transformation myth whereby nature is transformed into culture: the naked corporeal body is transfigured into the nude form, the perfect subject for the work of art. The nude in Western art becomes, then, *the* form for *framing* the female, transforming and limiting her shape through male hands. Such a concept, pushed to its limit, sees the stylus or writing (or painting, sculpting, photogravure) tool as a process which inscribes its marks on the soft earth, metaphorically representing the woman's body.[5] Arguing that there can be no 'naked' corporeal body outside of representation, Nead concludes that "we must be content to investigate the diverse ways in which women's bodies are represented and to promote new bodily images and identities" (p.16). It seems rather obvious to point out, here that this already goes on through fashion which mediates the body through the nude/naked binaries.[6]

Nead then goes on to make a case that the beauty/sublime binary, the very plank that forms modernist aesthetics and at the core of Kantian aesthetics, is yet another variation of the nude/naked binary.[7] The representations of the female body that escape such framing are said to be ob-scene, in excess—literally—to be seen/scene from the side, "what is off, or to one side of the stage, beyond presentation" (p.25). Here is where the sublime is to be found—in excess, in pornography as the other of art, in action, in excitement, rather than contemplation. For Nead this deviant or transgressive nature of the sublime means that there is room for a bodily feminist aesthetic to be played out; one which is past the reach of masculinity. Once more a "*sinthomic* possibility" reveals itself.

After reviewing how the nude has been studied, written about, and taught, Nead, in her next two sections tackles the question of transgression; i would say, following Žižek, her search is for a feminist *jouissance*, her symptom as *sinthome*—as a sense of enjoyment. In her section "Breaking the Boundaries," Nead essentially supports the argument being questioned here. The strategies of the nude that play into a sexual liberation of the female body, and thereby celebrating a liberalist feminist position, are easily co-opted. In her following section, "Redrawing the Lines," Nead identifies feminists who, i would argue, have dropped the liberalist chant and have recognized the problematics it brings. As brought forth in the two previous vignettes, identity as a contradictory sight/site/cite where gender, sex, ableism, color, class, all come into play, requires feminist strategies not so easily identified. Still within the confines of the academy, Nead points to the well-known works of Mary Kelly and Jo Spense as positioning their bodies in their artworks in such a way that the discourses that impinge on them become visible.[8] In Spense's therapeutic projects, it is the health, medical, class, and psychic discourses that have shaped her body. For Kelly, the representation of the female body is displaced through her use of emblematic objects, characteristic of her two main projects: *Post Partum Documentation* and *Interim*. Both reveal the socioeconomic, psychoanalytic, and medical discourses at work: the first during motherhood, and the second during middle age. Nead also develops the work of Chila Kumari Burman and Mary Duffy. The former artist is representative of the difficulties women of color and different ethnic backgrounds have in establishing identity through their bodies, while the latter artist who is disabled and a paraplegic, demonstrates the formations of identity in a artistic tradition that desires wholeness, beauty and health. It is the last section of her book, "Cultural Distinctions" which leads the reader outside the hallowed walls of the high institution, outside its frames into the seedy, perverse, and obscene world of pornography as art's other

Pornography as Art's Other:
The Domestication of "Smut"

There is no problem making the more important distinction between scenes that depict hatred, contempt, and degradation from those that do not—not even if the lesbian sadomasochists are right that "I love you" can be expressed just as well with a slap across the face as with a tender kiss on the forehead.

(Soble, 1986: 187)

Pornography and the art world do not *normally* mix. However, this state of affairs has been shaped by a moral discourse generated by the middle-to-upper classes since the eighteenth century. Museums, at that time, were the first institutions to control the viewing of sexual imagery because abundant sexual imagery had been found during the archaeological excavations of Pompeii. These sexually explicit artifacts (vases, stone phalluses, scenes of intercourse on walls of a satyr with a goat) were removed from the site/cite/sight to a "secret museum" at the National Museum of Naples. This "pornographic" collection was only open to educated men of science and letters; so-called "gentlemen" who studied these works from the proper perspective of scientific sensibility, and deemed them unfit for the general public, especially poorly educated persons who couldn't adequately "protect" themselves from the effects of the images. By the nineteenth century, middle-to-upper class morals had created an entirely new genre paradigmatically illustrated by Victorian England. The public display of sexual imagery and the sexual discrimination of taste began to be governed and censored by a body of (White) middle-to-upper class males who became the defenders of the public "good."[9]

There came into existence an in-between zone which acted as a political, social and legal buffer to settle disputes as to what could or couldn't be publicly shown. The term for such a zone is often referred to as "erotic art."[10] Such art was said to have redeeming qualities. "The erotic represents aestheticized sexual representation; it marks out the limits of the sexual within legitimate culture. 'Erotic art' is the term that defines the degree of sexuality that is permissible within the category of the aesthetic" (Nead, 1992:103). Regularly then, art exhibitions are closed down as a result of artists crossing over the border. An exhibition's "redeeming quality" is questioned by government-sponsored commissions whose power as the defender's of public taste has been a right of inheritance since the nineteenth century. At the time of this writing, the most infamous incident has been the homosexual 'erotica' of the late Robert Mapplethorpe—deemed pornographic by United States Senator Jesse Helms, the same senator who spearheaded a campaign to prohibit the use of public funds from the National Endowment for the Arts against the publication of explicit safe-sex comics for gays (Crimp, 1988). No less notorious has been the 1990 exhibition of lesbian feminist 'erotica,' *Drawing the Lines* (published ingeniously as a series of postcards by Press Gang Publishers, Vancouver, B.C.), organized by a three-woman collective called 'Kiss & Tell' from Vancouver, Canada,[11] and their recent *Much Sense: Erotics and Life* (1992). Sylvie Gilbert from the catalogue of the exhibit writes:

> Unlike the 'secret garden,' this exhibition presents in pub-
> lic view the works of artists who are trying to understand
> the power of sexual desire and its relation to life as we
> experience it with all of its complexity and paradoxes.

Kiss & Tell, like Mapplethorpe, push at the boundaries of what might be acceptable display of explicit sexual imagery. An art history of such transgressions would chart the criss-crosses of competing discourses that lawfully identify what is and what isn't pornographical. At one time such pornographic figures would never have been allowed to hide in the "Garden of Eden," i.e., today's museum system, or given protection by the high priests of art–the museum curators. The conditions under which sexuality is displayed, disseminated and consumed raises its status and recontextualizes the meaning of its receptions. The museum is the most powerful space for its legitimation.

Paul Morrison (1991) makes the point that Mapplethorpe's s/m photographs appeared within the context of an academic journal, and *not* in a gay porn magazine where he had also been featured. Analyzing three of Mapplethorpe's photographs, *Bill, New York, 1976-77*, *The Slave* (1974), and *Brian Ridley and Lyle Heeter* (1979), Morrison makes the case that these photographs participate and subvert the museum discourse that is already in place, predicated on the way paintings have been historically consumed in this space. *Bill, New York, 1976-77* forces the viewer to inadvertently participate in a masturbatory experience; a mirror divides the two side panels of a man pursuing his pleasure and the viewer literally and figuratively, and inadvertently, gives "head" through his/her ensuing reflection. *The Slave* plays on the border between high-minded art and its implicit sadomasochism, as well as reversing the order of an art exhibition and the accompanying art catalogue process. *Slave* is a mounted opened book of two self-portraits of Michaelangelo's *Dying Slave* explicitly focusing on the pleasure of their bondage. The last photograph, *Brian Ridley and Lyle Heeter*, domesticates the practice of s/m by photographing both men in leather and chains as if they were posing for a family portrait in their living-room; making it appear as if this photograph belonged in a coffee table (art) sex book.

Like museum paintings, Mapplethorpe is given the signature of style; his photographs are differentiated from "mere" snapshots by an amateur. The museum "collection" of photography establishes a code through which Mapplethorpe's images are able to intervene. The whole understanding of "Perfect Moment," Mapplethorpe's name for the controversial retrospective exhibit at Cincinnati's Contemporary Arts Centre, trades on such an understanding. Morrison concludes with a perceptive comment: "It is difficult to know how the retrospective could have been judged obscene, which the law defines as lacking in serious artistic content or redeeming social value, when museum existence is itself proof positive of serious artistic content. To date, no museum or exhibit show has ever been so judged by a U.S. court, so absolute is the power of the museum in conferring aesthetic value" (p. 32). Galleries were said to be subject by market forces, whereas museums were elevated to the status of dealing with aesthetic issues, preserving the illusion that there really is a difference in kind between the two forms of cultural institutions.[12]

There is yet another way to legitimate exhibits that push the limits of pornography, this being the claim of reception aesthetics which states that the denotative meaning of the visuals change, depending on who is looking at them, and the surrounding identity politics of the artist who produces them. It then becomes a matter of the politics of interpretation: whose view will becomes inscribed by law? Kobena Mercer's (1992, 1993) and Jane Gaines's (1992) meditations on the images of Black men photographed by Mapplethorpe's *Black Book* bring out the limitations of this deconstructive move. In 1986/1993, "Imagining The Black Man's Sex," Mercer reads Mapplethorpe's *Black Book* as representing the discourse of an "imperial" eye, erotic and exotic racial fetishism at its ugly best. The pornography of the Black body is caught by two contradictory ways of seeing: "the nude, which eroticizes the act of looking, and the stereotype, which fixes the flux of experience. This ambivalent colonial fantasy allows for the cancellation of the threat posed by a Black body with one of docility and amusement" (p.64). Hence this denigration and idealization are typical of the structure of the disavowal of fetishism. Black nudes bodies are being fetishized since there is a denial of their lack (i.e., they are idealized) and the acceptance of it (i.e., they are stereotyped).

In 1986, Mercer saw these pictures as little else than the objectification of the Black male body by a White gaze. In 1989/1993, "The Mirror Looks Back: Racial Fetishism Reconsidered," Mercer argued that the contexts of his viewing had changed. Mapplethorpe's death, the Jesse Helms initiative to close down his exhibitions, and the emergence of new aesthetic practices in the late '80s among Black lesbian and gay artists required Mercer to revalue the fetishistic aspects of the Black nudes. He finds this re-evaluation by examining the subject position he took while looking at those photos, not realizing that there were other positionalities which he repressed. His anger, raised by identifying with the Black models as the White racial Other, made him collapse the subject position of the artist with the enunciated subject (the spectatorial subject) of the photographs taken by a White male subject. The result: Mercer had set up a Black/White binary which gave him the analysis of his dominant reading. What he dismissed was his own homoerotic fascination with these photographs as a gay black critic (ironically, he was occupying the same space as Mapplethorpe, the gay White photographer). In this subject position he was inhabiting the fantasy and power of what he had accused a White male gay subject of doing. Mercer admits to a touch of envy, an effect of an imagined rivalry for these unobtainable objects of desire. Now he reinstates the importance of the author, praising Mapplethorpe for his avant-gardism of turning the photographic discourses in-on-themselves to the point where the two discourses (racial stereotypes and the nude) now become high and low culture that present us with the "deconstruction of the ethnocentrism that binds the two systems of representation together" (p.322).

Should we be a little skeptical of this change of heart ? This (rare) self-confession and self-reflexion by a critic is a confirming example as to how the *sinthome* functions. It points to the real kernel of Mercer's enjoyment: his desire for the Black bodies himself. His critique was structured around this void. Mercer admits the issue as "undecidable," or "unresolvable," a good Derridean escape for it, once again, dissolves his identity that was at play in 1986. But that identity never went away; he only begins to recognize it six years later. Nevertheless, the interdependency of the two discourses (racial stereotypes and the nude) and their deconstruction are said to be demonstrable by Mapplethorpe's representing the underclassed gay Black nude in a classical aesthetic, thereby challenging the acceptable canon. Mercer finishes his essay showing us the difficulties of the criticism of difference with a promise to explore this more completely in his "Skin Head Sex Thing" (1992). In this essay we find Mercer being even more introspective, continuing to pursue "close reading" of the said photographs (this time he makes explicit the replacement of White females of the nude convention with Black males as a transgressive move); but the bulk of this essay is a review except towards the end in a section called, "different degrees of othering." It appears all along Mercer has been bothered how is it that a White gay male photographing Black male models could have caused such an ambivalent disruption within himself. This self-interrogation of his experience does not lead him to explore his own fascination of the Black body as a gay critic, as it might have; rather it leads him to eventually question "Whiteness" by raising the question of the different degrees of othering that manifest themselves. If "different practices of racial representation imply different positions of identification on the part of the white subject" (p.21), then what might be the more progressive identities? Was Mapplethorpe after all, non-racist? Mercer ends by reflecting on the image of the 'White Negro.' Is this simply another form of "racial romanticism" he asks? "At what point do such identifications result in an imitative masquerade of White ethnicity? At what point do they result in ethical and political alliances? Mercer seems to be caught in a vicious hermeneutic circle.[13] Jane Gaines (1992) adds to these ambivalences by comparing the charges made against Mapplethorpe's racism as repeating many of the same mistakes feminists have made against pornography. The charges of 'objectivism' and 'stereotypage,' says Gaines, still buy into an outdated humanism and liberal individualism. Black male bodies are "reduced to," or "nothing but," or "only body." In a typical deconstructive move, Gaines argues that behind this charge of typage (generic categorization) is the assumption that what is individuated is the 'real' which misses the point that such images are always socially constructed. There is no empirical 'real' or an 'ideological' real where the positive image is fixed once and for all. Towards the end of her essay Gaines avoids questioning her own fascination, facing her own void, and hence her own desires, mentioning in passing that these images are enjoyed by Black and White women alike.

Unlike Gaines and Mercer, Yingling (1990) is more certain of Mapplethorpe's racism and his pornographical intent. Unlike lesbian representation, gay pornography "has historically served as a means to self-ratification through self-gratification" (p.6). By appropriating masculinity as a representational strategy for self-empowerment, the political commitment by gays has been limited to achieving this liberatory status. But again this "heroic male image" is a co-optive subject, and it is questionable whether it is an attainable object of desire. In Yingling's terms, Mapplethorpe can't possible escape the charge of racism that Mercer had at first been sensitive too. Despite Mapplethorpe's subversiveness Yingling is correct to note Mapplethorpe's slippage during his *Vanity Fair* interview where he says, "Most of the blacks don't have insurance and therefore can't afford AZT. They all died quickly, the blacks" (p.23). As "individualist" as his models were, in the end Mapplethorpe lumps them together into a generic category—the Blacks. Is this too harsh? i don't think so. "[F]or all their occasional power and astonishing beauty, these images too often stage racial difference in order to insure their own status as controversial texts. And that staging seeks to bypass the social history that has made it both necessary and possible, limiting its interventions in the social construction of the erotic to a problematic aesthetic effect" (ibid.).

If i were to get back to my reason for reviewing Mercer's criticism of Mapplethorpe in the first place, this was to demonstrate how complicit the critic is (like the gallery owner) for furthering a political agenda for the gay community and pushing the limits of pornography. Yet for Butler (1990b) this is precisely what is required. Having made a sustained analysis of the fantasy structures as they apply to Mapplethorpe, and the surrounding controversy by the antiporn coalition and Helms's reaction, she concludes:"My recommendation is not to solve this crisis of identity politics, but to proliferate and intensify this crisis. This failure to master the foundational identity categories of feminism or gay politics is a political necessity, a failure to be safeguarded for political reasons" (p.121). Chaotic multiplicity of representations or "rifting" can take place at the level of production and criticism.

Nevertheless, the nude in the gallery and the museum remains "in the body"—self-contained and framed, coded by the aura of high art, unique and priceless. Her counter part—the fallen woman, the prostitute lies somewhere "out of the body," walking the sidewalk, outside the art institutional walls—mass produced, cheap, available and still unable to fully escape her pimp. At least that's the image often presented. Catherine A. MacKinnon (1988) who is herself vehemently antiporn, notes: "... by all reports it [prostitution] is women's best economic option—that is, it is the only thing, with modelling, for which women as a group are paid—by men—more than men" (p.109).[14] Money, sex, power, self-autonomy and personal control all go together in a capitalist patriarchy. The female prostitute as "bad girl" helps men *testify* (from 'testicle' which is derivative of the Latin *testis* or witness and thus related to 'testimony' and 'testify,' see Kaite, 1987:154) their superior economic position, but also helps men discipline the "good girl" by valorizing and making it appear normal that women's sexual services should be given freely and without economic compensation; after all, prostitution represents dirty and exploitive sex. "If he doesn't get it at home, he will find it elsewhere," so the saying goes. "Bad girls" do it for money; "good girls" do it for free! Again, that's the image often presented. If this good girl/bad girl binary is presided over by phallocentrism, perhaps the ambiguities surrounding the best sex, which is both paid and unpaid at the same time, is negotiated through the exchange of gifts?

The policing of the boundaries of art and obscenity relies on imagined viewers and audiences, and the invocation of norms of moral and sexual values. This realm is all but impossible to police today as the explosion of the home video market has not only made x-rated movies available to children of all ages, but pornographic movies of all varieties are easily rentable at regular video outlets, not to mention the easy accessibility of computer porn. Is this too alarmist a view? i shall pick up this question after a personal exploration of my own "pornographic" imagination.

1 These quotations come from the opening page of Wolff's essay "Reinstating Corporeality: Feminism and Body Politics" (1990). In this essay she argues that, although difficult, a feminist body politics is possible, especially in postmodern dance where the Brechtian device of laying bare the medium becomes possible by deconstructing dance, i.e., turning dance in-on-itself and making the operations of the body self-evident. A body politics "must speak *about* the body" (p. 138). The quotes are useful since i shall be using the strategy that the "naked" female body, already heavily coded by the male gaze, cannot act in the capacity she claims. The quotes in order are Peter Gidal quoted by Mary Ann Doane (1988:217); Mary Kelly, quoted by Rosemary Betteron (1987b:206); Parveen Adams (1986:29) and Mary Ann Doane again (1988:226).

2 Lynda Nead's (1992:9) comment on the photography of Lisa Lyons by Robert Mapplethorpe.

3 Women's departments have not developed in European universities, although a percentage of a university's curriculum is mandated for courses specific to women's issues. Feminists teaching those courses are more likely to be in contact with the public sector than in Canada or the United States; but this is a personal observation only.

4 In cinema, the early Hollywood avant-garde films of Maya Deren (*Meshes of the Afternoon,* 1943 and *Ritual in Transfigured Time,*1946) tried to mitigate the classical apparatus of representation that objectified women by subverting the filmic and editing processes (see Deren, 1992/1960).

5 Nead (p.56-57) draws on Derrida's discussion of the relation between style and stylus as a tool of phallic inscription in *Spurs: Nietzsche's Styles* (1979). In another context Thompson (1981:22) makes the same argument concerning cuneiform writing of the Neolithic period where a reed-like stylus, cut diagonally at an angle across its stem, was pressed into the soft clay, making an impression which resembled the triangle of a woman's genitalia. The inference is that men began writing to wrestle power away or to compete with the power of the oral tradition controlled by women.

6 The most interesting literature in this direction has come from feminists who argue that it is precisely through fashion and the masquerade that they negotiate and clear their own social spaces; hardly are they overdetermined by a capitalist consumerist society or caught by a male spectatorial 'look.' The narcissistic pleasures of homo or auto-eroticism of the body's dress has been underestimated. See Hollander's *Seeing Through Clothes*(1975) and Alison Lurie's *The Language of Clothes* (1983), as early attempts leading to this direction. More recently see Jane Gaines and Charlotte Herzog's *Fabrications: Costume and the Female Body* (1990). More provocative are Marjore Garber's *Vested Interests: Cross-Dressing & Cultural Anxiety* (1992); Juliet Ash and Elizabeth Wilson (eds.) *Chic Thrills: A Fashion Reader* (1993), and Jennifer Craik's *The Face of Fashion: Cultural Studies in Fashion* (1994).

7 This is by now a well-established argument in feminist aesthetics. See Timothy Gould (1990, 1991); Paul Mattick, Jr. (1990). At issue here is also the possibility of a "feminine sublime" as opposed to a masculine one. This is developed by Yaeger (1989) and Rod Giblett (1992). Giblett's gives the feminine sublime an interesting spin by referring to it as "slime" which is the embedded limit of the masculine s(ub)lime. See also footnote 5, in "Give Me a Little Sign."

8 These two paradigmatic artists have been discussed previously in "Give Me a Little Sign."

9 This argument is developed by Kenrick's *The Secret Museum: Pornography in Modern Culture* (1987). Both Linda Williams (1989: 12-14) and Lynda Nead (1992:92-94) accept the usefulness of Kenrick's account, with modifications of course.

10 The distinction as to what is erotic and what is pornographic cannot be analytically maintained. The analytic philosopher Alan Soble (1986), in the last chapter of his book, "Feminism, Pornography, and Erotica," positively disseminates this distinction, carefully arguing against the claims of Gloria Steinem and Andrea Dworkin. Part of the dispute centers around the conceptualization of love. Erotic arts depict love, while pornography is said to be devoid of it. Soble's argument against such a distinction is to note that the emphasis on love merely reintroduces the conservative and bourgeois thought that feminists had condemned as oppressive in the first place. Further, he explains, there is no way to authenticate love simply by looking at a couple's sexual performance (lesbian, gay or hetero). The better term, as he sees it, should be "acceptable pornography" (p. 179). Linda Williams, in the last chapter of *Hard Core* (1989), reiterates Soble's views. This time it is Kate Millett who is deconstructed. Appearing on *Not a Love Story* (Bonnie Klein, 1982), Millett, sitting on the floor surrounded by her own erotic drawings of women, says, "We got pornography, and what we needed was eroticism," implying that the drawings of women she owns are what should replace hard core. But then she goes on to say, "There is some usefulness in explicitness," it can help us get over "dreadful patriarchal idea that sex is evil and that the evil in it is women" (p. 265). Williams latches onto those words and begins to indicate how *Not a Love Story* merely reverses Millett's statement, making hard core pornography as the evil in men; a very reductionist proposition

given Williams's thoughtful historical account of pornography.

11 *Drawing the Lines* is mentioned by Nead (1992:106-108) and Harmony Hammond (1994:120-121). The range of sexual or sexualized photographed activities ranged from "hugging, making love in a bathtub, kissing and cunnilingus to butch/femme role-playing, fist-fucking, S/M, and bondage" (p.120).

12 An indicator how the "shock" value of "the poetics of perversion" has worn off in todays more permissive climate can be seen by the recent exhibition (until May 7, 1994) of the French artist Pierre Molinier's (1900-1976) photographs curated by Wayne Baerwaldt and co-sponsored by Buddies in Bad Times Theatre and Queer Culture at the Toronto Photographers Workshop. Molinier, a transvestite and Satanist, provides his viewers a panoramic view of the erotics of lust and evil. However, as John Bently Mays, Toronto's visual arts critic for the *Globe and Mail* points out, this exhibition is unlikely to be raided by the morality police, or picketed by "White Normals." Thanks to Robert Mapplethorpe, who "has been turned into gay America's Grandma Moses," transgression against "the hegemony within contemporary liberal culture of 'normative sexual activity'—whatever *that* means anymore," is a hard sale (see Mays, 1994).

13 Mercer does come out of this circle in his rather ingenious essay," '1968' Periodizing Postmodern Politics and Identity" (1990a). By using the influential developments in political semiotics of Laclau and Mouffe (1985) Mercer offers his readers the challenge of "sameness." By this he means the problems that arise when differing ideological factions form alliances around specific issues, often making them strange bedfellows. Historically, how do you assess the progressive from the regressive alliances?

14 Ronald Dworkin, in "Women and Pornography" (1993), carefully reviews the key arguments presented by Catherine MacKinnon's latest book, *Only Words* (1993), where she argues that the First Amendment (the right to free speech) should be balanced against the Fourteenth Amendment (all people should be treated equally) when it comes to pornography because that balance has become too liberal. Like the government's action to prohibit discrimination to assure equality, pornography also needs to be banned or punished on this same ground. Ronald Dworkin points out the consequences of such a position, arguing that the government could then forbid the graphic or emotionally charged expression of any opinion or conviction which might reasonably offend a disadvantaged group, i.e., films about professional women who neglect their children, or parodies of homosexuals in nightclub routines could be banned through such logic. In the end the First Amendment protects equality in the processes through which the moral and political climate is formed. Freedom of speech is the other side of equality. See MacKinnon's vehement response (MacKinnon, 1994) and Dworkin's equally provocative response (1994).

TRUE CONFESSIONS OF A HARLEQUIN SOFT-PORN EATER:

Or, What's a Heterosexual to do?

Desire is what we do not control;
goodwill and desire are perhaps,
peculiarly and sadly, twins that
sit incompatibly in the
domestic sphere.

(Naomi Segal, 1992:35)

Does sex have to be dirty?
Yes, if it's done right.

(Woody Allen quoted by Forrester, 1992:106)

There are important differences
between the concealment of female
and male genitals in mainstream
cinema and the ritualistic exposure
of both male and female genitals
in hard-core pornography.

(Anne McClintock, 1993a:18)

This section must be one of the most difficult to write. It shall soon
become evident as to why. In the many brilliant theorizations of feminists
applying psychoanalytic theory towards cinema—Mulvey, Butler, Modleski,
Silverman, Williams, Doane, Adams, Fuss, Penley, Grosz—no personal understanding of their own sexual fantasies and pleasures are ever given. i find this
an odd omission, especially by women who make it their business to have a
thorough working knowledge of the limitations of Freud and Lacan. Their
scholarly work is usually performed on the text side of things; the reader *rarely*
has any glimpses into how feminist critics deal with their own identification
and sexual object choice in the very films they watch and discuss. What about
the men or women they love? What are their solutions to living with a part-
ner(s) of the opposite or same sex? Do they believe in marriage? If so—what
are the arrangements? How do they raise their sons and daughters to avoid
the traps that they claim to know? Their complicity with, or the pleasure of
resistance against, the patriarchal order is never made explicit through any
kind of self-reflective discussion (in public print at least) despite all the talk
about the necessity of examining women's experience. But perhaps it is too
dangerous to do so, given this homophobic society? Or perhaps the admit-
tance of contradictions in their own lives weakens the critique they are making? The elision of personal praxis is approached obliquely, often enough, by
referencing subject positions that are made available by the various genres
under discussion. But how *their* personal imaginary is formed remains a mystery. The phenomenology of their lived bodily pleasures are, on the most part,
left in silent. Within their writing the "I" often appears, but it is distanced and
analytic. There are notable exceptions, of course.[1] My quote by Naomi Segal
in the introduction to this section raises such a question for me, in my personal life, as it did for her.[2] Perhaps the issue is even more fundamental? As
Butler (1991) maintains, "part of what constitutes sexuality is precisely that
which does not appear and that which, to some degree, can never appear. This
is perhaps the most fundamental reason why sexuality is to some degree always
closeted" (p.25).

i must confess, it becomes fascinating for me to "read" the body comportment of internationally known feminists when they visit my campus since so much theorizing about the body appears in feminist literature. Knowing that Gayle Rubin appears dressed in leather when she presents her views on lesbian s/m, or watching the obvious narcissistic performance of Paglia presenting a public lecture, or noting Gloria Steinem's reserve makes a difference. i was surprised by Jacqueline Rose's and Alice Jardine's fashionable presence. Both could easily appear within the covers of a *Vogue* magazine. Am i voyeuristic in this regard? i suppose i am. But is my confession of an erotic attraction any different from bell hooks (1993) admitting to an erotic attraction for a Black student in her class? Only the most prudish would say so.[3] Their masquerades vary in surprising ways. Often their sexual object choice and their personal identification seem to be at odds. My perceived disparity between what they write and speak, and how they "act" and "look" speaks volumes about the naïveté of my own expectations and perceptions. It tellingly reveals how much identity and knowledge are expressive of sexuality and gender roles. If there are contradictions between their public sexual politics and their private lives (and there *may* well be), then these are shared in private—amongst close friends. "My life is not for public consumption," shouts Catherine MacKinnon. In other words, "get out of my face!"[4] Their public face remains "different." This applies equally to men who claim to be in feminism. The contradictions men share about their own sexual lives with women and other men in men's groups are not often laundered in public. The I can't recall one instance in the past 15 years as a university professor where a heterosexual speaker theorized about his own homophobia, or dealt with his own homosexual experiences in a public lecture. i am struck, therefore, by any slips that do take place. A quote taken from Soble (1986:151) on the sexual politics practiced by Andrea Dworkin (from her book *Woman Hating* (1974) which is now considered a classic of radical feminism) is one such slip.

[The European pornographic newspaper *Suck*] has made positive contributions. Sucking is approached in a new way. Sucking cock, sucking cunt, how to, how good. Sperm tastes good, so does cunt. In particular, the emphasis on sucking cunt serves to demystify cunt in a spectacular way— cunt is not dirty, not terrifying, not smelly and foul; it is a source of pleasure, a beautiful part of female physiology, to be seen, touched, tasted.

How am i to read this? Perhaps it was meant to be read ironically, knowing that (today at least) Dworkin has become a leader in the anti-porn movement. Or perhaps it is a "true confession." Her lesbian desires made manifest? Perhaps both. Who knows? Often, it is much later that the reader finds out that Judith Butler or Diana Fuss were writing from a feminist lesbian standpoint, or that Camille Paglia goes it both ways, happier now in a lesbian relationship since, according to her, no man could possibly match her wit and intelligence—for very long, that is! Should such elisions even matter? But to say they don't matter is to deny what was long held to be a central tenet of feminist sexual politics: the belief that the personal was the political—was the theoretical. The academic game of print pushes most of this aside. It exists as gossip, yet another exclusive, yet oxymoronic form of knowledge since it's supposed to be idle and informal. Vulnerability and the academic star system do not mix—easily.

Hysterical jitters: School days, School days

Have i been conditioned by a pornographic imagination? i suppose the answer to that question is an unqualified—yes. While reading the anti-pornographic literature, trying to understand how my own sexuality had been constructed, eventually led to feelings of guilt. Looking at a "beautiful" woman somehow became "wrong." Here, i don't mean the 'objectifying stare' that was said to mentally strip a woman off her clothes, i mean the sexual attraction that was felt immediately on the body by the way someone of the opposite or the same sex physically carried themselves, spoke, laughed. The I became very confused as to what should be a "correct response" to lovemaking as a heterosexual male if i was seriously to accept what the anti-porn movement was telling me—that my subject position as a male was always one of sadism, domination and objectifying women's bodies. How was i to avoid fetishizing my partner's body? Did this mean no play with undergarments, no "wild" sex in unlikely places? woman always on top, i on the bottom? in other words, no playing out our erotic fantasies together, no matter how "crazy," if my partner was willing? How was i to restructure my male psyche so as to feel comfortable again? (All this sounds rather comical and silly as i read it over—a form of denial i suppose—but it wasn't at the time!)

This problem began to bother me so much that doubts began to flood my mind each and every time i made love. The more the I read psychoanalysis, feminist critiques, spoke about sex/gender constructions, the more "confused" the I became. The I went through a period where my heterosexual libido seemed to wane. For the first time i could see the possibility of how impotency could, perhaps does, happen. The I suffered a loss of my sex drive—no image for my sexual fantasies could be found. i consciously kept "dirty pictures" out of my mind. It raised for me how difficult it might be for men to break the connection between "power" and "pleasure." But what 'power' and whose pleasure? Throughout my twenty some odd years of sexual activity i cannot recall ever forcing myself sexually on anyone. But seduction ... well, that was a definite libidinal economy i could relate to. But what is a search for desire without seduction and passion? Perhaps rape.

It has been well-documented that heterosexual masculinity is socially constructed, in western culture at least, in schools. Paul Willis's study, *Learning To Labour* (1981), an ethnographic description of White male, working class identity in Britain, is often cited/sighted/sited as a demonstration of just how a positive working class identity of manual labour in school becomes coterminous with machismo masculinity. Raphaela Best (1983), in her ethnographic study of an elementary classroom, refers to this social construction of sex euphemistically as the 'third curriculum.'[5] Best describes the interaction between boys and girls and tries to pay close attention to how heterosexual sex roles come to be defined through kissing games that go on in the playground; through the "tent club" activities of the boys who keep girls out so they can develop their own macho code based on strength and domination; and through both sexes playing "house" and "doctor" and "spin the bottle." Through note passing and telephone calls during the evening amongst classmates, a class hierarchy emerges as to who "loves" who, who is the most popular (receives the most Valentine cards), who is a nerd, a goody-goody and so forth. Tomboyism is acceptable, while the gylandrous behavior exhibited by "sissy" or "mother's boys" is strictly policed. The macho code is strictly enforced by what it is not—not feminine and not homosexual. Non-feminine girls are said to look like a man. A heterosexual masculinity embodies personal characteristics such as success, status, toughness, independence, aggressiveness and dominance.

The percentage of teenagers engaged in sexual intercourse has been steadily increasing, as has violent behavior, including an increase in the incidences of rape in junior high schools. It is not my intention here to develop the socio-historical reasons as to why this is the case, nor what can or should be done about it; rather simply to point out that this is the sex "norm" which emerges in the school's institution in both Canada and the U.S. Given this situation, it should not be a surprise to anyone as to why rape, prostitution, and the varieties of pornography (child, gay, lesbian, s/m, hetero) are the manifestations of a heterosexual hegemony, and why homophobia continues to reinforce this state of sexual relations.[6] These obverse manifestations are intrinsically related to the very institutional forces that wish to censor them. As a father of a thirteen-year-old son, i see this sex curriculum unfolding in front of my own eyes, virtually every day.

Put bluntly and startlingly, (some) girls and (some) boys learn to play the heterosexual game by reproducing the very stereotypes that we've all learned to spout as litany in casting the woman as man's Other: passive/active; good/bad; mind/body; nature/culture. Girl's passivity develops as they learn to police and survey their bodies. This is not to deny the active side of narcissism, rather to note that a masquerade has to be learned. They learn that kissing is bad, and that they shouldn't let themselves go, to take sex too far. As a controlling devise they make boys feel badly about their sexual desires. The idea is to stay chaste and virginal until prince charming arrives which exchanges their sexual favours for "things"—nice house, car, kids. To ward boys off, girls call them names—usually animals. They learn to "use" their sex rather than enjoy it. This profile constitutes the "good" girl scenario. The "bad" girl engages in her own sexual explorations and consequently is labeled as "easy." The double bind is obvious. Boys, on the other hand, learn that aggressive behavior is the only way to achieve results. Although their egos may be fragile in the inside, they have to act bravely on the outside. Meeting the other sex is an anxiety laden encounter, for fear of being turned down—castrated. In both cases sexual pleasure is denied in different ways. Boys "get off" most often if they are aggressive and dominant, in full display of this form of masculinity, bragging about their physical display, and use their sex sadistically. While girls sexual pleasure is most often achieved through a masochistic display. Even in situations where (some) girls have no difficulties in competing with the boys, they have to defer their place if they continually wish to be desirable.[7] Any reversals of these roles places the girl as a "slut"—loose with her slit—a "whore," and the boy as a "sissy," peeing his pants when faced with a challenge or a dare. He is a wimp—he can't get it up.

This sketch is only meant to be a cartoon for the complexities of an exchange which can never be so reductively described. Yet this cartoon pushed to an extreme, offers the exposure of its so-called "perverse" or "abnormal side." The denied sexual pleasure for men by women can lead to rape. The profile of a male emerges who is unable to play the sexual game, denied accessibility to women because of his own social inadequacies; he has learned only to take things aggressively. Violence and abuse of his spouse and children are the only way he can assert control and reconfirm his masculinity. Testimonies of convicted rapists are fraught with feelings of powerlessness, anger and inferiority (Levine and Koenig, 1980). Such men present extreme pathology of the heterosexual code. Prostitution exists as a form of release for them. As "sex-workers" these women service all sorts of male desires which cannot be fulfilled through a straight heterosexual imperative, i.e, their inability to ever posses the phallus. Pornography exists ersatz for the real thing. For most men power is denied in the workplace and in politics; therefore pornographic consumption *may* provide compensatory fantasies of power in the domain of sexuality.

If such an explanation is accepted then anti-censorship of pornography usually takes the liberal feminist stance for sexual liberation. Their sexuality is something that has been *repressed*, usually by middle-class capitalist values where touching yourself is prohibited.[8] Bodily contact and nakedness are frowned upon. Sex is mostly in the bedroom—away from the prying eyes of the children. Even kissing and fondling in front of children is forbidden. In analogous fashion, all the games that Raphaela Best mentioned, i.e., playing doctor and nurse, have to occur in places of seclusion and out of sight from adult's prying eyes in case the kids are caught and punished. So prohibitions, restraints, the secrets of sex shrouded in mystery and obscurity shape the profile of the middle-class. Moral panic is sounded now that video rental has transgressed this public/private division. All the adult secrets are out and can be viewed on television (see Meyrowitz, 1986). Pro-pornography supporters wish to regain the pleasures that have been repressed—to become liberated and free to explore their own sexual freedoms. As adults, women are to seek ways of finding their own pleasures, given that they were repressed throughout their childhood. Fashions in lingerie and swimwear epitomize the tensions between the body and this internalized shame frontier; but the nudity barrier is a difficult one to "lift" because it is impossible to do away with culture that installs the barrier in the first place. In Prince Rupert, British Columbia several women walked around publicly bare-breasted as a protest for their rights and freedoms which allow men the same privilege. It wasn't a successful strategy.[9] However, pornography made specifically for women's pleasure, as opposed to male pleasure supports this liberalist tenant of *repressed* sexuality.

Although not quite a "sissy" boy myself, the I was a "soft male" with the occasional show of courage when it was needed. "Sissiness" was beaten out of me through sports, through the dares of going to horror movies, and after-school fights. A hard-working student, who kept out of "trouble," winning the "Christian award" each year in elementary and junior high for the most helpful and friendly student, my place was somewhere in the middle of the pack, between macho and a complete nerd (although i do not recall that term being used during my high-school days in the '60s.). As an immigrant in the early grades the I was called a DP—displaced person. Like most students, the I could identify which boys were the sport heroes, and which boys were a little slow and needed extra help. They were usually much older, mostly boys who had failed grades or had recently immigrated to Canada. As Best describes, girls flirted and boys teased as various secret whisperings went on as to who was with whom. Apart from the few fondling incidents, and the attempts to fondle breasts—often unsuccessfully—i remained a virgin throughout high school, somehow oblivious it seemed, to the recognition that there were sexually active teenagers in my midst. i could imagine "doing it," but couldn't actually *do it*. It all seemed underground to me, although in my mind the I knew that so-and-so was definitely "getting some," and so i admired such classmates. i looked up to their sexual exploits and consoled myself that i was smart. Talk about a mind/body split. Meeting girls and asking them out for dates was a high anxiety experience for me. Somehow the I never stacked up. The I felt possible rejection. By the end of grade twelve the I was seriously thinking about entering a catholic seminary, but the costs were too high for my parents and the I ended up in university—studying honors physics. When I finally did "step out"—discovering women and losing my virginity— it cost me my education. Either body or mind, it seemed. The I failed my second year of university, an unimaginable experience for me. My life changed.

This brief profile of mine is not unique, nor is it complete. It is representative of a particular strata of boy's experiences in school—a generation of Albertan prairie boys (in my case of immigrant kids), many whom were from Slavic backgrounds, Catholic or Greek Catholics, who did as they were told in the late '50s and early '60s to get ahead in life. "Good boys," raised as good Catholics with high moral standards. My parents never sat me down and told me about the "facts of life." This was to happen through osmosis. i can still recall the excitement and shock of seeing my five-perhaps six-year-old neighbor, lift up her dress to show me "hers," if I would show her "mine;" or was it the other way around? My curiosity went wild. Her "difference" excited me. Little was the I to know that in my unconscious this difference was being censored, disavowed. News to me! But my curiosity about women would never be satisfied. Bed wettings from "dirty" dreams, masturbating in the bathroom—hoping my parents wouldn't find out or accidentally walking in on me while i was stroking myself (the I always checked to see if the bathroom door was really shut) were all part of my sexual exploration. The I took the "normal" route to heterosexuality. Looking through *National Geographic* magazines at bare-breasted exoticized women (who knows what the residual effects of this were, given what i have read since about the National Geographic[10]), looking at women's underwear in the Sears catalogues, and then progressing to *Playboy* and then *Penthouse* which (at last) showed genital nudity, so called 'beaver' nudity. All these, i'm sure (?) were fetishized substitutes for my curiosity, and ersatz for my inability to have or to do "the real thing." For Freud, fetishism was considered the most satisfying of the sexual perversions. Compared to the route of psychosis, i suppose the I should rejoice in this (?). Grosz (1989:56-60) has made it understandable for me as to why this should be so, since i've already bought into the phallogocentric order. Had i become psychotic, rather than simultaneously affirming and denying the sight of my mother's genitals (as i did to sustain my fantasy of her maternal phallus), i would have "foreclosed" or "repudiated," that is, negated my observation, "and, with it, the registration of representation of the father's law" (p.58). Because the maternal castration is not registered in psychosis, the father's castration threat is not operational, so to speak; no exclusion of the key-signifier, *le point de capiton* (the Name-of-the-Father). The psychotic is unable to operate in accordance with the symbolic but is caught in the imaginary pre-Oedipal maternal space. His identity is confused with that of the mother. Whereas the fetishist retains a libidinal attachment to the Mother, "the psychotic strives to be her ..." (p.58). Should i be thankful about this?!

When i read Grosz's account (several times in fact) what immediately came to mind were the horror films like Hitchcock's *Psycho* which paradigmatically present us with the fear of the castrating mother—the overpossessive mother who has dominion over her children, particularly the male child. She is the mother who discourages any forms of illicit sexual desire; overprotecting her boy from dirty sex; making all the moral decisions for him. It is not my intention here to explore the psychoanalytic readings of such films;[11] rather to note within myself satisfaction for a fetishistic resolution. Clover's (1987; 1992) study on the horror genre provides a satisfying solution to this crisis by having the "Final Girl" kill the pursuing monstrous psychopath, but as Williams (1983:88) so succinctly points out, the "Final Girl" is always the "good girl" who is allowed to kill her male pursuant. In the end, the Law is restored at the expense of the "good girl" becoming a monster herself. Yet how precarious this maleman's journey must be? How easy might it be for psychotic men to go over the edge and sadistically murder their mothers, like Henry, in *Henry: Portrait of a Serial Killer* (John McNaughton, 1989), a psychopathic killer completely outside the Symbolic Order. He has no fear of the Law. He has not been "properly" oedipalized. Raised by an absent father and a prostitute mother who made him watch as she "did" her johns, Henry hated her. As a castrating mother she beat him senseless. Eventually Henry kills her and any woman who remotely comes close to him. He fears the feminine so completely that his only response is to kill, seemingly without passion or rage. For him it is a crime of self-defence. He simply leaves a trail of bodies, each a symbolic killing of his mother. Love is impossible for Henry.

Soft Core/Hard Core

To speak then of ocular penetration is to penetrate the working of this visual imagery (Kaite, 1987:153).

Pornographic soft core is what i consumed. Berkeley Kaite (1987) provides a careful "penetrating" analysis of how such soft pornography is consumed by men through the solicitous look by a model; involving an exchange of looks between them which circulate within a libidinal economy. Her analysis recalls many of the problems with the masculine gaze developed earlier. She points out that, far from being an object for the male viewer, a view that is so often argued by radical feminists, the models of *Playboy, Penthouse, Hustler* have more agency than at first "glance." The privileged masculine position is first challenged by a discourse of insatiability that surrounds these pictures. These "girls" tell their viewers that they can't get enough; there just isn't any *one* man (nor *one* woman) that can satisfy them. The fantasy of excessive pleasure shows a female in active pursuit of her own pleasure. Her 'sexual fix' (Heath, 1982) is therefore transgressed. Kaite argues that the 'look' is contradictory and oscillating. "The look is possessed by both the reader and the subject of the representation; thus subject positions of male/female are only as good as their discourses: i.e., when talking of the power of the gaze, designations of masculine/feminine do not represent a picture of unity but are themselves unstable, shifting and rife with cross-currents" (p. 152). The viewer also risks becoming the object of the look. At the point of her seductiveness is the boundary of his horror. The male's desire, through the "penetration" of her eyes and his surrender, can be swallowed up, bitten off, taken away by the model's insatiability. He can be made to feel totally inept and stripped of his bodily properties. "Next," she says.[12] Within the pornographic discourse, the power for the woman's desire is captured for me by an image whereby men watching a peep-show crouch down... down ... down; contorting their necks; hoping to catch a last glimpse of the woman's body in the dying seconds as the door closes over the peep-hole, and their time runs out. Time to reach for another dollar and another three minutes of pleasure to stare, fascinated by "that" which they want to possess, but can't.[13]

The exchange of glances reveals the interplays of heterosexual fantasies of (heterosexual) love. The model's gaze only penetrates when her eyes are open: the moment when his denial of her castration is lost and he allows himself to be penetrated/castrated by her gaze. How often is it that lovers "stare" into each other's eyes in full passion and desire? With her eyes shut, absorbed in auto-eroticism, her body is offered up for ocular penetration by him. "It [the woman's look] does suggest that the woman looks, knows she is being looked at, and in doing so encounters her double who is already inscribed in his own drama involving the 'pleasure of passivity, of subject-ion'"(p.158). Katie is suggesting that if the model is the bearer of both pleasure and penetration—her look formally elaborates voyeurism and identification in that she controls the gaze and is, at the same time, a self-conscious display—then it may be that the male's surrender when he is castrated by her sends him back to a moment when his own subjectivity was formed. In Dinnerstein's (1976) description, making love is going back to the mother's body characterized by both plenitude and loss.

i never made it to "hard core" in any big way, compared to the extent the I consumed soft core (erotica). In my mind there was this division between magazines that made it on the newsstand and all that underground stuff that was more inaccessible. Any "hard core" i might have seen were usually at stags, but i do recall viewing *Deep Throat* as part of a philosophy class in aesthetics in the mid-seventies. Therefore, reading Linda Williams's *Hard Core* (1989) helped a great deal in trying to understand "the frenzy of the visible," which was what hard core was all about: the maleman's quest to understand the "truth" of female sexuality, of "figuring the visual knowledge" of women's pleasure. Williams's study makes it abundantly obvious the impossibility of men ever capturing their fantasy Woman; she remains the whole/hole he circles around—existing as plenitude and emptiness at once. The history of pornography which Williams provides, marks the stages of the genre through technological specular innovation; each stage hoping for greater clarity for the impossible visibility of a Woman's desire—"the frenzy of the visible."

Beginning with the optical inventions of the nineteenth century—cameras, magic lanterns, zoetropes, kinetographs and kinetoscopes (the early precursors of the movies)—to the present time where every conceivable variety of pornography is available—couples, s/m, lesbian, gay—the porno eye has sought to expose and lay bare the pleasures of women's *jouissance* which are unrepresentable. With the stag film, the limits of penetration were encountered. For the performer to penetrate the wonders of woman was to make it impossible for the viewer to see *what* was penetrated. To extend visibility required the 'money shot,' the ejaculation of the penis as the climax. But female wonders remain mysterious; the visual extension was more like a self-reflective mirror (*mise-en-abyme*). Only the mechanics of ejaculation were learned.

As Baudrillard (1990) notes in *Stereo-Porno*, "Modern unreality no longer implies the imaginary, it engages more reference, more truth, more exactitude—it consists in having everything pass into the absolute evidence of the real. As in hyperrealist paintings (the paintings of the 'magic realist') where one can discern the grain of the face's skin, an unwonted microscopics that lacks even the charm of the uncanny" (p.29). And so it was with porno: sex as *scientia sexualis* (cf. Foucault,1980a).

If there ever could be a remotely "progressive" form of pornography given the circumstances of patriarchy, Williams points to *Femme* films directed by Candida Royale which provide the best attempts at representing pornographic desire for couples and female desire on its own terms. Williams dismisses Andrew Ross's (1989) argument that these fall into the category of erotica, defending her conclusion that it is the eroticism of the mother that is missing, but provided in *Femme* productions. *Femme* productions provide a feminine desire that is all too often denied. Following the influential theory of women's desire by Jessica Benjamin (1986), Williams sees this genre providing an "intersubjective" fantasy space that is a substitute for the phallus because it attaches women to an exciting world on the outside-in freedom. This fantasy space of feminine desire is "a space of exchange between people in which, by being with the other, one also experiences a profound sense of self" (p.260). She writes: "When hard core begins to probe the nature and quality of male pleasure with the same scrutiny that it devotes to female pleasure, when erection, penetration, and ejaculation [the so called 'money shot' that is visible evidence of male prowess] are no long primary, self-evident measures of male pleasure, then a realm of female pornotopia may be at hand. . . . If this is possible, then feminist re-vision [and not revision] might revise obscenity itself. For obscenity is simply the notion that some things—particularly the dirty confessions of female difference—must remain off the scene of representation. If those 'sexual things' are no longer dirty, if sexual desire and pleasure are no more unseemly in women than in men, then perhaps pornography will serve women's fantasies as much as it has served men's" (p.277). Obviously, patriarchal society is along way from this realization but it points to the tenets of sexual liberation in Williams's terms.

The historical analysis of the pornographic genre, i.e., how its internal dynamics have changed with the social changes brought about by the women's movement and feminism, has made me realize that there are many masculinities, as well as femininities, which consume different forms of pornography for their sexual pleasure. Perhaps this statement seems banal right now, but not when i was having my own crisis of masculinity. Williams mentions several times throughout her study that pornography is the only genre where women's sexual desires are made explicit. And it seems clear to me that there are forms of pornography i would avoid consuming. The consumption of "snuff" films seems absolutely untenable. As Williams notes, the "unthinkable thing in the specter of snuff is not the sadism of the viewer who identifies with the torturer, but the masochism of a woman viewer identifying with her annihilated surrogate" (p. 227). Although pornographic sadomasochism isn't "the diff'ernt strokes" that i would be looking for, Williams discussion of this genre provides valuable insights as to the blurring of subject positions that take place between the dominated and dominator, stressing all along that s/m occurs between consenting partners, yet still within the confines of a patriarchal system. Especially important is her lucid discussion as to how the figure of the mother underlies masochistic fantasy and pornography, while the figure of the father underlies sadistic fantasy. She makes it clear that masochism is not simply the obverse of sadism but a complex masquerade played by the superego and designed to give the appearance of passive submission.[14]

Drawing on the body of recent work on masochism (Silverman, 1988b; Studlar, 1988; Modleski, 1988b; Rodowick, 1982 and 1991; Deleuze, 1971) as a corrective to the sadistic male look of Mulvey, Williams advocates the oscillatory positions of the gaze. The recent writings of Slavoj Žižek (1993a) have extended this discussion on masochism by developing a Lacanian insight as to how the contract of masochism permeates the whole notion of courtly love which still persists today. Of special significance is the realization that the knight's Lady (like Dante's Beatrice, Cyrano's Roxanne, Valmont's Marquise de Montreuil), contrary to the common sense view, should *not* be mistaken as a sublime object of desire, a spiritually elevated figure of ecstatic longing. In Lacan's reading, the Lady is a cold, distanced and inhuman abstraction (as Deleuze suggests as well). This is the dark side of the Mother often represented by the mysterious black hole which signifies female genitalia. The masochistic pact made with the Lady places her in the role of the "dominatrix in the theatre staged by man" (p. 96 n.5). But in doing so, she becomes an impossible object of desire, a Thing, in Lacanian terms, "the 'black hole' around which desire is organized" (p. 102). This can be read as the 'archaic mother' or parthenogenetic mother who signifies sexual difference *prior* to the phallic economy of the Symbolic order. She is not castrated, nor does she 'lack,' for her womb signifies a fullness or an emptiness which is its own point of reference. The black hole is the blackness of extinction. There is always a presence of death (see Creed, 1990:136). The idealization of the Lady is therefore a secondary phenomenon, a smokescreen if you will, "to render invisible her traumatic, intolerable dimension" (p. 96); an intolerable dimension on two levels—at the level of the archaic mother and at the level of the phallic mother. Like Williams, Žižek describes the economy of desire within this matrix in terms of the variations that it can take. The most troubling is of course sadomasochism. Through a series of readings on popular literature and films, Žižek shows how breaches of this pact make the transference of pain and pleasure so complex and so controversial. i prefer to use the homology hole/whole as the paralogical signifier, an *ur*-binary if you will, for the unreachable *sinthome* of Woman which conveys this sense of her presence and absence (see pretexts to the title).

In Williams's discussion of hard-core utopias, it is possible to see how the contradictions of masculinity in patriarchy are worked out by the possible pornographic utopias that become available. Men, whose lives are conditioned by "exhausted," "limited," "dreary," and economically "manipulated" sex lives; in other words, an existence whereby men have little control and power over their lives, are more likely to consume what Williams (after Dyer, 1982) calls a *separated pornographic utopia*. The pleasure is found in its potential to transform "dreariness and scarcity into phallic and commodity intensity and abundance" (p. 159). Such a genre presents a strict separation between the narrative and the sexual fantasy which is often sadistic. Rape is presented in crass terms of sadistic power. The victim wants to be victimized and enjoys it. In contrast, *integrated utopias* present the working out of sexual fantasy on the claims of equality but still under phallic rule. Here the narrative and the sexual fantasies are mixed, but the problems of gender, class, and race are addressed in terms of the power imbalances that they represent. The negotiation that occurs between the traditionally active males and passive females ends in a resolution within the acknowledged structure of power, i.e., a better partner is found; the woman is sexually free to have lovers like her husband or former boyfriend, and so on. Popular during the "sexual liberation movements," Williams concludes that: "Where for men it meant more sex, for women it was the beginning to mean better sex, a notion that ultimately entailed a redefinition of the heterosexual act itself" (p.171). Lastly, in *dissolved pornographic utopias*, the film minimalizes the "distinctions between sexual fantasy and narrative reality" (p.174). In all such escapist fantasy the woman becomes an insatiable desiring object who can never get enough. Patriarchal power is banished from the narrative, leaving only the phallic organ to be played with as she pleases. She now occupies a position of power, i.e., Madonna.

Perhaps what i appreciated most was Williams's discussion of pornography and violence. Presenting "the other side of the issue" (Christensen, 1987), was her avoidance of any simple behavioral models, which argued for causality. The sheer variety of pornography made me hesitate to arrive at any rash condemnations as to their amoral "perverse" nature. In contrast, then, when i read about the structures of homosexual pornography for men i was presented with an entirely different agenda. Gay porn remains the main source of representations of male homosexuality. Following one of the last essays by Paul de Man, "Aesthetic Formulation: Kleist's *Über das Marionettentheater*," Pendleton (1992) usefully argues that porn can be conceptually read in three distinct ways: mimetically, hermeneutically and as a system of rhetorical figures. Anti-porn feminists read film mimetically. They declare pornography dangerous based on its openly visible display of masculine sexuality as sadistic. The text's meaning is read literally. In a similar way pro-porn feminists read pornography as a liberating experience which can even reeducate desire once certain regressive and reactionary elements are removed. Pendleton assigns a hermeneutic reading to Linda Williams's reading of pornography. Meaning is no longer on the surface but can be disclosed by a labor of interpretation and decoding. Both of these reading positions, however, often end up in normative moral pronouncements and answer to political correctness; both are subject to a reinstatement of the discourse of *scientia sexualis*. In contrast, Pendleton reads gay porn as an allegorical staging of grammatically construed figures. He plays this ruse, i believe, in order to keep gay porn out of any romantic appropriations. He is clear that their structure, with their sparse plots, no closure, and lack of hermeneutic coding, but assertive and combinatory sex scenes that often have no narrative time line about them, are modern Sadeian texts. They can be read within the context of a Sadeian grammar. Why should this be celebrated? According to Pendleton they are to be read allegorically. But to what ends? "[G]ay porn's usefulness lies in its uselessness, its excess" (p.167). It strength lies in its "insignificance." Sex cannot signify in any fixed and stable way and thereby it "begins to strip sex of the demand for meaning placed on it by *scientia sexualis* ... ." (ibid.). This might be interpreted then as a "radically free act free of any compulsive [Kantian] doubt" (cf. Žižek, 1993b:71). The pervert knows perfectly well what he is doing and what the Other wants from him. Perhaps this is Pendleton's way of recognizing the *sinthome* of homosexual desire? To which Jonathan Dollimore (1991) would add,"we are all perverts."

My Undergarment "Thing": What Level is this?

Paul Gebhard suggests that sexual fetishism can be conceptualized along 'a continuum of intensities' as follows: Level 1: A slight preference exists for certain kinds of sex partners, sexual stimuli or sexual activity. Level 2: A strong preference exists for certain kinds of sex partners, sexual stimuli or sexual activity. (Lowest intensity of fetishism). Level 3: Specific stimuli are necessary for sexual arousal and sexual performance (Moderate intensity of fetishism). Level 4: Specific stimuli takes the place of a sex partner (High level fetishism). (in Gamman & Makinen, 1994:38).

My kind of pornographic consumption is perhaps hardly surprising given my Judeo-Christian upbringing. It seems rather banal and uninteresting compared to the variety that's out there; not a good market indicator when it comes to selling books. Yet, i found some clues as to how this scenario had been constructed for me by reading Jennifer Craik's (1994) study of fashion. She accepts the historical evidence that the eroticization of undergarments only happened during the nineteenth century. According to several interpretations, undergarments became more and more elaborate as the "shame frontier" reached newer heights during the Victorian age. High morals drove sexuality under the skirt, so to speak.[15] In her "States of Undress: Lingerie to Swimwear" (1994:115-152) she examines the contradictory interplays that go on between the body as a site/sight/cite of sexual conduct (which requires the discipline to control sexual impulses) and the site/sight/cite of the body as the focus of sexual desire of the other (which requires protection). This dialectic leads to a complex variety of scenarios depending on social context and culture. In western cultures, at least, this contradiction between the inner and outer messages repeats the public/private divide of bourgeois society. The corset mediated the private desire of the Victorian woman with the public face of respectability by highlighting shapes as to how the outer clothes should fall. "[T]he period from 1890 to 1910 was the great epoch of underwear and dishabille" (V. Steele, 1985 in Craik, p.121). Underwear was the site/sight/cite of contestation and secret pleasures. Femininity (for underwear) was "ascribed through the use of special fabrics, through decoration, line of cut, and associated symbolism"(p.127). Underwear concealed "the body, but the design of women's underwear [was] calculated to display the fashionable contours of the female forms" (ibid.). It highlighted the female genitalia and buttocks as well. Variants of these undergarments formed the basis of the wardrobes of prostitutes and showgirls. Folded within this binary of under/ outer codes of dress was the swimsuit. "The swimsuit constitute[d] a barometer of standards of sexual and social morality" (p.136). Like erotica, it was the limit case or border that mediated public from private.

This brief digression into the fashion discourse sensitizes me to the historical roots of its construction, and how my own fetishism for such garments has been discharged. This interplay between inner and outer play of clothes remains with us today, constantly transgressed on countless billboards and lingerie shops, at least this seems to be more the case in Europe. In countless fashion magazines the *mise-en-scène* created around the garment and the model creates new registers of fetishism. The lesbian gaze that these fashion magazine solicit offer new contradictions for feminism to sort through (see Fuss, 1992). In a recent art exhibit in Vienna which the I attended in 1993, called, "The Erotic Body of Palmers," featured a historical survey of the changes that Austrian-owned Palmers undergarments had undergone since the '50s. Known internationally for their triptych billboards which pose a model in various daring states of auto-eroticism, Palmers must be seen as the leader in pushing, blurring and often erasing the line between erotica and soft porn. Today, when even underwear can become outerwear—as in the corset collection of Madonna—and satiny slips can be worn as evening wear, the boundary of respect, romance and femininity on one side, and eroticism on the other side, easily conflate. This binary is sent shimmering by destabilizing the look as models now become stars (Wiseman, 1993).

Historically, as has been mentioned, the female model has been construed as raw material for (male) artistic whims (photographic or otherwise). She did not authorize her text, and even if she did so (i.e., as in Expressionist group, *der Blaue Reiter*), she could never displace the power of the artist. Stars on the other hand, even though they are "models," are given much more agency. They are known for their distinctive styles despite the power of the director. Arguments between directors and stars as to the staging of a shoot form the gossip of Hollywood.(You can see where this argument is going.) Who you are looking at changes the context of viewing. The model reaching star status legitimates her "private" exposure. You no longer "stare" at just any flimsily clad or nude body. You are staring at a personality which brings in extra-textural implications. It collapses that private/public divide. Sex *belongs* to the star body. In the Palmers' exhibition, the names of well-known International models appeared in the catalogue and in the explanations of the billboard posters that featured them. Cindy Crawford figured prominently. Often the models quote Hollywood stars themselves in makeup and hair do. Marilyn Monroe and Sophia Loren are the most recognizable favorites.

Hard-core porn is no exception; not so much Linda Lovelace, who might have reached star status had she not renounced the industry, but Marilyn Chambers of *Insatiable* fame, who made hard core 'more respectable' by making as many possible forms of pleasure available to sexually questioning females. In transvestism it was Sekula. More so in soft porn, models and stars interchange between the centerfold's of *Playboy* and *Penthouse* and their stage careers—either on the catwalk (e.g., Cindy Crawford who has appeared in *Penthouse* and discreetly nude on *Rolling Stone's* front cover), or on screen (too many here to mention) or on the concert stage (i.e., Latoya Jackson, Madonna, Pia Zadora). In this regard, it is interesting to note where and when the barrier does come up. In 1983 the first Black Miss America, Venessa Williams, was stripped of her title in July of 1984 for having appeared in *Penthouse*. The pageant's "moral" leverage was used since the pageant's contract said nothing that forbade her to pose nude. However, the contract between *Penthouse* and Williams allowed them to publish photographs of her whenever they so pleased. Williams did not have any textual authorization. They could use her representation as they pleased. It is this legal understanding of the body which separates the opposition of the female nude to pornography.[16] In fine arts the exchange of money is a marker of status. If you are hired to pose for a drawing class, your worth is judged against the artistic privilege of painting or photographing "famous" people *pro hac vice* and *pro gratis*—for free and for this occasion *only*. In short, you're not worth very much. The astronomically high prices paid for model-stars and the exotic locations for the shoot are there to keep the divide of cheap nudity of the "skin" magazine from high fashion apart. The same applies to "ladies of the evening." The more removed from the "domestic space" of a brothel, hotel or apartment, the more expensive the escort service. The photographs of Williams were done prior to the pageant. Had she reigned for a year, with her status, especially as a Black Miss America growing, and then, if she decided to pose nude within any "skin" magazine, her reception would have been entirely different. Become famous first, and then "expose yourself," like k.d. lang's lesbianism, and unlike this scriptease!

On the extreme side of this ledger is Madonna and her recently wrapped book in silver mylar—*Sex*, quoting and at the same time reversing the transgressive appeal of the (once?) seedy and clandestine pornography market. Madonna is its author; her own body is its text. She writes her own contract with it, directs it and sets its design. Her photographer, Steven Meisel, takes a second seat. Sex promotes a permissive ethic under the consent of soft-porn values; a utopian world were fantasies can be released without the fear of AIDS or the use of condoms.[17] It's soft porn but a hard sell; but money is never discussed— the divide remains unspoken. It is Wiseman's (1993) argument that Madonna deconstructs the art/obscene binary through the interplay of contradictory written texts, the control of her images, and her own star status. Once removed from pornography, and contra- to Playboy, sex is an open liberal text. "[I]t can be read as liberating women's fantasy, as concentrating on women's pleasure, as offering in equal status heterosexual and same-sex representations or, alternatively, as exploiting real differences by annexing all images to marketability for a mass audience" (p. 110). If the *repressed sexuality* thesis of liberalism is maintained, then Madonna is paradigmatically the quintessential liberated woman of capitalist patriarchy. The masochistic pact has been made. You are her adorning fans, who love and worship her, eager to open her "mylar bag." And you men? you too are "liberated," for included in the Palmers' exhibit was their recent line of sexy men's underwear which now emphasizes your penis size, a trend began by Calvin Klein and his display of the sexually, muscular active male body. Now your breasts (pectorals) can be grabbed, squeezed, felt, and stroked over the airways. You have joined the ranks of becoming "feminine" consumers, unable to pull away from the allure of your own jock-straps—or is it your bikini briefs?

So what's a soft-porn eater to do if eroticism cannot be chased so far away that it vanishes into a state of indifference and impotence? How is masculine desire to be reformed so that it is perpetually disturbed "at the peep- hole" into shame and guilt? Often the I catches glances of women whose "presence" seems larger than life; whose body is carried with confidence, strength and attractiveness; knowing full well that my "peeped look" has been structured by my Imaginary fantasy of her. Not every woman catches my "look," not every woman carries "the look, " but the phallogocentric Symbolic Order of Western culture sets up those structures so this sight/site/cite of subjectivity can be occupied. To answer this, the I can only introduce his little i and become aware how that screened image of Woman has been constituted by the discourses of the Symbolic Order; to try to replace his stretched out penile (I) with a more deflated one (i), changing the relationship of my (I)(i)s that stare so as to side-step my focus. In other words, i must recognize that woman is my *sinthome*, but work within and against the complicity of this recognition of a phallocentric order; to call other men on their own complicity (this can take on different forms, not only men's support groups but outright interventions in misogynistic behaviours), to undermine it from an impossible anamorphic space created by the disjuncture of these two (I)(i)s. i think feminists do the same with their masquerades; they work within and against the patriarchal Symbolic Order that tries to position them in certain ways—in this way we both need each other to displace the phallus (and maybe the "two-lips?) "elsewhere."

So i got over my "hysteria" but developed something else, but that "something else" will have to wait till the end of the performance. It's time to drop another garment.

1 Eve Kosofsky Sedgwick's chapter, "Divinity: A Dossier, A Performance Piece, a Little-Understood Emotion," a conversation with Michael Moon in her *Tendencies* (1994) is an exception. This chapter explores the filmic texts of John Waters (*Pink Flamingos, Desperate Living, Mondo Trasho, Multiple Maniacs, Female Trouble, Polyester*). Both Moon and Sedgwick attempt to relate their own lives as "fat" lesbian and gay academics to the representational performances of the 'divine couple' John Waters and Divine (Glenn Milstead)—unusual for its theoretical and personal reflexions. Lynne Segal (1987) also reflects on her "sexual liberation" in the '60s.

2 i do not wish to appear ignorant of the phenomenal amount of autobiographical material written by women, nor the recent psychoanalytic analyses by various feminists of Simone de Beauvoir's autobiographical writings and her relationship to Sartre. There have been a number of such studies, i.e., recently (April, 1994) the Department of English at the University of Alberta hosted Toril Moi who presented her own Lacanian reading of their relationship from her most recent book (1994). Rather i am singling out that body of feminist psychoanalytic scholarship which applies itself to films and television. There is a remarkable void to discussing personal experiences to the films discussed. It's as though the theoretical and analytical examination are a way of "mastering" the very contradictory pleasures they bring, a theoretical masquerade perhaps.

3 hooks opens her self-refective essay with, "Professors rarely speak of the place of eros or the erotic in our classrooms" (p.58). The body of the essay speaks to the way mind and body are separated when teaching. Transformative changes require passion, love and caring which are also forms of the erotic.

4 As reported by Justine Picardie (1994) in a telephone interview with MacKinnon over her recent book *Only Words* (1993) which fueled considerable debate in the U.S., especially by Carlin Romano in *The Nation* (November 1994) who "rapes" her with words in his article.

5 The other two being the official syllabus and the so-called "hidden curriculum," which might be simply defined as the sub-text a teacher inadvertently teaches his/her students through the values, beliefs, body comportment, ways of behaving; in brief the ideology that are unconsciously conveyed by the teacher to students. Best's study is only the tip of the iceberg in the understanding of the sex curriculum;but her study is representative of the findings. and her contribution is reinforced by her perceptive descriptions.

6 On the hegemony of heterosexuality see Katz (1990).

7 One example of many will suffice. Popular culture provides an interesting illustration. Horror films are typically the acid test of manhood for boys. The dare is to look straight into the eyes of your worst nightmare and not be afraid. Girls, who also find this a challenge and are not scared, soon learn to play the social game. They pretend fright so as to get "protection" from their dates. If they don't, it is less likely that they will be asked out again. What those imaginings of horror are for boys in relation to feminism has been effectively explored by Barbara Creed's *The Monstrous-Feminine: Film, Feminism, Psychoanalysis* (1993).

8 This line of thinking begins with Wilhelm Reich's *The Sexual Revolution: Towards a Self Regulating Character Structure* (1945), furthered by Reimut Reiche's *Sexuality and Class Struggle* (1971), and then expanded by Herbert Marcuse's *Eros and Civilization* (1962), and most recently developed by Soble's *Pornography: Marxism, Feminism, and the Future of Sexuality* (1986). In a future communist society, Soble argues, pornography would not be contaminated by power. It would be liberated and free. From a similar theoretical context the French film director Jean-Luc Godard and the American feminist film director Liz Borden see prostitution as an emblem of the exploited worker in capitalism (see Godard's *Two or Three Things I Knew About Her and Every Man For Himself* and Liz Borden's *Working Girls*). For a brilliant Marxist analysis of Freudian middle-class roots from which his psychoanalytic theories emerged, see Richard Lichtman's *The Production of Desire: The Integration of Psychoanalysis into Marxist Theory* (1982).

9 Wolff (1990) offers a similar anecdote of a protest by women against a bathing area at Sandycove, Dublin where men often swam naked. Removing their swim suits brought only laughter and stares by young boys.

10 See the section. "Proleptic Installations of the Exotic Gaze."

378

11 The is a wide body of literature in this area. Chapter 10,"The Castrating Mother: Psycho" in Creed (1993) provides an excellent review. On a different level it would be interesting to compare Slavoj Žižek's reading of Hitchcock films in his *Looking Awry: An Introduction to Jacques Lacan through Popular Culture* (1992) with the feminist Tania Modleski's account of Hitchcock films in *The Women Who Knew Too Much: Hitchcock and Feminist Theory* (1988a).

12 The pornographic 'look' and the 'look' of the fashion model often collapse on one another. However, Lacanian psychoanalytic readings of this 'look' differ widely. For example, Diana Fuss agues in, "Fashion and the Homospectatorial Look" (1992), that the female fashion model presents one of the few social sanctioned occasions where women are allowed to look at other women. In other words, straight women must look *as* if they were lesbians. The series of facial advertisements Fuss examines 'look' very much as if they were produced by the soft-porn industry, Fuss provides a tight and complex argument as to how these images take the woman viewer back to the pre-mirror stage; back to her own specular and fictive origins. The woman is positioned by the photographic codes of production to endlessly rehearse the introspection of the (M)other's imago to reassure her of the moment of identification that her own subjectivity "took."

13 The image of Marcel Duchamp's *Etant Donnes: le La Chute dÉau; 2e Le Gaz dÉclairage* (1946-66) comes to mind. When i first saw this "installed room" with a peep-hole on the door (i believe it was at the Philadelphia Museum of Art, but i am not sure), i recall placing my eye up to it to see what i could. Duchamp had strategically placed a nude *mannequin* (Fr. for fashion model) in such a way that "she" could not be comfortably "gazed at." I kept trying to adjust may body to get a "better view." i interpret this as Duchamp's play on the peep-show gaze of masculine desire.

In another context Martin Roberts (1991) does an excellent analysis of how the capitalist gaze of commodity fetishism became historically structured through the "show window" of large department stores (vitrines). He makes the following insightful comment about peep-shows. "The peep-show *vitrine*, however, in reality collapses the distinction between looking and buying, window-shopping and shopping *tout court*, by making the act of looking itself conditional on payment: the peep-show shifts the act of consumption one step back, to its preliminary stage, as it were, making the act of looking itself, rather than what is looked *at*, the object of purchase, as if a department store started charging its customers for browsing; it turns the image displayed in the vitrine itself into the commodity, thereby displacing the 'actual' commodity which it ostensibly displays. In effect, the image of the commodity *becomes* the commodity [pay for your fantasy, or pay the phone bill for your fantasy] making the commodity itself in a sense redundant. Since the goal of the peep-show's customers is masturbation rather than coitus—or even physical contact—the image of the woman [fantasy], rather than the woman herself, is sufficient, and it is accordingly only this which is commodified" (p. 223). Roberts also shows how Wim Wender's film, *Paris, Texas* deconstructs the peep-shows voyeurism in a scene when Travis talks, by telephone, to Jane who is in a peep-booth. "In *Paris, Texas*, ... the glass window of the peep-show functions as a *vitrine* for the display of commodified female sexuality. But in Wender's film, the *vitrine* is also a *screen*. Whereas the booth from which Travis watches, invisible, is in darkness, the image of Jane which he sees through the glass is flooded with light: structurally, then, the peep-show reproduces *en abyme* the audience's experience of watching the film itself (p.224).

14 i used this same argument to defend the "masculine gaze" of the Surrealists. See "The Masculine Desire of the Imaginary."

15 Craik draws on the thesis developed by Norbert Elias in his study of the rise of bourgeois etiquette and taste, *The Civilizing Process* (1978). Until the 16th century the sight of the total naked body was an everyday occurrence. With the rise of civility and etiquette a 'shame frontier' became established. Special clothing was devised to make the body respectable in situations of intimate contact. Bathing costumes, underclothes and nightdresses came into fashion.

16 Ten years later, the original contract and photographs which made the pageant committee decide to strip her of her title appeared in *Penthouse*, April, 1993: 40ff. It speaks to the control such magazines have over 'their' models. Williams has gone on to have a successful singing career.

17 The recent book edited by Lisa Frank and Paul Smith, *Madonnarama: Essays on Sex and Popular Culture* (1993) provides a concentrated look on Madonna's book *Sex*, by such well known figures as Andrew Ross, bell hooks, Douglas Crimp, Pat Califia.

THE
PORNOGRAPHY
DEBATES

The public/private distinction of liberalism makes pornography and prostitution particularly troublesome for feminist critique confined to a politics within humanism. Can a distinction ever be made between pornography and eroticism, for instance? (see Soble, 1986:175-182) Or is eroticism, as the radical feminist Andrea Dworkin (1981) says, merely a variation of high-class or fine art pornography? The genealogy of the female nude in bourgeois art history moved from *"femme honnête* to *fille publique"* (Clark, 1980:24), then replaced by the prostitute in modern avant-garde art, like cubism and surrealism (Caws, 1985; Gubar,1987). Since the Second World War, pornographic images have "spread,"if you will excuse perhaps an unexcusable pun.[1] Soft porn presentations as the photographing of swimsuit models that appear on the front covers of *Sports Illustrated* is "illustrative" of the way the *gaze* of the connoisseur and the *glance* of the pleb can be collapsed together to maintain the fiction of a magical union between lens and body, brush and sight.[2] When "shooting" the model, she can be captured "obliquely," so to speak; slyly, randomly in movement, at a glance, and then exposed, developed, cropped, fixed, and gazed at, as a body part if need be. In the "shooting," she can appear "natural," seemingly untouched and not caught by the cinematic apparatus, but free to frolic about with an abandoned sense of freedom. Her photographer often acts as her surrogate father, brother, cousin, or even sister; someone like family who has seen her body or bodies like her thousands of times before to make it seem all "a matter of fact," common, even blasé, so that her body becomes relaxed and ready for action. At other times, the photographer must "work" to seduce her, act "professionally" and "draw out" her sensuality. When properly approached, depending on her mood, she will perform for the camera and entertain her "fantasy man." Does a pimp act in any other way? Is there a qualifiable difference between the pact made by the model and her photographer and the pimp and his ring of prostitutes? There is a willing exchange for money, for fame, and for the demands of her own narcissism (de Lauretis, 1987a:131, ft.9, 146). Yet money and power are intimately linked. The model is self-employed, exchanging her eroticism and image for personal control and autonomy, perhaps laughing all the way to the bank. The difference seems a question of degree not kind.

Literally thousands of photographs are examined to find the right 'look.' It is the 'look' of hyperreality. The male's voyeurism is now compressed into a nanosecond, shaped by an oxymoron of a "natural hyperreality" within the flicker of a glance, like the shutter mechanism itself. Thus Myers (1982) points out, the porn image and the fashion image may be remarkably similar; but it is the context of viewing, the condition of production and consumption which position the viewer in a legitimated space. For Barthes (1981:40-41), a pornographic image as opposed to an erotic photograph had no *punctum*—no shock, no surprise, paradoxically no prick (not to miss the pun), or just too much prick—just plain boring, unary, banal. So, what might you say to feminist pornography (Laura Fraser, 1990), which sounds like an oxymoron!? videos which cater to a particular market where the woman initiates the action, meets her own needs and satisfies her own pleasure rather than that of the male-typical of male pornography. Or what do you think about "Christian fundamentalist" erotica? sex manuals and marriage guides which help get that "zip" back into a relationship within what appears to be a straight jacket of normative morals (Ehrenreich, 1986). Then there are porn videos made specifically for gay men, lesbians, transvestites, submissive male partners, dominant female partners, sadomasochists and illegal 'snuff' films where actual torture and killing take place.

Soft-porn novels such as *Lace, A Woman of Substance, Hollywood Wives, Mistral's Daughter* Lewallen (1989) argues, represent the contradictory position of women bound up by a patriarchal discourse. On the one hand, they actively desire their own pleasure within it. On the other hand, they must deal with the danger of having their bodies inadvertently objectified. These erotic novels, and made for T.V. serials based on them, present a subject position made acceptable by the Women's Liberation Movement who have successfully challenged the traditional male views of female sexuality. "Through the discourse of bourgeois liberalism it [Romance novel] offers the possibility of change for women, but only through existing structures: as a sort of mirror image of the *Cosmopolitan* type of magazine produced by characters in the novel itself" (p.101). i am reminded of *Flash Dance* and *9 1/2 Weeks*: both films illustrate the paradoxes of female narcissism in the context of capitalism and patriarchy. In the first film, in the end, the dancer realizes she needs the support of a man all along in order to make it into a prestigious ballet school despite her extraordinary abilities, thus reinforcing the Cinderella story once more; the only twist being that Cinderella has now become a steel worker and welder rather than a cleaning lady. In the second film, the protagonist must leave her lover for he continues to exploit her narcissism to the edges of sadism. She is his unwilling partner.

The contradictory positions women find themselves in capitalist patriarchy are often worked out through woman's genres like soap operas, Gothic and Harlequin Romances. (My own subject position as a maleman in the previous vignette is caught up (differently) in the same matrix.) Modleski (1982) has treated each genre as a special case with a specific fantasy, i.e., the fisty heroine (Harlequin Romance), the absent mother (Gothic), and the community of "Another World" (Soaps). Each fantasy enables women to both cope with and resist what are often inescapable contradictions of being dependent on men and acting as housewives who must be ever vigilant to the moods of their families. Marriage is interrogated at the same time as it is celebrated. Extramarital affairs become points of identification and pleasure as "soap" wives challenge the power of their husbands and find their own happiness because they have been neglected (Seiter, 1982). Incest, abortion, test-tube babies, interracial marriages are themes whose boundaries are often explored in soaps. Fiske (1987:185-87) notes that soap operas are a form of feminine pornography. The male "hunk" fantasy is not just body but a question of interpersonal relationships. A tremendous amount of cultural work continues to be done on these genres to overturn the naive view that women are mere dupes of the mass media market.[3]

Perhaps most dramatically, lesbian romances and detective stories provide representational role models for teenage girls to explore their own sexuality that otherwise would be denied them, especially in the school system. Such novels become points of resistance for them. JoAnn Pavletich (1992) provides a lucid analysis how lesbian detective novels have rewritten the country-house, i.e., Agatha Christie, and the hard-boiled detective traditions of Raymond Chandler, Dashiell Hammett and Elmore Leonard.[4] When the "dick is a dyke" Pavletich argues, one learns that social issues that not only deny a lesbian's search for justice, but impact an entire community or the social order, are up for progressive questioning. Criminals are "typical" members of society whose crime is one of male privilege in their attempts to enforce obedience to patriarchy. The lesbian detective does not stand out in a crowd of otherwise mundane and incompetent women; rather "she is one woman among many who are competent, creative, sexual [but not predatorily sexual], interesting, sometimes amusing, and sometimes moving" (p.97). Pavletich readily admits that most of the protagonists are liberal White middle-class lesbians who may be complicit with racist and classist dominant order; however, they also find themselves victims of the same order. Like television melodramas, the endings of these murder mysteries remain inconclusive and unresolved. If traditional authority is reinstated it remains obviously oppressive. Often the endings remain at the level of critique.[5]

Beginning with Janice Radway's (1983; 1984) study of women readers of romance novels who identify with a particular feisty heroine who fights against her domineering, brutal, sometimes murderous male antagonist and transforms him into a tender lover, audience research has proliferated. Caught by further contradictions of male dominance, Radway's readers identified with the heroine and denied the reality of male hostility felt towards them by their husbands. The study of women's psychological resistance to patriarchy through popular culture has continued to increase. Ien Ang's development of a textual theory around the "melodramatic imagination" in *Watching Dallas* (1985), is widely sighted/cited/sited. But more importantly, since Radway's study, the "romance revolution" has come into being (Thurston, 1987). The sexually conscious female *hero* is adventerous, no longer passive. It is she who initiates the action and the male target of her desire must be sensitive and vulnerable. This "revolution" is repeated in the soap operas of today. She is an "achieving woman" who actively fights patriarchy. Martha Nochimson's study, *No End To Her* (1992), unapologetically claims that the soaps are where feminine sensibility is extolled. A writer, consultant and editor of no less than five soaps, Nochimson unabashedly follows the theories of Nancy Chodrow, Mary Field Belensky, Carol Giligan, Jean Baker Miller. The soaps, in contrast to Hollywood cinema (of any kind it seems for her), become *the* sight/cite/site where women mediate their roles between their mothers and the men they love.[6] Evoking the Persephone myth, and not Oedipus, Nochimson argues that soaps display the very virtues of Demeter's daughter. There are always reconciliations, unity, cooperation, closeness and inclusiveness.[7]

If the new "revolution" in soaps and romances are a barometer of the changing patriarchal order with the emergence "new" woman, then Williams' comment seems particularly apropos:

> As female readers of mass-market romance came to recognize the politically unacceptable masochistic self-deceptions of the genre's heroines, they began to demand new fictions in which men would be more like women and women more like men. The result was narratives with female heroes knowingly engaged in sadomasochistic games of power and pleasure with more "vulnerable" male love objects (1989: 219).

A strong reading of the therapeutic fanciful success of soap operas makes it appear that women have made gains within the structures of capitalist patriarchy. What is often forgotten is that such gains can be attributed to a very small strata of middle class usually White women who are represented in these melodramas. Issues of class, color, ableism obviously complicate maters. Reception of soaps by working-class women and by women in the Third World, as well as what were once one-party state communist countries, i.e., Russia, find American soap operas fanciful projections of life styles they could never hope to achieve. They read them as being "unrealistic," confirming more what they don't have than what they hope to have (Brown, 1990a,b). Joyrich (1990:162-63) is especially perceptive in her account of showing how the gendered consumption, tropes of female proximity, fluidity, and "nearness" which are codes of "feminine textuality" offered as subversive alternatives to masculine models of identity, support the psychology of the perfect consumer. And, as forcefully argued by Rosemary Hennessy (1993), this emergent "new woman" is the exemplar of the logic of late capitalism.[8]

Issues surrounding pornography are far from being settled. What should be my posture as a male to the Anti-Censorship Taskforce (Ellis et al., 1988) whose publication *Caught Looking* is a celebration of pornographic images so that female sexual pleasure is not denied? Are such women deluding themselves, living in false consciousness, like my own confessional vignette? Is the pornography issue about the liberalist feminist discourse standardizing sexual desires, universalizing and disclaiming difference amongst women's sexual desires by moralizing and constricting sexual practices and fantasies to valorize the "nice girl" image?

In Canada, the national organization of *Real Women* act as watchdogs to ensure that the bourgeois family values are maintained, and that public respectability be a primary concern for women. Homosexuality and lesbianism are condemned as pathological behaviors. There is an enforced image that the girl/woman should *always* appear "respectable," with no bra straps visible, or with not *too* much make-up on. Sex is, once again a shameful, disturbing, guilt-provoking area of life. Echols (1983) draws me to see a certain parallel between 19th century feminists like Susan B. Anthony and Elizabeth Cady Stanton, who were active in the temperance movement, holding conservative views on marriage, the family and sexuality, against prostitution, with current radical (Echols names them cultural) feminists like Mary Daly, Catherine MacKinnon, Andrea Dworkin, Adrienne Rich in their anti-pornographic stance. In their indictment, fantasies are to be abolished, since they are conflated and correlated with reality: masochistic fantasies reveal women's powerlessness and socialization while sadistic fantasies are said to confirm a male's fundamental murderous nature. Male and female sexuality are said to be dichotomous. As summarized by Echols: "Male sexuality is driven, irresponsible, genitally oriented and potentially lethal. Female sexuality is muted, diffuse, and interpersonally oriented. Men crave power and orgasm, while women seek reciprocity and intimacy ... For men, sex and violence are intimately linked and find their cultural expression in pornography" (p.47). Sexual intercourse for men is now said to be a mere euphemism for rape; it is selfish, violent and misogynist. In contrast women's sexuality is more spiritual than sexual, and less central to their lives than men, e.g., "gay male sexual subculture of s/m and cross-generational sex" is said to "demonstrate male rapacity" (ibid.).

Violence/Rape

In their struggle against anti-pornographic feminists, women (in American and Canadian contexts) who make their living providing sexual excitement to themselves and to men, wish to be supported rather than being ostracized and ghettoized by the law and by women in general. In other countries, notably Holland, Germany, Austria, Sweden, prostitutes are unionized, receiving regular medical examinations by the state. McClintock (1992, 1993b), a strong advocate of sexual workers' rights maintains:

The whore stigma and the constructed ignorance that enshrouds the public's understanding of sex work foster the misconception that prostitution involves no more than a woman "selling her body" to a man, for a certain period, to wantonly do as he pleases. Far from "selling their bodies" to men, sex workers ... exchange specific services, often for very good money, carefully negotiating the time, the terms, the amount, and the exact service, demanding, though too seldom receiving, the respect that other workers in the social service sector can receive. ... Empowering sex workers empowers all women, for the whore stigma is used to discipline women in general; and encouraging society to respect sex workers encourages society to respect all women" (p.2-3).

Other feminists, those who are also against anti-pornographic legislation, maintain that censorship has always served to defend established power relationships. By avoiding censorship, they claim that the discourse on sexuality will be open for continual examination and debate. "Anti-pornographers have a short memory," writes Lynne Segal (1990:229-230). It wasn't that long ago that feminist books were banned in many parts of the world. Birth control information and any references to abortion were defined as being pornographic in Britain and the United States. "Looking historically and cross-culturally, we see that when sexual expression is confined to the private sphere, women become more vulnerable to sex practices, and women's concerns have a harder time claiming space in the realm of public discussion" (Ellis et al., 1988: 8). In an age of exposure, when all the secrets have come out of the confessional, there is resistance to put them back underground, as American radical feminists Andrea Dworkin and Catherine MacKinnon would want it through their *Anti-pornography Civil Ordinance Bill*.

Is violence and rape fundamental to the causes of sexism, rather than child-rearing practices or economic inequalities? One of the arguments of the anti-porn activists has been the isolation and exaggeration of sex at the exclusion of a myriad of other factors. These contradictions seem particularly difficult to sort out. Yet sex radicals who are against anti-pornography want more freedom for women; they need to distance themselves from their mothers. In asserting their independence and breaking from their bonds of dependency, they often identify more with their male counterparts. The rhetorical force of this argument seems contray-to Chodorow. There are more similarities between male and female sexual needs and male and female eroticism. Cultural (radical) feminists who are anti-porn, like Dworkin, MacKinnon, Adrienne Rich, Jean Baker Miller, see this as a denial of their connectedness to their mothers and want more protection for women. The mother is again split as either good (the breath and milk of the Mother as nurturer) or bad (the smuther of the Mother).[9]

In reaction to Griffin's (1982) universal category of the "pornographic mind," which is the desire of men to dominate their suppressed female part within themselves by dominating women, Ellis (1988) writes:

> [I]f men project, in fantasy, a culturally tabooed part of themselves onto women in order to simultaneously indulge and control it, why should we assume that women do not project onto men the aggression that is as culturally taboo for women as in the feminine side of men? (p. 42).

Women are capable of rage and violence as well as men. Many have displayed an authoritarian attitude: Margaret Thatcher, Golda Meir, Indira Gandhi, Cora Aquino and Imelda Marcos, to name a few. Their responses are more a question of social function and position rather than some biological innateness. Segal (1990:262) singles out the reports *Naming the Violence: Speaking Out About Lesbian Battery* (Lobel, 1986), which documents the daily, almost ritual-like episodes of violence in lesbian bars in the U.S.A.. Virtually every violent act committed by heterosexuals repeats itself in the dynamics of lesbian battering—including involuntary prostitution, pimping, rape, sex on demand and forced sex with others. Segal goes on to mention fighting which is common amongst working-class girls in London, Liverpool and Oxford. Women use force and violence when they are placed in analogous jobs to men, sometimes more so than men, as is the case of women prison officers (p.268). Segal reminds her readers that women have been passionate supporters of war and active in military engagement and that White women have in the past, and still do in the present, oppress Black women. The thrust of Segal's arguments concerning both male and female violence is her continual non-neglect of class, color and the workings of inequalities in a capitalist patriarchy. *The single most pronounced characteristic of victims of violence is poverty.* "[F]amily violence is affected by material deprivation, interacting with women's dependence and powerlessness and men's assumptions of their right to control women" (p. 256).

Given such examples, this weakens if not entirely dismisses Mary Daly or Susan Griffin's claim that women are "universally" superior as caregivers and peacemakers.[10] After reviewing her own convictions on the pornography debate and the Ginny Foat trial (Foat was found not guilty for the murder of her brutal, alcoholic wife-battering husband.) Stimpson (1988) writes, "For feminists, the Foat case involved a survivability of two Utopian representations of women: that they are essentially innocent, essentially good, and that they are, like the women in violent pornography, essentially victims, an image that the image of innocence makes logically necessary" (p.193). What Stimpson, whose writings are indicative of a committed feminist who has consistently examined issues with great wit, humor, passion and intellectual vigor, objects to is Andrea Dworkin's or Foat's (for that matter) "right to speak for all women," thereby clouding the issues of differences under the cultural space of women's essentiality. "Woman as victim, or woman as innocent lamb," as Stimpson says, is simply "wrongheaded."

Pornography is ripe for deconstruction. It confronts me with the binary opposition between illicit and licit sex, each being complicit with the other. To what extent does pornography police heterosexuality? What is perverse, incestuous, homosexual, lesbian becomes marginalized as pre-oedipalized polymorphous sexuality. The I is led back to recognizing other Oedipal resolutions and fantasies which, once more, begs an ethical question: are we to conclude then that all such sexual resolutions treat women as objects, or only some do? How would social relationships change on both sides of the current opposition as family structures change from their predominant nuclear arrangement? Questions such as these find no easy answers. Cross-culturally a wide variation of familial patterns is known to exist; incestuous relations and homoerotic love amongst member of the same sex were not forbidden although culturally demarcated and specified. i am reminded of Morris Berman's(1984) historical assessment of bodily erotics: "It is quite clear" he writes, "that the history of increasing ego-development in the West is also the history of increasing repression and erotic deprivation, manifested over the centuries by a drop in the body contact and sensual enjoyment that normally occurs during the first two years of life. Ego-development is not merely purchased at the expense of sensual enjoyment (the classical theory of sublimation); more significantly, it has repression (i.e., sexual alienation) as a condition necessary—and possibly even sufficient for its development" (p.158). Following Ariès's *Centuries of Childhood* (1962), Berman charts the eventual desensualization of child-rearing practices to the sixteenth century with the emergence of the nuclear family; this desensualization comes to full expression in the seventeenth century. Late capitalism has now reached this apogee with the development of reproduction technologies, i.e., test tube babies, artificial insemination, surrogate motherhood. In this line of reasoning, if the Oedipal conflict is given historical articulation specific to capitalism and the bourgeois family, pornography and promiscuity now become the excessive spaces of "touching," acts of abjection (as in the repression of the anal), ironically in opposition to the clean, pure, moral and rational mind of the Enlightenment. Another split occurs between *touching* (auto-eroticism and hetero and homoeroticism) and *seeing* as spectacle, including the passiveness of voyeurism—the dirty/clean distinction. In this line of reasoning it could be argued that Irigaray's writings are "pornographic!" Pornography focuses and fixates the sexual economy of exchange at the genital level. In this sense it is passive, becoming active only when looking is displaced by masturbation. Masturbation, as the active Derridean supplement to the fantasy of love making, is supported by the passive supplement of pornography.

Paradoxically, the liberalist commitment to liberty and the inviolability of private life favors same sex desire, abortion and contraception, creating a contradictory space for the interplay between anti-censorship and anti-pornographic discourse, making *public* sex education in some school districts still a contentious issue despite the rising levels of teenage pregnancies and the spread of AIDS. Andrew Ross (1989) explores the potential of this pornographical space for change, naming it *liberatory* and *libertinist* imagination as compared to the traditional liberal values of tolerance and pluralism.[11] Structured by this distinctive public/private status makes issues of same sex desire and women's bodily rights *both* marginal *and* central at the same time; marginal in the sense that many gays and lesbians feel safer in the closet (the privacy of their own homes), and central in that the door to the privacy of the home must be opened if wife battering, wife "rape," and incest are to be stopped. However, contradictory forces are at work. Wife battering, rape and paedophillia are a violation of human rights, which allows for state intervention and incarceration of its offenders, but even here there are incredible contradictions and ambiguities. Gruesome cases such as the recent (Dec. 7, 1989) slayings of 14 women at the University of Montréal, or the infamous case of the Yorkshire Ripper, (examined by Ross (1987b) in *Men in Feminism*), and numerous battered-wife murder cases which never make it to the front page, point to the contradictions of masculinity. Pathological serial slayings provide a 'nodal point' (a conflation of floating signifiers, fixed by a sign that stops them from sliding, cf., Laclau and Mouffe) to reinforce radical feminist accusations that all men are inherently violent even when the pitiful lives of such sadistic murderers are made public where "the return of the repressed" seems to be at work.[12] If the courts were to support the universality of such male violence it would serve only to naturalize such phenomena, leaving men and women in fixed sexual categories.[13] A battered-wife murder defense serves only to further the institutionalization of sexual inequality. "For such provision would recognize not only an 'essential' and 'natural' relation between every woman and 'the universal weakness of women,' but also between any woman and the 'essential' and 'natural' phenomenon of male violence." In short, the universalistic basis of this claim demands that "to be defined as a woman is to be helplessly abused by a violent man" (Ross, 1987b: 91).[14]

The above discussion helps to clarify why many feminists wish to change the law from rape as a sexual crime, to one of *power*, a logical outcome of political, economic, and social processes that foster men's domination. However, this does not escape the problematic of how one goes about separating sex from power. If power is derived from the social, then sex must pre-exist the social and the reasoning is once again caught up in a biological fix; male aggressivity is fueled by an uncontrollable sexual need which can be claimed as innate. Such a conclusion cannot be tolerated under liberalist law but supports the claim that the essence of masculinity is violence (e.g., Dworkin). Such reasoning can lead to the treatment of men as mere "material," fodder for the killing fields in the name of national defence; after all, men are inherently "fighting machines." The machisimo code allows this abuse by a system of representation which permits men's bodies to be slashed, killed, blown apart and counted as mere numbers on war memorials. There is little sympathy for pacifists, none for cowards.

Roped Tight: The Contradictions of Masculinity

Judith Mayne (1987) provides the contradictions of this masculine dilemma in popular culture. In her provocative analysis of the Dirty Harry series—in *Tightrope*—she says that the Hollywood narrative works male desire *between* sexuality and violence. Wes Block (Dirty Harry-Clint Eastwood) is a split character who must face up to his violent side as represented by the killer he is after. But, claims Mayne, "*Tightrope* is as unsure of what rape is, as it is of what a hard-on is" (p.69). This ambiguity of Block's character is analogous to the contradictory ways in which rape has been articulated as a theoretical and ideological issue within feminism. "One feminist argument is founded on the incompatibility of sex and rape, and thus defines rape as a crime of violence and not a crime of sex. Another argument claims rape to be the very paradigm of male sexuality, rather male heterosexuality" (ibid.). For Mayne, sexuality is rescued either in the name of lesbianism (the first option), and thus lies outside male desire, or sexuality is given over to a utopian hetero-sexuality where both agents are said to be free and equal in their relationship. *Viva la differance!* If the first resolve is taken, men cannot find themselves *in* feminism since they are irrelevant—not "needed." This narrative is rarely enter-tained, rather it is the latter resolution which is taken; a narrative modeled on the traditional male desire with a beginning, middle, end. The ambiguity ends in a heterosexual relationship. In the case of *Tightrope*, Beryl Thibodeaux, (por-trayed by Geneviève Bujold) "Hollywood's representative feminist" (in 1987 at least!), writes Mayne, "is comforted and affirmed in the end by Harry." Her feminism has little to do with the problematic nature of masculine sexuality. She has no relationships with other women in the film except Block's daugh-ters. As Alice Jardine (1987) emphasizes in another context, the presence of feminism is seen as a minor irritation or intrusion. "End of struggle," she writes, "Odor di Uomo" (p.59).[15]

This doubled contradictory discourse on male violence is, of course, ubiquitous throughout the popular media. Men are charged with *both* being innately violent *and,* at the same time, find themselves the victims of that vio-lence brought on by not living up, nor giving up a masculine ideal. Men are expected to take the hardships, hazards and risks which come with such a masculine characterization. They must "bear" the pressures and stresses of the workplace, the effects of which are evident statistically in terms of heart attacks, suicides, and an earlier death compared to women. Yet, in her essay in *Men in Feminism* (1987) Judith Mayne transfigures Robin Morgan's controversial statement, "pornography is the theory and rape the practice," (1980:139) into popular cultural terms: "*Tightrope* is the theory, *Dirty Harry* is the the prac-tice"(1987:64). This is surprising given that Morgan was in the forefront of male bashing in the '70s, and given the questionable dichotomization con-cerning a male's nature, the corollary should be read with the utmost cau-tion, if not simply a rhetorical gesture. Thus far there is *no* conclusive evi-dence which *causally* relates watching pornography with male violence, i.e., aggressive behavior, rape, murder. i found numerous references in support of this, even by researchers themselves who have been paid to find precisely those connections (Donnerstein and Linz, 1986; Donnerstein et al., 1987; Williams, 1989:187-188; Hodge and Tripp, 1986, chap. 10; Christensen, 1987: Segal; 1987, chap. 3:110-11 and chap. 4; Segal, 1990, chap. 9). There are even stud-ies that claim pornography may provide a cathartic experience actually *reduc-ing* violence (Gillian, 1978). However this is hardly the whole story. The entire question of how structural violence works itself throughout a capitalist patri-archal society requires an understanding how its use in the mass media, in pornography and its (possible?) increase in child abuse and wife battering is a symptom of the larger inequities between classes, between heterosexual men and women, and between heterosexual men and their homosexual counterparts (esp. Fiske, 1993: Chap.6). The summary statement by Carrigan et al., 1985), i believe is entirely correct in its assumptions:

> It [the history of homosexuality] forces us to recognize the importance of violence, not as an expression of subjective values or a type of masculinity, but as a constitutive practice that helps to make all kinds of masculinity—and to recognize that much of this violence comes from the state, so the historical construction of masculinity and femininity is also a struggle for the control and direction of state power (p.589).

Violence remains a heterosexual male problem that is intimately tied up with sexual politics, the division of labor, and the "structure of cathexis— the social organization of sexuality and attraction" (p. 590). Although causality between violence and behavior cannot be proven, there is a feeling that there is something "wrong" with a society where violence (structural and physical) is so ubiquitous. It is telling, therefore, to read a content analysis of American television media violence which reveals that what is almost an *inverse* relationship between simulated violence on prime time television and the "real" violence on the streets, in the homes, and in the institutions (Lyon, 1990). Who commits violence on television and who are its victims are in disparate disaccord to the daily news reports i hear and read. Televised violence is initiated by predominantly White, middle-class males. Lyon's study showed that those classified as "good" violents were both female and upper-class, while those classified as "bad" tended to be lower class. Lyon also found that a larger percentage of upper-class females than males were violents. The number of non-White violents was far too small for this particular analysis, however she notes, "there was *not one* 'good' Latino in the sample" (p. 147). Victimization was equally dramatic. The data on victims revealed that women and upper-class characters were "disproportionately vulnerable to violence, especially upper-class women" who were predominately "good" or "innocent victims" (ibid.). Lower-class characters (to a lesser extent men) were more likely to be violents than victims who "deserve" violence because they were "bad."

From this evidence Lyon draws several conclusions: First, there is a "virtual absence on television of minority members as both violents and victims" when it is well known that "Black males have the highest victimization rates of any group. Further, the overwhelming majority of violent crimes is intraracial" (p.149-150). Second, there is a disproportionate representation of the upper class as victims when the majority of known victims of violent crime come from the lower classes. Third, although family violence is pervasive, rarely are there any portrayals of wife battering and child abuse. Lyon's final concern is with the over-exaggerated dangers of violence. With the exception of family violence, the incidents usually ended with death, whereas in reality threats of physical injury are more the case.[16] Lyon concludes with,

> Upper-class violents are "good" characters, lower class violents are "bad." Lower-class victims are "bad," and are likely to be killed, while upper-class people are vulnerable, but not consequentially so. Women are more likely to be victimized by violence than to commit it, but their victimization is relatively harmless. Black, Latino and other minority group members are infrequently seen in violent incidents, but are seen more frequently as violents than as victims, thus removing them from public view as among the victims deserving sympathy and support. Family violence is infrequent and, when it occurs, is relatively without impact. Finally, television violence disproportionately leads to death (p. 151-152).

Notwithstanding the methodological problems of her study, such results do suggest a paranoia by the middle-to-upper classes of the lower classes; the same paranoia targeted at pornography and neo-racism by the Moral Right. There is almost a denial it seems, so when these fears are brought to the surface in the cinema there is outrage as happened with the recent film *Falling Down* (Joel Schumacher, 1993), starring Michael Douglas as D-FENDS, a middle class unemployed civil servant who becomes psychotic, killing those who threaten his former (American) way of life.[17]

What and who is *exscribed* from television violence is as important as what is shown if the general public attitudes towards the order of things are to be shaped and reproduced. This remains true of gender representations of masculinity and femininity on television. *Exscribed* from the male world of action shows are women, work, and marriage (Fiske, 1987:204), and, it might be added, any representations of gay men unless they are the butt of a joke, as the masculine other. Themes of becoming a 'man'—maturity, responsibility, leadership, physical strength, individualism, power and control—are played out by any number of interrelated male characters which form the matrix of masculinity as a team or in partner relations. In the former case, the team mirrors the dynamics of men's competitive sports, while in the latter case, the questions of rivalry (good guy vs. bad guy), friendship and socially permissible displays of homoerotic attraction provide clever narratives for breaching racial tensions (i.e., the White and Black partnerships in police and detective stories), and for accepting women into male dominated work places (i.e., male and women partnerships in law enforcement, crime, medical institutions and *film noir*). The most common heterosexual male narrative is the hero story, the prowess of ONE man. The hero provides the dominant heterosexual identification especially for young boys whose bodies are not physically strong enough and who have yet to be "granted" positions of social power, being relatively powerless in the family or at school. The physical strength of heroes is usually extended by technological gadgetry (i.e., "suped" up cars with electronic defensive options, special weaponry) while their social strength comes from fighting villains, big business corporations, communism, the enemy, the System, ersatz for the Oedipal father. Young boys relate particularly well to this "self against the System" scenario which presents the world in black and white terms. (i play this myself.) Hodge and Tripp (1986) mention in their study of television viewing how junior high schools boys interpreted the *Prisoner* (an Australian series about prison life) as being a mirror of school life, restaging the overbearing father and a defiant son.

When the repressed women is introduced into these heroic narratives (representing commitment, caring, emotion, nurturing, sentimentality, emotion), she is often rejected so that masculinity can be preserved, or she becomes his adoring fan and the narrative comes to a close (you are to assume that they live together forever in bliss). This was the objection Judith Mayne made to *Tightrope*. Its narrative closed in bliss rather than exploring the feminist character of Bujold who ran a rape crisis center and told Block about his own psychological problems with sex and violence. It is this wide array of narratives, in various combinations and genres, which allow for the identification of many hetero masculine subject positions to play out male fantasies.[18]

1 Lise Vogel's (1988) and Carol Duncan's (1988) review articles offer many examples from the history of modern art.

2 This follows Norman Bryson's (1983) excellent study on the logic of the gaze in Western art. Bryson makes a distinction between the aristocratic gaze of the connoisseur, which held up until modernism and the glance of late modernism, which is more plebian, random, not as violent or penetrating as the "framing" stare of the gaze. Both are superimposed in the art of fashion photography. This is, of course, a rich area of examination. In this regard see essays edited by Victor Burgin's *Thinking Photography* (1982). Burgin attempts next to deconstruct these very photographic codes that are explored in that text through an exhibition and catalogue by the same name, *Between* (1986).

3 Fiske (1987, chap. 10) provides an excellent review of the soap genre. Recognizing the work of Modleski, Fiske points to the use of close-ups in soaps which place more value on the act of communication between people (conversation and facial expressions), thereby allowing for greater viewer identification and accommodating more of a contemplative aesthetics (gaze), rather than a glance, which is the characteristic of action genres with their many editing cuts and exaggerated action.

4 For the same development in heterosexual detective novels inspired by the *film noir* crime fiction that deal with women's oppression, e.g. Sara Paretsky's V.I. Warshawski, Sue Grafton's Kinsey Milhone, Katherine V. Forrest's Kate Delafield, and Sarah Caudwell's Hilary Tamar, see Landry and MacLean's chapter 5, "How PC Can a White Girl Be?" (1993). These heroines disobey their fathers and transgress rather than uphold the law in the name of liberalist principles—truth, personal liberty, and tolerance for differences.

5 My intention is not to develop this very complex area. i do not have the cultural competence, but i do wish to recognize the importance that such 'soft porn' plays in lesbian subcultures.

6 An interesting thesis might emerge from Nochimson's claim, which is diametrically opposed to what Eve Kosofsky Sedgwick in *Between Men* (1985) called the homosocial contract. For Sedgwick the homosexual love between men as rivals is played out over the woman's body. In contrast, is Nochimson unintentionally suggesting that lesbian love between women is played out over men's bodies in soap operas? By this i mean the whole process of women man-ipulating men in the figure of the vamp; and the contradiction that brings when women viewers *both* admire the vamp's resistance and in the next episode, perhaps wish that the man-ipulator be punished for her scheming ways because she has carried her manipulations just too far; even though such schemes are resistances to patriarchy. This struggle is never-ending as the title of Nochimson's book suggests—*No End to Her*. Like homosexuality, lesbianism is a discourse that is omitted from the soaps, but this is also changing.

7 For a strong critique of these positions see Lynne Joyrich, "All that Television Allows," (1988). Joyrich, while recognizing that resistance to TV melodramas is possible, also calls for more critique. She makes a distinction between the subversive potentials of film and TV melodramas. The former has at times been more politically progressive calling attention to contradictions in class and gender. She is less sure that TV melodramas allow a similar response.

8 See "The Third Vignette: The Unhappy Marriage of Marxism & Feminism."

9 Historically such feelings by boys and girls may be displaced from the real biological mother onto a nanny or wet nurse, nevertheless this split is still subject to repetition.

10 To continue to cite such examples and claim that women are therefore not subordinated in general would be crass. That's not the point being made here, although studies have shown that women (mothers) hold power over their young sons in many middle-class households (Dowsett, 1985). The point is that contradictions between local situations and the global situation of women's oppression will always be found. Class, color and economic stability are major factors when determining the levels of violence. Where women are said to be "universally" superior as caregivers and peacemakers it is more a question of their social location, as teachers, nurses, mothers, than biology. See "Vignettes Three and Four."

11 The "erotic warfare" that goes on in these various institutions through the "logic of late capitalism" about sex is carefully explored by the late Linda Singer, *The Erotic Welfare: Sexual Theory and Politics in Age of Epidemic* (1993).

12 Lynne Segal (1990:250-253) gives an account of the Yorkshire Ripper's (Peter Sutcliffe) background. What struck me in her account was the uncertainty of his masculinity, exhibiting characteristics of what might be perceived to be a gentle, lovable family man. From an early age he was small, weak, shy and gentle. The son of a violent and bullying father and an unhappy mother, teased and persecuted in school, Sutcliffe would not fight with tough, aggressive working-class boys around him. His father perceived him as a "mother's boy." He was a gentle husband who always listened to what his wife said. His feminist biographer writes that Sutcliffe had no support to deal with his own homosexuality. A strong Roman Catholic upbringing made him believe that there was a direct link between sex and sin.

13 This is further developed by de Lauretis (1987a:16) in her examination of Foucault's contradictory position when he argued for the decriminalization of rape, and supported that rape should be treated as an act of violence rather than a sexual act. de Lauretis claims that his *History of Sexuality* "may be understood as an effort to counter the technology of sex by breaking the bond between sexuality and crime; an effort to enfranchise sexual behaviors from legal punishment, and so to render the sexual sphere from the intervention of the state" (p.17). His position was contradictory in that it furthered the cause of male oppression, for it was men who battered wives and, no doubt, it was wives who verbally abused their husbands. It was perhaps Foucault's avowed alliance with the mad, the imprisoned, and the sexually deviant which made him turn to such a position. An out of the closet activist gay, Foucault wrote from a position of apparent gender neutrality, which allowed him to make the claim that sexuality is not a property of bodies, as something which is originally existent in a human being, but a product of certain technologies, i.e., since the 18th century these have been the sexualization of children and female body, the control of procreation, and the psychiatrization of anomalous sexual behavior as perverse. This stance has especially irritated feminists, like de Lauretis who see Foucault as presenting a circular argument: "Sexuality is produced discursively (institutionally) by power, and power is produced institutionally (discursively) by the deployment of sexuality (ibid.)." The issue of gender is avoided. However, Foucault's desire to "desexualize" sexuality, to multiply and diffuse pleasures, was for him, the key strategy to oppose power and the law. If women attempt to spell out or live out an "authentic" sexuality, as many feminists would have it, then they are buying into the very discourses of power that have shaped their lives since the 18th century (see Woodhull, 1988). i shall return to Foucault in my text to point out the difference between a *repressed* view of sexuality by the liberalism i have been reviewing (see foontote 8, "True Confessions of a Harlequin Porno Eater") and sexuality as a discourse.

14 From a similar perspective societal homophobia provides the "homosexual panic" defense strategy for a person (typically a man) who has been accused of anti-gay violence, even to the point of homicide. The crime is diminished because homophobia is treated as a pathological psychological condition which rarely happens. It is oxymoronically perceived as normal behavior for a heterosexual to hit back when he has been sexually approached without consent.

15 It so happens that Jardine was rhetorically answering Paul Smith's contribution to *Men in Feminism* by an essay of his with the same title. Interestingly, Smith has gone on to discuss at length Clint Eastwood's masculinity and discusses the interrelationships between male sexuality and violence in *Tightrope* as being a self-reflexive one. Despite the ending and chase scene at the end, and the loss of a gendered politics brought by the happy ending, Smith defends the script: "the proposition that the 'amongst men' within which both masculine imaginaries and male lives [Block's and the killer's] are caught cannot be so easily divided into a 'good' and an 'evil' camp, and that both camps play out their aggression across the bodies of women" (1993:135).

16 The 1994 story of Lorena Bobitt, who cut off the penis of her abusive husband with a "space age knife," which was then sewn back on through the wizardry of postmodern medical technology, became sensationalized throughout the media as CNN brought daily coverage of the trail. i would read this "event" as historically paradigmatic, not only of an act of a castrating woman within the dynamics of a heterosexual relationship, but also for the display of the force of technology which can sew "it" on almost as easily as "it" can cut "it" off; suggesting that "its" restorative patriarchal function is always "at hand" when the need arises. By the way, Lorena was judged "not guilty."

17 The film is a good example of this paranoia, perhaps the decline and decay of the middle classes. D-FENDS, played by Michael Douglas (named after his personalized license plate; his real name is William (Bill) Foster) is a laid-off defence worker who becomes psychotic on June 12, 1991, the hottest day of the year in Los Angeles (filmed, ironically, during the time of the L.A. riots!). Wedged between upper-class snobbery and lower-class impoverishment, he goes about committing a series of vigilante outrages; all of which are ironic gestures of middle-class hate which, in his psychotic state, he considers to be mere self-defence. Koreans who can't speak proper English; grocery prices which are too high; roads which require no repair; gang members who harass innocent victims; neo-Nazis who foster hate; the hypocritical hospitality of fast food establishments; the ostentatious display of wealth (private golf courses and huge homes) by wealthy business men and plastic surgeons; all come under his f(ire). D-FENDS is divorced and alone, living with his mother. "I just want to go home," he laments throughout the film. But"home" is a nostalgic look at old video tapes of by-gone days when the family was still intact. At the end of the film he asks incredulously, "... you mean *I'm* the bad guy?" This ending lays bare the social contract that underwrites D-FENDS violence by assuming the position of the *feminine* male masochist (in both action and appearance in this case), and then reversing that role into a sadist. Kaja Silverman accurately describes the male masochist,

[H]e acts out in an insistent and exaggerated way the basic conditions of cultural subjectivity, conditions that are normally disavowed; he loudly proclaims that his meaning comes to him from the Other, prostrates himself before the Gaze even as he solicits it, exhibits his castration for all to see, and revels in the sacrificial basis of the social contract. The male masochist magnifies the losses and division upon which cultural identity is based, refusing to be sutured or recompensed. In short, he radiates a negativity inimical to the social order" (1993/1988b:53).

The sociopolitical climate was ripe for such a display. D-FENDS begins by being a passive spectator of life's hardships. He just wants to get along, but soon he is brought to a boiling point and "flips out." In the end he is perceived as being crazy, the very embodiment of the anger and insanity that scandalizes the social order, but he is a hero to all those that secretly side with him. To survive D-FENDS has to wage violence on others so that he can assume a sadistic position of a terrorist to wreak havoc on the social order, but he can not be *too* sadistic. There are limits. He bluntly differentiates himself from a neo-Nazi, the only victim he kills. Arnold Kopelson, the film's producer put it this way, " ... with the economy in disarray, massive unemployment, crime on the increase and general discontentment with living conditions, I believe the moviegoing audience will respond to the character of D-FENDS and his frustrations and experiences with contemporary life, yet appreciate the irony with which they are presented." It is difficult to read the irony in such a field of urban decay. i found little to laugh at, yet there were members of the audience who did laugh. Was this then a sign of their progressive resistant popular culture and my ignorance?

18 The literature in this area is rapidly growing. Routledge knows a good market when it sees it. I mentioned Fiske (1987) as an exemplar of "resistance" theory in media studies. Recent titles that develop the construction of masculinity in the cinema (not television) are: Tasker's *Spectacular Bodies* (1993b); Steven Cohan and Ira Rae Hark's *Screening the Male* (1993); Paul Smith's study on *Clint Eastwood* (1993) and Warner's political analysis of Rambo (1990).

S/M

The Lesbian Bar as the Dildoed Body

Mapplethorpe's counterpart in the lesbian community is Della Grace whose *Love Bites* (1991) is also a "coffee-table art book" (Lewis, 1994:76), but unlike Mapplethorpe there is no museum to run to for shelter. *Love Bites* was intentionally banned from London's feminist bookstores to avoid casting disfavor with the censor. Its radical position had to be sold and advocated on the streets. Because of the paucity of S/M representations, Reina Lewis argues that Della Grace's photographs may well be overvalued in their potential to be subversive of both feminism or mainstream/vanilla lesbianism. What troubles Lewis about these representations are the unquestioning moral concerns that remain unanswered.[1] Unlike Mapplethorpe these "models" have no names. Viewers are unsure whether these photographs are enactments—simply staged sex—like those of Madonna. Her book provides no mention of consensual non-exploitative conditions. Can one be sure that the 'bottom' is indeed in charge of her own subjugation by the use of a code word to end the activity? To be tacky for a moment, this reminds me of the "holo-deck" on board the USS Enterprise (*Star Trek, The New Generation*) where the word, "freeze program," stops the titillation from turning into disaster. In S/M the voyeuristic gaze ersatz for porn is welcome, the antithesis of the feminist complaint. The lesbian gaze in S/M redeploys the same subject position of male heterosexuality, making the photographs equally enjoyable by a male heterosexual. Rather than being de-objectified, the *assertion* of lesbian identity is in the viewer looking. The objectification of the female body is an aim of the images "in keeping with the S/M theory of liberation through the embrace of objectification and subordination" (Lewis, 87).

Della Grace defends her position as the bad girl outside the lesbian ranks, the sexual outcast by naming herself as a "xenogenetic dyke" (1993). Coining the world herself, Grace sees dykes like herself as those who embrace the Otherness within themselves; this being a homeopathic remedy for xenophobia. Grace is quite clever delineating the breadth of this self-naming. She recognizes the evolutionary process of the changing 'iconic' lesbian image by extending the word's usage to "xenomorphosis," which includes the idea of transformation (i.e., *morphing*). When Doc Marten's shoes no longer function as a lesbian code because everyone is wearing them, it's time to change! Plus, Grace even harnesses the toothed vagina complex, the oral-sadistic mother that refers to pre-Oeidipalization. Her play is on the word "isis," the Egyptian Goddess, rather than "oisis" which denotes the condition. All in all, this is a clever justification for her subject position which is heartily endorsed by Parveen Adams (1993).

Adams' support is premised on doing Lacan one better, rethinking his seminar on ethics which, as i have previously referred to, has given Žižek(and me holding onto his coat-tails) so much mileage when positing 'woman' as an ideal unobtainable object in romantic or courtly love. Like Lacan, who had offered the category of anamorphosis as a project to disturb the illusions of perspectively organized pictorial space (it becomes significant precisely at the moment when the representation of space is mastered), Adams identifies the *dildo* as an anamorphic projection, which calls into being the gap between the phallus and the penis. The dildo severs the connection between the two. Very imaginative! As Reina Lewis reminds me, "sex with a woman wearing a dildo is sex with a woman and a dildo not sex with a man" (p.85). The sublimation here is not 'woman' as the unreachable 'Thing' (cf. Lacan), woman in that case placed in a position of power as the dominatrix by the will of man; rather Adams makes a seemingly outrageous claim that an object—a dildo—releases the woman from "what she wants" to "how she wants." In butch-femme relationships, June Reich (1992) argues, the heterosexual structural masquerade which this relationship seems to mimic, is subverted by "camping it up"; made even more ironic by the use of the dildo. Perhaps i have found my answer to Amelia Jones's fascination with Benglis[2] "The dildo is a sutured phallus. ... It is the law of the Daddy Butch. As a phallus, it assures difference without essentializing gender" (p.120). In this sense it is pure artifice, a "supplement" to the "natural" body. Within butch-femme roles it becomes a strategy of appearance that replaces any claim to a truth, for the gendering of desire for the dildoed-girl and the dicked-boy is different even though structurally they seem the same. The dildo performance is "queer" because it doesn't respect the hetero/homosexual dichotomy. In June Reich's terms, it makes a "genderfuck" possible for it makes the signifying practices in a libidinal economy of multiple sexualities unstable. It produces a genderfuck body as a "*drag* anchor" (p.126, emphasis added).[3] Like drag, it enables a performance that interrupts the circulation of the phallus which attempts to fix, that is, anchor signification. "A drag anchor, far from centering a soul, casts a body loose in a queer sea of love" (ibid.).

It must be added that the dildoed couple act in privacy—in the invisible social spaces, whereas the butch-femme couple are marked through public display. It seems that their *duoism* is absolutely necessary if the kind of aesthetic disruption that the well-known argument in lesbian literature by Sue-Ellen Case (1988-1989) is to take place. Case maintains that the butch-femme couple "do not impale themselves on the poles of sexual difference or metaphysical values, but constantly seduce the sign system through flirtation and inconstancy in the light fondle of artifice, replacing the Lacanian slash with the Lesbian bar" (p.57). But if the femme enters the frame of representation alone, without her butch escort, she looses her visibility, swallowed up by the codes of feminine heterosexuality (de Lauretis, 1988). The performance of butch-femme requires that both partners be clearly marked within the hetero-hegemonic social fabric. The parodic possibilities of pro-porn lesbianism, it seems to me, are confined to private spaces of the closet. For instance, Bensinger (1992) makes an issue of the parodic "mas*queer*ade" of a photo series that appeared in *On Our Backs* as a third generation copy of lesbian pornography. The first copy is heterosexual; the second copy of this copy is homosexual, and now this third variety: a copy of the homosexual presents Heron as a large and muscular woman dressed in gay leather drag wearing a dildo, positioned above and behind, about to fuck Lucille who is dressed in a white tank top and underwear. But this raises questions of reception and ethics. The photograph is derived from a heterosexual model and from the perspective of the man, and not the women involved in this relationship. This is a clear case of lesbo-porn meant for private consumption, for the issue of the "lesbian bar" is made more difficult in Bensinger's next example where reception of lesbian identification is more public. Bensinger remarks on a full page film still of Lois Weaver, who plays the part of the femme protagonist in Sheila McLaughlin's film, *She Must Be Seeing Things*. (This still appears in de Lauretis's essay (1988) on lesbian identity.) "For the astute reader of (sub)cultural codes, Lois Weaver/Sheila McLaughlin is unmistakenly a femme" (p.79). Perhaps for the "astute reader" but, as i've admitted elsewhere in this text, i cannot tell the "difference." In this regard, it seems that "assumed" lesbian lovemaking which appears within the confines of soft-core magazines like *Penthouse* and *Playboy* can easily be accommodated into heterosexual male fantasies. This 'straight' lesbian porn is read predominantly for its comedic effects by pro-porn lesbians (Bensinger: 82). The dildo remains conspicuously absent. Peter Benson (1993) tries to make sense of this by claiming that "[l]esbianism is here phantasized within the dimension of narcissism. The women (with their similar looks) receive desire from their own image, becoming self sufficient. As Freud noted, it is narcissistic women who hold the greatest fascination for men" (p.423). With the introduction of the dildo, however, the male voyeur is reminded that he is redundant.

Lesbian desire challenges both Freudian and Lacanian formulations of fetishism and the universalism of the 'phallic signifier' by way of the "genderfucked body." This challenge is brilliantly and lucidly argued by the recent theorizations by Anne McClintock (1993a,b,c), a theorist with Foucaultian leanings. Lacanian universalism is quickly dispatched and deconstructed by questioning the very 'split' Lacan posits at birth; the child as an alienated self condemned to a life of finitude in search for, in the end, delusionary objects of desire that would fill that original lack, satisfying a return to the all-embracing oneness with the mother. McClintock reads this as a humanistic binaric residue of Hegelianism, i.e., Hegel's split subject who is defined in relation to the Other as that which 'it' is not, wedded to Freudian psychoanalysis which offers a perpetual insoluble resolution to this fundamental split. "The 'phallic signifier' is the mark of illusionary objects of desire that humans, in the inevitable act of misrecognition, desire as being able to satisfy and resolve the impossible split" (1993a:10). In other words, Lacan is caught by his own essentialism which his entire psychoanalytic theory is against simply by positing a universalistic, and therefore essentialist, claim that the condition of humanity is marked by a self-division and a lack-of-being organized around a transcendental phallic signifier (a signifier without a signified).[4] Theorized from this position, Lacan seems to be repeating the logic of Western philosophical thought once again. Lacan has displaced God, as the previous transcendental signifier who assured all of humanity *plenitude* and the teleological promise of heaven, with the metonymical phallic signifier for Man. It can be so interpreted that the condition of *lack*, claims McClintock, as the obverse of the previous plenitude which the phallic signifier represents, is yet another disguise for the will to power, or will to knowledge, the irresolvablity of which simply repeats the modernist assumption of the uncertainty of knowledge and Kantian reflexive critical philosophy in general. Desire, read in this way, becomes the perpetual gap that must always be filled between certainty (oneness with the Mother), and the striving for uncertainty which paradoxically is always deferred when striving to get back to oneness in plenitude. It is not difficult to metaphorically see this as man's striving to know his mother. McClintock calls it a "maternal signifier." To follow this path can also lead to nostalgia, the other side of the post-modern reaction. The solution to the crisis of modernism is then to be found in the stability of past traditions, repeating once more the danger of the maternal signifier as the "homeland" to be kept free from foreign infiltration.[5] As Jance Doane and Devon Hodges (1987) read it, there is a retreat to more stable gendered positions presented by any number of Hollywood films. Lesbian theory would have none of that.

The issue of gay and lesbian art-pornography is especially crucial for feminism simply because such pornography is one of the principle means through which their identity as men or as women who engage in sexual relations with the same sex is expressed, confirmed and legitimated. Mapplethorpe's homoerotic photographs are explicit in this desire. So when Adrienne Rich (1980), who is anti-porn and pro-motherhood, argued for a 'lesbian continuum'— the erotic and the sexual were interpreted as various levels of friendship between women (i.e., mother-daughter, sister-sister, daughter-grandmother etc.)—the very specificity of a lesbian identification which centers on having sex with another woman seemed to drop out. As Sedgwick (1985:3) points out, the homosocial bonds across the continuum between "women loving women" and "women promoting the interests of women" is far more uniform than the diacritical opposition between homosocial bonds between men and homosexuality. But such bonds are in terms of promoting egalitarian and loving relationships between women. What happens to lesbian sadomasochism and its visual display, a sexual practice of domination and submission which Sedgwick acknowledges herself to practice? Is S/M a re-enactment of patriarchal relationships? Such questions were part of the "sex wars" (also "sex debates," "porn wars") which split the lesbian community, those for ("sex radicals") and against pornography and S/M practice.[6] S/M presented the limit case to a lesbianism which tried to liberate the "lesbian" in every woman along feminist maternal lines, for its practice paradoxically disrupted this claim. It became a "daughter's revolt" against the Mother who tried to contain her. The issue was, therefore, a question of ethics.

Identity Problems: the Sex Wars

Gayle Rubin (1975), herself a lesbian sadomasochist and a "sex radical," is usually singled out as having written a very influential essay calling for the separation between sex and gender, identifying what has summatively been called the "hegemony of heterosexuality" or "compulsive heterosexuality" (see Frank, 1987). In Rubin's (1984) view, modern Western societies hierarchize sexual acts with marital reproductive heterosexuals on top "of the erotic pyramid." These individuals are certified as mentally healthy; they have respectability, social and physical mobility, and legal institutional support. Sadomasochism, on the other hand, is low on this pyramidal scale. It is perceived as abnormal. So what makes S/M so subversive and pleasurable, since it goes against so many feminist and "primary lesbian" rhetorical sensibilities such as care, sensitivity, kindness, equality? There seem to be several explanations offered. i begin with one of many "queer" readings.[7]

Parveen Adams' (1989) "Of Female Bondage" is often referred to as providing one such meditation. Working with Catherine Millot's (1990a) Lacanian explanations of a girl's entry into desire, Adams usefully begins by outlining three fates of Oedipal resolutions for girls: retreat from sexuality, or movement towards femininity, or masculinity. Once castration has been realized, the girl is driven from her mother to her father by her desire for the male organ. If she is dissatisfied with her own genitals, traumatized by her castration, then she may renounce sexuality altogether ("retreat from sexuality"). Those girls who turn to their fathers and demand the phallus ("penis envy") are given two options: still caught by Oedipalization they can either have a baby as a substitute for the phallus, and therefore detach themselves from the father by looking for another man ("femininity"), or they can deny their own castration and identify with the father ("masculinity complex"). With the denial of their own castration, they emerge from Oedipalization (often, but not inevitably so) into homosexual desire. In any case, the Oedipus complex pathologizes femininity so that "woman does not exist." Montrelay, a Lacanian revisionist (1978/1990, in Silverman, 1983:186-188) offers one of the best explanations as to why this is so. The key to understanding why woman is assigned *jouissance* outside the phallic order is Montrelay's claim that those drives which constitute "femininity" are "*censored*" rather than *repressed* (p.260). The censoring of female sexuality means that it is non-represented and outside cultural structuration.[8] But female sexuality which is *not* Oedipally organized is what Adams is after. Until the girl believes in her mother's castration, she *will not* enter the Oedipus complex; rather she will answer to the demands of the mother. She remains at the level of pre-Oedipalization. To disavow her mother's castration the girl fetishizes an object or a location on the mother's body to deny that there is any difference between mother and father. Such a disavow of sexual differences is a perversion (the opposite of neuroses which are repressions). The fetishist, sadomasochist, and the homosexual are the most common perversions.

The Lacanian theorist Elizabeth Grosz (1991/1993) provides a lucid explanation of what lesbian fetish might be, particularly as it relates to the girl's masculine complex. Her early discussion of Freud's explications of fetishism is to make the point that the fetish is *not* an "equivalent to the maternal or female penis because it both affirms and denies women's castration" (p. 43). Nor is a fetish the last object seen (i.e., shoes, stockings, underwear, etc.) before witnessing the missing organ which is registered as a phallus (as authority in the symbolic order). These objects are still veiled. The fetish is rather a substitute for the phallus, a talisman for the phallus. "The fetish thus plays the role of the veil, both outlining and yet covering over woman's castration" (p.44). In her next section Grosz deals with disavowal, distinguishing it form two other defense mechanism—negation and repudiation—and concluding that it exists mid-way between them both, as two attitudes that exist side by side as "the denial of woman's lack and its recognition and acceptance" (p.46). With this preliminary work aside, she deftly and skillfully draws out the implications for female fetishism.

To begin, then, Grosz makes it emphatic that the girl's disavowal of castration is not that of the mother's but her own. This can take three forms: heterosexual (secondary) narcissism, hysteria, and the masculinity complex. With heterosexual narcissism the "feminine subject (whether male or female) loves an object according to its resemblance, identity, or connection with the self" (p.48). As a compensation for her lack she invests in her body, "treating it as the corresponding male would an external love-object" (ibid.), phallicizing her whole body. This response to disavowal is the "normal" path of femininity. "[I]f man believes he has the phallus (the object of desire), then woman believes she is the phallus. The man's penis and the whole of the woman's body are rendered psychically equivalent". In Lacanian terms "he has the object of desire while she is the object of desire" (ibid.). In the case of hysteria the acceptance of the castrated position results in the woman's sexuality being displaced to a non-genital body part or "hysterogenic zone." In this way the hysteric gains a self-defined status as phallic. Hysteria is a rebellion against the passivity usually associated with femininity and unlike the narcissist, the hysteric invests her desire with the mother in memory of a pre-Oedipal attachment. In the third-masculine position, the woman refuses castration and takes the female-mother substitute as the desired object of choice.

There is, i should think, great pleasure in theorizing this position for lesbian theoreticians like Grosz since it offers even more forms of resistance. Grosz notes that the "normal" transformation into Oedipalization transforms the leading sexual organ from the clitoris to the vagina (active to passive). Unstated, the assumption is made that this is not the case with a lesbian position. She gives a description of what might be called the "primary" lesbian relationship which repeats the structural positions of a patriarchal heterosexuality, "distinguishing a narcissistic (female) lover from an anaclitic (masculine) lover. Here the latter disavows her castration, while the former accepts her castration but refuses to convert her love object from maternal to paternal" (p.50). Retaining the masculinity of her pre-Oedipal position, with the mother as love-object, the latter is also the "phallic" woman, while the former position, in her acceptance of a castrated status, requires a "temporary taking on of the father as a love-object as in 'normal' femininity; but instead of transferring her attachment from the father to a suitable male father-substitute" (p. 51), i.e., a masculine woman.[9] Whereas the love-object for a masculine lesbian is a feminine love-object, the love-object for a feminine lesbian woman is a masculine love-object who may be male or female. Grosz draws to a conclusion by connecting lesbian fetishism primarily with the masculine lesbian. Having denied her own castration, like a fetishist, she takes on a substitute for the phallus as an "object outside her body." Whereas the narcissist and the hysteric phallicize or fetishize their own bodies, the masculine woman "takes an external love-object—another woman—and through this love-object is able to function as if she has, rather than is, the phallus. ... Her 'fetish' is not the result of a fear of femininity but a love of it..." (p. 51).

This background i find very useful to sort out the difficulties of S/M. Adams's thoughts on sadomasochism come in the last three pages. She wants to exonerate the perversion of S/M from being a pathology by marking the differences between it and clinical heterosexual male masochism. Lesbian sadomasochistic practices are said to construct many fetishes, many fantasies and pleasures amongst consenting parties where there can be play with identity and genitality. By celebrating the bodily pleasures that come with transgressive excitement leads Adams to what, seems to me, a difficult claim to maintain: "She has succeeded in detaching herself from the phallic reference and in orienting her sexuality outside the phallic field; which in turn suggests that the question of sexuality has finally been divorced form the question of gender" (p.263). Nowhere does she mention, as Grosz points out, that the masculine woman remains the least content. Since she loves femininity she is also most susceptible to "widespread social homophobia" (p.51). Nor does the duoist structure that accompanies their refusal escape Lacan's logic of sexuation. I turn now to Julia Creet's assessment in "Daughter of the Movement: The Psychodynamics of Lesbian S/M Fantasy" (1991).

In view of what Grosz has articulated, Creet's meditation has given me a little more insight than Adams. Creet identifies why an uneasy relationship exists between lesbian S/M and the feminist community. In her view, "feminism acts as a kind of symbolic mother, a locus of law" (p.138). In this regard S/M might be perceived as a daughter's revolt against anti-pornography lesbians who make this oppression felt from a ground of moral superiority, an advanced ethics as in the writings of Sarah Lucia Hoagland's *Lesbian Ethics* (1988). "Perhaps the most striking feature of lesbian S/M writing ... [is] a transgression against the feminist Mother ('woman' as morally superior), or what I would call the Law of the Mother. For, while 'Mom' may be the strongest source of disapproval of our being lesbians, it is the Symbolic Mother vested in feminism that functions as the repressive force acting in the lesbian S/M fantasy"(p. 145).[10] Through feminist moralizing there seems to be a loss in the necessity of maintaining the *imago*, the introjected image of a powerful mother. Outsider status can no longer be maintained which is required if castration is to be disavowed and the eroticism of breaking taboos recuperated. Ethics and erotics are both required conditions for lesbian identity. In other words, if i've got it right, the pre-Oedipal mother introjected by feminism has become too restrictive and confining, or "monstrous" towards lesbian sex radicals, but not powerful enough against patriarchy. In S/M lesbian fictions, Creet reiterates Parveen Adams' observation that the most popular fantasies are masochistic. The woman on the "bottom" is in control at all times. There is a concern for the partners throughout such fantasies. In this sense they are every bit as "moral" as those who would chastise them. The woman on the "bottom" can end the scenario at any time. Unlike Adams, these S/M scenarios are not so free and playful as she had theorized, which brings me to Modleski's account (1991a).

Modleski's account, begins by following Deleuze, as did Adams, and ends with a startling statement: S/M rituals beat and mock out of women "*the law of gender itself*, in its patriarchal form—the law that dictates the subordination/humiliation of women to be the very essence of her role" (p.155, emphasis in original).[11] So what is going on here, it seems, is a disruption within a lesbian relationship which is presently replicating the structural positions of patriarchal heterosexuality. The unacknowledged power plays are made visible by various rituals. It is this 'internalized' feminine woman within patriarchy who is the love object of this sacrificial ritual. For the subordinated or "bottom woman," an S/M ritual becomes a self-disavowal for her own acceptance of femininity within patriarchy. This contradiction of her positionality within patriarchy needs reminding, which is what S/M rituals precisely do. Trust comes, Modleski explains, because as a fetish object of the dominant masculine woman—the woman on "top"—the submissive woman sees her as a "symbolic mother" who can affirm her even in seeming degradation because it is the dominant woman who is transforming the symbolic order "into a realm of difference presided over by women" (p.157). Existing gender arrangements are preserved only so as to be 'inverted' in ritual. To put the matter in tacky terms, S/M rituals are a way for lesbians to resist being fucked-over by patriarchy. In this sense S/M are performative repetitive rituals (in the closet) which attempt to stave off an acceptance of the phallic signifier. But Modleski sets limits. The ethical question remains in the foreground as she outright dismisses Susie Bright's (the lesbian editor of *On Our Backs*) lecture on pornography with its explicit show of sexual violence on the grounds that 'actors' are in control and in consent with one another.

How far then should a ritual be pushed, and what forms should it take if fantasy and suspense, guilt and punishment (morals), pleasure and pain are to be considered? Indeed! i end this section by referring to yet another meditation on S/M; that provided by Mandy Merck (1993). Merck points to an elision in the above accounts by Adams, Creet, Modleski, and that is the abstinence of sadism. Sade is nowhere mentioned. In a footnote (f. 39) she quotes Pat Califia's "The Limits of the S/M Relationship" (1992:17): "It's a truism in the S/M community that bottoms outnumber tops about ten to one," a revealing anecdote that there are more dangerous practices to be had. Bringing Sade into the picture is a vivid reminder to what those limits might be. As Merck concludes, his *Philosophy in the Bedroom* gives us the 'top' girl, as the daughter who commits unspeakable acts of cruelty to her mother, perhaps *the* indefensible ethical position. Where, then, does the boundary lie between unbridled sadism—the 'top' girl in 'top' form—and the social subculture of consensual fetishism when the 'bottom' girl shouts, reaching the borders of her psyche, the code word to stop? i submit that S/M solicits the limits for an answer.

Perhaps the most perceptive discussion to date concerning heterosexual S/M are those of Anne McClintock (1993c). In a stunning essay, McClintock offers a lucid and historicized explanation as why ritualistic conversions, i.e., slave to master, adult to baby, pain to pleasure, man to woman, exist. First, she makes the point that the majority of men who participate in these "conversion" rituals are masochistic and not the sadists of the popular media who like to beat women up. Her explanation for the willingness to be dominated by a domina can be explained by the way men must divorce themselves from their mothers so that they may recognize their masculinity through a negation of the feminine. Like lesbian S/M, the rituals recognize the dominance of the phallic mother:

> By cross-dressing as women or as maids, by paying to do "women's work," or by ritually worshipping dominas as socially powerful, the male "slave" relishes the forbidden feminine aspects of his own identity, furtively recalling the childhood image of female power and the memory of maternity, banished by social shame to the museum of masturbation ... For men [in Western culture], the disjunction between women as object-choice, and women as desirable to identify *with*, is split and unresolved, policed by social shame and stigma" (pp.95-96).[12]

To ask a tacky question: does this mean the more "masculine" and more "authoritative" a man is, the more likely he desires a "strong" woman to "smarten" him up? Did sadists like Hitler or Mussolini play this game? Klaus Theweleit (1987) doesn't deal with this point. It requires more research. From this basic premise McClintock is able to explain some "conversions" in both historical and class terms. The fetishism for dirt, for instance, emerges from the nineteenth century as the counterpart to the commercial commodity which is symbolically clean and legitimate. In opposition, dirt avoids commercial value and transgresses the "normal" commercial market. If commodity fetishism is an overvaluation of the commercial exchange of goods, then Victorian obsession with dirt marked the undervaluation of human labor of the working class. If, as children fetishists, were punished for being "out of control" of their "dirt," then reenacting an "excess of control" over dirt in a scatological (scat) ritual gives them great pleasure. "S/M is haunted by memory. By reenacting loss of control in a staged situation of excessive control, the S/Mer gains symbolic power over perilous memory" (p. 101). This seems to be the basic release mechanism. So in male "babyism" or "infantilist" rituals, wherein the man-*as*-baby, or baby-*as*-man is enacted, men are surrendering to the memory of female power. "[I]n babyland or Fem Dom they fleetingly relinquish their stolid control, surrendering responsibility and authority in an ecstatic release of power " (p. 102).

Perhaps the most startling revelation for me was McClintock's analysis as to how S/M was the inverse of the Law—the justice system. Drawing on the parallels between S/M rituals and the rituals that go on in the law courts, she concludes: "the trial displays illicit pleasure and power for punishment; S/M displays illicit punishment for pleasure and power. The trial exists to produce the sentence of rational Truth, while in S/M Truth becomes orgasm, the word is made flesh. S/M thus emerges as a private parody of the public trial: the public punishment converted to private pleasure" (p. 105). Extending this insight historically, McClintock draws on Foucault's *To Discipline and Punish*, to identify the end of the eighteenth century as the historical period when S/M first appeared, the very time frame when punishment and discipline began to change from public spectacles to the surveillance methods of modernity. [13] Like the *tableaux vivants* of floggings, restraints and deprivations carried out in institutions like the school, S/M became a practice that borrows from this same judicial model but "radically *disarranging* the right-to-punish. S/M stages the right-to-punish, not for the civic prevention of crime, but for pleasure, parading a scrupulous fidelity to the scene and costumery of the penal model, while at the same time interfering directly with the rules of *agency*" (p. 108). In this sense, especially with gay and lesbian S/M, punishment is purposefully exhibitionistic and voyeuristic, which brazenly flaunts the state's penal monopoly. Situating the practice historically and knowing the model of discipline and punishment it draws from goes a long way in enabling to comprehend the prevalence of this practice. Given that the law, as the right-to-punish, was in the hands of men (until recently), i.e., judges, juries, prison governors, executioners, wardens, schoolteachers, army courts, fathers, heterosexual S/M subverts this gendered economy by placing the woman in charge. (Does this mean the almost all male cabinet under Thatcher enjoyed their tongue lashing?) Since S/M is pervaded by the contradictions that surround authority, it seems no longer a mystery as to why so much of its fetishized ritualistic object are signs of power: images, words, costumes, uniforms, scripts, handcuffs, badges.

It is perhaps with some relief for me that McClintock ends her discussion by pointing to the dangers of S/M and comes out against the extreme libertarian argument that S/M is always beneficial, avoiding extremes of anger and hate. Because it involves "rituals of recognition" and "reenactments of social violations to selfhood" requiring a great deal of trust between partners, the dangers are obvious and they should not be down-played. Yet, like the previous discussions by Modleski, Creet, Adams, the name of Sade and the possibility of radical evil (Žižek,1993b,Chap 3) does not appear. McClintock does however make a distinction between "reciprocal" S/M and "consensual" (or commercial) S/M. In the former, there is more likelihood that the S/M is motivated by love, whereas in the latter there is more likelihood of sadistic tendencies of women sex workers to show themselves. Her conclusion is therefore vital for the future of human(e) relations in general; "S/M thus brings to its conceptual limit the libertarian promise that individual agency alone can suffice to resolve social dilemmas" (p. 114).

Some Pornographic Conclusions:
Sex in an Age of an Epidemic

> *To see pornography as some special set of representations is to miss the extent to which pornography is the master genre for late capitalism, the literature for a society of perpetual incitement. In this sense, pornography is not an aberration, but an intensification of its productive logic, its generative grammar* (Singer, 1993:44).

Throughout the last four sections i have been trying to make sense of the virtually indescribable ways the sexualization of the body permeates Western culture and trying to understand how the I has been shaped by it. It seems obvious that a major achievement of feminism has been based on the rhetoric of sexual liberation and the new representations of strong women throughout various genres.(i am reminded of a very funny scene where Eveyln (Kathy Bates) examines her labia with the aid of a mirror during an all women's sex therapy session in *Green Fried Tomatoes*. Evelyn, a middle-aged, 'large,' house-bound wife, living with a 'fat' slob of a husband, tries desperately to rekindle her marriage with little success. She finally gives up. If husbands and lovers don't come around it's time to look elsewhere.) Entirely new characters have begun to appear in familiar fairy tales to re-write them from a feminist perspective, a certain indication that the social mores are once again changing (see esp. Zipes, 1982; Davies, 1989b).The beauty is no longer afraid of the Beast in the latest version from Walt Disney Studios. From the "Mae West" Piggy in *The Three Little Pigs* of Sherry Duval's *Storybook Theatre* to the loud mouth, somewhat pushy Miss Piggy of the Muppets, a middle-class white woman's voice has been strongly heard. As Stallybrass and White (1986:44-59) explain, the "pig" has had a long history as a figure of transgression, both celebrated and despised, a grotesque ambiguous figure in Western thought that has undergone changes in its semiotic functions. In the early records of Greek and Latin slang, female genitalia were described as " *porcus* or *porcellus*" (p.44).The description of the female genitalia as pig was an aggressive form of degradation or violence. Prostitutes were called pig merchants. Given this cultural background, the hybrid grotesque figures of Miss Piggy, large actresses like Marianne Sägebrecht (*Sugar Baby, Bagdad Cafe, Rosalie Goes Shopping*) and transsexual, large figures like the late Divine (*Hairspray*) are apt disruptions into established sex/gender binaries.

Against the repression theories of sexual liberation, the discourse theories of Foucault have been influential in understanding how sexuality becomes inscribed on various bodies. Queer theory, cultural studies, feminism, and men's studies are intertwined contradictory discourses which define the (my)nefield of sexuality. In this regard it is impossible not to notice the way "panic" sex affects all of us today.[14] The discourse of sexual liberation is very seductive in its claims for self-expression, self-exploration, and pleasure. Under its rubric all but the most violently sadistic forms of pornography are condoned, from lesbian and hetero S/M—as expressions of symbolic reenactments of social violations to selfhood, to gay porn—as allegorical statements of excessive pleasure for identification. From stag films to femme porn productions, the sex industry is held up as a liberatory model of freedom. Caught up in this dance, it is difficult to pull back and make some sense of it all. In this regard, i have found the late Linda Singer's (1993) analysis, "Sex and the Logic of Late Capitalism," especially rewarding as one such overview of this (my)nefield. Singer has not lost her critical edge; the post-Marxist discourse is very much a part of her analysis. She brings in a sobering mood to such celebratory proclamations. For her, the sex industry, defined as two separate, but not oppositional sectors—*reproductive technologies* (contraception, abortion, birthing instruments and services) and *erotic technologies and services*——are better understood as the two profit centers of late capitalism. The logic of late capitalism relies on erotic excess, "summarized under the sign of pleasure" (p.36). The genius of late capital is the way it has been able to develop strategies for managing and profiting from the perpetual promise of pleasure along two basic axes—"genital gratification and satisfaction through consumption"—both of which converge in the construct of leisure time, that space which exists outside work. McClintock's call for the unionization of sex workers would simply disrupt profit for the sex industry which is defined by its various forms of resistance to work as discipline. Patriarchal capitalism needs the porn industry even though it claims to oppose it. The 'high cost' of sex is therefore an overvaluation for an unrecognized and unpaid form of labor: as a form of non-alienated labor. The sex worker controls the product, and the sex industry exists within the realm of leisure. Compared to alienated labor of the market, leisured sex is coded as resistant, transgressive, oppositional and therefore free. The liberalist rhetoric reappears.

Singer's article attempts to describe the management and the construction of the capitalist sexual political economy in a time of the AIDS crisis. "[O]ne ironic consequence of the sexual epidemic is that sexual services and commodities have been a real growth area in the 1980s. At a time when uncommodified sexuality has been constituted as a high-risk zone, the zone of sexual commodification expands as a profit center" (p.37). Epidemic sexuality has produced "new and enlarged mechanisms for commodifying the sexual body, erotic and reproductive, and for profit by the fact that in catastrophic conditions which place the sexual body in question, value is intensified" (p.40). The other side of this is to circulate the notion of "safe sex" as being "synonymous with the family, preserving and protecting incest and intra-marital rape as forms of safe sex" (p.42). In this age of epidemic there has been a social urgency in discovering sexual criminals—especially those who exploit children, i.e., incest by parents, child-care workers, baby-sitters.

Epidemic prostitution, addiction and pornography are the three strategies of late capitalist logic "for maximizing and consolidating the socially useful, profitable excess produced as sexual energy, excess desire" (p.39). The commodity system, the medical profession and the media together have found a way to make the sexual epidemic profitable. "That which is prohibited works to sustain hegemonic social structures: the regulation of prostitution preserves marriage and the sexual and reproductive exploitation of women; pornography preserves advertising; addiction preserves brand loyalty and repeat-purchasing consumer patterns" (p.42).

Singer develops the complicity between advertising, marketing, and pornography: the way the spectacularization of the body has created erotic needs which are then displaced onto other commodities, from one object to another in an endless series. From this emerges an addiction to commodities. Addiction being "the ultimate extension of the logic of discipline—the production and regulation of needs—through the double gesture of incitement and enslavement in the name of pleasure" (p.38). Addiction assures a repetitive, routinized and predictable body which can then be managed. Panic sex fuels sexual commodification to hysterical proportions which, of course, is good for business. Designer sex makes it possible to consume sex anytime, anywhere—at home, in bed, at the office, through the computer network, through the telephone, at the sex club. Marketing strategies have made pornographic films and texts available to every shade of desire, to any number of specialized audiences. Taking sexual services out of red light districts and into the home normalizes and destigmatizes them. Mass marketing of sexual apparatuses and services, contraceptive devices, hygiene produces, sexual accessories also normalizes "the commodification of sexual functions and the integration of sexuality into a capitalist market system" (p.48).

Singer's historization of the pornographic imagination within the logic of late capital is also helpful to see why the publishing industry, especially Routledge (which fills up so much of my bibliography) working the centers of London and New York (and to a lesser extent the University of Minnesota Press), has profited so well on the growing discourses in cultural studies, queer studies, gender and women's studies which have penetrated virtually all institutions. The commodification of sex/gender and culture studies throughout the academy has become yet another way to manage that which it writes about; to ease the anxiety of the current epidemic and to further the discourse of *scentia sexualis*. The discussions surrounding the "hysterical male" of the '90s, part of which the I had experienced earlier, has been documented by Author and Marilouise Kroker (1987; 1991;1993). It is to this "hysteria" that i now turn.

1 These photographs are often compared with the well-known book edited by Tessa Boffin and Jean Fraser's *Stolen Glances* (1991), which was published during the same year. In contrast to *Love Bites*, *Stolen Glances* is theoretically astute; its contributors recognize the discourses that are already at play.

2 i refer to my puzzlement over a statement Jones makes with Benglis' photo with a huge dildo. See Vignette Five; Splitting Ourselves Apart, The Contradictions of the Pornographic Body.

3 Reich borrows the term from Roland Barthes' (1975), *The Pleasure of the Text*, p. 65.

4 i do not want to argue McClintock's misreadings of Lacan here. Defenders of Lacan, like Copjec (1990:16) tackle this accusatory essentialism head on. The split subject is what makes the self a historical subject to begin with because the split can never be closed; it's what makes the system open. The 'essential' nature of the signifier is the very source of human history. It is that material which makes the Symbolic Order historical.

5 This relates back to Kristeva's warning about the dangers of the avant-gardism that can fall into a fascism. i think of Marinetti and the Futurist movement here. See Keith Tester's chapter "Nostalgia" (1993) for the analysis of the responses to the certainty and uncertainty of knowledge within a postmodern context.

6 Arlene Stein's "Sisters and Queers: The Decentering of Lesbian Feminism" (1992), presents an overview of the changing lesbian identities since the '60s.

7 Teresa de Lauretis (1991) explains that she used this term to problematize the terms "lesbians" and "gay" that designate "distinct kinds of life-styles, sexualities, sexual practices, communities etc." (p.iii). She distinguishes her use at that time from Queer Nation which engages in similar rhetorical and political tactics as ACT UP: confrontation and direct action, which is opposed to more assimilationist liberal appeals by gay and lesbian groups. The term "queer" attempted to separate questions of sexuality from gender. Lisa Duggan's "Making It Perfectly Queer" (1992) reviews the historical background and emphasizes the constructivist stance of Foucault as being central to queer theorizing. Steven Seidman (1993) provides a historical review of gay and lesbian identity politics.

8 This way of theorizing is very reminiscent of Baudrillard's (1990) notion of seduction which he identifies as feminine.

9 Although i'm sure they, themselves would never tolerate the label, but this distinction that Grosz makes provides the distinction made between Cixous and Wittig—Cixous extolling the former position, while Wittig the latter.

10 In a footnote (n.6) Creed recognizes that the law of the Father prevails over all and that the law of the Mother would only uphold the same symbolic order, just another version of the "phallic mother," but she wants to identify the Law of the Mother at work during pre-Oedipalization.

11 Modleski points to Parveen Adams' "Of Female Bondage" (1989), for a description of the decisive separation of sex from gender and the possibilities of S/M's subversive potential. Adams in turn has developed her theories from the Lacanian psychoanalyst Catherine Millot, "The Feminine Superego" (1990a).

12 An earlier version of this essay appeared in *Dirty Looks: Women, Pornography, Power*, edited by Pamela Church Gibson and Roma Gibson (1993).

13 Foucault makes this point that S/M appears at the end of the eighteenth century in *Madness and Civilization* (1965:97).

14 See the series published by the Krokers (1987,1991,1993) and with Cook (1987,1989).

GENDER B(L)ENDING AND THE POLITICS OF THE SCULPTURED BODY

Foucault and the History of Sexuality

[M]en still have everything to tell
us about their sexuality.

(Cixous, 1981, Laugh of the Medusa)

[T]he postmodern body is the
body of the mythological
'Trickster,' the shape-shifter: 'of'
indeterminate sex and changeable
gender .... who continually alters
her/his body, creates and recreates
a personality ... [and] floats
across time' from period to
period, place to place.

(Smith-Rosenberg, 1985:291, in Bordo, 1990b:144)

The Trickser and the Cyborg
invite us to "take pleasure" in the
"confusion of boundaries."

(Haraway, 1990:191)

As men have been closely
identified with ... rationalist
tradition, they have often remained
strangely ignorant of themselves,
while rarely appreciating how this
ignorance forms the character of
their experience and relationships.

(Seidler, 1989a:85)

In my own case, it seems that i have unconsciously changed my code of dress. My 'costume' has become a runner's T-shirt underneath (masculine, macho, sportive) with a loose, flowing shirt on top which is generally colorful (feminine, loose, limpid). Shirts are generally collarless, or have a small limp collar. I never wear a tie, regardless of how formal the occasion. Pants are loose and bulky, textured with a coarse weave when i can find them. Shoes are usually different colored running shoes. I will wear black and a suit (without tie) at funerals. Hair is now long, often worn as a pony-tail, sometimes even braided, yet the beard remains; side-burns, however, are a definite NO. I wear two [three, 1990] pierced earrings in my left ear. i changed my name from John to jan. My name is now entirely spelt with lowercase letters. The contradictions of my gender blending are per-haps all too obvious (written in 1989).

Michel Foucault and His Retractors

The well-known works by Foucault, which make up his *The History of Sexuality*, question 'sexuality' from another position than that of the repression hypothesis. He asked, how have institutionalized discourses shaped sexual politics historically? Foucault's position has received as much controversy as praise from a wide range of interpretations.[1] From the point of view of masculinity, Seidler's (1989b) critique of Foucault is to claim that he was still caught within a rationalist discourse, and he did not provide a transformative or *affirmative* sense of power. Peter Dews' (1987:61 ff.) critique of Foucault is that he lacked a theory of the "libidinal body"—a body that could resist. In contrast Jana Sawicki (1988) sees *The History of Sexuality* as providing a theoretical position to justify a politics of difference amongst the various discourses in feminism; while Schor (1987a), defending a more universalist sense of woman, comes up with yet another interpretation: Foucault's displacements of indifference and desexualization meant the loss of "feminine specificity" (p. 110). After reviewing his micro-physics of power she writes: "The practical implication of this model is that resistance must be carried out in local struggles against the many forms of power exercised at the everyday level of social relations" (p.28). Hartsock (1990b) is also unhappy with Foucault for he did not offer a transformative conceptualization of power, only the possibility of resistance. There is the further reading of Fraser (1989: Chap. 2) who is concerned with Foucault's inability to demonstrate the failure of dialectical criticism of the human sciences, notably critical theory. John McGowan (1991:128-139) is particularly hard-hitting and succinct in his analysis of Foucault's conceptualization of power, calling his sense of freedom "empty" for his lack of making differentiations between resistances. All resistance was given positive valence. Foucault had no way of evaluating "successful purposive action that different social orders afford their subjects" (p. 131). Yet for lesbian theorists like Elspeth Probyn (1993, esp. chap. 5) Foucault's "technologies of the self" as the "care of the self" offer a way to recover the experience of the self within an epistemological/ontological tension. These conflicts of interpretation are troubling. Towards the end of his career Foucault, realizing his own lacunae, began to move into the issues of resistance and personal transformation through his case study analysis of the life of the hermaphrodite, Herculine Barbin (Foucault, 1980b), and his last volume, *The Care of the Self* (1988).

Foucault's work will remain controversial. Yet his oeuvre is worth reading for it raises, once more, the variety of sexual relations possible, and reiterates the "frenzy" of the visible which characterizes "panic" sex today.

For males in particular, he forces us to question our own construction of masculinity. Foucault's *History of Sexuality* Vol. 2 (1985) and 3 (1988) are especially significant in this regard. Foucault examined the relationships between older and younger men, developing themes of austerity as they related to the attainment of wisdom through the appropriate measure and quantity of food, drink and sex. In the last chapter of Volume Three, entitled 'A New Erotics,' the theme of love amongst men as a "virtuous community" was raised once again (as it was at the end of Volume Two). Older men, he warned, should not abandon their sons. The reciprocity in relationships between older and younger men must be worked out. This seems to be a powerful message since men have *repressed (Verdrängung)* their homoerotic love and displaced it into competitive sports.[2] Accusations are often made of fathers for abandoning their sons because of the hyper-speed world of work today. i am not entirely exempt from such an accusation. Few men are.

Foucault's examination of the discourse on sex has provided a paradoxical platform for "liberation." Knowledge of sex was confined to the closed space of the confessional. "The analyst's couch, "writes Bartkowski sarcastically, "mirrors the space of sex itself—the silent closed bedroom of the heterosexual couple" (p. 45). The body and words become the property of the discourse of power and sexuality for the listener (priest or psychiatrist). "It is produced through voyeurism or sanctioned eavesdropping. The listening men then recirculate the desire(s) of women into the economy of power and knowledge. The voices of resistance are translated into witchcraft and, later, into hysteria as medical institutions take over the function of the church" (Bartkowski, 1988:46). And here lies the paradox. It is precisely this discourse, once confined to the clos(et)ed space between inquisitor-victim, confessor-confessant, analyst-analysand, which has become exposed—marketable through countless T.V. talk shows (and perhaps texts such as this one!), but in this very marketability and exposure the sexual discourse seems hardly equipped to be a liberating experience.

How did certain institutions and cultural practices produce individuals through the disciplinary power that came with the rise of nineteenth century human sciences? Throughout the corpus of Foucault's work, in each case and each period, he explains how bodies were acted upon in discursively constituted institutional settings. One of his most dramatic examples comes from the seventeenth and eighteenth century: absolutist rule was reproduced by cruel public rituals of torture—a mnemonics of pain, written directly on the body through physical cruelty. Enter Modernity. Punishment now changes to a discourse of the applied sciences of Man. Knowledge is power and resistance—hence, techniques of surveillance, examinations, disciplines—as ways of knowing exercise power over individuals. Disciplinary practices create the divisions of healthy/ill, sane/mad, legal/delinquent. Through the discursive practices of medicine, psychiatry, criminology–the hospital, asylum, and prison are instituted. By extension one can think of the discourse of art separating high from low art—fine art from kitsch—through the institution of the museum and art gallery (see Crimp, 1983) and, by extension, education as the institution which defines knowledge from propaganda, the literate from the illiterate, the educated brains from the dropouts.

While Foucault has taught us that discursive practices historically construct their 'objects' and has shown us that history can be shown as a series of 'events' (*énoncés*) or disruptions wherein a 'principle of singularity' is at work (Rabinow, 1984:386) since such events are unpredictable and bring with them unprecedented changes and new possibilities, and his geneology (following Nietzsche) focused, not on the origins of things (*Ursprung*), but on the critical analysis of their emergence (*Entstehung*) and decent (*Herkunft*), what is still missing from his oeuvre by his dismissal of the *repression hypothesis* is an avoidance of non-discursivity, i.e., of existence without predicate which, in some ways, pre-supposes and underlies an 'event.' This is a point that Soper (1995) brings up for feminism. While Foucault is able to reveal the discursive machinery that makes up the 'events' in the history of sexuality, his account avoids any reference to a prediscursive reality. Therefore an 'event' such as feminism (described only discursively) "carries no obvious prescriptive force either in favor or against the project of female emancipation" (p. 24). In this regard Foucault remains at the level of a constructivist humanist subject (pre-Fruedian) as his 'technologies of self' testify. "The tasks of testing oneself, monitoring oneself in a series of clearly defined exercises, makes the question of truth-- the truth concerning what one is, what one does, and what one is capable of doing—*central to the formation of the ethical subject*" (Foucault, 1988:67-68).

As Copjec (1994c: Introduction) has argued, Foucault disavowed any reference to a principle or a subject that 'transcended' the regime of power he analyzed, and hence produced a historicist view which reduced society to a network of relations and power. What Foucault failed to acknowledge was a general principle at the level of the Real, at the level of fantasy that was the cause of society's 'being.' By leaving micro-politics on the level of appearances—on the surface as discourses, Foucault had no way of dealing with the 'unspeakable,' i.e., existence without a predicate. Dismissal of the repressive hypothesis leaves Foucault with no way of getting at the 'being' of society. As a result, the view of power 'from below,' dissipative and 'everywhere,'comes to a halting contradiction with his notion of the panopticon as developed in *Discipline and Punish* (1977). The device of the panopticon becomes a structuring principle that 'disciplines' the various institutions throughout the nineteenth century: the prison, school, hospital, factory and offices. But to assume that surveillance is so central and so powerful contradicts the very hypothesis of decentralized power Foucault had maintained. As Žižek (1994c: 198–199) points out, what avoids the inconsistancy is to recognize that it is the notion of *fantasy* that makes the uniform matrix of the panopticon possible. What holds the pluralities of power together, i.e., the networks of discourses at the level of appearance requires a principal that operates in the Real—beyond language. Lacanians like Copjec and Žižek insist that this transendental realm of a society's 'being' must be problematized. For Freud, existence without a predicate was theorized through his positing of the Father of Enjoyment and his notion of the 'death drive.' Both were principles which *negated* the institutions they established. In other words, they were unthinkable and unspeakable occurrences if the institution was to function as it did. To question the fantasy structures which install the system is to directly attack its very 'being:' the act of a heretic in former times, an act of postmodern ideology today. The killing of the Father of Enjoyment ('real' or imagined), as developed in Freud's *Totem and Taboo,* installed the Oedipal father and thereby ensured a society of equals—*brotherly* equals as MacCannel (1991) has demonstrated. The death drive as developed in Freud's *Beyond the Pleasure Principle* accounted for the centrality of the pleasure principle. Each transcendental term at the level of fantasy was the repressed negative cause that 'closed' the system. Unbinding these fantasy structures releases the terror and danger of *jouissance*—as in the 'laugh' of Medusa, for instance.

i am of the opinion that Foucault did away with the repression hypothesis so as to play another game which opened the floodgates of narcissism. His ethics present a 'stylistics of existence' (1988:71) whereby the self-surveying-the self becomes like so many discourse to be worked on, a kind of human geography of the skin's surface. His call to pleasure against desire, where the self is not lacking, tried to do away with Otherness interpreted by Lacanians as identification with the not-I—as a *negation*. The Other for Foucault becomes more fluid and heterogeneous—not a negation, but rather a 'quasi-negation' that holds multiple possibilities (see Golding, 1995). From this arises the possible reason why Foucault has been embraced by gay and lesbian theorists (especially Elspeth Probyn (1993) who makes his ethics central to her postmodern view of subjectivity) since such an ethics tries to escape the 'straight-jacket' of heterosexual society presided by the killing of the Father of Enjoyment and the resultant castration. In this sense, i read Foucault as playing Freud's grandson Hans' *other game* in the mirror (see the section After the Fort/Da Game: The Danger of a "Simulacred" Perverted Gaze) with a modification. Rather than a completely self-satisfactory narcissism that the game brings, where the choice of the drive cedes desire, Foucault wants the pleasure and the seduction of the Other watching and engaging in the body's "use"; consistent, i should think, with S/M practices examined earlier. This is a perverted ethics. Foucault is advocating a "designer-self" that is consistent with postmodern commodity fetishism: Foucault's 'ethical demand of an ecstatic fetish' as Golding (1985) characterizes it. This is the thesis i would like to both question and maintain in the following sections.

Sculpting the Body

The New Man and the New Woman of the postmodern advertising pose—a 'pose' which denies an apotropaic politics—a problem etc. that is a problem for me as i question my role in feminism. For women "[t]he current body of fashion is taut, small-breasted, narrow-hipped, and of a slimness bordering on emaciation; it is a silhouette that seems more appropriate to an adolescent boy or a newly pubescent girl than to an adult woman" (Bartky, 1988:64). Does Bartky's description still hold? or has it morphed elsewhere? The new hysteria is bulimia and anorexia (Bordo, 1990a), the evaporating or evaporated body. Surprisingly enough, women body builders have the same psychic affliction as anorexics—"will, purity, perfection, control." The body is treated as alien—not belonging to the self. It is meant to be sculpted, which is the very opposite to that of the anorexic who literally cannot see her body as any other 'thing' than what her inner reality dictates. She is relentlessly driven by an ideal image of ascetic slenderness. But the anorexic and the body builder are intimately linked. "The technology of dictating to nature one's own chosen design for the body is at the center of the bodybuilder's mania, as it is for the anorexic" (Bordo, 1990a:99).[3] Are these, then, also responses to Foucault's 'technologies of the self'?

How much of these developments are confined to White middle-class women and men? It is claimed that few Black women suffer from anorexia (unless, of course, they have taken on the same middle-class values). Is this because historically they have always been displaced as body? The wet nurse, the nanny, the aunt Jemimah stereotype, cooking and cleaning for her living, make her huge bulked-body a sign of strength and resistance. Anorexia and bulimia, on the other hand, confined to images of conformity and idealized beauty play into the 'gaze' of others that are absent; the contortions of narcissism, by and large, are White middle-class preoccupations. These same concerns hold for men. This I jogs for many miles. This I loves to "sweat." This I is proud to have won five marathons. This is done for more than mere health reasons. My male narcissism is clearly visible, striving for perfection offered by the sport's "fix." My description of the "costume" i wear is a walking semiological sign system that projects my intentional "designer" cross-dress. It is a sartorial awakening visible everywhere. Holly Devor's (1989) *Gender Blending* provides a sampling of women who play with their gender identities in their style of dress and in their sexual preferences. It should be of no surprise that Foucault is not far from "call," as Butler (1990a:96), coming from the performing and dramatic arts, eagerly notes. It is a position of an ethics he himself maintained throughout his life; an *ethics* that rested on familiar modernist aesthetic ground, the art of choosing or inventing oneself, turning the body into a work of art.

Against this background, the anorexic and the body builder are the limit responses to this "call": one makes the body disappear while the other blows it out of its "feminine" proportions. The woman looks like a man. Perhaps their modernist analogues were "hysterics" and female heterosexual and lesbian artists who wore male drag as an extension of the male dandy, e.g., Romaine Brooks, Radclyffe Hall, Frida Kahlo. i say "no surprise" to this development because the postmodern once again repeats the crisis of sexual identities (Butler's "gender trouble") at the turn of the century when an artistic avant-garde were consciously forming their identities (see Tickner, 1992). "From the idea that the self is not given to us, I think that there is only one practical consequence: we have to create ourselves as a work of art" (Foucault, 1983:237). Foucault desired an ethics of aesthetic self-creation, like Nietzsche and the dandyism of Baudelaire,[4] as a posture against the world. "The 'new' ethics," writes Rosemary Hennessy (1993), "is less a code of conduct than a strategical indeterminacy that allows uncertainty, the position of being 'elsewhere,' a focus on the limits of language, and its unspeakable grounding in the unsignifiable" (p.58).[5]

Foucault's comment, taken seriously, can lead to some fairly bizarre conclusions and forms of sexual practices, at least by Western standards. Judith Butler (1990a) for example, argues that the Oedipal story can be read as a narrative of a binary disjunction with only two heterosexual or homosexual desires, yet in fantasy a variety of positions are possible, all of which are *not* culturally intelligible possibilities. In fantasy life, excesses are possible that lead beyond any *one* consciously lived identity. Identity and fantasy are *not* mutually exclusive. It is possible to internalize a figuration through imagination that yet does *not* exist, or one which may be artificially manipulated through cosmetic surgery (e.g., Michael Jackson, Orlan). If, as Deleuze and Guattari (1983) have suggested, it is possible to internalize "parts" of others (like an assemblage), it becomes possible to identify with figures from the past, not as empirical figures but as fantasy impersonations. In this sense, Elvis will never die. He is "alive and well" in his thousands of clones! Such desire introjects fantasied figures that literally 'figure' the body. They constitute the "genealogy of that embodied/psychic identity" (Butler, 1990b:333). Fantasies condition and construct the specificity of the gendered subject within the discourse of cultural sanctions and taboos (see Caplan, 1989). "If gender is constituted by identification and identification is invariably a fantasy within a fantasy, a double figuration, then gender is precisely the fantasy enacted by and through the corporeal styles that constitute bodily significations" (p.334). This conclusion reached by Butler has enormous social implications for it virtually claims that the Other is continually constructed through discourses which produced alien body types distinguished by shape, color, voice and so on. Here we have then a postructuralist, antiessentialist, 'writing on the body' (i shall pick her arguments again).

Foucault's *History of Sexuality, Volumes Two and Three* (1985, 1988) had already charted the shift from pederasty of Classical Greece to virginity and marriage in Rome. It can be surmised from this study that it is the very discourses on sexuality in the context of the changing material conditions which change the Imaginary and the Symbolic Order, the internalized imagery of the gendered body. The austerity associated with the 'good' or 'proper' uses of pleasure are explored in regards to food, drink, and sex; taken together they re-design body type. All this is suggestive of the malleability of gender and sexual relations. One can imagine a prehistory when incest taboos were not yet in place, allowing for many sexual resolutions.[6] Clinical cases of "sex reassignment" make us aware of sex-gender malleability, and the need, as argued earlier, for questioning the limits of such malleability (Shepherdson, 1994; Millot,1990b). "[I]n unusual cases, a child of one biological sex is raised as the other sex because of such bizarre accidents like the removal of male genitalia in circumcision" (Doyle, 1983:128). Even more bizarre are the practices of "body artists" who perceive themselves as "modern primitivists" (Vale and Juno, 1989). The most sensational cases are those where the artist's death occurs through self-mutilation of his own genitals. Fakirs, tattoo artists, piercing, scarification and the complex eroticism that accompanies such bodily contortions reach back to the practice of many indigenous tribes.

Surprisingly, there is no systematic account of the psychic consequences of this with Foucault. Foucault offers no psychological accounting of desire. Identity formations are left as subject positions formed by the intersections of various discourses. The subject is always a construction of discourse through the workings of the micropolitics of power. Of the many critiques of Foucault's limitations, this seems to be a crucial one. Joan Copjec (1990) argues that by rejecting the "repression hypothesis," the originary repression that splits the subject, Foucault does not analyze "the *positive operation* of negation, ... he is instead *eliminating* negation and replacing it with a purely positive force of 'construction' " (p.13, my italic). For Foucault that which is repressed is shaped by the psychiatrist's discourse, which in turn shapes the analysand's discourse. The law for Foucault does not operate negatively by forbidding, censoring, or neglecting to acknowledge the subject; rather it becomes a discrepancy between different subject positions, an internal force. In this sense, every negation of the law (as a transgression) becomes an affirmation of it. The law, according to Foucault, does not forbid a desire that already exists (as in the repression hypothesis); rather a desire is constructed which did not exist before through us speaking about it.[7] This may be partly the reason why so little commentary by Foucault's own aestheticization of his body appears throughout his work. i think Butler (1990a) recognizes this lacuna in Foucault and attempts to rescue him by incorporating Freud's theory of melancholia with aspects of parodic performance in order to retrieve desire into identity formation.

Butler's position, close to the anti-oedipal theorizations of Deleuze and Guattari, does not condemn drag queens as have other feminists (e.g. Showalter and Munster). If the "inner truth of gender is a fabrication and if true gender is a fantasy constituted and inscribed on the surface of the bodies, then genders can neither be true not false but are only produced as true effects of a discourse of primary and stable identity" (p. 337). There is no self to be alienated from since there is no "truth" of self as such. Referring to Esther Newton's (1972) study on female impersonators, the drag becomes the perfect parody of a true, that is, the assumed 'natural' gender identity, deconstructing the inner and outer psychic space. The drag, according to Newton, is a double inversion: the 'outside' appearance is feminine, but the 'inside' essence (body) is masculine. The opposite inversion holds as well. The appearance on the outside (body and gender) are masculine but the essence inside is feminine. Both appear to be claims to truth and contradict one another, which seems to me, *is* the deconstructive move of "neither/nor." Butler considers cross-dressing, butch/femme lesbian identities (which mime the sex-role stereotyping), and drag to be infinitely more complex than the theories i have read which have been critical of this masquerade.

A "milder" extension of the "art of the body" is developed by Dick Hebdige (1983) through his studies of various sub-cultures—the youth gangs,

426

juvenile delinquents, skinheads and punks who effectively resist the surveillance gaze of society.[8] Scarification and the practice of the grotesque are their forms of display. It is their "resistant" body which "poses back" at the shaping effects of discursive "microphysical technologies of gender," thus forming the social abjected Other. What may be their desires as transgressors of the law? Historically, the well-known theories of Mikhail Bakhtin on the carnivalesque body chart similar occurrences. In such contexts the female grotesque body of the old pregnant hag is opposed to the classical, monumental static body. The hag's state of abjection undermines the narcissism and imaginary identities of perfection (see Russo, 1986). What all this suggests is that gender and the body are extremely malleable. The practices which go on the fringes of "normal" gender definitions at the micropolitical levels infectiously change the drift of gender identifications. In England, punk hairdo's became chic with the middle-classes. "That the gendered body is performative suggests that it has no ontological status apart from the various acts which constitute its reality, and that reality is fabricated as an interior essence, that very interiority is a function of a decidedly public and social discourse, the public regulation of fantasy through the surface politics of the body" (Butler, 1990b: 336). The ethical relationship, however of performative masks is raised by transgression. How one plays with the established masks or creates new ones must be judged against the "progress" of human sexual relationships, class, gender, age, racism and so forth.

Hebdige makes it clear that there is great anxiety surrounding the urban crowd for its non-conformity. The masses may be threatening if they remain "illegible" or are found "ungovernable." When this happens, the crowd is 'policed' and 'contained.' Hebdige provides the historical example of the 19th cen. *costermongers*, boys who, as street traders, made a precarious living selling perishable goods from wheelbarrows. They had their own identifiable style of dress and slang. "Copper," which the I remembers using as a school boy in England, became the term for policemen whom they attacked because their street economy was being disrupted through public space supervision. Reformatory schools for delinquents were then instituted as part of the need to control the streets. Dress, slang, gender bending may be an adversarial stance which forms a postmodern micropolitics of resistance, subverting existing regimes of discourse. Although i am not romanticizing the pain surrounding marginality, in a world which appears out of control the body's skin has become the new battleground. It may manifest itself in a tolerable cross-dress such as my own within the institutional site/cite/sight of a university, or it can take on the extreme forms of mutilation, body building, anorexia, and bulimia. i believe the scarification that is increasing becoming more and more popular in schools is a symptom of this pain of a marginalized youth who have few jobs and less hope for a future. This "nihilistic" side of postmodernity (Roseneau, 1992) points to the so-called "thirteenth generation" of baby busters who have been let down by the promises of modernity.

Whose Dress is it Anyway? Madonna is to Michael Jackson as Pornography is to Childhood

Dress is yet another major aspect of feminist critique; after all, clothing and ornamentation make the body culturally visible. The semiotics of fashion, a fascinating area for feminist analysis (Barthes, 1985; Hollander, 1975). Currently, women wearing padded shoulders to simulate a male's broad shoulders, making their waists appear proportionately thinner to the rest of their upper torso, wearing blue jeans or pant suits, seem to be direct borrowings from the male signification system in order to gloss the real material inequalities of the workplace. In the '90s leggings have become so popular in the workplace that the sale of panty hose is down to "loss of profit" proportions. The equating of women's dress in relation to the male's suit allows for the appearance of equality, when in reality, power relations lie in the hands of men. These gestures are not transgressive gender performances as much as they are liberal attempts at gender "equality." Like my own dress, such signifiers are what Garber (1992) calls "synecdochic quotation[s] of transvestism" like the gold necklaces worn by Mr. T of the once-popular TV series, *The A-Team,* or the pony-tails and earrings that have (like the taming of punk culture before by the middle class) become a widespread male fashion. The potential of their cultural disruption has been exhausted. Adolescent clothing, by mimicking adult styles, seems to fuel the same consumer market. Inequality exists because women are expected, for economic reasons, to spend large amounts of money on make-up, hair, diets, figure salons, and alluring clothing since they are relentlessly "made-up" as sexual objects who carry the burden of spectacular appearance.

Rosalind Coward, (1985) in her book *Female Desires,* examines body parts (the mouth, the voice, the instinct, the look, the story) as manufactured by the media industry which are continually subjected to the male gaze, while a German feminist collective, organized by Frigga Haug (1987), does collective memory work to recall how their own sexuality had been constructed by analyzing the memories of their formative years. The Body now becomes a viable strategic 'tool' for feminist posturing. Makeup is 'wedded' to an aesthetics of ornamentation. There is no need to rehearse a truism that the application of cosmetics through advertising industry today continues through the same use of rhetoric premised on the metaphysical principles of ideal beauty. What has changed, however, is the overlay of yet another discourse manufactured by the "health" industry which pushes for a perfect, toned body through aerobic exercise, a hyped reality in hyper time and space. The fetishization of the entire body displaces the high heels. In the swim suit competitions of today, beauty contestants walk to center stage in their bare feet to mimic the 'natural' look. After all, who wears high heels to the beach? Is this more than a hint of a changed narcissism?

At all levels, argues French (1985), 'natural' women, as against distinctively 'cultured' men, control the expression of women's sexuality and define the order of power and morality. In this sense women are alienated from the process and product of their labor like all workers in a distinctively capitalist system (see Sandra Lee Bartky, 1982). To what extent women's sexuality is developed only for men's enjoyment rather than their own, once more recapitulates the arguments that surround pornography. When does one dress for oneself as against dressing for the Other is a difficult question.[9] Does the 'authentic' feminist display the 'natural' look—the absence of make-up and the presence of body hair? Or is this yet another costume? another binary like that of the naked/nude? Is it the generation gap between feminist mothers and their daughters who have differing views as to what the politics of dress are today? Is the new generation of daughters less prudish, not believing in an essential 'natural' woman as Elizabeth Wilson (1987:231) argues? One answer is offered by Kaja Silverman (1986) who has examined this 'scopic' ocularcentric discourse. She cleverly points out that it was at the end of the eighteenth century when the 'Great Masculine Renunciation' took place. Men's dress changed from the lavish display of the aristocracy to the somber, harmonizing, and homogeneous uniform. This change occurred in order to level the hierarchical distinctions of the aristocracy. It came with the disappearance or 'absorption' (cf. Freud) of the subject and the birth of the *citizen*. A 'uni-form' provided the possibility of integrating male members of the moneyed classes with the new capitalists of industry. With the inhibition of the narcissistic and exhibitionist impulse in men, Flugel (in Silverman, 1986:141) argued that their desires were displaced into a "professional" showing off—especially in spectator sports. Scopophilia, as a means of mastering the female subject, and the woman-as-spectacle were further repercussions. The male associated himself with a beautiful, well-dressed woman or in a more deviant form, actually adopting female mannerisms and dress: cross-dressing, transvestism, or engagement in various fetishes of heterosexual voyeurism.

As Silverman points out, since the 18th century class distinctions have softened while gender distinctions have hardened. While men's dress remained sartorial for the past 200 years, women were given a new 'look' each year which fed the competition between classes and fed the fashion industry. Maureen Turin (1983) provides a historical analysis of this fashion industry, showing the collusions between the fashion industry and Hollywood film industry. In 1945, a typology was drawn up which listed six types of women (the exotic, outdoor, sophisticate, womanly woman, aristocrat, gamine) and the costume each type was to wear. Turin outlines three fashion trends in the 20th century which literally changed the fashion industry. The "slit" aesthetic, as might be expected fetishizes the female body through exposure of flesh, while transvestite designs extend the sculptural presence of the body and emphasized composure and self-possession of the wearer. Lastly, sportswear freed up the woman's body. It could be argued that it charts a changing comportment of the female body to the present. And while Iris Young's (1989) essay, "Throwing Like a Girl" argues for the hampering of 'femininity' in relation to sport, there is also the counter trend of women enjoying their bodies more and more through active involvement in sport brought on by the discourse on health. i am, of course, not naïve enough to fully endorse this without the ideological recognition that "fat *is* a feminist issue," which leads to all sorts of anorexic and bulimic complications, and that contemporary dance styles reflect a more active and frenzied lifestyle. Body movement can be as oppressive as being caught by its sheer weight. There is, in my mind, a ceaseless oscillation between the two—to the degree that i am caught by the disciplinary technologies which idealize my body as the perfect male or female.

Not all feminists read clothing through psychoanalytic semiotic lenses. There are differing views amongst feminists as to the sexual politics of costume and dress. Gilbert (1980) has persistently argued that male modernists drew a sharp distinction between masks and the 'true self,' between false costumes and true garments, and even opposed costume as artificial or false compared with nakedness which was said to be natural. Feminist modernists, in contrast, regarded all clothing as costume and all costuming as false. Nakedness was just another costume. While modernist male costume imagery (e.g. Joyce, Lawrence, Yeats, Eliot) was considered conservative in order to assert gender distinctions, for feminist modernists costume was radically revisionary in both a political and literary sense.

Gilbert is suspicious of any androgynous cross-dressing by men, claiming that, as in the sixteenth century, men impersonated women in order to dominate them. Through sexual inversion, the sixteenth-century man was able to achieve sexual strength by co-opting sign values from the female signifying systems. Since women were defined as "the lustier sex"—the "sex made for sex" (p.397), men who displayed feminine characteristics were more virile, better in bed. (This brings to mind the question whether the use of wigs by men was a related issue?) Gilbert claims, following Robert Stoller, that the transvestite shows mastery over women by claiming that he is not "just" like a woman; rather he is *better* than a woman because "he is a woman with a penis" (p.397). Impersonating femaleness into his maleness and *not his androgyny*, he mysteriously owns the power of both sexes.[10] The arguments are complex and the question as to whether a psychoanalytic explanation of transvestism is transhistorical in its formulation, or whether it holds good only for our postindustrial society, is always in order.

A further contradictory position is presented by Lichtenstein (1987) whose developed thesis raises the same question of costume and masquerade but couched in the context of ornamentation.

> If adornment is necessary for beauty, too much ornament distorts nature and truth: we can summarize thus an aesthetic principle, current until France's classical period and still shaping our own discourse. The principle implies an essential distinction that constitutes all metaphysical aesthetics, allowing one to separate the wheat from the chaff: a distinction between ornament and makeup, between a regulated and unregulated use, between lawful employment and abuse—its use to excess. Ornament becomes makeup, which conceals rather than elucidates truth (p.78).

Such a discussion recapitulates the distinction between primary and secondary characteristics of classical philosophy. In drawing, color would hide the figure (the foundational lines), thus blurring the pure ideas which the rationalists were seeking to discover. The use of sesquipedalianistic languages (excessive tropes) again takes away from what might be simply said as fact, as essence, in clarity. Rhetorical figures, ornament, and colors clouded the issues. Excessive ornamentation was identified through metaphors of femininity. Indulges of the refinements of brush stroke and the use of color as a cosmetic art—through its heavy application or staining and feigning (p.79) were given over to the seductive artifice of the colorings and allures used by prostitutes and courtesans. The borders of ornamentation "make-up" the masks of social play.

Recently, this narrative of the masquerade and the mask has been brilliantly reformulated with cross-cultural comparisons by Jennifer Craik (1989) and Hilary Radner's (1989) argument that late capitalism has tapped what she calls a 'rhizomorphic discourse',[11] which exploits not the male gaze of the 'look,' but a "feminine position in which [the woman] is the subject of her own pleasure" (p.301). In late capitalism, the beauty industry began to redirect its discourse from women as objects of the male gaze to promoting the independent, autonomous 'career woman.' Bare feet during swim suit competitions was an obvious concession to the New Woman. Femininity became a discourse, not under male possession, but under the New Woman's possession, heralded as post-feminism (see Janet Lee, 1989: Hennessy, 1993). i would argue that the recognition of feminine narcissism and the new libidinal economy dovetails with the anti-pornographic discourse. Feminine pleasure and feminine autonomy apply equally to both: one legitimates libidinal economy legitimately through the beauty industry while the other is an illegitimate libidinal economy which continually plays off and exaggerates that industry, i.e., underclothing, makeup, stiletto heels - as a phallic symbol served to 'give' the woman her missing phallus (see Wright,1989). The line between good/bad girl is continually collapsed with someone like Madonna presenting both sides simultaneously.

In our postmodern society there has been an explosion in clothing/costumes/uniforms. Oppositional clothing has become a form of contestation. Men appear to be trying to reclaim spectacle through the glitter of rock music and MTV. Is this another masculine assertion? i think it is. But the rebels have been tamed. Brown and Campbell (1986) claim that only one-fifth of rock videos may be identified as social protest songs; the rest are about heterosexual love and sex, or have no clear theme at all. Male opposition against their Fathers, which was found in rock, has become "music for pleasure," and music videos produced for star-conceit (Frith, 1988: Afterwards). Past oppositions like that of the Teds, the Mods, and the punks and skinheads who purposefully ridicule dress, is gone. Again i am drawn to such a contradictory figure like Madonna, whose very name is the antithesis of her stage antics. Her clothing are often undergarments worn on the outside, or inappropriately such as a wedding dresse worn for everyday use. Is she then able to keep the rebelliousness alive? Her stare is given right back to those who try to humiliate her by turning the sign system in on itself. No one can deny her manipulations of her *screen* image.

E. Ann Kaplan (1987:116-126) has dubbed this "ambiguous" stance as "postmodern feminist." When discussing Madonna's video "Material Girl," she notes that it is a parody, a take-off on the classic Hollywood style as presented by the film *Gentlemen Prefer Blondes*, with Marilyn Monroe singing 'Diamonds Are a Girl's Best Friend.' Yet this pastiche provides a questioning of "materialism." Madonna seems to be split in two. There is the Madonna who is the material girl, desired by her director, all performance, a "bad" girl, (a socialized I); and the Madonna off-stage, who rejects the riches of her suitors, a "good" girl who searches for true love. This second Madonna plays off a narrative that is barely visible in the video, thus reversing the classical Hollywood musical which is but a small interlude in the larger love story (an ironic i). However, this bad/good reversal becomes blurred and confused at the end of the video. Which Madonna is the "real" or "fictitious" one? Kaplan's characterization of Madonna "as a cross between a bordello queen and a bag lady" allows teenagers, and 12-year-old girls, to "protest against their mothers and the normal feminine while still remaining very much within those modes" (p.126) by spending a great deal of time, money and energy on the Madonna "look." In the video 'Papa Don't Preach,' Kaplan comments that Madonna wants to keep her 'illegitimate' child. She blurs the line between whore and virgin and yet "the heroine is *neither*, but rather a sexy young teenager, in love and pregnant, and refusing to conform to social codes and give up her baby (as her friends, she says, tell her to)" (p.132). She is split again as bejeaned teenager and a sexy woman in black. The New Man appears to be as much a victim of fashion and the designed look as the new women's narcissism. Jean Ash's (1989) article, "Tarting Up Men: Menswear and Gender Dynamics" presents a brief but insightful examination of the history of men's clothing claiming that the new clothes emerged in 1984/5, marketed for the Yuppie males who had the money and the desire to become an object of envy, hardly a rebellious posture and highly apolitical, i.e., men as spectacles.

Madonna's antics display quite well, i think, one expression of where Foucault's 'technologies of the self' can lead. Her re-signification of key cultural signifiers, not only the reversal of undergarments and wearing men's clothing, but re-significations of Church symbols such as the cross and the rosary, and the ambiguity of her good girl/bad girl image taken up by teenage "girlie culture," disrupt accepted cultural norms of feminine gender. Her morphing image is continually reconstructing itself to the point where Kaplan was refused to utilize a photograph of Madonna on the book's cover in fear that her identity would be fixed, once and for all.

Madonna's transvestism partakes in what Marjorie Garber (1992) in *Vested Interests* called a 'category crisis': "... a failure of definitional distinction, a borderline that becomes permeable, that permits border crossings from one (apparently distinct) category to another... The binarism male/female ... is itself put in question or under erasure in transvestism, and a transvestite figure, or a transvestite mode, will always function as a sign of overdetermination—a mechanism of displacement from one blurred boundary to another" (p. 16). Like Homi Bhabha (1990), Garber sees this hybrid category as a disruptive "third" term between binary positions that cannot be fixed, and whose meaning is always in flux. However transgressive Madonna's transvestism might be, her *sex* seems less malleable and subject to construction, perhaps because her past history was already shaped by a pornographic discourse (e.g., her earlier appearances in *Playboy* before she became a star), and her mimetic identification with leading Hollywood 'ladies,' quoting such famous stars as Marilyn Monroe, Jessica Lange, Judy Holiday, and Carole Lombard. Consequently, her claimed bi-sexuality (in her book, *Sex*) seems staged and unconvincing as a cultural disruption, while her "pederast" quotes (appearing as a little girl in various stages of undress in *Vogue*) were even more problematic, bringing disgost rather than shock to the sensibility of the Other. The ethics of such acts trade on the very limit of the psychic Law and the subsequent pleasure (*jouissance*) this transgression brings.

Perhaps the paradigmatic example of what Foucault means by 'technologies of self' is embodied by the figure of Michael Jackson, who is not only a 'work of art in progress' but seems to be *the* constructivist dream of such theorists as Judith Butler (1993) where *both* sex and gender seem malleable and subject to reversals and inversals. But is such a total construction 'truly' or 'really' possible? (see Grosz, 1994, 1995) Awkward (1995) identifies Jackson as being engaged in *transraciality*: a "mode of negotiating American racial boundaries which,... can be said potentially to highlight race's constructedness. ...[T]ransraciality as a mode of masquerade necessitates the radical revision of one's natural markings and the adoption of aspects of the human surface (especially skin, hair, and facial features) generally associated with the racial other" (p. 180). In other words, transracial 'texts' both challenge and clarify the arbitrariness of racial notions of essential difference. Apart from Jackson's straightened hair, which as Mercer (1990b) argues, is a "key 'ethnic signifier' because, compared with bodily shape or facial features, it can be changed more easily by cultural practises such as straightening" (p. 250); and apart from his "fortuitous" (and psychologically painful) affliction with the dermatological condition vitiligo which "whitens" his skin color, Michael Jackson's surgical interventions seem to 'feminize' his appearance to the point where the question of transsexuality becomes a possibility. But despite these cultural interventions, which seem like the ultimate anti-essentialist gestures, Awkward points out that there are times when Jackson returns to racial essentialism that is at odds with this conclusion. In an interview with Oprah Winfrey, Jackson makes it explicit that he is "proud to be a black American," and "proud of my race" (p.179). On another occasion he admits that he is a "slave to rhythm" (p.190) bringing to the surface all the nuanced meanings this sentence implies. What emerges is a form of essential deconstruction, the same ruse played by Luce Irigary, i.e., both essentialist and obviously socially constructed. Jackson must play "in and between" a discourse that was 'already there,' installed by the big Other before Jackson's 'birth.' Rather than repeating an Afrocentric discourse, he performs a mimetic intervention—or innovation which puts it to question. In this sense Judith Butler and Homi Bhabha's assertions regarding the disruptive potential of performance at the level of race and gender are in order. (Bhabha problemizes the forms of performative masquerades by pointing out that during the French colonial occupation of Algers, a number of Muslim women purposefully began to remove their veils so as to identify with their capturers in order to act as spies for the cause of Algerian nationalism.)

When it comes to sex, however, the term seems non-negotiable (cf. Shepherdson). Despite Jackson's effeminate speaking voice, long processed hair, make-up, eyeliner, and surgically feminized features that contribute to his *transsexual* image, there are enough contradictions within his own career that indicate an essential deconstruction at the level of sex is not "in progress." The most obvious 'performance' to observe here is the separation between Jackson's public/private life which has collapsed lately. In private Jackson appears to be a de-sexualized eunuch (unthreatening to racist White-male fantasies). Soft spoken and caring, Jackson comes across as *the* lover of children all over the world, living in his 'Never-never Land' mansion where the Peter Pan figure never wants to grow up—a case of arrested childhood (see Rose, 1984). On stage he presents the opposite image—a crotch-grabbing sexual object of excitement, full of macho gestures (pelvis thrusts and shirt rippings), exuding sexuality in his dancing while females faint over his stage eroticism. While it may be, following Butler's hypothesis, that the two selves of Jackson's personality present us with a 'gender confusion,' there seems to be no contradiction at the level of sex. When asked why the surgery was done, Jackson responded that he was trying to minimize his resemblance to his verbally and physically abusive father, Joseph Jackson (in Awkward, ft. 10, pg.217 as reported in Randy Taraborreli's biography, *Michael Jackson: The Magic and the Madness*). Whether this is 'true' or not, it seems that his oedipally driven efforts are a psychic flight to transcend his abusive father, rather than a flight towards becoming transformed into a 'woman.' And if Rose (1984) is correct regarding her psychoanalytic exposé of the Peter Pan fantasy, Michael Jackson continues to struggle against his Oedipalization. This is why the allegations over his pederasty with a twelve-year-old boy and the eventual settlement were so damaging to him physically (not to mention his career and public image). The attack was directed at the very structures of his own fantasy—the man-boy who identifies with children on the verge of adolescence who have not yet come to grips with their own Oedipalization, who live in a state of (seeming) virginal innocence. This is why Ann Powers in the *New York Times* can write: "his music has always communicated *sexuality*, but he has failed to confidently incorporate *sex* into his person" (in Awkward:189, my emphasis). His subsequent marriage to Lisa Marie Presley, which soon followed the child abuse incident, should come as no surprise. It was a reaffirmation to himself (and his fans) that he was after all, a 36-year-old virile "man." Nor should it be surprising what one of the most popular questions asked by his fans after the marriage: "do they sleep together?" Can Jackson consummate the marriage? (They are now divorced.)

Designer personae (Madonna), like plastic surgery (Jackson), seem to open only to very thin strata who are rich. However, there is no doubt that this is the tip of a larger floating iceberg. Felski (1989:126), for example, identifies yet another strand of feminist *Bildungsroman* which may be identified as a genre that overlaps both liberalist and social feminist emancipatory women's movements. The feminist *Bildungsroman* "is characterized by a historical and linear structure; female self-discovery and emancipation is depicted as a process of moving outward into the public realm of social engagement and activity, however problematic and fraught with difficulties this proves to be" (p.127). This genre is strongly represented through a realist feminist fiction. Its narrative model of history is progressive, emphasizing the activist and participatory dimensions of politics which are necessary for change in the public sphere.

All this is indicative of the emergence of a strong, middle-class woman —autonomous and independent—searching for her own pleasure (*Nine and a half Weeks, Desperately Seeking Susan*[12]), who wishes to share equal power with the male within the context of a late capitalist system. By and large the New Man and the New Woman are middle-to-upper class, mostly White, who occupy university positions, middle management or have executive capacities. Jameson (1984) argues that this aspect of the postmodern plays admirably into the post-Fordian capitalist information system.

Back To Orlan

Earlier in my journey, i mentioned how problematic working with the body in feminism might be. I mentioned the work of Orlan at this time (Fifth Vignette) as presenting perhaps the most problematic position possible.

436

What follows then is a synthetic moment of re-evaluation as this i now tries to speak to that I, back then. i had the good occasion to meet Orlan at the end of May, 1994 in Salzburg, Austria—during a symposium on the body related to an exhibition and symposium, *Suture - Phantasmen der Vollkommenheit* (Suture - Phantasms of Perfection) organized by Silvia Eiblmayr. Eiblmayr brought together artists and theoreticians to talk about the concept of "suture" and the changing, hybridized body in postmodern art. What i want to do is talk about the way the I experienced Orlan and what this says to me as a male caught in the field of vision when experiencing her as a personality. The symposium was late in beginning because Orlan had not yet showed up, so everyone waited ... nervously, in anticipation to "see" what she looked like. Finally she came, and i did all that i could do not to look or stare at her in any way: to glare at her or stare at her as if she were a "freak." The I was very conscious in trying to act normal within the confines of the seminar. Yet admittedly i kept trying to catch glimpses of her without being conspicuous. Two things struck me—first were her extraordinary sunglasses which provided a mask of impenetrability: they had studs in their rims; and second was her choice of heels which were high, but not stiletto. They had allusions to the clogs European women wore so as not to get their dresses caught in the mud. Whether she was quoting this through her choice of shoes, i could not say. She also wore a girdle—a very wide girdle that seemed to shrink her waste/waist. Ultimately, what i write here cannot possibility justify her description, which also included blond hair with a predominant accent of blue hair in the front. i could, from a distance, make out two protrusions or bulges along both sides of her temples.

Kaja Silverman began the symposium with an earlier paper on suture, Valie Export, a prominent German performance artist spoke next, followed by John Miller, an American artist interested in this same question. Then there was a break while everyone left for lunch. i stayed in the Hörsaal writing some of this text you are reading now. As the technicians were checking to see that all the media apparatuses were functioning (they were students at the university), they played with the mike (the males did) mimicking what Orlan was going to do with her talk, "I Have Given My Body to Art." Testing whether her video would function or not, her operation appeared on the screen, along with the sound. The video clip showed her temples being operated on—like any number of plastic surgical operations. Orlan was conscious and talking all the time. A model skull was placed on a television monitor in front of her bed; the procedure was recorded and broadcast to various intellectuals watching in various major cities throughout the world. The skull was a model for the insertion of what looked like four plastic inserts—two where the temples were and two on the cheek bones: hardly the "beauty operation" that i had commented upon earlier. The I tried looking at this video. How to face the rawness of the open body being cut during this interval, alone, with only a few people around? As the technicians played with the video, often it would stop and there came this sense of relief.

Eventually the symposium started again and Orlan came back to speak; she spoke in French—i tried to listen to the German translation with some success as my French has faded away. The video in all its rawness was playing as she spoke. I tried to look at this video; i tried the macho thing—this wasn't going to get to me; i tried distancing myself—but as she spoke i tried desperately not to look at her. There was this oscillation between her face and the screen as i scanned back and forth. The operation was so graphic that i began to get hot; as much as i tried facing the operation my body began to feel so hot that i took off my jacket. I knew that i was close to fainting—very close as the feeling of going limp came over me; thankfully the video shut off and i recovered—concentrating on the translation.[13]

Later, through forms of happenstance, i ended up having a small meal with her and some others. As i awkwardly tried to speak my awful French—with little success—the German kept getting in the way—i began to relax more and more with her presence; she did not consciously wish to pose a threat, but to be heard about her attempt to deal with the discourse of plastic cosmetics with its impulse to idealized beauty[14] and the difficulties that meant for feminism—not only the physical suffering, but what i feared most when i wrote about Orlan in that vignette: the insatiable desire of the media wanting to co-opt her body for themselves, i.e., the problematic that she had in fending herself from journalists and their misquotes which formulated their own fantasies as to what she was doing.

Orlan is a contested zone of feminist body politics. She is a postmodern hysteric, for it is her body which speaks. Her voice is disembodied. She speaks while she is operated upon, but it is a frenetic, nervous voice. She uses her body to encode and articulate psychic pain and psychic suffering. i could feel that suffering. i almost fainted. Yet, she has no desire to continue this brutalization on her body. It takes everything out of her to go through one of these operations. Orlan is perhaps the antithesis of the cult figure of Michael Jackson and Madonna who are representatives of the logic of late capitalism. As Eiblmayr (1994) says, " [Jackson] reflects the fundamental 'fantasies of totality' prevalent in Western society. The contrasts that social reality is based on, i.e., those of class, race, age and gender, seem to have been abolished in him" (p. 3). i think now of Orlan, at this moment, and i suffer for her and with her. It is a tormented body that must now negotiate between the seductions of appropriation and the convictions that what she is doing can make a critical difference. But there are no guarantees.

My son has also had his body disciplined by the institution of education. My performance in the appendix speaks to this utilizing Foucault's disciplinary regimes.

1 The variety of feminist interpretations may be found in the edited edition *Feminism & Foucault: Reflections on Resistance* (1988) by Irene Diamond and Lee Quinby. Such an earlier collection of feminist positions can be compared with Caroline Ramazanoglu's (ed.) *Up Against Foucault* (1993) which presents a similar uneven reception of Foucault by feminists five years later. See also footnote 13 in "The Pornography Debates."

2 i want to alert the reader to my use of "repression" (*verdrängung*) here which is more in keeping with the split subject. Where a distinction is made between it and foreclosure (*Verwerfung*) where the Real is primordially repressed (*ur-verdrängt*). The Real as Thing is a repression which is not a historical variable but constitutes symbolic historicity (Žižek, 1994c:199, original emphasis). Foucault would claim that which is repressed is shaped by the psychiatric discourse. He sociologizes repression. In other words, for Foucault the power/knowledge couplet is neither ontological nor epistemological; rather an historical construction of the concept. So whereas power for Marcuse would be repression, that is, as a neo-Marxist he sees power as a negative force used to dominate, coerce, manipulate, insert authority, Foucault, the Nietzschean ,wants to produce positive and negative effects. Staying with a negative sense of power leads to concepts like false consciousness and the critique of ideology whereby it is possible to gain a way of thinking non-ideologically and possess a true authentic consciousness. Foucault sees this a wrong-minded. Foucault is a nominalist concerning power. Like the Lacanian notion of the phallus or the gaze, power "does not exist," only site/sight/cite specific exercises of it are 'real'. Power in this sense is not a property, possessed by a dominant class or given as a privilege; rather it is a strategy that spreads throughout a social system. This is where i personally get off the Foucaultian band-wagon. i would rather follow the repression hypothesis in the sense that it is possible to locate power more specifically in an empirical inquiry as to exactly who exercises power over whom. Hoy (1986b:135) provides a useful analogy for my difference. For Foucault, the capturing of any piece in a chess game, as an example of 'micro-power,' depends upon the over-all arrangement of the pieces at any given time, as well as the strategy that leads up to and including the capturing of a piece. Power relationships in this sense are ubiquitous and changing all the time. The capturing of any one piece is therefore an expression of power where one piece takes another piece (dominates). But there is a possible resistance to being captured. Perhaps this might be named as a tactic (cf. de Certeau). This exercise of power does not have to be taken. Opportunities are sometimes delayed for future gains, or simply left overlooked, except for the possibility of a check-mate. The problem with Foucault's model is that it is not empirical enough and hence power /knowledge couplet can become vacuous. Without some assessment of repression at an empirical level, progress has no meaning. One power/ knowledge configuration is relation with another. The question of human(e) freedom is left unanswered. It should be remembered that there is a king and queen on the chessboard and some pieces can move more "freely" than others. Freedom remains both the condition and the effect of power, and life is often more than just a 'game'. Perhaps the singularity of an *event* can disrupt the game. See John Rajchman (1991) who has compared the differences between Foucault and Lacan views of ethics points out their differences when theorizing the subject. Whereas Lacan, following Freud posits the Real, a non-discursive realm that insists on an external psychic Law, Foucault does away with this making 'techne' or 'being used' central to his ethics (see Golding, 1995). The law remains internal and historical; pleasure is pitted against desire. i would argue that Foucault's aestheticization of ethics is still embedded within a humanist-elitist individualistic tradition of mastering the 'uses of pleasure.' The subject has to invent the self by harmonizing and self-mediating the antagonistic forces within one's self, thereby creating an image of the self and finding one's own art of living. This is why marginal lifestyles, like the S/M homosexual practices, fascinated him (Žižek, 1989a:2; Copjec, 1994a).

3 i pick this discussion up in Male Hysteria, the next to the last vignette.

4 A recent attempt has begun to chart this is the *Zone* series 3,4 and 5 under the editorship of Michel Feher: *Fragments for a History of the Human Body* (1989).

5 Hennessy's critique of Foucault is his missing politics. "Although Foucault's notion of discursive practice situates discourse in a social field, because that social field is conceptualized in terms of a logic in which one force merely asserts its difference from another, the relation between social conflict and the

discourses that construct meaning can only be vaguely formulated as local tensions within and between discursive practices" (p.42).

6 The implications of this assumption are discussed from a cross-cultural comparative basis as well as the Greek context by Hodge and Kress's 7th Chapter, "Transformations of Love and Power: The Social Meaning of Narrative," in their *Social Semiotics*, 1988.

7 For a deconstructivist philosopher of the law, like Drucilla Cornell (1991, 1992) Foucault doesn't even appear in her index. For someone with such a command of theory, this certainly is not an oversight but perhaps a recognition of his under-theorization of the subject.

8 Angela McRobbie and Jenny Garber (1975) have done a similar analysis on girls. (See also McRobbie, 1980; McRobbie and Nava, 1984).

9 Silverman (1986) develops the great sartorial refusal by men during the industrial revolution with the subsequent spectatorial "burden" carried by women.

10 It might be noted that this is the same argument Showalter (1987) used in her 'cross-dressing' article; and it is worth pointing out, as Owens does (1987:222), that both Gilbert and Showalter, in supporting Stoller's research who regards homosexuality as a gender disorder, are polarizing gay men and women. Gilbert alludes to such a disclaimer when she mentions that the transsexual may be Other than the transvestite (p.397). i believe she is careful in differentiating this phallic woman from painting all gays with the same brush. Stoller claimed that the transvestite converted his original humiliation of being denied his masculinity, which often occured before the Oedipal phase when he was treated as a little girl by his dominant mother or older more powerful sister. Dressing up as a woman was his way of psycho-logically overcoming this repressed humiliation by showing that he can he a 'better' woman than a woman herself.

11 This comes from the anti-Oedipal musings of Deleuze and Guattari that will be discussed later in this journey. In contrast to a phallocentric libidinal economy which is hierarchical and fixed, the rhizomatic economy is" multi-branched, interconnected dynamic economy of associations" (Radner, 1989:301).

12 See Jackie Stacey's (1989) review of this movie in the context of the female gaze, women looking at women. At the end of the film she says "Roberta's [played by Rosanna Arquette] desire to become more like her ideal [Susan-played by Madonna]—a more pleasing co-ordinated, complete and attractive fem-inine image—is offered temporary narrative fulfillment. However, the pleasures of this difference and otherness cannot be collapsed into simple identification, since difference and otherness are continually played upon, even when Roberta 'becomes' her idealized object" (p. 129).

13 Approximately two years later i came across Parveen Adams (1996) psychoanalytic exposé of Orlan's *Omnipresence*. As a keynote speaker for the conference she had witnessed the same operation as I had. Her analysis reconfirmed the horror i felt and provided a theoretical justification for it. Adams reads Orlan's *cosmimetic* operation as an anamorphic distortion which disturbs the inside/outside isomorphism of normal centered perception. During the operation her face is literally detached from her head, as a gap or abyss opens up behind her curled ear by the cut of the scalpel. This immediately destroys a viewer's normal narcissistic fantasy that the face "represents" something. Such a facial detachment reveals a pure exteriority with no signifying interior to be discovered. In this newly created space, when her face becomes "unmade," a horrifying moment opens up which I could not "bear" to look at. It almost made me pass out. Such a new space is created when "there is an emptying out of the object" (p.154), which means "that the structure of representation has collapsed" (p.156). I found myself unhinged by a spatial gap which was no longer organized by isomorphism but by a sudden realization that there was "noth-ing" behind her facial mask.

14 The film, *Death Becomes Her*, with Goldie Hawn and Marilyn Streep is a spoof on this very question.

THE SIXTH VIGNETTE

Deconstructive Contortions

Is the position of men to feminism marginal, an individualism? I think it is, and at best, despite the difficulties of the terms; not meaning by that to exclude shared actions and relations, simply saying that feminism has decentered men, something else they must learn, and that means that there is no simple position, only a shifting marginal-ism, a new individualism in the sense that collective identity of man is no longer available (no longer available once you listen and respond to feminism).

(Heath, 1987:24)

For the past eight years i have been fortunate enough to teach a graduate seminar course entitled 'Gender and the Curriculum' (which has changed its title to "Postmodernism: Gender, Culture and the Curriculum" in 1991-1992). With the help of caring and concerned students, their questioning has fueled my own energy to continue examining my own relation to the feminist discourse. Yet on one of those occasions, the seminar was, to my mind, a complete disaster. To explain why would take some doing. Every time the I initiates this course i have deep pangs of doubt. Should a woman be teaching this course, rather than me? I am haunted by Moore's (1988) daunting critique of Barthes and Baudrillard—am i just another "a pimp of postmodernism?" Am i treading in forbidden waters?

Much of the material written in education from a feminist perspective falls under the liberalist rubric, although there are emerging exceptions. In 1989 the reader could be referred to only one reference in feminist post-structuralism—the Australian Bronwyn Davies.[1] Phenomenological-existentialist applications held the field (see Grumet,1988) and, of course the area of critical theory has been explored (see Katheleen Weiler,1988). Other names might be proliferated here to identify the network of defined bodies of knowledge but that has masterfully been done by Pinar et al. (1995). Those who will chronicle such names will form the mythological canon for the next generation who reads it. Within the liberalist discourse, then, Bern (1983) is known for her reputed attempts at raising "aschematic children," children with androgynous modal personalities. Bern is just the tip of the iceberg, if what floats underneath is envisioned as liberalism. In my course, many concerns stated in this text have been redirected from an artistic discourse to an educational one. It is not my intent, in this vignette, to rehearse the feminist discourses in curriculum theory. i'm sure such a book is being written or already finished within the confines of a doctoral thesis.[2] Recognizably, the amount of men writing in this area are far and between. Nevertheless, several men writing in the area of feminism and its applications to education may be found in the *Journal of Curriculum Theorizing*, where the early essays by Bill Pinar (1983), Peter Taubman (1982), James Sears (1985), and Jesse Goodman (1985) have introduced a gendered male discourse. Both Pinar and Sears have raised the issue of male homosexuality: the need to deal with the traditional masculine role of the authoritarian teacher in the school. Pinar's recently published essays *Autobiography, Politics and Sexuality* (1994) show clearly his early involvement and leadership in theorizing sexual politics of the school curriculum. Perhaps, not surprisingly, as a male heterosexual, the homosexual and lesbian discourses in education did not have my full attention, which they should have.[3] It seemed in my case, it was necessary to know the various praxiological positions of feminism, so well reviewed by Tong (1989),[4] so that a broad spectrum of positions could be introduced into this course. The I stayed away from opening up the discussion in any sort of depth, other than mentioning 'non-man and non-woman' positions did exist. i didn't "no" a way into the complexity of these positions.

In *Men in Feminism*, it is Craig Owens who shatters the underlying heterosexual unity of the previous essays, taking Showalter's exemplary essay to task, providing a defense for an entire different representation of homosexuality. In the artistic literature, this is a perspective which has been kept out of the frame of art history. The artist is almost always represented as the archetypal masculine personality: egomaniacal posturing, over-identified with sexual prowess, sacrificing everything and everyone for something called his art. Van Gogh's madness is played up, his homoerotic desire for Gauguin rarely mentioned (Bradley Collins, 1988). The temperament of the male gaze to that of forcing the position of viewing across the boundary of the woman's gaze has hardly begun to take place. The most outstanding works on homosexuality and art, such as those in Saslow's (1986) study of *Ganymede,* are not informed by a psychoanalytic discourse but rely on conventional criticism. Feminists have been far more successful in pointing out a lesbo-erotic love amongst women and the potential of a women's culture then men. Adrienne Rich, for instance, calls for the desexualization of the categories "woman" and "man" and "homosexual" as a 'lesbian continuum.' Craig Owens (1992) and Douglas Crimp (1987, 1988) are probably the best-known critics writing in the area of gay criticism. Crimp's activism to make art into a socially relevant cultural practice in the struggle to transcend the AIDS epidemic is exemplary. Recently, the *Village Voice* carried a story by Carr (1990) on the struggle with AIDS by the New York artist David Wojnarowicz, himself not only a "victim" of AIDS,[5] but with an entire list of horror stories ranging from child abuse, hustling through to almost being killed. In contrast, male heterosexual critics have not done work on themselves. The connection between sexuality and art is there for exposure.

As discussed earlier, lesbian writers have been sensitive to their exclusion, to *indifference* as de Lauretis (1987a;1988) claims. In 'The Straight Mind' Wittig (1980) argues that "lesbians are not women... it would be incorrect to say that lesbians associate, make love, live with women, for 'woman' has meaning only in heterosexual system of thought and heterosexual economic systems" (p. 110). Her Nietzschean characterization of a feminist who is masculine and (in this case) misogynistic in a perverse way, a Second Woman, by Nietzsche's count, is the one who has no need or use of the phallus; who implicitly critiques the entire Lacan psychoanalytic system as phallic centered, speculogic and heterosexual in its gender formulations. It appears that the binary couplet man/woman is best deconstructed from the position of this *negative* Oedipal position. But there are yet other possibilities which will be discussed below.

In an important speculative essay, Heather Findlay (1986) argues that Derrida's dismissal of Nietszche's second (lesbian) woman, because she is unable to challenge patriarchy, is quite mistaken. Findlay claims that the *specificity* of the lesbian woman exists in the *second stage* of Derridean deconstruction. Derrida's first stage or space, as specified in his *Positions* (1981) interview, is to identify the binary oppositions that operate in the discourse to be deconstructed. The *second* movement is to overturn this hierarchy in the given moment, and the third movement is then to dismantle the opposition by showing the dependency of one term upon the other. This third movement is gendered as bisexual. The first movement is gendered as presence, phallocentric, whereas the second movement is split. As lesbian, the 'second' woman is doubled. She is both same and other. In the third stage, the deconstructed text produces a 'bifurcated' writing—Derridean undecidables (i.e., dissemination, the trace, invagination, the gram, the supplement) and the 'affirmative,' bisexual, or is it polysexual woman? Findlay claims that this last phase de-politicizes his discourse, and it is yet another form of heterosexuality. The third woman's theoretical success occurs at the expense of the second woman, and polysexuality excludes lesbian specificity. Findlay goes on to show how Wittig's *Lesbian Body* is claimed as an exemplar of the second woman who is "stuck" in the phase of inversion (Derrida's second phase), yet escapes being appropriated by phallocentric discourses and the "truth of castration" which Derrida claims "she" is implicated in.[6]

Unlike lesbianism, which has gained holistic politicization under "women's culture," homosexuality has been formed by a different discourse (Taubman, 1982). Medical, psychiatric, and psychological discourses have represented homosexuals as perverts, cruisers, or wimps. Historically they have been subsumed under the traits of a woman—as pansies, fairies, queens—narcissistic, vain, hypersensitive, fragile, fearing old. For the heterosexual imagination, the voyeurism of lesbianism is more palatable/palette-able than the eroticism associated with homosexuality. Homosexuality plays on the border of man and non-man (same and other), but unlike women's love, homosexuality is sexually charged as sex between men. A gay-life-style is now firmly linked with cruising and AIDS in the popular imagination.

A radical homosexuality discourse exists which tries to show that homosexuality is a social construct.[7] It may well be that a discursive formation must begin to evolve around male homo-erotic love if another image of

444

the 'male' is to emerge.[8] There is, for example, the disavowal within the gay community that homosexuality is necessarily an essential or natural way of being. The author's stance in the edited work by Plummer (1981) is entirely Foucaultian. The "modern homosexual subject" has been produced discursively, *not naturally*, across a whole range of discourses. Fuss (1989:108) outlines the various theories which have tried to locate historically the construction of the homosexual subject. Contending narratives situate the site/sight/cite in the 17th century; others claim the 18th century with the rise of industrial capitalism to be the critical period, while Foucault laid claim to the 19th century with the "professionalization of medicine and the social organization of sexual types."

The problems with constructivist theories, like those of Jeffery Weeks (1985), avoid issues of homophobia and are dismissive of psychoanalysis as simply a part of the heterosexist hegemony. Diana Fuss argues that this weakens his case. Her point is that homosexuality, as a form of 'identity politics,' must be seen as a moment within heterosexuality. Weeks (1989), while still supportive of an identity politics, has continued to avoid playing the Oedipal game. In 1978, Weeks had written an introduction to Hocquenghem's book, *Homosexual Desire (1972),* whose theoretical roots lay in the anti-Oedipal theories of Deleuze and Guattari (1983).[9] Weeks has not forgotten the possibility of separating 'desire' from a "subject position that is [in] identification with a particular social position and organizing sense of self" (p.44). Identity politics takes on agency and *choice* rather than being confined to sexual preference alone, and foremost to the discourses of sexologists. In other words, Weeks does not want to get caught in this field of vision but continues to side-step it. Weeks is trying to redirect the discourse of homosexuality from one based on the exclusive fixation on sexual practices, which may be varied just like the heterosexual community—from promiscuity to partners for life— to that of brotherhood. Weeks thus tried to emulate the lesbian discourse, where at one time sisterhood, solidarity and affection formed their culture free of men; so as to "weeken" the causal link between sexual practice and sexual identity, if you will excuse the pun. Weeks' position is close to Foucault's 'new eroticism.' He raises the need for the quality of relations amongst men. Not all 'sexual identities' are of equal value. He calls for a 'relationship paradigm' where there is 'quality of involvement' and the freedom of relationships; in so doing he himself recognizes that identity must remain a 'fiction.'

Teresa de Lauretis (1988), like Weeks, has mapped out the "critical efforts [of lesbian writers and artists] to dislodge the erotic from the discourse of gender" (p.159), but it appears a highly paradoxical task to maintain two senses of homosexuality and *hom(m)o*-sexuality;[10] the former term keeps collapsing into the latter one, creating sexual (in)difference (cf. Irigaray). de Lauretis' review attempts to show how lesbian writers escape gender (i.e., the effeminate man and the mannish woman) by "disguis[ing] erotic and sexual experience so as to suppress any representation of its specificity"(ibid). Unfortunately such a tactic is often *not* successful. The opposite view, to embrace gender by entering the male world as a lesbian in male body drag (butch-femme) as a form of "reverse discourse," is certainly an assertion of sexual agency and feelings, but it too does *not* escape in separating sex and gender as "distinct areas of social practice," and as Butler (1990) would have it. Representational contexts remain difficult to identify and theorize. A woman either passes as a lesbian or straight unless she is seen "*as or with* a lesbian in male body drag" (p.177). Teresa de Lauretis is more impassioned with Wittig's work, claiming that her text(s) *do* go beyond gender, positing the theoretical space of neither man nor woman, but then again it must be asked (cf. Diana Fuss) whether Wittig's "lesbian body" is as much a fiction as the "heterosexual body" existing in an ahistorical space—an overstated fictitious subject. i have come to the conclusion in my text that it is.

Deleuze and Guattari's Postmodern Desiring Machines

Weeks' refusal to play the Oedipal game, and his attempt to escape the trapping of gender, is part of a strategy of the late '60s when Hocquenghem wrote his defence of homosexual desire borrowing heavily from Deleuze and Guattari. What is striking about their work is that they provide an entirely contradictory discourse to that of Lacan which is repeated endlessly in feminist journals. Their appeal has been in their historization of desire. The recent wrath of articles concerning the various positionalities of the gaze in popular culture as was discussed in a previous vignette, drew me to conclude that Deleuze and Guattari's initial insights are more pertinent to theorizing late capitalism—designer identities if you like—rather than the neo-Freudian, object relations theories and Lacanian theorizations about the split. It has often been remarked throughout my text that the family has changed in the late capitalist mode of production. No psychoanalytic theory, not even post-Lacanians, has managed to re-theorize what this means for desire. Deleuze and Guattari provide one such attempt. Here we have a fragmented subject as it were, but that subject is perceived as an 'assemblage,' a montage of cathected others.[11]

Deleuze and Guattari[12] (1983) are interesting in the sense that their works directly relate to feminist discourse, especially since for them desire holds no 'lack.' In their words: "The Women's Liberation movements are correct in saying: We are not castrated, so you get fucked" (p. 61). Further, because they "denaturalize bodies" and sexuality, especially its polarized genders, it provides another possibility to theorize lesbian and homosexual desire. In their argument, Oedipalization belongs to the capitalist mode of production, hardly a universal form. It marks the latest of three "territorializations" of desire within a historical civilized or capitalist socious (community); the other two being primitive or tribal socious and barbarian or despotic socious. Desire is postulated as a material libidinal flow, "molecular," a *hylé* (p.36). As a continuous flux "it" is 'interrupted' by bodily 'machinations,' which cut and divide "it" into partial objects below the level of language. Molecular flow becomes 'molar.' In this sense, homosexual desire is subject to the "abyss of nonpersonalised and uncodified desire ... desire as the plugging in of organs subject to no rule or law" (Hocquenghem, 1978:81). Desire is created by the id. It is grounded in the Real; therefore its foundations are material.[13] We, you, (I)(i) are all 'desiring-machines' in a 'machined' or 'machinist' discourse.

Deleuze and Guattari's are *not* introducing a 17th century machine metaphor here, but a way to characterize the functioning of the Unconscious, and a way to avoid the representational discourse of the Oedipal tragedy; to jolt us out of our bourgeois centered I. "Machine" has yet another meaning. Because it is pre-personal (pre-Oedipal), it becomes a metaphor for the Unconscious. It is an assemblage (montage would be better) "made up of moving parts that have a capacity to form new machines with other parts, it can dissolve these connections to form other productive connections." This 'molecular force' is then the workings of the unconscious. Its basic function is to *produce* desire. Against the 'lack' of an object, desire is in search of a subject since it "exists before the opposition between subject and object, before representation and production" (p.57).

Deleuze and Guattari critique Freud and Lacan's universal Oedipalism—the idea that all phenomena of the Unconscious are reduced to a triad: mother-father-baby (girl/boy)---as being reductive. The reliance on incestuous sexual desire of the 'natural family' is what's at issue. For them, there is no inherent incestuous desire or fear of castration. This is confined to the bourgeoisie family of capitalism. The Unconscious, rather, is a collective public experience—a group fantasy. To avoid the familial complex, Deleuze and Guattari argue that the mother and father exist only as fragments, parts in a constellation with a myriad of agents which break up that initial triangulation. They view the family as decentered, interrupted by current political and historical events that are the register of the Unconscious as dreams; therefore the Unconscious registers the events of the political and historical period. Their theory is more compatible with the decentered family today. No wonder Foucault wrote an introduction to their book.

Kathy Myers (1984), in her review of the various contending conceptualizations of desire, teases out their opposition to Lacan. If the theoretical psychoanalytic discourse were to shift over to anti-oedipal orientation, radical potential is given over to desire. Rather than a lack, its capacity is "to sweep over outmoded institutions such as family, monogamy, heterosexual compulsion" (p. 37). To "deterritorize" them.[14] Being a drive, rather than a finite object or experience, means that desire must be managed, checked, regulated and is done so through the repression of violence in the Oedipalized family structure. Deleuze and Guattari conclude their book by making a distinction between two types of desiring machines which are the two poles of desire in general. The first is a reactionary paranoia machine whose essential operation is to fix and stratify the flows of desire; the other is a revolutionary schizo machine which intensifies the flow and generates a process of psychic deterritorialization.

Rather than the Name of the Father of Lacanian analysis, Deleuze and Guattari posit a history of names (p.86). The fragmented I is hypothesized as a complex of forces that "determine persons as so many intensive states" which are registered on the *body* as *effects* through proper names. Such names are not holistic representations but the "effects" of specific states of parts of races, cultures and gods. i imagine them seen as a collaged individual of multiple identifications; almost a pastiche of bits of meanings (*signs*) gleaned from this history of names, carefully juxtaposed for overall effect, always in process like a multi-perspective postmodern self-portrait composed of collaged parts of the self (see Kearny, 1988:14). It is the schizophrenic, not the child or the primitive, which best exemplifies such conceptualization. Split personalities and identification with particular celebrities, subject to hearing voices and receiving messages from God, for instance, are the hallmarks of the schizophrenic disorder. Paradoxically, for them, this is the unconscious norm. The schizophrenic is both anti-social as well as social at the same time. Such a description seems to identify the postmodern artist living on the borderlines, capable of transgression (criminal behavior?) and accommodating to the situation; living in the Lacanian Symbolic, yet not being completely swallowed up by it. Boundaries are there only to be transgressed.[15] Codes are continually reversed. And, significantly in terms of this study, the schizophrenic's body is experienced as ambiguously gendered.

Hal Foster (1985:176-178) draws on Deleuze and Guattari's concept of the *minor*. "A minor literature is not the literature of a minor language but the literature a minority makes in a major language" (Deleuze and Guattari in Foster, note 45, p. 228). Such cultural practice is said to be "an intensive, often vernacular use of a language or a form which disrupts its official or institutional functions" (p.177). It is collective in its form, a mishmash that calls for deterritorialization. The minor connects itself to minor practices in the past, thus becoming 'untimely' and disruptive. Foster points to reggae, surrealist Latin American fiction, Black gospel, and i suppose one could include rap. Such practices are not "marginal" as in opposition to the central discourse; they simply refuse to believe major culture. There are many novels and films which play off this same fluctuation, which might be perceived as *minor*. Four movies come to mind: *House of Games, Blade Runner, Kiss of the Spider Woman,* and *Blue Velvet*. Although perhaps not in the calibre of the writings of Kafka, a paradigm example of a minor cultural practice for Deleuze and Guattari, each of the above-mentioned films questions and deconstructs the limits of a particular sign. *The Kiss of the Spider Woman* deconstructs masculinity; *Blade Runner* puts to question the boundary between artificiality and life; *House of Games* presents us with the dilemma as to who 'understands' human nature better—a psychoanalyst (the legitimated societal representative of the psyche) or a 'confidence man,' who operates outside the law; lastly, *Blue Velvet* plays with many binary oppositions, questioning voyeurism and taking us into the world of our primary fantasies. Life in each text is led somewhere between tragedy and comedy. As in many postmodern fictions, a well-known genre is rewritten to present the text in an entirely novel form. The detective story serves as a backdrop for *Blue Velvet* and *Blade Runner* while *House of Games* is a reflective journal told by the protagonist. Yet, in each case, ontological questioning becomes the dominant in contrast to the epistemology of modernism (McHale, 1987). New "worlds" are created and the boundaries between them are violated as in the recent movie *Alien Nation*, its title playing with the double meaning of the text's message, questioning how to live with the alien Other.

An ambitious attempt to apply Deluzean and Guattarian concepts to cinema comes from Steven Shaviro's *Cinematic Body* (1993). In his chapter, "Masculinity, Spectacle, and the Body of *Querelle*", Shaviro turns to Fassbinder, like Silverman, to write gay male eroticism. For Deleuze (1972:78), *all desire is homosexual* (Shaviro, 74) and *Querelle* is the right film for such an assessment for its anti-bourgeois sentiments regarding sex. Fassbinder aestheticizes "the most troubling moments of his narrative, those when male sexuality is explicitly associated with power and domination, with violence, and with death" (p.159). There is no redemption in this film. It is a film which presents all the ambivalences and transgressive sexuality that has nothing to do with liberation nor transcendence, but "abjection, denial, and ultimately murder" (p.160). Unlike Silverman (1992), who reads Fassbinder in Lacanian terms, Shaviro wants to go back to the mirror image that is so characteristic of Fassbinder, and spin the doubled image that is produced towards infinity. In other words, Fassbinder wants endless duplication and doubling, as if one were standing in front of a mirror, angled on either side, which splits the viewer in so many duplications. Each image rebounding in the mirror, incorporating the traces of the gazes that it attracts. Shaviro has a different description: "It is as if our eyeballs were turned inside out, as if the virtual images in our retinas were themselves exteriorized and imprinted on the screen, alongside the images that originally stimulated them. To look at an image is to lose oneself within it, to be oneself transformed into an image" (p.168).

Such postmodern antics of fiction are more compatible with anti-oedipal readings of the body. Unconscious meanings are meanings worked on the body, not images or signifieds of an inner mental state or stage, but as a 'thinking body.' Deleuze's schizodynamic of the body follows Artaud. It is a 'body without organs.' By this Deleuze and Guattari mean that we experience our bodies non-organically, although bodies are perceived to be organic totalities.[16] "The unconscious is a desiring-machine and the body parts, components of that machine" (Theweleit, 1987:211). A quote from Jessica Benjamin(1986) seems appropriate here since she repeats current psychoanalytic discourse:

> The mode of representing intrapsychic events, the symbolic use of the body that psychoanalysis discovered, does not distinguish between real and imagined, inside and outside, introjective-projective processes and interaction. It does not distinguish between you as an independently existing subject and you as a fantasy extension of my wishes and desires (p.92).

The above difficult passage in Deleuze and Guattari's paradigm can be best understood in the following way: "First, 'figures' are recorded on the surface of bodies which correspond to the part objects (anus, the breast, the penis) of desiring-machines themselves" (Lash, 1984:10). These should be cathected literally, as a real and material investment, rather than metonymi-

450

cally as a part of a larger whole. This is the productive mode of the unconscious. The child experiences various parts of the mother's body, but not her
as a *whole* person. Second, 'figures' are recorded from the outside world on
the body. There is a real and material investment of the libido in significant
parts of Others. Machinic production is therefore formed by joining part to
parts, which are then later dissolved. Thirdly, 'the decentered subject' "serially
identifies with a number of real and historic subjects in whom psychic energy
is invested" (ibid.), as mentioned above. These internalized subjects are 'phantasms,' not constituted by language but by 'intensities of difference.' Lastly are
the body's sense organs which should be perceived as confronting art similarly to the way a hysteric perceives his or her body. "This means that for
example when we listen to music, the ear should be distorted to take the shape
of a 'polyvalent organ' which not only hears but sees and feels" (ibid.).

As admirably exemplified by Coward's (1985) examination of manufactured female desire, this libidinal economy has been historically repressed
in the interests of state politics, coercion and patriarchal interest. But have
they now been released with the new narcissism? As 'desiring machines' in a
capitalist society, Deleuze and Guattari argue that sexual and political economy have become one and the same thing. We consume symbols and codes
to fulfill our desires, to close the gap between the subject and object. If one
were to link these anti-oedipal theorizations with the social imaginary as they
are at play in the various institutions through a theory of seduction, such as
Baudrillard's (see Burchill,1984), fact and fantasy begin to blend together.
What is "real" and what is original are subsumed as simulacra. It is the code,
the symbol, the mark that is desired. There is no lack—merely an over-aes-
theticization of society. In this gambit, then, the North American late capital
commodity fetishism has closed the gap between art as entertainment and
everyday life once and for all. This is a Baudrillardian world.

Deleuze and Guattari's anti-oedipal insights have been applied in
the works of Klaus Theweleit's *Male Fantasies* (1987), which is a materialist
account of fascist fantasy. Theweleit outlines why Freudian Oedipal theories
fail to explain the fascistic fantasy because the Freudian discourse is confined
to "clearly defined boundaries and names" (Theweleit, 1987: p.205). The fascistic fantasy wants something more than mere incest "which is a relationship
involving persons, names and families. They want to wade in blood; they want
an intoxicant that will 'cause both sight and hearing to fade away.' They want
a contact with the opposite sex—or perhaps simply access to sexuality itself—
which cannot be *named,* a contact they can dissolve themselves while forcibly
dissolving the other sex. ...they have a desire for incest, it is, at the very least,
with the earth itself ('Mother Earth').... Here we are faced with something

that cannot be subsumed under the heading of 'Incest,' or the concept of 'object relations' (p. 207). Following Delueze and Guattari, the symbolism that appears in fascist textual analysis goes beyond person-to-person object relations.

Theweleit identifies the pre-Oedipal period, pre-linguistic period when the ego is not yet developed. These men are psychotic; they cannot yet name themselves. Theweleit goes on to explain that the discourse of their autobiographies does not repress incestuousness nor castration. "[I]n situating the real and fantasized bodies of women as the channels through which all desires of the 'soldier males' are to made to flow—Theweleit invests femininity with a fullness which it cannot attain within the Freud-Lacanian organization of culture around the law of the phallus" (Carter and Turner, 1986:205).

Hocquenghem's *Homosexual Desire* (1978/1972/1993) offers the reader a developed radical homosexuality, which relies heavily on this anti-oedipal stance. Although his arguments are numerous, it might be briefly pointed out that desire for him is a promiscuity freed from guilt. As the homosexual frees himself from guilt he becomes like the schizophrenic in Deleuze and Guattari's work. He has a revolutionary potential. There is also a historical argument made by Hocquenghem that the homosexual as a identifiable fugitive is only 'discovered' during the 19th century with the rise of capitalism. Bill Pinar (1983) has taken some of Hocquenghem's ideas and applied them to school curriculum, arguing for its de-oedipalization so that resistance and patriarchy would not be reproduced. "Exposing its oedipal ties and functions suggests another moment coming, one in which we sons and fathers work to become brothers and lovers" (p.48). What Pinar suggests is too radical to be put into practice, although i am told, there is a school in New York, N.Y. only for gays. Similar to Adrienne Rich, Pinar's ruse is to suggest a male culture which would help destabilize the centrality of the Phallic signifier. Because of the current heterosexual/ homosexual divide, such a possibility seems almost inconceivable. "Homosexuals are often embarrassed over the relative prominence of sadomasochistic sexuality in gay life, not realizing that they only act out concretely and privately what 'straight' men do to each other abstractly in the public domain. In schools, as in homes and offices, men get women to do their dirty work" (p.48). Bill Pinar's condemnation and radical suggestions are less than a hush in curricular circles. Theweleit and Hocquenghem's studies which employ the anti-Oedipus thesis present the difficult case when the Father-of-enjoyment (primal Father) is released as the psychic presider, and a narcissistic self is allowed to run amuck without control—rather the control is redirected onto the body as parts. The critique by the Lacanian Slavoj Žižek of Deleuze and Guattari is precisely the danger as what a schizo transgressive anti-Oedipal psychoanalysis releases—an unremmiting *jouissance* without ethical checks, as in Nazism and in Hocquenghem's case—unbridled sex. "What Deleuze and Guattari fail to take into account is that the most powerful anti-Oedipus is *Oedipus itself*: the Oedipal father—father reigning as his Name, as the agent of symbolic law—is necessarily redoubled in itself, it can exert its authority only by relying on the superego figure of the Father-of-Enjoyment" (1991:24). But, if Linda Singer (1993) is right in her assessment, late capitalism is a time that the psychic hold of the Father-of-Enjoyment is breaking down, causing "moral panic" with yet a further commodification of sex and addiction. Shaviro's (1993) 'cinematic body' hypothesis also supports such a possibility. The screen image offers a cornucopia of "materially open bodies" ready for consumption in whatever "part" we so desire. Deleuze and Guattari present late capitalism's psychic symptoms which historically repeat a similar psychic breakdown during the *fin de siècle*. Freud's psychoanalytic foundation was to be inherited by Wilhelm Reich, who was advocating a similar release of sexual pleasure and enjoyment of the body orgasm in America before controversies began to emerge.

A recent film, *The Road to Wellville* (1994), written and directed by Alan Parker, provides a parody of this possibility. From the perspective of a queer reading, the film appears to exemplify the issues raised in this and the previous vignette concerning Foucault's 'technologies of the self.' Set in 19th century America, during its capitalist *electric* industrialization, the European psychiatric sanitarium has been transformed into a health spa cum-grand-hotel-cum-hospital-cum-religious cathedral ('the Temple of Health') called The Battle Creek Sanitarium, affectionately known as the 'San,' where the wealthy come to take the "cure." Located in a fashionable city ('The Cereal Bowl of the World') somewhere on the east coast (Boston, in all probability, judging from the references to Bluepoint oysters and Beacon Hill, e.g.,'Be a beacon of good health'), this is where the good doctor John Howard Kellogg (played by Anthony Hopkins), as its "head" and high priest, preaches his philosophy: not only to his guest-patients but to a flock of trained nun-like matron nurses who lean on his every word. The "cereal philosophy" that he preaches is like pablum for the rich, both metaphorically and literally. The allusions to baby food and soiled diapers are vividly present, for the good doctor is anally fixated. He is an expert on stools and bowels. Paradigmatically he exhibits Deleuze's claim: "all desire is homosexual" (the opening scene has the good doctor sitting on a "toilet-like" chair, which turns out to be an exercise machine, answering to journalist's questions about his methods). As a cure he offers his patients a vegetarian diet (a steady diet of "Kellogg corn-flakes" which he had invented, but whom his brother, W. K. Kellogg has developed into an enterprise using the family name), abstinence from sex (masturbation, 'the sin of Onans,' is strictly forbidden—'an erection is a flag-pole on your grave'), the use of the most up to date "electric" machinery where no exercise is necessary to remove flab (a literal allusion to D+G desiring machines), and lots and lots of enemas (5 a day) to keep the bowels clean. Guest-patients are "infantized." They must go to bed early; eat regular meals; wear diaper-like underwear; are allowed to fart at the dinner table; are bathed, washed and given enemas by the nurses; and must participate in group sing-songs and exercises. Everything is rationally and scientifically controlled and professionally regulated.

Throughout the film this *anti-Freudian, anti-Reichean, anti-Oedipal* figure displaces the unconscious Mind with Body, an unconscious pre-linguistic experience which D+G regard as being crucial (in this sense they differ from Lacan whom the unconscious does not exist before language.) The staff are treated as mere bodies, extensions of the electric machines they attend and the guests they are assigned to. When Kellogg's principle assistant, Mr. Poult, dies of a heart attack on the San's grounds, the good Doctor chastises and then kicks him for being "unprofessional" as to the choice of where he died. Even death is to be controlled (with journalists watching, the good Doctor dies at the end of the film in mid-air of a heart attack while diving off a high platform into a lake at the age of 70). In the operating room the slogan reads: 'Life is death postponed,' thereby reversing Freud's principal of the 'death wish' which installs pleasure as a life principle. Wilhelm Reich's 'organon boxes,' which were simplistic in their design, are replaced with complicated electric machines that give men "shock" treatments capable of giving them erections. As a measure of his own refusal of sexual desire and pleasure the good Doctor has *adopted* 40 children! (an allusion perhaps to D+G's idea of a 'history of names,' i.e., "the unconcious is an orphan" (1983:49). No "family romances" are allowed, nor developed in the film. 'Featherbeds and romance novels' are forbidden in the San. Relationships among spouses and relatives are non-existent in the diegesis (i.e., in its fictional world). Sex is reserved for procreation. When it does happen in the narrative, it is presented in a variety of contradictory forms. There is strictly the "body to body" contact as when Will Lightbody (ironically, like his name suggests, Will 'doesn't eat much'), one of the protagonists, has sex with Mrs. Ida Muntz (who suffers from green-sickness or chlorosis, an anemic condition suffered especially by young women brought on by a lack of iron deficiency; perhaps also an allusion to the fact that she probably has had too little to eat, and only vegetables at that!) because she is "cold," or performs cunnilingus for her under the cover of a sheet. In both cases her head is removed from the site/cite/sight of this experience, suggesting a mind/body separation. In another instance Eleanor, Will's wife, also a patient at the San, visits a 'massage therapist' (somewhat illegally) to have her "womb manipulated." She struggles to keep her mind apart from her body in the proper clinical manner she had learned at the San as she reaches orgasm. Eventually the gap between the two can't be maintained, and she begins to "let go." And then there is the case of Virginia, Eleanor's friend at the San. The irony of her name is at play here as well. As a staunch feminist, she is always thinking about sex and her own self-gratification.

Dr. Kellogg totally disregards the possibility that symptoms are caused by repressed traumas, even when they are obvious to the most naive viewer of the film, i.e., that each "ill" patient suffers from some former repression. Anything "German" is perceived as being suspiciously unhealthy and charlatan as when the name of Dr. Kuntz, an expert on "free love," is brought up (the slippage to Cunt-zz occurs in the film), or when Dr. Hans Spitzvogel's "massage therapist" practices of 'Handhabungstherapy' (literally hand-bugging, sexual stimulation which leads to pleasurable orgasms, the one act that is strictly forbidden in the health-prison of "San Quentin") are discussed. Another instance is when Will is humiliated in front of an inquisition of nurses for having worn a 'Düsselberg Belt,' a mechanical devise that gives electric shocks to the penis stimulating an erection and ejaculation. There is even the conflation of the signifier flesh/Fleisch (Gr. for meat). As Seventh-Day Adventist vegetarians, their anti-cannabilistic slogan reads: 'Eat not the Flesh.' Spitzvotel's "manipulations" are a spoof on the (anal)yst-(anal)ysand's transference experience and Willhelm Reich's techniques of releasing the bodys pent-up repressions and erotic energies through breathing techniques, body manipulations and primal screaming, as well as the practise of gynaecology by male doctors. These therapies are literalized in the film as sexual stimulation. Rather than psychiatric dialogue between patient and doctor, Spitzvogel (as the name suggests) sings German songs to his patients as he "manipulates" their breasts and "wombs."

The sub-text throughout the film is that the authoritative Oedipal Father, the good Dr. Kellogg suffers from the trauma which one of his rebellious (adopted) sons, George had caused, i.e., George's refusal to obey his Father's demand, and his son's subsequent refusal of the phallic signifier, and to play the Oedipal game. Like D+G's note about the psychotic child 'Dick' (1983:45), the good Doctor tries to position George within the Oedipal family rather than listen to his *anoedipal* desires. We are told he was found by the side of his dead prostitute mother. George never knew his "natural" father, and he does everything to avoid entering into the Symbolic Order of the Father. He refuses to talk back to the Doctor and refuses to eat his food. When he does speak it is always as a *demand* which never turns to desire. His Father never lacks. No love has ever been established between them, only hate. As a child he demanded 'proper food,' and as a grown-up that demand has changed to money. In the flashbacks when the good Doctor recalls these problems, Freud's concept of unconscious *repetition* is literalized and made conscious. George continually repeats an action—a temper tantrum (e.g., closing the door and hanging up his coat endlessly; or banging on his dinner plate through the night to protest the quality of the food) until the Father's authority has been broken.

George's sexual desires are somewhat ambivalent. As a child he comes across as nerdy and physically frail, but as a grown-up he has a virile body underneath his filthy clothes. There is a scene where it looks as if he is about to rape Eleanor (Bridgit Fonda) in the style of his undress, and he tells her he likes to look at the nude bodies of the new ladies. But his demeanor as an impish, immature brat makes it seem as though he is not capable of sex. George is the One Body the good Doctor cannot manage. He literalizes the Thing the good Doctor keeps trying to expel from his health clinic, but the Thing keeps coming back as a "return of the repressed"—as abjected *shit*. In proper schizo fashion, the Thing is materialized and literalized. Shit is voiced throughout the entire film, and graphically (i.e., "materially") presented as a site/cite/sight in all its possible appearances. His abjected son is dishevelled and has a "piggish" appearance, who slings boxes of shit at the San's guests. Shit, as unprocessed cereal, also becomes the baptismal liquid in the next to last scene when Father and son finally unite while the San burns to the ground. In contrast to this shit, the good Doctor is always impeccably dressed in a white suit wearing white gloves. Only his 'gigantic' stools don't smell!

A queer reading of this film is difficult to miss. The good Doctor's possible aversion to heterosexuality is marked throughout the film. Lionel Badger is presented as his opposite: also an advocate of vegetarianism, but with a healthy dose of lust, practising the philosophy of "free love." Obviously the "ass-hole" is Kellogg's erogenous zone. In this case the Doctor is not a "fruit" but a "vegetable." He performs rituals of self-buggery by administering enemas to himself. There is even a joke told between Will and Charles Ossining, a young entrepreneur looking to make it big in the cereal business: 'With a friend like you, who needs enemas?' There is a similar reference to 'Bu(l)garians' who live longest by giving themselves yogurt enemas. Men's asses are in prominent display throughout the film. While there are a few voyeristic looks at women's breasts, these are brief. Female nudity is usually presented in the background as so many blurred bodies, while the heterosexual Big Other is sent spinning, hysterical and confused, i.e., the police are comically presented like the Keystone Cops who are always furiously running around chasing criminals.

Father and son come finally together in one of the last scenes. When George is drowning in a vat of unprocessed cereal, having fallen in when chased by Kellogg, he stretches out his hand as a call for help. The good Doctor grabs it and pulls him out, and then says: "George, speak to me." A child's voice is heard coming from George's mouth, "give us a cuddle daddy," presenting that "other" demand that Kellogg never heard, but which George always desired. The good Doctor kisses him and they hug. From a heterosexual reading, this is a son finally accepting the Symbolic Order of the Name of the Father. But is it? A tell-tale sign is the unprocessed cereal—shit, as brown, foul-looking liquid—which forms a ring around the lips of Dr. Kellogg after kissing his son on the forehead. This scene may also be read with all the allusions to "pederastic practices" Foucault talks about in *The Care of the Self*. What should have been the homosexual ethics between an older man and a boy? between George and Kellogg? George, after all, was adopted. Technically and potentially speaking there would have been no incestuous relationship here. Were the 'technologies of the self (body)' that the good Doctor preached the ones which assured them both "health"? What are the ethics now in a time of AIDS when Foucault himself said, a year before his death in an intrerview given in Berkeley before entering the BART station: "How can I be scared of AIDS when I could die in a car?...If sex with boys gives me pleasure. . . Don't cry for me if I die" (in Treichler,1988:68). "Is the rectum a grave?" asks Bersani (1988).

Paradigmatically, *The Road to Wellville* is an allegory about D+G's postmodern desiring machines where the commodification of the packaged Kellogg boxes of corn-flakes are the signifiers of processed shit, a schizophrenic literalization of the Thing—material libidinal flow that has been digested, cut up by the unconcious, and processed out through the body. The Body has become a site/cite/sight caught in a schizo flux between a Deleuzean 'phallus of co-ordination' (pre-castration as represented by George who *cannot* co-ordinate his erogenous zones into a unified field. He is a ' body without organs'; he has not yet been subjected into a single unit within a state-system; rejecting the phallus he remains scattered in parts as various *forms* of processed shit. There is an ambivalence as to what his sexual orientation is) and 'the phallus of castration' (as represented by Dr. Kellogg himself, where his *desexualization* in proper schizophrenic fashion is presented for us *literally* as well. But, here too the castration complex has been rejected. The phallic signifier cannot act as a guarantee of his desexualization in the Real so that "normal sexuality" can be performed. It functions not as a 'signifier-*without-*

signified' as the Lacanians would have it. Rather it is materialized and displaced by the "ass-hole," and the penis—like the lesbian dildo---now converts to the good Doctor's artificial one that is attached—erect,rigid and perpetually ready—at the end of his enema apparatus). In D+G's terms, George exhibits the schizophrenic pole of unconcious desire and potential 'deterriorialization,' while the good Doctor occupies the paranoic pole of order and wholeness; both characters, however, are anti-social and social at the same time (they distinguish between schizo/normal and paranoic/mad. George, in their system has escaped bourgeois repression by the signifier). The father kissing and hugging his adopted son suggests the fantasy of a homosexual resolve where the phallic signifier has been escaped, although a Lacanian would say that both still suffer the trauma of the Thing that cannot be articulated in the signifying chain. In this case it is its odour Kellogg avoids and refuses to smell.

The very last scene presents a couple, Will and Eleanor, whose marital problems we've been following throughout the story, as being well again, integrated back into society, sitting and relaxing on their lawn—a large southern mansion looms in the background as their four young daughters play in the foreground. Eleanor reads a letter from Charles Ossining, which has enclosed in it a cheque for 1000 dollars paying back a old dept to Will. The young entrepreneur has finally made it, not selling cereal (Per-fo Cereal), but by selling a soft-drink whose name and allusions to Coca-Cola and cocaine are unmistakable—*Coka-Kane*. By adding the leaf of the coca plant to the drink's *contents* he has made millions—not on the health industry but on pleasure and addiction industry, raising yet another question about the 'technologies of the self.' Throughout the film's diegesis addiction plays a subtle sub-text, raising another aspect of D+G's desiring machines. There was Eleanor's guilt that she had turned Will into an opium addict by feeding him 'Hot Bitters' to put an end to his drunkenness which had turned him into a 'love-machine' (she felt she was just a "hole" in the bed); there was Will's own addiction to alcohol; there was the addiction to enemas and the addiction to meat. Every addiction holds "the Real Thing"—Coke's "Real taste," or Coke's "The taste is IT." This "it" is precisely what escapes signification and what "makes" the product. In Lacanian *it* is the negative signifier or phallic signifier (i.e., signifier-without-signified). But here, again in proper schizophrenic fashion, the "it" has been literalized, materialized, embodied as the leaf of the coca plant. The secret to late capitalist entrepreneurship is to tap this fantasy dimension *at the level of the body, at the level of contents, at the level of results—real or imagined*. D+G's schizophrenics escape such capitalist exploitation because they are not fooled by the "package." They literalize *contents over form—substance over aesthetics*.

Charles always dreamed of money and making it big. His partner (in crime) Goodloe Bender was a master at creating illusion and appearance as his name suggests ('behind every great enterprise lurks the shadow of a lie'). But the *form* of the package isn't IT. Despite the well-designed and attractive cereal boxes they had printed, no one rushes to buy Per-Fo Cereal. Their enterprises end in failure. Aesthetic form wasn't enough. Bartholomew Bookbinder, hired by Charles and Goodloe to find a "magic" corn-flake recipe, couldn't do it. As his name suggests, his rational attempts (21 in all), recorded carefully in a book, all tasted like shit. The good Doctor performed his own feats of illusion through a number of spectacular experiments in front of his guest-patients where he "proved" that a steak, like horse dung, was covered with dangerous bacteria, and that a wolf fed on a vegetarian diet was rid of all its 'wild instincts' to become the San's pet. All this is suggestive that the *contents* as "the negative body" (the IT at the level of the Real which is inside the commodity—"that" which gives the body pleasure) as opposed to *form* (formalist aesthetics) is what finally *unifies* the body's parts into its ego ideal. The guest-patients consumed Dr. Kellogg's anal fantasies in exchange for money and a desired "body cure." Like diets that don't work, his patient-guests would return each year to take the "cure" again and again, confirming Linda Singer's (1993) thesis that *addiction* is one of the fundamental corner stones of late capitalism.

Reading Deleuze and Guattari selectively i almost think that their rhetoric was a deliberate attempt to "stand Descartes and Rousseau on their heads," in an attempt to reverse the mind-body split of Western rationalism and to validate the Noble Savage as a natural substratum of "polyvocal, non-personalized relations among organs." It is the machinic body of late capitalism which needs to be theorized. Such a theoretical ruse appears, at first, distasteful, yet when reading Haraway's (1990) celebrated essay, "A Manifesto for Cyborgs,"[17] there is a resonant sound. The "body without organs" is the cyborg, and, as i concluded earlier, even the French feminists spoke to its fragmentation. The blurring of the animate and the inanimate, the animal and the human, the "hard-won recognition of their social and historical constitution, gender, race, and class cannot provide the basis for belief in 'essential' unity. There is nothing about being 'female' [or male for that matter] that naturally binds women" (p.197). "The cyborg is a kind of disassembled and reassembled, postmodern collective and personal self. This is the self feminists must code" (p.205). Haraway's socialist cyborg sounds a lot like Deleuze and Guattari's "nomad." "Cyborg gender is a local possibility taking a global vengeance. Race, gender, and capital require a cyborg theory of wholes and parts. There is no drive in cyborgs to produce total theory, but there is an intimate experience of boundaries, their construction and deconstruction. ... It means both building and destroying machines, identities, categories, relationships, spaces, stories." (p.223). Haraway's essay draws me to write another vignette and another personal elision.

1 It should be noted that, in terms of educational praxis at the elementary and secondary schools this perspective is virtually absent. The reference to Bronwyn Davies (1989a) is merely an explorative essay that offers directions and possibility as to what might be done. Respondents to her essay were generally negative. Davies has also applied poststructuralist strategy to fairy tales, *Frogs and Snakes and Feminist Tales: Preschool Children and Gender* (1989b). In higher education, as might well be expected, the situation isn't nearly as glum, although glum enough. I am aware of Ulmer's attempt at a grammatological education based on the work of Derrida, Lacan, Eisenstein and Joseph Beuys, but it appears to have no feminist discourse informing its theoretical basis. In contrast, the special issue 63 in the *Yale French Studies*: -The Pedagogical Imperative: Teaching as Literary Genre incite/insight/insite possibilities, and recent works give an inkling of what is being done in deconstruction but are not specific enough in curricular orientation. In brief, this perspective has not yet become 'paradigmatic' in the Kuhnian sense in the late '80s. (Since this assessment in 1989-1990 the literature in this area has increased at a staggering rate. *The Journal of Curriculum Theorizing*, which always had its conference at Bergamo Center in Dayton, Ohio, generated a number of scholars who were willing to explore the question of deconstruction. In art education the situation is much worse. Few have made this initiative. See Pinar and Reynolds, 1992).

2 This indeed turned out to be the case with the publication of Luke and Gore's *Feminisms and Critical Pedagogy* (1992).

3 This is changing as well within the Bergamo Conference on Curriculum Theorizing. See Deborah P. Britzman's "Is There a Queer Pedagogy?: Or, Stop Being [Acting?] Straight!" (1993) (unpublished).

4 Tong's (1989) listing includes liberal feminism, marxist feminism, existential feminism (exclusively Simone de Beauvoir) and postmodern feminism.

5 i use "victim" in the sense of being exploited. ACT UP has changed that terminology to "people with Aids" (PWA).

6 Grosz's (1989:32-36) discussion of the figure of 'Woman' on Derrida's writings is helpful here. It is probably one of the more lucid discussions around.

7 See Diana Fuss (1989) Chapter 6, "Lesbian and Gay Theory: The Question of Identity Politics" for an account between those theorists who hold on to an essentialism—what homosexuality *is*, versus the social constructivists who develop the Foucaultian notion of how homosexuality is historically produced.

8 As in the recent work of Silverman's male marginality (1992).

9 In the most recent update of this book from Duke University Press (1993), Michael Moon tries to situate Hocquenghem's book within the 1968 Gay Liberation Front in France—FHAR (the *Front Homosexuel d'Action Révolutionnaire*). Hocquenghem died of AIDS-related illness in 1988.

10 Teresa de Lauretis (1988:156) borrows this play of words for Irigaray whereby *homo* in the Latin means 'man' while in the Greek it means "same." Hommo-sexuality, written as hom(m)osexuality, implies that lesbianism is once again collapsed under the 'one' signifier. Hom(m)o-sexuality is (in)different to homosexuality. The question becomes: is it possible to clear a conceptual space between the two so that homosexuality is given its own specificity?

11 John Ellis' (1983) speaks of shifting identifications between images on the screen and the various positionalities—both active and passive offered by a screen's narrative: "Identification is therefore multiple and fractured, a sense of seeing the constituent parts of the spectator's own psyche paraded before her or him" (p. 128). Such a view of the decentered ego fits comfortably with Deleuze and Guattari's articulations. i might also mention the social semiology of Hodge & Kress. Their views follow the pioneering work of Volosnov's wherein the process of semiosis posits an active subject who produces and interprets signs giving him/her a sense of identity. They, however, say little as how identity may be subverted.

It might be interesting to develop the spectrum of male and female character types as outlined by Jean Bolen (1985, 1989), Jungian archetypes in this context. Perhaps, if the masculine and feminine archetypes she identifies in the Greek and Roman context could be historicized to understand how identity takes place with them in particular lived contexts, then a good deal of her mysticism could be eliminated. What appear as ontologically innate categories could be historically changing. Zeus, Apollo, Athena, etc.

live with us today in other forms and characters. There would be the need to write in missing archetypes which the lesbian and homosexual discourses revealed. The range of character types which existed during Greek times have yet to be articulated. Bolen's analysis is entirely heterosexually biased.

12 An understanding of Deleuze and Guattari can be gleaned from the writings of Wright (1984:162ff.) as well as Samuel Kimball (1986), Erica Carter and Chris Turner (1986), Lash (1984) and Theweleit (1987: esp. 205ff.). Jardine (1985) Chapter 10, "Becoming a Body without Organs: Gilles Deleuze and His Brothers" (208-223) provides a difficult read. She underscores "D+G's" theorizations of wanting the world to become Woman, which is, as i understand it, an allegorical fiction that goes beyond any gender of man or woman. Jardine critique is that such a view vanishes 'women' first because men, who are already the majority, must follow her lead into becoming-Woman. According to Jardine, D+G have not escaped their phallocentric bias.

13 Deleuze and Guattari's notions of desire have had little impact in education. A rare exception have been the musings of Jacques Daignault and Clermont Gauthier (1982) and Gauthier (1986). Written during a time when curriculum theory was in flux, before the pull back to current neo-conservative positions, Daignault (who had studied with Deleuze) and Gauthier, his colleague at the Université du Québec at Rimouski, have gone the furthest in theorizing desire in education by drawing more on Deleuze's "logic du sens." In an elaborate and playful analysis of the curriculum field, they chart a 'paradoxical' course between curriculum as terrorism and nihilism; to develop a curriculum which is all process, operating in the gap between theory and practice. A recent book by Pinar and Reynold's *Understanding Curriculum as Phenomenological and Deconstructed Text* (1992) has an essay by each of them.

14 In *Mille Plateaux* Deleuze and Guattari develop an ethics of the "nomad" and the "war machine." Both concepts must be understood as allegorical constructs which attempt to identify a "rhizomatic existence" whose "lines of flight" are the creative power of deterritorialization (see Patton, 1986). This idea is similar to Bordo (1990b) who argues that the transcendental body of the Enlightenment which exists *nowhere* has been replaced by a postmodern body that is always moving but whose own unity is shattered by the choreography of multiplicity to the extent that it exists *everywhere*. For Bordo, both positions make the body disappear.

15 The ethical considerations of Deleuze and Guattari are discussed by Patton (1986:139).

16 i wonder how much Deleuze and Guattari (D + G) were influenced by Surrealism? Caws (1985:278) speaks of the Surrealist's celebration of body parts. Man Ray's photographs of Méret Oppenheim entitled *Erotique-violeé* is a suggestive example. Here the disjunction of her body parts may be read as pleasurably liked to the printing machine; her nude body is pressed against, or read as being caught up in its mechanisms. This double reading of her desire echoes the polarities of D+G's schizophrenic self: the reactionary paranoia machine and the revolutionary schizo machine, while her 'body without organs' points to the malleability of the body before it becomes territorialized.

17 i am reminded of an earlier book by Landers (1966) who explores the thesis that we now live in a 'dybosphere' where what is human and what is machine has been blurred through the continual intervention of medical technologies. As Haraway (1990) puts it, "the difference between machine and organism is thoroughly blurred; mind, body, and tool are on very intimate terms" (p.207).

461

THE
SEVENTH
VIGNETTE

The *Fin de Millénium* and the End of Ends

It was not only my heterosexual bias and the elisions of color and ethnicity which had brought me to the limitations of my understanding of feminism and the possibilities of men *in* feminism, but the continuous reoccurrences of certain limitations that women themselves have begun to recognize. An internal critique of their discourse has begun by a third generation of articulate professors who have benefited from the shelter of Women's Studies programs. Unlike the lone dissidents of the first generation, such as Virginia Woolf or Simone de Beauvoir, and unlike a whole host of second generation feminists who helped establish those very departments, this new generation must and does continue to problematize difference. Yet, Bordo (1990b) warns that the recent "gender-skepticism" and wave of feminist fragmentation through the deconstruction of gender analysis is repeating the 1920s and 1930s fragmentation and dissipation of feminist consciousness and activism after the social results of the first wave of feminists had been realized. Such a "postfeminism" for her is unsettling for it ushers in, once again, male universalism, particularly at the universities where this third generation of women scholars has gained acceptance. i have already pointed out the emergence of the 'New Woman' (her positionality displayed in such magazines as *Elle* and *Cosmopolitan*), and the links of that positionality to the late capitalist aesthetic of consumer style. But this fragmentation is also occurring in "the men's quarters" as well. The New Man competes with the New Woman and the rash of conservatism on universities campuses (Hirsch, Jr., Bloom, Kramer, Greenberg)[1] is matched by neo-conservative programs like Discipline Based Art Education (DBAE) and the efficiency accountability movements in educational discourse, like those of Madeline Hunter.

As i read recent feminist criticism, it appeared that each author was proposing a new direction for the end of the journey. What follows is sort of an end "of ends," knowing full well that the "end" shall never be reached. i should like to articulate some of these "ends" in this vignette, which did not emerge so much from interrogating a personal experience as from a "thoughtfulness" about the "ends" as they have registered with me as a clumsy dancer on this (my)nefield. i shall, *where applicable*, continue the discourse in relation to art.

The End of Avant-garde Feminism and the Problems of Postmodernism

The turn towards the narrative in the arts has initiated new directions. It is the avant-garde aspects that have become problematic. You might recall Peter Bürger's (1984: 49 ff.) analysis of the avant-garde as an attempt to refine the concept of art from its bourgeois moorings: the Kantian-Schillerian-Hegelian notion of an autonomous art form which stands outside the social order, outside of competition, individually produced, viewed, and interpreted so that it might exemplify a moral-aesthetic imperative of how things ought to be. This is its uncoerced freedom. Standards are thereby fortified and taste is institutionalized. It becomes, in Marcuse's formulation, an 'affirmative artwork' where once more a moral order is projected, distinct form the technical rationality of society.

This Enlightenment idea, from the position of a feminist discourse, merely recapitulates the male-centered rationalist concerns of the Masterpiece which must be given a fixed pedigree to ensure ownership. The signature or style marked that ownership and insured its currency (profit). The first generation of avant-garde artists tried to redintegrate art back into society but failed to do so. Bürger argues it is because they adopted a 19th-century Aestheticism—that is, the content of art became art itself. The avant-garde "assent[ed] to the aestheticists' rejection of the world and its means-ends rationality. What distinguishes them from the latter is the attempt to organize a new life praxis *from a basis in art*" (p. 49, my emphasis). And here is where the problems began since such an art, if it is absorbed by technical rational society, has no space from which to critique the existing order. To do away with the distance between art and life, and still have a contradictory stance in its production, reception and function (purpose), turned out to be an impossibility. One solution is to aestheticize the body. Art and life would once more be restored if the critique begins anew from an existing frame of place.

The problem of what the social purpose of art should be, once art became redintegrated into social life, became problematic. Duchamp's Ready-Mades effectively questioned the artistic signature and negated individual production, but the provocation could only be done once, and this within the gallery system of meaning. The question of what is a "work" of art became problematic for it did not fit the bourgeois notion of 'work.' The protest of the historical avant-garde against bourgeois art itself became institutionalized as *art*. The elimination of the distinction between the producer and recipient was also a failure. Dadist provocation ended with recipes and automatic texts as part of a liberating life praxis, but then both the producer and recipient "no longer exist[ed]" (Bürger, 1984:53). Eventually, Bürger concludes: "the neo-avant-garde institutionalizes the avant-garde as art and thus negates genuinely avant-garde intentions .... It is the status of their products, not the consciousness artists have of their activity, that defines the social effects of works" (p.58).

This quick review seems to be part of the problem of feminist avant-garde art. To develop a non-organic art in opposition to the organicism of bourgeois consumption has not proven to be the political force intended. Felski (1989) is sensitive to this problem. In her final chapter, "Realism, Modernism, and the 'Death of the Avant-Garde' " (p.156 ff.), she develops a defense of realism for feminist politics. Keenly aware of the critique made of realism by well-known critics such as Barthes, McCabe, Catherine Belsey, she defends 'readerly,' as opposed to 'writerly,' texts on the grounds that they able to offer as many multiple interpretations as 'writerly' texts which then may be used for political ends once the social context of reception is accounted for. Felski rehearses and echoes Bürger's thesis above (p.158 ff.). Feminist avant-garde art relies on the historical definition of art in order to negate, defamiliarize and deconstruct its form. This already presupposes a sophisticated viewer; one who must have the necessary cultural capital to understand the sophistications of the discipline of art history. My valorization of particular feminist artworks presented from the poststructuralist position falls under this criticism. This position, placed in the larger social context, affects very

465

few people.[2] Like Duchamp's Ready Mades, Felski claims the " 'revolutionary' effects of change in formal techniques grow ever more short-lived" (p. 159). Because of this Danto called for "an end of art"; Docherty (1993) called "an end of the avant-garde"; and Hans Belting (1987) called for the "end of art history."[3]

For Felski, therefore, the question of reception emerges as the crucial issue for theorizing distinctive features of feminist culture. A *feminist counterpublic sphere* has been created with a plurality of public-spheres; each specific site/cite/sight of oppositionality is related to gender, race, ethnicity, age, and sexual preference. There are then "coalitions of overlapping subcommunities" (p. 171). Yet what holds this heterogeneous mass is a common identity of "gender-based oppression" (p. 166). This same conclusion is reached by Fraser and Nicholson (1988) in their discussion of Lyotard and postmodernist feminism. How to effectively politicize the process of reception and production with a feminist audience is becoming increasing more important. Decentralized and collectively organized projects is one way (day-care, publications, women's groups, health centers, bookstores) (p.170), while at the institutional and bureaucratic levels, the creation of women studies departments, affirmative action projects and refuge and advisory centers, are others. The organizational structure through which texts are "produced and disseminated" remains unchanged despite independent feminist presses and journals. The greatest impact made by feminist criticism is the way literature and art are viewed and read.

The lesson to be learned, claims Felski, is that feminist "cultural politics" cannot privilege the avant-garde aesthetic over the political potential of popular forms such as television, rock music, popular novels and women's magazines. It is here that there is an incorporation of art with life that the historical avant-garde failed to accomplish, making their art entirely one of negation. Romance fiction and soap opera may be a potential source for change. i think of Roseanne Barr's tremendous success as a television personality: here is someone who is overweight, not beautiful by male standards, has a blue collar accent and shoots from the hip, yet has a tremendous following. What is the desire to be her fan? to identify as a blue-collar worker? (Jenkins, 1992). "The model of a feminist public sphere provides a theoretical justification for feminist interest in *both* popular and more esoteric forms in relation to the cultural interests and needs of different segments of an actual or potential feminist public while avoiding the problems inherent in the existing attempts to theorize a 'feminist aesthetic'" (Felski: 174). "Rather than privileging the aesthetic, a feminist cultural politics should concern itself with addressing the potential value of forms from both high and mass culture in relation to the objectives of a feminist public sphere" (p. 181).[4]

This ambivalency, of having it both ways, is repeated by Flax (1990a:55) who argues that women should preserve both autonomy and being-in-relations, and not fall into one or the other categorizations. The ambiguity is deliberate as postmodernism is entrenched in the dilemmas of difference in modernist and anti-modernist alternatives (see di Stefano, 1990:77-78). The same argument is rehearsed with Krauss's (1981) discussion of Sherry Levine's anti-modernist and anti-avant-garde "style." The signed photographs are produced from originals and then destroyed. Or Frampton's (1983) stance that "Architecture can only be sustained today as a critical practice if it assumes an *arrière-garde* position, that is to say, one which distances itself equally from the Enlightenment myth of progress and from a reactionary, unrealistic impulse to return to the architectonic forms of the preindustrial past" (p.20).

Throughout my readings it appears that French poststructuralism is being questioned. Flax (1990b) argues that "such an approach obscures the projection of its own activity onto the world and denies the existence of the variety of concrete social practices that enter into and are reflected in the constitution of language (e.g., ways of life constitute language and texts as much as language constitutes ways of life)" (p. 47). It is the lack of attention to concrete social relations and the distribution of power that bothers her. Felski and Flax are not alone in these conclusions. Pollock (1988) ends her study with a similar proposal. She too seems to see the public as crucial for feminist emphasis.

Realism seems to be the issue. Like Adorno, Brecht had also dismissed Lukács' Realism, but on different grounds. 'Distanciation' or 'defamiliarization' was turned against Realism so that the viewer would become an active participant in the production of meaning across an event which was representing contemporary social reality (Lunn, 1982). Whether Brechtian distanciation, which relied on montage, the mixing of popular and high culture, the use of comic and tragic, song, images sounds and so on, spurred extensions to non-organic allegorical forms like performance, installations, and videos, is still questionable (Wright, 1992). Critical realist practices most often put to doubt a reflected reality and replace it with an public recognition that it is a constructed one. Yet, significantly, Brechtian theatre also wanted an art form that stood paradoxically in and out of life's praxis at the same time. The audience was always imagined as socially specific, a concrete social group in relation to whose position and needs pleasure and instruction would be calculated. Easier stated than performed, nevertheless this issue of a feminist audience is also Pollock's (1988) concern with perhaps one difference: if an avant-garde work is not understood, the viewer might be forced to ask:

> What knowledge do I need to have in order to share in
> the productivity of this work? This becomes crucial for fem-
> inist interventions because their difference lies precisely in
> negating the knowledges and ideologies which are dom-
> inant [e.g., realism] and have become normalized as the
> common sense about art and artists, about women and
> societies (p.183).

There is need to mention yet another "end." In Rosa Lee's (1987) review of painting and postmodernism, she notes the direction Sarah Kent and Jacqueline Morreau had taken in their exhibition-book *Women's Images of Men* (1985). Devoid of a tradition, both artists returned to the *figure* by establishing a new subject matter: women's representation of men. "Although deconstructive feminist art provided invaluable insights into the less visible workings of patriarchy it failed to offer a scheme for the radical reconstruction of artistic language" (p.24). Introducing women's representation of men into an already existing structured sexual division produced further differences which, hopefully, questioned the current discourse of male representation. Lee also mentioned that a radical reconstruction of artistic language may be possible by women re-writing the male artistic tradition, but as discussed earlier, this may be a patriarchal repetition. Lastly, Lee discusses the artistic work of Oulton who has attempted to re-animate material—the actual paint. "[T]raditional conventions of 'reading' a painting are thwarted through subversive use of those conventions: chiaroscuro is used, for example, to imply modeling, but simultaneously does not refer to any visible, easily apprehensible object" (p. 22).

The difficulty of describing Oulton's work is telling, thereby matching the difficulty of her theoretical project. During an interview (Kent, 1986), Oulton was asked to describe her process and her dialogue with the Masterly male tradition. She replied by saying:

> ...there's hope that through an exploration of language [of
> paint— specifically central European traditions — Venetian,
> Spanish and German], base matter again, you can be intro-
> duced to a spiritual dimension. Part of the problem for me
> was the concept of duality, which sets you in opposition
> to everything that is outside your own skin, which is par-
> ticularly relevant if you are using shreds of landscape
> imagery. Landscape is treated as inanimate, which has had

468

drastic results for the actual landscape. I am trying to change that approach to landscape—not to place it 'out there,' taking on all your sins, and the meanings that you put into it. Landscape 'out there' is dying because of that treatment, as though it had no life but were mute, victim. I'm trying to develop a method that allows that which is mute—the paint—to have a voice (p.43).

That voice is found by treating paint like a piece of skin. The intimacy is in Oulton's touch. Paintings are worked with a very small touch and the vastness grows out of smallness. Each brush mark is visible—nothing is hidden. They're one-skin deep. The brush marks are about joining opposites, for they are never on top of one another.

The Direction of Popular Culture

Oulton's intentions could easily support a spiritual materialist ecological consciousness in terms of her approach to matter; at the cosmological level this is an important undertaking. But another direction has been taken by some feminists. What is perhaps a most interesting development is the need to incorporate 'high art,' like Oulton's, with life in a critical way, via popular culture. Postmodernism has blurred the distinction between high and low. "One of the few widely agreed upon features of postmodernism is its attempt to negotiate forms of high art with certain forms and genres of mass culture and the culture of everyday life" (Huyssen, 1986:203). Yet this has brought on other dimensions to the "end of art" thesis: art's disenfranchisement (Danto, 1986) i.e., the nihilism of anything goes as long as one can provide a theoretical justification and the aestheticization of everyday life (Featherstone, 1991). "The aestheticization of everyday life to be seen in contemporary America does not limit itself to the commodity sphere. It refers instead to the universal disappearance of an outside to art. There is no pre-aesthetic dimension to social activity, since social order has become dependent on aesthetic organization" (Christa Bürger, 1986 quoting Berman, 1984/85:99). With the autonomy of art eliminated, the critical potential is lost. Art appears to be trapped by this predicament.

All aspects of the artistic impulse as defined by Gowans (1981), beautification, persuasion, story-telling and self expression, have been t(r)apped into the aestheticization of everyday life. As E. Kaplan (1987) admirably showed, montage techniques of the avant-garde, strategies of self-reflexivity, and narrative fragmentation have become standardized features of rock videos and television. It becomes more difficult to separate out the *kitsch* from popular artforms that try to incorporate social critique. Often, as it has happened to me, i am left in undecidability and ambiguity as my discussions regarding the art of Cindy Sherman and Madonna scattered throughout this 'scriptease.' Mass culture, which had been traditionally associated in the nineteenth century with women (Huyssen, 1986; Modleski, 1986a), while authentic culture rested with men, has now become excessively "feminized."[5] We are, in Postman's (1986) turn of phrase, "amusing ourselves to death." It may appear from the above synopsis that popular art merely reproduces the patriarchal subject since our television appears riddled with "the look" while avant-garde feminist art has little impact. Is the only space left for feminist work the *Bildungsroman* that Felski supports? Mass culture seems an unlikely place for critique and yet it may be the very place of regeneration and reexamination as the emergent field of cultural studies has shown (Grossberg et al, 1992).

Huyssen (1986), as noted, sees the relationship between woman and mass culture developing in the 19th century. "The fear of masses in this age of declining liberalism is always also a fear of woman, a fear of nature out of control, a fear of the unconscious, of sexuality, of the loss of identity, and stable ego boundaries in the mass" (p.196). In Huyssen's view, Modernism becomes a reaction formation to such developments—which is, as he admits, no longer the case. Nevertheless the rationalization and the subordination of women's leisure under patriarchal capitalism is a familiar one (Dawson, 1988). Mass culture is always a potential source of resistance. For critics of the left who continue the Frankfurt critique of mass culture fail to realize the myriad of differences in and amongst the public. Jim Collins's *Uncommon Cultures* (1989) presents an interesting case against Jameson's and Eagelton's all too pessimistic view of mass media as the commodification of late capitalism. There *is* a critical social discourse in any number of films. i have already mentioned several, however *Wall Street, We Live, Broadcast News, Talk Radio, Do the Right Thing*—the list of critical main stream movies is endless. It is possible to argue that in a decentered society, the critic may turn any film into a trenchant critique if a critical reception aesthetic stance is taken. Even a blockbuster hit like *Batman* can be used to ask the question why the Joker is not joking and Batman has a dark side (Ross, 1990a). Radical readings are always possible and necessary as long as they are not sociologically reduced, but include the formation of fantasies.

This same social discourse is identified in rock videos by Kaplan (1987:66-88). Themes which explore the computerized man and address the confusion of the boundary between human/non-human in an advanced technological era; the dystopias of cyberspace fantasies; themes which deal with foreign policies or specific social injustices such as poverty, the re-hashing of the Vietnam war, the ecological disasters, provide constant grist for the critical mill. There have also been a string of spectacular social events: International 'Live Aid' event (which brought rock stars from America, Europe, and the Soviet Union to raise money for people starving in drought worn Ethiopia), Sun-City Video against apartheid, USA/Africa event/video, Farm AID Event, Fashion Video for victims of AIDS and a recent rock spectacle for Nelson Mandella. As might be expected, these events enter into the Baudrillardian world of the simulacra, of the TV image and the "ecstasy of communication," and i wonder, along with Kaplan whether Baudrillard (1983b) isn't right in claiming "the end of the social" as we now know it, with the shrinkage of public spaces. Like the 'telethons" or World Vision television broadcasts of starving African infants, politics have been changed by the new "cold" universe.

Further limitations: The Two Jocks/Jacques

Perhaps one of the most striking limitation's of the discussion of feminism, my own included, is the near total reliance of Lacanian and Derridean discourse. Again, there is no one interpretation of either of these 'figures' by the authors cited throughout this study. Both Jacques have spawned their defendants and critics, yet i cannot *help* in *not* recognizing the ahistorical nature of the Lacanian paradigm and the almost religious acceptance of deconstruction, without perhaps Derrida's own subtleties and wit. Ralph Flores (1984) is re-mindful of Derridean warnings "that we must be 'careful,' 'rigorous,' 'vigilant,' moving by 'perilous necessity,' 'avoiding regressions' into the 'naive concepts' or 'uncritical oppositions' being deconstructed or, inversely, too easy an escape to a place mistakenly 'outside the classical oppositions' " (p.34). For instance, David Lehman (1992) devotes two chapters to the various definitions that "deconstruction" has taken. Few, of which, are respectful of a "close reading."

The main difficulty for many critics who oppose a deconstructivist position appears to be its 'missing' link to 'reality,' i.e., reality is forever 'detoured' (Lacan) or 'deferred' (Derrida) (see Rankin, 1987). Reality for Derrida, writes Flax (1990b), "is somewhat contradictory. On the one hand any finite, unitary concept of the Real is said to be merely an effect of a delimited set of (deconstructable) philosophic strategies or metaphysical claims about the nature of Being. On the other hand Derrida does make ontological statements about the Real. It is 'really' heterogeneous, fluctuating, infinitely open, and governed by chance, not logic or an immanent telos infolding in and over time" (p.199).Confusions occur between what Derrida takes for 'real' and what Lacan takes for Real. Other voices, like Fraser (1989: Chap.4) who has participated in French Derridean circles, also claim it as an apolitical gesture.

This makes for an uneasy politics which, in Ryan's (1982) analysis at least, admits to an apolitical practice.Yet, upon reading both Caputo (1988) and Robertson's (1986) defense of Derrida's alterity, his privileging of underprivileged terms is charged with political and ethical overtones. It is "responsible anarchy" for Caputo and "deconstructive contortion" for Robertson. i wonder if Derrida's deconstruction is the more non-violent form of criticism, particularly when the relationship, in the Levinasian sense, between the same and Other is not treated on equal footing but *curved*. "The other is both lower and higher: lower because excluded, higher because his/her exclusion cries out, calls for, claims my response" (Caputo:1988:69). This has serious implications for other fantastic identities of non-male and non-female gendered positions. Such positions currently fall into that category as both same (i.e. man or woman) and/or other (homosexual or lesbian).

The question as to what constitutes praxis continually surfaces and teeter-totters between by now a familiar opposition, modernism and postmodernism. As Sabina Lovibond (1989) characterizes the schism: "The Enlightenment pictured the human race as engaged in an effort towards universal moral and intellectual self-realization, and so as the subject of a universal historical experience; it also postulated a universal human reason in terms which social and political tendencies could be assessed as 'progressive' or otherwise (the goal of politics being defined as the realization of reason in practice). Postmodernism rejects this picture: that is to say, it rejects the doctrine of the unity of reason. It refuses to conceive of humanity as a unitary subject striving towards the goal of perfect coherence (in its common stock of beliefs) of perfect cohesion and stability (in its political practice)" (p.6). Lovibond, after reviewing three themes of postmodernism: 'dynamic pluralism', 'quiet pluralism' and 'pluralism of inclination,' concludes that neither of these positions are suitable for feminism. Her essay ends on a familiar note: feminism must work both at the local and at the universal levels, echoing Felski's belief in the possibility of a 'heterogeneous public life.'

To historicize or to put to question the universal sense of Lacan's Imaginary and Symbolic Order would be a marked change of orientation. The revisionary Marxist Castadoriadis' concept of the 'social imaginary' (1984/1975) as it is related to ideology and the maverick *anti*-psychoanalytic oeuvre of Deleuze and Guattari, whom i have referred to, are two texts which might (and have?) proved useful in questioning and displacing, in some circles at least, the Lacanian notions of desire and identifying his possible heterosexual bias. Both texts are fixated in the French context and extend the poststructuralist paradigm yet again, but i wonder how transferable their Eurocentric bias is to the North American context where a narcissistic subject is in the making (Lash, 1979). Žižek's innovations of the Lacanian Real have been discussed. His application of the Lacanian Real to political questions have given Lacan a new lease on life.

Castadoriadis is interesting to the field of art and art education since the Imaginary and the Symbolic Order are subject to change. Each society, when it becomes instituted in the fullest sense, "posits a new *eidos* that could not be deduced from or produced by a prior state of affairs" (Thompson, 1982: 663). The social imaginary, as the symbolic frameworks of representation through which cultural meanings are produced and disseminated, becomes a realm of ideological clashes. These are given material effect in the real world of events. History is therefore always at balance, and change is potentially around the corner once the rooted imaginary metaphor is displaced. However, the displacement must happen at the level of the Real, which is underdeveloped by Castadoriadis. As the recent events of the Eastern bloc indicate, the formation of a counter-imaginary *eidos* finally erupted as the plurality of repressed civil societies emerged victorious, displacing the central *imago* of an authoritarian state with a centralized bureaucracy. This seems also to support Castadoriadis' contention that the imaginary is created *ex nihilo*. Figures and forms come from nowhere, it seems, non-reflecting one may say, echoes that mysterious dimension of non-discursivity. It displaces bourgeois notions of time as development and progress with "genuine time" as the "emergence of *new* and *other* determination," "the auto-alteration of what is" (Thompson, 1982:663). These are different notions of time, those which fall into dimensions of mysteriousness, the feminine, the mythological and the chaotic like Foucault's historical event. Stephen-Paul Martin (1988) has recently outlined what may be an emerging "feminine" *eidos*. Whatever its limitations may be, it forces the male reader to read across the feminine gaze, displacing the ingrained imagination of patriarchy and capitalism which denies *effective* temporality (incessant rupture and recurrent crisis) by managing, standardizing, and rationalizing the conquest of nature.

Some More Doubts, Poststructuralism Revisited

The disparity within the psychoanalytic discourse available and the problematics which surround it for the men in feminism have been referred to throughout my journey. The question of essentialism proved to be a major difficulty. Anna Munster's (1986) analysis of the difference between Irigaray and Gallop's critique of Irigaray's position has further vivified this for me. According to Munster, Gallop's (1983) renouncement of Irigaray's position as playing into the Oedipus complex by being a "revolting" daughter," *is* the very Oedipal complex she detests. Hysteria, obedience and seduction are all strategies of expectation under the Law of the Father. Like Foucault, by giving up the repression thesis, every transgression against the law simply seems to affirm it. Iragaray's disavowel becomes an avowel by its very focus on the prohibition.

In Gallop's summation, Irigaray has repressed her *heterosexual* desire, but Munster chastises Gallop for maintaining a "difference *within* the subject at the expense or in place of sexual difference: at the cost of sexual indifference" (p.120). Gallop, by arguing for the position of the third woman, the bisexuality of every subject, brings out Munster's ire: "Masculinity and femininity would be free-floating representations, lacking any reference to the male or female body. Like an outer layer of clothing to be worn and/ or discarded, Gallop's conception of gender and her notion of sexual difference accommodate themselves to the recent fad for cross-dressing or 'gender-blending'" (p.120). For Munster, cross-dressing is a fad; hardly disruptive of patriarchy. As a male then, it is much more palatable to accept Gallop's (1982b) difference *within* the subject. Such a 'feminine' position remains disruptive of phallocentrism through a non-identity to the Law (Symbolic Order), and a refusal of pornographic desire within a phallic text. It is the position of a masochist. As a male, the I could 'read' like a woman from this position. By dismissing Lacan, as Irigaray has, is to discard 'feminine' men who are attempting to rethink their own power base and form new masculine relationships. The position represented by 'feminine' men, for Munster, is still caught by phallocentrism. In her ironic tone: "He [the masochist] is the man who flashes, exposes his penis; feminine because he has challenged the veiled law of phallocentrism" (p. 125).

For Gallop the realm of the Law, (the Symbolic order, language) can be separated from the site/cite/sight of the sexed body. It is not the sex of the person who 'speaks' the phallocentric discourse, hence there are many strategies, tactics by both men and women to 'expose' the prick. The political consequences of this conception of male 'femininity' has led to a profound skepticism i have already referred to in the work of Schor and de Lauretis. "If the feminine is always critical, the woman is again located on the negative side of a dichotomy, doomed to be indefinitely other; what is not present, full or complete" (p.125). Such a male is a "gag queen" (ibid).

Irigaray's game is therefore to play both dutiful and revolting (in its double sense) daughter, simultaneously "homo" and "hetero," maintaining a difference *between* them, i.e., essential deconstruction. To clear such a space, the body is not to be anchored as natural or purely anatomical; rather it is a body to be questioned in the way it is represented and meaningfully constructed. Since such a space does not currently exist, especially within the psychoanalytic discourse (woman remains the castrated Other), female sexuality and feminine desire requires its own morphology. Irigaray's biological discourse is 'written' over and through the sexual and discursive metaphor of "two lips" (vaginal and oral). "[T]he lips are not the essence of woman or her sexuality. Instead they are a strategic representation defying the logic of definition and identity; lips can never be reduced to the one and its mirror image. There are always at least two, speaking, desiring, in an exchange where one gains no more profit than the other" (p. 121-122). It is Irigaray's way to avoid the specificity of identity as what a woman is. The implication for men in this analysis is that they must play their own essential deconstructivist game.

My dismay felt as not being able to participate as a "feminine" male was further confirmed by Scholes (1987) who makes a similar critique as Munster but from yet another position in this debate. Scholes' claim is to expose the incompatibility between deconstruction and feminism and to show why "feminism is right while deconstruction is wrong" (p.205). Scholes does this by placing woman as a "class" which deconstruction attempts to dismantle. By class Scholes means members who are a cultural categorical creation because of "necessity and interest," like Jews in Hitler's Germany or the "class" of Blacks in South Africa. If such a definition is applicable to women as a whole because of patriarchy, despite the differences amongst them (race, color, age), then it becomes possible for Scholes to critique both Derrida and Culler's (1982) position in "Reading Like as a Woman," as denying their experiences which form the bonds of their necessity and interest within that class. Deconstruction, as the ability of men to read texts *like* or *as* women, is legitimated because Derrida must deny any significant difference between speech and writing. "The fundamental in the edifice of deconstructive thought is the denial of any significant distinction between speech and writing, on the grounds that the apparent distinction between the co-presence of speaker and listener in speech and their mutual absence in writing is not a real distinction, there being no such thing as pure presence" (p.211-212). So says Scholes: "The same line of thought, if accepted, must lead us to the conclusion that there is no significant difference between reading about an experience and having an experience, because experience simply never occurs" (p.212).

The relationship between deconstruction and feminism is not so easily dismissed as Scholes believes (see Fuss, 1994). Mary Robertson (1986) is a strong supporter of deconstruction, claiming that its reception and application has fallen under abuse. She also mentions Culler's "reading like a woman" (p. 708-709) and dismisses it as being "uninteresting" because of its chastisement of "experience" as not being the absolute ground of Truth, by now a familiar ruse. But this does *not* mean that experience is *not* the site/cite/sight of reality and truth. For Robertson, deconstruction in the hands of French feminism have hypostatized "the play of difference into Difference" (p. 710). Woman's experience is perceived as irrational and incoherent. Deconstruction, on the other hand, never has left the empirical ground of experience. It examines experience as (non)rational. For Robertson, feminism should remain faithful to Derridean practice as a deconstructive "contortion" on the grounds that, unlike any forms of pragmatism (e.g., Rorty), it is able to maintain a paradoxical logic. The presentment of limits through the exposure of both binaries, which maintains a tension between opposing terms, is said to initiate quiet and patient revolutionary change without violent overthrow through simple inversion. Robertson tries to bridge deconstruction without dismissing experience. Modleski's (1986b) comments on Culler are not as kind: "[H]e treats feminism as a man would his wife who supports him through professional school and then is discarded once she has served her purpose..." (pp.131-132).

To avoid the reproachment of essentialism, the feminist rhetoric (de Lauretis, 1994a: Fuss, 1994) has been to adopt the definition of a *nominal essentialism* after Locke's *An Essay Concerning Human Understanding*. In that essay essence, rather than being defined as an unchangable Aristotelian universal, is redefined as a linguistic convenience, more of a utopian ideal, and a classificatory fiction to categorize and label reality. In this sense, "woman" as a linguistic gendered category solves her historical changeability, but it still must answer to the category of sex which still seems to support an Aristotelian universalism. But the category of sex is not so easily changed as has been argued (Shepherdson, 1994: Millot, 1990b). This suggests that men may become 'feminists' but not 'feminine' males, which, as the history of coveting such traits shows, has been to the woman's disadvantage (Battersby, 1989).

Shoo-ing/Shoeing Out the "Ladies" Man

Throughout this study, beginning with the preface, the role that Derrida plays concerning his stance towards women has been forever problematized. Janet Todd's (1988) review in her next to last chapter, "Men in Feminist Criticism," concludes that deconstruction "fails to read her texts or notice her corporeal presence in the present or the past" (p.129). In Jardine's (1985) text, his is a "pornosophical wink" (p. 180). Writing which operates outside metaphysical discourse is "the feminine operation," what she called gynesis, "the putting into discourse of 'woman' as that *process* diagnosed in France as intrinsic to the condition of modernity; indeed, the valorization of the feminine, woman, and her obligatory, that is, historical connotations, as somehow intrinsic to new and necessary modes of thinking, writing, and speaking" (p. 25). Yet this discourse puts "a woman-in-effect that is never stable and has no identity" (ibid.). By deconstructing man/woman, writing initiates the transvaluation of values. In a similar move, Braidotti (1991: 98-108) is particularly vehement when chastising the Derrida of *Spurs* for his ignoring the "reality of women," as is Scholes (1994); while Barbara Johnson (1987) says that he "may sometimes see himself as philosophically positioned as a woman, but he is not politically positioned as a woman. Being positioned as a woman is not something that is entirely voluntary" (p.2-3). In Flax's (1990b:212) terms, this would mean body over mind; feeling over thought; the pre-oedipal over the oedipal; the mother over the father; pleasure over work and production; the non-cultural other over culture; style over truth. Naming is a violence, but asks Jardine, is "being un-named through a re-naming-in-parts any less violent?" (p.183). The woman's body is evaporated into "female voices, hymens, veils, vaginas, *tocseins*, traces and texts,[6] *déja vue* of Magritte. In *Spurs*, Jardine notes Derrida's deconstructive lever is the word 'veil,' and that Nietzsche's styles are most consistently separated from themselves here. The text [Nietszche's Women and their Action at a Distance] is a realm of sexual undecidability (*le viol, la viole, le voile, la vole*) where the Truth is not to be decided because 'the text veils itself by itself unveiling itself'—like a woman. The text is veiled—both open and closed, like a flower, like a woman. But it would be a mistake to think that something lies behind its veils. The text hides neither truth nor untruth, but operates an uncertainty of vision which is no longer anguished, an uncertainty as to castration or non-castration—a dissimulation that, in its effect, is female to the extent that it is affirmative (that is, not anguished)" (p.198). This indictment reaches back to René Margritte (*Le Viol*) as a display of Derridean undecidability, as well to the preface and Žižek's "synchronicity" of the *cogito*. For Derrida, the ques-

477

tion of woman suspends a decidable opposition between the true and the non-true. However, to recall Rabine's (1990) critique, she will have none of that "hymian" ruse of the "between." Rather "[s]he hopes many people will heed Derrida's call to reduce the gap between philosophical deconstruction and political action; she hopes that this "between" will be thoroughly explored, and she hopes it will *not* be called a *hymen*" (p.37, my italic). Derrida is like a Flaubert who fetishized his own imaginary femininity but was still caught by his society's hostility towards women (Huyssen, 1986:189).

Flax's (1990b:212-216) own review of Derrida's ruse of the 'affirmative' woman, of 'writing' as opposed to 'style,' the *éperon* or spur, is a proposition she will not buy. "Woman as writing/other/style is 'outside' all concrete history and bodily experience or determination .... The specificity of being a woman in locatable and discrete cultures is lost" (p.214). Her arguments raise the spectre of the Romantic genius, the male who has taken on the 'feminine' and yet denies that experience for women (Battersby, 1989). And yet another feminist, Ruth Salvaggio (1990), borrowing the concept of "downmanship" from Barbara Johnson's frame of reference when she reviewed the two "Jocks/Jacques": "I wonder myself if it is this very sense of 'downmanship' —this stepping down from the assertion and quest of certitude associated with the masculine position—that makes Lacanian psychoanalysis and Derridean deconstruction into discourses which want to seduce the woman without themselves being seduced, that is, without themselves coming to any sexual or analytical conclusions" (p.152). For Derrida, woman remains an "untruth," for she cannot be "inscribed, imprinted, fixed." "They have named woman as the very process that disrupts closure in both its sexual and discursive sense" (p. 154). As Salvaggio concludes, woman's experience is still denied since writers like Gallop and Jardine are not speaking subjects; rather they speak "through the agency of a womanly man to reach her own woman..." (p.158).[7]

This denial of women's experience in deconstructive reading leads me to think of de Lauretis' last chapter in *Alice Doesn't* to reinstate the importance of recognizing the need to theorize "experience" as a process of semiosis. Semiosis is the work or activity that constitutes and transforms individuals through codes. Using Peirce's work she locates the active subject in the discursive intersection between Peirce's semiotics and psychoanalysis. Following Eco's rereading of Peirce's semiology as "pragmatic realism" and then extending both his and Eco's arguments, de Lauretis forcefully presents the necessity of bridging the gap between discourse and reality; between the sign and its referent; between signification and concrete action by examining an innocuous passage in *A Room of One's Own* by Virginia Woolf where Woolf describes an incident where she is motioned off a path in Oxford by a "Beadle." de Lauretis goes on to argue the code that was embedded in that very gesture by interrogating the semiotic discourse that was played over Woolf's body.

Peircean semiosis is able to give credence to practices that do make a difference to the grounding of perceptual and ideological codes: consciousness raising groups, alternative forms of labor organization, familial or interpersonal relationships. Both the interpretation and production of signs based on 'lived experience' does change the unconscious 'habits' (Peirce's term for the emotional, muscular and mental exertions and conceptual representations) so that the codes may be resisted and changed. Social practice becomes crucial for such self-analyses. "Since one 'becomes a woman' through the experience of sexuality, issues such as lesbianism, contraception, abortion, incest, sexual harassment, rape, prostitution, and pornography," (p.184) these become crucial themes. Such issues go beyond social and sexual (private) concerns. They are the very political and epistemological "immediate objects" of lived experience. Such reception theory tactics form in Umberto Eco's (1979) view the very last phase of semiotics—the "semiotics of reading." In *Technologies of Gender* de Lauretis solidifies her position, calling for a "multiple subject," a position i have criticized for its sociological reductions.

Benjamin (1986) has attempted to present the experience of a woman's desire as an alternative to the phallic structures of Lacan by drawing on D.W. Winnicott's work. Benjamin maintains that intersubjectivity provides the concept for such a conceptualization. "Intersubjectivity refers to what happens between individuals, and within the individual-with-others, rather than within the individual psyche" (p. 92). She tries to articulate and locate female desire in the 'transitional area' between mother and child. Within this space, which is a balance between holding and union, the child feels safe to be alone, explore, and be creative. Similarly, in a loving relationship where that same space is enacted, there is a heightened sense of self and pleasure with the other because each is allowed to 'be.' More exactly: "this experience of inner space [of women's desire] is in turn associated with the space between self and other: the holding environment and transitional experience" (p. 96). "[W]hat is experientially female is the association of desire with a space, a place within the self, from which this force can emerge. This space is in turn connected to the space between the self and other" (p.97). Woman's desire is not found in *freedom from,* but in *"freedom to,* freedom to be both with and distinct from the other" (p.98). Benjamin's strong call on women's culture strikes me very maternalistic and subject to the charges of essential womanhood.[8]

It may be recalled that Moi (1988) summed up the necessity of experience and the need of politics in particular. Feminism, for her, is (also) an impossible undertaking. From a liberalist stance feminism must engage itself in struggling for equality, that familiar position whereby women want to be *like* men. To become equal with men, women must paradoxically rest their case on *difference*, arguing not so much for equality but equity given to different social roles. They don't want to be just *like* men, but enjoy equal benefits. Such reasoning makes the jump to radical feminism and the danger of essential womanhood. Since patriarchy constitutes to oppress women *as women*, blacks as blacks etc., the local political situation is crucial to make Otherness specific. Participatory, not representative, democracy plays at both ends of the macro/micro continua. Moi's 'non-solution' to this is to "hold all three positions simultaneously... live out the contradictions of all three feminists and agonistically take sides" (p. 7). Ultimately it requires the need to make some hard decisions and accept the "pain, sacrifice and closure" that comes with it. Or in Flieger's (1990) accounting, to be at times the "Prodigal Daughter." But i am reminded of Hal Foster's (1985:143) words: "Clearly, the politics of representation is strictly a contextual affair: what seems radical in SoHo may be counterrevolutionary in Nicaragua. To rethink the political, then, is not to rule out any representational mode but rather to question specific uses and material effects—to question the assumption of truth in a protest poster, of realism in the documentary photograph, of collectivity in the street mural" (p. 143). Differences are at work, not *différance* in this case.

The strongest defence of Derrida (and deconstruction) for feminism has come from the stunning work on law by Drucilla Cornell (1991, 1992), Elam's (1994) rethinking of feminism along the ethics of a "groundless solidarity," and Renata Salecl (1994), a member of the Lacanian circle in Ljubljana, Slovenia, who has re-thought the question of democracy along the lines of the feminist logic of the non-all (see Preface). What binds these women together is their search for an activist feminist ethics that draws inspiration from Lacan (Salecl), Derrida (Cornell and Elam) and Levinas (Cornell).

The 'High' Art of Cindy Sherman
and 'Low' Art of Madonna:
The Material Girl Meets the Affirmative Woman

i should like to leave this discussion by returning once more to the Baudrillardian world hinted in the above section, this time with the *musings* of Cindy Sherman, that well-known chameleon and master of the masquerade who freeze-frames the cinema in photographs of herself in various disguises, and to the multiple gendered gazes of MTV as developed by Kaplan (1987) in *Rocking Around the Clock*. Cindy Sherman addresses one current of postmodernist 'high art' while the other, Madonna, comes "willingly" into households through MTV. To discuss these two women and their postmodernist art forms is perhaps to demarcate the distance between them and late modernism, where the feature-length film, relying on the narrative form was and continues to be the apotheosis of modernism. In contrast video, especially rock video, is a highly fragmentary, alinear form. Quantitatively, at least in measurable time, the distance between these two forms (cinema and video) can be seen as the gap between 3-4 min. and 2 hours; the gap itself is indicative of the increased density of communication for it requires less and less physical time to "read" hieroglyphic-like images whose intertextualities have been built by two decades of television and cinematic viewing. The implications are enormous as the spectator enters Baudrillard's (1983b) "ecstasy of communication." i have already discussed the research of Walkerdine who has provided the reader with a "sneak preview" as to how feature length video films may function as a form of resistance, at least in two specific sights/cites/sites. In contrast E. Ann Kaplan has tried to analyze rock video, not through the lived reality of reception aesthetics, but through a typological analysis of MTV's video hits. But before i turn to her study, it is first necessary to turn to Cindy Sherman for an understanding of the postmodern decentered ego as it is exemplified through her photographs.

"Will the real Cindy Sherman, then, please stand up!" Not present you say?! Absent. Gone for a walk perhaps? Hiding behind the photographic surface? If she truly *is* hiding, and it *is* not her essence that we see in her photographs, what *is* 'she' doing? scheming? flirting? being cute? What? And *where* is she? Williamson (1993) calls her art a *"process* of the 'feminine' as an effect, something acted upon" (p.104); but it may also be argued 'her' art shows the loss of voice, no language to speak, just a multiplicity of masquerades. The ultimate decentered subject, who *knows* what she's doing!? So Cindy Sherman does *not* exist as a Proper Name as Derrida might argue; rather she exists only as an intersection of femininity linked with eroticism. She is this one fragment 'split' off the mirror of her personality, a deconstructed *image* which, paradoxically, holographically contains the whole. The emotions of her narratives are " fear, suspicion, vulnerability, anxiety, or at best, uncertainty," which says Williamson, place the woman in a vulnerable and threatening position as if she is caught in a horror film—perpetually terrified and screaming on the inside. She invokes the interplay between death and sexuality.

Sherman is, i believe, in Sarah Kofman's (1985) threefold schema, the castrating woman.[9] "She castrates the metaphysics of truth, cuts its power, by playing it against itself. Like a chameleon, she changes to protect herself from threats in the environment, which undermines the fixity of the meta-physician's reality" (Oliver, 1984:191). Notes Derrida (1979:97), she plays with truth at a distance, "as if it were a fetish, manipulating it, even as she refuses to believe in it, to her own advantage." "She poses playfully to her own advantage. ... she cuts off the authority of the dogmatic truth by asserting equally believable illusions—she poses as the truth, but never takes herself seriously. As the artist the castrating woman cuts the power of the metaphysics of truth by replacing it with equally convincing disguises" (p.192). The will-to-truth, characteristic of the castrated woman who wishes to be like a man by search-ing for objective knowledge, is replaced by an Apollonian will-to-illusion. Appearance is chosen over reality, and effects over the truth of the woman as represented by man. Williamson's (1983) review of Cindy Sherman's art is equally castrating. "[W]e women" writes Williamson, "don't have to get trapped trying to 'be' the depth behind a *surface,* and men just might bang their heads up against it and stop believing in that reflected space" (p.106). She revels in the way a man was upset over how sexist Sherman's images were. Williamson was "certain his anger must have come from a sense of his own involvement, the way those images speak not only *to* him but *from* him—and he kept blam-ing Sherman herself for it" (p. 103). Later, she takes delight in criticizing Waldemar Januszczak's critique that Cindy Sherman is only a "small, scrawny girl from Buffalo" wanting to project herself as a sexy heroine like Marilyn Monroe. Here we have a male critic believing that all women wish to be desirable for men, not recognizing that Sherman may well be playing a dou-ble masquerade: first as that scrawny girl who positions her own look by reject-ing the male gaze and, secondly, by photographing herself as Marilyn she is able to cause confusion in the male gaze itself.[10] In Nietzsche terms:

> But after the inventive genius of the young female artists
> has run riot for some time in such indiscreet revelations of
> youth ... then they at last discover, time and time again,
> they have not been good judges of their own interest; that
> if they wish to have power over men the game of hide-
> and-seek with the beautiful body is more likely to win than
> naked or half naked honestly (in Oliver, 1984:192).

This is a ruse played often in the rock scene, where men have now become 'groupies' to female rock stars. But, perhaps unlike the female rock star, Sherman avoids what Nietzsche saw to be the castrating woman's downfall: being caught by her own illusions. "She is the actor as the hysterical little woman. She mistakes the means, her illusion, for an end. The castrating woman becomes [just] another version of the castrated woman" (Oliver, 1984:193).

Cindy Sherman will not be castrated. She cannot "stand up" for she, as in Derridean logic, is all and none of those images in her photographs. The 'artificial' and the 'real' Cindy Sherman are imbricated, like the zero in the number '10.' Zero is a number and yet not a number, yet zero forms the system of numbers and hides in them as well, becoming a place holder for the digits one through nine. The original Cindy Sherman is likewise hidden, existing perhaps in her capacity to control the lighting, the angle of the lens, the artifice of photography. Is this what makes her, in Nietzsche's sense, an 'affirmative woman,' driven by a will to power? Is she outside the discourse of truth? the "self-perpetuating Dionysian force who has no need for a foundation" (p.194)?

As Dionysus, her powers can be both destructive and creative, and judging by the way Sherman's art has been interpreted by men and women alike, she is continually affirming herself, needing no metaphysical foundation, nor creating one to which she may be trapped in her own 'light,' so to speak. Once more Williamson points to Sherman's most recent photographic series where the interplay between the castrating woman and the affirmative woman presents itself as Cindy Sherman the *performer* and Cindy Sherman the *photographer*. In these recent images there are some stills with only the barest hints of who is represented. They are bathed in darkness rather than light. It is as if these refer to that Dionysian force, the will to power, oscillating between masculine and feminine, and appropriating both at once. "Yet it is a myth, an origin which does not exist. The will to power is layer after layer of masks with no face behind the costumes. The will to power is the affirming woman. She is layer upon layer of marks, 'a papier-mâché balloon' " (p. 196), a Goddess with a thousand faces, each face a facet to a centerless whole/hole. "She is hollow like a womb. She is the space, the womb, from which everything originates. This space *is* distance: the affirming woman is not an object *in* the distance: rather she *is* distance. Her power is distance. As distance, as space—pure womb— she does not exist. Just as there is no woman, there is no truth" (p.196, my emphasis).[11] These passages echo Lacanian formulae of sexuation.

Yet again, the question is provoked whether art must play an *empty* game of hide and seek. If distance can never be closed—truth and woman forever unknown—then, says Nietzsche, it can only be bridged by the artist/castrated woman for the 'eternally feminine face,' "the eternal torrent of the will to power/affirming woman is too horrible a sight unless masked" (p.197). Michael Phillipson captures this dilemma of no hiding and no seeking, the dialectic between the second and third Nietzschean woman:

> Apparently in the cultural conditions of late modernity modern art increasingly realized itself as a project that had to work within the paradox of being both against and for the culture that supported it; it sought to retain traces of the self-alienation that defined the modern project in its heyday whilst recognizing the inescapable appropriations of the culture's all-pervading institutions (especially those whose very work was that of 'representation' itself). Art thus began to gather itself around 'values' standing aside from preceding 'aesthetics.' ... In this de-aesthetizing work of art appears to have represented its project through its impotence, its placelessness, its decomposing and withholding of 'meaning,' its undoing of the self and of the culture's conventions or representation (1989:viii).

This leads to the logic of Cindy Sherman as the affirmative woman who has no where to hide and no place to seek, in a culture that has no place for the 'real' her. Yet, a paradox manifests itself: just like Cindy Sherman offers the male spectator many fantasies, the dumb blonde, the punker, the fallen woman, *femme fatale*, the little-girl-lost, and so on, by creating a "potentially" politically charged image, this may well prove to be that part of a postmodernist sensibility which still retains a *critical* stance in a climate of high tech commercialism. Sherman, as a unified subject, has to disperse herself over several 'fields,' enter into the coded circuits of representation in order to disrupt their flows. Cindy Sherman joins Susan Holzer, Hans Haacke, Barbara Kruger as artists whose artistic statements try to find a place in amongst the crowded commercial images; but their images, and Sherman's, can be easily lost amongst the crowded noise of information.

In late capitalism the logic of the commodity and the logic of the sign are part of the same process of abstraction, one that traverses all fields of social production, and it is this process that constitutes ideology in advanced capitalist society today. Given this state of affairs, by which culture may no longer be an autonomous sphere (to negate), or no longer serves a consensual function (to expose) and in which the ideological may no longer simply be a mystification (that can be demystified), the definition and deployment of cultural resistance becomes difficult to pose (see Foster, 1985:159-169). For Foster, political art in a postindustrial society must play the role of "resistance" as a subcultural practice rather than a countercultural or transgressive one of the '60s. There may be no limits to transgress or no 'one' structural code that is defended by the hegemonic culture which would provide a definitive target for a unified critical avant-garde.

Drawing on the work of Baudrillard, Foster points to the changed conditions of late capitalism. "[P]olitical art is now conceived less in terms of the representation of a class subject ... than of a critique of social representations (gender positioning, ethnic stereotyping etc.)" (p.141) "Marxism, then, is faced with two displacements—from a concept of an (apriori) class subject of history (of subjectivity as subjection); and from a focus on the means of production (on use and exchange value) to an interest in the processes of circulation and the codes of consumption (sign value exchange)" (p. 143). Crucial to his position is the further recognition that there are technologies of control that 'discipline' our behavior (cf. Foucault and Baudrillard). "[C]onsumption defines the stage where the commodity is immediately produced as sign, as sign value, and where signs (culture) are produced as commodities" (p.145). So, argues Foster, through techniques of recuperation signs from other registers are appropriated and incorporated into a second-order semiological system to function as mere signifiers. In this innocuous manner, cultural industry generates what Barthes (1973) had identified as 'second-order myths.' Because of this, Foster (1985:169 ff.) argues that new strategies are required for resistance. One such strategy is to "rob myth of its myth," and then to have this "myth-critical art circulate with mass-signs so as to be socially current, but remains tactical, neither complicit with media functions nor anarchic only, neither a stylistic ruse nor a 'true' representation of its own" (p.170). This recoding of cultural signs offers "a parodic collage of the privileged signs of gender, class, and race, that are contested, confirmed, 'customized'" (Hebdige, 1979:116). What Hutcheson (1989) was to call 'dedoxification.' Having said this, the I can now return to Kaplan.

Kaplan (1987) has identified a particular genre of "postmodern feminism" in MTV video which in many respects repeats Cindy Sherman's ruse and satisfies Foster's call for the 'art' of a resistant art.[12] In her discussion of Madonna's videos,[13] she shows how the usual bipolarities are violated by the new postmodernist feminists: male/female, high art/pop art, film/TV, fiction/reality, private/public, interior/exterior. Kaplan points to Cindi Lauper, Donna Summer, and Pat Benatar as three postmodern feminists who "came in on the coat-tails of the 1970s feminist movement" and have gone on to make "socially conscious" statements. Benatar plays the "tough-woman image," Lauper has a "woman-identified space," while Donna Summer is explicitly "feminist." A strong "anti-parental sentiment" is evident, which deliberately "ridicules" adults. Tina Turner is said also to play the "tough" Black woman who "gains control over her own sexuality through enticing male desire" (p.137). Her struggle against sexual abuse in her own life are written into her songs. As Kaplan points out in her "Afterward," the image of each male and female star is constantly changing and refuses to be "fixed." Each is a subject in process, shedding and changing identities seemingly at will.

Madonna, in the "Open Your Heart Video," presents a critique of 'carousel porn parlors' of 42nd St. by rescuing an innocent boy by herself, running away from the parlour and escaping into "innocent boyhood." Susan McClary (1990) praises Madonna for dealing with tabooed themes, and for her "counternarrative of female heterosexual desire". Yet there is no original "Madonna," no original "Sherman"; their photographs and videos are ephemeral simulacra. They exemplify the assemblaged ego described by Deleuze and Guattari. "In Baudrillardian terms it [like postmodern feminists] reinvents signs and commodities with a symbolic ambivalence that threatens the principle of equivalence on which our social and economic exchange is based. It [like postmodern feminists] knows it cannot transform the code, but it can fetishize it to the point that it becomes apparent as such" (Foster, 1985:171). And if Cindy Sherman, Madonna, Cindi Lauper, Pat Benatar... do exist "off-stage," can the hyper-reality of *that* time provide anything but costume changes for the next show or the next video?

But how critical *is* all this? Anne Friedberg (1990), to illustrate "the narrow differences in the politics of appropriation between *recuperative* parody and *transgressive parody* (p.51), compares Madonna as the 'feminist Marilyn' in her "Material Girl" video to Sherman's photographic stills that quote Marilyn as a "to-be-looked-at object." Friedberg concludes that the question of transgression is undecidable between the two. Perhaps Marilyn continues to be "fucked" by both Sherman and Madonna in light of what i said earlier about the psychiatric profession's abuse (see Conundrums with the Gaze). Her quote has become a metonymic fetish available to anyone who wishes to use it. The "critical side" of the postmodern offers many conflicting and contradictory positions. At the 78th Annual Conference of the College Art Association meeting held in New York, Rosetta Brooks,[14] a critic for the art journal *ZG*, made the startling point that Robert Mapplethorpe had been acclaimed as a 'postmodern Master.' At the tender age of 32, Mapplethorpe, whose photographs play with similar conceptualizations as Cindy Sherman, put to question conceptualizations of masculinity, homosexuality and pae-dophilia, died of AIDS. Apparently, it no longer takes the 'historical test of time' to be written into the history books. Art criticism has now become somewhat redundant in its capacity to ratify who does and doesn't belong in the canon of art. Dealers have become crucial in creating and managing images and reputations. Music and art consultants play the market game. The Getty Foundation for the Arts can virtually control the market value of paintings that are available for auction. Again Kaplan's "Afterwards" gives an interest-ing anecdotal accounting as to the impossibility of fixing an image of a rock video star on the front cover of her book in fear that the image would be 'fixed' forever. From this perspective the 'deconstructed,' de-centered, assem-bled subject is a product of consummerist late capitalism. Its morphing capa-bilities generate good profit dollars! Hence, some art critics, like Donald Kuspit,[15] valorized the German Neo-Expressionist movement as a recovery of socially relevant art so as to overcome "the contradictory character of post-modernism" he outlined in an earlier paper (Kuspit,1990). He takes this move-ment to be a direct contrast to the vacuous world of American art which has lost its artistic tongue. Feminist critics were quick to point out that German neo-Expressionism centers with and ends with men in a frantic attempt to recover the fetishization of the signature and the painterly brush 'stroke,' repeat-ing the '60s phenomenon when men's masculinity was tied to a sexual 'out-burst' of paint over the large canvas.[16]

Foster's Baudrillardian thesis is tempting. It is difficult to identify which subcultural practices are *enabling* in their capacity to critique or to pro-mote values that further democracy. Resistant styles are not necessary enabling. Hebdige's (1979:113-127;1990:17-36) study of punk subcultures marked the point of postmodern nihilism. "The punks wore clothes which were the sar-torial equivalent of swear words, and they swore as they dressed—with cal-culated effect, lacing obscenities into record notes and publicity releases, inter-views and love songs. Clothed in chaos, they produced Noise in the calmly orchestrated Crisis of everyday life in the late 1970s ..." (p.114). But already by the time of the '80s, the punk culture had become 'transfunctionalized' into a 'third stage' of semiosis (Gottdiener, 1985:996), wherein the culture industry has 'tamed' and transmuted the rebelliousness as 'New Wave,' and then No Wave, and today 'Rap' and Hip Hop. By the time Kaplan (as part of her rock video typology) points to a category which she called nihilistic (a youth culture which actively fights against appropriation), this category has already gone into "receivership;" it has become a second-order mythology whose signifiers have been poached and appropriated by the entertainment industry. Every transgression against the law only helps to affirm it. Despite the similarities of appearance, Billy Idol is a long way from Johnny Rotten and Sid Vicious. In Willis'(1990a) account, youth culture must continually play a poaching game and stay one step ahead of appropriation.

In recent videos, it is the male who dons a new masquerade—that of the "androgynous look." "A Bakhtinian reading of this might argue that the adoption of female traits and clothing manifests a beneficial carnivalesque gender reversal" (Kaplan, 1987:93). How 'beneficial' is a moot point. The androgynous masquerade can be interpreted as a denial of any separate sexual difference. By possessing the feminine, the androgynous male has no desire for the feminine outside himself. Kaplan contributes one form of this androgyny to heavy metal bands and their nihilistic response to the world. "The nihilistic video...seeks to eliminate or to master the mother, displacing desire for her into sadistic possession" (ibid.). Such an aggressive phallic stage in the heavy metal, claims Kaplan, "deplores humanistic solutions and speaks violence and destruction without compunction" (p.102). The desire is to master and posses the Mother. "The hero will do anything for her only if she will succumb to him and worship his phallus as much as he does himself" (p.106). Heavy Metal band names, like Billy Idol, reinforce this self-fetishization. Despite Kaplan's useful analysis, there are always exceptions that put the generalities of psychoanalytic interpretations to the test. What would Kaplan say about Christian rock cast in the decor of Heavy Metal, bands like Stryper, Petra, and The Daniel's Band song, *Walk on Water*? There are fifty such bands in Britain alone, representing a pastiche of styles, all in the name of Christianity.[17]

In contrast to this nihilistic genre, Kaplan describes the romantic genre of video, coming from the '60s soft rock and operating at the pre-Oedipal level of bliss. Here, the infant-mother's gaze is inscribed in the video's aesthetic. Close-ups and preoccupation with the face are given. There are filmic dissolves that suggest regression to the moment when the mother's face represented plenitude, oneness, pre-Oedipal pleasure. Bi-sexuality as opposed to androgyny is played with. There is a desire to merge with the object of the lost mother as most of these videos premiere love songs. Bonding and attachment seem to be primary values. There are also what she calls, 'socially conscious' videos which come out of the late '60s and '70s acid rock Woodstock days. Phil Collins's *Another Day in Paradise,* about New York's homeless, is an example. These socially conscious songs deal with anti-establishment, working class identification, anti-authoritarian stance, anti-parental themes. It seems that the typology Kaplan outlines, romantic, socially conscious, nihilistic, classical (pastiche style that still rely on narrative story format), and postmodern outline a listening public which may be dated in generational shifts, the classical and the postmodern forming the two ends of its continuum.

Given that the primary emphasis of MTV is commercialism, given that postmodern feminists and socially conscious singers are given less air time in the never-ending 'flow' of entertainment, i am hesitant and ambivalent in following Foster and other critics, notably Linda Hutcheon (1988,1989), into supporting a parodic and ironic artform as being critical. Kaplan points out the various postmodern devices used by "resistant" political art have found their way into MTV: parody of previous signifying chains (especially Hollywood), pastiche, self-reflexivity, alinearity of time, self-criticism of MTV itself, frames within frames (*mise en abyme*), screens within screens, and play with images such as scrunching it up into balls. Rock videos are discourses and not history in that they foreground their sources of enunciation and comment on their processes of production. Abigail Godeau (1987), an influential art critic of photography, for example, discussing artists who use the "photographic quote" for political practice (Sherry Levine, Richard Prince, Victor Burgin, Cindy Sherman, Sarah Charlesworth, Silvia Kolbowski, Barbara Kruger, Vikkie Alexander, Martha Rosler[18]), to criticize the "institutional frame" have, in her opinion, lost their edge. Commenting on a 1985 exhibition in New York called "In the Tradition of: Photography at the Light Gallery," where both modernist and postmodernist photographs were displayed simultaneously, she concludes: "postmodernist photography, once conceived as a critical practice, had become a 'look,' an attitude, a *style*" (p. 12). Just as the painting of exposed women's crotches have outworn their tactical (political?) effects, so too has the "quote."

Yet much of what i am saying is coming from my own "reading formation;"[19] as an academic, someone who believed/believes in culture critique from a historical perspective and who still believes in the ecological movement and some form of 'spiritual materialism.' Having said this, the redeeming feature of parodic guerrilla warfare in specific sights/cites/sites where borderline games are fought, may be the few tactically games available for many artists today. Yet the danger of "chic" socialism begun by Live Aid, is always there. How do i answer to Sting's crusade to save the Amazon Jungle? Certainly i'm not against it, yet the spin-offs for records, books, promotion are good for business, aren't they? Am i dating myself: 'social criticism' is what i recall of the acid music that i used to listen to. Am i then, truly deaf and blind to it all—like Lukács was to Expressionism—in not recognizing that it's the only oppositional game in town? One need only to think that the bourgeoisie in a dependency position to the Church and Monarchy had to make tremendous concessions before their values could come to fore and their constitutions instituted. If i were to think on the 'sunny side' of things, i have to believe that these oppositional movements imbedded in the multinational popular cultures of late capitalism, like rock, rap and critical film present one more possible global strategy towards participatory democracy. Certainly these voices are buried in the institutions they critique, but their texts offer the teacher a Deleuzian and Guattarian "*minor*." If a 'strong' reading is able to draw out and 'screen' the critique through critical consumption by 'freeze framing' the flow, not to find the TRUTH or THE ANSWER, but to heighten responsibility and participation into the reconstruction of new possibilities, then there is hope for a critical education in a postmodern world.

That was then (1989-1990), this is now (1994).

1 Stanley Fogel's (1988) *Postmodern University*, is an enjoyable roll through the edges of dissent which wish to emerge in the universities but are kept down by current forces of conservatism and budgetary restraints.

2 Eugene Lunn's (1982) study of the different reactions to modernism by the four key aestheticians of the Left, Lukács, Brecht, Benjamin and Adorno, points out that a recurrent theme amongst all four was just how an oppositional art could 'outrun' its demise as just another new commodity form. By 1972 the art critic Rosenberg argued that the 'heroic phase" of the avant-garde was over (p. 282). Recently, Diane Crane (1987) has provided a definitive analysis of the absorption of the avant-garde into it current commodity status.

3 More importantly the exhibition curated by Tucker & Olander (1986), *The Art of Memory: The Loss of History*, at the New Museum of Contemporary Art in New York attempted to unravel the problems of the loss of a cumulative history.

4 Tallis's (1988) defence of the realist novel still recognizes the need for anti-realist novels to make us conscious of the artifice of all "writing."

5 By feminized i mean this in the double sense. In Donna Haraway's (1990) sense: "the family of the 'homework economy' where the work is being literally female and feminized whether performed by men or women. To be feminized means to be made extremely vulnerable; able to be disassembled, reassembled, exploited as a reserve labour force; seen less as workers than as servers; subjected to time arrangements on and off the paid job that make a mockery of a limited work day; leading an existence that always borders on being obscene, out of place, and reducible to sex. Deskilling is an old strategy newly applicable to formally privileged workers" (Haraway, 1990: 208). "[T]he 'family" of this home economy with its oxymoronic structure of women-headed households and its explosion of feminisms and the paradoxical intensification and erosion of gender itself" (p.209). The second sense of 'feminized' is totally antithetic. Elenor Lenz and Barbara Mayerhoff, in *The Feminization of America* (1985), s e e all aspects of culture becoming feminized because of the women's movement. This, over-optimistic thesis glosses over the real poverty and oppression Haraway brings out.

6 In her review of Jardine's *Gynesis*, Toril Moi (1988) chastises Jardine's valorization of the French postmodernist theory (i.e, Lacan's 'la femme'; Derrida's 'double chismic invagination,' Deleuze's 'becoming woman') as a form of positive *gynesis* (p.11) which fails to develop the material conditions for which a particular feminism Jardine supports. The repression of Otherness must have some sort of specificity otherwise Derrida's 'feminine writing' loses its political force and once more the oppression of women's lived lives is avoided.

7 Four years later, after the above commentary was written, the issue of Derrida's 'women' continues to be hotly debated. Sally Robinson (1990) commentary seems to overlook Derrida's "third woman" entirely. Drawing heavily on Luce Irigaray's essay (1983), "Veiled Lips." trans. Sara Speidel, *Mississippi Review* (Winter-Spring), Robinson reads Derrida's Woman as a feminine textual space that is divorced from "woman's femininity," "female sexuality," and even female subjectivity. Following Irigaray, woman becomes an item of exchange between Derrida, Nietzsche, Heidegger. Irigaray evokes the figure of Athena as a "man's woman" whose legend historically replays a position between men in the patriarchal pan-

theon of Zeus's relationship to Hera. Irigaray could have just as easily evoked the figure of the Virgin Mary who equally mediates an in-between position between men: Christ and God the Father. Her Greek example is aimed at Nietzsche.

In yet another attempt to come to terms with Derrida's Woman, Jennifer Thomas (1993) articulates how Derrida might have been misread by Irigaray by initiating a close reading of his essay which points to the non-discursive play of the French language. It becomes obvious, when reading her essay, that the ability to attend to the nuances Derrida provides in his essay in *Spurs* is beyond the capabilities of most scholars. One would have to be sensitive to the grammatical changes in French stylistics, which Thomas is—dwelling on Derrida's use of the exerque and pointing to Derrida's change to the conditional tense when remarking on the *figure* of woman—as well as having a razor sharp mind for argument. Personally, the whole debate is rather arcane and disheartening, for no matter how much i try to comprehend the nuances between Derrida, Irigaray, Doane, and all those others who are certain that the third woman is a failed ruse, in the end, it becomes little more than an academic game.

8 Linda Williams's *Hard Core* (1989) calls on Benjamin to provide a re-orientation to female desire in the new women's porn of Candida Royale.

9 In Sarah Kofman's *The Enigma of Woman* (1985), threefold schema was as follows: The first woman is the hysteric who is need of psychoanalysis. Hence she is linked to 'the mask or the lie.' Kofman claims the second woman to be Freud's Mother who teaches him the law of difference. It is she who teaches him the science of psychoanalysis. She is also the narcissistic woman who separates herself from the masculine world. Because she remains mute and silent, a blank page, it is the male who speaks her truth for her. Hers is an enabling position, but feminism has been effectively appropriated by man (i.e. Derrida and company?). Lastly, the third woman in Kofman's reinterpretation of Nietzsche is the one who breaks the bondage of the first and second woman. She refuses castration and hence holds bisexual powers. She has an undecidable sexual difference, oscillating between the masculine and the feminine. She affirms her femininity by refusing to be castrated. This is made possible by playing the phallic mother. She possesses and does not possess the phallus (Berg, 1982). She is Dionysiac and "scandalous."

10 Sherman is therefore the very antithesis of the Marilyn figure, which in my mind at least, was "fucked" by the patriarchal system as i vehemently wrote earlier. See Fucking Marilyn Over... and Over ... after 1962: The Necrophilic Practices of Psychiatry in "The Conundrums of the Gaze."

11 Such logic fits Silverman's (1992) call to play with the masks of the screen.

12 Kaplan has outlined a typology of five different types of videos: romantic, socially conscious, nihilistic, classical and postmodernist. It is this last category where a number of 'postmodern feminist' singers are categorized.

13 See Vignette three for Kaplan's discussion on Madonna's "Material Girl", "Papa Don't Preach".

14 The session was entitled, "Significant Directions in the 1980s" and was held on Saturday, Feb 17, 1990.

15 In a talk entitled "The Primacy of German Art in the 1980s," given at the College Art Association, 1990, New York in a session entitled: Significant Directions in the 1980s, chaired by Jeanne Siegel.

16 The polemics, for example, between Kuspit and Benjamin Buchloh over German expressionism may be found in Brian Wallis's (1984) excellent edited overview of postmodernist art (up to 1984), *Art After Modernism: Rethinking Representation*. Kuspit's essay is entitled, "Flak from the "Radicals":The American Case against German Painting," while Buchloh's essay reads as,"Figures of Authority, Ciphers of Regression." A delightful short film which explores the relationship between New York Abstract Expressionist artists of the '50s sense of virility and sexual prowess in relation to the size of their canvasses and paint strokes can be found in *New York Stories*. (See, footnote 13 in "Pretexts to the Title.")

17 Featured on the television series *Man Alive*, Sept.15, 1989.

18 This is a good example of the anxiety brought on by "listing" those artists who will fit the category. Has Godeau missed someone? Are these friends she has come in contact with as a critic of photography? Have this particular group been written about in one of the thousands of museum catalogues which have limited distribution, and hence are only available to those who are aware of the scene/seen? Does Godeau, in criticizing the re-appropriation of the quoted image as a new style, indeed help to make it a style through her writing and publishing? am i, then complicit to all this by recognizing that she is someone who has written about this postmodern confusion?

19 By reading formation, i mean "a set of discursive and intertextual determinations which organize and animate the practice of reading, connecting texts and readers in specific relations to one another in constituting reading subjects of particular types and texts as objects to be read in particular ways" (Tony Bennett, 1986, in Kaplan, 1987:26).

491

HONEY
I SHRANK ...!

Male Hysteria

Lacanian psychoanalysis is, I
suggest, a rearguard attempt to
rescue the potency of the 'law of
the father' as an abstraction, at the
very moment when it is
disappearing as a political force.

(Anne McClintock, 1993a:15)

It should have become obvious to
the reader by now that this is a
hysterical text.

The two Disney films, *Honey, I Shrank the Kids* (d. Joe Johnson, 1989) and its sequel, *Honey, I Blew up the Kid* (d. Randel Kleiser, 1992) were perhaps meant as a warning (by the moral Right?) that parents had neglected their kids. Rick Moranis plays Wayne Szalinski, the somewhat *ex*-centric nerdy inventor whose technology does the dastardly deed—it shrinks and blows up his kids. (After all, don't they have their heads buried in computer games already?) But no one is held responsible, only the effects of nature's chaos. Szalinski's machinery does it accidentally, and without feeling. There is no "sorry." A Lacanian, with a twist of Žižek (1992:3-20), might read these films as the paradox of *objet petit a*, the object of desired fantasy. Parents either *over*look their children, unable to find them– children must undergo the trials and tribulations of life by themselves–or their monstrous disproportionality makes them impossible to communicate with. The paradox of parenting, it seems, is that they can never *attain* their children—pull up beside them, communicate with them on some equal plane. At any given moment, the (parent and/or child) is either too small or too big. The child as the *objet petit a* is the impossible object for the parent, near and yet far away, monstrous yet familiar at the same time. It is difficult not to enjoy applying such philosophical banter. Its applicability seems to be found everywhere: feminine desire is said to be too close, too near to gain critical distance, hence the need for a masquerade—feminine, queer or "otherwise"; masculinity is said to be too distant, objective, requiring forms of softening. The first is coded low; the second is coded high. Again the object is overlooked—or perhaps found in hybridity as has been already argued. Fantasy designates the subject's impossible relation to *objet petit a*, the object-cause of its desire, i.e., the child. Parents are condemned forever to "search" for their children. Some stop and give up.

While it may be possible to continue this meditation on parenting (i will return to this later), for now i want to draw your attention to the filmic titles: that a penile metaphoric displacement is at work here seems likely. Ejaculatory power! The films span a three-year gap, from the late '80s to the early '90s, the approximate time frame when this "book" was written. i want to offer and develop a thesis in this section, part of which will return me to parenting, but the bulk of which will discuss the shrinking phallus, and then its sudden ejaculation into monstrous size as it recovers from its shock. Either way the *objet petit a*—the phallus-remains an impossible object of male fantasy. The thesis to be explored is simply this: as women continue to enter the workforce into areas which were typically male dominated; and as technology makes it possible for women to do jobs which previously required muscle and upper body strength; and as gay and lesbian rights become more and more visible,[1] dominant heterosexuality with its concomitant view of masculinity is/has been(ing) threatened. Two years ago, Modleski (1991a) had written how male-to-male desire had been either so obviously repressed (e.g., *The Dead Poets Society*) or so obviously flaunted (e.g., *Lethal Weapon*) that this balance between openness and secretness was impossible to negate, and i would add navigate.[2] To overcome such threats traditional masculinity as represented in a capitalist patriarchy has had to regroup its forces and regroup family values.[3] In the following section i shall develop just how it has done this.

Hypermasculinity: The Penile Body "Pump" or, It's Not Just in the Shoes

To begin then, it is interesting to note the following phenomena. First, superheroes have been revived, not only on the big screen but in comics. With the death and resurrection of the comic book Superman, several super-*men* are now available. Superman has been splintered into several personalities. In the new television series *Lois and Clark: The New Adventures of Superman*, Lois's name is billed ahead of Clark, and she has an equal role to play. Lois is now unabashedly free to chase Superman's 'bod' in search of her own pleasure. Her character is stern, calm in the heat of action, coded as masculine. Batman has lost his sidekick Robin, supposedly for homosexual innuendoes, although Robin is about to be revived in the movie *Batman II*, while his début on the screen revealed his dark and vulnerable side.

The second phenomena will take some space to work out. The phenomenal increase in the fitness revolution, especially weightlifting—body building for both men and women. The question here has to do with body image. In Western culture the mesomorphic (well-proportioned, average build) is a desirable body for heterosexual men (Mishkind, et al.,1986). "This physique is the 'muscleman'-type body characterized by well-developed chest and arm muscles and wide shoulders tapering down to a narrow waist" (p.547). A rippling set of abdominal muscles is also desirable. Such bodies are typical of superheroes. Women call such men "hunks," calendar "beefcake"—the male equivalent of the model pin-up.[4] Men carry with them images of both their own body and their ideal body which are non-identical. They are often in constant pursuit to close this gap. This is an extremely important point since it is at the heart of sex/gender identity formations. This primacy of the imaginary may be explained by considering the structural lack of any signifier of femininity or masculinity in the unconscious. This lack of a symbolic prop (some however do claim there is a biological prop attributable to the genes) requires an act of choosing from what constitutes a man or a woman's being, made from the differences that are socially available to "it." Often this is an ideal conformity that appears "natural." This also applies to a gay male subculture which places an elevated importance on all aspects of a man's physical self—grooming, body building, dress and handsomeness (Kleinberg, 1980, in Mishkind et al.). If women suffer from anorexia and bulimia when they try to close the gap to achieve ideal beauty, men suffer from an addiction to sports and fitness to achieve their ideal body type.[5] Achieving such a body often brings with it the rewards of being confident, powerful, strong, independent, and efficacious. Lifestyle change and self-management have become the new religion for promoting health and *inward* growth as self-improvement.[6] The specularization of the body in the consumer logic of capitalism and its subsequent narcissistic practices (plastic-surgery, hair-transplants, therapy, diet, aerobics, body-building) are well-known themes taken up by Christopher Lash's (1979) concept of cultural narcissism.

Mishkind and his colleagues believe this to be symptomatic of the crisis of masculinity in general. Once a man could be assured of his masculinity by virtue of his occupation, interests, or certain personality characteristics. Times have changed. The five traditional archetypes of masculinity—soldier, frontiersman, expert, breadwinner, and lord—are now archaic artifacts, although their images remain. By process of elimination, the expert and breadwinner are no longer exclusively male, and the frontiersman and lord are no longer viable; only the "soldier archetype" remains as an image males have held since youth. Body building becomes a way of recovering such an image. The performed body is intensely stylized, making its purest existence "show" especially at the competitive level.[7] Tasker (1993a:242), following Zavitzianos's (1977) notion of "homeovestism"—defined as "a perverse behavior involving wearing clothes of the same sex" (p.242/p.489) —recognizes the wearing of uniforms associated with paternal authority (sports and military) as a way to "stabilize the body image, to relieve anxiety and to raise self-esteem" (ibid.). In Lacanian terms, Tasker continues, the concept of male parade (i.e., wearing ties and medals) are "the accouterments of phallic power, the finery of authority, belie the very lack that they display" (ibid.).

If Mishkind's premise is extended to today's video games and the cyberpunk genre, which feature lots of muscle as well, traditional masculinity is thereby preserved with the additional roles of frontiersmen and policemen making a comeback as "space cowboys," *Robocops*, and *Demolition Men*.[8] The masculine frontier has been displaced off the earth and into space of the future, and onto other planets by the trajectory of what Romanyshyn (1989) has called "the symptom and dream of technology," the desire to become the human homunculus in the machine. Throughout numerous sci-fi films the

496

hypermasculinized performed body is at "work," playing out male fantasies of the law enforcer, solitary hero soldier, frontier explorer *(Robocop, Running Man, Terminator, Outlander, Last Action Hero, Free Jack, Demolition Man* etc.) in what Fred Glass (1990) calls the "New Bad Future" (NBF). In these films body-building remains the single most obvious site/sight/cite of this hysterical hypermasculinization. Muscle, the traditional signifier of physical work, has become decoration, a signifier of aesthetized narcissism. Arnold and Sylvester compete on a regular basis, quoting each other across the screen surfaces for the year's best cultural object of fetishism. As has often been remarked, their bodies offer a point of narcissistic identification. "A male movie star's glamorous characteristics are thus not those of the erotic object of his gaze, but those of the more perfect, more complete, more powerful ideal ego conceived in the original moment of recognition in front of the mirror" (Mulvey, 1975:12).

Steve Neale (1983/1993) extends Mulvey's remark about the male protagonist and the extent to which his image is dependent upon the narcissistic phantasies of the "more perfect, more complete, more powerful ideal ego" by pointing out (after Rodowick, 1982) that there is a certain amount of frustration and inadequacy (castration) that goes along with this identification, as well as an eroticism with the body itself. In other words, the frustration means a masochistic deferral of identification with the male star, i.e., he is "bigger" than me, while the eroticism presents a homoerotic object choice. The I can contemplate and admire his "bigness." The homoerotic look, however, presents problems for heterosexuality. It threatens male masculinity and consequently needs to be repressed. Neale argues that the economic libidinal exchange of sadomasochism works throughout these heroic genres to do precisely that. The hero's body is tortured, shot, mutilated so that it can be disqualified as an object of erotic contemplation and desire. The sadistic role of violence is to police homosexuality. On the other hand, the *pure* spectacle of the fight: the duel, the sword-battle, hand-to-hand combat (pure in the sense it stops the forwarding of the narrative) intertwine both voyeuristic and fetishistic gazes (both farness and closeness), which allow the display of the body for pleasurable looking through a socially acceptable masculine ritual. Violence in this form is on the side of "good." Homoerotic identification of the combative spectacle is now more allowable since it displays the masculine body on the side of justice.[9] Torn shirts, tank tops, and sporting a more effeminate sartorial code, like Steven Seagal's pony tail, have become common. Spectatorial violence offers both pleasure and pain, the every enactment of sadomasochism.

Neale (1992) also supports (after Mulvey,1981) the way heroic masculinity is further split into a social compliance and integration with the law—narratives either close with the hero marrying, i.e., his coming together with the woman of his dreams and thereby accepting responsibility to the family—or remaining an outsider to the law; what Neale and Mulvey consider to be a form of "nostalgic narcissism." The hero stands alone, refusing to accept the social standards of fatherhood. Like the Lone Ranger, he rides off into the sunset, leaving responsibilities behind and the woman longing for his return. Nostalgia here polices the threat of the feminine and the threat of entrapment: not being free to do what he wants, whenever he wants. So when these bodies are torn apart, riddled with bullets, often in slow motion, as in the last sequence of *Butch Cassidy and the Sundance Kid*, they "can be viewed at one level at least as the image of narcissism in its moment of disintegration and destruction" (Neale,1983/ 1993:15) or, in another instance, as a moment of suspended animation as when 'Solo' of *Star Wars* fame is frozen in molten metal, or John Spartan (Sylvester Stallone) is thawed from cryogenic imprisonment to do battle in the future with Simon Phoenix (*Demolition Man*, d. Joel Silver, 1994). In its 'purest' and most refined state then, narcissistic nostalgic hyper-masculinity must be guarded from both homosexuality and femininity. Compassion and gentleness are only shown in moments when heroic action has been accomplished; the weak have been defended. These are celebratory moments which continually reaffirm and justify heroic work.

Perhaps a more fruitful way to theorize violence and heroic action is to go back to Lacan's 'mirror phase' once again, recalling that the infant's anticipation to achieve control and unity by assuming an image of itself in the mirror (metaphorical or actual) is caught up in misrecognition. The ideal image the child sees is but a mirage. The child, when captured by its ideal image, is alienated by a fundamental discord between its physical body and the ideal ego of the mirror image. This 'crack' or 'split' is experienced as a fundamental lack (as *objet a)*. The imaginary overcoming of this division within the self as a split subject ($) can occur only in fantasy through the Other, as a pursuit of the lost *objet a* in its imaginary mode within another person. Hypermasculinized heroes who are strong and self-sufficient seem to lack nothing; they present an ideal image in the mirror, and seem to desire nothing. In other words, they mask the demand of desire, seemingly not needing anyone, which is a fundamental impossibility. (It may be recalled that the good Doctor Kellogg in *Wellville* was "heroic" in precisely this way.) To recall this "impossibility," Lacan drew distinctions between need, demand, and desire to theorize how desire emerged from the other two terms. A biological *need* became an articulated *demand* when the child moved into the symbolic order of language. On the level of demand the child asks its m(other) for a specific object to fulfill its need, but the articulation of that need as a demand brings with it an *additional demand* for love and attention. *Desire* is this excess of demand over need (e.g., that "something" which Doctor Kellogg never gave to his adopted son George). It is the remainder in very demand that cannot be reduced to a need. When the m(other) is unable to wholly fulfill the child's demand for love, anguish arises. In the child's desire to have the m(other) fulfill its lack, it encounters the lack in the m(other). At that moment the child learns that the mother is not all-powerful and not the perfect other that will guess what it wants. As is well-known, Lacan terms the object that embodies the surplus of demand over need as *objet petit a*. This object stands for the emptiness which the child encounters when its demands remain unsatisfied (e.g., George in *Wellville*). So objet a is what the m(other) lacks, what the child imagines it wants but can't get.

Hypermasculinized heroes, therefore, deny this anguish and deny that they lack anything. They shun pain and feelings. They need no one for support and pretend that their mirrored reflection is self-sufficient. Perfection has no desire. Its *jouissance* is the amassment of power, the fascistic dream of omnipotence. In its "cyborgian form" this perfection simply becomes a *drive* (*Trieb*), a demand that avoids being caught up in desire. It is simply a "mechanical" insistence that continually and perpetually comes at you. As Sarah Connor tells Kyle Reese in *Terminator*, "it can't be bargained with, it can't be reasoned with, it doesn't feel pity or remorse or fear and it absolutely will not stop, ever, until you are dead" (in Springer, 1993:95). But the cost of such completeness, as the impossible mastery of the mirror image, is aggression towards anyone who comes between the hero and his desired image of unity, (his ideal image), or to anyone who provides the hero with a romantic possibility of unity (usually a woman), whereby his weakness as lack is exposed and his wholeness threatened. Traditionally it is the woman who is situated at the sight/cite/site of lack by being beaten, attacked, raped, threatened, or killed. Violence is dished out because of the lack in the Other, the very lack that the hero cannot face himself. Hence, paradoxically, he converts his very narcissism into aggression.

Villains who are terrorizing society offer yet another way that the hero can mask his own lack. They represent an obstacle to social harmony and order which blocks his desire for a perfect ego ideal. In short, they are the ones who lack, and their elimination fills the very hole the hero himself lacks. In some instances the violence is directed at the killing of his counterpart, his very complement—a Doctor Jekyll and Mr. Hyde complex. It's as if he can no longer stand looking at himself *looking*, facing his own "flaw" so to speak, which is what his counterpart enables. When the counterpart gets "too" close, and exposes the hero's mask, suicide is inevitable with the "loss of face," the very face the hero cannot bear to expose. The counterpart must die in the end, as in the ridiculous film *Double Impact* (d. Sheldon Lettich, 1991), where Chad's (played by Claude van Damme) evil twin brother Alex (played by Claude van Damme) must die if good is to triumph. A form of suicide is also inevitable when the hero chooses (often a heroic) death in preference to an existence which he has (or will have) that is intolerable, e.g., Patrick Swayze's plea to take his "last" surf ride during a hurricane at the end of *Point Break* rather than spend his life in jail; Sam Peckinpah's filming of the suicidal stance of the "wild bunch" against countless Mexican soldiers at the film's end (*Wild Bunch*); the stereotypical soldier-hero-leader who would rather die with his platoon than face the responsibility for his failure (see Lapsley and Westlake, 1992/1993:186-187).

In a highly complex article, Jonathan Goldberg (1992) attempts to apply a psychoanalytic reading of Schwarzenegger's passion for body-building and how this relates to his cyborgian fame on the "big" screen. In relation to what has been discussed so far concerning hypermasculinity,[10] the patrolling of homosexuality is evident throughout all of Schwarzenegger's films; however, Schwarzenegger openly accepts the gaze of the gay man! There is no contradiction here. For Schwarzenegger, it is analogous to a straight man looking at a women. In this way homosexuality, as same sex preference, is dismissed within a heterosexual/sexist construction of gender. Gender difference here is defined by gender opposition. In other words, the homospectatorial gaze is allowable at the same time it is denied by incorporating it within a phallic economy, i.e., gay men worship he-men because they themselves are wimps. Men, while body building, are constantly looking in the mirror, at themselves and at other men. But within this look Goldberg finds a fundamental anxiety of masculinity that circulates around the concept of size, i.e., bigness and smallness. Size now replaces gender, which may help explain how it is that women body builders have become accepted in this traditional male enclave. The body of both sexes is reified as a thing, judged by the aesthetics of size and full development. Schwarzenegger is quoted as saying, "You don't really see a muscle as part of you, in a way. You see it as a thing. You look at it as a thing and you say well this thing has to be built a little longer ... And you look at it and it doesn't even seem to belong to you. Like a sculpture" (in Goldberg, p.176).

The phallus is an imaginary object, *objet petit a* which is impossible to attain. The equation of the penis with phallus can never achieved so it (the penis) is displaced throughout the entire body as a "pump." The pump makes the body grow hard (and jump higher!). Like a woman's pump, her walk is heightened, hardened and exaggerated. The "pump" is a supplement to the phallus/penis, the total body in masturbation. A paradigmatic example of this is illustrated by a photo of Carl Lewis. Carl Lewis (fig. 18), the Olympic gold medal winner for the U.S., is dressed in his racing uniform, wearing red high-heel pumps. His legs look as good as any model's and could easily pass as such. Photographed by none other than Annie Leibovitz herself, Lewis was paid a million German marks (a little less than a million US dollars) to advertise a tire company whose name is not even mentioned. The obvious sensationalism is enough to divert the eyes.

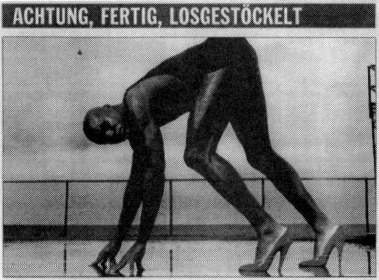

ACHTUNG, FERTIG, LOSGESTÖCKELT

Eine Million Mark kassierte der Weltklassesprinter Carl Lewis dafür, daß er sich von der Weltklassefotografin Annie Leibovitz in Stöckelschuhen ablichten ließ. Der tiefere Sinn des Spektakels: Werbeaufnahmen für eine Reifenfirma.

fig. 18 Carl Lewis, *Achtung, Fertig, Losgestöckelt*
(Ready, Set, "Strut")

Creed (1987) has this summary comment:

Both actors [Stallone and Schwarzenegger] often resemble an anthropomorphized phallus, a phallus with muscles, if you like ... They are simulacra of an exaggerated

501

masculinity, the original completely lost to sight, a causality of the failure of the paternal signifier and the current
crisis in the master narrative (p. 65).

Paternalism is something that always haunts Schwarzenegger, Goldberg
tells us. In *Pumping Iron*, he occupies "the father's place in every possible locale"
(p. 175). But, as you shall see, his role as a paternal signifier is about to change
and relocate in yet another place. The transition of the he-man body to that
of the cyborg is a complicated one, cleverly described by Goldberg analysis
of the *Terminator*, the movie which furthered Arnold's career. "The Terminator
embodies a 'new order of intelligence' that is resolutely anti-human and anti-
reproductive" (p.185). It would seem that Schwarzenegger's paternity is for-
feited, or should i say "terminated?" But not so, for after all, it is Schwarzenegger,
a flesh and blood "pumped" body and a star, who *is* the Terminator. There is
a triple conflation here: the body of the bodybuilder, machine and star are
ONE. The paternal is now replaced by a cyborg whose reproductive technologies are a new combination of flesh (the 'humanized' body of hypermasculinity) and machine (alluding to the repetition and iron used in creating such an excessive body[11]). This is confirmed when the
Terminator/Schwarzenegger cuts into his arm to reveal the machinery underneath. He even removes one of his *eyes*, not to become a dumb Cyclops with
just one eye. No! But to repair himself, to build his eye back to its normative
function.

The cyborg is, in effect, an inverted bodybuilder. The technologies
that made his outer appearance what it is (physical and psychological) have
displaced his organic being. Goldberg brilliantly notes that: "The simulated
'real' eye is displaced by another 'real,' the red light that will signal life to the
end of the film. This artificial life realizes a dream of the bodybuilder" (p. 186-
187). That dream, Goldberg tells us, is never to get old, never age, to remain
"infinite," ageless—to perhaps live in the suspended animation of nostalgic
narcissism. This dream of never aging, is to forever push back the death instinct,
to stop the work of nature; it is the dream of unlocking the secret of every
single gene through biogenetic research which is believed to control our physical and emotional conscious processes, and then grafting, recording, imprinting, that information back onto the machine to give it flesh. And the result:
Data from the *Starship Enterprise*, "The new generation." The creators of these
cyborgs are either benevolent, kind scientists, like Dr. Sung, or the evil
McCandless of *New Jack* (d. Geoff Murphy, 1992), or Tyrell himself in *Bladerunner*
(d. Ridley Scott, 1982). Dr. Sung dying, in need for a healthy body, builds one
so as to transfer his consciousness; McCandless dying, in need for a healthy

body, steals one so as to transfer his consciousness; and Tyrell, living off the bodies he has built, is killed by them. The anxieties of technologies end in dystopias. But wait! There is a way to save us yet. Why, it's ... it's Arnold Schwarzenegger! He's come back, new and improved, to save humanity ... yet again?

In *Terminator 2* Jeffords (1993) argues, the "inverted cyborg" has become both the father and the mother of humanity. In a world where traditional masculinity is being threatened, male viewers, particularly White male viewers may feel "increasingly distanced from what they understand to be traditional males forms of power and privilege can be empowered through the assertions of the role male individualism must play in the future of humanity. *Terminator 2* can offer these viewers not only a panacea for their feelings of disempowerment, but it can reinforce the culturally-designated culprits of that scenario in the guise of technology, machines, non-passive women, and managerial blacks as well" (p.257-258). Most importantly, for my purposes here, is the way Jeffords identifies the trajectory of Sarah's demise as a mother as the Terminator slowly, throughout the narrative, takes over the role of parenting John Connor, her son. This new emergent role for the Terminator in the sequel is meant to introduce to the viewing audience the "new," more internalized man of the 1980s, "who thinks with his heart rather than with his head—or computer chips" (p.253). T2 offers the "ostensible explanation for why men of the 1980s are changing their behavior: they have learned that the old ways of violence, rationality, single-mindedness, and goal-orientation ... were destructive, not only for individual men, but for humanity as a whole" (ibid.). The death of the "old" masculinity is presented at the film's end when the Terminator is lowered into the melting iron. John Connor now represents the "new" masculinity, having chosen his own biological father (Kyle Reese), and having reprogrammed his "mechanical father into the 'kinder and gentler' Terminator" (p.260). Jeffords' (1989) earlier account of the "remasculinization" of America presents a similar argument; however, it should be noted that hers is a textual analysis. Robert Deming (1992) questions this "remasculinization" thesis, first by reviewing the sheer variety of television shows in the '80s targeted for various "masculinities," and second, by arguing that there are many subject positions that can be taken while viewing these shows, many of which are occupied by a female audience as well. A more adequate way of assessing the situation, he says, is to recognize that patriarchy "is always working against itself, always setting up more 'difference' from what it wants to be, always dismantling itself from within" (p.133).

i can agree with Deming yet recognize that theorists like Jeffords have identified the narratives of the masculine dispersal. Claudia Springer

(1993) makes a similar case as Jeffords on the premise that sexual difference of the cyborg is presented on the opposition between a two-sex model. Whereas the women's genitals are described as internal, hidden, and inert, and thus associated with the interior spaces of the body—the fluid and fluctuating internal systems, men are defined by the aggressive penis—dry solid and hard physical strength. Hypermasculinity in her mind is an "anachronistic industrial-age metaphor of externally forceful masculine machinery, expressing nostalgia for a time when masculine superiority was taken for granted and an insecure man needed only to look at technology to find a metaphor for power of phallic strength" (p.96). However, electronic technology has become feminized: "its bodily equivalents are concealed as fluid internal systems," and its interaction with humans "no longer fortifies physical prowess." *Terminator 2: Judgment Day*, Springer says, demonstrates the clash of the two metaphors: T-800 (Schwarzenegger) vs. T-1000 (Robert Patrick), hard vs. liquid metal. While the cyborg Eve 8, in the film *Eve of Destruction* (d. Duncan Gibbins, 1990), has also been "feminized"—literally, but for a different reason. As Springer argues, Eve 8 (Renee Soutendijk) "continues a misogynistic tradition exemplified by the 1926 film *Metropolis* (Fritz Lang) of associating technology with women's bodies to represent the threat of unleashed female sexuality" (p.97). She is equipped with a nuclear bomb located "deep inside her womb, at the end of a tunnel inside her vagina" (ibid.). As the fetishized phallic woman who is a killing machine, Eve 8 "evokes patriarchal fascination with and fear of that which is concealed and mysterious" (p.97). Fuchs' (1993) assessment is similar to Springer. "Finally, Dr. Eve plunges the nozzle of the weapon into Eve VIII's already bloody socket, a gesture which is simultaneously self-penetrating, self-destroying, and self-redeeming" (p.126). In Fuchs' review of *Robocop* and *Terminator* series, and in her discussion of *Eve of Destruction* and *Hardware* the thesis of a male hysteria that offers no resolution is repeated.

Perhaps a more insidious reading of the T-1000 cyborg is that of Albert Liu (1993) who also concurs that the old masculinity is in its "last days." "T-1000's gender," says Liu, "is readable only in the way that we assign genders to certain worms with no regard for their sexual characteristics" (p.108). Described as a "boneless," "postcybernetic," "pure material" body, characterized by the "serene coldness of a self-healing organism" that is "not organ-ized in cellular formations," T-1000 is the apotheosis of the BwO (Body without Organs). But there is more. According to Liu, this "trans-being" emerges as none other than Hollywood's Oscar come to life, morphed as a nonbiological consciousness to become its "Filmic Intelligence." In Lacanian terms it is the Thing in the field of vision, the "site[cite/site] of an alien gaze" (p.110). If this is so, Hollywood is engaged in a kind of "feminizing of the phallus" which provocatively characterizes "the new man," a Carl Lewis in pumps. But we have not arrived at the terminal end. There is more.

Queering T2

As a gay viewer of the Terminator, Goldberg ends his evaluation of Schwarzenegger's masculinity with what could be called an "inverse" or queer reading, as opposed to a perverse one. For him, at least (following Haraway's well known "Cyborg Manifesto"), Terminator offers a disruption along sexual difference that avoids an Oedipal resolution as presented by Constance Penley (1986) who relies on gender difference. In his case *Terminator* offers the sadomasochistic pleasure of gay leatherspace identification, while in *Total Recall* these pleasures are to be found in the confusions of cross-gendered identifications. His queer reading, while clever, does not mitigate Jeffords' or Springer's equally clever analysis of "out with the old, in with the new-old," recalling Hennessy's strategies of "transference" of late capitalism (see the Third Vignette).

From a similar sexual political position, Chris Holmlund (1993) claims to do a queer reading of Sylvester Stallone's male masquerade by examining movies where his clone appears: *Tango and Cash* (Stallone/Kurt Russell) and *Lock Up* (Stallone as Frank Leone/Larry Romano as First Base). Holmlund maintains that the ambiguous (or straight, i should think) as opposed to the inverted gay and lesbian masquerades have been underdeveloped in the theories of Doane, Riviere and Butler. Inverted masquerades, i.e., lesbian butch, the drag queen, the cross-cultural dresser, focus on visible differences; as do Doane's White heterosexual women and Franz Fanon's Black heterosexual men, in *Black Skins, White Masks,* who don the White mask even though it may not guarantee them authentic passage into White culture.[12] In contrast the gay butch clone (who passes for a heterosexual straight man), the lesbian femme (who passes for a straight heterosexual female), and the passing Black are non-visible masks which subvert racial and/or sexual identities. Holmlund's strength is trying to recognize class, color, race and religious markers that also are at play on these bodies. Dressing up (embellishment), putting on (parody, critique), and stepping out (affirmation, contestation) are three forms of the masquerade which are linked to power and resistance. Holmlund tries to apply these forms in the two "buddy pictures" mentioned above. In my opinion she is not successful in *explicitly* making clear *how* First Base or Cash, read as gay butch clones of Stallone, are resistant masks that "step out." With a slight twist, a queer reading suggests that First Base and Cash are slightly more effeminate (but not to the point of drag of course), and there are scenes where the buddies look long and hard at each other not entirely in competitiveness, but also in admiration and affection.[13] Yet, the "doubled" image of the two hunks, especially in *Tango and Cash*, and the strong policing of homophobia throughout the film makes such a reading barely visible. This not to say it isn't there; the power of the clone's disruption is at issue for me here.[14] Holmlund admits to the quandary, "Thus, though I may talk about Stallone and the clones' masculinity and heterosexuality as masquerades, most people do not see them as such. ... [T]here is always the risk that the specificity of homosexual pleasures will disappear within speculation about homoeroticism in what are, in this case, basically heterosexual male genre films" (p.225). And disappear they do. With the male body becoming more and more of an acceptable site/cite/sight for homospectatorial view, the specificity of homosexual pleasure is surely reduced on the textual side of things.

As Tasker (1993a,b) points out, today's hero (policeman or soldier) is "expendable," perhaps even a "dying" breed. But such heroes never "really" die; they only *Die Hard*. Such heroes act outside the law, unofficially and in vengeance. Their "*specific form of transgression of the Law, of its suspension*" (Žižek, 1993a:98) is sanctioned by the very social order that they protect. In this way the community is held together. As Slavoj Žižek so perceptively points out, the state and bureaucracy they fight is sadistic in its very being; it always requires a"code red" (e.g., *A Few Good Men*, d. Rob Reiner, 1992) which operates outside the Law. The "code red" for postmodern cinematic heroes is to get even with big business, coded foreign (Asian) or otherwise. They are the contradictions to a liberal democracy for they have become a Law unto themselves and need to be symbolically punished so that some kind of justice is secured in the world.

Freak Shows: Making Bev Francis "Figure"

The flip side of this hypermasculinity, Mishkind and his colleagues suggest, is the thin female body which connotes the stereotypic feminine traits of smallness, weakness, and fragility. This bipolarity may be a reaction against sexual equality, "an expression of a wish to preserve some semblance of traditional male-female differences" (p.556). So what can be said of those women who oppose such traits? Those who develop their own "muscle," so to speak? Before developing the third phenomena concerning the thesis of a shrinking penis/phallus, a paragraph or two must be devoted to this phenomena simply because it is another site/cite/sight of the body erotic.

If the anorexic and the female body-builder are the extreme responses to the images of capitalist patriarchy, the former being a refusal of food—a *literal* response to *escape* the perfect image of patriarchal desire of an emaciated phallic-like body (Caskey, 1986; Orbach, 1986; MacLeod, 1981; Bordo, 1990a, Mahbobah, 1992),[15] while the latter— supplementing food with steroids, depleting the skin of water with diuretics—is an *exaggerated* response to *literally* possess masculine desire through the body, a patriarchal feminine if you will, then are these to be taken as forms of resistance threatening capitalist patriarchy? The answers seems to have mixed reviews. To gain autonomy the former ends in death while the latter staves death off to an impossible utopian moment. In Catherine Clément's (Clément and Cixous, 1986) words, "These women, to escape the misfortune of their economic and familial exploitation, chose to suffer spectacularly, before an audience of men: It is an attack of spectacle, a crisis of suffering" (p.10, in Mahbobah, p. 91). If the anorexic stares at her "skeletal frame" in the mirror, a contradictory sight of both narcissism and estrangement from that body, how different is that from the woman body builder who stares into the gym mirror, having replaced her "skeletal frame" with objectified muscle? Are not both responses defaced spectacles "of a socially endorsed prosopopeia of male perfection" (ibid.)?[16] Both have aversions to fat, both forego menstruation as a result, and both appear asexual; one is socially acceptable, the other isn't. Apparently, even anorexics feel that being female in a Western culture is an unjust disadvantage that deprives them of options and choices. Both the anorexic and the body builder desire to achieve masculine attributes, to forego the qualities of a woman's body.

Perhaps one last comparison is in order. Mahbobah mentions the work of Helda Bruch who describes an anorexic's speech as a form of theft of the Other, usually the parent's speech; this "verbal kleptomania" results in a confusion of identities. The anorexic's voice seems to be dispersed in amongst Others, empty and absent. Analogously, the voice of a woman body builder is also a theft of sorts. The deep masculine voice one often hears comes from months, often years, of steroid use while the dispersion of self is spread throughout the muscular body as it concentrates and hallucinates the growth of each muscle. If the former purloins the voices of Others, the latter skews the feminine voice by lowering it and turning it on itself. One is an outward movement of self-abandonment of the waif; the other is an inward movement of the over-exaggerated will of "the muscle." Both are grotesque, distorted reminders of women's "lack of a lack" in patriarchy, psychotic responses to maintain identity through bodily *jouissance*.

Women's body building and exercise are therefore especially confusing sites/sights/cites for such analysis of resistance. It is time to recall Lynda

Nead's (1992) study of the female nude in Western art, for she has some very clever things to say concerning Robert Mapplethorpe's 1983 photographs of Lisa Lyons who was the first to have won the World Women's Bodybuilding Championship in 1979. Nead argues that women's bodybuilding is easily contained by patriarchy. Moreover, in Lyons' case, this is a doubled gesture. First, as a self-acclaimed performance artist Lyons strives to sculpt her body into a classical ideal where two dimensions of the idea of the bodily frame converge: "the skeletal frame that forms the body's *outside* frame tightening around the skeletal frame that forms the body's *inside*" (p.10). Her inner ideal form is to be matched with an equally ideal outer form so that no contradiction exists between them. For Nead, this epitomizes the way the female body has been regulated, contained and controlled in the West, making sure that the female body doesn't issue forth any filth or pollution. The stoppage of menstruation and the inability to become pregnant are often the result of prolonged strenuous exercise. Within this aesthetic, boundaries are set and a formal integrity maintained. Excess fat must be gotten rid of since it is part of a false boundary. Stripping it away reveals the true frame of the body. Secondly, Lyons is contained through Mapplethorpe's photographic techniques which deliberately frame her poses through an aesthetics of logic, precision and order. Nead concludes:

> Lisa Lyons has been 'framed.' By contouring her own body she turns its surfaces into a kind of carapace, a metaphorical suit of armor. But what may start out to be a parody of ideals of masculinity and a claim to a progressive image of femininity is easily appropriated. Rather than transgressing sexual categories, Lyons simply re-fixes the boundaries of femininity. The surface of her body has become a 'frame,' controlling the potential waywardness of the unformalized female body and defining the limits of femininity (p.9).

Judith Butler's (1987) review of Mapplethorpe's book on Lyons, *Lady*, comes up with the same conclusion as Nead. "For his elaboration of the image of Lisa Lyon the body builder as a glamorous 'lady' successfully assimilates the unfamiliarity of the body-building aspect to a familiar ideal convention, that of the *femme fatale*, represented here in images ranging from Harlow to *Maitresse* kinds of evocation. The threat of feminine independence is thus converted into the traditional male projection of the dangerous lady, with her black widow beauty that lures only to destroy" (p. 124).

Jane Fonda has called this exercise of power over oneself as: "I like to be close to the bone" (ibid, p.10), a comment Susan Willis (1991) explores in her analysis of exercise as a contradictory site/sight/cite for women in a capitalist patriarchy. In Willis's argument, women's exercise is a contradictory synthesis of work and leisure, and it "may well represent the most highly evolved commodity form yet to appear in late twentieth-century consumer capitalism" (p.69). According to Willis, there has been a shift towards privatization of the work(out) into private spas and clubs, and away from the community minded exercise programs of the YMCA (YWCA) and community recreation centers which had offered a place for women to meet and get to know one another as they mutually exercised. In contrast:

> The workout focuses women's positive desires for strength, agility, and the physical affirmation of self and transforms these into competition over style and rivalry for a particular body look and performance. Body rivalry has long been a feature of men's exercise. Men flexing for themselves and each other in front of a mirror is the single most expressive metaphor of masculinity and exercise. The workout puts women in contention with one another for the right look. For women, poised body line and flexed muscles are only half the picture. Achieving the proper workout look requires several exercise costumes, special no-smudge make-up, and an artfully understated hair-do (p.70).

The flip side of this argument is to claim that women bodybuilders deconstruct the totemic phallus by presenting its limit case, its *aporia* through a feminine representation that scandalizes the very phallic power it strives to covet. Schulze (1990) begins by entertaining such a possibility but ends in hesitation. No doubt, there is a lesbian story to be told about women's bodybuilding as another site/sight/cite from which the identificatory transgression of *not* being a woman can be maintained. There is a subculture here that parallels gay body builders and, as Schulze points out, women bodybuilders themselves take great pains to guard against such homophobia, and often reassert that they are heterosexual. A film like *Red Sonja* (d. Dino de Laurentis, 1985), starring Schwarzenegger and Brigitte Nielsen, becomes an action movie which tries to reaffirm any rumors of being "otherwise." Muscle magazines such as *Flex* have a "power & sizzle" section—a full page of a well-known woman champion bodybuilder (e.g., Heather Tristany, Debbie Muggli, Lendra

Murray, Marie Mahabir, Laura Binetti, Laura Creavalle, Skye Ryland, Sue Price, Dorit Kearns etc.) seductively posed wearing Nylons, stiletto heels, corsets, bikini swim suits, and lacy g-strings to show off her "real" or more "natural" side as a "woman" (see Aoki, 1995). It is interesting to note in this context that in *Pumping Iron II, The Women* (1984), the Australian Bev Francis was denied winning the title in Caesar's Palace, Las Vegas because her aesthetic proportions were considered (at that time) too "manly" by the judges. She was just too "big" in comparison with the other runners-up: Rachel McLish and Carla Dunlap (the only Black contestant). Francis came in at a disappointing 8th place; her implied lesbianism acted as a disruptive force. Holmlund's comment on Bev Francis' physique explores the consequences of this lesbian disruption:

> [T]he association of muscularity, masculinity, and lesbian-ism invokes these fears of a loss of love for spectators of both sexes, though in different ways. If heterosexual men see Bev as a lesbian, she is threatening: lesbians incarnate sexual indifference to men. If heterosexual women see Bev as a lesbian they must reject her: to like her would mean admitting that they might themselves be lesbian, which would in turn entail the abnegation of traditionally feminine powers and privileges (Holmlund, 1989:43, in Tasker, 1993b:146).

The butch-femme body of Bev Francis was inadequate as an object of sexual desire. As de Lauretis succinctly says:

> The fantasy of an unlovely and unlovable body… not feminine or maturnal, not narcissistically cherished, fruitful, or productive, nor, on the other hand barren (as the term goes) or abject, but simply imperfect, faulty and faulted, dispossessed, inadequate to bear and signify desire. Beacause it is not feminine, this body is inadequate as the object of desire, to be desired by the other, and thus inadequate to signify the female's desire in its feminine mode; however, because it is masculine but not male, it is also inadequate to signify or bear the subject's desire in the masculine mode (de Lauretis, *The Practice of Love*, 1994b:212

510

Bev Francis's cancellation or negation of femininity as a lesbian (imagined or real) puts the heterosexual binary into question which is determined along sex/gendered lines. Such a disruption forces the hetero viewer to disavow the displacement of his/her looking onto the register of genital sexual economy. This poses a threat to sex/gender identification for it *ex*-poses and makes self-evident the artificiality of sex/gendering.[17] The judges' refusal to award Bev Francis the title is analogous to them recognizing their own disavowal. The persona of the butch-femme in Francis's case placed the accent too much on the butch and not enough on the femme side which suggests that there are drags which are not as threatening to compulsory heterosexuality.[18] As Kuhn (1988) surmises:

First prize, in fact goes to Cara Dunlap, whose body is represented in the film as a midpoint between Bev's and Rachel's [the most feminine]. But there is more to this resolution than mere compromise. Carla is set up as an outsider, as different from the other contestants—and not just by virtue of race [she is black]: she is the most articulate of the group, a self sufficient loner, the only one with no man to coach her and provide moral support. ... The issue of the appropriate body for a female body-builder is not actually resolved: rather it is displaced on a set of discourses centering on— but also skirting—race, femininity and the body, a complex of discourses which the film cannot acknowledge, let alone handle" (p.18).

For Aoki (1995) the female bodybuilder such as Bev Francis presents a crisis of optical antilogy. Her image cannot be represented in the heterosexual terms of sexualized display. It is "unsymbolizable" and "illegible." Calling on Žižek, Butler, and de Lauretis, such an abjected body, maintains Aoki, represents the fantasy object of the Thing—a fantasy object constructed to hide a lack of the Symbolic Order. "[T]he singularity of *das Ding* is that it is at once fascinating and repellent: the female bodybuilder looks some-Thing like a woman and some-Thing like a man" (p.11). The sex/gender identity of Bev Francis remains 'open,' subject to ambiguous recognition. As the Thing, existing in the Real, her body does double-duty both uncovering and masking sexuality all at once. Such a double-gesture, Aoki conlcudes, places the bodybuilder as a Symptom/*Sinthome* for the mainstream subject (e.g., the judges at the contest). Bev Francis is "a traumatic Object with whom no relationship is possible" (Žižek, 1994c, p.102, in Aoki, p.12). In this sense, the Symbolic Order can maintain its heterosexual bias. As *Thing* she covers up its lack.

What is disturbing for me in this discussion is the uncomfortable conclusion that *only* the figure of a "freak" within the heterosexual/homosexual binary can cause rupture with any degree of *certainty*. The "freak" is the thing that both fascinates and repulses us. Further, this "freak" must *expose the ambivalency of sexuality* itself, not *only* gender.[19] The "freak" is often the figure of the hermaphrodite, like the bearded lady who is only allowed to live within the confines of the carnival. In her description of tv (transvestite) porn, Kaite (1987) describes the transvestite/transsexual in just these terms; that of a freak. "She possesses the gaze, sharp and penetrating: s.he has phallic insight. This look of critical perception accompanies a body which is a discursive play of transgressive sexual positions and which competes with the look of the model for the reader's attention" (p. 161). The voyeuristic heterosexual stare by men at transvestites is "doubled," predisposed by their expectations along gendered lines. Kaite tries to describe a male reader's confrontation of this "horror vision" of his own body. "[T]he freakishness of the "TV" body is its phallic protrusion " (ibid.). "A man having sex with another man who is made to look like a woman," Kaite informs her readership, "is judged as one of the more exceptionally 'degrading' obscenity cases" (p. 168, ft. 34 from the *Montreal Gazette*, "Selling Sex, 8 April, 1987). i am immediately reminded of *The Crying Game* (d. Neil Jordan, 1993) where the figure Dil as a *transsexual* rather than as a *transvestite* causes this disruption. By this i mean that one of the allusions of the film's title, the "crying game" refers to Dil's oscillation between these two possibilities since it is never made certain which s.he leans to, but overwhelmingly it would seem to be transsexuality. Here are Millot's (1990b) helpful distinctions: "[T]he dividing line is unclear between transvestite, who, in the terms of the specialist, is careful to hide the wherewithal to dumbfound his neighbor, and the transsexual, who despises and detests the burden of a virility that he has always refused with all his strength" (p.12).[20] According to Stoller (1979), she says, "what characterizes male transvestism and distinguishes it from transsexuality is the sexual excitement generated by wearing clothes of the opposite sex, as well as the ever-present dimension of the onlooker, who can be stymied by the revelation of the transvestite's male organ. This dimension is entirely lacking in women transsexuals, and in this sense there is no such thing as female transvestism for them. Women dressed as men experience no *frission*. Moreover, discovery of their biological sex is more often than not a source of confusion or shame. For Stoller, there is no doubt whatsoever that a woman who permanently dresses as a man is not a transvestite, but a transsexual" (p.108).

"The freakishness of the 'TV' display is the 'T' to rupture the 'V' façade always slipping away to reveal the 'TS' (transsexual) underneath. To be totally stripped, however, would be the death of language [after Pacteau, 1986] ... and the death of desire" (Kaite, p. 161). With plastic surgery and the advent of sexual transplant technologies, such anxieties can be eased. Today's transsexuals are also walking cyborgs. "With us, science fiction becomes reality," confides one transsexual to Millot. She-men have no need to procreate, lactate, nor menstruate. It is a masculine artifact, a typical male fantasy. "For transsexuals a book may be read by its cover, and the bodily frame is thought of as another article of clothing, to be retouched by will [by the plastic surgeon]" (p.116). Shades of Orlan.

Bev Francis' persona cannot totally disrupt as a transsexual; a posing bra and bikini do not a drag costume make! She has already "stripped" down to the barest minimum. It is her muscles that make her man, all save one that is. Should she have pulled down her "bottoms" and given her judges a look? If she had, in all likelihood, she would have been dismissed from the contest; not for obscene behavior but for (perhaps) representing an impossible category. Were this to have been the case, Bev Francis would have been akin to Herculine Barbin, the hermaphrodite studied by Foucault (1980b; Butler, 1990a:93-106) whose trial exposed the regulative strategies of sexual characterization and whose suicide is a tragic reminder how repressive the effects of those strategies must have been. The law (in France) will soon clearly differentiate *sex* (organ) and *gender* (identity). But this is perhaps, too simple. "To be sexed for Foucault," writes Butler," is to be subjected to a set of social regulations, to have the law that directs those regulations reside both as the formative principle of one's sex, gender, pleasures, and desires and as the hermeneutic principle of self-interpretation" (p. 96). Given the historical location of body building, it was enough that Bev Francis's body represented the *aporia* of women's body building at that time. What are you to make, then, of Catherine Millot's (1990b) description of a TS wrestler who wears a feminine drag, but who does not hesitate to use his fists in defense of militants?

Now back to *The Crying Game*. In the game of masochistic courtly love (i.e., paradigmatically illustrated as the lady/knight relationship, played out in Gothic novel), the ideal Lady as the sublime object of love, is cold, distanced and inhuman. In Lacanian terms, she represents *das Ding*, the Thing; what he fears most is her Otherness.[21] Here we have another form of its manifestation, i.e., the freak's opposite–the Lady. Her elevation to a spiritual, eternal Ideal is merely a cover, a way not to become traumatized by the Thing. In this sense, like the question of the child for the parent which opened up this section, the Lady is an inaccessible object. "The place of the Lady-Thing is originally empty: she functions as a kind of 'black hole' around which the subject's desire is sutured" (Žižek, 1993a:100). The artifice of courtly love is 'inverted' in *The Crying Game* as the reluctant IRA soldier, Fergus (Stephen Rea), discovers that the beautiful Black woman he is in love with, Dil (Jaye Davidson), is a transsexual. H.er masquerade of feminine transvestism hides his membership. Yet, as Kaite quoting Russo (1986:43) says, "This is femininity with a vengeance, suggest(ing) the power of taking it off" (p.165). This has everything to do with *seduction* before the undressing. S.he eludes a semantic anchor. Desire is continually oscillating in deferred possibility. Fergus's "gaze sliding down the naked male body towards the sexual organ is shocked by the fact that there is nothing where one expects to see something (penis); in the case of *The Crying Game*, the shock is caused by the fact that the eyes sees *something* when it expected *nothing*" (Žižek: 105). Yet, after this initial shock, and especially after his resolve with a former love affair (a sadistic woman who is also an IRA soldier, which results in her spectacular death), Fergus extends his hand back to Dil and answers the call to love. What form this love will take remains undecided at the end; nevertheless, this is one of those rare feature movies which presents a seemingly distinct, but *impossible* reconciliatory gesture of a "sensitive" heterosexual man with an idealized feminine transsexual, suggesting that this is also a social acceptable arrangement, as long as "it" doesn't show. The subjectivization of the object which lacked (e.g., the knight, Fergus) through the acknowledgment by the Lady (e.g., Dil), as Žižek argues, remains caught within the same structure of courtly love by an insoluble solution. In prison, partitioned by a glass which prevents physical contact, Fergus and Dil speak about a day that will never come as he, correcting Dil to call him Fergus again and not Jimmy, paradoxically says—"only 2,335 days to go." This last scene "is the exact equivalent to the obstacle which courtly love renders the object inaccessible. .." (p. 106).[22] Compare this ending with Jennie Livingston's (a White Jewish lesbian from Yale) *Paris is Burning* (1991), a film documentary about drag balls in New York City, in Harlem. When Venus Xtravaganza's "little secret" is revealed, she is mutilated and killed by a client for having seduced him. Here ethnicity, racism, poverty, homophobia are not so easily smoothed over as in *The Crying Game*.

To come back to the previous discussion, it seems that the accept-able body within hegemonic heterosexuality is occupied by the butch-*femme* of the emergent action hero(ine), paradigmatically in the figure of Linda Hamilton as Sarah Connor in *Terminator 2* and Sigourney Weaver in the *Alien* series. Since 1979 with *Alien*, the fisty heroine has emerged in all popular genres. Why? Both offer enough feminine characteristics to make them plea-surable and complementary to their bulked and not so bulked male co-stars. SF hero(ines) seem to be a cross between a health club and a body-building gym. In the case of Connor, Jefford's has already argued, she has been dis-placed by the Terminator as both mother and father of John Connor, while in the case of Weaver—shaved head, in military fatigues as Ripley—has to kill herself in the final sequence so that what was alien inside her was finally destroyed (*Alien 3*). Why? What is *Alien*? In Kavanagh's (1990) reading "the voracious phallic monster [is] forced on her [Ripley] by Mother [the ship's computer] as the representative of the will of the appropriately absent Father (the Company)" (p.77). Three different and distinct femininities are at play here: Ripley, Mother and the phallic monster. i look at each one separately.

Newton's (1990) reading of Ripley seems succinct. *Alien* serves two fantasies, says Newton. First, all the de-humanizing anxieties that belong to late-capitalist labor are inflected into the *Alien*, so when it is blasted into space through a heroic individualistic effort, social and economic horrors are relived. And second, White middle-class women will save us from such dehumaniza-tion once they have been integrated into the work force. Their higher moral values will make the difference, an ideology maintained since the nineteenth century. To a White middle-class audience, *Alien* offers a utopian fantasy of women's liberation, "a fantasy of economic and social equality, friendship, and collectivity between middle-class women and men" (p.84). Both Newton and Kavanagh agree that Ripley is the "new" woman. Their ideology critique claims that in the end Ripley is just another Company woman despite her feminism. The film is a "triumphant rebirth of humanism, disguised as pow-erful, progressive, and justifying feminism" (Kavanagh, p.73). 'Mother' the ship's computer is no problem here as well. 'She' represents the company's "new" maternalism, supposed to be looking after her workers. However, she is caught completely by patriarchy since she is programmed for the Company wishes. That leaves the *Alien*. Why would Mother let her in on the ship? and why would she do battle with the "new" woman?

Newton and Creed (1990) have different readings. For Newton the *Alien* is the "perfect organism for the Company purposes. It is in fact a kind of ultimate Company Man, and the Company means to use it in its own defense, as part of the weapons division" (p.83). The *Alien* is perfectly adaptable, perfectly defended, "unclouded by conscience, remorse, or delusions of mortality" (ibid.). In almost direct contrast, Creed reads the *Alien* as the "monstrous-feminine" ersatz for the phallic mother, the all-devouring vagina.[23] The ambiguity of the Alien might be interpreted as the contradictions which surround the "new" woman in the workforce of the '80s. On the one hand she is pressured to have children, and on the other hand she must have a career. Both are in conflict. The monstrous-feminine is not only feared by men—their controllable Mother is represented by the ship's computer—but also feared by women. This 'mother' possesses an imaginary phallus which endows her with power and authority. Ripley faces a non-castrated mother.

The *Alien* series may be interpreted as a girl's pre-oedipalization process. The father (the Company) is physically absent, but psychically present in the symbolic order of the *Nostromo* run by the castrated Mother who knows her lack. How is the "new woman" to answer to the call to the dark side of the Ancient Mother-Goddess, or pre-Oedipal Mother? In *Alien* she temporarily wins the battle, she continues to deny her castration. In *Aliens (2)* Ripley has a daughter. It is uncertain how that came to pass, but certainly the reproductive technologies that would be available in the future is one possibility, adoption another. Is Ripley now facing the contradictions between "natural" and "reproductive" motherhood, forms of parenting—single, lesbian? The *Alien* mother is once more a reminder of Ripley's transgression? In the last sequel, *Aliens 3*, Ripley is definitely *butch*-femme. Her transformation complete, she has decided to be the masculine woman and refuse castration, even if that means her death (which it does). Here the *Alien* may be any number of things, even feminism, as has been discussed, for its uneasy relationship with lesbian s/m women.

Finally, a Lacanian reading of *Alien* (Žižek, 1989a:78-79) presents it as yet another version of *Das Ding*. Its changeability "confirms it's *anamorphic* status: it is a pure being of semblance" (p.79). The Alien is the traumatic kernel of "the maternal body, of the living substance of enjoyment" (ibid.). Cast in Creed's terms, the phallic Mother as Ripley's symptom, cast as the Thing, is both horror and pleasure at once—the Real of enjoyment. "From this perspective of *sinthome*, truth and enjoyment are radically incompatible: the dimension of truth is opened through our misrecognition of the traumatic Thing, embodying the impossible *jouissance*" (ibid.).

The Mutant is Not the Cyborg and It's not Crying

i want to end this discussion on transsexuality and transvestism by pointing to first, what seems to be under-theorized, if not a gaping omission, in the many discussions of the cyberpunk genre, especially *Total Recall* discussed by Goldberg and Glass (1990); and second, to identify how transvestism (and not transsexualism) has been appropriated as a safety value so that "normative" sex/gender distinctions are maintained and the "new order" reinstated. To the first concerns then, and that is the existence of the colony of mutants on Mars. It seems that they have an identity which is the very embodiment of transsexuality. They could easily represent the "third sex" of the future, a collection of "its" that join the New Man and the New Woman.[24] Glass reads the mutants as the distortion of human potential under authoritarian rule. Their image of deformity "brings the inside of the body erupting out of its skin, presents a literal sense of the pressures toward rebellion experienced by an oppressed people or class. Their solidarity with one another is partly based on their shared misfortune; it is also clearly rooted in their political understanding of who has done this to them and the reasons why" (p.4). You might interpret this statement as a "collective crying game" of all those "freaks" living in a capitalist patriarchy under a heterosexual hegemony. Of course the symbolic weight of the mutant theme can be extended to include all current revolutionary skirmishes, as Glass does, caught as it were, "underground' (ersatz for the artificial atmosphere of Mars not in their control) and at the mercy of transnational corporations.

The leader of the resistance is the mutant Kuato who emerges out of a man's stomach as a mutant child, half imbedded in the man's flesh, neither completely external nor completely internal to his body—a very complicated image. This is suggestive of the birthing desires of transsexual men to bear children physically. The figure plays once again into the theme of men giving birth to themselves with no need for women, and lastly, the mutation seems organic, repressing the connotations of the machine.[25] Kuato is brilliant, clever, and psychologically sophisticated, more than any cyborg can ever be—it is an It. This is the return of repressed nature in all It's mutant forms. But it is a most forceful resistance, one which completely rejects the surgeon's scalpel and the endocrinologist's analysis which would sculpt the mutant back into the existent binaries of man/woman. Kuato is the very embodiment of unrenounced transsexual desire; not surrendering to the Other of science, nor to the Other of heterosexuality, but trying to find its own voice of resistance based on the radical potential of its sexuality. The mutants speak metonymically for transsexualism but their voice is muffled by "other carnivalesque characters." This point brings me to my second concern, transvestism.

To summarize this thesis thus far, it seems that the hystericalization of both men and women through the disruptions of the feminist and gay and lesbian liberation movements have worked themselves through into reestablishing quite traditional roles through cyborgian technologies. Hypermasculinization (body building) and its lesser varieties (sports, running, triathlons) have been the way to ease the anxiety amongst men to reestablish their masculinity. The specularization of their bodies through advertisements and action cinema (as cyborgs, policemen, soldiers) has displaced homophobic fears along a homosocial narcissistic axis. Men can now look at men and themselves. Even transvestism, which is supposed to be so disruptive of patriarchy, has sale value today, as the exemplified by the photograph of Carl Lewis. Transsexuality is also placed into the advertising motion as well. Kaite (1987:168, ft. 34; Kolbowski, 1984) draws my attention to the phenomenon of the androgynous cleavages which are given expression in Calvin Klein underwear ads. "A woman with a boy's body (lean, taunt, without feminine voluptuousness), save for partial exposure of one breast, sports 'his' (Klein's underwear)." Transvestism is also in play, but it is usually the woman who steals and poaches from the man. "Wear something of his and you'll fascinate him even more," Kolbowski's quote from an ad for a Klein clone called "Swipes."

Men are caught by similar contradictions living within a capitalist patriarchy.[26] Jonathan Rutherford (1988) identifies the Retributive man and the New Man; the former "represents the struggle to reassert a traditional masculinity, a tough independent authority" (p.28).[27] The latter, "is an expression of the repressed body of masculinity. It is a fraught and uneven attempt to express masculine emotional and sexual life" (p.32). Advertising has gone after the New Man. The male body can now be gazed by women playing into the liberalist assumption that sexual inequality can be found in the denial of women's aggressivity by asking men out and courting them. Commercials now "equally" fetishize his body.

Perhaps, the quintessential image of what i have been exploring appeared as a Benetton advertisement in 1994 (fig. 19). The viewer is presented with two *almost* identical men, possibily twins, hugging each other, their eyes facing the camera. I say *almost* identical because on closer examination we are looking at the *reverse* mirror image of just one man. To put this another way: if you imagine that the left side, or the right side is a mirror, then the opposite image is its reverse. In effect, this one man is hugging his *own image* in a mirror. There is a "give away" sign to the eye which makes you hesitate that your first glance has been fooled. It's as if such a reading was expected, so that you might then hesitate, and think about another possibility. Each hand contains a slight reddened cut, or pimple. This might or might not be the same hand which appears on both sides of the mirror. This perceptual aside, which elicits close scrutiny, is meant to add more uncertainty, so that other readings become possible. Another closer look and you realize that these two figures are not looking at you from the same point of view. The figure on the left is looking slightly up, while the figure on the right looks slightly down. The implied viewer's point of view is placed directly eye to eye with these figures, so as to participate directly in their look, and to experience the parallax of their looking; as if one were being viewed by two sets of eyes, causing a slight fracture in the plane of vision, or *fault* line. The slash in vision caused by that fault, forces the viewer's eyes to dart up and down, back and forth, incessantly. Meaning cannot be easily stabilized. Benetton has managed to play with the very homospectatorial narcissism that i have been discussing, as well as appropriating the homosexual look. It's as though the very "fault" that the picture presents implies the possibility of a nervousness that a homophobic gaze produces. A less startling version of this appears on the front cover of a recent *Der Spiegel* (Nr. 22/30, 1994, fig. 20). Here it is clear that the man kisses his own image in an ornately framed mirror, announcing the feature article which is on the narcissistic society.

fig. 19 United Colors of Benetton, 1994

fig. 20 Die Ego-Gesellschaft, *Der Spiegel*

The Tears of the Softened Male:
General Schwarzkopf Cries with
Robert Bly On the Planes of Television Land

If the above description provides the physical forms of men's feminization, then the emotional form is not far behind, for the New Man has now been given the ability to cry. Male melodramas, such as *Thirtysomething,* are a recent genre, appearing in the late '80s (Joyrich, 1988). Yet, as Boscagli (1992-1993) argues, often these new "sensitive" men cry media tears that are worn like jewels around their necks. "Male tears are not a chosen feminization, or a form of androgyny, a case of postmodern gender blending. We need to consider male emotions as a particular formation of power and as a symptom of male anxiety in a period of crisis" (p.67). In his discussion of Robert Bly's interview on TV with Bill Moyer in 1991, and General Schwarzkopf's interview with Barbara Walters in March 1991, after the Gulf War, Boscagli lays bare how "emotional masculinity" (both men displayed earnest feelings and publicly shed tears) is a strategy of self-defense for crisis of the masculine subject. What televised masculine emotions do in Western culture is violate the taboos of privacy by making public what is shameful and secretive, and thus breaking with established gender boundaries, i.e., men do not emote their feelings or cry in public. When they do so, it is to confirm "authentic," humanly warm feelings. To make these interior feelings sell, however, can only be done in the most public way through the electronic eye of the TV camera.

Televised masculine emotions, by using the conventions of melodrama, become a way to recuperate the lost inferiority and intimacy brought on by the technologies of postmodern culture—especially television (Deming, 1992). The proliferation of talk-show hosts, where tears and confessional modes are a steady diet, seems to confirm Boscagli's observation of a simulacra world where the self has been fragmented and dissolved in the hyperreal (cf. Baudrillard).[28] Given this context General Schwarzkopf and Robert Bly represent two different responses of recovering the masculine myth of mastery through melodramatic forms of "oversimplification" and "the language of home and domesticity." The former makes distinction between good and bad immediately recognizable, while the latter personalizes social and ideological conflicts in terms of the family and personal relationships.

> Both the postmodern, self-induced hysteria of Bly's men and the 'personal side' of General Schwarzkopf which was disclosed in the interview with Barbara Walters hinge on the figure of the Father as the character capable of restoring a lost order to an emasculated age. While Bly's men endlessly rework their fractured relation to the paternal figure, Schwarzkopf's humanity and paternal tone have the effect of translating the authoritarian structure of the military into family terms (p.72).

So, while Boscagli fingers the melodramatic representations of men's emotions as a clever way to universalize male tears as "humanity" so as to reinstate the aura of authenticity for the subject, he also reminds me that women are excluded from this "new home produced by male tears" (p.74). Men do not make a spectacle of themselves crying in public. Their subjective distance is preserved. It is perhaps not unlike the moment after an S/M ritual; the man gets dressed and acts as if nothing had happened, his emotions purged so that he can continue his work. Schwarzkopf, voted TV Personality of the Year in 1991, likewise returns to the homophobic camp of the army.

Schwarzkopf and Bly are one and the same in yet another way. Zipes (1992) cleverly points out that once the eighth and final phase has been reached by Bly's wild man, called "the wound by the king's men," he receives a new heart. The wound symbolizes for Bly "the memory of a primeval wound, grief, and the *womb* within the male body" (p.7, my emphasis). We have here the transformation of the man to a man-woman. The "new heart" is a way for men to regain pride in themselves and, as a consequence, in the American nation. In this regard, Iron John is a contemporary American myth that wants to celebrate how men can regain their self-respect and become soulful leaders of their nation. "*Iron John* is our Desert Storm book" (Sharon Doubliago, in Zipes, p.16). A close reading of *Iron John* (1990; Bly and Thompson, 1985) by Zipes unravels the "nightmare" it harbors. Contrary to the pre-Greek roots that Bly claims for the tale, Zipes traces the various versions to the Middle Ages in Europe. It turns out that the tale is an initiation process that a young aristocrat was expected to undergo in order to become a warrior and a king. In this version, the wild man is not a mentor but a demonic figure. Wilhelm Grimm rewrote the tale, replacing the motif of the conflict with the devil with that of a mentor relationship, thereby, according to Zipes, fulfilling his own psychological needs for the quest of a father figure which he lost at the age of ten. These tales, contrary to celebrating a new heart, celebrate violence and killing as a means to establish male identity.

Zipes makes it clear that there is no place for women in Bly's world either. As men are given archetypal masculinity, *à la* Jung and Joseph Campbell, so are women. "He wants to establish, or re-establish, a world where men are so great that women *like* being lorded over. ... Women are reified into archetypal figures representative of phases that a man must pass through in order to reach a goal of self-fulfillment with a distinct orientation to a Christ-like hairy figure, who is in touch with God and sexuality, and whose advice is sought by rulers and common people" (p. 15-16). In the end, Zipes concludes, *Iron John* is a mythopoetic tale that is a form of "depoliticized speech" (cf. Barthes), an essentialist tale that avoids all discussion of a material analysis of the "wounds" that men *cause* as opposed to *have*. There is no discussion of the "manifold disturbances in family caused by the development of capitalism, no class, gender, or racial distinctions in Bly's diagnosis of the malaise affecting men, no consideration of the economic factors of unemployment and bureaucratization that cause violence in and outside the family, no consideration of why men have become more soft and violent at the same time, leaving women more victimized than ever since the 1970s" (p.18). *Iron John* is like CNN's coverage of the Gulf War, hiding and masking the true horror that was being perpetuated under the noble claim of global leadership to eliminate a lesser tyrant.

Masculinity on Parade: A Review of the Jitters

In his discussion on the way men view violence on television, Fiske (1993) tries to make sense of how meaning is created by audiences that are positioned in society because of their status in a capitalist society, a status dependent on race, color, ethnicity, money, ableism. He vividly demonstrates his thesis by describing how a group of homeless men watched Bruce Willis in *Die Hard* struggle against a group of terrorists, who were about to rob a Japanese multinational, its building located in New York. The homeless men watched with interest in the beginning as Willis, the lone action hero, made daring attempts to even-up the score. But as he slowly overcame his enemy he also began to cooperate more and more with the law. As soon as that began to happen, the homeless men shut off the video and popped in another cassette. Fiske reasons that this phenomena, which happened time and again, reconfirmed the dignity and sense of agency these men tried to maintain by resisting their identification with authority and bureaucratization: the very authority they struggled against daily. Thereby they identified with John's (Willis) heroic, but violent struggle against all odds.[29]

Violence is ubiquitous throughout western society as men have become unmoored from their traditional rolls, feeling helpless as the economic crisis of capitalism makes so many homeless, jobless, deskilled. In capitalist patriarchy, masculinity is still defined by agency—an ability to act in the world. Each "maleman" tries to find his own way to maintain that agency and sense of self, no matter where he finds himself on the social scale. With the lessening of manual labor because of technology—a shift from proletarianization to deskilling, sometimes called "*cog*-nitization"—exercise through sports and bodybuilding has become a way to displace work by turning to the body itself. Working class men can build their bodies up as a way to reassure their worth; middle class can gain health benefits, and sports can be perceived as the great equalizer of color, ethnicity and race as the filmic comedy *White Men Can't Jump*[30] aptly shows. Joyrich (1990) has usefully extended the category of masculine hypermasculinity to television to counteract what she argues to be the "feminized" world of TV. Sports shows, series like *Magnum, p.i.* and *Miami Vice* specularize the male body and hence provide the traditional anchoring of masculinity, and help to cope with homophobia for there has also been a freeing up space to allow for gay pride.[31] The straight gay identity is more likely to be accepted than the invert by heterosexual hegemony (Halperin, 1990). On the other side of the ledger, ideal notions of femininity have been restored through exercise, aerobics, and through the technologies of plastic surgery and the cosmetic industry. As Fuss (1992) has argued, fashion modeling has also been an acceptable site/sight/cite for the lesbian gaze. The perfect penis is matched with the perfect body. In addition ts and tv sex transplants have introduced another group to disrupt any easy stable sex/gender definitions, as sexually transformed men call themselves feminists, others call themselves lesbians, while yet others wish to be gendered as feminine women.

The increase of pornography is a further indicator of masculine anxiety. Lynne Segal (1990:218) perceptively notes that the fictions of manliness: erection on demand (as often as manageable), penis size (longer and thicker, the better), and a skilled performance (taking a woman to orgasm) has led to a variety of sexual dysfunctions—premature ejaculation, inhibited or loss of sexual desire, inability to become erect—are the exact inversions of the fictions of pornography. Segal reasons that these sexual frustrations, fears and anxieties are exploited by the porn industry with its expansion into porn for gay men, lesbians, transvestites, sadomasochists and so on. Since the 1970s the explosion of the porn industry in the West happened precisely when women had been successfully "*objecting* to men's violence against them" (p.22). The porn industry is the flip side of feminist activity as male anxieties have risen. Leonore Tiefer's (1986) research indicates that there has been a total disappearance of the term "frigidity," a term with pejorative connotations in its use from the 1940 to 1970. Since 1970 the term "impotence" has replaced it. This dramatic displacement is indicative of the shattering of the "virility myth" and the medical search of the "perfect penis," as she puts it.

There has been a paternal crisis in the home and in the church as well, which brings me back to my opening paragraph. The new fathering role is ubiquitous throughout the movies: *Three Men and a Baby, Look Who's Talking, Terminator 2, One Good Cop, Regarding Henry, Boyz N the Hood, Ms. Doubtfire,* and even a call for dishevelled and imprisoned fathers to find their children, as in *American Heart.* Vivian Sobchack (1991) has tried to chart the landscape of the changing family from the late '70s to the present, beginning with the horror genre that began to dramatize the terror of patriarchy without power— the bad dad. "[T]he repressed is patriarchal hatred, fear, and self-loathing. As the culture changes, as patriarchy is challenged, as more and more 'families' no longer conform in structure, membership, and behavior to the standards set by bourgeois mythology, the horror film plays out the rage of a paternity denied the economic and political benefits of patriarchal power" (p.10). On the other side of the ledger is the "good" dad of *Kramer vs Kramer*. As women began to move out of the home into the work-world, abandoning their children—the "bad moms" emerged. The new family melodramas appeared right around the same time when the horror film Father began his active and hostile return from the repressed, and the special powers of his furious and alienated children began to weaken in the face of his paternal hostility. "In direct contradiction to the horror genre film Father, the 'good' Dads in the family melodrama are powerless, harmless. The patriarchal authority lessens as they paternally assume more and more the genre's traditionally 'maternal' functions. Initially they are figured as 'soft' and 'weak' in visible contrast to the 'hard,' 'strong,' and 'selfish' wives" (p.11).

This situation, Sobchack argues, leaves the family with the problem of the horror film where there is patriarchal impotence or rage, or with patriarchal weakness and confusion, generated by the presence of children (the melodrama). "If the child is figured as powerful at the 'expense' of the Father, then patriarchy is threatened; if the Father is figured as powerful at the "expense" of his child, then paternity is threatened" (p.13). Sobchack has taken me back full-circle to where i began this vignette, but now it the Father who is either blown up, threatening paternity or miniaturized, threatening the loss of patriarchy. How is this to be solved? Sobchack points to an ingenious solution:

A child is born.

But it no longer belongs to the earth, and no longer is it a child, although it is marked with innocence. The conflation of paternity and patriarchy happens at the extraterrestrial level: to a phantasm who is at once patriarchy empowered and paternal child-like.

E.T.

E.T. is a transported and transformed dad. The powerful/child/alien/father is the symptomatic figure of bourgeois familial crisis, a sort of mutant Michael Jackson who has somehow grown up, living in the Disney World theme park in Orlando, Florida telling kids how to survive their hysteria. After all, the world has become a Disney set.

1 To the point where *Philadelphia*, despite all its problems of representing a gay lawyer dying of AIDS, was nominated as one of the *best* pictures of the year (1994), with Tom Hanks (who plays the lawyer) and Bruce Springsteen ('Streets of Philadelphia' is one of the films main songs) *winning* the best actor and best song category respectively.

2 The literature i am alluding to here is the whole question of the representation of AIDS. Broadly speaking the policing begins with the representations of AIDS 'victims' as untouchables in a state of moral and physical decay; then moves to an 'invisible' phase of panic where your next door neighbor, school chum, or your partner who looks perfectly healthy may have AIDS. Abstinence, monogamy or safe sex were given as the 'solutions.' In the '90s, if one were to follow Crimp, Patton, and Singer, Treichler, Grover on this, a humanistic discourse recuperates AIDS in the name of liberal tolerance and humanitarianism.

Christian fundamentalism and the Moral Majority see the disease as a wrath brought on by God for the sins of the flesh. Nevertheless, such sinners need to be shown mercy, kindness and forgiveness (provided they repent, of course). The key texts in this area which specifically deal with the photojournalistic and artistic representation of AIDS as i know them are: Douglas Crimp, ed., *AIDS: Cultural Analysis, Cultural Activism* (1988); Tessa Boffin, and Sunil Gupta, eds., *Ecstatic Bodies: Resisting the AIDS Mythology,* (1990); Simon Watney, *Policing Desire: Pornography AIDS and the Media* (1987); Douglas Crimp, *"Portraits of People With Aids"* (1992); James Miller, *Fluid Exchanges: Artists and Critics in the AIDS Crisis,* (1992), and a special on AIDS in the journal *camera obscura*, Paula A. Treichler and Lisa Cartwright, eds., Imagining Technologies, Inscribing Science: Special Issue, (1992); Cindy Patton's *Inventing AIDS* (1991); Linda Singer, *Erotic Welfare* (1993). This reading list provides a general review.

3 The late Linda Singer's (1993) analysis of *Fatal Attraction*, "Just Say No: Repression, Anti-Sex, and the New Film," is excellent in this regard. She explains the popularity of the film in the way it manages anxieties surrounding the permissiveness of sex and its dangerous consequences to the stability of the home. This is "Panic Sex" (cf. Krokers, 1987, 1989, 1991, 1993). Much like the moral panic surrounding AIDS, and its policing in the '80s by claiming you could be "infected" unknowingly by your healthy looking date, Michael Douglas has chosen (has been "infected") the wrong woman to have an affair with. The narrative makes it seem as if he had little to do with it. Singer argues that this narrative exonerates the man (Douglas) and presents a backlash to strong, independent women in the work place (the character of Alex played by Glenn Close) by having them killed by the protective "housewife." From another perspective Modleski's (1991b)"Three Men and Baby M," an analysis of male parenthood, provides another strategy to preserve the nuclear family. This is just the tip of the iceberg in the number of films in this genre, and speaks to the two Disney films which introduce this section.

4 See Richard Dyer's "Don't Look Now: The Male Pin-Up" (1982/1992), for an analysis of the way the male pin-up is photographed as compared to that of women. Dyer also discusses the exchanges of looks and how these are gendered along the active/passive axis. Ten years later, Dyer's article still seems current. One still finds men presented in magazines as if they are self-assured with eyes averted away from the camera. Their "profile" is what's important. If they stare into the camera lens they seem capable of action. Women models in contrast invite surveillance.

5 There are now self-help magazines in sports stores that help you get off being addicted to running and weight lifting. The abundant use of steroids amongst high school boys and in sports gyms testify to men's desire for such bodies.

6 The same "make-over" of transformed well-being through physical exercise, body building or any number of Asian self-defense techniques (karate, Tai-Kwon Do) is offered to women's fantasies as well. In the television film *Getting Physical* (1984), Kendal, the film's protagonist, undergoes this transformation in every facet of her life. See Tasker (1993: 143). There is also the television series, *The New You*.

7 The book by Sam Fussell's *Muscle: Confessions of an Unlikely Bodybuilder* (1991), is such an example. Fussell specifically identifies with Arnold Schwarzenegger as his ideal body. See Leng's "Muscle: Or How to Impress With Flesh and Be a Social Theorist Too" (1993), who argues that such musclemen like Fussell can never attain the long sought after phallus, but in doing so they come to a point where they become caricatures of the very ideal they are trying to achieve. At that point they realize the futility and the frailty of the performing self. After all, Fussell wrote a book about it, didn't he?

8 A small remark may be made here regarding the movie *Toys* (Barry Levinson, 1992) which features Robin Williams as Leslie, an adolescent male who never grows up. This Peter Pan like figure with many effeminate characteristics is pitted against his uncle, a three-star general (General Leyland) who takes over running the toy factory from his deceased brother (Leslie's father). Bringing with him a new ideology of efficient work and the mentality of a military camp, the very fabric of children's play as metaphorically represented by the old toys becomes transformed. (A similar argument is made about 'modern' toys by Barthes' in his "Toys," in *Mythologies* (1976/1973.) The dominant reading of the story is that Williams has to "grow up" in order to fight the evil that comes with war video toys and the hypermasculinity i have been discussing. On the other hand, *Toys* disrupts and splits masculinity in two, asking the viewers to question their assumptions about what it means to "be a man." Although 'Leslie' (Williams) portrays a heterosexual —he seems certain of his sexuality—he is a 'soft' male who is extraordinary cautious and sensitive in his approach to the woman he loves, almost virginal and adolescent. There is no apparent gay bashing in this film. Male feminine characteristics are displaced on the whole notion of children's play. In a way, this film took me back to my experiences in daycare and kindergarten in my opening vignette

9 Neale, writing in 1982-1983 before the more open eroticization of the male body became available on the screen, felt that this explicit erotic look was not obviously available except in genres like the musi-

cal and the occasional display of Rock Hudson's feminized body. Combat scenes were heavily marked by fear, hatred or aggression which didn't open themselves up for fetishistic looking. This has changed dramatically with the "rule" of Schwarzenegger, Stallone, Jean Claude Van Damme, Bruce Willis, and Seagal.

10 This term is quite common throughout literature on gender. See Joyrich (1990) for one such use.

11 There is another repetition at work here as well, discussed by Susan Jeffords' "Can Masculinity Be Terminated?"(1993). Both Constance Penley (1986) and Karen Mann (1989-90) identify the importance of "the repetition of reproduction" where the future son reaches back to the past in order to chose the father to give birth to himself. This is an old theme, as de Certeau (1984) informs us, of spontaneous male births, reaching back from Zeus to Duchamps, The Bride Stripped Bare By Her Bachelors. Even. Jeffords' article extends this to include the repetition of rewriting and sequels of the block-buster heroic genre, and shows how Terminator 2 changes Swartzenegger into a protective father and mother. Displacing the father is what Schwarzenegger was doing since Pumping Iron, and so he's good at it. "Everything is altered [in Terminator 2]," Jeffords writes, "if only slightly ... in a way that offers clues about how repetition, reproduction, and self-production are working in the shift from the masculinity of the 1980s to the 1990s, how, ... masculinity is currently reproducing itself, i.e., through inversion rather than duplication" (p.248). Following Goldberg, i would say that this inversion leads to the conversion of the cyborg itself. In T2 the old Terminator not only becomes the protector of human life, but also its generator "[b]y 'giving' John Connor his life, the Terminator takes, in effect, Sarah Connor's place as his mother. In one of the film's most astounding inversions, the Terminator can now be said to give birth to the future of the human race" (p.249). This provides a new wrinkle as to why Schwarzenegger was appointed by US President Bush as the ambassador of sports! And makes one wonder why it is possible for Schwarzenegger to play a father who delivers his own baby in Junior (d. Ivan Reitman, 1994).

12 Holmlund does note the well known writings of Homi Bhabha in extending Fanon's racial masquerade. Bhabha's mimicry of colonial authority is at the peak of its terrifying threat only when there is something hidden behind (or under) the mask, i.e., bomb, a knife, gun. However, this doesn't deal with the whole issue of compradorism or spying. Surely here is where passing off as a (post)colonial invader by speaking the same language and sharing the same culture, is indistinguishable from the very people the comprador or the spy is trying to oppress, either by supporting a transnational company, stealing advanced technology or military secrets. No doubt there is pleasure in this danger as well.

13 It is surprising that Holmlund makes no mention or comparison with The Kiss of the Spiderwoman which, like Lock Up, is about prison life but with the obvious intent to deconstruct masculinity as Molina the femme gay seduces Valentine, the revolutionary Left macho man who proudly wears his scars. Admittedly, Molina's masquerade is 'visible,' however it is the scheming that goes on behind his masquerade which makes the "kiss" such a pivotal moment in this film. In this film the effect of the signifiers make both gay and hetero men question the performance markers of their own masquerade. i don't 'see' any of this in Lock Up or Tango and Cash.

14 It has been well-documented by Liz Ellsworth (1986) that lesbians read film "otherwise" as do gay men.

15 Albaraq Mahbobah's "Reading the Anorexic Maze"(1992) makes the case that the anorexic tries to subvert the convergence of anorexia with "normal" femininity as defined by psychoanalysis as a "lack of a lack." The anorexic asserts she is not lacking, although she lacks the sense of a lack of food. He further observes Catherine Clement's comments that Lacan himself was like an anorexic who tried to find independence by defining himself away from his students who showered him with love. It is the anorexic daughter who is unable to break with her parents who is then showered with love by her parents. The "escape" i refer to is the eventual renouncement of sexual attributes and the devastation of the body to look as though you are endowed by taking on masculine attributes.

16 Mahbobah quotes J. Hiller Miller's meaning of prosopopeia: "the word comes from the Greek prosopon, mask or face, and poein, make, confer. The trope of prosopopeia uses language to ascribe a voice or a face to the absent, the inanimate, or the dead." (p.91).

17 See Tasker's discussion (1993b:141-146) and Butler (1990a:122-125). As Butler says of such theatricality of Bev Francis, "it mimes and renders hyperbolic the discursive conventions that it also reverses" (1993: 239).

18 Yvonne Tasker mentions the case of Catherine Tramell in Basic Instinct. Here there seems to be an absence of any masculine markers, no drag whatsoever. Tramell's bisexuality can't be read in her character. In other words, she's too straight to cause any disruption of sex/gender boundaries, perhaps one of the reasons why the film was picketed by gay and lesbians and had such a popularity amongst the

heterosexual public. Dil, in the *Crying Game*, would be another such figure since s.he is an outed gay. The shock of her identity comes with the exposure of her *primary* organ. In Bev Francis' case, it is her *secondary* characteristics that make her "look like a man," and so the ambiguity of her sex/gender identity remains open.

19 Butler's (1990a:94-96) discussion of Foucault's shift to treat "sex" as an effect rather than an origin, calling for "sexuality" as an open and historical system of discourse and power is helpful here. For this reason, the repression of sexuality, as argued by emancipatory and liberalist models of sexuality is dismissed by Foucault on the grounds that sex is considered an originary category restricted by the binaries of gender. The problem is, however, that there are limits to how "sex" might be altered (cf. Shepherdson).

20 Catherine Millot is a Parisian professor of Lacanian psychoanalysis at the University of Paris, VII, who works with transsexuals. The book i am referring to is her *Horsexe: Essay on Transsexuality* (1990b). i shall be drawing most of my attempts to comprehend transsexuality from her. Millot's book is organized as an interrogation of transsexuality by juxtaposing what two notable experts have identified as defining transsexuality, along with autobiographical written accounts and interviews with male and female transsexuals of her own choosing. The clinical work of Robert Stoller (1979) is especially considered, while that of Harry Benjamin less so. Stoller's account is considered normative. He distinguishes the transsexual from the transvestite and the effeminate homosexual. According to him, the later two feel themselves to be men who find pleasure in the penile organ, whereas this is abhorred by the transsexual. The transsexual is someone who has always felt himself to be a woman caught in the body of a man or visa versa. The male transsexual is feminine but not effeminate. Stoller's explanation for this involves a "more-than-perfect mother." i.e., a mother who does not separate from her son—almost *never*; she has no interest in seducing him nor being hostile to him. Hers is a perfect love. The father is not a rival. He is virtually absent. Her son becomes the mother's "feminized penis." Stoller reasons that the transsexual abhors his penis because it symbolizes the "splinter in the blessed mother-child symbiosis" (p. 53). The transsexual is caught up in this pre-Oedipal feminine with the mother having castration wishes for him. The *entourage* that would 'normally' intervene during Oepidalization, doesn't or can't "get through" to this mother/child dyad. In contrast to male transsexuals, female transsexuals are more likely to be fathered with their mother almost entirely absent. Female transsexuals identify with their fathers and grow up seeing themselves as boys.

Millot then goes on to discuss Soller's explanation of female transsexuals and the claim that they are often identified as denying their lesbianism since a woman loving another woman (as a man) can be so interpreted. To understand this difference between a transsexual and a lesbian, a case history of Sandor/Sarolta, a Hungarian count is undertaken. Millot points out that transsexual women inevitably choose heterosexual women as their libidinal object choice. Often they do not let their partners touch their genitals. Perhaps these are dubious distinctions? Yet Millot calls on Freudian distinctions to argue that a lesbian relationship doesn't rely on virility; which is to say, two women love each other in full recognition of their own 'lack'. For them "the male organ is in no way indispensable." In contrast women transsexuals are "more or less excluded from this dialectics of lack: virility is something they must possess" (p.112).

This, fortunately, is only part of the story. All along Millot has *not* judged Stoller's account, merely showing—through case histories and autobiographies—points of similarity and difference, and thereby leaving the reader with a conscious recognition of the complexity of what's at hand. She then changes her tact to include historical examples where transsexuality and the practice of sacrificial acts of castration shed light on one another. Examining the Cybele of pre-Greek times and the Skoptzy (meaning "castrates") of the 18th century, Millot concludes that such sacrifices were made on the demand by the Other (Mother, God, lover, Lady, Great Goddess), and that demand required the sacrificing of one's own desire. Those who sacrifice the object of their desires (i.e., castrate themselves, their son, their lovers) become the symbol of *jouissance* of the Other, i.e., God sacrificing his son Jesus Christ for salvation of the people.

Millot saves the best for last. She concludes her discussion by identifying Stoller and Benjamin as inventing the term "transsexual." Both male and female transsexuals are caught by their relationship to an imaginary phallus. This impossible identification results in the demand for a surgical sex-change. It is only after the surgery that this impossible relation is realized. Sex-change gives them an opportunity to act out their fantasy and in doing so they give up their own desire (having been castrated) to be the object of the Other's *jouissance*. Male transsexuals identify with The Woman who replaces the Name-of-the-Father (Symbolic Order), while female transsexuals who identify with the Name-of-the-Father, is the more difficult situation simply because the gap which separates the penis and the phallus is less of an illusion for them. They are unable to acquire a functional penis. In both cases, says Millot, transsexual desire is further usurped by discourse of science which wants to install them into the phallic economy of either/or gender identifications. At present they are denied their own desires of "difference." Given Millot's account, Foucault's anti-repression stance seems at risk. For Millot, the medical profession, like the cosmetic surgical profession, merely reinscribes the gender oppression that is already there (see also Grosz, 1994 a,b,c, 1995).

21 i am following the Lacanian reading as given by Žižek (1993a).

22 Millot provides yet another Lacanian explanation of the "crying game" in her discussion of Gabriel, a female transsexual. Gabriel finds himself in an ambivalent position after her operation. He feels that his "difference" lies somewhere between the accepted notions of being a man and a woman. He is uncertain that he can provide a woman what she lacks—the penis, and therefore he is "different" from a "real" man in this way, but also he considers himself superior to men in that he is closer to women, having been one. Millot interprets this identification with what is lacking in a woman—the phallus which is neither male nor female, but an imaginary signifier. Gabriel is situated "outside sex" (horsexe).

23 Creed makes a dubious assumption that the archetypal Mother is pure difference; there is no masculine. She bears her own children with out help of a man. But such a pre-originary space cannot be materialized for this archetype exists prior to culture itself. It remains a black hole; for Derrida one of its names is *différance*. Creed slips back and forth from this pre-originary impossibility to pre-Oedipalization. However, this child-mother dyad cannot remain as a utopian ideal. Such an imagined unity only exists in fantasy for the mother is sadistic as well as loving and kind. Has Creed posted the Other of the Other—the generative mother, the pre-phallic mother, the being that exists prior to the knowledge of the phallus?

24 Millot develops the notion of the 'third sex' towards the end of her book. Interviewing Gabriel, a male transsexual, he says, "Transsexuals are mutants, different from women when one is all woman, and different from men when one is all man. I feel and know that I am not a woman, and I have the impression that I am not a man either. The others are playing a game, they playing at being men" (p.130). Because there is no 'third sex' society forces Gabriel to choose to gender himself within a polarity.

25 This alludes to the birth of *Alien* (d. Scott, 1979) which takes places in the gastrointestinal of Kane. A phallus born from the stomach of a man.

26 An interesting example of an art that fits this playfulness see Mark Kostabi in Kroker's *Panic Encyclopedia* (1989), pp. 18-25.

27 Rutherford's article should have been "*Whose* That Man?" not "Who's that Man?" Given the mind/body distinction of humanist liberalism one can't prostitute the body in public, but prostituting one's mind and one's art is perfectly fine. Capitalism, after all, is built upon the free exchange of ideas for a price, is it not?

28 The melodramatic world of emotions as sold to us through television has been described by Lynne Joyrich's "All That Television Allows: TV Melodrama, Postmodernism and Consumer Culture" (1988). The "melodramatic screen" is the postmodern medium *par excellence* expressing "ideological and social conflicts in emotional terms. Action then largely takes place within the context of the home or in sites at the intersection of public and private space that are central to personal concerns (the hospital room, hotel, the private office available for intimate conversations, etc.)" (p.131-132). It "figures social turmoil in the private, emotional terms of self and experience, it rejects the psyche as a realm of inner depth" (p.139). Unlike a host of feminist writers like Radway, Brown, Seiter, Ang, Nochimson, who celebrate melodramas as feminine desire, Joyrich is much more critical of the way patriarchal capitalism manages women through this genre. "While feminist theorists [Luce Irigaray, Michèle Montrelay] may posit such nearness as a subversive alternative to the male model, proximity is also bound to consumer desires. The same closeness that ruptures the boundary between subject and object, allowing women a multiplicity of identifications and a self-embracing eroticism, also makes the female subject susceptible to the lure of consumerism which plays on her fluctuating position and the narcissism it implies" (p.144).

29 This same point is reiterated with Walkerdine's (1986) study of a working class family watching *Rocky*.

30 In *White Men Can't Jump* physical and economic differences between "Black &White" are inverted to produce an ironic play of signs. The "White' man'" is poor, being chased by crooked money lenders and is always on the hustle, living with a Hispanic-American girl friend. The "Black' man'" is at least middle class, owns his own tile business and is trying to move "on up" into a better neighborhood. The scene/seen is played out on the beach basketball courts of Los Angeles, while the discourses that crisscross on this space are analogous to the boxing ring. Wesley Snipes (Black white) is the king of the court—Woody Harrelson is the "White black." Throughout the film the usual assignment of the signs begin to

wander over the established "B&W" borders. The viewers are never quite sure (until the end), which of the two antagonists is physically&mentally the better ball player. Nor is it clear who can out hustle who (until the end), nor is it clear who understands Black music more fully (until the end), nor is it certain who can understand 'his' woman better (until the end). The film holds off the resolutions to these ambiguities for a long, long time by Hollywood standards, but eventually collapses the suspense into another wish fulfillment scenario. African-American's come out ahead as the smooth talking "hipsters" that they are, capable of out playing, out jumping, out hustling, (and out loving 'their' women), surpassing the best the White'man' has to offer. Towards the end, the irony of the film goes even further. Woody Harrison's "Chicana" girlfriend (played by Rosie Perez) wins big on the gameshow *Jeopardy* because she has memorized cultural trivia. The reward for such cultural knowledge is the exchange for money (another wish fulfillment). The irony is apparent. She must assimilate (melt into) culture that is 'trivial' to her, which holds little or no meaning for her, but which she must nevertheless learn in order to achieve wealth; thereby becoming "culturally literate" by E.D. Hirsch Jr.'s cultural standards. She wins, by the way, by knowing all the words of fruits that begin with the letter "e." She is then free to leave Woody who, in turn, becomes dependent on his newly found Black "friend." Score "two" for the African-American male and "three" for the Hispanic-American female for her long "outside" shot.

31 For an overview of the gains made see Jeffrey Escoffier's essay, "Sexual Revolution and the Politics of Gay Identity" (1985).

530

THE
EIGHTH
VIGNETTE

The Last Garment

Nothing is less certain today than
sex, behind the liberation of its
discourse. And nothing today is less
certain than desire, behind the
proliferation of its images.

(Baudrillard, *Seduction, 1990:5)*

Given the enormous amount of changes that have taken place in
the area of feminism and queer studies since my naïve attempts at problematizing my own masculinity five years ago, the promise of my title *then* (in
1989) was both a serious and a playful gesture. i feel today that its promise
cannot be fulfilled nor adequately lived up to. Questioning yet another title,
"the last garment," the reader expects to find an exposure of some dark, deep
secret that has been withheld all along until now. This, however, is not the

case, although there are aspects of my life that have not been mentioned nor exposed (my divorce for instance, as yet another nodal point for questioning). Rather, it leaves me with one last reflection as to the question of the performative aspects of sex/gender which is "now" the current academic rage, especially with the way Judith Butler's two important books *Gender Trouble* (1990) and *Bodies That Matter* (1993) have been received by the queer and feminist communities. The issues surrounding the performative sexed body was little understood when the I first wrote down the title, thinking it was a quite clever thing to do at that time. The last garment is a thinking through of the failures and successes of that title.

The Body in Question

It is heard often enough, and echoed throughout my text, that gender/sex is a performative act which, if not repeated and reassured within the prevailing regimes of sexual discourses, can create major disturbances in the way the very core of sexuality is defined. Butler (1993) makes the claim that hegemonic heterosexuality "is itself a constant and repeated effort to imitate its own idealizations" (p.125); such heterosexuality, sustained through the imitation of an idealization, is anxiety-ridden, for no such idealization is impossible to achieve. Homosexuality must be continually policed. From the start of this sojourn i have referred to this "performative" aspect of identity by the homology site/cite/sight to be mindful of the complex history of disciplines, punishments, regulations that are at play on *any*body. A similar position is maintained by Butler (1993) by what she refers to as "citationality."

As Terry Threadgold (1990) concludes in her introduction to *Feminine, Masculine and Representation*, "theorists of sexual difference are not talking about the physical body, the anatomical body. They are talking about a body which, in Freudian terms, is both biological and psychical, a hinge between nature and culture, and about a biology which is always already cultural. The meaning the biological body has for human beings, the significance of the body as lived, varies with ideas about bodily functions in a given culture. This significance is learned and developed in a milieu of social meaning and value and constitutes what Gatens (1983) called the imaginary body" (p.31). Threadgold wants to differentiate that notion of the body against discursively and Foucaultian influenced feminist analyses (for instance, Probyn, 1993). The difference is subtle, but it seems to me that Gatens's "imagined body" incorporates a non-discursive affective dimension, referred often as the fantasmatic or phantasmatic identification, which remains problematic for these discursively based theories since the body's *imago* exists 'beyond' discourse. Discursive constructions of identity, such as the one proposed by Foucault, do not sufficiently meet the complexity of identification. The affective aspect of the psychical or libidinal mapping of the body is crucial as well. It is this other side of discourse which provides for us the lived body so valuably described by someone like Merleau-Ponty.[1] What anecdotes i have tried to describe here and there call forth that affected lived body within the material discourses that impinged on me. It is the reason why (no matter how problematic the whole issue of "experience" continues to become) experience is not likely to be *entirely* abandoned by sexual politics, for it embodies the *rule* of the signifier as Lacan argued in his reading of Edgar Allan Poe's "The Purloined Letter" (see Muler and Richardson, 1993). The "sex wars" amongst s/m lesbians and feminists are a testament to how important this non-discursive and hence more mysterious and unexplainable aspect of the body is. The "technologies of gender" (de Lauretis, 1987) of the *effected* body, in and of themselves, are not enough, but require the supplement of lived life of the *affected* body. In this regard, each of us has a story to tell of the body's remembrances.[2] Literature is continually analyzed for the disruptive body images it projects as possibilities. Jeanette Winterson's novel, *Written on the Body* (1993), for example, presents the reader with a love story wherein the narrator's gender remains undecidable.

   Threadgold's summary of a discursive and social semiotics of the body as text which sees "physical, sexual and socially inscribed attributes, accouterments and behaviors as the material instantiations of systems of significance, or discourses, which construct and are constructed by a regime of sexual difference, and which participate in the resilience and persistence of that regime" (p.33), should be supplemented by the non-discursivity of language itself, as the Lacanian Real that 'insists' from 'beyond.' This non-discursiveness—that which informs the materiality of the body like the spacings of the grammar we use—might be likened to a "soul." As Butler (1993), following Foucault says, "it is an historically specific imaginary ideal (*idéal speculatif*) under which the body is effectively materialized. ... [It] is the effect and instrument of a political anatomy ..." (p.33, 34). Obviously another history of sexuality could be written which might identify the paradigmatic shifts of this imaginary body such as that begun under the editorship of Zone Books. Three books, edited by Michel Feher, have been published to date in the series *Fragments for a History of the Human Body*. While there is no systematic historical paradigmatic tracings of the body's imaginary, the multiplicity and cultural variability that emerges throughout the various essays makes the body's malleability startlingly obvious.

Performative Non-discursivity:
Lacan with a Post-Kantian Twist

Phantasmatic identification remains a central issue for the politics of gender studies.[3] Often racial, class interests, able-bodiness concerns seem to drop out as ahistorical psychoanalytic explanations engulf the discussions. Such, however, has not been the case by recent writers such as Silverman, whose study of Lawrence of Arabia (1992/1989c) tries to combine insights of psychoanalysis along with an historical examination of discourses of "Arabness" so that a particular masculinity is identified and informed by specific racial and class interests. More so, Butler's *Bodies That Matter* tries to explore phantasmatic identification by moving the debate from 'construction to materialization'; first, by avoiding 'discursive monism' which reduces sex/gender to a linguistic construction and thereby overlooks "the constitutive force of exclusion, erasure, violent foreclosing, abjection and its disruptive return within the very terms of discursive legitimacy" (p.8). It is this 'constitutive outside,' as the unthought, which is internalized. Second, by replacing construction with "*a process of materialization that stabilizes over time to produce the effect of boundary, fixity, and surface we call matter*" (p.9, in italics). In this view the body still remains a text, a historical and socially specified construction of sexuality and biology. However sex, which is erased through the social constructions of gender, is recuperated by Butler, as materialized processes which are considered to be its regulatory norms of fixity. Following Foucault, sex is thereby both produced and destabilized at the same time through the course of this reiteration of norms over time. It is both a *performative* and a *performed body*: the former reiterates discursive categories while the latter is able to imaginatively disrupt them. i have tried to chart some of those discursive norms in the section on the "hysterical male" as the recuperation and construction of both the hypermasculine and "soft" melodramatic masculinities during this postmodern transition. The proliferation of feminist science fiction bodies is yet another contestation of 'citationality' (Wolmark, 1993). Barbara Duden's (1991) account of how women experienced their bodies, especially as expectant mothers in the eighteenth century compared with today, makes this process of materialization startlingly visible as the new reproductive technologies have offered completely new phantasmatic identifications. These intelligible morphological possibilities are sighted/cited/sited and thereby historically produced.

Butler is interested in the way that the symbolic law has been tutored by materialist sightations/citations/sitations of hegemonic racist heterosexuality at the exclusion of homosexuality. More importantly, she is interested in questioning the possible transgressive and disobedient sex/gender *performances* that can offer challenges to the interpellation to the symbolic order. In response to Althusser she writes,

> The law might not only be refused, but it might also be ruptured, forced into a rearticulation that calls into question the monotheistic force of its own unilateral operation. Where the uniformity of the subject is expected, where the behavioral conformity of the subject is commanded, there might be produced the refusal of the law in the form of the parodic inhabiting of conformity that subtly calls into questioning of the command, a repetition of the law into hyperbole, a rearticulation of the law against the authority of the one who delivers it. Here the performative, the call by the law which seeks to produce a lawful subject, produces a set of consequences that exceed and confound what happens to be the disciplining intention motivating the law (1993:122).

This stance is not unlike the parodic 'dedoxification' of postmodern politics articulated by Linda Hutcheon (1989:31). But Butler is quick to add that parodic drag performance is *not* necessarily subversive and that it may well be used for both "denaturalization and re-idealization of hyperbolic heterosexual gender norms" (p.125). Its imitative powers are a reminder that heterosexuality is not natural nor original. Butler comments on the recurrent question of this book's title. Films like Julie Andrews' *Victor, Victoria*, Dustin Hoffmann in *Tootsie*, and Jack Lemon in *Some Like it Hot* perform a *recuperative* drag which concedes its lack of naturalness and originality in order to have cultural power over homosexual anxiety. Homophobia and "homosexual panic" in army camps, prisons, monasteries, boarding schools are negotiated by a long tradition of cross-dressing and transvestism, especially in theatre. Marjorie Garber (1992:40) provides a historical list of such drama, as in ancient Greece, the public theatre of the English Renaissance, Kabuki and Noh theaters in Japan and in Chinese opera. In "Breaking the Code: Transvestism and Gay Identity," (chapter 6) Garber quite clearly identifies the common misperception that male cross-dressers are gay, when empirically this is *not* the case. She offers a very explicit explanation of how "homosexual panic" works, and why cross-dressing may be potentially threatening.

In mainstream culture it thus appears just as unlikely that a gay man will be pictured in non-transvestite terms as it is that a transvestite man will be pictured in non-gay terms. It is as though the hegemonic cultural imaginary is saying to itself: if there is a difference (between gay and straight), we want to be able to *see* it, and if we see a difference (a man in women's clothes), we want to be able to *interpret* it. In both cases, the conflation is fueled by a desire to tell the difference, to guard against a difference that might otherwise put the identity of one's own position in question. (If people who dress like me might be gay, then someone might think I'm gay, or I might get too close to someone I don't recognize as gay; if someone who is heterosexual like me dresses in women's clothes, what is heterosexuality? etc.) Both the energies of conflation and the energies of clarification and differentiation between transvestism and homosexuality thus mobilize and problematize, under the twin anxieties of visibility and difference, all of the culture's assumptions about normative sex and gender roles (p.130).

Butler thinks that drag can be disruptive precisely because gender is undecidable, traced "as the play *between* psyche and appearance (where the latter domain includes what appears *in words*)" (p. 234) and where "play" is defined by heterosexual constraints. i shall return to the question of performative drag shortly.

It is well-known that both Mapplethorpe and Andy Warhol, as gay artists, turned to Marcel Duchamp as a way of problematizing the instability of the sex/gender boundary. Duchamp created his alter ego, "Rrose Sélavy," as a way to divide himself into an 'I' and a 'you' (see Krauss, 1985:200ff). T(his) homophonic name was a multiple pun in French, *Éros, c'est la vie,* inscribing life as a vicious circle of eroticism (Jay, 1994:167). Throughout this book two (I)(i)'s have been at work: questioning the I to oppose its construction, meant that "i" had to, in some sense, draw from that very construction to articulate its oppositions. Butler offers a similar ruse when she writes, "You will note that in the making of this formulation, I bracket the "I" in quotation marks, but I am still here" (p. 123). How this "I" had been interpellated through ideology requires a certain disinvestment by the performative "i," which draws its strength from a different phantasmatic identity. Agency is thereby created to push back "subjection." Yet how this happens is often a mysterious process. Butler's discussion of Žižek's thoughtful rethinking of subjectivity which steers a course between Althusser's notion of ideology as interpellation, and Lacan's symbolic, is very helpful in understanding this process. Only hinted by Terry Threadgold's objection to the total hegemony of discourse theories in subject formation, Žižek is lucid in his opposition to the poststructuralist theory of Foucault and Derrida by not accepting that the subject is a unilateral effect of prior discourses. In poststructuralist accounts there is no conceptual means of tracing linguistic effects back to self-identity of speaking subjects. All meaning is derived from a play of absolute differences internal to language. Such a totalization of differences reduces individuals as the effects of "subjectivization," overdetermined through discursive formations such as habituation, familiarization, socialization, enculturation, and acculturation. The human subject becomes an effect of pre-subjective processes, like the text for Derrida, or power in the case of Foucault, or desire as in the anti-oedipal formulations of Deleuze and Guattari. "The subject is therefore to be strictly opposed to the effect of subjectivization: what the subjectivization masks is not a pre-or trans-subjective process of writing but a lack in the structure, a lack which *is* the subject" (Žižek, 1989a:175, emphasis added).

In contrast to these "subject-position" accounts, Žižek draws on Lacan and theorizes the subject produced in language through an act of foreclosure (*Verwerfung*), and not only repression (*Verdrängung*). He stresses *that* which remains outside the subject; *that* which is refused or repudiated in the formation of the subject. This defining "negativity" is therefore never coherently self-identified because of these foreclosures and repressions which can continually disrupt the lived unity. This "constitutive outside" is the non-discursive background, if you like, which is non-symbolizable; an abyss that we, you, and (I)(i) know exists which presents for us the 'difficulty' of writing, and which, i would add, makes syntactical constructions never before encountered so mystical. Referred to as the Real in Lacanian liturgy, it is *that* which constitutes the lack in any discourse formation. It is *that* which cannot be accounted for any account of "reality." Throughout Žižek's explanations of Lacan through popular culture, i.e., *Enjoy Your Symptom*, *Looking Awry*, he continually evokes the Thing as *that* which cannot be theorized. It is difficult *not* to interpret this as yet another clever name for the creative "something" that goes beyond the intentionality of any artist: Lacan with a post-Kantian twist seems to say it for me since, in Kantian aesthetics, art is something which *cannot* be subsumed under a concept. As Butler puts it,

> In Žižek's view, every discursive formation must be understood in relation to that which it cannot accommodate within its own discursive or symbolic terms. This traumatic 'outside' poses the threat of psychosis and becomes itself the excluded and threatening possibility that motivates and, eventually, thwarts the linguistic urge to intelligibility (1993:192).

This social constitutive antagonism on the 'outside' can be mistaken as simply the outcome of conflictive subject-positions. Žižek wants to show that this misrecognition presents the impossibility of ever fully realizing self-identity as a teleological purpose, i.e., the belief that once capitalism or patriarchal oppression is overcome, a utopian telos will have been reached. Such a totalizing thought posits the other as "capitalist" or "male chauvinist" who prevents the realization of the human potential, and hence gives rise to class and gender conflicts. In stark contrast, Žižek's starting point (see the "pretexts of the title") is the fundamental split of desire within individuals themselves which will never be sutured sometime in the future. This split remains as a fundamental lack which is perpetually satisfied and emptied through ideology until death. We are back to *that* which is beyond Althusserian interpellation; to *that* which prevents the account of ideology from lapsing into socialization. The Lacanian order of the *Real* functions as the cause of desire and thereby accounts for a subject's identifications with ideological meanings. The reception of ideology is traversed by the unconscious, the Real of desire.

Problematically Butler argues, Žižek's Real repeats the Lacanian Real, understood as the threat of castration, typically bringing into existence the difference between "having" the phallus and "being" the phallus. Ideology in this case is a social fantasy which sutures this ahistorical and essentialized Lacanian "lack," for it (ideology) is an idealized vision of a "society" which in reality cannot exist.[4] The challenges to the recognition of this Real, i.e., feminism, Foucault and poststructuralism, which Žižek discusses and dismisses, become his way of easing the anxiety of the threat of a collapse of the masculine into the abjected feminine, keeping homosexuality at bay. Ultimately, however, because the Real remains as the impossible "outside" to discourse, Butler argues, it institutes a permanently unsatisfactory desire for the ever-elusive referent—no matter how it is 'figured.' In the end this impossible referent, as "the sublime object of ideology," is politically ineffectual; rather, not effectual enough.

To some degree, Butler has misunderstood the radical political potential of the Lacanian Real and its related concept, the *sinthome* which Žižek has developed. The book series, *Wo Es War* (Turia & Kant, Wien), edited by the Slovenians Mladen Dolar and Slavoj Žižek, which has a listing of six publications to date, is a testament to the praxiological power of these conceptualizations, where topics of nationalism, racism, and feminism are discussed applying such psychoanalytic "tools." Žižek takes Freud's *"wo es war, soll ich werden"* to be the very heart of ideological identification. The subject must identify with the place where the symptom already was, i.e., to recognize the 'pathological particularity' which gives consistency to one's being. Lacan's "third period," beginning in the late '50s with the seminar on *The Ethic of Psychoanalysis* according to Žižek (1989a:132), is the dividing line for the conceptualization of this 'pathological particularity' as Freud's *das Ding*. The Thing is the traumatic kernel which lies beyond the Symbolic Order and hides its lack. It is the horror that fascinates. The Thing belongs to the Real—as the real-traumatic kernel in the midst of the Symbolic Order.

The corollary to this formulation reads that the Real is *jouissance* par excellence—impossible enjoyment which paradoxically has traumatic effects. The prohibition of incest, as installed by the Father of Enjoyment, is the fundamental of the Thing which attests to the existence of the impossible Real. Given this situation, sex takes on a radical ontological status of a symptom conceived as a *sinthome*, i.e., it is that point which gives consistency to the subject. Sex does not belong to the level of sense, but a limit to reason as Lacan's 'formulae of sexuality' demonstrate (see Copjec, 1994c).

Butler argues that this formulation is politically ineffectual. i shall come back shortly as to why i believe she dismisses its formulations, but for now, i would like to point out where there is a fundamental agreement between her notion of performance and Lacanian theorists such as Žižek. In Žižek's three-fold catagorizations of Lacan's periodical developments, Butler's Lacanian appropriations closely resemble his second period where the Imaginary and the Symbolic play the central roles concerning self-identification. Enjoyment, rather than conceived as the incarnation of an impossible *jouissance*, i.e., his third and last period, is instead focused on the Imaginary level. Governed by the pleasure principle, this Imaginary self-identification strives for a homeostatic balance against the Symbolic Order which continually disrupts its homeostasis. As a blind mechanism the Symbolic is 'beyond the pleasure principle.'

Identification on the imaginary level is with the self—what I would like to be. It is an image that makes me feel good and self-loved—the enjoyment I have of my self. Here an ideal ego (*Idealich*) is generated. Symbolic identification takes another logic. What is at stake is the formation of an ego-Ideal (*Ich-Ideal*) conferred by the Symbolic Order or Big Other; its existence is assured by the place from where the self is being observed by the Big Other. This place is where we look at ourselves as subjects conferred by the Symbolic Order. The difference between how we see ourselves and the point from which we are being observed, is the difference between the Imaginary and the Symbolic. The difference speaks to the play of masquerades and screen images that have been referred to throughout this text. The Symbolic identification—the point from which I am being observed—dominates and determines the imaginary form in which I appear to like myself.

The most important aspect to recognize in this formation, then, is that this Imaginary ideal ego (*Idealich*) is subordinated to the ego-Ideal (*Ich-Ideal*) of the Other, i.e., the Other confers meaning on the self (lacks a mandate or interpellates the self) since it is perceived as non-lacking (e.g., the Father, the king, the social order as the Big Other). The ideal ego fantasizes a wholeness to the Other, i.e., the Other is more than the self. The fantasy covers any inadequacies or inconsistancies in the (Big) Other—it "fills out a void" that is there. Finally, Imaginary identification is made with the Other at the point where it is possible to imitate(e.g., resemble)—but symbolic identification is made at the point which eludes resemblance—the point which is inimitable—the Big Other is more than us and doesn't lack.

Up to this point Butler is consistent with such Lacanian reasoning. In fact her distinction between 'performativity' (related to ego-Ideal (*Ich-Ideal*), Symbolic Order, symptom) and 'performance' (related to ideal ego (*Idealich*), Imaginary, fantasy) merely repeats the distinction Jacques-Alain Miller made between 'constitutive' (Butler's performativity) and 'constituted' (performance) identification respectively (see Žižek, 1989a: 105). At this level there is no disagreement that there may be "gender trouble" when the two disparate logics are put into a dislocation or disruption within a social formation to break the reputation that glosses over the gap of potential difference between ideal ego and ego-ideal. For example, the juxtaposition of a lesbian with a transvestite to present a "lesbian transvestite" performance where the stress is placed on the first term *lesbian*. A *lesbian* transvestite would be a woman who dresses up as a man, who dresses up as a woman, and who might then desire a sexual partner dressed up as a man; or the other contorted accent, the lesbian *transvestite* is a man dressed up as a woman who might desire a subject dressed like a woman (Glynos, 1995). The undecidable oscillation plays with the socially accepted sex/gender pact between the ideal ego and the ego-Ideal.

With imaginary or performance identification, i.e., the way I see myself in fantasy, the way I am 'constituted,' is shaped by a certain gaze in the

Other. The performance is done for the Other's gaze whose lack is covered over. What makes this process repeatable is the "performativity" or "constitutive identification" which is an identificaton with the gaze—the place from where we are being observed. When this place of observation is matched with our own ideal ego's then there is a comfirmation. We appear to like ourselves—loved. But the mandate of the ideal ego is always arbitrary, and part of Žižek's project has been to expose its lack as *das Ding*; to show that there is nothing "behind" the Symbolic Order—the paranoia which results in believing there is an Other of the Other, e.g., as in conspiracy theories.

To return to the rejection of the Lacan's 'third period' by queer theorists like Butler. What Butler proposes in Žižek's stead, therefore, is to turn to (not surprisingly) performative acts in her last chapter, "Critically Queer."[5] For Butler, the Real drops out. The body becomes rhetorical and discursive (see Dean, 1994). Here Butler begins by outlining what performative power is. Performative acts are forms of authoritative speech which perform an action and confer a binding power on the action performed, i.e., legal sentences, baptisms, inaugurations. For the performance to achieve binding power it needs to be done through the invocation of a convention—through citation.

> Where there is an "I" who utters or speaks and thereby produces an effect in discourse, there is first a discourse which preceded and enables that "I" and forms in language the constraining trajectory of its will. Thus there is no "I" who stands behind discourse and executes its volition or will through discourse. On the contrary, the "I" only comes into being through being called, named, interpelled, ... and this discursive constitution takes place prior to the "I"; it is the transitive invocation of the "I" (p.225).

The power of the performative succeeds "not because an intention successfully governs the action of speech, but only because that action echoes prior actions, and *accumulates the force of authority through the repetition or citation of a prior, authoritative set of practices*" (p.227, original emphasis). This "citation," however, can be disrupted through a performative act as well. Butler is careful to clarify her position so as *not* to claim that all performative drag as gender parody is necessarily subversive. This is especially examined in her chapter four, "Gender is Burning: Questions on Appropriation and Subversion," which examines the film *Paris is Burning* (d. Jennie Livingston, 1991). Here she is rather critical as to the subversiveness of such drag balls, but later makes the point that it is the "*reformulation of kinship*" (p. 240) by the various "houses" to which numerous members of the gay and lesbian community belong which is the radical innovation. These 'houses' are forms of collectivity, of 'mother-ing,' of 'mopping' (stealing clothes and accessories to effect their look), and of 'reading' the hetero-culture from which certain figures emerge as 'legends.' Such a structure rewrites the kinship meaning in dominant culture. 'Children' are the younger performers, 'legends' refer to the experienced drag artists who have won trophies, while 'mother' and 'father' refer to the older generation.[6] But "a house is not a home; the film reconstiututes what that fabled term means" (Goldsby, 1993;109). This is a different kind of performative than drag where 'citationality' can be disruptive through miming existing heterosexual law "*and its expropriability*" (p.232). Queer discourse is performative in the very same way, e.g., the play on "It's a girl!" is replaced by "It's a lesbian!" "This kind of citation will emerge as *theatrical* to the extent that *it mimes and renders hyperbolic* the discursive convention that it also *reverses*. The hyperbolic ges-ture is crucial to the exposure of the homophobic 'law' that can no longer control the terms of its own abjecting strategies" (p.232).[7] As has been argued, Bev Francis presents an example of such a hyperbolic gesture. In *Paris is Burning*, the contrast can be made with the masquerade of 'passing.' The trope of 'real-ness' derives its charge from the gesture of erasure precisely because the marks of the race, class, and sexuality limn images indelibly and cannot be suppressed *no matter how hard the children try*" (Goldsby, 1993:110, emphasis added).

In another context Butler notes "gay is to straight not as copy is to an original, but rather, as copy is to copy [*simulacrum*]. The parodic repetition of 'the original,' ... reveals the original to be nothing other than a parody of the *idea* of the natural and the original" (Butler, 1990a:31). Garber (1992) makes a clarifying example that marriage "*is* a dress." (p.142) Consequently gay "marriage" is contrasted with "wedding," performing another cita-tional/sitational/sightational disruption. The disruptions of *mimicry* and *hybrid-ity*, as developed by Homi Bhabha discussed earlier within the context of postcolonialism and the tourist gaze, are underwritten by the same perfor-mative argument.

Melancholic Drag and Masculine Balls

Gender-as-drag, according to Butler, might be theorized in terms of melancholia, that is, as an ungrieved loss of the Other with the conse-quence of heightened identification with that Other. This is a theme Butler began to explore in her *Gender Trouble* (p. 61 ff.) and continued in her "Imitation and Gender Insubordination" (1991) essay. Lacan's alienated subject (which Žižek follows) takes on the specific form of melancholia. As she writes:

> In my view, the self only becomes a self on the condition that it has suffered a separation (grammar fails us here, for the "it" only becomes differentiated through that separation), a loss which is suspended and provisionally resolves through a melancholic incorporation of some 'Other.' That 'Other' installed in the self thus establishes the permanent incapacity of that 'self' to achieve self-identity; it is as it were always already disrupted by that Other; the disruption of the Other at the *heart* of the self is the very condition of that self's possibility (p.27, emphasis added).

The "heart," it may be argued, can be likened to Lacanian concept of the *sinthome*, drawing Butler closer to Žižek's theorizations than she admits. The self-critical attitude of the melancholic, according to Freud, results in the internalization of a lost love object. Such an internalization within the ego results as a critical voice or agency. The original anger felt for the object is *reversed*. The melancholic's refusal to let go of the lost object, engages in a strategy to resuscitate it. Given that the relationship to that object remains ambivalent, this resuscitation scolds the ego. The affective state of depression comes from fighting to resolve the lost object within one's own self. Under these terms the performing of femininity for a "man," or masculinity for a "woman," means "an attachment to and a loss and refusal of the figure of femininity by the man, or the figure of masculinity by the woman. ... In this sense, drag allegorizes some set of melancholic incorporative fantasies that stabilize *gender*" (p. 235, org. italic). Drag as a negotiated effort of cross-gendered identification is *not*, however, the best way to think through homosexuality, since such cross-dressing applies most often to the straight crowd as Garber's (1992) study illustrates. For Butler, drag "allegorizes heterosexual melancholy, the melancholy by which a masculine gender is formed from the refusal to grieve the masculine as a possibility of love; a feminine gender is formed (taken on, assumed) through the incorporative fantasy by which the feminine is excluded as a possible object of love, an exclusion never grieved, but "preserved" through the heightening of feminine identification itself. In this sense, the 'truest' lesbian melancholic is the strictly straight woman, and the 'truest' gay male melancholic is the strictly straight man" (p.235). The drag of "strictly straight" heteros, in Butler's argument, is a performance which avoids the full passage of

543

grievement by refusing to work through their childhood loss of the mother's or father's love in the formation of their self-identity. In other words, the "Other" does not remain as their problematic *sinthome*. Being a "strictly straight" hetero can now be interpreted as a form of pathological behavior since the anger for the lost love object remains. (Does this mean my three earrings keep me sane!?) In this context, i wonder how a "truly *straight* melancholic woman"—pejoratively called a "lipstick lesbian"—would answer to this? or for that *matter*, what would a "truly *straight* melancholic gay man" say? Drag, as cross-dressing, emerges as a performative ambivalency regarding sex/gender identification. In light of what has been said concerning bulimia and anorexia throughout this sojourn, drag, or *masquerade,* appears to be their sartorial and fashionable equivalent, and the logic of Lacan's formulae of sexuation cannot be escaped.

Why has Butler turned to melancholia for psychoanalytic justification to answer the (permanent) crisis of "gender trouble"? It may be recalled that "melancholia" was what poets and artists were said to have suffered during the time of the "Copernican revolution," a transitional period of decentering much like postmodernity is today. A related experience to melancholia has been accounted for by the recent work of Celeste Olalquiaga (1992). In *Megalopolis: Contemporary Cultural Sensibilities*, she argues that many people today suffer from psychasthenia. This condition is a disturbance in the relations between the self and one's surrounding territory. Could melancholia and psychasthenia be related conditions on a continuum? One with the centering of identity, the other with its dissimulation?

> [P]sychasthenia is a state in which the space defined by the coordinates of the organism's own body is confused with represented space. Incapable of demarcating the limits of its own body, lost in the immense area that circumscribes it, the psychasthetic organism proceeds to abandon its own identity to embrace the space beyond. It does so by *camouflaging* itself into the milieu. This simulation effects a double usurpation: while the organism successfully reproduces those elements it could not otherwise apprehend, in the process it is swallowed by them, vanishing as a differentiated entity (p.2-3, added emphasis).

Olalquiaga applies this description to the experience of the "megalopolis." "Architectural transparency, for example, transforms shopping malls into continuous window display where the homogeneity of store windows, stairs, elevators, and water fountains causes a perceptual loss, and shoppers are left wandering around in a maze" (ibid.). Kowinski (1985) describes this effect as *mal de mall*; one eventually becomes a walking Zombie due to its (an)aesthetic effects. This disorientation lingers as the shopper comes out of a mall, into the parking lot, and has forgotten just where the car has been parked! These dislocations, caused by *trompe l'oeil* effects, force one to find a place to center oneself. This, Olalquiaga claims, is most often found in the concreteness of the food and the goods one buys, or as in Butler's meditations on drag, in the very masques that are worn, as is the case of the masquerade balls and "vouging" where a "second skin" is worn as a way to master the experience of self-disintegration (Bick, 1992-1993:88-89). Olalquiaga's basic thesis is that spatial and temporal coordinates have collapsed in a megalopolis. Time has shrunk, and space is no longer defined by depth and volume, but rather by a temporal repetition. Everything mirrors itself. Like Butler's performative self, all is artifice—a performative repetition as well as an attempt at a performed disruption of the copy, the same position Gamman & Makinen (1994:217) arrive at in their study of female fetishism. Such a postmodernist condition speaks to a 'decline' hypothesis or 'apocalyptic imagination' (Jay, 1994) that has had many past repetitions: pre-Fascist Europe for neo-Marxists like Horkheimer and Adorno; a pre-technological age in the case of Marcuse; T.S. Eliot's old south; and expressed recently in the agentic hopelessness of Baudrillard's (1983b) "ecstasy of communication." Is melancholia being recalled here to remind us of the decline? Is the performative disruptive mode a way to stave off this apocalyptic imagination that pervades the *fin de millénium* jitters? The reviews seem mixed.

In light of Butler's insights, what can be made of the hyperbolic "macho" gay style of the seventies? (Altman, 1980). Richard Dyer (1981) reads this style as subversive, while Leo Bersani (1988:207-208) confirms it as an identification and idealization with the very representational standard which oppresses the homosexual man. As Butler often notes, the potential of any crossed-sartorial dress to be disruptive depends upon the context, which is fleeting and changeable, dependent on the discursive "winds" so to speak. How quickly codes are read, broken and reappropriated. This is the side of consumerist postmodernism so often lamented as capitalism's greatest gain for profit (Baudrillard, 1983c, Mike Featherstone, 1991, Davidson, 1992). Within my figurative homology cite/*site*/sight needs to be emphasized when answering such undecidability, and only then with a subversive potential in mind. My earlier example of Carl Lewis wearing red high-heel pumps, dressed in a track suit, would not be a disruptive citation/sightation given the site of the photograph and its reception. His attire is not a "travesty."[8] However wearing a tuxedo, smoking a cigarette, having a cropped haircut and sporting a monocle would be, *if* you were a lesbian living in Paris in the twenties (Garber, p.153). And what of Madonna? Again, the marketability factor collides with the shock of signification. Yet she is "acute to the power of travesty... sporting a monocle (as well as a pinstriped suit strategically slashed to let her peach satin brassiere poke through, another literalization of the 'double-breasted suit') in her 1990 'Blond Ambition' tour" (p.155). i'm not convinced of this context. It's like me wearing my bikini briefs, not particularly subversive of sex/gender differentiation. The fashion industry, like the rock industry, has cross-blended clothing to such a degree that gay sartorial difference has become invisible. In some degree Madonna's cross-dressing has taken away the power of drag so influential in its disruptive power since the 1969 Stonewall Rebellion.

Another interesting example in this regard is Silverman's reference to Don Mager's (1985) description of the "Castro Street clone," a look which has many masculine signifiers such as leather, denim, work boots, military clothes. Yet, they are worn with a feminine "accent." Without this "accent" there would no difference between the gay man and his heterosexual counter part. He would pass as a straight male. Such a performance could not be *read*; there is no exposure at the level of appearance, simply a divestment of theatricality (Watney, 1988/1987). That's if you believe "clothes make the man," as Butler quips. "The publication of *Gender Trouble* coincided with a number of publications that did assert that 'clothes make the woman,' but I never did think that gender was like clothes, or that clothes make the woman" (p.231).

What then am i to make of this discussion in light of the way my own sartorial dress changed over the past ten years as the I shed many of the accoutrements of the signs of 'macho' masculinity and took on some feminine ones, e.g., the shaving of the long sideburns; the refusal to wear suits, cravats and polished leather shoes other than runners; shirts always chosen without collars; the long hair—sometimes in a pony-tail, occasionally braided, earrings which continue to proliferate; more flowing shirts and looser fitting pants? These are signs that cut into the established code of masculinity. When i first wore an earring, i recall a number of my colleagues sent me "singles" their wives had around the house as a joke. When my pony-tail came in, no one said a thing, except some remarks like the I had began to look like some of my students. Should all this be seen as a direct 'softening' of hysterical masculinity? Underneath, the body remains taut, well exercised, yet never narcissistically flaunted by tight T-shirts and exposed V-neck shirts. Is this my way to deal with gendered contradictions and accept my melancholia ?

Bodily affective *investments* are performed through (often visible) vestments (clothing, skin scarification, mutilation). The earring did mean something. i thought that it was a conscious recoding of bodily adornments, from wearing a wedding ring—a sign of confinement—to opening up the ear to the "other." Ideology is always interwoven with the imaginary investments of subjects. Only through "disinvestmenting" from particular ideological forms can there be an imaginary reorganization of the self and its related objects. These disinvestments are often tense and painful experiences because of the intensity of the affective intensity of desire itself. i can still recall the fear that simple ear piercing brought, wondering what my department colleagues would think, not to mention the more conservative school principals i often taught. Yet such disinvestments can "only proceed *from* a careful reconsideration of self-identity, developed *through* the creation of new imaginary relations between self and others" (Elliot:1992:198, my emphasis).

You might call me somewhat "soft" on the outside, and "hard" underneath, producing one variation of an effeminate (not *sensitive*) body. But the sight of the body underneath that i desire has also been effeminatized (not *sensitized*), for the image the I carries around is not of a muscle builder but one "shaped" by the site of middle-class activities of a professional male in his mid-forties: the body of a runner, biker and a swimmer. What then is my 'citationality'? Is it predominantly *white?* for there are Black powerful athletic masculine bodies which i recognize, but they provide incommensurate possibilities. And no matter how much the I would like to distinguish between effeminate and sensitive, such differentiations cannot hold. The I falls continually back into a yuppie-baby-boomer. As soon as i saw that pony-tails had begun to proliferate amongst my age cohort, i cut mine off. i'm beginning to think that a particular colleague of mine, a few years younger than myself, who teaches in the philosophy department, sports a suit and a bow-tie that changes color daily, is *more* radical in his statement than i "pretend" to be. His nostalgic parody reverses the signs within the masculine code rather than disseminates cross-gendered signs as i did (do).

In another context, a sport like boxing—a performance naked in its visual brutality—elicits in me a confirmatory sadness that licensed and ritualized violence between and against men, whose racial overtones are clearly marked by the any number of combinations of bodies of color and ethnicity doing battle, continues to signify a predominant motif in the way men settle their accounts. Phallus and fist come together in a struggle for power. In this sense boxing is "real" while wrestling is entertainingly "fake." In a review of Martin Scorsese's *Raging Bull*, the story of Jack La Motta's rise and fall as the world's middle-weight champion, Robin Wood (1987) develops how La

Motta's repression of his homosexuality is characterized by four Freudian forms of paranoia, three of which are clearly evident in the film. They are worth reviewing since they hold insights to male violence and aggression. The first, "I do not *love* him- I *hate* him," refers to the hate that comes from delusions of persecution which must be justified on rational and moral grounds. Here ritualized boxing can play into racism of the "Great White Hope"; the second, "I don't love at all," and its corollary, "I love myself," connects paranoia with megalomania, e.g., the self-overevaluation of the sport hero. The third, "I don't love men—I love women." This can be interpreted as the denial of homosexuality manifesting itself as an obsessive pursuit of women. The last, "It is not *I* who loves the man—*she* loves him," refers to the paranoia surrounding the contradictions of jealousy where violence is asserted against other men and to the partner on the assumption that neither have been "faithful."

When this I meets a male who is "full of himself," a braggart, displaying his phallic power in all its glory, i am likely to become confrontational. Telling, is it not? It points back to the fragility of my own masculinity; to my childhood when one learned to fight or learned to run; where the I was picked on, or the I learned to joke and talk my way out of a confrontation. The always-present fear of humiliation from other men who might be potential enemies and competitors repeats the boxing motif. i am reminded of the viciousness of this violence in academia where "points" are scored during presentations and confrontations are a way of conference life. There is an unwritten rule that graduate students defending their thesis must be made to feel that they have really been grilled during their oral hearing, otherwise no ritual had taken place, no "write/rite/right" of passage performed. Physical or mental bruises are part of the masculine affective code so forcefully exemplified by a film like *Glengary Glen Ross* (d. James Foley, 1992) which casts New York real estate salesmen as (con)fidence men, who would do anything for money, including break and entry with theft. Sadistically punishing the phallic signifier seems to be a way men both remind themselves and police themselves of their capacity to act out the "father of enjoyment" who is capable of rape, incest and murder. The law of the father is, therefore, maintained. Whereas boxing keeps the other at bay, at striking distance, sports like Greco-Roman wrestling, and to a lesser extent jujitsu, bring bodies close to one another whereby the homoerotic bond of closeness and attraction between men becomes displaced by competition. Men's violence against other men, especially through contact sports, is one of the significant ways patriarchal society simultaneously allows and denies the homoerotic attraction of men to other men and polices the phallus. The various ways in which "balls" come into play throughout men's sports, in both their visible and invisible forms, would provide a fascinating study of the degrees by which homosexuality is policed. In this sense, drag balls and 'vouging' provide the extreme examples of gay men coping with the humiliation that underwrites heterosexual law.

In another context, Modleski (1988b) argues in her, "A Father is Being Beaten: Male Feminism and the War Film," that the very gesture that underwrites the journey of this book repeats a masochistic alliance with the mother (ersatz feminism) by equating women with the law *in order* to reinstate the law of the father by punishing the woman. Whereas sadism involves the alliance with the father against the mother, as performed by the rituals of 'blood' sports like boxing, Modleski claims that war films about Vietnam during Reagan's U.S. presidency (*Top Gun, Heartbreak Ridge, Platoon* and even Kubrick's *Full Metal Jacket*) attempted to reinstate the law of the father either through a sadistic or masochistic male subject position. Either way, homosocial and heterosexual bonds remain unchanged.

Gentrified Anti-homophobia?

According to Butler, "The straight man becomes (mimes, cites, appropriates, assumes the status of) the man he 'never' loved and 'never' grieved; the straight woman becomes the woman she 'never' loved and 'never' grieved. It is this sense, then, that what is most apparently performed as gender is the sign and symptom of a pervasive disavowal" (1993:236). If i am to seriously entertain this claim within the context of my own lived reality as a heterosexual male, the word "never" seems particularly harsh and uncalled for. Silverman's (1992) last chapter, "A Woman's Soul Enclosed in a Man's Body: Femininity in Male Homosexuality," is a thoughtful examination as to how the "feminine" figures in gay identities. Her close reading of Freud develops at least three 'models' of male homosexuality (she names these as the negative Oedipus complex, the 'Greek' model, the 'Leonardo' model) with the further recognition that this is only the beginning of unraveling such complexities. Each model has within it a different emphasis on femininity—some forms are hyperbolic wherein the feminine *appears* to express a hatred for femininity itself, as in the bitch drag performances of Hollywood stars; still others take themselves as their own sexual objects. They proceed from a narcissistic basis; looking for young men who resemble themselves; loving them just as their mothers loved them. Why should 'straight' men be exempt of analogous variations? It has often been brought out by Butler, Silverman,

Grosz, Rodowick *et al.* that Freud's Oedipus complex includes its positive and negative variations: constitutional bisexuality. Every subject goes through both a heterosexual and a homosexual version of the Oedipus complex. The subject desires the father as well as the mother, and identifies with the mother as well as the father. The intricacies of this complexity, as has been argued, is exactly what has decentered Mulvey's masculine gaze. "Successful" oepidal-ization requires that homosexuality be repressed, but it can never be con-tained nor annihilated: it will always strive to return in the disguised forms of dreams or as neurotic symptoms.[9]

i have "always" identified myself as heterosexual, but having read Silverman's (1992) various accounts of homosexuality it seems that this descrip-tor, like homosexuality itself, is limited.[10] But before i explore what this means in my own life so that i may end with the complexities explored by the title of this book, a remark by Bristow and its subsequent discussion seems appro-priate. Bristow (1992) writes: "They [straight (White?) males] might, for a start, consider how the 'homosocial continuum' locates them within a pho-bic space (like a bathroom cubicle) with misogynistic pictures of women on the one side set against homophobic accusations on the other" (p.75). Bristow is referring to Eve Kosofsky Sedgwick's (1985) well-known and important formulation of the 'homosocial continuum' in her book *Between Men*. This "male homosocial desire" describes a variety of male-to-male relations which slip and slide along a continuum between homosocial and homosexual desire. She shows, through a reading of a number of poems, fictions, and plays, why in the middle of the nineteenth century there was a decisive break between 'homosexual' and 'homosocial' relations with increased, virulent forms of homophobia. Sedgwick argues against the 'repressed homosexuality' hypoth-esis and proposes that genital contact between men is policed by forms of regulated homophobia that demonstrate how difficult it is to maintain either a straight or a gay identity (psychically and politically).[11] What regulates the 'homosocial continuum,' argues Sedgwick, is this regulative mechanism of homophobia and the traffic of women in the form of misogyny as played out through the gender asymmetries of erotic triangles: the bonds of "rivalry" between two active members of an erotic triangle and the love each has for the third. It is the fear of other men, especially the fear of weakness and pas-sivity in relation to other men, which helps create a strong dependence on women, thereby meeting men's emotional needs for expression.

Writing in 1985, Sedgwick was convinced that the bonds amongst women (straight and gay) were not dichotomized as they were for men. 'Love for women' informed their entire 'lesbian continuum' (as articulated by Adrienne

Rich, 1980). In her account, homosexuality becomes the limit case of heterosexuality, making it play a (Derridean) supplement to the dominant discourse.[12] She makes the point that even when men were allowed to love men, as in classical Greece, it was still women (and slaves) who remained subjugated. Patriarchy did not go away. Sedgwick's claim is that the relationship between the homosocial and the homosexual is historically contingent. Sometimes it abets patriarchy; at other times it may threaten it. Currently, the potential is for gays to critically subvert patriarchal ideology. It was Sedgwick's hope that gays and lesbians might join forces to overcome the hegemony of both heterosexuality and the patriarchy it supports.

Leaving the hetero/homo divide in tact, as her study did, seemed to confirm that male heterosexuality had no redeeming values, while homosexuality became simply a detestable remainder. Like Butler's melancholy musings, male heterosexuality ends up as a pathology, for instance, when another writer, John Forrester (1992) rhetorically asks, "what do men want?" He answers with a list of 'perversions' against the all-powerful mother: "sadism, masochism, necrophilia, coprophilia, fetishism, rape, paedophilia, exhibitionism, voyeurism *and going to the cinema*" (p. 111, my emphasis).[13] In her second book, *Epistemology of the Closet* (1990), Sedgwick provides a lengthy introduction to clear up some of the concerns of her first book. She makes it clear that the "the only imperative... the book means to treat as categorical is the very broad one of pursuing an antihomophobic inquiry" (p.14). She now extends her deconstruction of hetero/homo divide to cover a one hundred-year period, from the 1880s to the 1980s. Through a number of "axioms," Sedgwick answers to some early criticism. In this book she makes clear that sexual preference ("sexuality") and gender are two analytic axes which may be productively imaged as being distinct from one another, "so every issue of gender would necessarily be embodied through the specificity of a particular sexuality and visa versa ..." (p.31). She is particularly careful not to be caught by the nature/nurture binary, arguing that the concept of gay origins should remain inconclusive and in flux given the recent homophobia of finding a "homosexual gene." Her interest is not to show the paradigmatic changes in homosexuality historically; rather to argue for their present complexities of form which include both *gender transitive homosexuality*, i.e, Foucault's analysis of the construction of homosexuality at the turn of the century (ca.1870) in the form of feminized man or virilized woman, and *gender intransitive homosexuality*—the straight acting and appearing gay male, Halperin's (1990) characterization of homosexuality accepted by the dominant heterosexual culture today.[14]

This detour through the writings of Bristow, Sedgwick, Halperin leads me back to one last reflection on the homo/hetero divide, and the promises and failures of this book's title. i believe that i can say, with conviction, that this I is not homophobic. Halperin and Silverman's account of the 'Greek' model of homosexuality suggests that, if historical circumstances were different, homosexual activity would be a 'normal' activity men engaged in without the "psychic" suffering that this brings today. Freud in his, *The Ego and the Id*, maintained that the dissolution of both the negative and positive Oedipus complex eventually worked themselves out, but never to the point of absolute assurance. Reflecting on this process, perhaps it should not come as a surprise to me that throughout my youth and university years i was constantly approached by gay men. Yet there was no indication of a conscious homosexual desire on my part. The acid test came when the I was about twenty-five years of age. A close male friend, of about three years, tried to "rape" me in bed. We were both sleeping together on a trip away from university, when suddenly i woke up in the middle of the night while he was attempting to "jerk me off." When compared to the more violent and forceful persistences that do happen, i realize that this incident is a rather "mild" form of sex abuse suffered often enough by women who have to constantly say "no" to unwanted advances by overly aggressive men. This writing might have been *otherwise* had i been anally raped. In the morning he was more upset about this incident than i was, feigning illness to avoid conversation. Telling him in a state of calmness that i was not gay should not have dissolved our friendship. However, it was his denial that forced our eventual break-up. Since then i have had other close friends who have tried to "make me" under different circumstances. As long as the situation doesn't progress to sexual relations, i remain accepting of their friendship.

i'm not sure what this means entirely. Some would identify this as a potential homosexual latency. To have been able to reach a moment of possibility where i could imagine having the capacity to love both men and women sexually has given me an awareness of the bi-sexuality that constitutes every human being. This, however, is not to claim bi-sexuality as a sexual practice for myself; rather it reinforces the conflicts of identity that the I experienced in assuming my own sex/gender. From this position, Butler's accusatory downgrading of melancholy 'straightness' seems misguided whereas Lacanian 'formulas of sexuation' of a never ending "gender trouble" seem more appropriate (Žižek, 1994c: 146-161). If the social imaginary were to change social relations to such a degree that all those negative aspects of patriarchy would disappear, i would be all for it. Perhaps such disruptive performative "family" relationships are possible but certainly dangerous (as experienced by Wilhelm Reich for instance), given the current erotic warfare on the "embattled family" to release its secrets of incest, wife and child abuse, and paedophilia. The question concerning the 'father of enjoyment' and the indulgencies of postmodernist narcissistic society hinted throughout this narrative remain open as to the disruptive potential of its "futurological effects" on the social imagination. My love of men who display a specific form of masculinity and my physical attraction to them in my capacity to kiss them, put my arms around them and hug them, while certainly homosocial, would not lead to anal penetration. i *simply* would not find it pleasurable, but i would not deny other men the right/write/rite to do so.

In this regard, i am taken by the figure of Craig Owens. Long admirer of his theoretical writings, a strange sadness overcame me when i read of his death after his struggle with AIDS. My "strange sadness" can be attributed, as Butler might suggest, "to the absence of cultural conventions for avowing the loss of homosexual love" (p.236). Remembering the name, as in the NAMES Project Quilt, is a way to counter this loss (Nunokawa, 1991). He must have been an outstanding human being. Both Silverman and Sedgwick acknowledge his contribution to gay and lesbian struggles.[15] What struck me was his insight, following Foucault, *that historically the disappearance of male friendship took place at the same time that homosexuality was declared a socio-political and medical problem.* i recall that Linda Williams's study of the earlier forms of pornography (as "stag" films) occurs at the turn of century when homosexuality was "invented." Heterosexuality and the stag film go hand in hand in assuring that this dichotomy could be sustained and reproduced. Male friendship was also inimical to the smooth functioning of the modern institutions like the army, university, schools, administration and bureaucracy. As i outlined earlier, the pernicious policing of homosexuality continues in our schools today. As Owens says, homophobia was the primary weapon against male friendship, and today it remains as a double-bind. "For a man to be a man's man is separated only by an invisible, carefully blurred, always-already-crossed line from being 'interested in men' " (Sedgwick, 1985: 89). Perhaps this provides the historical backdrop to what was happening to me as the I began to explore my own negative oedipalization? If men's friendships do not take other forms than their current combative phallic structures inherent in corporate capitalism, surely the homophobia will persist. A recent Benetton advertisement showing a man's bottom with HIV positive tattoed on it was forbidden to be shown in Germany. The burgeoning literature in queer theory *is* changing the social fantasmatic. Historically the sexual imaginary will change, and perhaps Lacanian 'formulas of sexuation' will require modification? In what direction this change will take place no one knows, for equally at work are reactionary nostalgic moral movements of "postfeminism," and an equally burgeoning "virtual reality" porn industry that both fuels and thrives on the AIDS panic itself. Although such a pessimism can be registered, the changed power relations amongst and between the sex/genders as a result of the politicization through feminism, men's studies and queer writing, identified by the awkward signifier "pheminism" in my subtitle, remains unstoppable.

So ends my scriptease. Throughout my performance i have tried to speak to the changes in art, introducing aspects of cultural studies, film studies, fashion, postcolonialism, and psychoanalytic theory to help further my questions concerning my self-identity. Whatever movement and changes in self-identification i have made over the last fourteen years as a direct confrontation with feminism and, to a lesser extent, with men's studies and queer writing, my cross-dressing and re-dressing are certainly small, almost insignificant steps when compared to politicized feminists, gays, and lesbians i have read or talked with. It seems as a "whyte" academic maleman concerned with the pejorative sounding signifier "pheminism," my autobiography is hardly sensational; however i think it is probably indicative of many heterosexual men who are questioning their masculinity in relation to the fields they are working in. i do recognize that a "book" such as this may appear too self-serving, so i do thank the reader for having participated in its indulgences.

1 Merleau-Ponty's phenomenology of perception has been recently applied to film theory by Vivian Sobchack's *The Address of the Eye: A Phenemenology of Film Experience* (1992).

2 Such an attempt can be found in Ulmer's concept of "mystoriography" in his *Teletheory* (1989).

3 Butler develops the concept of "phantasmatic identification" in chapter three, "Phantasmatic Identification and the Assumption of Sex" (1993).

4. Anthony Elliot offers a lucid critique of the inadequacies of the work of Laclau/Mouffe and Žižek in their neglect of the agency of the self and their Lacanian appropriation of the imagination as a negative alienation of Self from Other. See his *Social Theory & Psychoanalysis in Transition: Self and Society from Freud to Kristeva* (1992:183-199).

5 Butler has developed an earlier essay of this chapter. See, "Imitation and Gender Insubordination" (1991).

6 It should be pointed out that Owens' (1992:226-232) examination and potential rewriting of the kinship structures as presented by Lévi-Strauss by reviewing the role of the maternal uncle is also a performative act. He refers to the potentiality of such theorizing of Sedgwick's examination of the avunculate which now appears as a chapter, "Tales of the Avunculate," in her *Tendencies* (1993).

7 Examples mentioned by Butler include hyperbolic theatrical display (cross-dressing, drag balls, street walking, butch-femme spectacles, the sliding between the "march" in New York City and the parade in San Francisco): die-ins by ACT UP, kiss-ins by Queer Nation; drag performance benefits for AIDS.

8 Garber (1992: 155) develops the point how Lacan uses the term 'travesty' when discussing anamorphic projections. She identifies the "monocle" at the turn of the century as a phallic anamorphic instrument. "An indication at once of supplement and lack, both instrumental and ornamental, connoting weakness (in the eye) and strength (social position, as well as class and style), the monocle both *reflects* and *peers into* or *through*. Simultaneously a signifier of castration (detachable, artificial, made to be put on and taken off) and of empowerment, the monocle when worn by a *woman* emphasizes, indeed parodies, the contingent nature of the power conferred by this instrumental 'affectation'" (p.154).

9 Queer filmic studies like that of Richard Dyer's *Now You See It: Studies on Lesbian and Gay Film* (1990) provides queer cultural analysis of filmic sub-texts, especially rethinking notions of authorship. See his "Believing in Fairies: The Author and the Homosexual" (1991). Alexander Doty's *Making Things Perfectly Queer* (1993), is a good overview of what has transpired in this area. His reading of Pee-Wee/Paul Reubens is especially important as he answers feminist accusations of gay misogyny, i.e., Modleski(1991c) and Penley's (1989) reading of Pee-Wee.

10 It should be pointed out that Butler criticizes Silverman's typology as too simplistic, despite Silverman's own recognition of this. She argues that such typologies conform with ease "to the regulatory requirements of diagnostic epistemic regimes." See her "Imitation and Gender Insubordination" (1991:27).

11 Sedgwick is particularly good in her account of showing how the policing of non-homosexual-identified men occurs institutionally through homophobic "blackmail," and with the shape of the entire male homosocial spectrum and its effects on women during the last third of the nineteenth century. Barbara Ehrenreich (1983:24-28) provides an example of this sliding scale in the changes to masculinity that were occurring from the mid '50s to the mid '60s. Men who were fleeing from their familial and work responsibilities, i.e., failures as breadwinners and husbands, were labeled first as "pseudo-homosexuals" because they showed a lack of initiative, did not have a competitive spirit and were "immature," and then they became "overt homosexuals." Such men were making a subconscious slide toward a homosexual identity. The equation was as follows "*I am a failure = I am castrated = I am not a man = I am a woman* follows *= I am a homosexual* (Lionel Ovesy, 1969, quoted in Ehrenreich, p. 25). This is a particularly good illustration as to how homophobia and the 'trade on women' policed men back into the home and work force.

12 To reiterate the logic of the Derridean supplement: in the apparent *symmetrical* dynamic of heterosexual/homosexual binary, heterosexuality maintains its hierarchical (natural) status only if homosexuality is both included, and at the same time, excluded as an inferior sexual characteristic in the definition of heterosexuality. Homosexuality needs to be included in heterosexuality in order to identify difference, and then it needs to be excluded to retain a (pure) heterosexual identity: to *really* be a man, or in the lesbian dynamic — to *really* be a woman.

13 The critique of Sedgwick's thesis has been her inability to explain the various manifestations of desire. Why do some men end up on one side of the scale and not the other? even though there is a recognition that a both/and logic is at work, i.e., the homosocial is already in the homosexual and visa versa. Why is lesbian desire left out of her account? and why is homosexuality presented so dichotomously? Bristow (1992:63-64) reviews these issues referring to the exchange that took place between Sedgwick and David van Leer in *Critical Inquiry* 15 (1989).

14 Halperin's provocative and ground breaking essay, "One Hundred Years of Homosexuality" (1990), (his title refers to the existence of "homosexuality" for a century) points out that the word "homo-sexuality" was first coined into the English language in 1892 by Charles Gilbert Chaddock in order to render a German cognate twenty years its senior. "Before 1892 there was no homosexuality, only sexual inversion" (p.15). In other words, same sex choice was lumped together with other deviant behaviors that were non-conformist to the culturally defined sex-role. The bulk of the essay examines, in stark contrast, the Athenian context where sex was a masculine discourse polarized by the distribution of phallic pleasure interpreted as passive (penetrated) and active (dominated). The sexual system was intimately related to the social and political life of Athenian citizens. Male citizens had legitimate sexual access to women, boys, foreigners and slaves. Halperin specificity points out that gender roles were not at issue in Athenian Greece. In another context Herek (1986) points out that in many New Guinea societies it requires incorporating the semen of other men into one's body through homosexual acts to become a heterosexual man. This most important relationship is accomplished between a boy and his mentor—usually the maternal uncle—his mother's brother (cf. G. Herdt,; 1982). However, in other cases sexuality is often determined by gender roles. "In some indigenous American societies, biological males could assume women's occupations and be socially recognized as women; some men in this 'berdarche' role married (biological and social males)" (p.569-570). The other side of this has been examined by Jonathan Ned Katz, "The Invention of Heterosexuality" (1990).

15 "In Memory of Craig Owens: Outlaw in Feminism," (book dedication, Silverman, 1992). "Memorial for Craig Owens," in *Tendencies* (Sedgwick, 1993).

A GRAND
FAILURE?
1989-1990

a feminist intellectual is one
who seeks to stress her own
politics, not one who seeks to
replace it with geography.

(Moi, 1988:10)

Countless pages of books and articles, uncountable footnotes
later—is this not someone trying to master the discourse of feminism? Has
this not been a grand Herculean masculine gesture, hardly a invocational
dance, but a stomp up and over the material to overpower the networks of
those thousands of authored pages that weave in and out over the
(my)nefield of patriarchy? What adjectives can be used to describe my
'nomadic journey?' The I started out with a pretextual flourish, a confident
brashness, hardly a humbling gesture. And now? It seemed as if an insatiable

appetite could not be quenched, simply confirming the impossibility of Woman. Forever chasing the next book, the next article, thinking it would provide the answer, but the answer was forever deferred. i am reminded of Teresa de Lauretis's (1984:12) warning tale of the city of Zobeide, a city built from a dream of Woman. i too could not lay the trap. She always escaped. i only found authors echoing one another in the city's corridors, holding hands across the distances of 'named' and 'unnamed' journals, so that they may be confirmed. Does this make me just another "ladies man?" i am plagued with this thought. In my search i too wanted confirmation, not to feel castrated, intimidated. The nagging sensation is still there. Some of my traps were taxonomies so that some positions could be dismissed outright. Liberalism, in particular, was such a dumping ground. Yet, the more i read, the more i realized in certain postures there was a need to find a location for the city's dump. Without it the city could never cleanse itself. A site/cite/sight had to be located. As the typologies melted i began carefully stepping over a field of differences.

i am still bothered about the ladies, man, Derrida. It is quite possible to turn the tables around and ask: if some feminists are insistent that his Otherness evaporates specificity and corporeality, why should then any feminist bother to continue to draw her theoretical energy from him? should it not remain the task of a male to draw on the sense of the feminine—as that which remains absent? Derrida has been consistent in his rejection of a specific form of feminism which insists on binary inversions. He has consistently drawn on 'male' texts where the feminine was repressed. Should that not remain an important posture for men? i think so. What also bothers me is the indiscriminate use of patriarchy that i so glibly used throughout my text. What specifically comes to mind now is the monolithic sense of patriarchy that is used throughout the feminist studies i read, and my wholesale acceptance of the term often as an ahistorical category. The category stretches from the essentialism of Mary Daly (1978:28) as "males and only males are the originators, planners, controllers and legitimators," to Dinnerstein's (1976:276) view that patriarchy is *"the male-female collaboration to keep history mad,"* or Leyland's (1978:18) comment regarding William Burroughs' own proclamation: "the only patriarchal society that exists today is the Arab." It is quite obvious that "patriarchy" is quite a different object in each discourse discussed above: liberalism, essentialism, poststructuralism, socialism, Marxism. The most common characterization of patriarchy remains ahistorical. The central values of objectivity, linearity, rationality, logic, aggressivity, competitiveness, and a hierarchical chain of bureaucratic command have come to stand for patriarchy. Regardless of one's gendered persuasion, displaying such qualities positions you in the patriarchal driver's seat, and these have traditionally defined what ~~the~~ "man" is, but THE MAN does *not* exist either. The phallus is an unattainable figurative signifier.

At this moment of hesitation in my journey, it appears it may have been mis-spent energy, for the I knows that he avoided painful explorations that were not written in these pages—the coffee-stains that lay 'outside' the writing when they should appear in their accidental spillage. They have been deliberately wiped up and wiped out, repressed. The I deliberately avoided examining one semester of the Curriculum and Gender course which i have still not forgiven myself. All these vignettes are painful memories. It seems that in pain and scarification, memory lingers longest. They embody the remnants of the Lacanian Real. It is our finitude—our being towards death that vivifies life. How strange! "For feminism at its core is nothing less than a recasting of one's world view, a collectivizing of experience that may until then have seemed only individually painful" (Nelson, 1987:159). What has become rhetorically clear is that the I doesn't belong *in* feminism. i must pick up the trail of "men" who have tracked before me. Men must begin to do their own work on themselves. i still am lured by the ecofeminist movement and the question of a "spiritual" materialism, although Robert Bly's masculine archetype of the "wildman" bothers me. He seems to be trapped by ahistorical Jungian archetype. On one level, his poetry is wonderful, but vacant of the changing historical Imaginary. It seems an obvious statement to make that the heterogeneous positions of feminism repeat themselves in men's studies. The entire spectrum may be found.

In my gleefulness to outline what the I thought to be an innovative reflective way of writing, it seems that i have been kidding myself, and perhaps the reader, all along, for it indeed has been a script-*tease*. The I is only a little more aware of what 'feminism' is about. When i read Ellie Ragland-Sullivan's (1986) section of Lacan's view of the subject, it dawned on me what had happened. In answer to her opening question "What is "I"? Regland-Sullivan concludes by saying,

> [I]n conscious life two subjects appear: the subject of
> individuality and the subject of speech (which has the
> capacity to lie, deny and misrepresent). But the Real sub-
> ject is that of the unconscious, and it is beyond both *moi*
> and *je*. There will never, then, be only one subject, e.g.,
> the savant who looks at the ensemble and hopes one
> day to reduce everything to the game determined by
> symbols enveloping all the interactions between objects.
> Nor is the subject the identification and objectifica-
> tions—the *moi*——an ego or identity in the psychologi-
> cal sense. The subject is, instead, an unbridgeable gap
> between a person's perceptions and alienation in relation
> to an external *Gestalt*, an internal discourse, and Desire.
> Any "I" will mirror the history of its own structuration in
> the Other(A). The intermingling of the two apparently
> unmodified modes of meaning—the *moi* and the *je*—
> each already contingent and relative, establishes percep-
> tion and its "translation" in terms of tension, fading, dis-
> continuity, and incompletion, instead of as the
> developmental, objective, and linear process we assume
> it to be. (p. 66-67)

This sounds a lot like what (I)(i) thought i was doing, but never finding my Other in self-analysis completely satisfying. Just teasing myself, playing a performative game. The ten years of linear time was never linear. The I jumped all over the place to 'find' a dance-partner. The (my)nfield wasn't satisfying no matter where i landed. In Ross's (1990b) sense, it was a "politics of impossibility." Since feminism can never be seen from some single viewpoint, the I played an anamorphic contingency game. My identity as university professor, as father, as artist, as citizen, as consumer of movies and popular culture, dispersed in the field of institution the I inhabits—the university, the family, the artistic community, are in as much flux as the dispersed field of feminism. i am continually changing clothes, and have come to realize that this study has been only one clumsy step in that understanding, with my own rusty chains wrapped around my feet. The i tripped the I/eye and fell flat on its face, blinded but relieved that it could still smell the humus!

The epitaph by Moi, which opens this last vignette, has an uncomfortable ring of truth to it. By her definition the I/i cannot be a male intellectual *in* feminism after all!

But That was Then; This is Now

THE DILEMMA OF DISCIPLINE: SCHOOLING AND RESISTANCE

The whole secret lies in arbitrariness. People usually think it easy to be arbitrary, but it requires much study to succeed in being arbitrary so as not to lose oneself in it, but so as to derive satisfaction from it. One does not enjoy the immediate but something quite different which he arbitrarily imports into it. You go to see the middle of the play, you read the part of a book. By this means you insure yourself a very different kind of enjoyment from that which the author has been so kind as to plan for you.

(Kierkegaard, 1944:295)

As a father and professor in art education, two contradictory discourses often clash against one another. The first is the institutionalized discourse which can often snuff out the very sparks of interest that make discovery and learning a joyful experience. This is the down side of education characterized by a language of mechanization and objectification, efficiency and effectiveness; its stress is on careers and the job market. Embedded within this discourse is a sense of order and stilling of the body, the notion of doing "work" and being on time, and on task. It means having your body charted and graphed, computerized, and graded. This discourse is certainly not what I/i nor Carolyne wish for our son, Jeremy. As an artist, my experience of space/time is in direct contrast to such disciplining. A "discipline" is required here, of course, but one of a different order; Kierkegaard's quote points to the serendipitous and chaotic sense which belongs to it. These two discourses are therefore at odds with one another. The second might be interpreted as the binary of the first, in the sense that *resistance* to order is what keeps them both dichotomous.

Jeremy loves to draw. Every since he was tiny I/i would sit him on my lap and let him mess with colors and scribble to his heart's content. Like a "good" art educator I/i made it possible for him to be secure and have a playful and comfortable space to himself. But as parents, we give up our children to the school institution and lose control as to what will happen to them once they meet yet another twenty or more kids of the same age. Should trouble arise, the parental discourse clashes with what "society" as represented through the institution of education desires.

The following is a performance that I/i wrote and presented at several educational conferences between 1987-1989. It marks a crisis in the very discourses I/i have mentioned above: between school and parents; between order/disorder; between conditioning and resistance to that conditioning. Jeremy was too much of a socializer in school, and his work was "messy." After several meetings with his grade two teacher, it became clear to Carolyne and I/i that his teacher was very dissatisfied with Jeremy's overall attitude to school. In this performance I/i have tried to intertwine my biography as a student with that of my son. I have also drawn heavily on Michel Foucault's *Discipline and Punishment: The Birth of the Prison*, especially on the section where he talks about the relationship between discipline and schooling, in order to present the genealogy of the "stilled body" in contrast to Jeremy's constant "moving" one. Foucault is the perfect choice as an anamorphic or oblique voice in this text. He has argued that the mechanisms which organize us into the disciplined subjects required by capitalism work ultimately through the body. He has tried to grapple with the problem as how it is possible, in this highly elaborated social system of late capitalism, to maintain inequalities and conflicts of interest without coming to an all-out revolution. Centralized management control by the agencies of the state, as we have seen recently in the burning and looting in Central Los Angeles (1992), only becomes too visible when major trouble is happening. Otherwise, Foucault has argued, we must understand the micro-technologies of power which produce, organize, and control social differences. The direct correlation between schooling and the class system, as argued by the early neo-Marxist critics (especially 'early' Michael Apple) does not seem to hold.

It is the body that replaces the subject (as an individual) in these micro-systems of control; on the body are imposed the social norms which cure or punish those that exceed them, and it is within these norms the organization of the body behavior in space and time which forms the basis of the social order. The body must occupy certain "work stations" which are individualized so that any body not occupying them properly can be identified and disciplined.

> Similarly, every body's individual history, his or her accumulation of behaviors, is recorded and rated in school records and grade sheets, work records, credit ratings, criminal records, driving records—our society works on a highly elaborated system of surveying, and recording, ranking, and individuating our everyday behaviors. Individuality of this sort is a top-down product: individuals are differentiated according to the demands of the system, and individuation becomes a disciplinary mechanism. Its technologies of differentiation do to measure individual differences that pre-exist them, but actively produce those differences as part of the operation of its power. This continuous process of individuation is power-in-practice, is discipline-in-practice. It is not the power of one class over another, nor the discipline of officers over subalterns; it is a social technology of control that organizes the behaviors of everyone within it, the big cogs as much as the little cogs. The social order, as Foucault analyzes it, depends upon the control of the people's bodies and behaviors: it couldn't give a damn about their subjectivities (Fiske, 1992:161-162).

Lastly, there is a strong feminist discourse which weaves in and out of the performance. This discourse speaks on several levels. The first is to foreword women's experience as a counter to a patriarchal schooling system. This voice speaks to the ethics of caring and the potential s(mother) of the mother.

The second, is the sense of the feminine as the other of masculinity. Here the voice speaks to affect which is associated with creativity, the right brain and the imagination—the other of cognition and rationality.

It will be quickly apparent there is a great deal of word and number play which attempts to put the "visible" into play along with the textually written. This is my attempt to put the *figural* force into play, following Lyotard's (1971) sense of deconstruction in his *Discours, figure* (1971). There is a blocking together which is a mode characteristic of the *figural*, in which two incommensurable elements (in this case the visible and the textual) are held together, impossibly, in the 'same' space. This is a kind of 'superimposition without privilege' (Readings, 1991: xxx). There is also a deconstruction of subjectivity. Throughout the performance several graphic forms of the personal pronoun "I" are used. "Eye" refers to the position of omniscience, a small "i" refers to a subject position of reflection, and "ja" is the Polish personal pronoun for "I." i use this to refer to my "ethnic" sense of self.

Members of the audience were given The Script/ The Score to follow as visuals were simultaneously shown. Two projection screens and a video tape were set up. On the left project screen appeared photographs of myself as a child along with close-ups of my report cards. On the right projection screen, photographs of Jeremy as a child were shown and close-ups of his report cards, along with teacher's comments, were shown. Between the two projection screens a video recorder and a television were installed. A video tape of *Evil River*, a made for television film based on the Keegstra affair[1] was shown. I/i had selectively used scenes from this film in conjunction with the script of the performance. A tape recorder with the voices of myself and Carolyne read the script.

1 Jim Keegstra was a high-school teacher and ex-mayor of Elkville, Alberta, Canada. He was tried and accused for teaching Nazis propaganda that the Holocaust was a hoax, and that there was a world-wide Jewish conspiracy to take over the world.

DISCIPLINE/ DISCIPLE;

THE **CHOREOGRAPHY** OF THE PUNISHED BODY
READING FOUCAULT THROUGH THE VOICE
OF OUR SON JEREMY

The following is the text of a performance piece which had four separate 'showings.' Three of those occasions were conference meetings of educators. It is not possible to include the visuals and audio which went along with this piece. Nevertheless, the reader will have an idea of how I/i am attempting to translate some of my concerns about men *in* feminism through performance art. The incident about which I/i—speak, talk, question—was the pain that our son went through in grade two when his teacher thought that he was inattentive and disruptive in class. It questions the broader discourse of education which has entrenched itself in conservative views of knowledge, discipline, and evaluation. Little has changed since 1987; in fact it has become worse.

Below is a newspaper article which I/i read in an authoritative, news-like voice behind a podium before the performance began.

Doc's goof costly

STOCKHOLM (AFP) — A Swedish surgeon who had confused two patients cut one testicle off a man and almost removed the second, a newspaper reported yesterday.

The error occurred in February 1986 on a day when two men were booked for urological operations in adjacent rooms, *Aftonbladet* reported. One man was suffering from prostrate cancer. The other was there for minor surgery.

To avoid any confusion, the nurse gave each patient a number. The trouble was she gave both the same one.

The surgeon and the nurse have been <u>disciplined</u>.

568

The Script/ The Score

(re-righting **spell-**ing)

Several fonts have been used to indicate the voices which speak the text in keeping with the textual, non-subjective 'I'. Michel Foucault's celebrated work, *Discipline and Punish: The Birth of the Prison* (1977), forms the bulk of the citations/sight-ations/ site-ations, specifically pps. 135-185. They are presented in **Geneva font**. The voice of jan is represented in Americana font. Every so often insights, as separate paragraphs appear. These hint at the intertextual issues that lie beyond the pages of this text, the issue of patriarchy and the curriculum. These are presented in a **Courier** font which has been bold faced, shadowed and outlined to indicate the seriousness I/i attach to these **fragments.** The voice of excellence in teaching has been given a Bembo font.

The Sight/ The Site/ The Cite

(re-seeing sight)

The images presented on the viewer's **reading left** screen will speak the images of jeremy and jan. They are deconstructed photographs; the sentimentalism of family snaps, which in the art world are perceived as kitsch and sentimentalism—not real art. The images presented on the **trailing right** will be the slick images of the disciplined body. Their suture is hidden, and hence present to you as polished photography, the **sly**de) The made-for-television movie in the **center** is run silently, without sound. It is a **silent** movie. *Evil River* is based on the Keegstra a(**ffair**). The movie has been deconstructed; its **grain** has been produced by aiming a video camera at the television while the movie was on. This silent movie is a movie of a movie—a **dub.**

Discipline/disciple .... is a fiction, and its content derives entirely from my imagination. Where I have used real names or what seem to be physical descriptions of real people, it is done purely in the interest of fiction. In any serious sense any similarities between this story and the real lives of any person living or dead is unintended and coincidental.

ja-ja

no rights reserved

Ja means "I" in Polish

DISCIPLINE/ disciple,

the **Choreography** of

the **Punished Body**:

Reading Foucault through the **Voice** of Our Son Jeremy

jan**ja**godzinski—jeremy—carolyneperri
university of alberta, Canada

In 1956, as Russian/Polish/English immigrants we arrived on the shores of Montrèal. Having been denied an education, my parents had high expectations and wanted me to succeed in school in the worst way. After a series of tests and interviews   i /ja was placed in a grade two class. New to the country   i/ja remember vividly how diligent   i/ja   was: obedient, punctual, perserverate, wanting to get good grades, to win the teacher's approval, to be at the top of my class. i/ja wanted to succeed in the worst way. Each year we were ranked from :

1 through 2 3 4 5 6 7 8 9 10. the rest were o's. 1(one) remembers, 1 was proud to think that 1 had never dropped below a 3 ranking. 1ndependent, 1 did what was expected of me, got along nicely with everyone. 1 was a loner, creative, and dependable, my homework was always completed and neatly done. My experience as an immigrant was not unique in this regard. i/ja   did what   (aye, aye, sir—-ja/ja)   was told in order to move ahead through good grades and good citizenship.

571

The historical moment of the *disciplines* was the moment when an art of the human body was born, which was directed not only at the growth of its skills, nor at the intensification of its subjection, but at the formation of a relation that in the mechanism itself makes it more obedient as it becomes more useful, and conversely. What was then being formed was a policy of coercion that acts upon the body, a calculated manipulation of its elements, of its gestures, its behavior. The human body was entering a machinery of power that explores it, breaks it down and rearranges it. (Foucault:137-138)

As **(eye)** look back at **Ja**, the conceptualization of discipline has always been associated with control, order, following rules and punishment "for your own good," to quote Alice Miller's (1983) words as to why children have been beaten throughout the centuries. Any book one picks up today on educational discipline is defined by analogous binary terms: pain/pleasure, behavior/misbehavior, success/failure. work/pleasure.

> Discipline is a language of re(**enforcement**), re(**ward**), co(**erection**), re(**habilitate**)ation; of enforcement, wards, erections, and habilitations - to [re]qualify oneself (as for teaching at a university).

The language tells you that classroom **MAN**agement means keeping a particular form, a particular 'being' through instituted techniques, or procedures. That form is characterized by behavior, enforcement, ward, erection, habit- a sterile and **kl**inical **kl**imate of business. What sort of teacher/child relationship allows such a form to exist ? What is the nature of that form? Is it gendered?

(eye)

knew **ja** was in a privileged position. Teachers were far more lenient with me than others, even when **ja** transgressed the rules. During reading period, in particular, someone would be repri**MAN**ded/re(**made**) for not concentrating on their reading. During work periods the teacher would walk up and down the aisles correcting mis(**takes**) or sit in the desk at the front of the class and every so often lift **the** head up from correcting/**erecting** to see who was not doing their work. A **stare** would soon follow. If that failed, detentions were handed out. Perhaps the most vivid memory was the strapping which took place in front of the class. We were all spectators to the punishment. Secretly **ja** was glad that it wasn't me that was being punished, but someone else. **Ja** was a good boy. Later, because my grades were so good, **Ja** had free periods and was exempt from final exams. **I** played at what **eye** liked. **Eye** was a success.

It is abundantly clear, "(avoiding the pitfalls of rhetoric)" that all disciplines defined by the hierarchy of the above binary oppositions which privilege order, become norm based. The exceptions are non-observable, such spaces provide transgression—eye "played." The whole notion of discipline suggests a defined corrected body (of knowledge), a personality type whose boundaries are clearly defined—tight, clear, erudite. To discipline is

to hold one's/ 1 's form, to be **erect** to be a disciple of the teacher. Yet this adds nothing to knowledge, to gnoseology. Paradoxically, knowledge happens outside the center, during the transgressions of serendipitous play (Feyerabend, 1970). Where then is knowledge to be found? Where is its space of breathing? To '**be**' disciplined is (**main**)tain form. To **be** disciples means to internalize

one's/ 1 's self-will: to surrender to the will of the Other, be that a religious Order, a Creed of a country or an Author. Remaining disciplined within the self suggests self-control, self-restraint, particularly of mind and body. Excessiveness, self indulgence, being out of control- hyper, would be actions that are intolerable. Being disciplined means re(**main**)ing obedient to Authority since you have suppressed your own will to be re(**place**)ed by the will of the Other. When **should** you surrender your will? and to **whom**?

> To discipline means to 'be,'
> to deny change in
> Order to remain the same.

There are two main ways children hold form. The first form of discipline is where you have internalized your own will-to-power through the conscious denial of Self to gain approval by the **Other** in(**order**) to feel complete. Motivation, your desire to feel purposeful, is fulfilled by meeting your 'lack' through the **Other**. Such an internalized desire fulfills that original split all of us have felt from our **M**(Other)s, that moment when the baby realizes that s/he is a(**1**)one, that s/he is not the **M**(Other) but exists outside her body. It is that moment when a fundamental 'lack' has been established (Lacan, 1977).

You

always desire that moment when **you** might be whole again and enter a period when **you** were **supplemented** by parts of your **M**(other)'s body- a non-time when **you** were not an independent bounded 'being' but a non-bounded, non-being, swept away in your **M**(other)'s arms. The creation of such desire, to restore your original 'lack,' to put yourself right, manifests itself in this internal control to please the feminine side of yourself, the voice of your, **M**(other) still inside **you.** It is when **you** obey in **order** to make the Other happy. In return one is stroked, fondled and loved. Children are disciplined in this way through soft words and gentle persuasion - please and thank you's and as long as the model is still in keeping to the form the teacher wants, all is ordered, non-chaotic. This form of modeling creates the gentle'-man' and the gentle 'wo/man' (the lady). It lives on the premise that **we**= is a junction between the "**I**" and the non-"**I**"; the non-**I** which is personal as in **me + you** or impersonal **"me" + them**. **WE** all ought to behave with etiquette and politeness, in consensus, in norms, in disciplines:

To S(Mother) the Other

In discipline, punishment is only one element of a double system: gratification-punishment. And it is this system that operates in the process of training and correction. The teacher must avoid, as far as possible, the use of punishment; on the contrary, s/he must endeavor to make rewards 0 more frequent than penalties, the lazy being encouraged by the desire to be rewarded in the same way that the diligent, rather than by fear of punishment; that is why it is very beneficial, when the teacher is obligated to use punishment, to win the heart of the child if s/he can before doing so.

The other way to discipline turns to the Voice of the Father. One 1 obeys because of **Authority**, -Law, the rules of the social order as instituted by patriarchy. Here there is unquestioned attention. One 1 knows the rules and therefore the limits of acceptable behavior. Obeying the Voice of the Father allows one 1 to be identified as being good and being rewarded for good behavior. If the **S**(mother) of the **m**(other) fails, then the Voice of the Father, as represented by the principal, vice-principal is called upon to establish the Law. The power to challenge such **A**uthority is continually deferred by the child. When their will-to-power is not given up to the leadership of the Father, form breaks down and deviancy declared.

eye

remember **I**, when still attending school in England, in 1954, sitting on top of cold dustbins, my calves pressed tightly against their sides. My body stilled, feeling the sting of the cane **I** had received for doing—**eye** knew not what? The feel of the cold tin against my burning flesh was marvelously soothing. First **we** beat our children, then **we** are stroked; that is the Voice of the Father.

The form of discipline which we have come to assume as the most conducive for learning is one **1** where the body is stilled so that the stilted mind can learn. The stilling of the body is done either through the S(Mother) of the M(other) or through the Voice of the Father. The child is continually played off between these two forms as instituted by the bourgeois family. These forms reproduce themselves in the school setting. Such forms suggest a well-bounded space- the classroom/home, which can be easily surveyed for its order, where the parts inside this field have freedom, but degrees of freedom only to the point where the classroom/home wouldn't disperse and become out of hand, out of control. Small group work, the assignment of desks, schedules, timetables, period changes— re(present) such a form. Deviations from such a form are perceived as chaotic, mis(behaviors) where students seek attention. (One **1** asks sarcastically, why shouldn't a child seek attention?) Everything points to Logos, to Order, Sequentially, Linearity, Reason, Rationality. As a gender issue?

In almost every cultural myth, Woman
has been associated with chaos.

What is specific to the disciplinary penalty is non-observance, that which does not measure up to the rule, that departs from it. Whatever is non-"con"forming is punishable. Chaos is punishable, woman is punishable.

Children who do not fit the normalization patterns are perceived as either mad/bad. They have learning disabilities, are considered hyper-active—the polite word is exceptional. Today the number of classifications and remedial programs are growing so rapidly that the norm is becoming an absurdity.

The organization of serial space was one of the great technical mutations of elementary education. It made it possible to supersede the traditional system (a pupil working for a few minutes with the master, while the rest of the heterogeneous group remained idle and unattended). By assigning individual places it made possible the supervision of each individual and the simultaneous work of all. It organized a new economy of time of apprenticeship. It made the educational space function like a learning machine, but also a machine for supervising, hierarchizing, rewarding.

Jeremy is in grade 2. He is **our** son. Carolyne and **i** have been told that he is not doing his work, not keeping up. **We** talk first to his teacher. **We** are told he is not paying attention to her, moves out of his desk too much, wants to socialize with others, writes too many sentences, does sloppy work, and is messy (dirty). His teacher, on the other hand, is perfectly made-up, manicured nails, wears tight clothes and is super well-organized.

Dirt,
the Earth, has always been associated with
Woman. Women value relationships. They are gatherers.
Rather than serialization, since recorded time, their signs
have been labyrinthine.
Is Jeremy being denied his feminine
side, that side we have taught him to dream in?

In the first instance, discipline proceeds from the distribution of individuals in space. To achieve this end, it employs several techniques.

1. Discipline sometimes requires *enclosure* , the specification of a place heterogeneous to all others and closed in upon itself. It is the protected place of disciplinary monotony.

the desk

strappings no longer take place in Jeremy's
school. Because of his talkative behavior his
desk was moved to the front of the class. He
now stares at the board and feels that his
classmates are looking at him,

laughing behind his back.

**2. But the principle of *enclosure* is neither constant,
nor indispensable, nor sufficient in disciplinary
machinery. This machinery works space in a much
more flexible and detailed way. It does this first of
all on the principle of elementary location of *parti-
tioning* . Each individual has his own place, and each
place its individual. Avoid distributions in groups,
break up collective disposition; analyze confused,
massive or transient pluralities. Disciplinary space
tends to be divided into as many sections as there
are bodies or elements to be distributed. One must
eliminate the effects of imprecise distributions, the
uncontrolled disappearance of individuals, their diffuse circulation, their unusable and dangerous coag-
ulation...Its aim was to establish presences and
absences, to know where and how to locate individuals, to set up useful communications, to inter-
rupt others, to be able at each moment to supervise the conduct of each individual, to access it, to
judge it, to calculate its qualities or merits. It was
a procedure, therefore, aimed at knowing, mastering and using. Discipline organizes an analytical
space.**

the attendance sheet, the cumulative record,
the seating arrangements, the daily register

Jeremy's *Mon carnet de conduit* - literally translated as his book of behavior- metaphorically his "ticket to ride" -his pass-book, a passport into the school system, is filled with unhappy faces. The teacher's symbol of her displeasure which, we as parents must acknowledge through the presence of our *signature*. The signature confirms of our approval, our contract between the home and the school.

3. The rule of *functional sites* would gradually, in the disciplinary institutions, code a space that architecture generally left at the disposal of several different uses. Particular places were defined to correspond not only to the need to supervise, to break dangerous communications, but also to create a useful place.... By walking up and down the central aisle in the workshop, it was possible to carry out a supervision that was both general and individual: to observe the worker's presence and application, and the quality of his work: to compare workers with one another, to classify them according to skill and speed; to follow the successive stages of the production process. All these serializations formed a permanent grid; confusion was eliminated: that is to say, production was divided up and the labour process was articulated, on the one hand, according to its stages or elementary operations, and on the other hand, according to the individuals, the particular bodies, that carried it out.

Hey dad, guess what I got today? What Jeremy?
- I got a star for speaking French!

4. In discipline, the elements are interchangeable, since each is defined by the place it occupies in the series, and by the gap that separates it from the others. The unit is, therefore, neither the territory (unit of domination), nor the place (unit of residence), but *the rank* ; the place one occupies in a classification, the point at which a line and a column intersect, the interval in a series of intervals that one may traverse one after the other. Discipline is an art of rank, a technique for the transformation of arrangements. It individualizes bodies by location that does not give them a fixed position, but distributes them and circulates them in a network of relations.

Jeremy's teacher shows us his printing. She complains how little care he has taken and then proceeds to show what the best printers in class are doing. Carolyne and i are silent. [Now he writes so small, nobody can read it.]

In the eighteenth century, 'rank' begins to define the great form of distribution of individuals in the educational order: rows or ranks of pupil in the class, corridors, courtyards; rank attributes to each pupil at the end of each task and each examination; the rank he obtains from week to week, month to month, year to year; an alignment of age groups, one after another; a succession of subjects taught and questions treated, according to an order of increasing difficulty. And in this ensemble of compulsory assignments, each pupil according to his age, his performance, his behavior, occupies sometimes one rank, sometimes another.

Jeremy tells me he feels the dumbest in the class because all the rest of the kids are finished and playing at recess while he is still writing. [Now he rushes to get things done FIRST.]

The distribution according to ranks or grade has a double role: it marks the gaps, hierarchizes qualities, skills and aptitudes; but it also punishes and rewards. It is the penal functioning of setting in order and the ordinal character of judging. Discipline rewards simply by the play of awards, thus making it possible to attain higher ranks and places; it punishes by reversing this process. Rank in itself serves as a reward or punishment.

Jeremy tells me he doesn't want to be put in the other English class - the dumb class. **We** are told by the teachers that there is no difference. All the kids **no** better. **We** refuse to move Jeremy. But the teacher feels betrayed and treats him accordingly.

At École Militaire, a complex system of 'honorary' classification was developed;...The first class, known as the 'very good,' were distinguished by a silver epaulette;...The second class, 'the good,' wore an epaulette of red silk and silver;...The class of 'mediocre,' had the right to an epaulette of red wool;...The last class, that of the 'bad,' was marked by an epaulette of brown wool.

The research on effective teaching conducted since 1974 has yielded a pattern of instruction that is particularly useful for teaching a body of content or well-defined skills. This pattern is a systematic method for presenting material in small steps, pausing to check student understanding and eliciting active and successful participation for all students. (Rosenshine,p.60)

The digestion of such material is a dead matter.
Our children are being fed dead meat, which
makes them ill without knowing why.

Jeremy tells me he only got two stars this week in English. ✳✳✳ ✘✳✘✦✎✳▲☐✳

Although this method was delivered primarily from reading and mathematics research conducted in elementary and junior high schools, the results are applicable to any "well-structured" discipline where the objective is to teach performance skills or mastery of a body of knowledge. (Rosenshine, p. 60)

In summarizing the studies on effective teaching, I have divided the results into six teaching functions: review, presentation, presentation of new materials, guided practice, feedback and corrections, independent practice, weekly and monthly reviews. (Rosenshine, p. 64)

WE

realize something horrible. i must pull Jeremy out of school if he is to survive into the 21st century. Bit melodramatic, don't you think? i realize that the Name of the Father is being acted out on him. He must become linear, rational, serial, and reasonable. The three subjects that claim priority (reading, writing, arithmetic) demand that of him. He must submit to a matron teacher who believes that she is doing the best for her students. Children do learn to spell, read and write in her class. They make the proper gaps between words, they are clean and perfect, not messy. Eventually the b's and d's are distinguished and the play is over.

> **Discipline is a political anatomy of detail. The meticulousness of the regulations, the fussiness of the inspections, the supervision of the smallest fragment of life and of the body will soon provide, in the context of the school, the barracks, the hospital or the workshop, a dissected content, an economic or technical rationality for the mystical calculus of the infinitesimal and the infinite.**

WE

talk to the teacher for the second time. She has arranged the plusses and minuses of Jeremy's behavior neatly on his file.

WE

are told in detail what is right and what is wrong with him. He sits with us listening.

Do you have anything to say Jeremy?

Jeremy is silent, just shakes his head. The checklist is worked from top to bottom. There are awkward moments to be sure. The traits put together make Jeremy into the right sort of adult.

> **In organizing 'cells,' places,' and 'ranks,' the disciplines create complex spaces that are at once architectural, functional and hierarchical. It is spaces that provide fixed positions and permit circulation; they carve out individual segments and establish operational links; they mark places and indicate values; they guarantee the obedience of individuals, but also a better economy of time and gesture.**

i realize something more horrible. Jerry is messy, unordered, mixes up his b's with d's. He sometimes uses his left hand, sometimes his right. His 6's and 7's are backwards (**even this Mac SE cannot show you this!**), in short, all his mistakes, his wonderful chaos is being stripped away from him. What is the cost? He is entering the Age of Reason where there is only order. Only the beleaguered space of the fine arts offers him some freedom. Jeremy is told he is a good artist. He does his art longer than others when he has a chance.

> **In the eighteenth century, the *table* was both a technique of power and a procedure of knowledge. It was a question of organizing the multiple, of providing oneself with an instrument to cover it and to master it; it was a question of imposing upon it an 'order.'**

We are now frantic about what we should do with Jeremy. In this Age of Reason there is so little creative madness left. i come to the conclusion that he will become one among the living dead, either the right arm or the left will be stilled. i know few people who are ambidextrous. Yet i know better. The flight away from school by our youth is evident everywhere. They live within album covers, magazines and movies. i realize that madness is alive and well and that i will lose Jeremy to that chaos, a chaos which adults just don't understand.

582

1. The *time-table* is an old inheritance. The strict model was no doubt suggested by the monastic communities. It soon spread. Its three great methods- establish rhythms, impose particular occupations, regulate the cycles of repetition- were soon to be found in schools, workshops and hospitals,

In the elementary schools, the division of time became increasingly minute; activities were governed in detail by others that had to be obeyed immediately:' 'At the last stroke of the hour, a pupil will ring the bell, and at the first sound of the bell all pupils will kneel, with their arms crossed and their eyes lowered..,

eye ask i,

why is it that the most creative people
don't operate by bells, change day into night,
in a time card,

at least the last i heard —— hadn't.

The workshop, the school, the army were subject to a whole micro-penalty of time (latenesses, absences, interruptions of tasks), of activity (inattention, negligence, lack of zeal, of behavior (impoliteness, disobedience), of speech (idle chatter, insolence), of the body (incorrect attitudes, irregular gestures, lack of cleanliness), of sexuality (impurity, indecency). At the same time, by way of punishment, a whole series of subtle procedures was used from light physical punishment to minor deprivations and petty humiliations.

"Who's making that stupid noise?"
asks the teacher. (Jeremy is growling
like a bear) Jeremy, ... Jeremy, two

students state with accusing voices. "Jeremy, if you can't settle down and be responsible I'll have someone else read the part of the bear!" (from one of my classroom observations in Jeremy's English class)

In the correct use of the body, which makes possible a correct use of time, nothing must remain idle or useless: everything must remain idle or useless; everything must be called upon to form the support of the act required. A well-disciplined body forms the operational context of the slightest gesture. Good handwriting, for example, presupposes a gymnastics- a whole routine whose rigorous code invests the body in its entirety, from the points of the feet to the tip of the index finger.

Jeremy tells me he is improving. The next meeting with the teacher. She tells us he is improving. He is becoming cleaner, neater, more tidy. Now i'm getting nervous. Is the trade off worth it? Carolyne and i become runners.

We start searching for another school.

We are desperate.

We have sleepless nights.

A disciplined body is the pre(requisite) of an efficient gesture.

Jeremy had never had a bad nightmare. He had *sort* of one the day before. He always giggles in his sleep. He has no fears. He isn't afraid of the dark. We have given him a chance to sleep with us whenever he wanted if he ever became afraid. **We** didn't mind if he peed his bed. Since he started grade two

584

he has less energy. He wants to sleep in longer, reluctant to go to school. i wonder how much darkness is being suppressed by his unconscious that makes his body so heavy. Last night he dreamt of flying space toilets. i wish he could flush some school out his mind.

The disciplines, which analyze space, break up and rearrange activities, must also be understood as machinery for adding up and capitalizing time. This was done in four ways, which emerge most clearly in military organization. 1. Divide duration into successive or parallel segments, each of which must end at a specific time...2. Organize these according to an analytical plan— successions of elements as simple as possible, that instruction should abandon the principle of analogical repetition...3, Finalize these temporal segments, decide on how long each will last and conclude it with an examination, which will have the triple function of showing whether the subject undergoes the same apprenticeship and of differentiating the abilities of each individual...4. Draw up series of series; lay down for each individual, according to his level, his seniority, his rank, the exercises that are suited to him; common exercises have a differing role and each difference involves specific exercises.

Most of our teacher education has been based on these principles, commonly referred to as a curriculum rationale based on behavioral objectives.

Is *this* a gender issue?

Exercise is that technique by which one imposes on the body tasks that are both repetitive and different, but always graduated. By bending behavior towards a terminal state, exercise makes a perpetual characterization of the individual either in relation to the term, in relation to other individuals, or in relation to a type of itinerary.... In any case, the idea of an educational 'programme' that would

**follow the child to the end of his schooling and which
would involve from year to year, month to month,
exercises of increasing complexity, first appeared,
it seems, in religious group, the Brothers of Common
Life.**

i often wondered why organized religions,
run by men,
fear women 'priests.'
Now i know.

Is the curriculum gender
specific?

We are doing homework together, Jeremy, Carolyne and i. Jeremy hates homework. He thinks he is being punished. Endless repetition, one work sheet after
another.

**Exercise, having become an element in the political
technology of the body and of duration, does not
culminate in a beyond, but tends towards a subjection that has never reached its limit.**

**The examination combines the techniques of an
observing hierarchy and those of a normalizing judgment. It is a normalizing gaze, a surveillance that
makes it possible to qualify, classify and to punish.
It establishes over individuals a visibility through
which one differentiates them and judges them. That
is why, in all the mechanisms of discipline, the examination is highly ritualized. In it are combined the
ceremony of power and the form of the experiment,
the deployment of force and the establishment of
truth. At the heart of the procedures of discipline,
it manifests the subjection of those who are perceived as objects and the objectification of those
who are subjected.**

Jeremy is collecting his things. He is leaving the school. He has collected a small number of names and telephone numbers. He intends to call them all up. The teacher asks me if i want to take away his file with the test results to show his new teacher. i am reluctant to take it but i know there is no escape. The file, the report, the cumulative record is only the beginning of Jeremy's subjugation. i take them in silence.

The examination also introduces individuality into the field of documentation. The examination leaves behind it a whole meticulous archive constituted in terms of bodies and days. The examination that places individuals in a field of surveillance also situates them in a network of writings; it engages a whole mass of documents that capture and fix them.

We have found another teacher. She is very disorganized, chaotic. The electronic age has changed all our concepts of reasoning, Writing and .... ..**We** live in a world of the child/adult. All our adult secrets have been let out. We dress and think as children. Some say we are entering into a **new** Dark Age, a neo-medievalism which is melting down our dictionaries and replacing them with non-linearity. **We** live in an Age where the Earth is dying and the nuclear Shadow covers her face. **We** need an education where the wonderment of the cosmos needs to be rekindled. Unless such an education is found Jeremy, Carolyne and i will be always running. But running away from **what**?

And to **where**?

The danger of the direct
questioning of the subject
about the subject and of all
self-reflection of the spirit lies
in this, that it could be useful and important for one's
activity to interpret oneself
falsely" (Nietzsche, *The Will
to Power,* p. 356).

ja - ja

jeremy never had a voice
carolyne never had a voice

it is perhaps a Father's neurosis,caught in the web of the real-ations of
Author-izing
Father/sun

it is perhaps a M(other)'s neurosis, caught in the real-ations of
S(mothering)

Mother/son

Other Voices

Feyerabend, P. Against Method. in M. Rader and S. Winokur (eds). *Analysis of theories and **methods** of physics and psychology*. University of Minnesota Press, Minneapolis, 1970.

Foucault, Michel. *Discipline and punish: The **birth** of the prison*. Trans. Alan   S h e r i d o n . Penguin Books Ltd., Harmondsworth, Middlesex, England, 1977.

Jeremy Jagodzinski, _____. Edmonton, Alberta, Canada, July, 31, 1980

Lacan, Jacques. *Écrits: A Selection*. Trans. Alan Sheridan. W.W. Norton & Company, New York, 1977

Miller, Alice. *For your own **good**: Hidden cruelty in child-rearing and the roots of violence*. Trans. Hildegarde and Hunter Hannum. Toronto: Collins Publishers, 1983.

Nietzsche, F. *The **Will** to power*. (Ed. Walter Kaufmann). Alfred A. Knopf., 1967.

Rosenshine, Barak V. " Synthesis of Research on Explicit Teaching," *Educational **Leadership**,* April 1986, pp. 60-69.

BIBLIOGRAPHY

Voices Cited/Sighted/Sited and Summoned

Abel, Elizabeth, ed. (1982). *Writing and Sexual Difference*. Chicago: University of Chicago Press.

Abel, Elizabeth (1990). Race, Class, and Psychoanalysis? Opening Questions. In *Conflicts in Feminism*. Marianne Hirsch and Evelyn Fox Keller, eds. pp. 184-204. New York and London: Routledge.

Abels, Gabriele Joscijka (1990). Whar-nehmung und Sinn-gebung: Theoretisher Diskurs und Gang durch die Spiegel. In *Sprung im Spiegel: Filmisches Wahrnehmen zwichen Fiktion und Wirklichkeit*. Christa Blümlinger, ed. pp. 51-80. Wein: Sonderzahl Verlagsgesellschaft m b.H.

Adams, Parveen (1986). "Versions of the Body," *m/f*, 11/12.

Adams, Parveen (1989). Of Female Bondage. In *Between Feminism & Psychoanalysis*. Teresa Brennan, ed. pp. 247-265. London and New York: Routledge.

Adams, Parveen (1991). Per Os(cillation). In *Male Trouble*. Constance Penley and Sharon Willis. eds. pp. 3-26. London and Minneapolis: University of Minnesota Press. Also in *Psychoanalysis and Cultural Theory: Thresholds*. James Donald, ed. pp. 68-88. Houndmills, Basingstoke, Hampshire and London: MacMillan Education Ltd.

Adams, Parveen (1993). "THE THREE (DIS)GRACES," *New Formations*, 19 (Spring).

Adams, Parveen (1994). Father, Can't You See I'm Filming. In *Supposing the Subject*. Joan Copjec, ed. pp. 185-200. London and New York: Verso.

Adams, Parveen (1996). Operation Orlan. In Adam's *The Emptiness of the Image: Psychoanalysis and Sexual Differences*. pp. 141-159. London and New York: Routledge.

Adams, Parveen and Elizabeth Cowie, eds. (1990). *The Woman in Question, m/f*. An OCTOBER Book. Cambridge, Massachusetts: The MIT Press.

Alcoff, Linda (1988a). "Cultural Feminism versus Post-structuralism: The Identity Crisis in Feminist Theory," *Signs: Journal of Women in Culture and Society*, 13, 3:405-436.

Alcoff, Linda (1988b). *Cultural Feminism versus Poststructuralism: Identity Crisis in Feminist Theory*. Chicago: University of Chicago Press.

Allen, Jeffner and Iris Marion Young (1989). *The Thinking Muse: Feminism and Modern French Philosophy*. Bloomington and Indianapolis: Indiana University Press.

Allen, Paula Gunn (1986). *The Sacred Hoop: Recovering the Feminine in American Indian Traditions*. Boston: Beacon Press.

Alpers, Svetlana (1983). *The Art Of Describing: Dutch Art in the Seventeenth Century*. Chicago: University of Chicago Press.

Althusser, Louis (1971). Ideology and Ideological State Apparatuses: Notes Towards an Investigation. In Louis Althusser's *Lenin and Philosophy and Other Essays*. pp. 121-176. Trans. B. Brewster. London: New Left Books.

Altman, Dennis (1980). What Changed in the Seventies. In *Homosexuality: Power and Politics*. Gay Left Collective, eds. London: Allison and Busby.

Alvarado, Manuel, Edward Buscombe, and Richard Collins, eds. (1993). *The Screen Education Reader: Cinema, Television, Culture*. New York: Columbia University Press.

Amos, Valerie and B. Pratibha (1984). "Challenging Imperial Feminism," *Feminist Review*, 17:3-19.

Ang, Ien (1985). *Watching Dallas*. New York: Methuen.

Aoki, Doug (1995). She Looks Like a Man. Paper presented to the Canadian Sociology Anthropology Association: Lacanian Indirections in Social Theory (June 4) 1-12. 30th Annual *Learned Societies*, Montréal, Quebec, Canada.

Ang, Ien and Joke Hermes (1991). Gender and/in Media Consumption. In *Mass Media and Society*. James Curran and Michael Gurevitch, eds. pp.307-328. London, New York, Melbourne, Auckland: Edward Arnold, A div. of Hodder & Stoughton.

Ariès, Phillipe (1962). *Centuries of Childhood: A Social History of Family Life*. Trans. Robert Baldick. New York: Vintage Books.

Armstrong, Carol (1988). "Reflections on the Mirror: Painting, Photography, and the Self-Portraits of Edgar Degas," *Representations*, 22 (Spring): 108-141.

Armstrong, Nancy (1987). *Desire and Domestic Fiction: A Political History of the Novel*. New York and Oxford: Oxford University Press.

Ash, Jennifer (1990). The Discursive Construction of Christ's Body in the Later Middle Ages: Resistance and Autonomy. In *Feminine, Masculine and Representation*. Terry Threadgold and Anne Cranny-Francis, eds. pp. 75-105. Sydney, London, Boston, Wellington: Allen & Unwin.

Ash, Juliet (1989). Tarting Up Men: Menswear and Gender Dynamics. In *A View from the Interior: Feminism Women and Design*. Judy Attfield and Pat Kirkham, eds. pp. 29-38. London: The Women's Press.

Ash, Juliet and Elizabeth Wilson, eds. (1993). *Chic Thrills: A Fashion Reader*. Berkeley and Los Angeles: University of California Press.

Ashcroft, Bill, Griffiths, Gareth and Helen Tiffin (1989). *The Empire Writes Back*. London and New York: Routledge.

Atwood, Margaret (1985). *A Handmaid's Tail*. Toronto: McClelland and Stewart.

Awkward, Michael (1995). *Negotiating Difference: Race, Gender, and the Politics of Positionality*. Chicago and London: The University of Chicago Press.

Balbus, Isaac D. (1982). *Marxism and Domination: A Neo-Hegelian, Feminist, Psychoanalytic Theory of Sexual, Political, and Technological Liberation*. Princeton, New Jersey: Princeton University Press.

Balibar, Etienne (1991). Is There a 'Neo-Racism'? In *Race, Nation, Class: Ambiguous Identities*. Etienne Balibar and Immanual Wallerstein, eds. Trans. Chris Turner. pp. 17-28. London and New York: Verso.

Bandura, Albert (1972). Modeling Theory: Some Traditions, Trends, and Disputes. In *Recent Trends in Social Learning Theory*. Rodd. D. Park, ed. pp. 35-61. New York: Academic Press.

Banner, Lois (1989). "Book Review," *Signs*, 14, 3:703-707.

Bannet, Eve Tavor (1992). "The Feminist Logic of Both/And," *Gender*, 15 (Winter): 1-21.

Bannet, Eve Tavor (1993). *Postcultural Theory: Critical Theory after the Marxist Paradigm*. London: MacMillan.

Barber, Benjamin R. (1992). "Jihad vs. McWorld," *Atlantic Monthly*, (March):53-63.

Barbosa, Anna Mae (1993). From Gaugin to Latin America: Where are We? Session 1. In *Official Program of the International Society for Education Through Art. 28th World Congress*. Montréal, Quebec, Canada.

Barkowski, Frances (1988). Epistemic Drift in Foucault. In *Feminism & Foucault: Reflections of Resistance*. Irene Diamond and Lee Quinby, eds. pp. 43-60. Boston: Northeastern University Press.

Barnes, Clive (1974). "Homosexuality in Dance," *New York Times*, November 3: D8.

Barrett, Michele (1980). *Women's Oppression Today: Problems in Marxist Feminist Analysis*. London: Verso. Reprinted with a new introduction and new subtitle, *The Marxist Feminist Encounter*, 1988.

Barrett, Michele (1982). Feminism and the Definition of Cultural Politics. In *Feminism, Culture, and Politics*. Rosalind Brunt and Caroline Rowan, eds. pp. 37-58. London: Lawrence & Wishart.

Barrett, Michele (1987a). "The Concept of Difference," *Feminist Review*, 26 (July): 29-41.

Barrett, Michele (1987b). "Max Raphael and the Question of Aesthetics," *New Left Review*, 161: 78-97.

Barry, Judith (1980). Women, Representation and Performance Art: Northern California. In *Performance Anthology: Source Book for a Decade of California Performance Art*. Carl E. Loeffler and Darlene Tong, eds. pp. 439-462. San Francisco: Contemporary Arts Press.

Barry, Judith and Sandy Flitterman-Lewis (1988). Textual Strategies: The Politics of Art-Making. In *Feminist Art Criticism: An Anthology*. Arlene Raven, Cassandra Langer and Joanna Frueh, eds. pp.87-98. London and Ann Arbor: University Microfilms Inc. Research Press.

Barthes, Roland (1973). *Mythologies*. Trans. Annette Lavers. Frogmore, St. Albans: Granada Publishing Ltd. Paladin. (reprinted 1976).

Barthes, Roland (1973). The Face of Garbo. In *Mythologies*. Trans. Annette Lavers. pp. 56-58. Frogmore, St. Albans: Granada Publishing Ltd. Paladin. (reprinted, 1976).

Barthes, Roland (1975). *The Pleasure of the Text*. New York: Hill and Wang.

Barthes, Roland (1979). *A Lover's Discourse: Fragments of an Autobiography*. New York: Hill and Wang.

Barthes, Roland (1981). *Camera Lucida: Reflections on Photography*. Trans. Richard Howard. New York: Hill and Wang.

Barthes, Roland (1985). *The Fashion System*. London: Jonathan Cape Ltd.

Barthes, Roland (1986). To Write an Intransitive Verb. In *The Rustled Language*. Trans. Richard Howard. pp. 11-21. New York: Hill and Wang. (original, 1970).

Bartky, Sandra Lee (1982). "Narcissism, Femininity and Alienation," *Social Theory and Practice*, 8, 2 (Summmer): 127-143.

Bartky, Sandra Lee (1988). Foucault, Femininity, and the Modernization of Patriarchal Power. In *Feminism & Foucault: Reflections of Resistance*. Irene Diamond and Lee Quinby, eds. pp. 61-86. Boston: Northeastern University Press.

Battersby, Christine (1989). *Gender and Genius: Towards a Feminist Aesthetics*. London: The Women's Press.

Battersby, Christine (1995). Just Jamming: Irigaray, Painting and Psychoanalysis. In *New Feminist Art Criticism*. Katy Deepwell, ed., pp. 128-137. New York and Manchester: Mamchester University Press.

Baudrillard, Jean (1983a). *In the Shadow of Silent Majorities. . . Or, The End of the Social and Other Essays*. Trans. Paul Foss, Paul Patton and John Johnson. New York: Semiotext(e).

Baudrillard, Jean (1983b). The Ectasy of Communication. In The *Anti-Aesthetic: Essays on Postmodern Culture*. Hal Foster, ed. pp. 125-136. Port Towsend, Washington: Bay Press.

Baudrillard, Jean (1983c). *Simulations*. Trans. Paul Foss, Paul Patton and Philip Beitchman. New York: Semiotext(e).

Baudrillard, Jean (1990). *Seduction*. Trans. Brian Singer. New York: St. Martin's Press.

Bauman, Zygmunt (1989). *Modernity and the Holocaust*. Ithaca, N.Y.: Cornell University Press.

Belensky, Mary Field, McVicker Blythe Clinchy, Nancy Rule Goldberger, and Jill Mattuck Tarule (1986). *Women's Ways of Knowing: The Development of Self, Voice, and Mind*. New York: Basic Books.

Belsey, Catherine (1980). *Critical Practice*. London: Methuen.

Belsey, Catherine (1985). Constructing the Subject: Deconstructing the Text. In *Feminist Criticism and Social Change: Sex, Class and Race in Literature and Culture*. Judith Newton and Deborah Rosenfelt, eds. pp.45-64. New York: Methuen.

Belting, Hans (1987). *The End of Art History?* Chicago: University of Chicago Press.

Benhabib, Seyla and Drucilla Cornell, eds. (1987). *Feminism as Critique: On the Politics of Gender*. Minneapolis: University of Minnesota Press.

Benjamin, Andrew (1991). *Art, Mimesis and the Avant-Garde: Aspects of a Philosophy of Difference*. London and New York: Routledge.

Benjamin, Jessica (1986). A Desire of One's Own: Psychoanalytic Feminism and Intersubjective Space. In *Feminist Studies/Critical Studies*. Teresa de Lauretis, ed. pp. 78-101. Bloomington and Indianapolis: Indiana University Press.

Benjamin, Walter (1973). The Work of Art in An Age of Mechanical Reproduction. In *Illuminations*. Trans. Harry Zohn. Hannah Arendt, ed. N.Y.: Shocken Books. (original, 1935).

Bennett, Tony (1983). "Text, Readers, and Reading Formations," *The Bulletin of the Midwest Modern Language Association* 16,1 (Spring): 3-17.

Bennett, Tony (1986). Texts in History: The Determinations of Reading and Their Texts. In *Post-Structuralism and the Question of History*. Derek Attridge, Geoffrey Bennington and Robert Young, eds. Cambridge: Cambridge University Press.

Bensinger, Terralee (1992). "Lesbian Pornography: The Re/Making of (a) Community," *Discourse*, 15,1 (Fall): 69-93.

Benson, Peter (1993). "Between Women: Lesbianism in Pornography," *Textual Practice*, 7, 3 (Winter): 412-427.

Bentov, Itzhak (1977). *Stalking the Wild Pendulum: The Mechanics of Consciousness*. New York: E.P. Dutton Co.

Benveniste, E. (1971). *Problems in General Linguistics*. Trans. Mary Elizabeth Meek and Coral Gables. Miami: University of Miami Press.

Berg, Elizabeth (1982). "The Third Woman," *Diacritics*, 12 (Summer): 11-20.

Berger, John (1972). *Ways of Seeing*. Harmondsworth: Penguin.

Bergoffen, Debra (1996). Queering the Phallus. In *Disseminating Lacan*. David Pettigrew and François Raffoul. New York. State University of New York.

Berman, Morris (1984). *The Reenchantment of the World*. New York : Bantam Books.

Berman, Morris (1989). *Coming To Our Senses: Body and Spirit in the Hidden History of the West*. New York: Bantam Books.

Berman, Russell (1984-85). "Modern Art and Desublimation," *Telos*, 62 (Winter): 31-57.

Bern, Sandra Lipsitz (1983). "Gender Schema Theory and Its Implications for Child Development: Raising Gender-aschematic Children in a Gender-schematic Society," *Signs*, 8 (Summer): 598-616.

Bernheimer, Charles (1987). "Degas's Brothels: Voyeurism and Ideology," *Representations*, 20 (Fall): 158-186.

Bersani, Leo (1988). Is the Rectum a Grave? In *AIDS: Cultural Analysis, Cultural Activism*. Douglas Crimp, ed. pp. 197-222. An OCTOBER Book, Cambridge, Massachusetts and London: The MIT Press. (reprint of October, No. 43, 1987).

Best, Raphaela (1983). *We've All Got Scars: What Boys and Girls Learn in Elementary School*. Bloomington and Indianapolis: Indiana University Press.

Betterton, Rosemary, ed. (1987a). *Looking On: Images of Femininity in the Visual Arts and Media*. London and New York: Pandora Press.

Betterton, Rosemary (1987b). New Images for Old: The Iconography of the Body. In *Looking On: Images of Femininity in the Visual Arts and Media*. Rosemary Betterton, ed. London and New York: Pandora Press.

Bhabha, Homi (1985). "Signs Taken For Wonders: Questions of Ambivalence and Authority Under a Tree Outside Delhi, May 1817," *Critical Inquiry*, 12, 1:144-165.

Bhabha, Homi (1987). Interrogating Identity. In *Identity: The Real Me, Post-Modernism and the Question of Identity*. ICA Documents, 6, pp. 5-12 London: ICA.

Bhabha, Homi (1988). "Commitment To Theory," *New Formations*, 5 (Summer).

Bhabha, Homi (1990). The Third Space: Interview with Homi Bhabha by Jonathan Rutherford. In *Identity: Community, Culture, Difference*. Jonathan Rutherford, ed. pp. 207- 221. London: Lawrence & Wishart.

Bhabha, Homi (1992). Postcolonial Authority and Postmodern Guilt. In *Cultural Studies*. Lawrence Grossberg, Cary Nelson and Paula Treichler, eds. pp. 56-68. New York and London: Routledge.

Bhabha, Homi (1994a). On Mimicry and Man: The Ambivalence of Colonial Discouse. In Homi Bhabha´s *The Location of Culture*. pp. 85-92. London and New York: Routledge. (also in *October; Anthology*. Boston, Mass. :MIT Press, 1987).

Bhabha, Homi (1994b). Signs Taken For Wonders. In Homi Bhabha´s *The Location of Culture*. pp. 102-122. London and New York: Routledge. (also in *Race, Writing and Difference*. Henry Gates, Jr., ed. Chicago University Press, 1985).

Bick, Ilsa J. (1992-1993). "To be Real: Shame, Envy, and the Reflections of Self in Masquerade," *Discourse* 15, 2 (Winter): 80-93.

Biehl, Janet (1991). *Finding Our Way: Rethinking Ecofeminist Politics*. New York and Montréal: Black Rose Books.

Binder, David and Barbara Crossette (1993). "As Ethnic Wars Multiply," *New York Times*, 7 Feb.: A1, A12.

Bird, Jon, Curtis, Barry, Mash, Melinda, Putnam, Tim, Robertson, George and Lisa Tickner eds. (1996). *The BLOCK Reader in Visual Culture*. London and New York: Routledge.

Blazwick, Iowana, Mark Francis and Seclan McGanagle (1987). *Nancy Spero*. Brighton: ICA/Fruitmarket Gallery/ Foyle Arts Project.

Bleier, Ruth (1984). *Science and Gender: A Critique of Biology and Its Theories on Women*. New York: Pergamon Press.

Bloom, A. (1987). *The Closing of the American Mind: How Higher Education has Failed Democracy and Impoverished the Souls of Today's Students*. New York: Simon & Schuster.

Bly, Robert and Keith Thompson (1985). What Men Really Want. In *Challenge of the Heart: Love, Sex, & Intimacy in Changing Times*. John Wellwood, ed. pp. 100-116. Boston: Shambhala.

Bly, Robert (1990). *Iron John: A Book About Men*. Reading, MA: Addison-Wesley.

Bobo, Jacqueline (1988). The Color Purple: Black Women as Cultural Readers. In *Female Spectators: Looking at Film and Television*. E. Deidre Pribram, ed. pp. 90-109. London and New York: Verso.

Boffin, Tessa and Sunil Gupta, eds. (1990). *Ecstatic Bodies: Resisting the AIDS Mythology*. London: Rivers Oram Press.

Boffin, Tessa and Jean Fraser (1991). *Stolen Glances: Lesbians Take Photographs*. London: Pandora.

Bois, Yves-Alain (1988). "Painting as Trauma," *Art in America*, 76, 6 (June): 131-139, 172-173.

Bornstein, Kate (1994). *Gender Outlaw: On Men, Women, and the Rest of Us*. London: Routledge.

Bolen, Jean (1985). *Goddesses in Everywoman: A New Psychology of Women's Lives and Loves*. San Francisco: Harper & Row Publishers.

Bolen, Jean (1989). *Gods in Everyman: A New Psychology of Men's Lives and Loves*. San Francisco: Harper & Row Publishers.

Bookchin, Murray (1982). *The Ecology of Freedom*. Palo Alto: Cheshire Books.

Boone, Joseph Allen (1989). Of Me(n) and Feminism: Who(se) is the Sex that Writes? In *Gender & Theory: Dialogues on Feminist Criticism*. Linda Kauffman, ed. pp. 158-189. Oxford: Basil Blackwell Ltd.

Boone, Joseph Allen and Michael Cadden, eds. (1991). *Engendering Men: The Question of Male Feminist Criticism*. London and New York: Routledge.

Bordo, Susan (1990a) Reading the Slender Body. In *Body/Politics: Women and the Discourses of Science*. Mary Jacobus, Evelyn Fox Keller, and Sally Shuttleworth, eds. New York and London: Routledge.

Bordo, Susan (1990b). Feminism, Postmodernism, Gender-Scepticism. In *Feminism/Postmodernism*. Linda J. Nicholson, ed. pp. 133-156. New York and London: Routledge.

Borzello, Frances and Natacha Ledwidge (1986). *Women Artists: A Graphic Guide*. London: Camden Press Ltd.

Boscagli, Maurizia (1992-93). "A Moving Story: Masculine Tears and the Humanity of Televised Emotions," *Discourse*, 15, 2 (Winter):64-79.

Boulding, Elsie (1976). *The Underside of History: A View of Women Through Time*. Boulder, Colorado: Westview Press.

Bourdieu, Pierre (1984) *Distinction: A Social Critique of the Judgement of Taste*. Trans. R. Nice. Cambridge, Mass: Harvard University Press. (original, 1979).

Bové, Mastrangelo Carol (1984). "The Politics of Desire in Julia Kristeva," *boundary, 2*, XII, 2 (Winter): 217- 228.

Bovenschen, Silvia (1985). Is There a Feminine Aesthetic? In *Feminist Aesthetics*. Trans. Harriet Anderson. Gisela Ecker, ed. pp. 23-50. London: The Women's University Press.

Bowlby, Rachael(1989). Still Crazy All These Years. In *Between Feminism & Psychoanalysis*. Teresa Brennan, ed. pp. 40-60. London and New York: Routledge.

Božovič, Miran (1993). "The Bond of Love: Lacan and Spoinoza," *New Formations* 23 (Summer):69-80.

Braidotti, Rosi (1987). Envy: Or With My Brains and Your Looks. In *Men in Feminism*. Alice Jardine and Paul Smith, eds. pp. 233-241. New York and London : Methuen.

Braidotti, Rosi (1989). "Organs Without Bodies," *differences: A Journal of Feminist Cultural Studies*, 1 (Winter):147-161.

Braidotti, Rosi (1991). *Patterns of Dissonance*. Trans. Elizabeth Guild. New York: Routledge.

Braidotti, Rosi (1994). *Nomadic Subjects: Embodiment and Sexual Difference in Contemporary Feminist Theory*. New York : Columbia University Press.

Bredbeck, George W. (1992). Body Odor: Gay Male Semiotics and *l'écriture féminine*. In *Between Men and Feminism*. David Porter, ed. pp. 80-104. London and New York: Routledge.

Brennan, Teresa, ed. (1989). *Between Feminism and Psychoanalysis*. London and New York: Routledge.

Bristow, Joseph (1992). Men After Feminism: Sexual Politics Twenty Years On. In *Men and Feminism*. David Porter, ed. pp. 57-79. London and New York: Routledge.

Britzman, Deborah (1993). Is There a Queer Pedagoy?: Or, Stop Being [Acting?] Straight! Paper presented to The Curriculum Theory Conference, Bergamo Conference Center. October 28th. Dayton, Ohio.

Brittan, Arthur (1989). *Masculinity and Power*. Oxford: Basil Blackwell.

Brod, Harry, ed. (1987). *The Making of Masculinities: The New Men's Studies*. Boston: Allen & Unwin.

Brodribb, Somer (1992). *Nothing Mat(t)ers: A Feminist Critique of Postmodernism*. Toronto: James Lorimer & Company Ltd. Publishers.

Bronfen, Elizabeth (1992a). Castration Complex. In *Feminism and Psychoanalysis: A Critical Dictionary*. Elizabeth Wright, ed. pp. 41-44. Oxford and Cambridge, MA: Blackwell Publishers.

Bronfen, Elizabeth (1992b). *Over Her Dead Body: Death, Femininity and the Aesthetic*. Manchester: Manchester University Press.

Brooks, Peter (1993). Gauguin's Tahitian Bodies. In Peter Brook's *Body Work: Objects of Desire in Modern Narrative*. pp. 162-198. Cambridge, Massachusetts and London: Harvard University Press.

Brooks, Rosetta (1984). "The Body of the Image," *ZG*, 10 (Spring).

Broude, Norma and Mary D. Garrard (1982). *Feminism and Art History: Questioning the Litany*. New York: Harper & Row, Publishers.

Brown, Mary Ellen (1990a). Comsumption and Resistance: The Problem of Pleasure. In *Television and Women's Culture: The Politics of the Popular*. Mary Ellen Brown, ed. pp. 201-210. London, Newbury Park, New Delhi: Sage Publications.

Brown, Mary Ellen (1990b). Motley Moments: Soap Operas, Carnival, Gossip and the Power of Utterance. In *Television and Women's Culture: The Politics of the Popular*. Mary Ellen Brown, ed. pp. 183-200. London, Newbury Park, New Delhi: Sage Publications.

Brown, Beverly and Parveen Adams (1979). "The Feminine Body and Feminist Politics," *m/f* 3:35-50.

Brown, Jane and D. Campbell (1986). "Race and Gender in Music Videos: The Same Beat But a Different Drummer," *Journal of Communication*, 36, 1 (Winter): 94-106.

Brownmiller, Susan (1984). *Femininity*. New York: Fawcett Columbine.

Bryson, Norman (1981). *Word and Image: French Painting of the Ancient Régime*. Cambridge: Cambridge University Press.

Bryson, Norman (1983). *Vision and Painting: The Logic of the Gaze*. New Haven, Connecticut: Yale University Press.

Bryson, Norman (1984). *Tradition and Desire: From David to Delacroix*. Cambridge: Cambridge University Press.

Bryson, Norman, ed. (1988a). *Calligram: Essays in New Art History from France*. Cambridge: Cambridge University Press.

Bryson, Norman (1988b). The Gaze in The Expanded Field. In *Vision and Visuality: Dia Art Foundation Discussions in Contemporary Culture: Number 2*. Hal Foster, ed. pp. 87-114. Bay Press: Seattle.

Bryson, Norman (1990). Painting, Text and Sexual Difference: 1) Women, the French Revolution and Jacques-Louis David, 2) Géricault and Masculinity, 3) Stendhal and David. *Henry Kreisel Lectures on Literature and the Visual Arts*. University of Alberta, Edmonton, Canada (Jan. 12, 15, 16). Tapes available through the Department of English.

Bryson, Norman, Ann Michael, and Holly Keith Moxey, eds. (1991). *Visual Theory*. Cambridge: Polity Press.

Buchloh, Benjamin H.D. (1984). Figures of Authority, Ciphers of Regression. In *Art After Modernism: Rethinking Representation*. Brian Wallis, ed. pp. 107-136. The New Museum of Contemporary Art, New York in association with Boston: David R. Godine, Pub.,Inc.

Budge, Belinda (1989). Joan Collins and the Wilder Side of Women. In *The Female Gaze: Women as Viewers of Popular Culture*. Lorraine Gamman and Margaret Marshment, eds. pp. 102-111. Seattle: The Real Comet Press.

Buhrich, Neil (1996). A Heterosexual Transvestite Club. In *Blending Genders: Social Aspects of Cross-dressing and Sex-changing*. Richard Ekins and David King, eds. pp. 63-69. London and New York: Routledge.

Bukatman, Scott (1993). *Terminal Identity: The Virtual Subject in Postmodern Science Fiction*. Durham and London: Duke University Press.

Burchill, Louis (1984). Either/Or: Peripeteia of an Alternative in Jean Baudrillard's *De La Séduction*. In *Seduced and Abandoned: The Baudrillard Scene*. André Frankovits, ed. New York: Semiotext(e) Inc.

Bürger, Christa (1986). "The Disappearance of Art: The Postmodernism Debate in the U.S.," *Telos* 68 (Summer): 93-106.

Bürger, Peter (1984). *Theory of the Avant-Garde*. Trans. Michael Shaw. Minneapolis: University of Minnesota Press.

Burgin, Victor, ed. (1982). *Thinking Photography*. London: MacMillan.

Burgin, Victor (1984). Man-Desire-Image. *Desire*. Lisa Appignanesi, ed. pp. 32-34. London: Institute of Contemporary Arts Documents.

Burgin, Victor (1986a). *Between*. New York and London: Basil Blackwell, Institute of Contemporary Arts.

Burgin, Victor (1986b). *The End of Art Theory: Criticism and Postmodernity*. Atlantic Highlands, NJ: Humanities Press International, Inc.

Burke, Carolyn (1981). "Irigaray Through the Looking Glass," *Feminist Studies*, 7, 2 (Summer): 288-306.

Butler, Judith (1988). "Performative Acts and Gender Constitution: An Essay in Phenomenology and Feminist Theory," *Theatre Journal*, 40, 4 (December):519-531.

Butler, Judith (1987). Revising Femininity? Review of Lady, Photographs of Lisa Lyon by Robert Mapplethorpe. In *Looking On: Images of Femininity in the Visual Arts and Media*. Rosemary Betterton, ed. pp. 120-126. London and New York: Pandora

Butler, Judith (1990a). *Gender Trouble: Feminism and the Subversion of Identity*. New York and London: Routledge, Chapman & Hall, Inc.

Butler, Judith (1990b). "The Force of Fantasy: Feminism, Mapplethorpe, and Discursive Excess," *differences: A Journal of Feminist Cultural Studies*, 2, 2:105-125.

Butler, Judith (1990c). Gender Trouble, Feminist Theory, and Psychoanalytic Discourse. In *Feminism/Postmodernism*. Linda J. Nicholson, ed. pp. 324-340. New York and London: Routledge.

Butler, Judith (1991). Imitation and Gender Insubordination. In *Inside/Outside: Lesbian Theories, Gay Theories*. Diana Fuss, ed. pp. 13-31. New York and London: Routledge.

Butler, Judith (1993). *Bodies That Matter: On the Discursive Limits of "Sex"*. New York and London: Routledge.

Byars, Jackie (1988). Gazes/Voices? Power: Expanding Psychoanalysis for Feminist Film and Television Theory. In *Female Spectators: Looking at Film and Television*. Deidre Pribram, ed. pp. 110-131. London and New York.

Byars, Jackie (1991). *All that Hollywood Allows: Rereading Gender in 1950s Melodrama*. London: Routledge.

Califia, Pat (1992). "The Limits of the S/M Relationship," *Outlook*, 15 (Winter).

Callen, Athea (1979). *Angel in the Studio: Women Artist of the Arts and Crafts Movement, 1880-1914*. London: Astragal Books.

Cameron, Debra (1992). *Feminism and Linguistic Theory*. 2nd. Edition. London: MacMillan Press. Ltd.

Caplan, Pat, ed. (1989). *The Cultural Construction of Sexuality*. London and New York: Tavistock.

Caputo, John D. (1988). "Beyond Aestheticism: Derrida's Responsible Anarchy," *Research in Phenomenology*, XVIII:59-73.

Carby, Hazel (1987). *Reconstructing Womanhood: The Emergence of the Afro-American Woman Novelist*. New York: Oxford University Press.

Carr, C. (1990). "David Wojnarowicz: Portrait of the Artist in the Age of AIDS," *Village Voice*, XXXV, 7 (February, 13): 31-32, 34-36.

Carrigan, Tim, Bob Connell, and John Lee (1985). "Toward a New Sociology of Masculinity," *Theory and Society*, 14: 551-604.

Carrier, David (1987). *Artwriting*. Amherst: The University of Massachusetts Press.

Carroll, David (1987). *Paraesthetics: Foucault, Lyotard, Derrida*. New York: Methuen.

Carroll, David (1990). "The Temptation of Fascism and the Question of Literature: Justice, Sorrow, and Political Error (An Open Letter to Jacques Derrida)," *Cultural Critique*, 9 (Spring): 39-81.

Carroll, Michael (1986). *The Cult of the Virgin Mary: Psychological Origins*. Princeton University Press.

Carroll, Noël (1988). *Mystifying Movies: Fads and Fallacies in Contemporary Film Theory* . New York: Columbia University Press.

Carroll, Noël (1990). "The Image of Women in Film: A Defense of a Paradigm," *The Journal of Aesthetics and Art Criticism* 48, 4 (Fall):349-360.

Carter, Erica and Chris Turner (1986). Political Somantics: Notes on Klaus Theweleit's *Male Fantasies*. In *Formations of Fantasy*. Victor Burgin, James Donald and Cora Kaplan, eds. pp. 200-214. London and New York: Methuen.

Case, Sue-Ellen (1988-89)."Towards a Butch-Femme Aesthetic," *Discourse*, 11, 1 (Winter):55-73. Reprinted in (1989). *Making a Spectacle: Feminist Essays on Contemporary Women's Theatre.* Lynda Hart, ed. pp. 282-299. Ann Arbor: UMI Press.

Caskey, Noelle (1986) Interpreting Anorexia Nervosa. In *The Female Body in Western Culture: Contemporary Perspectives.* Susan Rubin Suleiman, ed. Cambridge, Mass.: Harvard University Press.

Castoriadis, Cornelius (1984). The Imaginary Institution of Society. In *The Structural Allegory: Reconstructive Encounters with New French Thought.* John Fekete, ed. pp. 6-45. Minneapolis: University of Minnesota Press. (original, 1975).

Caws, Mary Ann (1985). Ladies Shot and Painted: Female Embodiment in Surrealist Art. In *The Female Body in Western Culture: Contemporary Perspectives.* Susan Rubin Suleiman, ed. pp. 262-287. Cambridge, Mass. : Harvard University Press.

Caws, Mary Ann, Rudolf E. Kuenzli, and Gwen Raaberg, eds. (1991). *Surrealism and Women.* Cambridge, Massachusetts and London: MIT Press.

Chadwick, Whitney (1988). Women, Artists and the Politics of Representation. In *Feminist Art Criticism: An Anthology.* Arlene Raven, Cassandra Langer and Joanna Frueh, eds. pp.167-186. London and Ann Arbor: University Microfilms Inc. Research Press.

Chapman, Rowena and Jonathan Rutherford, eds (1988). *Male Order: Unwrapping Masculinity.* London: Lawrence & Wishart.

Chave, Anna C. (1990)."O'Keeffe and the Masculine Gaze," *Art in America,* 78, 1 (January): 115-125.

Cherfas, Jeremy and John Gribbin (1984). *The Redundant Male.* London: Bodley Head.

Chodrow, Nancy (1978). *The Reproduction of Mothering.* Berkeley, California: University of California Press.

Chow, Rey (1993). *Writing Diaspora: Tactics of Invention in Contemporary Cultural Studies.* Bloomington and Indianapolis: Indiana University Press.

Christensen, F.M. (1987). *Pornography: The Other Side.* Calgary: Research Unit for Socio-Legal Studies, Faculty of Social Sciences, University of Calgary.

Christian, Barbara (1987). "The Race For Theory," *Cultural Critique,* 6: 51-63.

Cixous, Hélène (1981). The Laugh of the Medusa. In *New French Feminisms: An Anthology.* Elaine Marks and Isabelle de Courtivron, eds. pp. 245-264. New York: Schocken Books.

Cixous, Hélène and Catherine Clément (1986). *Newly Born Woman.* Minneapolis: University of Minnesota Press.

Clair, Jean (1979). "Seven Prolegomenae to a Brief Treatise on Magrittian Tropes," *October, 8* (Spring): 89-110.

Clark, Kenneth (1956). *The Nude: The Study of Ideal Art.* London: John Murray.

Clark, T.J. (1980). "Preliminaries to a Possible Treatment of 'Olympia' in 1865," *Screen,* 21, 1 (Spring).

Clark, T. J. (1984). *The Painting of Modern Life: Paris in the Art of Manet and His Followers*. London: Thames & Hudson.

Clifford, James and George E. Marcus, eds. (1986). *Writing Culture: The Poetics and Politics of Ethnography*. Berkeley: University of California Press.

Clifford, James (1988). *The Predicament of Culture: Twentieth-Century Ethnography, Literature, and Art*. Cambridge, Massachusetts, and London: Harvard University Press.

Clover, Carol (1987). "Her Body, Himself: Gender in the Slasher Film," *Representations*, 20 (Fall): 187-228.

Clover, Carol (1992). *Men, Women and Chainsaws: Gender in the Modern Horror Film*. Princeton, New Jersey: Princeton University Press.

Cockburn, C. (1986). The Relations of Technology. In *Gender and Stratification*. Rosemary Crompton and Michael Mann, eds. Cambridge: Polity Press.

Cocks, Joan (1989). *The Oppositional Imagination: Feminism, Critique, and Political Theory*. London: Routledge.

Cohan, Steven and Ira Rae Hark, eds. (1993). *Screening the Male: Exploring Masculinities in Hollywood Cinema*. London and New York: Routledge

Collins, Bradley (1988). "Van Gogh and Gauguin on the Couch," *Art in America*, 77, 12 (Dec.): 59-62.

Collins, Georgia and Reneé Sandell (1984). *Women, Art, and Education*. Reston, Virginia: National Art Education.

Collins, Jim (1989). *Uncommon Cultures: Popular Culture and Post-Modernism*. New York and London: Routledge.

Conley, Christine (1989). "Hot Tramp, I Love You So!" *Fuse*, XIII, 1 + 2 (Fall): 53-54.

Conley, Verna Andermatt, ed. (1993). *Rethinking Technologies*. Minneapolis and London: University of Minnesota Press.

Connell, Robert (1987). *Gender and Power: Society, the Person, and Sexual Politics*. Cambridge: Polity Press.

Cook, Pam (1982). "Masculinity in Crisis?" *Screen*, 23, 3/4 (Sept.-Oct.): 39-46.

Coombes, Annie E. (1992). "Inventing the 'Postcolonial' Hybridity and Constituency in Contemporary Curating," *New Formations*, 16 (Spring): 39-52.

Copjec, Joan (1989). "The Sartorial Super Ego," *October* 50:58-72.

Copjec, Joan (1990). m/f, or Not Reconciled. In *The Woman in Question, m/t*. Parveen Adams and Elizabeth Cowie, eds. pp. 10-18. Cambridge, Mass.: MIT Press.

Copjec, Joan (1991). "The *Unvermögender* Other: Hysteria and Democracy in America," *New Formations*, 14 (Summer): 27-41.

Copjec, Joan (1993). The Phenomenal Nonphenomenal: Private Space. In *Shades of Noir*. Joan Copjec, ed. pp.167-198. London and New York: Verso.

Copjec, Joan (1994a). *Read My Desire: Lacan Against Historicists*. Cambridge, MA: MIT Press.

Copjec, Joan (1994b). "The Cogito, The Unconscious, and the Invention of Crying," *New Formations*, 23 (Summer): 1-12.

Copjec, Joan (1994c). Sex and the Euthanasia of Reason. In *Supposing the Subject*. Joan Copjec, ed. pp. 16-44. London and New York: Verso.

Cornell, Drucilla (1991). *Beyond Accommodation: Ethical Feminism, Deconstruction and the Law*. New York and London: Routledge.

Cornell, Drucilla (1992). *The Philosophy of the Limit*. New York and London: Routledge.

Cottingham, Laura (1989). "The Feminine De-Mystique: Gender, Power, Irony, and Aestheticized Feminism in '80s Art," *Flash Art*, 174 (Summer): 91-95.

Cottingham, Laura (1994). The Masculine Imperative: High Modern, Postmodern. In *New Feminist Criticism: Art, Identity, Action*. Joanna Frueh, Cassandra L. Langer, and Arlene Raven, eds. pp. 132-151. New York: HarperCollins Publishers (IconEditions).

Coward, Rosalind (1983). *Patriarchal Precedents: Sexuality and Social Relations*. London, Boston, Melbourne, and Henley: Routledge & Kegan Paul.

Coward, Rosalind (1984). Julia Kristeva in Conversation With Rosalind Coward. In *Desire*. Lisa Appignanesi, ed. pp. 22-27. London: Institute of Contemporary Arts Documents.

Coward, Rosalind (1985). *Female Desire: How They Are Sought, Bought and Packaged*. New York: Grove Press, Inc.

Cowie, Elizabeth. (1978). "Woman as Sign," *m/f*, 1: 49- 63.

Cowie, Elizabeth (1990). Fantasia. In *The Woman in Question, m/t*. Parveen Adams and Elizabeth Cowie, eds. pp. 149-196. Cambridge, Mass.: MIT Press.

Craik, Jennifer (1989). " 'I Must Put My Face On': Making The Body and Making Out the Feminine," *Cultural Studies*, 3, 1 (January): 1-24.

Craik, Jennifer (1994). The Face of Fashion: *Cultural Studies in Fashion*. London and New York: Routledge.

Crane, Diana (1987). *The Transformation of the Avant-Garde: The New York Art World, 1940-1985*. Chicago and London: The University of Chicago Press.

Crary, Jonathan (1990). *Techniques of the Observer: On Vision and Modernity in the Nineteenth Century*. Cambridge: MIT Press.

Creed, Barbara (1987). "From Here to Modernity: Feminism and Postmodernism," *Screen*, 28, 2: 47-67.

Creed, Barbara (1990). *Alien* and the Monstrous-Feminine. In *Alien Zone: Cultural Theory and Contemporary Science Fiction*. Annette Kuhn, ed. pp. 128-144. New York: Verso.

Creed, Barbara (1993). *The Monstrous-Feminine: Film, Feminism, Psychoanalysis*. New York and London: Routledge.

Creet, Julia (1991). "Daughter of the Movement: The Psychodynamics of Lesbian S/M Fantasy," *differences: A Journal of Feminist Cultural Studies*, 3, 2:135-159.

Crimp, Douglas (1983). On the Museum's Ruins. In *The Anti-Aesthetic: Essays on Postmodern Culture*. Hal Foster, ed. pp. 43-56. Port Towsend, Washington: Bay Press.

Crimp, Douglas (1987). Strategies of Public Address, Which Media, Which Publics? In *Discussions in Contemporary Culture*. Hal Foster, ed. pp. 31-38. Seattle, Washington: Bay Press.

Crimp, Douglas, ed. (1988). *AIDS: Cultural Analysis, Cultural Activism*. Cambridge, Mass: MIT Press.

Crimp, Douglas (1992). Portraits of People With Aids. In *Cultural Studies*. Lawrence Grossberg, Cary Nelson, and Paula Treichler, eds. pp. 17-133. New York and London: Routledge.

Critical Art Ensemble (1994). *The Electronic Disturbance*. Brooklyn, N.Y.: Autonomedia.

Crowther, Paul (1993). *Critical Aesthetics and Postmodernism*. Oxford: Clarendon Press.

Crowder, Diane Griffin (1983). "Amazons and Mothers? Monique Wittig, Hélène Cixous and Theories of Women's Writing," *Contemporary Literature*, XXIV, 2:117-144.

Culler, Jonathan (1982). *On Deconstruction: Theory and Criticism After Deconstruction*. Ithaca: Cornell University Press.

Curnick, Marie (1993). "Techno-Sex Objects," *Australian Feminist Studies*, 17 (Autumn):46-66.

Daignault, Jacques and Clermont Gauthier (1982). "Indecent Curriculum Machine: Whose Afraid of Sisphe?" *Journal of Curriculum Theorizing*, 14, 4, 1:177-196.

Daly, Mary (1978). *Gyn/Ecology: The Metaethics of Radical Feminism*. Boston: Beacon Press.

Daly, Mary and Jane Caputi. (1987). *Websters' First New Intergalactic Wickedary of the English Language*. Boston: Beacon Press.

Danto, Arthur (1986). *The Philosophical Disenfranchisement of Art*. New York: Columbia University.

Davidson, Martin (1992). *The Consumerist Manifesto: Advertising in Postmodern Times*. London and New York: Routledge.

Davis, Mike (1990). *The City of Quartz: Excavating the Future of Los Angeles*. London and New York: Verso Press.

Davies, Bronwyn (1989a). "Education for Sexism: A Theoretical Analysis of the Sex/gender Bias in Education," *Educational Philosophy and Theory*, 21,1:1-20.

Davies, Bronwyn (1989b). *Frogs and Snakes and Feminist Tales: Preschool Children and Gender*. Sydney: Allen and Unwin

Dawson, Don (1988). "The Rational Subordination of Women's Leisure Under Patriarchal Capitalism," *Society and Leisure*, 11, 2: 397-411.

Dean, Tim (1994) "Bodies that Mutter: Rhetoric and Sexuality," *Pre/Test: A Journal of Rhetorical Theory*, Vol. 15, 1-2 (Spring-Summer): 80-119.

de Certeau, Michel (1984). *The Practices of Everyday Life*. Trans. Steven Rendall. Berkeley: University of California Press.

de Lauretis, Teresa (1984). *Alice Doesn't: Feminism, Semiotics, Cinema*. Bloomington and Indianapolis: Indiana University Press.

de Lauretis, Teresa (1986). Feminist studies/Critical Studies: Issues, Terms, and Contexts. In *Feminist Studies/Critical Studies*. Teresa de Lauretis, ed. pp. 1-19. Bloomington and Indianapolis: Indiana University Press.

de Lauretis, Teresa (1987a). *Technologies of Gender: Essay on Theory, Film, and Fiction*. Bloomington and Indianapolis: Indiana University Press.

de Lauretis, Teresa (1987b). "The Female Body and Heterosexual Presumption," *Semiotica*, 67, 3/4: 259-279.

de Lauretis, Teresa (1988). "Sexual Indifference and Lesbian Representation," *Theater Journal*, 40, 2 (May):155-177.

de Lauretis, Teresa (1990). Upping the Anti (sic) in Feminist Theory. In *Conflicts in Feminism*. Marianne Hirsch and Evelyn Fox Keller, eds. pp. 255-270. New York & London: Routledge.

de Lauretis, Teresa (1991). "Queer Theory: Lesbian and Gay Sexualities, An Introduction," *differences: A Journal of Feminist Cultural Studies*, 3, 2:iii-xviii.

de Lauretis, Teresa (1994a). The Essence of the Triangle or, Taking the Risk of Essentialism Seriously: Feminist Theory in Italy, U.S., and Britain. In *the essential difference*. Naomi Schor and Elizabeth Weed, eds. pp. 1-39. Bloomington and Indianapolis: Indiana University Press.

de Lauretis, Teresa (1994b). *The Practice of Love: Lesbian Sexuality and Perverse Desire*. Bloomington and Indianapolis: Indiana University Press.

Deleuze, Giles (1971). *Masochism: An Interpretation of Coldness and Cruelty*. Trans. Jean McNeil. New York: Braziller.

Deleuze, Giles (1972). *Proust and Signs*. Trans. Richard Howard. New York: George Braziller.

Deleuze, Gilles and Félix Guattari (1983). *Anti-Oedipus: Capitalism and Schizophrenia*. Trans. Robert Hurley, Mark Seem, and Helen R. Lane. Minneapolis: University of Minnesota.

de Man, Paul (1979). "Autobiography as Defacement," *Modern Language Notes*, 94, 5: 919-930.

Deming, Robert (1992). "The Return of the Unrepressed: Male Desire, Gender, and Genre," *Quarterly Review of Film & Video*, 14 (1-2):125-147.

Denizen, Norman K. (1991). *Images of Postmodern Society: Social Theory and Contemporary Cinema*. London, Newbury Park, New Delhi: Sage Publications.

Deren, Maya (1992). Cinematography: The Creative Use of Reality. In *Film Theory and Criticism: Introductory Reading*, Fourth Edition. Gerald Mast, Marshall Cohen, and Leo Braudy, eds. pp. 59-70. New York and Oxford: Oxford University Press. (original, 1960 *Daedalus*, 89, 1, Winter).

Derrida, Jacques (1973). *Speech and Phenomena And Other Essays on Husserl's Theory of Signs*. Trans. David B. Allison. Evanston: Northwestern University Press.

Derrida, Jacques (1975). "The Purveyor of Truth," *Yale French Studies*, 52: 31-113.

Derrida, Jacques (1977), The Question of Style. In *The New Nietzsche*. David B. Allison, ed. New York: Dell Pub.

Derrida, Jacques (1979). *Spurs: Nietzsche's Styles*. Chicago: University of Chicago Press.

Derrida, Jacques (1981) *Positions*. Trans. Alan Bass. Chicago: The University of Chicago Press.

Derrida, Jacques (1982a). White Mythology. In Jacques Derrida´s *Margins of Philosophy*. Trans. Alan Bass. pp.207-272. Chicago: Chicago University Press.

Derrida, Jacques and Christine V. McDonald (1982b). "Choerographies," *Diacritics, 12, 2* (Summer): 66-76.

Derrida, Jacques (1985). *The Ear of the Other: Otobiography, Transference, Translation*. Trans. Peggy Kamuf. New York: Shocken Books.

Derrida, Jacques (1987a). *The Truth in Painting*. Trans. Geoff Bennington and Ian McLeod. Chicago and London: The University of Chicago Press. (originally published 1978).

Derrida, Jacques (1987b). Women in the Beehive: A Seminar with Jacques Derrida. In *Men in Feminism*. Alice Jardine and Paul Smith, eds. pp.189-203. London and New York: Methuen.

Derrida, Jacques (1988). Afterword: Toward an Ethic of Discussion. In *Limited Inc*. Evanston, IL.:Northwestern University Press.

Derrida, Jacques (1993). The Purveyor of Truth. In *The Purloined Poe: Lacan, Derrida, and Psychoanalytic Reading*. John P. Muller and William J. Richardson. 4th Printing. pp. 173-212. Baltimore and London: The John Hopkins University Press.

Der Spiegel (1994). "Die Bombe von Nebenan," No.47 (Nov. 21):104-117.

Desmond, William (1987). *Desire, Dialectic, and Otherness: An Essay on Origins*. New Haven and London: Yale University Press.

Devor, Holly (1989). *Gender Blending: Confronting the Limits of Duality*. Bloomington and Indianapolis: Indiana University Press.

Dews, Peter (1987). *The Logics of Disintegration: Post-Structuralist Thought and the Claims of Critical Theory*. London and New York: Verso.

Dhillon-Kashyap, Perminder (1988). "Locating the Asian Experience," *Screen*, 29, 4 (Autumn): 120-127.

Diamond, Irene and Lee Quinby (1988). *Feminism & Foucault: Reflections of Resistance*. Boston: Northeastern University Press.

Diawara, Manthia (1988). "Black Spectatorship–Problems of Identification and Resistance," *Screen*, 29, 4 (Autumn):66-79.

Dijkstra, Bram (1986). *Idols of Perversity: Fantasies of Femininine Evil in Fin-de-Siècle Culture*. New York and Oxford: Oxford University Press.

Dill, Bonnie Thornton (1983). "Race, Class, and Gender: Prospects For an All-Inclusive Sisterhood," *Feminist Studies*, 9, 1 (Spring): 131-150.

Diner, Helen (1965). *Mothers and Amazons: The First Feminine History of Culture*. Trans. John Philip Lundin. New York: Julian Press.

Dinnerstein, Dorothy (1976). *The Mermaid and the Minotaur.* New York: Harper & Row.

Discover (1994). Special Issue: The Science of Race. 15, 11 (November).

di Stefano, Christine (1990). Dilemmas of Difference: Feminism, Modernity, and Postmodernism. In *Feminism/Postmodernism.* Nancy Frazer and Linda J. Nicholson, eds. pp. 63-82. New York and London: Routledge, Chapman & Hall, Inc.

Doane, Jance and Devon Hodges (1987). *Nostalgia and Sexual Difference: The Resistance to Contemporary Feminism.* New York: Methuen.

Doane, Mary Ann (1981). "Woman's Stake: Filming the Female Body," *October,* 17 (Summer):23-36.

Doane, Mary Ann (1982). "Film and the Masquerade: Theorizing the Female Spectator," *Screen,* 23, 3/4 (Sept.-Oct.):74-87.

Doane, Mary Ann (1984). The 'Woman's Film': Possession and Address. In *Re-Vision: Essays in Feminist Film Criticism.* Mary Ann Doane, Patricia Mellencap and Linda Williams, eds. pp. 67-80. Frederick, Maryland: The American Film Institute/ University Publications of America.

Doane, Mary Ann (1987). *The Desire to Desire.* Bloomington and Indianapolis: Indiana University Press.

Doane, Mary Ann (1988). Woman's Stake: Filming the Female Body. In *Feminism and Film Theory.* Constance Penley, ed. New York and London: Routledge and BFI Publishing. (originally published, 1981).

Doane, Mary Ann (1989). Veiling over Desire: Close-ups of the Woman. In *Feminism and Psychoanalyis.* Richard Feldstein and Judith Roof, eds. pp. 105-141. Ithaca, New York: Cornell University Press.

Doane, Mary Ann (1991). *Femmes Fetales: Feminism, Film Theory, Psychoanalysis.* New York and London; Routledge.

Dobie, Elizabeth Ann (1990), "Interweaving Feminist Frameworks," *Journal of Aesthetics and Art Criticism,* 48, 4 (Fall): 381-392.

Docherty, Thomas (1993). Postmodern: An Introduction. In *Postmodernism: A Reader.* Thomas Docherty, ed. pp. 1-32. New York: Columbia University Press.

Doerry, Martin (1994). "Baß Erstaunt im Zauberreich," *Der Spiegel,* 22 (Mai, 30):192-196.

Dollimore, Jonathan (1991). *Sexual Dissidence.* Oxford: Clarendon Press.

Donnerstein, Edward and Daniel Linz (1986). "Mass Media Sexual Violence and Male Viewers: Current Theory and Research," *American Behavioral Scientist,* 29, 5 (May-June):601-618.

Donnerstein, Edward, Daniel Linz, and Steven Penrod (1987). *The Question of Pornography: Research Findings and Policy Implications.* New York: Free Press.

Doty, Alexander (1993). *Making Things Perfectly Queer.* Minneapolis and London: University of Minnesota Press.

Douglas, Ann (1977). *The Feminization of American Culture.* New York: Knopf.

Douglas, Ann (1993). "Annie Sprinkle: Post Post Post Modernist: An Interview, Chicago, October 1991," *New Formations*, 19 (Spring): 23-36.

Dowsett, T. (1985). "Gender Relations in Secondary Schooling," *Sociology of Education*, 58 (January):34-48.

Doyle, James (1983). *The Male Experience*. Dubuque, Iowa: William C. Brown.

Duchen, Claire, ed. (1987). *French Connections: Voices From the Women's Movement in France*. Trans. Claire Duchen. Amherst: The University of Massachusetts Press.

Duden, Barbara (1991). *The Woman Beneath the Skin: A Doctor's Patients in Eighteenth-Century Germany*. Trans. Thomas Dunlap. Cambridge, Mass.: Harvard University Press.

Duggan, Lisa (1992). "Making It Perfectly Queer," *Socialist Review*, 22, 1 (Jan-March):11-32.

Duncan, Carol (1988). The Aesthetics of Power in Modern Erotic Art. In *Feminist Art Criticism: An Anthology*. Arlene Raven, Cassandra Langer, and Joanna Frueh, eds. pp.59-70. London and Ann Arbor: University Microfilms Inc. Research Press.

Dworkin, Andrea (1974). *Woman Hating*. New York: Dutton.

Dworkin, Andrea (1981). *Pornography: Men Possessing Women*. New York: Perigee Books.

Dworkin, Andrea (1983). *Right-Wing Women*. London: The Woman's Press.

Dworkin, Ronald (1993). "Women and Pornography," *New York Review of Books*, October 21.

Dworkin, Ronald (1994). "Reply to Catherine A. MacKinnon, *New York Review of Books*, March 3:48-49.

Dyer, Richard (1982). "Don't Look Now," *Screen*, 23, 3/4 (Sept.-Oct): 61-72. Reprinted in (1992). *The Sexual Subject: A Screen Reader in Sexuality*. pp. 265-276. London and New York: Routledge.

Dyer, Richard (1981). Getting Over the Rainbow: Identity and Pleasure in Gay Cultural Politics. In *Silver Linings: Some Strategies for the Eighties*. London: Lawrence and Wishart.

Dyer, Richard (1986). *Heavenly Bodies: Film Stars and Society*. New York: St. Martin's Press.

Dyer, Richard (1990). *Now You See It: Studies on Lesbian and Gay Film*. London and New York: Routledge.

Dyer, Richard (1991). Believing in Fairies: The Author and the Homosexual. In *Inside/Out: Lesbian Theories, Gay Theories*. Diana Fuss, ed. pp. 185-201. New York and London: Routledge.

Dyson, Michael Eric (1993). "Be Like Mike? Michael Jordan and the Pedagogy of Desire," *Cultural Studies*, 7, 1: 64-72.

Easthope, Anthony (1986). *What a Man's Gotta Do: The Masculine Myth in Popular Culture*. London: Paladin.

Easton, Richard (1992). "Canonical Criminalizations: Homosexuality, Art History, Surrealism, and Abjection," *differences: A Journal of Feminist Cultural Studies*, 4, 3:133-175.

Echols, Alice (1983). The New Feminism of Yin and Yang. In *Powers of Desire: The Politics of Sexuality*. Ann Snitow, Christine Stansell and, Sharon Thompson, eds. New York: Monthly Review Press.

609

Ecker, Grisela, ed. (1985). *Feminist Aesthetics*. Trans. Harriet Anderson. London: The Women's Press.

Eco, Umberto (1979). *The Role of the Reader*. Bloomington and Indianapolis: Indiana University Press.

Editors of Questions féministes (1980). "Variations on Some Common Themes," *Feminist Issues* 1, 1:15-17.

Ehrenreich, Barbara (1983). *The Hearts of Men: American Dreams and the Flight from Commitment*. Garden City, New York: Anchor Press/Doubleday.

Ehrenreich, Barbara (1986). Remaking Love: *The Feminization of Sex*. Garden City: Anchor Doubleday.

Eiblmayr, Silvia (1994). *Suture*–Fantasies of Totality. In *Suture–Phantasmen der Volkommenheit*. Silvia Eiblmayr, ed. pp. 3-16. Salzburg: Salzburger Kunstverein.

Eisenstein, Hester and Alice Jardine (1980). *The Future of Difference*. Boston: J.K. Hall.

Eisenstein, Zilah (1979). *Capitalist Patriarchy and the Case for Socialist Feminism*. New York: Monthly Review Press.

Eisenstein, Zilah (1984). *Feminism and Sexual Equality: Crisis in Liberal America*. New York: Monthly Review Press.

Eisler, Riane (1988). *The Chalice & the Blade: Our History, Our Future*. San Francisco: Harper & Row, Publishers.

Ekins, Richard (1996). The Career Path of the Male Femaler. In *Blending Genders: Social Aspects of Cross-dressing and Sex-changing*. Richard Ekins and David King, eds. pp. 39-48. London and New York: Routledge.

Ekins, Richard and King, Dave eds. (1996). *Blending Genders: Social Aspects of Cross-dressing and Sex-changing*. London and New York: Routledge

Elam, Diane (1994). *Feminism and Deconstruction: Ms. en Abyme*. London and New York: Routledge.

Elsaesser, Thomas (1988). "Desire Denied, Deferred or Squared?" *Screen*, 29 3:106-115.

Elias, Norbert (1978). *The Civilizing Process: The History of Manners*. Oxford: Basil Blackwell.

Elliot, Anthony (1992). *Social Theory & Psychoanalysis in Transition: Self and Society from Freud to Kristeva*. Oxford and Cambridge: Blackwell.

Ellis, John (1982). *Visible Fictions*. New York: Routledge, Chapman & Hall, Inc.

Ellis, John (1992). On Pornography. In *The Sexual Subject: A Screen Reader in Sexuality*. John Caughie and Anette Kuhn, eds. pp.146-170. London and New York: Routledge. (original, Screen, 1980, 21, 1:81-108).

Ellis, Kate (1988). I'm Black & Blue From the Rolling Stones and I'm not Sure how I feel About It: Poronography and the Feminist Imagination. In *Caught Looking: Feminism, Poronography & Censorship*. Kate Ellis, Beth Jaker, D. Nan Hunter, Barbara O'Dair, and Abby Tallmer, eds. pp.38-47. Seattle: The Real Comet Press.

Ellis, Kate, Beth Jaker, Beth, D. Nan Hunter, Barbara O'Dair, and Abby Tallmer, eds. (1988). *Caught Looking: Feminism, Poronography & Censorship*. Seattle: The Real Comet Press.

Ellis, Kate, O'Dair, Barbara and Tallmer, Abby (1988). Introduction. In *Caught Looking: Feminism, Poronography & Censorship*. Kate Ellis, Beth Jaker, D. Nan Hunter, Barbara O'Dair and Abby Tallmer, eds. pp.6-8 Seattle: The Real Comet Press.

Ellsworth, Elizabeth (1986). "Illicit Pleasures: Feminist Spectators and *Personal Best,*" *Wide Angle*, 8, 2:45-58. Reprinted in *Becoming Feminine: The Politics of Popular Culture*. Leslie G. Roman, Linda K. Christian-Smith, with Elizabeth Ellsworth, eds. pp.102-122. London, New York and Philadelphia: The Falmer Press.

Elshtain, Jean Bethe (1981). *Public Man, Private Woman: Women in Social and Political Thought*. Princeton, New Jersey: Princeton University Press.

Erkkila, Betsy (1985). "Greta Garbo: Sailing Beyond the Frame," *Critical Inquiry*, 11 (June): 595-619.

Escoffier, Jeffrey (1985). "Sexual Revolution and the Politics of Gay Identity," *Socialist Review*, 15 (82-83), 4 and 5 (July-Oct): 119-153.

Faludi, Susan (1991). *The Men Strike Back: The Undeclared War on American Women*. New York: Crown Publishers, Inc.

Farrell, Warren (1988). *Why Men are the Way They Are*. New York: Berkeley Publishing Group.

Fauré, Christine (1981). "The Twilight of the Goddesses or, The Intellectual Crisis of French Feminism," *Signs: Journal of Women in Culture and Society*, 7,11:81-86.

Fausto-Sterling, Anne (1985). *Myths of Gender: Biological Theories About Women and Men*. New York: Basic Books Inc., Pub.

Fausto-Sterling, Anne (1993). "The Five Senses," *The Sciences* (March/April):20-25.

Featherstone, Mike (1991) *Consumer Culture & Post-modernism*. London, Newbury Park, New Delhi: Sage Publications.

Feher, Michel, ed. (1989). *Zone 3; Zone 4; Zone 5: Fragments for a History of the Human Body: Part 1, 11, 111*. Cambridge, Massachussetts and London: MIT Press.

Felman, Shoshana (1977). "Turning the Screw of Interpretation," *French Yale Studies*, 55-56:94-207.

Felman, Shoshana (1987). *Jacques Lacan and the Adventure of Insight: Psychoanalysis and Contemporary Culture*. Massachusetts and London: Harvard University Press.

Felski, Rita (1989). *Beyond Feminist Aesthetics: Feminist Literature and Social Change*. Cambridge, Massachusetts: Harvard University Press.

Findlay, Heather (1986). "Is There A Gay Woman in the Text? Derrida, Wittig, and the Politics of the Three Women," *Subjects/Objects*, 4:1-22.

Finn, Geraldine (1988). Women, Fantasy and Popular Culture: The Wonderful World of Harlequin Romance. In *Popular Cultures and Political Practices*. Richard B. Gruneau, ed. pp. 51-68. Toronto, Ontario: Garamond Press.

Fiorenza, Elizabeth Schüssler (1985). *In Memory of Her: A Feminist Theological Reconstruction of Christian Origins.* New York: Crossroads Pub. Co.

Firestone, Sheshona (1979). *The Dialectic of Sex.* London: Women's Press.

Fiske, John (1987). *Television Culture.* London and New York: Routledge.

Fiske, John (1989a). *Understanding Popular Culture.* London and New York: Routledge.

Fiske, John (1989b). *Reading The Popular.* London and New York: Routledge.

Fiske, John (1992). Cultural Studies and the Culture of Everyday Life. In *Cultural Studies.* Lawrence Grossberg, Cary Nelson, and Paula Treichler, eds. pp.154-165. London: Routledge.

Fiske, John (1993). *Power Plays, Power Works.* London and New York: Verso.

Fitzgerald, Thomas K. (1992). Media, Ethnicity and Identity, Media. In *Culture and Power: A Media, Culture & Society Reader.* Paddy Scannell, Philip Schlesinger, and Colin Sparks, eds. pp. 112-133. London, Newbury Park, New Delhi: Sage Publications.

Flax, Jane (1990a). Postmodernism and Gender Relations in Feminist Theory. In *Feminism/Postmodernism.* Nancy Frazer and Linda J. Nicholson, eds. pp. 39-62 New York and London: Routledge, Chapman & Hall, Inc.

Flax, Jane (1990b). *Thinking Fragments, Psychoanalysis, Feminism, & Postmodernism in the Contemporary West.* Berkeley, Los Angeles, Oxford: University of California Press.

Flax, Jane (1993). "Multiples: On the Contemporary Politics of Subjectivity," *Human Studies,* 16:33-49.

Flieger, Jerry Aline (1990). The Female Subject: (What) Does Woman Want? In *Psychoanalysis and … .* Richard Feldstein and Henry Sussman, eds. pp. 54-66. New York and London: Routledge, Chapman and Hall.

Flores, Ralph (1984). *The Rhetoric of Doubtful Authority: Deconstructive Readings of Self-Questioning Narratives, St. Augustine to Faulkner.* London and Ithaca: Cornell University Press.

Fogel, Stanley (1988). *The Postmodern University: Essays on the Deconstruction of the Humanities.* Toronto: ECW Press.

Forrester, John (1992). What do Men Want? In *Men and Feminism.* David Porter, ed. pp. 105-120. London and New York: Routledge.

Forte, Jeania (1988). "Women's Performance Art: Feminism and Postmodernism," *Theater Journal,* 40, 2 (May): 217-235.

Foster, Hal (1984). "(Post)Modern Polemics," *New German Critique,* 33 (Fall): 67-78.

Foster, Hal (1985). *Recordings: Art, Spectacle, Cultural Politics.* Seattle, Washington: Bay Press.

Foster, Hal (1993). " 'Primitive' Scenes," *Critical Inquiry,* 20 (Autumn): 69-102.

Foster, Thomas, ed. (1993). Cyberpunk: Technologies of Cultural Identity, *Genders,* 18 (Winter).

Foucault, Madness (1965). *Madness and Civilization: A History of Insanity in the Age of Reason.* Trans. Richard Howard. London: Tavistock.

Foucault, Michel (1970). *The Order of Things: An Archaeology of the Human Sciences.* Trans. Alan Sheridon. New York: Pantheon Books.

Foucault, Michel (1977). *To Discipline and Punish: The Birth of the Prison.* Trans. Alan Sheridon. New York: Pantheon Books.

Foucault, Michel (1980a). *The History of Sexuality, Volume 1: An Introduction.* Trans. Robert Hurley. New York: Vintage Books.

Foucault, Michel (1980b). *Herculine Barbin: Being the Recently Discovered Memoirs of a Nineteenth Century French Hermaphrodite.* Trans. Richard McDougall. New York: Pantheon Press.

Foucault, Michel and R. Sennett (1981). Sexuality and Solitude. In *The Psychology of Society: Anthology 1.* London: Junction Books.

Foucault, Michel (1983). On the Genealogy of Ethics. An Afterword to *Michel Foucault: Beyond Structuralism and Hermeneutics.* H.L. Dreyfus and P. Rabinow. pp. 229-252. Chicago: University of Chicago Press.

Foucault, Michel (1985). *The History of Sexuality, Volume 2: The Use of Pleasure.* Trans. Robert Hurley. New York: Pantheon Books.

Foucault, Michel (1988). *The History of Sexuality, Volume 3: The Care of the Self.* Trans. Robert Hurley. New York: Vintage Books.

Fox-Genovese, Elizabeth (1991). *Feminism Without Illusions: A Critique of Individualism.* Chapel Hill and London: The University of North Carolina Press.

Fox-Genovese, Elizabeth (1993). "From Separate Spheres to Dangerous Streets: Postmodernist Feminism and the Problem of Order," *Social Research,* 60, 2 (Summer):235-254.

Frampton, Kenneth (1983). Towards a Critical Regionalism: Six Points for an Architecture of Resistance. In The *Anti-Aesthetic: Essays on Postmodern Culture.* Hal Foster, ed. pp. 16-30. Port Towsend, Washington: Bay Press.

Frank, Byle (1987). "Hegemonic Heterosexual Masculinity," *Studies in Political Economy,* 24 (Autumn):159-170.

Frank, Lisa and Paul Smith, eds. (1993). *Madonnarama: Essays on Sex and Popular Culture.* Pittsburgh, Pennsylvania: Cleis Press Inc.

Fraser, Laura (1990). "Nasty Girls," *Mother Jones* (Feb./March): 32-35,48-50.

Fraser, Nancy and Nicholson, Linda J. (1988). "Social Criticism Without Philosophy: An Encounter Between Feminism and Postmodernism," *Theory, Culture and Society,* 5, 2 and 3 (June): 373-394.

Fraser, Nancy (1989). *Unruly Practices: Power, Discourse and Gender in Contemporary Social Theory.* Minneapolis: University of Minnesota Press.

Freedman, Barbara (1988). "Frame-Up: Feminism, Psychoanalysis," *Theatre Journal,* 40, 3 (October): 375-397.

French, Marilyn (1985). *Beyond Power: On Women, Men and Morals.* New York : Summit Books.

613

Fried, Michael (1986). *Absorption and Theatricality: Painting and the Beholder in the Age of Diderot.* Berkeley: University of California Press.

Friedan, Betty (1981). *The Second Wave.* N.Y.: Summit Books.

Friedberg, Anne (1990). Mutual Indifference: Feminism and Postmodernism. In *The Other Perspective in Gender and Culture: Rewriting Women and the Symbolic.* Juliet Flower MacCannell, ed. pp. 39-58. Oxford and New York: Columbia University Press.

Friedrich, Heinz, Hans-Georg Gadamer, Elmar Budde Holthusen, Klaus Fußmann and Peter Sloterdijk (1984). *Ende der Kunst–Zukunft der Kunst.* München: Deutscher Kunstverlag.

Frith, Simon (1988). *Music For Pleasure Essays in The Sociology of Pop.* New York: Routledge, Chapman & Hall, Inc.

Fromm, Eric (1951). *The Forgotten Language: An Introduction to the Understanding of Dreams, Fairy Tales and Myths.* New York: Rinehart.

Frueh, Joanna (1988). Towards a Feminist Theory of Art Criticism. In *Feminist Art Criticism: An Anthology.* Arlene Raven, Cassandra Langer, and Joanna Frueh, eds. pp. 153-165. London and Ann Arbor: University Microfilms Inc. Research Press.

Frueh, Joanna (1994). Visible Difference: Women Artists and Aging." In *New Feminist Criticism: Art, Identity, Action.* Joanna Frueh, Cassandra L. Langer and, Arlene Raven, eds. pp. 264-288. New York: HarperCollins Publishers (IconEditions).

Fuchs, J. Cynthia (1993). " 'Death Is Irrelevant' : Cyborgs, Reproduction, and the Future of Male Hysteria," *Genders 18* (Winter): 113-133.

Fuss, Diana (1989). *Essentially Speaking: Feminism, Nature & Difference.* London & New York: Routledge, Chapman & Hall, Inc.

Fuss, Diana, ed. (1991). *Inside/Out: Lesbian Theories, Gay Theories.* New York and London: Routledge.

Fuss, Diana (1992). "Fashion and the Homospectatorial Look," *Critical Inquiry,* 18 (Summer): 713 - 737.

Fuss, Diana (1994). Reading Like a Feminist. In *the essential difference.* Naomi Schor and Elizabeth Weed, eds. pp. 98-115. Bloomington and Indianapolis: Indiana University Press.

Fussell, Sam (1991). *Muscle: Confessions of an Unlikely Bodybuilder.* London and Sydney: Cardinal.

Gaines, Jane G. (1988). "White Privilege and Looking Relations: Race and Gender in Feminist Film Theory," *Screen,* 29, 4:12-27.

Gaines, Jane and Charlotte Herzog (1990). *Fabrications: Costume and the Female Body.* New York and London: Routledge.

Gaines, Jane G. (1992). "Competing Glances: Who is Reading Robert Mapplethorpe's *Black Book*?" *New Formations,* 16 (Spring):25- 39.

Gallager, Catherine, Joel Fineman, and Neil Hertz (1983). "More about 'Medusa's Head'," *Representations,* 4 (Fall):55-72.

Gallop, Jane (1981). Phallus/Penis: Same Difference. In *Men by Women, Women and Literature,* vol. 2. Janet Todd, ed. New York and London: Holmes & Meier.

Gallop, Jane (1982a). *The Daughter's Seduction: Feminism and Psychoanalysis*. Ithaca: Cornell University Press.

Gallop, Jane (1982b). "Writing and Sexual Difference: The Difference Within," *Critical Inquiry*, 8:797-804.

Gallop, Jane (1983). "*Quand nos lèvres s'écrivent*: Irigaray's Body Politic," *Romantic Review*, 74, 1.

Gallop, Jane (1984). "Beyond the *Jouissance* Principle," *Representations*, 7 (Summer): 109-114.

Gallop, Jane (1985). *Reading Lacan*. Ithaca and London: Cornell University Press.

Gallop, Jane (1987). French Theory and the Seduction of Feminism. In *Men in Feminism*. Alice Jardine and Paul Smith, eds. pp.111-115. London and New York: Methuen.

Gamman, Lorraine and Merja Makinen (1994). *Female Fetishism: A New Look*. London: Lawrence & Wishart.

Gamman, Lorraine and Margaret Marshment (1989). *The Female Gaze: Women as Viewers of Popular Culture*. Seattle: The Real Comet Press.

Garber, Marjorie (1992). *Vested Interests: Cross-Dressing & Cultural Anxiety*. London and New York: Routledge, Chapman and Hall, Inc.

Garber, Marjorie (1995). *VICE VERA: The Bi-sexuality of Everyday Life*. N.Y.: Charles Scribner and Sons,

Garfinkle, Harry (1981). The Anthropological Foundations of Humane Psychology. In *Humanistic Psychology: Concepts and Criticisms*. Joseph R. Royce and Leendert P. Mos, ed. pp.185-234. New York and London: Plenum Press.

Garrard, Mary (1989). *Artemisia Gentileschi: The Image of the Female Hero in Italian Baroque Art*. Princeton, New Jersey: Princeton University Press.

Gasché, Rudolphe (1986). *Tain of the Mirror: Derrida and the Philosophy of Reflection*. Cambridge, Mass.: Harvard University Press.

Gates, Henry Lewis, Jr., ed. (1986). *"Race," Writting, and Difference*. Chicago: Chicago University Press.

Gates, Henry Lewis, Jr. (1987). *Figures in Black: Words, Signs, and the "Racial" Self*. New York: Oxford University Press.

Gauthier, Clermont (1986). "Postmodernism, Desire and Education," *Journal of Curriculum Theory Conference*, 1, 2:1-43.

Geyer, Michael (1993). "Multiculturalism and the Politics of General Education," *Critical Inquiry*, 19 (Spring): 499-531.

Giblett, Rod (1992) "Philosophy (And Sociology) in the Wetlands: The S(ub)lime and the Uncanny," *New Formations*, 16 (Summer): 142-159.

Giddens, Anthony (1979). *Central Problems in Social Theory: Action, Structure and Contradiction in Social Analysis*. London: Hutchinson.

615

Gilbert, Sandra M. (1980). "Costumes of the Mind: Transvestism as Metaphor in Modern Literature," *Critical Inquiry*, 6, 3 (Winter): 391- 417.

Gilbert, Sandra M. and Susan Gubar (1979). *The Madwoman in the Attic: The Woman Writer and the Nineteenth-Century Literary Imagination*. New Haven and London: Yale University Press.

Gibert, M. Sandra and Susan Gubar (1988). "The Man on the Dump versus the United Dames of America; or, What Does Frank Lentriccia Want?" *Critical Inquiry*, 14, 2 (Winter): 386-413.

Gillian, Patricia (1978). Therapeutic Uses of Obscenity. In *Censorship and Obscenity*. Rajeev Dhavan and Christie Davis, eds. New York: Roman and Littlefield.

Gilligan, Carol (1982). *In A Different Voice: Psychological Theory and Women's Development*. Cambridge, Massachusetts, and London: Harvard University Press.

Giroux, Henry (1988). *Schooling and the Struggle for Public Life: A Critical Pedagogy in the Modern Age*. Minneapolis: University of Minnesota Press.

Giroux, Henry (1993). "Living Dangerously: Identity Politics and the New Cultural Racism: Towards a Critical Pedagogy of Representation," *Cultural Studies*, 7, 1: 1-27.

Glass, Fred (1990). "Totally Recalling Arnold: Sex and Violence in the New Bad Future," *Film Quarterly*, 44, 1 (Fall):2-13.

Gledhill, Christine (1988). Pleasurable Negotiations. In *Female Spectators: Looking at Film and Television*. Deidre Pribram, ed. pp. 64-89. London and New York.

Glynos, Jason (1995). The Logic of Sex. Paper presented to the Canadian Sociology Anthropology Association: Lacanian Indirections in Social Theory (June 5). 30th Annual *Learned Societies*, Montréal, Quebec, Canada.

Godeau, Abigail Solomon (1987). "Living With Contradictions: Critical Practices In the Age of Supply-Side Aesthetics," *Screen*, 28, 3 (Summer): 2-22.

Goldberg, Jonathan (1992). "Recalling Totalities: The Mirrored Stages of Arnold Schwarenegger," *differences: A Journal of Feminist Cultural Studies*, 4, 1:172-204.

Goldenberg, Naomi (1979). *Changing of the Gods: Feminism and the End of Traditional Religions*. Boston: Beacon Press.

Goldenberg, Naomi (1982). *The End of God*. Ottawa: University of Ottawa Press.

Golding, Sue (1995). "The Politics of Foucault's Poetics, or Better Yet: The Ethical Demand of Ecstatic Fetish," *New Formations*, 25 (Summer):40-47.

Goldman, Shifra (1988). 'Portraying Ourselves': Contemporary Chicana Artists. In *Feminist Art Criticism: An Anthology*. Arlene Raven, Cassandra Langer, and Joanna Frueh, eds. pp. 187-206. London and Ann Arbor: University Microfilms Inc. Research Press.

Goldsby, Jackie (1993). Queens of Language: *Paris is Burning*. In *Queer Looks: Perspectives on Lesbian and Gay Film and VIdeo*. Martha Gever, Pratibha Parmar, and John Greyson, eds. pp. 108-115. Toronto: Between the Lines.

Gombrich, Ernst (1977). *Art And Illusion: A Study in the Psychology of Pictorial Representation*. Oxford: Phaidon.

Goodman, Jessie (1985). "Masculinity, Feminism, and the Male Elementary School Teacher: A Case Study Or Preservice Teacher's Perspectives," *Journal of Curriculum Theorizing*, 7, 2: 30-60.

Gordon, Linda (1992). "On 'Difference,'" *Genders*, 7, 2 (Spring): 91-111.

Gottdiener, M. (1985). "Hegemony and Mass Culture: A Semiotic Approach," *American Journal of Sociology*, 90, 5 (March): 979-1001.

Göttner-Abendroth (1982). *Die Tanzende Göttin: Prinzipien einer matriarchchalen Ästhetik*. München: Verlag Frauenoffensive.

Gould, Timothy (1990). "Intensity and Its Audiences: Notes Towards a Feminist Perspective on the Kantian Sublime," *The Journal of Aesthetics and Art Criticism*, 48, 4 (Fall):305-315.

Gould, Timothy (1991). Engendering Aesthetics: Sublimity, Sublimation and Mysogyny in Burke and Kant. In *Aesthetics, Politics, and Hermeneutics*. Gerald Burns and Stephen Watson, eds. New York: SUNY Press.

Gowans, Alan (1981). *Learning To See: Historical Perspective on Modern Popular/Commercial Arts*. Bowling Green: Bowling Green University Popular Press.

Graburn, Nelson (1970). The Eskimos and Commercial Art. In *The Sociology of Art and Literature: A Reader*. Milton C. Albrecht, James H. Barnett, and Mason Griff, eds. pp. 333-340. N.Y.: Praeger Publishers, Inc.

Graburn, Nelson (1976). *Ethnic and Tourist Art: Cultural Expressions from the Fourth World*. Berkeley: University of California Press.

Grace, Della (1991). *Love Bites*. London: Gay Men's Press.

Grace, Della (1993). "Xenomorphisis," *New Formations*, 19 (Spring).

Greer, Germaine (1979). *The Obstacle Race: The Fortunes of Women Painters and Their Work*. London: Secker & Warburg.

Greer, Germaine (1992). *The Change: Women, Aging, and the Menopause*. New York: Alfred A. Knopf.

Griffin, Susan (1982). *Pornography and Silence: Culture's Revenge Against Nature*. New York: Harper & Row.

Grimshaw, Jean (1986). *Philosophy and Feminist Thinking*. Minneapolis: University of Minneapolis Press.

Grossberg, Lawrence (1992). *We Gotta Get Out of This Place*. New York & London: Routledge.

Grossberg, Nelson, Cary and Paula Treichler eds. (1992). *Cultural Studies*. New York and London: Routledhge.

Grosz, Elizabeth A. (1986). Language and the Limits of the Body: Kristeva and Abjection. In *Futur*Fall: Excursions into Post-Modernity*. E. A. Grosz, Terry Threadgold, David Kelly, Alan Cholodenko, and Edward Colless, eds. pp. 106-117. Sydney: Power Institute of Fine Arts, University of Sydney.

Grosz, Elizabeth A. (1987). "Feminist Theory and The Challenge to Knowledge," *Women's Studies International Forum*, 10, 5: 475-480.

Grosz, Elizabeth A. (1989). *Sexual Subversions: Three French Feminists.* Wellington, London and Boston: Allen & Unwin.

Grosz, Elizabeth A. (1991). "Lesbian Fetishism?," *differences: A Journal of Feminist Cultural Studies,* 3, 2:39-54. Another version is found in (1993). *Fetishism as Cultural Discourse.* Emily Apter and William Pietz, eds. pp. 101-118. Ithaca and London: Cornell University Press.

Grosz, Elizabeth A. (1994a). Sexual Difference and the Problem of Essentialism. In *the essential difference.* Naomi Schor and Elizabeth Weed, eds. pp. 82-97. Bloomington and Indianapolis: Indiana University Press.

Grosz, Elizabeth A. (1994b). Experimental Desire: Rethinking Queer Subjectivity. In *Supposing the Subject.* Joan Copjec, ed. pp. 133-157. London and New York: Verso.

Grosz, Elizabeth A. (1994). *Volatile Bodies: Toward a Corporeal Feminism.* Bloomington and Indianapolis: Indiana University Press.

Grosz, Elizabeth A. (1995). *Space, Time and Perversion.* New York and London: Routledge.

Grover, Jan (1990). Dykes in Context: Some Problems in Minority Representation. In *The Contest of Meaning: Critical Histories of Photograph.* Richard Bolton, ed. Cambridge, Mass.: MIT Press.

Grumet, Madeline (1988). *Bitter Milk: Women and Teaching.* Amherst: University of Massachusetts Press.

Grüninger, Christain, Frank Lindermann, and Michaela Thier (1994). Rechte Bands auf dem deutschen Markt–Überblick und Bewertung. In *Rock von Rechts, Medienpädagogische Handreichung 3; Schriften zur Medienpädagogik 14.* Dieter Baacke, Michaela Their, Christian Grüninger, and Frank Lindermann, eds. pp. 32-121. Vorstand de Gesellschaft für Medienpädagogik und Kommunikationskultur in der Bundesrepublik Deutschland. Bielefeld: e.V. (GMK).

Guerrilla Girls (1995). *Confessions of the Guerrilla Girls.* New York: HarperPerrenial.

Gubar, Susan and Sandra Gilbert (1979). *The Madwoman in the Attic: The Woman Writer in the 19th Century Literary Imagination.* New Haven: Yale University Press.

Gubar, Susan (1987). "Representing Pornography: Feminism, Criticism, and Depictions of Female Violation," *Critical Inquiry,* 13 (Summer): 712- 741.

Hagan, Leigh Kay, ed. (1992). *Women Respond to the Men's Movement: A Feminist Collection.* Harper San Francisco.

Hall, Stuart (1987). Minimal Selves. In *Identity: The Real Me, Post-Modernism and the Question of Identity. ICA Documents* 6. pp. 44-46. London: ICA.

Hall, Stuart (1988). New Ethnicities. In *Black Film, British Cinema. ICA Document* 7, pp. 27-30. London: ICA.

Hall, Stuart (1990). Cultural Identity and Diaspora. In *Identity: Community, Culture, Difference.* Jonathan Rutherford, ed. pp. 222- 237. London: Lawrence & Wishart.

Halperin, David M. (1990). *One Hundred Years of Homosexuality: And Other Essays on Greek Love*. London and New York: Routledge.

Hamilton, R. (1979). *The Liberation of Women: A Study of Patriarchy and Capitalism*. London: Allen & Unwin.

Handler, R. (1989). Ethnicity in the Museum: A Culture and Communication Discourse. In *Negotiating Ethnicity*. S. Keefe, ed. pp. 18-26. Napa Bulletin, 8, National Association for the Practice of Anthropology.

Hansen, Miriam (1986). "Pleasure, Ambivalence, Identifications: Valentino and Female Spectatorship," *Cinema Journal*, 25, 4:6-32.

Haraway, Donna (1988). "Situated Knowledges: The Science Question in Feminism and the Privilege of Partial Perspective," *Feminist Studies* 14, 3:575-99. Revised version in Donna Haraway's (1991). *Simians, Cyborgs, and Women: The Reinvention of Nature*. pp. 183-210. New York: Routledge.

Haraway, Donna (1990). A Manifesto for Cyborgs: Science, Technology, and Socialist Feminism of the 1980s. In *Feminism/Postmodernism*. Linda J. Nicholson, ed. pp. 190-233. New York and London: Routledge.

Harding, Sandra (1987). *The Science Question in Feminism*. Ithaca: Cornell University Press.

Hammond, Harmony (1994). A Space of Infinite and Pleasurable Possibilities: Lesbian Self-Representation in Visual Art. In *New Feminist Criticism: Art, Identity, Action*. Joanna Frueh, Cassandra L. Langer and, Arlene Raven, eds. pp. 97-131. New York: HarperCollins Publishers (IconEditions).

Harvey, David (1989) *The Condition of Postmodernity: An Enquiry into the Origins of Cultural Change*. Oxford: Basil Blackwell Ltd.

Hartman, Geoffrey H. (1980). *Criticism in the Wilderness: The Study of Literature Today*. Conn., New Haven: Yale University Press.

Hartmann, Heidi (1981). The Unhappy Marriage of Marxism and Feminism: Towards A More Progressive Union. In *The Unhappy Marriage of Marxism and Feminism: A Debate on Class and Patriarchy*. Lydia Sargent, ed. pp. 1-42. London: Pluto Press.

Hartsock, Nancy (1983). *Money, Sex, and Power: Toward a Feminist Historical Materialism*. New York: Longman. Repr. (1985). Boston: Northeastern University Press.

Hartsock, Nancy (1990a). "Postmodernism and Political Change: Issues for Feminist Theory," *Culture Critique*, 14 (Winter 1989-1990):15-33.

Hartsock, Nancy (1990b). Foucault and Power: A Theory for Women? In *Feminism/Postmodernism*. Linda J. Nicholson, ed. pp. 157-175. New York and London: Routledge.

Hauser, Arnold (1951). *The Social History of Art, 4 Volumes*. New York: Alfred A, Knopf, Inc.

Haug, Frigga (1987). *Female Sexualization: A Collective Work of Memory*. London: Verso Press.

Hausman, Bernice L. (1995). *Changing Sex: Transsexualism, Technology, and the Idea of Gender*. Durham and London: Duke University Press.

Hayles, N. Katherine (1993).The Seductions of Cyberspace. In *Rethinking Technologies*.A. Conley, S.Verna, and B.Andermatt, eds. pp. 173-190. Minneapolis and London: University of Minnesota Press.

Hearn, Jeff (1987). *The Gender of Oppression: Men, Masculinity and the Critique of Marxism*. Brighton: Harvester.

Heartney, Eleanor (1988). "David Salle: Impersonal Effects," *Art in America*, 76, 6 (June): 120-129.

Heath, Stephen (1978). "Difference," *Screen*, 19, 3:50-112.

Heath, Stephen (1982). *The Sexual Fix*. London: MacMillan

Heath, Stephen (1986). Joan Riviere and the Masquerade. In *Formations of Fantasy*.Victor Burgin, James Donald, and Cora Kaplan, eds. pp. 45-61. London and New York: Methuen.

Heath, Stephen (1987). Male Feminism. In *Men in Feminism*. Alice Jardine and Paul Smith, eds. pp.1-32. London and New York: Methuen.

Hebdige, Dick (1979). *Subculture:The Meaning of Style*. London and New York: Methuen.

Hebdige, Dick (1983). "Posing ... Threats, Striking ... Poses:Youth, Surveillance, and Display," *SubStance*, 37/38: 68-88.

Hebdige, Dick (1990). *Hiding in The Light: On Images and Things*. London & New York: Routlege Ltd.

Heilbrun, Carolyn (1982). *Writing a Woman's Life*. New York: Ballantine Books.

Hennessy, Rosemary (1993). *Materialist Feminism and the Politics of Discourse*. New York and London: Routledge.

Herdt, G., ed. (1982). *Rituals of Manhood: Male Initiation in Papua New Guinea*. Berkeley: University of California Press.

Herek, Gregory M. (1986)."On Heterosexual Masculinity: Some Psychical Consequences of the Social Construction of Gender and Sexuality," *American Behavioral Scientist*, 29, 5 (May-June):563-578.

Hertz, Neil (1983). "Medusa's Head: Male Hysteria under Political Pressure," *Representations*, 4 (Fall):27-54.

Hirsch, Marianne and Evelyn Fox Keller, eds. (1990). *Conflicts in Feminism*. New York and London: Routledge.

Hirsch, E.D. Jr. (1987). *Cultural Literacy:What Every American Needs To Know*. Boston: Houghton Mifflin.

Hoagland, Sarah (1988). *Lesbian Ethics*. Palo Alto, CA: Institute of Lesbian Studies.

Hocquenghem, Guy (1978). *Homosexual Desire*.Trans. Daniella Dangoor. London: Allison & Busby. (original, 1972). Updated (1993) with a new introduction by Michael Moon. Durham and London: Duke University Press.

Hodge, Bob and David Tripp (1986). *Children and Television: A Semiotic Approach.* Cambridge and Oxford: Polity Press.

Hodge, Robert and Gunther Kress (1988). *Social Semiotics.* Ithaca, New York: Cornell University Press.

Holder, Maryse (1988). Another Cuntree: At Last, a Mainstream Female Art Movement. In *Feminist Art Criticism: An Anthology.* Arlene Raven, Cassandra Langer, and Joanna Frueh, eds. pp. 1-20. London and Ann Arbor: University Microfilms Inc. Research Press.

Hollander, Ann (1975). *Seeing Through Clothes.* New York: Viking.

Holmlund, Christine Anne (1989). "I Love Luce: The Lesbian, Mimesis and Masquerade in Irigaray, Freud, and Mainstream Film," *New Formations,* 9 (Winter): 105-123.

Holmlund, Christine Anne (1991). "Displacing Limits of Difference: Gender, Race, and Colonialism in Edward Said and Homi Bhabha's Theoretical Models and Marguerite Duras's Experimental Films," *Quarterly Review of Film and Video,* 13, 1-3:1-22.

Holmlund, Christine Anne (1993). Masculinity as Multiple Masquerade: The 'Mature' Stallone and the Stallone Clone. In *Screening the Male: Exploring Masculinities in Hollywood Cinema.* Steven Cohan and Ina Rae Hark, eds. pp. 213-229. London and New York: Routledge.

Holub, Robert C. (1984). *Reception Theory: A Critical Introduction.* New York: Methuen.

hooks, bell (1990). *Yearning: Race, Gender, and Cultural Politics.* Boston: South End Press.

hooks, bell (1993). "Eros, Eroticism and the Pedagogical Process," *Cultural Studies,* 7, 1:58-63.

Howard, Dick (1975). "Introduction to Castoriadis," *Telos,* 23 (Spring): 117-130.

Hoy, Couzens (1978). "Hermeneutic Circularity, Indeterminacy, and Incommensurability," *New Literary History,* 10, 1 (Autumn): 161-179.

Hoy, David Couzens (1986a). Must We Say What We Mean? The Grammatological Critique of Hermeneutics. In *Hermeneutics and Modern Philosophy.* Bruce R. Wachterhauser, ed. pp. 397-415. Albany, New York: State University of New York Press.

Hoy, David Couzens (1986b). Power, Repression, Progress: Foucault, Lukács, and the Frankfurt School. In *Foucault: A Critical Reader.* David Couzens Hoy, ed. pp. 1-26. Oxford: Basil Blackwell Ltd.

Hunter, Dianne (1985). Hysteria, Psychoanalysis, and Feminism: The Case of Anna O. In *The (M)other Tongue: Essays in Feminist Psychoanalytic Interpretation.* Shirley Nelson Garner, Claire Kahane and Madelon Sprengnether, eds. pp. 89-118. Ithaca and London: Cornell University Press.

Hunter, James Davison (1991). *Culture Wars: The Struggle to Define America.* New York: Basic Books.

Husserl, Edmund (1970). *The Crisis of European Sciences and Transcendental Phenomenology.* Trans. David Carr. Evanston: Northwestern University Press.

Hutcheon, Linda (1988). *A Poetics of Postmodernism: History, Theory, Fiction.* London and New York: Routledge Ltd.

Hutcheon, Linda (1989). *The Politics of Postmodernism*. London and New York: Routledge Ltd.

Huyssen, Andreas (1986). Mass Culture as Woman: Modernism's Other. In *Studies in Entertainment: Critical Approaches to Mass Culture*. Tania Modleski, ed. pp.188-208. Bloomington and Indianapolis: Indiana University Press.

Irigaray, Luce (1985a). *Speculum of the Other Woman*. Trans. Gillian C. Gill. Ithaca, New York: Cornell University Press (Orig.1974).

Irigaray, Luce (1985b). Così Fan Tutti. In *This Sex Which Is Not One*. Trans. Catherine Porter. pp. 86-105. Itaca, New York: Cornell University Press.

Issak, Jo-Anna (1987). "Seduction Without Desire," *Vanguard*, 16, 3. (Summer) 10-14.

Jacoby, Russell (1987). *The Last Intellectuals: American Culture in the Age of Academe*. New York: Basic Books.

Jagger, Allison (1983). *Feminist Politics and Human Nature*. Sussex: The Harvester Press.

jagodzinski, jan (1986-1995). *Narrating the "O" Between the Hominoid and the Hominid: The Proto-Cultural Esthetic Imagination*. (Unpublished Manuscript).

jagodzinski, jan (1987). Towards an Ecological Aesthetic: Notes on a "Green" Frame of Mind. In *Art in a Democracy*. Kristin Congdon and Doug Blandy, eds. pp. 138-164. New York: Teachers College, Columbia University.

jagodzinski, jan (1988). "Reawakening Aesthetic Insight," *Phenomenology + Pedagogy*, 6, 3: 119-146.

jagodzinski, jan (1989/1990). "A Wolf in Sheep's Clothing/ A Sheep in Wolf's Clothing," *Fine*, Winter: 4-20.

jagodzinski, jan (1991)."A Para-critical/sitical/sightical Reading of Ralf Smith's Excellence in Art Education," *The Journal of Social Theory in Art Education*, 11 (June, 1991): 90-137.

jagodzinski, jan (1992a). The Poetics of Green Esthetics: Situating "Green Criticism" in the Postmodern Condition. In *Pluralistic Approaches to Art Criticism*. D. Blandy and K. Congdon, eds. pp. 49-71. Bowling Green: Bowling Green University Press.

jagodzinski, jan (1992b). "The Nostalgia of Art Education: Back to the Future, Part Four," *Journal of Social Theory in Art Education*, 12 (Sept.): 35-56.

jagodzinski, jan (1997, August). *Postmodern Dilemmas: Outrageous Essays in Art&Art Education*. Vol. 1, and *Pun(k) deconstruction: Experifigural Writing in Art&Art Education*. Vol. 2, Mahwah, New Jersey: Lawrence Erlbaum Associates, Inc., Pub. (forthcoming)

jagodzinski, jan (1997). "The Nostalgia of Art Education: Reinscribing the Master's Narrative," *Studies in Art Education* (forthcoming).

Jameson, Fredric (1984). "Postmodernism, or The Cultural Logic of Late Capitalism," *New Left Review*, 146 (July-August): 53-93.

Janson, H.W. (1962). *The History of Art*. Englewood Cliffs: Prentice-Hall. Inc.

Jardine, Alice A. (1985). *Gynesis: Configurations of Woman and Modernity*. Ithaca and London: Cornell University Press.

Jardine, Alice A. (1987). Men in Feminism: Odor di Uomo or Comparnons. In *Men in Feminism*. Alice Jardine and Paul Smith, eds. pp.54-61. London and New York: Methuen.

Jardine, Alice (1989). Notes for an Analysis. In *Between Feminism and Psychoanalysis*. Teresa Brennan, ed. pp. 73-85. London and New York: Routledge.

Jardine, Alice and Smith, Paul, eds. (1987). *Men in Feminism*. London and New York: Methuen.

Jardine, Alice and Paul Smith (1987). A Conversation. In *Men in Feminism*. Alice Jardine and Paul Smith, eds. pp.242-263. London and New York: Methuen.

Jay, Martin. (1986). In the Empire of the Gaze: Foucault and the Denigration of Vision in Twentieth-century French Thought. In *Foucault: A Critical Reader*. David Couzens Hoy, ed. pp. 175-204. London: Basil Blackwell Ltd.

Jay, Martin (1993). *Downcast Eyes: The Denigration of Vision in Twentieth-Century French Thought*. Berkeley, Los Angeles, London: University of California Press.

Jay, Martin (1994). The Apocalyptic Imagination and the Inability to Mourn. In *Rethinking Imagination: Culture and Creativity*, eds. Gillian Robinson and John Rundell. pp. 30-47. London and New York: Routledge.

Jeater, Diana (1992). "Roast Beef and Reggae Music: The Passing of Whiteness," *New Formations*, 16 (Spring):107-121.

Jeffords, Diana (1989). *The Remasculinization of America*. Bloomington and Indianapolis: Indiana University Press.

Jeffords, Susan (1993). Can Masculinity Be Terminated? In *Screening the Male: Exploring Masculinities in Hollywood Cinema*. Steven Cohan and Ina Rae Hark, eds. pp. 245-262. London and New York: Routledge.

Jenkins, Henry (1992). *Textual Poachers: Television Fans & Participatory Culture*. New York and London: Routledge.

Johnson, Barbara (1980). *The Critical Difference: Essays in the Contemporary Rhetoric of Reading*. Baltimore: John Hopkins University Press.

Johnson, Barbara (1987). *A World of Difference*. Baltimore: John Hopkins University Press.

Jones, Amelia (1994). Postfeminism, Feminist Pleasures, and Embodied Theories of Art. In *New Feminist Criticism: Art, Identity, Action*. Joanna Frueh, Cassandra L. Langer, and Arlene Raven, eds. pp.16-41. New York: HarperCollins Publishers, Icon editions.

Jones, Ann Rosalind (1981). "Writing the Body: Toward an Understanding of L'Écriture Feminine," *Feminist Studies*, 7, 2:247-263.

Joyce, Joyce A. (1987a). "The Black Canon: Reconstructing Black American Literary Criticism," *New Liteary History*, 18, 2:335-344.

Joyce, Joyce A. (1987b). "'Who the Cap Fit': Unconsciousness and Unconsciousableness in the Criticism of Houston A. Baker, Jr., and Henry Louis Gates, Jr.," *New Literary History* 18, 2:371-384.

623

Joyrich, Lynne (1988). "All that Television Allows: TV Melodrama, Postmodernism and Consumer Culture," *camera obscura*, 16:129-153.

Joyrich, Lynne (1990). Critical and Texutual Hypermasculinity. In *Logics of Television: Essays in Cultural Criticism*. Patricia Mellencamp, ed. pp. 156-172. Bloomington and Indianapolis: Indiana University Press. (London: BFI Publications).

Jullian, Philippe (1975). *Dreamers of Decadence*. Trans. Robert Baldick. New York: Praeger Pub.

Julien, Isaac and Kobena Mercer (1988). "Introduction—De Margin and De Centre," *Screen*, 29, 4 (Autumn): 2-12.

Kahn, Douglas and Diane Neumaier, eds. (1985). *Cultures in Contention*. Seattle: The Real Comet Press.

Kaite, Berkeley (1987). The Pornographic Body Double: Transgression is the Law. In *Body Invaders: Panic Sex in America*. Arthur and Louise Kroker, eds. pp. 150-168. New World Perspectives, CultureTexts Series: Montréal.

Kamolz, Klaus and Peter J. Swales (1992a). "Die Verflixten Sieben Jahre," *Profil*, 28, 6 (July): 54-57.

Kamolz, Klaus and Peter J. Swales (1992b). "Ich Drehe Sicher Durch," *Profil*, 29, 13 (July): 63-65.

Kamolz, Klaus and Peter J. Swales (1992c). "Ich Habe Jesus Gefunden," *Profil*, 30, 20 (July): 60-62.

Kaplan, E. Ann (1983). *Women & Film: Both Sides of the Camera*. New York and London: Methuen.

Kaplan, Ann, E. (1987). *Rocking Around the Clock: Music, Television, Postmodernism and Consumer Culture*. London: Methuen.

Kaplan, E. Ann (1988). Introduction. In *Postmodernism and Its Discontents: Theories, Practices*. E.A. Kaplan, ed. London: Verso.

Katz, Jonathan Ned (1990). "The Invention of Heterosexuality," *Socialist Review*, 20, 1 (Jan-March): 7-34.

Kauffman, Linda, ed. (1989). *Gender & Theory: Dialogues on Feminist Criticism*. London: Basil Blackwell.

Kaufman, Michael, ed. (1987). *Beyond Patriarchy: Essays by Men on Pleasure, Power, and Change*. London: Oxford University Press.

Kavanagh, James H. (1990). Feminism, Humanism and Science in Alien. In *Alien Zone: Cultural Theory and Contemporary Science Fiction*. Annette Kuhn, ed. pp. 73-81. New York: Verso.

Kearney, Richard (1988). *The Wake of the Imagination*. London: Hutchison.

Keen, Sam (1991). *Fire in the Belly: On Being a Man*. New York: Bantam.

Keller, Evelyn Fox (1985). *Reflections on Gender & Science*. New Haven: Yale University Press.

Kelly, Mary (1983). *Post-Partum Document*. London, Boston, Melbourne and Henley: Routledge & Kegan Paul.

Kelly, Mary (1991a). Interm: Part I: Corpus, 1984-85. In *Psychoanalysis and Culurual Theory: Thresholds*. James Donald, ed. pp. 51-58. Houndmills, Basingstoke, Hampshire and London: MacMillan Education, Ltd.

Kelly, Mary (1991b). Re-Presenting the Body: On Interim Part I. In *Psychoanalysis and Culurual Theory: Thresholds*. James Donald, ed. pp. 59-67. Houndmills, Basingstoke, Hampshire and London: MacMillan Education, Ltd.

Kenrick, Walter (1987). *The Secret Museum: Pornography in Modern Culture*. New York: Viking Press.

Kent, Sarah, (1986). "Interview with Thérèsa Outon," *Flash Art*, 127, (April): 40-47.

Kent, Sarah and Jacqueline Morreau (1985). *Women's Images of Men*. New York: Writers and Readers Publishing.

Kerby, Anthony Paul (1991). *Narrative and the Self*. Bloomington and Indianapolis: Indiana University Press.

Kierkegaard, S. (1944) *Either-or: A fragment of life*. Trans. David & Lillian Sweson. New Jersey: Princeton University Press.

King, Katie (1990). Producing Sex, Theory, and Culture: Gay/Straight Remappings in Contemporary Feminism. In *Conflicts in Feminism*. Marianne Hirsch and Evelyn Fox Keller, eds. London and New York: Routledge.

Kimball, Samuel (1986). "Banning the Infant: Oedipus, Anti-Oedipus, and Reproduction: The Problematics of Autochthonous Desire," *Subjects/Objects*, 4:34-50.

Kirkland, Gelsey (1986). *Dancing on My Grave*. London: Penguin.

Kleinberg, S. (1980). *Alienated Affections: Being Gay in America*. New York: St. Martin's Press.

Kofman, Sarah (1985). *The Enigma of Woman: Woman in the Writings of Freud*. Trans. Catherine Porter. Ithaca: Cornell University Press.

Kolbowski, Silvia (1884). "(Di)vested Interests," *ZG*, 10 (Spring).

Kolodny, Annette (1980). "Dancing Through the Minefield: Some Observations on the Theory, Practice and Politics of a Feminist Literary Criticism," *Feminist Studies*, 6, 1 (Spring):1-25.

Konner, Melvin (1982). *The Tangled Wing: Biological Constraints on the Human Spirit*. London: Heinemann.

Korzenik, Diana (1985). *Drawn To Art: A Nineteenth Century American Dream*. Nanover, N.H.: University of Press of New England.

Kowinski, William Severini (1985). Mallaise: How to Know If You Have It. In William S. Kowinski's *The Malling of America: An Insider's Look at the Great Consumer Paradise*. pp. 337-42. N.Y.: William Morrow.

Krauss, Rosiland (1981). "The Originality of the Avant-Garde: A Postmodernist Repetition," *October*, 18 (Fall):47-66.

Krauss, Rosiland (1985). *The Originality of the Avant-Garde and Other Modern Myths.* Cambridge, Massachusetts: MIT Press.

Krauss, Rosiland (1988). The Im/pulse To See. In *Vision and Visuality: Dia Art Foundation Discussions in Contemporary Culture: Number 2.* Hal Foster, ed. pp. 51-78. Bay Press: Seattle.

Krauss, Rosiland (1993). *The Optical Unconscious.* Cambridge, Mass.; MIT Press.

Krauss, Rosiland and Jane Livingston (1985). *L'Amour Fou: Photography and Surrealism.* New York: Abbeville Press.

Kristeva, Julia (1980). *Desire in Language: A Semiotic Approach to Literature and Art.* Trans. Thomas Gora, Alice Jardine, and Leone S. Roudiez. New York: Columbia University Press.

Kristeva, Julia (1980). Motherhood According to Giovanni Bellini. In *Desire in Language: A Semiotic Approach to Literature and Art.* Trans. Thomas Gora, Alice Jardine, and Leone S. Roudiez. New York: Columbia University Press.

Kristeva, Julia ((1981). Woman Can Never be Defined. In *New French Feminists.* Trans. Marilyn A. August. Elaine Marks and Isabelle de Courtivron, eds. pp. 137-141. New York: Schocken Books.

Kristeva, Julia (1982). *Powers of Horror: An Essay on Abjection.* Trans. Leon S. Roudiez. New York: Columbia University Press.

Kristeva, Julia (1984). *Revolution in Poetic Language.* Trans. Margaret Waller. New York: Columbia University Press.

Kristeva, Julia (1986a). Women's Time (1979). In *The Kristeva Reader.* Toril Moi, ed. pp. 187-213. N.Y.: Columbia University Press. Also (1981). "Woman's Time," Trans. Alice Jardine and Harry Blake, Signs, 7, 1:13-35.

Kristeva, Julia (1986b). Stabat Mother. In *The Kristeva Reader.* Toril Moi, ed. pp. 160-186. N.Y.: Columbia University Press.

Kroker, Arthur and David Cook (1987) *The Postmodern Scene: Excremental Culture and Hyper-aesthetics.* Montréal: New World Perspectives.

Kroker, Arthur and Marilouise Kroker, eds. (1987). *Body Invaders: Panic Sex in America.* Montréal: New World Perspectives, CultureTexts Series.

Kroker, Arthur, Kroker, Marilouise and David Cook eds. (1989). *Panic Encyclopedia.* Montréal: New World Perspectives, CultureTests Series.

Kroker, Arthur and Marilouise Kroker, eds. (1991). *The Hysterical Male: New Feminist Theory.* Montréal: New World Perspectives, CultureTexts Series.

Kroker, Arthur and Marilouise Kroker, eds. (1993). *The Last Sex: Feminism and Outlaw Bodies.* Montréal: New World Perspectives.

Kruger, Barbara (1983). *We Won't Play Nature to Your Culture.* London: Institute of Contemporary Art.

Kuenzli, Rudolf E. (1991). Surrealism and Mysogyny. In *Surrealism and Women*. Mary Ann Caws, Rudolf E. Kuenzli, and Gwen Raaberg, eds. pp. 17-26. Cambridge, Massachusetts and London: The MIT Press.

Kuhn, Annette (1982). *Women's Pictures: Feminism and Cinema*. London: Routledge Kegan Paul, Ltd.

Kuhn, Annette (1985). *The Power of the Image: Essays on Representation and Sexuality*. London: Routledge Kegan Paul, Ltd.

Kuhn, Annette (1988). The Body and Cinema: Some Problems for Feminism. In *Crafts: Feminist Cultural Criticism*. Susan Sheridan, ed. pp. 1-10. London and New York: Verso.

Kureishi, Hanif (1985). "Dirty Washing," *Time Out* (November): 14-20.

Kuspit, Donald (1984). Flak from the "Radicals": The American Case against German Painting. In *Art After Modernism: Rethinking Representation*. Brian Wallis, ed. pp. 137-152. The New Museum of Contemporary Art, New York in association with Boston: David R. Godine, Pub., Inc.

Kuspit, Donald (1990). The Contradictory Character of Postmodernism. In *Postmodernism—Philosophy and the Arts*. Hugh J. SIlverman, ed. pp. 53-68. Routledge, Chapman, Hall, Inc.

Lacan, Jacques (1977). *Écrits: A Selection*. Trans. Alan Sheridan. New York and London: W.W. Norton & Company.

Lacan, Jacques (1979). What is a Picture. In *Four Fundamental Concepts of Psycho-Analysis*. Trans. Alan Sheridan. Jacques-Alain Miller, ed. pp. 105-122. London: Penguin Books.

Lacan, Jacques (1982). God and the *Jouissance* of Woman. In *Feminine Sexuality: Jacques Lacan and the École Freudienne*. Trans. Jacqueline Rose. Juliet Mitchell and Jacqueline Rose, eds. pp. 137-161. New York and London: W.W. Norton & Company.

Lacan, Jacques (1992). Courtly Love as Anamorphosis. In *The Ethics of Psychoanalyis 1959-1960. The Seminar of Jacques Lacan*. Trans. with notes by Dennis Porter. Jacques-Allain Miller, ed. pp. 139-154. London and New York: Tavistock/ Routledge. (First published by W.W.. Norton & Company, Inc., 1992).

Laclau, E. and Chantal Mouffe (1985). *Hegemony and Socialist Strategy: Towards a Radical Democratic Politics*. London: Verso.

Landers, Richard R. (1966). *Man's Place in the Dyboshpere*. New Jersey, Englewood Cliffs: Prentice-Hall, Inc.

Landry, Donna and Gerald MacLean (1993). *Materialist Feminisms*. Cambridge, Massachusetts and London: Blackwell Publishers.

Langer, Cassandra (1988). Against the Grain: A Working Gynergenic Art Criticism. In *Feminist Art Criticism: An Anthology*. Arlene Raven, Cassandra Langer, and Joanna Frueh, eds. pp. 111-132. London and Ann Arbor: University Microfilms Inc. Research Press.

Langer, Cassandra (1994). Transgressing Le Doit du Seigneur: The Lesbian Feminist Defining Herself in Art History. In *New Feminist Criticism: Art, Identity, Action*. Joanna Frueh, Cassandra L. Langer, and Arlene Raven. pp. 306-326. New York: Harper Collins Publishers (IconEditions).

627

Laplanche, J. and J.-B. Pontalis (1968). "Fantasy and the Origins of Sexuality," The *International Journal of Psycho-Analysis*, 49. Reprinted in *Formations of Fantasy*. Victor Burgin, James Donald, and Cora Kaplan, eds. pp. 5-34. London and New York: Methuen.

Laplanche, J. and J.-B. Pontalis (1973). *The Language of Psycho-analysis*. London: The Hogarth Press and the Institute of Psycho-analysis.

Lapsley, Rob and Michael Westlake (1992). "From Casablanca to Pretty Woman: The Politics of Romance," *Screen*, 33, 1 (Spring):27-49. Reprinted in (1993) *Contemporary Film Theory*. Anthony Easthope, ed. and introduced. pp. 179-203. London and New York: Longman.

Laqueur, Thomas (1990). *Making Sex: Body and Gender from the Greeks to Freud*. Cambridge: Harvard University Press.

Lash, Christopher (1979). *The Culture of Narcissism: American Life in an Age of Diminishing Expectations*. New York: Warner Books.

Lash, Scott (1984). "Genealogy and the Body: Foucault/ Deleuze/ Nietzsche," *Theory Culture & Society*, 2, 2:1-16.

Lauter, E. (1984). *Women as Mythmakers: Poetry and Visual Art by Twentieth-Century Women*. Bloomington and Indianapolis: Indiana University Press.

Lebeau, Vickey (1995). *Lost Angels: Psychoanalysis and Cinema*. London and New York: Routledge.

Lehman, David (1992). *Signs of the Times: Deconstruction and the Fall of Paul de Man*. New York: Poseidon Press.

Lee, Janet (1989). Care To Join Me In an Upwardly Mobile Tango: Postmodernism and the 'New Woman.' In *The Female Gaze: Women as Viewers of Popular Culture*. Seattle. Lorraine Gamman and Margaret Marshment, eds. pp.166-172. Seattle: The Real Comet Press.

Lee, John (1989). *The Flying Boy: Healing the Wounded Man*. Deerfield Beach, Fla.: Health Communications, Inc.

Lee, Rosa (1987). "Resisting Amnesia: Feminism, Painting and Postmodernism," *Feminist Review*, 26 (July): 6-26.

Leitch, Vincent B. (1983). *Deconstructive Criticism: An Advanced Introduction*. New York: Columbia Press.

Leng, Kwok Wei (1993). "Muscle: Or How to Impress With Flesh and Be a Social Theorist Too," *Melbourne Journal of Politics*, 21:55- 72.

Lentricchia, Frank (1987). "Patriarchy Against Itself—The Young Manhood of Wallace Stevens," *Critical Inquiry*, 13 (Summer):742-786.

Lentricchia, Frank (1988). "Andiamo," Critical Inquiry, 14, 2 (Winter):407-413.

Lenz, Elenor and Barbara Mayerhoff (1985). *The Feminization of America: How Women's Values are Changing Our Public & Private Lives*. Los Angeles: Jeremy P. Tarcher, Inc.

Le Pichon, Yann (1987). *Gauguin: Life, Art, Inspiration*. Trans. Mark Paris. New York: Harry Abrams, Inc., Pub.

Lerner, Gerta (1986). *The Ceation of Patriarchy*. New York: Oxford University Press.

Levin, Michael, ed. (1993). *Modernity and the Hegemony of Vision*. Berkeley, Los Angeles and London: University of California Press.

Levine, Sylvia and Joseph Koenig (1980). *Why Men Rape*. Toronto: MacMillan Press.

Lewallen, Avis (1989). Lace: Poronography for Women. In *The Female Gaze: Women as Viewers of Popular Culture*. Seattle. Lorraine Gamman and Margaret Marshment, eds. pp. 86-101. Seattle: The Real Comet Press.

Lewis, Reina (1994). "DIS-GRACEFUL IMAGES: Della Grace and Lesbian Sado-masochism," *Feminist Review*, 46 (Spring):76-91.

Leyland, Winston (1978). *Gay Sunshine Interviews*. San Francisco: Gay Sunshine Press.

Lichtman, Richard (1982). *The Production of Desire: The Integration of Psychoanalysis into Marxist Theory*. New York and London: The Free Press.

Lichtenstein, Jacqueline (1987). "Making Up Representation: The Risks of Femininity," *Representations*, 20 (Fall):77-87.

Lima, Costa Luiz (1988). *Control of the Imaginary: Reason and Imagination in Modern Times*. Trans. Ronald W. Sousa. Minneapolis: University of Minnesota Press.

Lippard, Lucy (1976). *From the Center: On Women's Art*. New York: Dutton.

Lippard, Lucy (1984). *Get the Message? A Decade of Art for Social Change*. New York: E.P. Dutton, Inc.

Lippard, Lucy (1983). *Overlays: Contemporary Art and the Art of Prehistory*. New York: Pantheon Books.

Liu, Albert (1993). "The Last Days of Arnold Schwarzenegger," *Genders*, 18 (Winter):102-112.

Lloyd, Genevieve (1984). *The Man of Reason: "Male" and "Female" in Western Philosophy*. London: Methuen.

Lloyd, Genevieve (1989). The Man of Reason. In *Women, Knowledge, and Reality: Explorations in Feminist Philosophy*. Ann Garry and Marilyn Pearsall, eds. pp. 111-128. Boston: Unwin Hyman.

Lobel, Kerry (1986). *Naming the Violence: Speaking Out About Lesbian Battery*. Washington: Seal Press.

Lovibond, Sabina (1989). "Feminism and Postmodernism," *New Left Review*, 178 (Nov-Dec): 5-19.

Lowe, Donald M. (1982). *History of Bourgeois Perception*. Chicago: Chicago University Press.

Luke, Carmen and Jennifer Gore, eds. (1992). *Feminisms and Critical Pedagogy*. New York and London: Routledge.

Lunn, Eugene (1982). *Marxism & Modernism: An Historical Study of Lukács, Brecht, Benjamin and Adorno*. London, Berkeley, Los Angeles: University of California Press.

Lurie, Alison (1983). The *Language of Clothes*. New York: Vintage Books, Random House.

Lutz, Catherine A. and Jane L. Collins (1993). *Reading National Geographic*. Chicago: University of Chicago Press.

Lyon, Eleanor (1990). Media Murder and Mayhem: Violence on Network Television. In *Marginal Conventions: Popular Culture, Mass Media and Social Deviance*. Clinton R. Sanders, ed. pp. 144–153. Bowling Green, Ohio: Bowling Green State University Popular Press.

Lyotard, Jean-François (1971). *Discours, figure*. Paris: Klincksieck.

MacCannell, Juliet Flower (1986). "Kristeva's Horror," *Semiotica*, 62, 3/4: 325-355.

MacCannell, Juliet Flower (1991). *The Regime of the Brother: After the Patriarchy*. New York and London: Routledge.

MacCannell, Juliet Flower (1994). Things to Come: A Hysteric's Guide to the Future Female Subject. In *Supposing the Subject*. Joan Copjec, ed. pp. 106-132. N.Y. and London: Verso.

MacKinnon, Catherine A. (1988). Desire and Power: A Feminist Perspective. In *Marxism and the Interpretation of Culture*. Carry Nelson and Lawrence Grossberg, eds. pp. 105-122. Urbana and Chicago: University of Illinois Press.

MacKinnon, Catherine A. (1993). *Only Words*. Cambridge, Mass.: Harvard University Press.

MacKinnon, Catherine A. (1994). "To the Editors: Reply to Ronald Dworkin," *New York Review of Books*, March, 3:47-48.

MacLean, M., Gerald (1989). Citing the Subject. In *Gender and Theory: Dialogues on Feminist Criticism*. Linda Kauffman, ed. Oxford: Basil Blackwell.

MacLeod, Shiela (1981). *The Art of Starvation*. London: Virago.

Mager, Don (1985). "Gay Theories of Gender and Role Deviance," *SubStance*, 46.

Mahbobah, Albaraq (1992). "Reading the Anorexic Maze," *Genders*, 14 (Fall):87-97.

Mann, Karen B. (1989-90). "Narrative Entanglements: The Terminator," *Film Quarterly*, 43, 2:17-27.

Marcuse, Herbert (1962). *Eros and Civilization*. New York: Vintage.

Marks, Elaine and Isabelle de Courtivron (1981). *New French Femininisms: An Anthology*. New York: Schocken Books.

Marin, Louis (1980). Toward A Theory of Reading in the Visual Arts: Poussin's The Arcadian Shepherds. In *The Reader In the Text: Essays on Audience and Interpretation*. Susan R. Suleiman and Inge Crosman, eds. pp. 293-324. Princeton: Princeton University Press.

Martens, Lorna (1985). "Saying 'I'," *Stanford Literature Review*, 2, 1:27-46.

Martin, Stephen-Paul (1988). *Open Form and the Feminine Imagination*. Washington, D.C.: Maisonneuve Press.

Martin, Wendy (1984). Another View of the 'City Upon a Hill': The Prophetic Vision of Adrienne Rich. In *Women Writers and the City: Essays in Feminist Literary Criticism*. Susan Merril Squier, ed. pp. 249-264. Knoxville: University of Tennesse Press.

Martin, Biddy (1988). Feminism, Criticism, and Foucault. In *Feminism & Foucault: Reflections of Resistance*. Irene Diamond and Lee Quinby, eds. pp. 3-20. Boston: Northeastern University Press.

Mattick, Paul Jr. (1990). "Beautiful and Sublime: Gender Totemism in the Consitution of Art," *Journal of Aesthetics and Art Criticism*, 48, 4 (Fall):293-303.

Mayne, Judith (1987). Walking the Tightrope of Feminism and Male Desire. In *Men in Feminism*. Alice Jardine and Paul Smith, eds. pp.62-70. London and New York: Methuen.

Mayne, Judith (1993). *Cinema and Spectatorship*. London and New York: Routledge.

Mays, John Bently (1994). "Prints of Perversion Expose Photographer's Humanity," *The Globe and Mail* (Toronto) (Saturday, April 23): C12.

McCabe, Colin (1978). *James Joyce and the Revolution of the Word*. London: MacMillan Ltd.

McCann, Graham (1991). Biographical Boundaries: Sociology and Marilyn Monroe. In *The Body: Social Process and Cultural Theory*. Mike Featherstone, Mike Hepworth, and Bryan S. Turner, eds. London, Newbury Park, New Delhi: Sage Publishers,

McClary, Susan (1990). "Living to Tell: Madonna's Resurrection of the Fleshy," *Genders*, 7 (Spring):1-21.

McClintock, Anne (1992). "Screwing the System: Sexwork, Race, and the Law," *boundary*, 2, 19, 2 (Summer):70-95.

McClintock, Anne (1993a). "The Return of Female Fetishism and the Fiction of the Phallus," *New Formations*, 19 (Spring):1-21.

McClintock, Anne (1993b)."Sex Workers and Sex Work," *Social Text*, 37 :1-10.

McClintock, Anne (1993c). "Maid to Order: Commercial Fetishism and Gender Power," *Social Text*, 37: 87-116. Also in (1993). *Dirty Looks: Women, Pornography, Power*. Pamela Church Gibson and Roma Gibson, eds. pp. 207-232. London: The British Film Institute.

McDonald, Christie and Jacques Derrida (1982). "Interview: Choreographies," *Diacritics*, 12 (Summer):66-76.

McGowan, John (1991). *Postmodernism and Its Critics*. Ithaca and London: Cornell University Press.

McHale, Brian (1987). *Postmodern Fiction*. New York and London: Methuen.

McLaren, Peter (1993). "Multiculturalism and the Postmodern Critique: Towards a Pedagogy of Resistance and Transformation," *Cultural Studies*, 7, 1:118-146.

McLelland, Jane (1983). "Now that the Muse is Writing: Écriture Féminine and Contemporary French Women's Poetry," *Contemporary Literature*, XXIV, 2:158-175.

McRobbie, Angela (1980). "Settling Accounts with Subculures," *Screen Education*, 34:37-49.

McRobbie, Angela and Jenny Garber (1975). Girls and Subcultures—An Exploration. In *Resistance Through Rituals*. Stuart Hall and Tony Jefferson, eds. pp. 209-222. London: Hutchinson.

McRobbie, Angela and M. Nava, eds. (1984). *Gender and Generation*. London: Macmillan.

Mercer, Kobena (1986). Imagining the Black Man's Sex. In *Photography/Politics: Two*. Patricia Holland, Jo Spence, and Simon Watney, eds. pp. 61-69. London: Comedia/Methuen. Repr. in (1993). *Fetishism as Cultural Discourse*. Emily Apter and William Pietz, eds. pp.308-318. Ithaca and London: Cornell University Press.

Mercer, Kobena and Julien, Issac (1988). Race, Sexual Politics and Black Masculinity: A Dossier. In *Male Order: Unwrapping Masculinity*. Rowena Chapman and Jonathan Rutherford, eds. pp. 97-164. London: Lawrence & Wishart.

Mercer, Kobena (1989). The Mirror Looks Back: Racial Fetishism Reconsidered (1989). In *Reading Racial Fetishism: The Photographs of Robert Mapplethorpe*. In (1993) *Fetishism as Cultural Discourse*. Emily Apter and William Pietz, eds. pp.318-329. Ithaca and London: Cornell University

Mercer, Kobena (1990a). "1968": Periodizing Postmodern Politics and Identity. In Cultural Studies. Lawrenge Grossberg, Cary Nelson, and Paula Treichler, eds. pp. 424-449. London and New York: Routledge.

Mercer, Kobena (1990b). Black Hair/Style Politics. In *Out There: Marginalization and Contemporary Cultures*. Russell Ferguson, Martha Gever, Trinh T. Minh-ha, and Cornel West, eds. New York, New York: The New Museum of Contemporary Art.

Mercer, Kobena (1992)." Skin Head Sex Thing: Racial Differences and the Homeoerotic Imagery," *New Formations*, 16 (Spring):1-23.

Mercer, Kobena (1993). Reading Racial Fetishism: The Photographs of Robert Mapplethorpe. In *Fetishism as Cultural Discourse*. Emily Apter and William Pietz, eds. pp.307-330. Ithaca and London: Cornell University Press.

Merck, Mandy (1993). *Perversions: Deviant Readings*. Candem Town, London: Virago Press.

Merrell, Floyd (1985). *Deconstruction Reframed*. West Lafayette, Indiana: Purdue University Press.

Metz, Christian (1982). *The Imaginary Signifier: Psychoanalysis and the Cinema*. Trans. Celia Britton, Annwyl Williams, Ben Brewster and Alfred Gezzetti. Bloomington and Indianapolis: Indiana University Press.

Metcalf, Amy and Martin Humphries, eds. (1985). *The Sexuality of Men*. London: Pluto Press.

Meyrowitz, Joshua (1986). *No Sense of Place: The Impact of Electronic Media on Social Behavior*. New York and Oxford: Oxford University Press.

Midgley, Mary (1988). On Not Being Afraid of Natural Sex Differences. In *Feminist Perspectives in Philosophy*. Morwenna Griffiths, and Margaret Whitford, eds. pp. 29-41. Bloomington and Indianapolis: Indiana University Press.

Miklitsch, Robert (1991). "Troping Prostitution: Two or Three Things about (Post)-Marxism/Feminism," *Genders*, 12 (Winter):120-139.

Miller, James (1992). *Fluid Exchanges: Artists and Critics in the AIDS Crisis*. Toronto, Buffalo, London: University of Toronto Press.

Miller, Nancy K, (1986a). Changing the Subject: Authorship, Writing and the Reader. In *Feminist Studies/Critical Studies*. Teresa de Lauretis, ed. pp.102-120. Bloomington and Indianapolis: Indiana University Press.

Miller, Nancy K. (1986b). Arachnologies: The Woman, the Text, and the Critic. In *The Poetics of Gender*. Nancy K. Miller, ed. pp. 270-296. New York: Columbia University Press.

Miller, Nancy, ed. (1986c). *The Poetics of Gender*. New York: Columbia Unversity Press.

Miller, Nancy (1987). Man in Feminism: A Criticism of His Own. In *Men in Feminism*. Alice Jardine and Paul Smith, eds. pp.137-145. London and New York: Methuen.

Miller, Nancy, ed. (1988). *Subject to Change: Reading Feminist Writings*. New York: Columbia University Press.

Millett, Kate (1969). *Sexual Politics*. New York: Ballantine.

Millot, Catherine (1990a). The Feminine Superego. In *The Woman in Question, m/f*. Parveen Adams and Elizabeth Cowie, eds. pp. 294-306. An October Book. Cambridge, Mass.: MIT Press.

Millot, Catherine (1990b). *Horsexe: Essay on Transsexuality*. Trans. Kenneth Hylton. Brooklyn, New York: Autonomedia.

Miner, Dorothy (1974). *Anastaise and Her Sisters: Women Artists of the Middle Ages*. Baltimore: Walters Art Gallery.

Mishkind, Marc E., Judith Rodin, Lisa R. Silberstein, and Ruth H. Striegel-Moore (1986). "The Embodiment of Masculinity: Cultural Psychological, and Behavioral Dimensions," *American Behavioral Scientist*, 29, 5 (May/June):545-562.

Mitchell, Juliet (1974). *Psychoanalysis and Feminism: Freud, Reich, Laing and Women*. New York: Vintage Books.

Mitchell, Juliet and Jacqueline Rose, eds. (1982). Jacques Lacan: God and the *Jouissance* of Woman. In *Feminine Sexuality: Jacques Lacan and the École Freudienne*. Trans. Jacqueline Rose. Juliet Mitchell and Jacqueline Rose, eds. pp. 137-161. New York and London : W.W. Norton & Company.

Miyoshi, Masao (1993). "A Borderless World? From Colonialism to Transnationalism and the Decline of the Nation-State," *Critical Inquiry*, 19 (Summer): 726-751.

Modleski, Tania (1982). *Loving With A Vengence: Mass-Produced Fantasies for Women*. Hamden, Connecticut: The Shoe String Press, Inc., an Anchor Book.

Modleski, Tania (1986a). Femininity as Mas[s]querade: A Feminist Approach to Mass Culture. In *High Theory/Low Culture: Analyzing Popular Television and Film*. Colin McCabe, ed. pp. 37-52. N.Y.: St. Martin's Press.

Modleski, Tania (1986b). Feminism and the Power of Interpretation. In *Feminist Studies/Critical Studies*. Teresa de Lauretis, ed. pp. 121-138. Bloomington and Indianapolis: Indiana University Press.

Modleski, Tania (1988a). *The Women Who Knew Too Much: Hitchcock and Feminist Theory*. New York: Methuen.

633

Modleski, Tania (1988b). "A Father Is Being Beaten: Male Feminism and the War Film," *Discourse*, X, 2 (Spring-Summer):62-77.

Modleski, Tania (1991a). Lethal Bodies: Thoughts on Sex, Gender, and Representation from the Mainstream to the Margins. In Tania Modleski's *Feminism Without Women: Culture and Criticism in a "Postmodern Age."* pp. 135-163. London and New York: Routledge.

Modleski, Tania (1991b). "Three Men and Baby M." In Tania Modleski's *Feminism Without Women: Culture and Criticism in a "Postmodern Age."* pp. 76-89. London and New York: Routledge.

Modleski, Tania (1991c). The Incredible Shrinking He[r]man: Male Regression, the Male Body, and Film. In Tania Modleski's *Feminism Without Women: Culture and Criticism in a "Postmodern Age."* pp. 90-111. London and New York: Routledge. (Reprinted in (1990) *differences: A Journal of Feminist Cultural Studies*, 2, 2 (Summer).

Mohanty, Chandra (1988). "Under Western Eyes: Feminist Scholarship and Colonial Discourses," *Feminist Review*, 30:61-88.

Moi, Toril (1985). *Sexual/Textual Politics: Feminist Literary Theory*. London and New York: Methuen.

Moi, Toril (1988). "Feminism, Postmodernism, and Style: Recent Feminist Criticism in the United States," *Cultural Critique*, 9 (Spring): 3-24.

Moi, Toril (1994). *Simone De Beauvoir: The Making of an Intellectual Woman*. London: Blackwell, Pubs.

Montrelay, Michele (1978). "Inquiry into Femininity," *m/f*, 1:83-101. (Reprinted in (1990). *The Woman in Question, m/f*. Parveen Adamsa and Elizabeth Cowie, ed. pp 253-273. Cambridge, Mass.: The MIT Press).

Moon, Michael (1993). New Introduction. In *Homosexual Desire*. Guy Hocquenghem. pp. 9-21. Durham and London: Duke University Press.

Moore, Henrietta L. (1988) *Feminism and Anthropology*. Basil Blackwell: Polity Press.

Moore, Robert and Douglas Gillette (1991). *King Warrior, Magician Lover: Rediscovering the Archetypes of the Mature Masculine*. San Francisco: HarperSan Francisco.

Moore, Suzanne (1988). Getting a Bit of the Other—the Pimps of Postmodernism. In *Male Order: Unwrapping Masculinity*. Rowena Chapman and Jonathan Rutherford, eds. pp. 165-192. London: Lawrence & Wishart.

Moore, Suzanne (1989). Here's Looking at You, Kid! In *The Female Gaze: Women as Viewers of Popular Culture*. Lorraine Gamman and Margaret Marshment, eds. pp. 44-59. Seattle: The Real Comet Press.

Morris, Megan (1987). "in any event." In *Men in Feminism*. Alice Jardine and Paul Smith, eds. pp. 173-181. London and New York: Methuen.

Morris, Megan (1988). "Banality in Cultural Studies," *Discourse* X, 2 (Spring-Summer): 3-29.

Morrison, Paul (1991). "Coffee Table Sex: Robert Mapplethorpe and the Sadomasochism of Everyday Life," *Genders*, 11 (Fall):17-36.

Morgan, Robin (1980). Theory and Practice: Pornography and Rape. In *Take Back the Night: Women on Pornography*. Laura Lederer, ed. New York: Morrow.

Muller, John P. and William Richardson, eds. (1993). *The Purloined Poe: Lacan, Derrida, and Psychoanalytic Reading*, 4th Printing. Baltimore and London: The John Hopkins University Press.

Mulvey, Laura (1975). "Visual Pleasure and Narrative Cinema," *Screen*, 16, 3 (Autumn): 6-18.

Mulvey, Laura (1981). "Afterthoughts on 'Visual Pleasure and Narrative Cinema' inspired by King Vidor's Duel in the Sun (1946)," *Framework*, 15, 16, 17 (Summer). (Reprinted in Laura Mulvey's (1989). *Visual and Other Pleasures*. pp. 29-38. Bloomington and Indianapolis: Indiana University Press).

Mulvey, Laura (1989). *Visual and Other Pleasures*. Bloomington and Indianapolis: Indiana University Press.

Munster, Anna (1986). Playing With A Different Sex: Between The Covers of Irigaray and Gallop. In *Futur*Fall: Excursions into Post-Modernity*. E.A. Grosz, Terry Threadgold, David Kelly, Alan Cholodenko, and Edward Colless, eds. pp.118-127. Sydney: Power Institute of Fine Arts, University of Sydney.

Myers, Kathy (1982). "Towards a Feminist Erotics," *Camerawork*, 24 (March).

Myers, Kathy (1984). Pasting Over the Cracks. In *Desire*. Lisa Appignanesi, ed. pp. 35-38. London: Institute of Contemporary Arts Documents.

Naficy, Hamid (1991). "The Poetics and Practice of Iranian Nostalgia in Exile," *Diaspora*, 1, 3 (Winter): 285-302.

Naficy, Hamid and Gabriel H. Teshome, eds. (1991). "Discourse of the Other: Postcoloniality, Positionality, and Subjectivity," *Quarterly Review of Film and Video*, 13:1-3.

Nead, Lynda (1989). *Myths of Sexuality: Representations of Women in Victorian Britain*. London: Blackwell.

Nead, Lynda (1992). *The Female Nude: Art, Obscenity and Sexuality*. New York and London: Routledge.

Neale, Steve (1983). "Masculinity as Spectacle: Reflections on Men and Mainstream Cinema," *Screen*, 24, 26 (Nov.-Dec.): 2-16. (Reprinted in (1993). *Screening the Male: Exploring Masculinities in Hollywood Cinema*. Steven Cohan and Ina Rae Hark, eds. pp. 9-22. London and New York: Routledge).

Neale, Steve (1982). " 'Chariots of Fire,' Images of Men," *Screen*, 23, 3/4 (Sept.-Oct.): 47-53.

Nelson, Cary (1987). Men, Feminism: The Materiality of Discourse. In *Men in Feminism*. Alice Jardine and Paul Smith, eds. pp.153-172. London and New York: Methuen.

Neuman, Shirley (1990). Your past...your future? Autobiography and Mothers' Bodies. 3rd lecture. *Edmund Kemper Broadus Lectures*. University of Alberta, Edmonton, Alberta. Monday, January 29.

Newton, Esther (1972). *Mother Camp: Female Impersonators in America*. Chicago: Chicago University Press.

Newton, Judith. (1990). Feminism and Anxiety in Alien. In *Alien Zone: Cultural Theory and Contemporary Science Fiction*. Annette Kuhn, ed. pp. 82-90. New York: Verso.

Nichols, Bill (1991). *Representing Reality: Issues and Concepts in Documentary*. Bloomington and Indianapolis: Indiana University Press.

Niranjana, Tesjaswini (1992). *Siting Translation: History, Post-Structuralism, and the Colonial Context*. Berkeley: University of California Press.

Nixon, Mignon (1992). "You Thrive on Mistaken Identity," *October*, 60 (Spring): 59-82.

Nochimson, Martha (1992). *No End To Her: Soap Opera and the Female Subject*. Berkeley, Los Angeles, Oxford: University of California Press.

Nochlin, Linda (1973). Why Have There Been No Great Women Artists? In *Art and Sexual Politics: Women's Liberation, Women Artists, and Art History*. Thomas B. Hess and Elizabeth C. Baker, eds. pp. 1-43. N.Y.: Macmillan Pub. Co.

Nochlin, Linda (1988). *Women, Art, and Power and Other Essays*. New York: Harper & Row, Publishers.

Nochlin, Linda and Harris A. Sutherland (1976). *Women Artists 1550-1950*. New York: Alfred Knopf.

Nodding, Nel (1984). *Caring*. Berkeley: University of California Press.

Norris, Christopher (1990). *What's Wrong With Postmodernism: Critical Theory and the Ends of Philosophy*. Baltimore: The Johns Hopkins University.

Norris, Margot (1985). Max Ernst: The Rhetorical Beast of the Visual Arts. In *Beasts of the Modern Imagination: Darwin. Nietzsche, Kafka, Ernst, and Lawrence*. pp. 134-169. Baltimore: John Hopkins University Press.

Nunokawa, Jeff (1991). 'All the Sad Young Men': AIDS and the Work of Mourning. In *Inside/Out: Lesbian Theories, Gay Theories*. Diana Fuss, ed. pp. 311-323. New York and London: Routledge.

O'Grady, Lorraine (1994). Olympia's Maif: Reclaiming Black Female Subjectivity. In *New Feminist Criticism: Art, Identity, Action*. Joanna Frueh, Cassandra L. Langer, and Arlene Raven, eds. pp. 152-170. New York: HarperCollins Publishers (IconEditions).

O'Brien, Mary (1981). *The Politics of Reproduction*. Boston, London, and Henley: Routledge & Kegan Paul, Ltd.

Olalquiaga, Celeste (1992). *Megalopolis: Contemporary Cultural Sensibilities*. Minneapolis and London: University of Minnesota Press.

Oliver, Kelly A. (1984). "Woman as Truth in Nietzsche's Writing," *Social Theory and Practice*, 10, 2 (Summer): 185-199.

Olver, Kelly A. (1993). Introduction: Julia Kristeva's Outlaw Ethics. In *Ethics, Politics, and Difference in Julia Kristeva's Writing*. Kelly Olver, ed. pp.1-22. New York and London: Routledge.

Oliver, Kelly A. (1995). *Womanizing Nietzsche: Philosophy's Relation to the Feminine*. New York and London: Routledge.

Olkowski, Dorothea (1985). If the Shoe Fits—Derrida and the Orientation of Thought. In *Hermeneutics & Deconstruction*. Hugh J. Silverman and Don Ihde, eds. pp. 262-270. New York: State University of New York Press.

Omi, Michael and Howard Winant (1986). *Racial Formations in the United States*. New York and London: Routledge & Kegan Paul, Ltd.

Ondaatje, Michael (1992). *The English Patient*. Vintage Books.

Opie, Anne (1992). "Qualitative Research, Appropriation of the 'Other' and Empowerment," *Feminist Review*, 40 (Spring): 52-69.

Orbach, Susie (1986) *Hunger Strike: The Anorectic's Struggle as a Metaphor for Our Age*. London: Farber & Farber.

Orenstein, Gloria Feman (1988). The Reemergence of Archetype of the Great Goddess in Art by Contemporary Women. In *Feminist Art Criticism: An Anthology*. Arlene Raven, Cassandra Langer, and Joanna Frueh, eds. pp. 71-96. London and Ann Arbor: University Microfilms Inc. Research Press.

Ortner, Sherry (1974). Is Female to Male as Nature Is to Culture? In *Woman, Culture and Society*. Louise Lamphere and Michelle Rosaldo, eds. Stanford, Caifornia: Stanford University Press.

Oresy, Lionel (1969). *Homosexuality and Pseudosexuality*. New York: Science House.

Owens, Craig (1982). "Representation, Appropriation & Power," *Art in America*, 70, 5 (May): 9-21.

Owens, Craig (1983). The Medusa Effect or, The Spectacular Ruse. In *We Won't Play Nature to Your Culture*: Barbara Kruger. London: Institute of Contemporary Arts.

Owens, Craig (1987). Outlaws: Guys, Men in Feminism. In *Men in Feminism*. Alice Jardine and Paul Smith, eds. pp. 220-232. London and New York: Methuen.

Owens, Craig (1992). *Beyond Recognition: Representation, Power and Culture*. Scott Bryson, Barbara Kruger, Lynne Tillman, and Jane Weinstock, eds. Introduction by Simon Watney. Berkeley, Los Angeles, Oxford: University of California Press.

Pacteau, Francette (1986). The Impossible Referent: Representation of the Androgyne. In *Formations of Fantasy*. Victor Burgin, James Donald, and Cora Kaplan, eds. pp. 62-84. London and New York: Metheun.

Paglia, Camille (1990). *Sexual Personae: Art and Decadence From Neferititi to Emily Dickinson*. London & New Haven: Yale University Press.

Paglia, Camille (1992). *Sex, Art, and American Culture: Essays*. New York: Random House, Inc, Vintage Book.

Parker, Rozsika and Griselda Pollock (1981). *Old Mistresses: Women, Art and Ideology*. London: Routledge & Kegan Paul, Ltd.

Parker, Rozsika and Griselda Pollock (1987). *Framing Feminism: Art and the Women's Movement: 1970-1985*. London: Pandora Press.

Parker, Rozsika (1984). *The Subversive Stitch: Embroidery and the Making of the Feminine*. London: The Women's Press.

Parks, Michael E. (1989). "Art Education in a Post-Modern Age," *Art Education*, 42, 2 (March): 10-13.

Patton, Cindy (1991). *Inventing AIDS*. New York: Routledge.

Patton, Paul (1986). Ethics and Post-Modernity. In *Futur*Fall: Excursions into Post-Modernity*. E.A. Grosz, Terry Threadgold, David Kelly, Alan Cholodenko, and Edward Colless, eds. pp. 128-145. Sydney: Power Institute of Fine Arts, University of Sydney.

Pavletich, JoAnn (1992). "Muscling the Mainstream: Lesbian Murder Mysteries and Fantasies of Justice," *Discourse*, 15, 1 (Fall): 94-111.

Pecheaux, Michel (1975). *Language, Semantics and Ideology*. New York: St Martin's Press.

Pendleton, David (1992). "Obscene Allegories: Narrative, Representation, Poronography," *Discourse*, 15, 1 (Fall): 154-169.

Penelope, Julia and Susan J. Wolfe (1978). "Towards an Feminist Aesthetic," *Chrysalis*, 9: 57-71.

Penley, Constance (1986). "Time Travel, Primal Scene, and the Critical Dystopia," *camera obscura*, 15:67-84.

Penley, Constance, ed. (1988). *Feminism and Film Theory*. New York, London: BFI Publishing.

Penley, Constance (1989). *The Future of an Illusion: Film, Feminism, and Psychoanalysis*. Minneapolis: University of Minnesota Press.

Penley, Constance (1992). Feminism, Psychoanalysis, and the Study of Popular Culture. In *Cultural Studies*. Lawrence Grossberg, Cary Nelson, and Paula Treichler, eds. pp. 479-500. New York and London: Routledge.

Penley, Constance and Andrew Ross, eds. (1991). *Technoculture; Cultural Politics, Vol. 3*. Oxford and Minneapollis: University of Minnesota Press.

Penley, Constance and Sharon Willis, eds. (1993). *Male Trouble*. Minneapolis and London: University of Minnesota Press.

Perkins, Roberta (1996). The 'Drag Queen' Scene: Transexuals in King Cross. In *Blending Genders: Social Aspects of Cross-dressing and Sex-changing*. Richard Ekins and David King, eds. pp. 53-62. London and New York: Routledge.

Petchesky, Rosalind Pollack (1987). "Fetal Images: The Power of Visual Culture in the Politics of Reproduction," *Feminist Studies*, 13, 2 (Summer): 263- 292.

Pheng, Cheah (1996). "Mattering," *Diacritics* 26, 1:108-39.

Phillipson, Michael (1989). In *Modernity's Wake: The Ameurunculus Letters*. London and New York: Routledge, Chapman and Hall, Inc.

Picardie, Justine (1994). "Viewpoint: Can Words Rape You?" *Vogue*, 5, 2350, 60 (May): 37-38.

Piercy, Marge (1991). *He, She and It*. New York: Fawcett Crest Books (Balantine).

Pinar, Bill (1983). "Curriculum as Gender Text: Notes on Reproduction, Resistance and Male-Male Relations," *Journal of Curriculum Theorizing*, 5, 1:26-52.

Pinar, Bill (1994). *Autobiography, Politics and Sexuality: Essays in Curriculum Theory: 1972-1992*. New York: Peter Lang, Inc.

Pinar, Bill and Bill Reynolds, eds. (1992). *Understanding Curriculum as Phenomenological and Deconstructed Text*. New York and London: Teachers College Press.

Pinar, Bill, Bill Reynolds, Patrick Slattery, and Peter Taubman (1995). *Understanding Curriculum: An Introduction to the Study of Historical and Contemporary Curriculum Discourses*. New York: Peter Lang.

Pleck, Joseph (1981). *The Myth of Masculinity*. Cambridge, Mass.: MIT Press.

Plessner, Helmut (1973). *Between Laughing and Crying*. Evanston: Northwestern University Press.

Plummer, Kenneth, ed. (1981). *The Making of the Modern Homosexual*. London: Hutchinson.

Pollock, Griselda (1985/1986). "Art, Art School, Culture: Individualism After the Death of the Artist," *BLOCK*, 11:6-18.

Pollock, Griselda (1986). "Art, Art School, Culture: Individualism After the Death of the Artist," *Exposure*, 24:20-33.

Pollock, Griselda (1987). Feminism and Modernism. In *Framing Feminism: Art and the Women's Movement: 1970-1985*, Rozsika Parker and Griselda Pollock, eds., pp. 79-124. London: Pandora.

Pollock, Griselda (1988). *Vision and Difference: Femininity, Feminism and the Histories of Art*. London and New York: Routledge, Chapman, and Hall, Inc.

Pollock, Griselda (1992a). Painting, Feminism, History. In *Destabilizing Theory: Contemporary Feminist Debates*. Michèle Barrett and Anne Phillips, eds. pp. 138-176. Cambridge: Polity Press.

Pollock, Griselda (1992b). "Trouble in the Archives: Introduction," *differences: A Journal of Feminist Cultural Studies*, 4, 4:iii-xiv.

Pollock, Griselda and Fred Orton (1978). *Vincent Van Gogh: Artist of his Time*. New York: Dutton.

Postman, Neil (1986). *Amusing Ourselves to Death: Public: Discourse in the Age of Show Business*. New York: Penguin Books.

Probyn, Elspeth (1990). Travels in the Postmodern: Making Sense of the Local. In *Feminism/Postmodernism*. Linda J. Nicholson, ed. pp. 176-189. New York and London: Routledge.

Probyn, Elspeth (1993). *Sexing the Self: Gendered Positions in Cultural Studies*. London and New York: Routledge.

Rabine, Leslie Wahl (1990). The Unhappy Hymen Between Feminism and Deconstruction. In *The Other Perspective in Gender and Culture: Rewriting Women and the Symbolic*. Juliet Flower MacCannell, ed. pp. 20-38. Oxford and New York: Columbia University Press.

Rabinow, Paul, ed. (1984). *The Foucault Reader*. New York: Pantheon.

Radway, Jance A. (1983). "Women Read the Romance: The Interaction of Text and Context," *Feminist Studies*, 9, 1 (Summer): 53-78.

Radway, Janice (1984). *Reading the Romance: Women, Patriarchy, and Popular Literature*. Chapel Hill: University of North Carolina Press.

Radner, Hilary (1989). " 'The Time's For Me': Making Up and Feminine Practice," *Cultural Studies*, 3, 3 (October): 301-322.

Ragland-Sullivan, Ellie (1986). *Jacques Lacan and the Philosophy of Psychoanalysis*. Urbana: University of Illinois Press.

Rajchman, John (1991). *Truth and Eros: Foucault, Lacan, and the Question of Ethics*. New York and London: Routledge.

Ramazanoglu, Caroline (1989). *Feminism and the Contradictions of Oppression*. London and New York: Routledge.

Ramazanoglu, Caroline, ed. (1993). *Up Against Foucault*. London and New York: Routledge.

Rankin, Aimee (1987). Legacies of Critical Practice in the 1980s. In *Discussions in Contemporary Culture*. Hal Foster, ed. pp. 91-98. Seattle, Washington: Bay Press.

Raven, Arlene (1994). The Archaic Smile. In *New Feminist Criticism: Art, Identity, Action*. Joanna Frueh, Cassandra L. Langer and, Arlene Raven, eds. pp. 1-15. New York: Harper Collins Publishers (IconEditions).

Raymond, Janice (1980). *The Transsexual Empire: Making of the She-Male*. London: The Women's Press.

Raymond, Janice (1994). Introduction to the 1994 Edition. The *Transsexual Empire: Making of the She-Male*. N.Y.; Teachers College Press. (1996) reprinted as The Politics of Transgenderism. In *Blending Genders: Social Aspects of Cross-dressing and Sex-changing*. Richard Ekins and David King, eds. pp. 39-48. London and New York: Routledge

Readings, Bill (1991). *Introducing Lyotard: Art and Politics*. London and New York: Routledge.

Rees, A. L. and Frances Borzello, eds. (1988). *The New Art History*. Atlantic Highlands, N.J.: Humanities Press International, Inc.

Rees, Mark (1996). Beoming a Man: The Personal Account of a Female-to-Male Transexual. In *Blending Genders: Social Aspects of Cross-dressing and Sex-changing*. Richard Ekins and David King, eds. pp. 27-38. London and New York: Routledge.

Reich, June L. (1992). "Genderfuck: The Law of the Dildo," *Discourse*, 15, 1 (Fall): 112-127.

Reiche, Reimut (1971). *Sexuality and Class Struggle*. Trans. Susan Bennett and David Fernbach. New York: Praeger.

Reich, Wilhelm (1945). *The Sexual Revolution: Towards a Self-Regulating Character Structure*. Trans. by Therese Pol Farrar. New York: Farrar, Straus and Giroux.

Rich, Adrienne (1980). "Compulsory Heterosexuality and Lesbian Existence," *Signs: Journal of Women in Culture and Society*, 5, 4:631-660.

Richman, Michèle (1980). "Sex and Signs: The Language of French Criticism," *Language and Style*, 13, 4:62-80.

Riddell, Carol (1996). Divided Sisterhood: A Critical Review of Janice Raymond's The Transexual Empire. In *Blending Genders: Social Aspects of Cross-dressing and Sex-changing*. Richard Ekins and David King, eds. pp. 171-189. London and New York: Routledge

Rieff, David (1993). "Multiculturalism's Silent Partner: It's the Newly Globalized Consumer Economy, Stupid," *Harpers*, 287, 1719 (August): 62-78.

Riley, Denise (1988). *"Am I that Name?" Feminism and the Category of "Women" in History*. Minneapolis: University of Minnesota Press.

Riviere, Joan (1986). Womanliness as a Masquerade. In *Formations of Fantasy*. Victor Burgin, James Donald and, Cora Kaplan, eds. pp. 35-44. London and New York: Methuen. (original, 1929).

Roach, Jacqui and Petal Felix (1989). Black Looks. In *The Female Gaze: Women as Viewers of Popular Culture*. Lorraine Gamman and Margaret Marshment, eds. pp. 130-142. Seattle: The Real Comet Press.

Roberts, Martin (1991). " Mutations of the Spectacle: Vitrines, Arcades, Mannequines," *FCS*, ii: 211-249.

Robertson, Mary F. (1986). "Deconstructive 'Contortion' and Women's Historical Practice," *Poetics Today*, 7:4: 705-728.

Robinson, Sally (1990). "Deconstructive Discourse and Sexual Politics: The 'Feminine' and/in Masculine Self-Representation," *Cultural Critique*, 13 (Fall): 203-227.

Rodowick, David (1982). "The Difficulty of Difference," *Wide Angle*, 5, 1:4-15.

Rodowick, David (1988). The *Crisis of Political Modernism: Criticism and Ideology in Contemporary Film Theory*. Urbana and Chicago: University of Illinois Press.

Rodowick, David (1991). *The Difficulty of Difference: Psychoanalysis, Sexual Difference, and Film Theory*. New York: Routledge.

Romanyshyn, Robert D. (1989). *Technology as Symptom & Dream*. London and New York: Routledge.

Roosens, E. (1989). *Creating Ethnicity: The Process of Ethnogenesis*. Newbury Park, Conn.: Sage Publications.

Rose, Jacqueline (1982). Introduction II. In *Feminine Sexuality: Jacques Lacan and the École Freudienne*. Trans. Jacqueline Rose. Juliet Mitchell and Jacqueline Rose, eds. New York and London: W. W. Norton & Company.

Rose, Jacqueline (1983). "Femininity and its Discontents," *Feminist Review*, 14:5-21.

Rose, Jacqueline (1984). *The Case of Peter Pan, or the Impossibility of Children's Fiction*. London and Basingstoke: The MacMillan Press.

Rose, Jacqueline (1986). *Sexuality in a Field of Vision*. London: Verso.

Rosenau, Pauline Marie (1992). *Post-modernism and the Social Sciences: Insights, Inroads, and Intrusions*. Princeton, New Jersey: Princeton University Press.

Rosenberg, Harold (1972). *The Anxious Object: Art Today and Its Audience*. New York, New York: Collier Books.

641

Ross, Andrew (1987a). Demonstrating Sexual Difference. In *Men in Feminism*. Alice Jardine and Paul Smith, eds. pp.47-53. London and New York: Methuen.

Ross, Andrew (1987b). No Question of Silence. In *Men in Feminism*. Alice Jardine and Paul Smith, eds. pp. 85-92. London and New York: Methuen.

Ross, Andrew (1989). The Popularity of Pornography. In *NO Respect: Intellectuals and Popular Culture*. Walter Kendrick, ed. London: Routledge. (Reprinted in (1993). The Cultural Studies Reader. Simon During, ed. pp. 221-242. London and New York: Routledge).

Ross, Andrew (1990a). "Ballots, Bullets, or Batmen: Can Cultural Studies Do the Right Thing?" *Screen*, 31, 1 (Spring): 26-44.

Ross, Andrew (1990b). The Politics of Impossibility. In *Psychoanalysis and …* Richard Feldstein and Henry Sussman, ed. pp. 113-128. New York and London: Routledge, Chapman and Hall, Inc.

Ross, Andrew (1991). *Strange Weather: Culture, Science and Technology in the Age of Limits*. London and New York: Verso

Ross, Andrew (1992). New Age Technoculture. In *Cultural Studies*. Lawrence Grossberg, Cary Nelson and Paula Treichler, eds. pp.531-555. New York and London: Routledge.

Rothenberg, Paula (1990). "The Construction, Deconstruction, and Reconstruction of Difference," *Hypatia*, 5, 1 (Spring): 42-55.

Rouse, Roger (1991). "Mexican Migration and the Social Space of Postmodernism," *Diaspora*, 1, 1 (Spring): 8-23.

Rowbotham, Shiela (1981). The Trouble With Patriarchy. In *People's History and Socialist Theory*. Raphael Samuel, ed. London and Boston: Routledge & Keagan Paul.

Rubin, Gayle (1984). Thinking Sex: Notes for a Radical Theory of the Politics of Sexuality. In *Pleasure and Danger: Exploring Female Sexuality*. Carole S. Vance, ed. Boston: Routledge.

Rubin, Gayle (1975). The Traffic in Women: Notes Toward a Political Economy of Sex. In *Toward an Anthropology of Women*. Raya Reiter, ed. pp. 157-210. New York: Monthly Review Press.

Rubin, Gayle (1984). Thinking Sex: Notes for a Radical Theory of the Politics of Sexuality. In *Pleasure and Danger: Exploring Female Sexuality*. Carole S. Vance, ed. London and New York: Routledge & Keagan Paul.

Ruether, Rosemary Radford (1983). *Sexism and God-talk: Towards a Feminist Theology*. Boston: Beacon Press.

Rushdie, Salman (1991). "Cover Quotation," *Diaspora*, 1, 2 (Fall).

Russo, Mary (1986). Female Grotesques: Carnival and Theory. In *Feminist Studies / Critical Studies*. Teresa de Lauretis, ed. pp. 213-229. Bloomington and Indianapolis: Indiana University Press.

Rutherford, Jonathan (1988). Who's That Man. In *Male Order: Unwrapping Masculinity*. Rowena Chapman and Jonathan Rutherford, eds. pp. 21-67. London: Lawrence & Wishart.

Ryan, Michael (1982). *Marxism and Deconstruction: A Critical Articulation*. Baltimore and London: The John Hopkins University Press.

Safouan, Moustafa (1981). "Is the Oedius Complex Universal?" *m/f*, 5/6.

Said, Edward (1978). *Orientalism*. New York: Vintage Press.

Salecl, Renata (1993). "Phantasmen des Krieges: Patriarchat und Mutterland—Heimat und Rassismus," *Lettre International*, 21:8-11.

Salecl, Renata (1994). *The Spoils of Freedom: Psychoanalysis and Feminism After the Fall of Communism*. London and New York: Routledge.

Salvaggio, Ruth (1990). Psychoanalysis Modern and Post-Modern. In *Psychoanalysis and* ... Richard Feldstein and Henry Sussman, eds. pp. 151-162. New York and London: Routledge, Chapman and Hall, Inc.

Sandoval, Chela (1991). "U.S. Third World Feminism: The Theory and Method of Oppostional Consciousness in the Postmodern World," *Genders*, 10:1-24.

Saper, Craig (1991). "A Nervous Theory: The Troubling Gaze of Psychoanalysis in Media Studies," *Diacritics*, 21, 4:33-52.

Sarap, Madan (1988). *An Introductory Guide to Poststructuralism and Postmodernism*. New York, London, Toronto, Sydney, Singapore: Harvester Wheatsheaf.

Sargent, Linda, ed. (1981). *Women and Revolution: The Unhappy Marriage of Marxism & Feminism*. London: Pluto Press.

Saslow, James M. (1986). *Ganymede in the Renaissance: Homosexuality in Art and Society*. New Haven: Yale University Press.

Sawicki, Jana (1988). Identity Politics and Sexual Freedom: Foucault and Feminism. In *Feminism and Foucault*. Irene Diamond and Lee Quinby, eds. pp. 177-192. Boston: Northeastern University Press.

Sawicki, Jana (1991). *Disciplining Foucault: Feminism, Power, the Body*. London and New York: Routledge.

Sawchuck, Kim (1987). A Tale of Inscription: Fashion Statements. In *Body Invaders: Panic Sex in America*. Arthur Kroker and Marilouise Kroker, eds. pp. 61-77. Montréal: New World Perspectives, Culture Texts Series.

Sayers, Janet (1982). *Biological Politics: Feminist and Anti-Feminist Perspectives*. New York: Tavistock.

Sayers, Janet (1986). *Sexual Contradictions: Psychology, Psychoanalysis, and Feminism*. New York and London: Tavistock.

Scarry, Elaine (1985). *The Body in Pain: The Making and the Unmaking of the World*. Oxford and New York: Oxford University Press.

Schade, Sigrid, ed. (1994). *Andere Körper—Different Bodies*. Passagen Verlag: Wien.

Schlafly, Phyllis (1981). *The Power of Christian Women*. Cincinnati, Ohio: Standard Publishing.

Scholes, Robert (1987). Reading Like a Man. In *Men in Feminism*. Alice Jardine and Paul Smith, eds. pp. 204-218. London and New York: Methuen.

Scholes, Robert (1994). Éperon Strings. In *the essential difference*. Naomi Schor and Elizabeth Weed, eds. pp. 116-129. Bloomington and Indianapolis: Indiana University Press.

Schor, Mira (1994). Patrilineage. In *New Feminist Criticism: Art, Identity, Action*. Joanna Frueh, Cassandra L. Langer, and Arlene Raven, eds. pp. 42-59. New York: HarperCollins Publishers (IconEditions).

Schor, Naomi (1987a). Dreaming Dissymmetry: Barthes, Foucault, and Sexual Difference. In *Men in Feminism*. Alice Jardine and Paul Smith, eds. pp. 98-110. London and New York: Methuen.

Schor, Naomi (1987b). *Reading in Detail: Aesthetics and the Feminine*. New York and London: Methuen.

Schor, Naomi (194). This Essentialism Which is Not One: Coming to Grips with Irigaray. In *the essential difference*. Naomi Schor and Elizabeth Weed, eds. pp. 40-62. Bloomington and Indianapolis: Indiana University Press.

Schor, Naomi and Elizabeth Weed, eds. (1994). *the essential difference*. Bloomington and Indianapolis: Indiana University Press.

Schulze, Laurie (1990). On the Muscle. In *Fabrications: Constume and the Female Body*. Jane Gains and Charlotte Herzog, eds. pp. 59-78. London and New York: Routledge.

Scott, Joan W. (1992). Experience. In *Feminists Theorize the Political*. Judith Butler and Joan W. Scott, eds. pp.22-40. New York and London: Routledge.

Searle, John R. (1980). "Las Meniñas and the Paradoxes of Pictorial Representation," *Critical Inquiry*, 6 (Spring): 477-88.

Sears, James T. (1985). A Personal Account of Coming to Grips With Gender in Research on Teaching: Rendering Silent What Must Be Spoken. Paper presented to the Seventh *Curriculum Theory Conference* (October, 15). Dayton: Ohio.

Sedgwick, Kosofsky Eve (1985). *Between Men: English Literature and Male Homosexual Desire*. New York: Columbia University Press.

Sedgwick, Kosofsky Eve (1990). *Epistemology of the Closet*. Berkeley and Los Angeles: University of Californai Press.

Sedgwick, Kosofsky Eve (1993). *Tendencies*. Durham: Duke University Press.

Segal, Lynne (1987). *Is the Future Female? Troubled Thoughts on Contemporary Feminism*. New York: Peter Bedrick Books.

Segal, Lynne (1990). *Slow Motion: Changing Masculinities*. New Bruswick: Rutgers University Press.

Segal, Naomi (1992). Why Can't a Good Man be Sexy? Why Can't a Sexy Man be Good? In *Between Men and Feminism*. David Porter, ed. pp. 35-47. London and New York: Routledge.

Seidler, J. Victor (1989a). Reason, Desire, and Male Sexuality. In The *Cultural Construction of Sexuality*. Pat Caplan, ed. pp. 82-112. London & New York: Tavistock.

Seidler, J. Victor (1989b). *Rediscovering Masculinity: Reason, Language and Sexuality*. London: Routledge.

Seidman, Steven (1993). Identity and Politics in a "Postmodern: Gay Culture": Some Historical and Conceptual Notes. In *Queer Politics and Social Theory*. Michael Warner, ed. pp. 105-142. Minneapolis and London: University of Minnesota Press.

Seiter, Ellen (1982). "Promise and Contradiction: The Daytime Television Serials," *Screen*, 23:150-163.

Seiter, Ellen, Hans Borchers, Gabriele Kreutzner, and Eva-Maria Warth (1991). Don't Treat Us Like We're So Stupid and Naive: Towards an Ethnography of Soap Opera Viewers. In *Remote Control: Television, Audiences, and Cultural Power*. Ellen Seiter, Hans Borchers, Gabriele Kreutzner, and Eva-Maria Warth, eds. pp. 223-247. London and New York: Routledge.

Shaviro, Steven (1993). *The Cinematic Body*. London and Minneapolis: University of Minnesota Press.

Shepherdson, Charles (1994). The Role of Gender and the Imperrative of Sex. In *Supposing the Subject*. Joan Copjec, ed. pp. 158-184. New York and London: Verso.

Shiach, Morag (1991). *Hélène Cixous: A Politics of Writing*. London and New York: Routledge.

Shiva, Vandana (1988). *Staying Alive: Women, Ecology and Development*. London: Zed Books.

Shohat, Ella and Robert Stam (1994). *Unthinking Eurocentrism: Multiculturalism and the Media*. New York and London: Routledge.

Showalter, Elaine (1979). Toward a Feminist Poetics. In *Women, Writing, and Writing About Women*. Mary Jacobus, ed. London: Croom and Held.

Showalter, Elaine (1982). Feminist Criticism in the Wilderness. In *Writing and Sexual Difference*. Elizabeth Abel, ed. pp. 9-36. Chicago: University of Chicago Press.

Showalter, Elaine (1987). Critical Cross-Dressing: Male Feminists and the Woman of the Year. In *Men in Feminism*. Alice Jardine and Paul Smith, eds. pp. 116-132. London and New York: Methuen.

Siebers, Tobin (1983). *The Mirror of Medusa*. Berkeley and Los Angeles: University of California Press.

Silverman, Kaja (1983). *The Subject of Semiotics*. New York and Oxford: Oxford University Press.

Silverman, Kaja (1986). Fragments of a Fashionable Discourse. In *Studies in Entertainment: Critical Approaches to Mass Culture*. Tania Modleski, ed. pp. 155-166. Bloomington and Indianapolis: Indiana University Press.

Silverman, Kaja (1988a). *The Acoustic Mirror: The Female Voice in Psychoanalysis and Cinema*. Bloomington and Indiana: Indiana University Press.

Silverman, Kaja (1988b). "Masochism and Male Subjectivity," *camera obscura: A Journal of Feminism and Film Theory*, 17:31-66. (Reprinted in Constance Penley and Sharon Willis, eds. (1993). *Male Trouble*. pp. 33-66. New York and London: Routledge).

Silverman, Kaja (1989c). "White Skins, Brown Masks: The Double Mimesis, or With Lawrence of Arabia," *differences: A Journal of Feminist Cultural Studies*, 1, 3. (Reprinted in (1992). *Male Subjectivity at The Margins*. pp. 299-338. New York and London: Routledge).

Silverman, Kaja (1992). *Male Subjectivity at The Margins*. New York and London: Routledge.

Silverman, Kaja (1993). "What Is a Camera? or: History in the Field of Vision," *Discourse* 15, 3 (Spring): 3-56.

Silverman, Kaja (1994) "What is a Camera? or: History in the Field of Vision." Lecture, *Das Kino*, Salzburg, Austria (May, 29). The Gaze, Look, "Screen": Lacan's Three Categories of the Visible World., Workshop. *University of Salzburg* (May, 30).

Silverman, Kaja (1996). *The Threshold of the Visible World*. London and New York: Routledge.

Sims, Lowery Stokes (1988). Aspects of Performance in the Work of Black American Women Artists. In *Feminist Art Criticism: An Anthology*. Arlene Raven, Cassandra Langer and, Joanna Frueh, eds. pp. 207-226. London and Ann Arbor: University Microfilms Inc. Research Press.

Singer, Linda (1993). *Erotic Welfare: Sexual Theory and Politics in the Age of Epidemic*. Edited and introduced by Judith Butler and Maureen MacGrogan. New York and London: Routledge.

Smith, Annie (1993). *Getting into Art History*. Mesquite, Lake Jackson, Texas: Barn Press.

Smith, Micahel Peters (1992). "Postmodernism, Urban Ethnography, and the New Social Space of Ethnic Identity," *Theory and Society*, 21:493-531.

Smith, Paul, (1987) Men in Feminism: Men and Feminist Theory. In *Men in Feminism*. Alice Jardine and Paul Smith, eds. pp. 33-40. New York and London: Methuen.

Smith, Paul (1988). *Discerning the Subject*. Minneapolis: University of Minnesota Press:

Smith, Paul (1993). *Clint Eastwood: A Cultural Production*. Minneapolis and London: University of Minnesota Press.

Smith, Ralph (1986). *Excellence in Art Education: Ideas and Initiatives*. Reston, Virginia: National Art Education Association.

Snyder-Ott, Joelynn (1978). *Women and Creativity*. Millbrae, California: Les Femmes Pub.

Snyder, Joel and Ted Cohen (1980). "Reflexions on Las Meniñas: Paradox Lost," *Critical Inquiry*, 7 (Winter): 429-477.

Sobchack, Vivian (1991) Child/Alien/Father: Patriarchal Crisis and Generic Echange. In *Close Encounters: Film, Feminism and Science Fiction*. Constance Penley, Elizabeth Lyon, Lynn Spigel, and Janet Bergstrom, eds. pp.3-30. Minneapolis and London: University of Minnesota Press.

Sobchack, Vivian (1992). *The Address of the Eye: A Phenemenology of Film Experience*. Princeton, New Jeresey: Princeton University Press.

Soble, Alan (1986). *Pornography: Marxism, Feminism, and the Future of Sexuality*. New Haven and London: Yale University Press.

Solanas, Valerie (1967). *The SCUM Manifesto*. Black Widow.

Sollors, Werner (1986). *Beyond Ethnicity: Strategies of Diversity*. Bloomington and Indianapolis: Indiana University Press.

Solomon-Godeau, Abigail (1989). "Going Native," *Art in America*, 77, 7 (July): 118-129.

Soper, Kate (1995). "Forget Foucault?" *New Formations* 25 (Summer): 21-27.

Spence, Jo (1988). *Putting Myself in the Picture: A Political, Personal, and Photographic Autobiography.* Seattle: The Real Comet Press.

Spense, Jo (1995). *Cultural Snipping: The Art of Transgression.* London and New York: Routledge.

Spivak, Gayatri Chakravorty (1976). Translator's Preface. In *Of Grammatology.* By Jacques Derrida. Trans. Gayatri Chakravorty Spivak. pp. ix-lxxxix. Baltimore and London: The John Hopkins Press.

Spivak, Gayatri Chakravorty (1981). "French Feminism in an International Frame," *Yale French Studies,* 62:154-184.

Spivak, Gayatri Chakravorty (1983). Displacement and the Discourse of Woman. In *Displacement: Derrida and After.* Mark Krupnick, ed. pp. 169-195. Bloomington and Indianapolis: Indiana University Press.

Spivak, Gayatri Chakravorty (1986). "Imperialism and Sexual Difference," *Oxford Literary Review,* 8, 1-2: 225-240.

Spivak, Gayatri Chakravorty (1988a). *In Other Words: Essays in Cultural Politics.* New York and London: Routledge.

Spivak, Gayatri Chakravorty (1988b). Can the Subaltern Speak? In *Marxism and the Interpretation of Culture.* Cary Nelson and Lawrence Grossberg, eds. pp.271-316. Urbana and Chicago: University of Illinois Press. (Reprinted in Spivak's *In Other Words: Essays in Cultural Politics.* pp. 197-221. New York and London: Routledge).

Spivak, Gayatri Chakravorty (1989a). Feminism and Deconstruction, Again: Negotiating With Unacknowledged Masculine. In *Between Feminism & Psychoanalysis.* Teresa Brennan, ed. pp. 206-224. London and New York: Routledge.

Spivak, Gayatri Chakravorty (1989b). "In Praise of Sammy and Rosie Get Laid," *Critical Quarterly,* 31, 2:80-88.

Spivak, Gayatri Chakravorty (1990). "Gayatri Spivak on the Politics of the Subaltern: Interviewed by Howard Winant," *Socialist Review,* 20, 3 (July-Sept.): 81-97.

Spivak, Gayatri Chakravorty (1992a). French Feminism Revisited. In *Feminists Theorize the Political.* Judith Butler and Joan W. Scott, eds. pp. 54-85. New York and London: Routledge.

Spivak, Gayatri Chkravorty (1992b). The Politics of Translation. In *Destabilizing Theory: Contemporary Feminist Debates.* Michele Barrett and Anne Phillips (eds). pp. 177-200. Cambridge: Polity Press.

Spretnak, Charlene (1982). *The Politics of Women's Spirituality: Essays on the Rise of Spiritual Power Within the Feminist Movement.* Garden City, New York: Anchor/Doubleday.

Springer, Claudia (1993). "Muscular Circuitry: The Invincible Armored Cyborg in Cinema," *Genders,* 18 (Winter): 87-101.

Stacey, Fances (l983). "The New Conservative Feminism," *Feminist Studies,* 9, 3 (Fall): 559-584.

Stacey, Jackie (1989). Desperately Seeking Difference. In *The Female Gaze: Women as Viewers of Popular Culture*. Lorraine Gamman and Margaret Marshment, eds. pp.112-129. Seattle: The Real Comet Press.

Stacey, Jackie (1994). *Star Gazing: Hollywood Cinema and Female Spectatorship*. London and New York: Routledge.

Staiger, Janet (1992). *Interpreting Films: Studies in the Historical Reception of American Cinema*. Princeton, New Jersey: Princeton University Press.

Stallybrass, Peter and Allon White (1986). *The Politics & Poetics of Transgression*. Ithaca, New York: Cornell University Press.

Stanton, Domna C. (1980). Language and Revolution: The Franco-American Dis-connection. In *The Future of Difference*. Hester Eisenstein and Alice Jardine, eds. pp. 73-87. Boston, Massachusetts: G.K. Hall and Co.

Stanton, Domna C. (1989). Difference on Trial: A Critique of the Maternal Metaphor in Cixous, Irigaray, and Kristeva. In *The Thinking Muse: Feminism and Modern French Philosophy*. Jeffner Allen and Marion Iris, eds. pp. 156-179. Bloomington and Indianapolis: Indiana University Press.

Steele, V. (1985). *Fashion and Eroticism: Ideals of Feminine Beauty from the Victorian Era to the Jazz Age*. New York: Oxford University Press.

Stein, Arlene (1992). "Sisters and Queers: The Decentering of Lesbian Feminism", *Socialist Review*, 22, 1 (Jan-March): 33-56.

Steinem, Gloria (1992). Foreward. In *Women Respond to Men's Movement: A Feminist Collection*. Kay Leigh Hagan, eds. pp. v-ix. HarperSanFrancisco.

Steinberg, Leo (1981). "Velázquez' Las Meniñas," *October*, 19 (Winter): 45-54.

Stimpson, Catharine (1988). Nancy Reagan Wears A Hat: And Its Cultural Consequences. In *Where The Meanings Are: Feminism and Cultural Spaces*. pp. 179-196. London and New York: Routledge, Chapman and Hill Inc.

Stoller, Robert (1979). *Sexual Excitement: The Dynamics of Erotic Life*. New York: Pantheon Books.

Stoltenberg, John (1984). "Refusing to be a Man," *Women's Studies International Forum*, 7, 1: 25-27.

Stockton, Kathryn Bond (1992). "Bodies and God: Poststructuralist Feminists Return to the Fold of Spiritual Materialism," *boundary*, 2, 19, 2:113-149.

Stone, Merlin (1976). *When God was a Woman*. San Diego, New York, London: Harcourt Brace Jovanovich, Publisher. (Originally published as *The Paradise Papers*).

Stone, Sandy (1991). The Empire Strikes Back: A Posttranssexual Manifesto. In *Body Guards: The Cultural Politics of Gender Ambiguity*. Julia Epstein and Kristina Straub. eds. pp. 280-304. London and New York: Routledge.

Storr, Robert (1988). "Salle's Gender Machine," *Art in America*, 76, 6 (June): 24-25.

Stuart, Andrea (1989). The Color Purple: In Defence of Happy Endings. In *The Female Gaze: Women as Viewers of Popular Culture*. Lorraine Gamman and Margaret Marshment, eds. pp. 60-75. Seattle: The Real Comet Press.

Studlar, Gaylyn (1988). *In the Realm of Pleasure: Von Sternberg, Dietrich, and the Masochistic Aesthetic*. Urbana: University of Illinois Press.

Suleiman, Susan Rubin, ed. (1986). *The Female Body in Western Culture: Contemporary Perspectives*. Cambridge, Mass.: Harvard University Press.

Suleiman, Susan Rubin (1990). *Subversive Intent: Gender, Politics, and the Avant-Garde*. Cambridge, Mass. and London: Harvard University Press.

Suzuki, Bob (1991). "Unity with Diversity: Easier said than Done," *Liberal Education*, 77, 1:30-35.

Tarabirrelli, Randy (1991). *Michael Jackson: The Magic and the Madness*. New York: Birch Lane Press.

Tagg, John (1988). *The Burden of Representaiton: Essays on Photographies and Histories*. Amherst: The University of Massachusetts Press.

Tallis, Raymond (1988). *In Defence of Realism*. London, Baltimore, Melbourne, Auckland: Edward Arnold, A div. of Hodder & Stoughton.

Tasker, Yvonne (1993a). Dumb Movies for Dumb People: Masculinity, the Body, and the Voice in Contemporary Action Cinema. In *Screening the Male: Exploring Masculinities in Hollywood Cinema*. Steven Cohan and Ina Rae Hark, eds. pp. 230-244. London and New York: Routledge.

Tasker, Yvonne (1993b). *Spectacular Bodies: Gender, Genre and the Action Cinema*. London and New York: Routledge.

Taubman, Peter Maas (1982). "Gender and Curriculum: Discourse and the Politics of Sexuality," *Journal of Curriculum Theorizing*, 4, 1: 12-87.

Taussig, Michael (1993). *Mimesis and Alterity: A Particular History of the Senses*. London and New York: Routledge.

Taylor, Lucien, ed. (1994). *Visualizing Theory: Selected Essays from V.A.R: 1990-1994*. New York and London: Routledge.

Tester, Keith (1993). *The Life and Times of Post-modernity*. London and New York: Routledge.

Theweleit, Klaus (1987). *Male Fantasies. Volume 1*. Minneapolis: University of Minesota Press.

Thomas, Jennifer (1993). "The Question of Derrida's Women," *Human Studies*, 16:163-176.

Thompson, John B. (1982). "Ideology and the Social Imaginary: An Appraisal of Castoriadis and Lefort," *Theory and Society*, 11:659-681.

Thompson, William Irwin (1981). *The Time Falling Bodies Take to Light: Mythology, Sexuality & The Origins of Culture*. New York: St. Martin's Press.

Threadgold, Terry and Anne Cranny-Francis, eds. (1990). *Feminine, Masculine and Representation*. Sydney, London, Boston, Wellington: Allen & Unwin.

Thurston, Carol (1987). *The Romance Revolution: Erotic Novels for Women and the Quest for a New Sexual Identity*. Urbana: University of Illinois Press.

Tickner, Lisa (1978). "The Body Politic: Female Sexuality and Women Artists since 1970," *Art History*, 1, 2 (June): 236-251.

Tickner, Lisa (1987). Nancy Spero: Images of Women and la peinture féminine. In Lisa Tickner's *Nancy Spero*. London: Institute of Contemporary Art.

Tickner , Lisa (1988). "Feminism, Art History, and Sexual Difference," *Genders*, 3: 92-128.

Tickner, Lisa (1992). "Men's Work? Masculinity and Modernism," *differences: A Journal of Feminist Cultural Studies*, 4, 3:1-37.

Tiefer, Leonore (1986). "In Pursuit of the Perfect Penis: The Medicalization of Male Sexuality," *American Behavioral Scientist*, 29, 5 (May-June): 579-599).

Todd, Janet (1988). *Feminist Literary History*. New York: Routledge, Chapman & Hall, Inc.

Tong, Rosemarie (1989). *Feminist Thought: A Comprehensive Introduction*. Boulder and San Francisco: Westview Press.

Torgovnick, Marianna (1990). *Gone Primitive: Savage Intellects, Modern Lives*. Chicago: University of Chicago.

Treichler, Paula (1988). AIDS, Homophobia, and Biomedical Discourse: An Epidemic of Signification. In *AIDS: Cultural Analysis, Cultural Activism*. Douglas Crimp, ed. pp. 31-70. Cambridge, Mass.: The MIT Press.

Treichler, Paula and Lisa Cartwright, eds (1992). "Imagining Technologies, Inscribing Science: Special Issue," *camera obscura*, 28 (January).

Trevathan, Wenda R. (1987). *Human Birth: An Evolutionary Perspective*. New York: Aldine de Gruyter.

Trible, Phyllis (1978). *God and the Rhetoric of Sexuality*. Philadelphia: Fortress Press.

Trinh. T. Minh-ha (1989). *Woman, Native, Other: Writing Postcoloniality and Feminism*. Bloomington and Indianapolis: Indiana University Press.

Trinh. T. Minh-ha (1991). *When The Moon Waxes Red: Representation, Gender and Culural Politics*. New York and London: Routledge.

Tseëlon, Efrat and Susan B. Kaiser (1992). A Dialogue with Feminist Film Theory: Multiple Readings of the Gaze. In *Studies in Symbolic Interaction, Volume 13*. Norman Denzin, ed. pp.119-137. AAI Press Inc.

Tucker, Marcia and William Olander, eds. (1986). *The Art of Memory / The Loss of History*. N.Y.: The New Museum of Contemporary Art, New York.

Tuft, Elenor (1974). *Our Hidden Heritage: Five Centuries of Women Artists*. New York: Paddington Press.

Turin, Maureen (1983). "Fashion Shapes: Film, the Fashion Industry, and the Image of Woman," *Socialist Review*, 71, 13, 5 (Sept.-Oct.): 79-96.

Ulmer, Gregory (1985). *Applied Grammatology: Post(e)-Pedagogy from Jacques Derrida to Joseph Beuys*. Baltimore: John Hopkins University Press.

Ulmer, Gergory, (1989). *Teletheory: Grammatology in the Age of Video*. London and New York: Routledge.

Vale, V. and Juno, Andrea, eds. (1989). *Modern Primitives*. Hong Kong: Re/Search Publications.

Venn, Couze (1992). "Subjectivity, Ideology and Difference: Recovering Otherness," *New Formations*, 16 (Spring): 40-61.

Vogel, Lise (1988). Fine Arts and Feminism: The Awakening Consciousness. In *Feminist Art Criticism: An Anthology*. Arlene Raven, Cassandra Langer, and Joanna Frueh, eds. pp.21-58. London and Ann Arbor: University Microfilms Inc. Research Press.

Walker, Alice (1983). *In Search of Our Mother's Gardens: A Womanist Prose*. San Diego: Harcourt, Brace, Jovanovich.

Walker, Barbara (1983). *The Woman's Encyclopedia of Myths and Secrets*. San Francisco: Harper & Row Publishers.

Walker, Barbara (1985). *The Crone: Woman of Age, Wisdom, and Power*. San-Francisco: Harper & Row Publishers.

Walker, Janet (1985). "The Problem of Sexual Difference and Identity," *Wide Angle*, 6, 3:16-23.

Walkerdine, Valerie (1986). Video Replay: Families, Films and Fantasy. In *Formations of Fantasy*. Victor Burgin, James Donald, and Cora Kaplan, eds. pp. 167-199. London and New York: Metheun & Co. Ltd.

Walkerdine, Valerie with June Melody (1993). Daddy's Gonna Buy You a Dream to Cling to (and Mummy's Gonna Love You as Much as She Can): Young Girls and Popular Television. In *Reading Audiences: Young People and the Media*. David Buckingham, ed. pp. 74-88. Manchester: Manchester University Press.

Waller, Marguerite (1987). "Academic Tootsie: The Denial of Difference and the Difference it Makes," *Diacritics*, 17, 1 (Spring): 2-20.

Wallis, Brian, ed. (1984). *Art After Modernism: Rethinking Representation. The New Museum of Contemporary Art*, New York in association with Boston: David R. Godine, Pub., Inc.

Wallis, Mieczyslaw (1983). *Sztuki i Znaki: Pisma Semiotyczne*. Warszawa: Panstwowy Instytut Wydawn.

Warner, William (1990). Spectacular Images: Rambo and the Popular Pleasures of Pain. In *Cultural Studies*. Lawrence Grossberg, Cary Nelson, and Paula Treichler, eds. pp. 672-688. New York and London: Routledge.

Watney, Simon (1987). *Policing Desire: Pornography, AIDS, and the Media*. Minneapolis: University of Minnesota Press.

Watney, Simon (1988). The Spectacle of AIDS. In *AIDS: Cultural Analysis, Cultural Activism*. Douglas Crimp, ed. pp. 171-87. Cambridge, Massachusetts and London: The MIT Press. (Reprinted from (1987) October, 43).

651

Watt, Ian (1957). *The Rise of the Novel*. London: Chatto & Windus.

Waugh, Patricia (1989). *Feminine Fictions: Revisiting the Postmodern*. London and New York: Routledge.

Weedon, Chris (1987). *Feminist Practice & Poststructuralist Theory*. London: Basil Blackwell.

Weeks, Jeffrey (1985). *Sexuality and its Discontents*. London: Routledge & Kegan Paul Ltd.

Weeks, Jeffrey (1989). Questions of Identity. In *The Cultural Construction of Sexuality*. Pat Caplan, ed. pp. 31-51. London & New York: Tavistock.

Weiler, Katheleen (1988). *Women Teaching for Change: Gender, Class, Power*. Hadley, Mass.: Bergin & Garvey Pub.

Weiskel, Thomas (1976). *The Romantic Sublime: Studies in the Sructure and Psychology of Transcendence*. Baltimore: John Hopkins University Press.

Wenger, Morton G. (1993-94). "Idealism Redux: The Class-Historical Truth of Postmodernism," *Critical Sociology*, 20, 1:58-78.

Wenzel, Hélène (1981). "The Text as Body/Politics: An Appreciation of Monique Wittig's Writings in Context," *Feminist Studies*, 7, 2 (Summer): 264-287.

West, Cornel (1990). The New Cultural Politics of Difference. In *Out There: Marginalization and Contemporary Cultures*. Russell Ferguson, Martha Gever, Trinh T. Minh-ha, and Cornel West, eds. pp. 19-38. New York, New York: The New Museum of Contemporary Art.

White, David (1992). 'The Soul is the Prison of the Body': Fabo on Foucault. In *Fluid Exchanges: Artists and Critics in the AIDS Crisis*. James Miller, ed. pp. 65-88. Toronto, Buffalo, London: University of Toronto Press.

White, Hayden (1980). "The Value of Narrativity in the Representation of Reality," *Critical Inquiry*, 6, 2 (Autumn): 5-27.

White, Hayden (1992). "Writing in the Middle Voice," *Stanford Literature Review*, 9, 2 (Fall): 179-187.

Whitford, Margaret (1988). Luce Irigaray's Critique of Rationality. In *Feminist Perspectives in Philosophy*. Morwenna Griffiths and Margaret Whitford, eds. pp. 131-151. Bloomington and Indianapolis: Indiana University Press.

Whittle, Stephen (1996) Gender Fucking or Fucking Gender? In *Blending Genders: Social Aspects of Cross-dressing and Sex-changing*. Richard Ekins and David King, eds. pp. 196-214. London and New York: Routledge

Williams, Linda (1983). When the Woman Looks. In *Re-Vision: Essays in Feminist Film Criticism*. Mary Ann Doane, Patricia Mellencamp and Linda Williams, eds. pp. 83-99. American Film Institute Monograph Series. Frederick, Md.: University Publications of America.

Williams, Linda (1984). " 'Something Else Besides a Mother': Stella Dallas and the Maternal Meoldrama," *Cinema Journal*, 24, 1 (Fall):2-27.

Williams, Linda (1989). *Hard Core: Power, Pleasure, and the "Frenzy of the Visible."* Berkeley, Los Angeles: University of Californai Press.

Williams, Linda (1993). "A Provoking Agent: The Pornography and Performance Art of Annie Sprinkle," *Social Text*, 37:117-134.

Williamson, Judith (1983). "Images of 'Woman'," *Screen*, 24, 6 (Nov.-Dec.): 102-116.

Willis, Paul (1981). *Learning To Labor*. New York: University of Columbia Press.

Willis, Paul (1990a) *Common Cultures: Symbolic Work at Play in the Everyday Cultures of the Young*. Milton Keynes: Open University Press.

Willis, Paul (1990b) *Moving Culture: An Enquiry into the Cultural Activities of Young People*. London: Calouste Gulbenkian Foundation.

Willis, Sharon (1987). *Margarite Duras: Writing on the Body*. Urbana and Chicago: University of Illinois Press.

Willis, Susan (1991) Work(ing) Out. In Susan Willis's *A Primer for Daily Life*. London and New York: Routledge.

Wilson, Elizabeth (1987). *Adorned in Dreams: Fashion and Modernity*. Berkeley: University of California Press.

Winant, Howard (1990). "Postmodern Racial Politics in the United States: Difference and Inequality," *Socialist Review*, 20, 1 (Jan-March): 121-147.

Wing, Betsy (1986). Glossary. In The *Newly Born Woman*. Hélène Cixous and Catherine Clément. Trans. Betsy Wing. pp.163-168. Minneapolis: University of Minnesota Press.

Winnicott, D.W. (1974). *Playing and Reality*. Harmondsworth: Penguin.

Winterson, Jeanette (1993). *Written On the Body*. Toronto: Vintage Books.

Wiseman, Sue (1993). *Rights and Permissions: Sex, the Model and the Star. In Deconstructing Madonna*. Fran Lloyd, ed. pp. 99-110. London: B.T. Batsford Ltd.

Withers, Josephine (1987). "Revisioning Our Foremothers: Reflections on the Ordinary. Extraordinary Art of May Stevens," *Feminist Studies*, 13, 3 (Fall): 485-498.

Wittig, Monique (1980). "The Straight Mind," *Feminist Issues*, 1, 1 (Summer).

Wolff, Janet (1981). *The Social Production of Art*. London and Basingstoke: MacMillan Press Ltd.

Wolff, Janet (1990). *Feminist Sentences: Essays on Women & Culture*. Cambridge: Polity Press.

Wolff, Janet (1990). Reinstating Corporality: Feminism and Body Politics. In Janet Wolff's *Feminine Sentences: Essays on Women & Culture*. Cambridge: Polity Press.

Wolff, Janet (1992) Excess and Inhibition: Interdisciplinarity in the Study of Art. In *Cultural Studies*. Lawrence Grossberg, Cary Nelson, and Paula Treichler, eds pp. 706-718. New York, London: Routledge.

Wolmark, Jenny (1993). *Aliens and Others: Science Fiction, Feminism and Postmodernism*. New York, London, Toronto, Sydney, Singapore: Harvester Wheatsheaf.

Wood, Robin (1987). Raging Bull: The Homosexual Subtext in Film. In *Beyond Patriarchy: Essays by Men in Pleasure, Power and Change*. Michael Kaufman, ed. pp.266-276. Toronto and New York: Oxford University Press.

653

Woolf, Virginia (1929). *A Room Of One's Own*. London: Hogarth Press.

Woodhull, Winifred (1989). Sexuality, Power, and the Question of Rape. In *Feminism & Foucault: Reflections on Resistance*. Irene Diamond and Lee Quinby, eds. pp. 167-176. Boston: Northeastern University Press.

Wright, Elizabeth (1984). *Psychoanalytic Criticism: Theory in Practice*. London and New York: Methuen.

Wright, Elizabeth (1992). *Postmodern Brecht*. New York and London: Routledge.

Wright, Lee (1989). Objectifying Gender: The Stiletto Heel. In *A View from the Interior: Feminism Women and Design*. Judy Attfield and Pat Kirkham, eds. pp. 7-19. London: The Women's Press.

Yaeger, Patricia (1989). Toward a Female Sublime. In *Gender & Theory: Dialogues on Feminist Criticism*. Linda Kauffman, ed. London: Basil Blackwell.

Yi, Sun-Kyung (1992). "An Immigrant's Split Personality," *The Toronto Globe & Mail* (April, 2): U1 (Facts & Arguments).

Yingling, Thomas (1990). "How the Eye is Caste: Robert Mapplethorpe and the Limits of Controversy," *Discourse*, 12, 2 (Spring-Summer): 3-28.

Young, Iris Marion (1989). Throwing Like A Girl: A Phenomenology of Feminine Body Comportment, Motility, and Spaciality. In *The Thinking Muse: Feminism and Modern French Philosophy*. Jeffner Allen and Iris Marion Young, eds. pp. 51-70. Bloomington and Indianapolis: Indiana University Press.

Young, Shelagh, (1989). Feminism and the Politics of Power: Whose Gaze Is It Anyway? In *The Female Gaze: Women as Viewers of Popular Culture*. Lorraine Gamman and Margaret Marshment, eds. pp. 173-188. Seattle: The Real Comet Press.

Zavitzianos, G. (1977). "The Object in Fetishism: Homeovestism and Transvestism," *International Journal of Psycho-Analysis*, 58: 487-95.

Zipes, Frank (1982). *Fairy Tales and the Art of Subversion: The Classical Genre for Children and the Process of Civilization*. London: Heinemann.

Zipes, Jack (1992). "Spreading Myths About Fairy Tales: A Critical Commentary on Robert Bly's Iron John," *New German Critique*, 55 (Winter): 3-19.

Žižek, Slavoj (1989a). *The Sublime Object of Ideology*. London and New York: Verso.

Žižek, Slavoj (1989b). "The Undergrowth of Enjoyment: How Popular Culture can Serve as An Introduction to Lacan," *New Formations*, 9 (Winter): 7-30.

Žižek, Slavoj (1991). *Looking Awry: An Introduction to Jacques Lacan through Popular Culture*. 2nd. Edition. An October Book. Cambridge, Massachusetts, London: The MIT Press

Žižek, Slavoj (1993a). "From Courtly Love to The Crying Game," *New Left Review*, 202 (Nov-Dec): 95-108.

Žižek, Slavoj (1993b). *Tarrying with the Negative: Kant, Hegel, and the Critique of Ideology*. Durham: Duke University Press.

Žižek, Slavoj (1994a). "Otto Weininger, or 'Woman Doesn't Exist,'" *New Formations*, 23 (Summer): 97-113.

Žižek, Slavoj (1994b). *For They Know Not What They Do: Enjoyment as a Political Factor*. London and New York: Verso. (Original, 1991).

Žižek, Slavoj (1994c). *The Metastases of Enjoyment*. London and New York: Verso.

Zukin, Sharon (1991). *Landscapes of Power: From Detroit to Disney World*. Berkeley, Los Angeles, Oxford: University of California Press.

Zupančič, Alenka (1994). "What's Love Got To Do With *ID?*," *New Formations*, 23 (Summer): 55-68.

INDEX

B

babyism 409
Bakhtin, Mikhail 51n.8, 125, 425, 486
Benglis 346-47, 399, 414
Benjamin, Walter 106, 259, 323
'beyond the phallus' 19-20, 25-27, 107, 151
Big Other 12, 17, 33, 52, 154, 166, 195-96, 238, 240, 435, 456, 540
Bildungsroman 87, 100, 158, 436, 470
binary (see logic) 13, 37, 70n.7, 77-78, 91, 110, 132, 134, 146-47, 149-50, 160, 185,
    193-94, 236, 289, 349, 354, 356, 372, 375, 377, 389, 424, 429, 434, 444, 449,
    510-12, 551
bisexual 22, 84, 115, 127-28, 142, 147, 488, 491, 527n.18
Black body (see also body) 290-93, 296-99, 353-54
Bly, Robert 12, 51n.7, 520-22
body (Black body) (bodybuilder) (transsexual body) (transgendered body) (porno-
    graphic body) (transvestism) (see also drag) 5, 11, 18, 36-38, 48, 54n.28, 85, 91-
    93, 105-07, 114, 116, 120, 122-27, 129-32, 144-55, 168, 174, 201, 223-25, 231-
    32, 246, 249-50, 253, 256, 304-06, 341-42, 345-49, 351, 353, 361-62, 370, 374,
    379n.15, 381-83, 401-02, 405, 411, 413, 417, 419-21, 423-24, 426-30, 436-38,
    444, 448-50, 452-54, 455-57, 459, 482, 494-98, 500-02, 506-15, 518, 523, 532-
    34, 541, 544, 546
Boone, Joseph 2, 49n.1
bulimia (see also anorexia) 68, 237-38, 422, 426, 496, 544
butch-femme (see also drag, body) 400-01, 406, 444, 510-11, 515-16
BwO's (see also Deleuze and Guattari) 132-33, 135, 245

C

castration (castrating women) (symbolic castration) (castration anxiety) 3, 5, 14, 16-
    17, 19-22, 24, 38, 59-60, 68-69, 114-16, 124, 134, 142, 154-55, 162, 172, 175-
    76, 178, 182, 184-85, 187, 194, 198, 206-08, 213, 222, 224, 226, 244-45, 250,
    252, 296, 314, 367, 369, 397n.16, 398, 404-07, 422, 444, 447, 452, 457, 477,
    497, 516, 538
cite/site/sight 42, 55n.36
Clover, Carol 201-08, 212, 366
common culture 276, 312
confession 2, 42-46, 55n.39, 70, 361
constructivism 298, 301
craft (see also low arts) 80, 82-84, 201, 267, 311, 317, 342-43
cross-dressing (see also drag, tranvestism) 2, 60, 406, 409, 426, 429-30, 440n.10, 474,
    535, 543-44, 546, 554
cultural studies 47, 145-46, 194, 229, 234, 275, 278, 284, 412, 470
cyberspace 92, 132, 212, 421
cyborg (see also Alien, Terminator, Schwarzenegger) 92, 106, 269n.7, 418, 459, 499-
    500, 502-06, 512, 516-18, 527n.11

D

deconstruction (deconstructive criticism) 23-26, 52n.16, 55n.35, 80-81, 110-12, 116-17, 127, 132-34, 138, 149-51, 154, 160-63, 180-82, 189, 219, 251, 254, 262, 264, 270, 280, 284, 298-99, 337, 349, 354, 389, 435, 444, 460, 463, 471-72, 475-78, 480, 550, 566

dedoxification 485, 535

desire (desiring machines) 1, 3, 6-7, 10, 13-14, 16, 20, 22, 33-38, 61-62, 68-69, 74-75, 82, 116-20, 132, 134, 146-47, 152-55, 157, 165-70, 172-76, 186-89, 197-99, 202-04, 209, 212-13, 219-40, 245, 252-53, 255-56, 260-61, 304-05, 321, 346-48, 350, 352, 254-55, 367-74, 382, 384, 385-92, 396, 400, 402-05, 409, 413, 422-29, 443-44, 446-48, 450-58, 479, 486-88, 494-99, 507, 509-10, 513-14, 524, 536-40, 548, 550-52

difference 2-5, 13-15, 21-22, 24-25, 30, 33, 37, 65-66, 74, 76, 92, 101, 103, 106, 110-14, 118-19, 128, 138-39, 141-42, 144-55, 164n.10, 176, 179, 183, 187-88, 195, 209-10, 220, 227-28, 235-36, 245-48, 256, 260, 262-63, 279, 298, 303-04, 306-09, 313-18, 320-22, 328, 330-36, 348, 353-55, 370-71, 400-02, 405, 408, 419, 434, 466-68, 474-76, 479-80, 536, 538, 546

différance 55n.35, 141, 220, 480, 529n.23

dildo 346-47, 400-02, 414n.2, 458

Dionysus 483

Dirty Harry 391-2

discursive subject 6-8, 10-11, 92, 143-44, 146, 228, 240n.4, 479, 532-33, 537

drag 6, 37, 147, 196, 202, 206-08, 401, 424, 426, 446, 505-06, 513-14, 527, 535-36, 541-46, 549, 554

dyke 132, 384, 400

E

ecofeminism 105-06, 134

ecology 105, 107n.1

écriture (écriture féminine) (écriture homosexuelle) 11, 36-37, 102, 109-16, 126-27, 138, 140

ego-ideal (*Ich-Ideal*) (ideal-ego, *Idealich*) 13, 18-19, 202, 209, 539-40

Encore 24, 118

Ernst, Max 32, 34, 177-79

erotic 73, 97, 126, 164n.7, 176, 180, 182-84, 186-87, 226, 256, 303, 306, 351, 353, 355, 357n.10, 361-62, 375, 378n.3, 382, 389, 396n.11, 403-04, 412-13, 420, 443-46, 455, 497, 506, 550, 553

essentialism (essence) (essential difference) (essential tactics) (essentialist difference) (essential difference) (anti-essentialism) (see also constructivism) 28, 37, 51n.2, 52n.10, 97-07, 116, 128-29, 138-39, 142, 145-46, 151, 153, 155, 261, 294, 298, 301, 314-16, 328, 402, 434, 474, 476

ethnogenesis 330, 335

K

Kant (Kantian dynamic sublime and mathematical sublime) 14-16, 23, 25-26, 44, 53n.24, 91, 164n.5, 200, 349, 403, 464, 534, 537

L

lack 14, 16, 22, 118, 126, 146, 161-63, 167, 182-84, 187, 189-90, 196, 199-200, 209, 212, 220-23, 225, 237, 264-65, 267, 371, 402-03, 405, 447-48, 451, 495-96, 498-99, 507, 516, 527n.15, 537-38, 540-41
Lady 41, 180, 371, 508, 512-14
lesbian (lesbianism) (lesbian fetish) (lesbian continum) 66, 74, 103, 105, 115, 119, 124, 128-29, 131-34, 147-48, 151, 154-55, 186, 224, 235, 300n.6, 346, 350-51, 375-76, 388-91, 399-410, 443-46, 509-11, 516, 533, 540, 542-44
liberalism (see also liberlist feminism) 42, 62, 64-67, 74-76, 80, 86-88, 283, 322, 342, 349, 369, 377, 381, 383, 385, 390-91, 412, 436, 442, 470, 480, 518
lingerie 365, 374-75
logic (both/and) (non-all) (antimony) (see also Kant) (see also binary) 11, 13-26, 28, 52n.13, 53n.16, 65, 91, 114, 116-17, 146, 148, 150-55, 157, 171, 210, 214n.7, 247, 281-82, 335, 349, 358, 402, 406, 411-13, 480, 484, 555n.12
look (male gaze) (see also gaze) 31, 33-34, 68, 165-67, 169, 171-72, 176, 178, 183-84, 186, 190-99, 208, 211-12, 216n.20,n.22, 222, 254-57, 259, 262-65, 267, 296, 348, 361, 368-69, 371, 379n.12, 382, 440n.13, 488-89, 509, 512, 518-19, 546
Lyons, Lisa 357n.2, 508

M

macho (machoism) 189, 201-02, 232, 293, 363, 365, 418, 435, 546
Madonna 38, 101, 238-39, 251, 254, 348, 372, 375-77, 379n.17, 399, 428, 432-34, 436, 438, 440n.12, 470, 480, 481, 485-86, 491n.13, 546
Magritte, René 34, 167, 169-76, 179, 180-82, 192, 208, 214n.2,n.6, 250, 261, 267
maleman 10, 136n.16
male hysteria (see also hysteria) 60, 493, 504
Mapplethorpe, Robert 351-58, 399, 403, 487, 508, 536
Marilyn Monroe 252-53, 375, 433-34, 482
Marx (Marxism) 5, 17, 42, 62-63, 104, 156, 264, 271-74, 277-81, 295, 329, 344, 378n.8, 412, 472, 485, 545, 565
master 79, 157, 169, 188, 224, 408, 487
master signifier (see also nodal point) 21, 224, 411, 502
masturbation 16, 52n.12, 117, 180, 352, 366, 379, 390n.13, 409, 454, 501
masculine (see also hypermasculinity) 2, 4, 14-20, 24-26, 30, 34, 36-37, 42, 44, 46, 65-66, 68, 172-73, 175, 178, 184, 186, 188-90, 206-07, 213, 223-24, 237, 342, 368, 377, 391-92, 395n.17, 397, 418, 429, 442-43, 474, 495-97, 503-04, 518, 520-21, 523-24, 527n.11, 529n.30, 542-43, 546-48, 550
masquerade 4, 45, 49-51n.2, 60-61, 68, 184, 188, 194, 196, 216n.20, 225, 240n.2, 254, 263, 347, 355, 357n.6, 361, 364, 371, 377, 400, 426, 431-32, 434-35, 481-82, 488, 494, 505-06, 514, 527n.12, 540, 542, 544-45
masochism (see also S/M) 61, 162, 178-79, 184, 204, 207, 209, 213, 225-26, 364, 371, 377, 385-86, 397-98n.17, 406-08, 474, 497, 513, 549, 551

U

unconscious 14, 25, 36, 44, 132, 143, 145, 157, 167, 172-75, 178, 182-83, 193, 220, 222, 237, 281, 345, 366, 418, 447-48, 450-51, 454, 456, 470, 479, 495, 538
undergarments 362, 374-75, 432-33

V

Velázquez (*Las Meninas*) 31-34, 53n.22, 157, 190-91, 194, 196, 199, 211, 265
violence 3, 7, 12, 175, 184, 187, 209, 213, 232, 240, 247, 290, 292, 295, 318, 321-22, 335-36, 364, 372, 386-88, 390-95, 408, 411, 448-49, 477, 488, 497-99, 503, 522-24, 547-49
virgin 38, 78, 101, 141, 175, 177-78, 186, 206, 208, 296, 364, 366, 425, 433, 436
vitrine (see also mirror) 379n.13
voyeurism (voyeuristic gaze) 184, 186, 213, 230, 232, 249, 252, 267, 361, 369, 379, 382, 390, 400, 410, 420, 429, 444, 449, 497, 512, 551

W

witchcraft 201, 317, 420
woman artists (see performance art, liberal feminism)
Women's Caucus 76, 98, 110-11
'woman does not exist' 13-14, 22, 28, 117, 126, 404
'*wo es war*' 27, 539

Z

Zeno's paradoxes 152, 256
Zeuxis and Parrhasius 166-67, 169-70, 174, 193

SELECTED
AUTHOR INDEX

Fox-Genovese, Elizabeth 70n.5, 87

Fuss, Diana 116-17, 131-34, 138, 151, 153, 186, 290-91, 294-95, 298, 300n.3, 360, 362, 374, 379n.12, 445-46, 460n.7, 476, 523

Gallop, Jane 7, 54n.28, 55n.38, 95n.16, 115-16, 129, 144, 186, 215n.11, 474, 478

Garber, Marjorie 147, 357n.6, 428, 433-34, 440n.8, 535, 542-43, 546, 554n.8

Grosz, Elizabeth A. 115, 120, 123, 136n.12, 152, 154-55, 360, 367, 405-07, 414n.9, 434, 460n.6, 550

Guatarri, Félix 132, 424, 426, 440n.11, 445-53, 459, 461n.12,n.13,n.15, 473, 486, 537

Hall, Stuart 292, 316, 318, 330-31

Hebdige, Dick 426-27, 485-86

Hennessy, Rosemary 280-83, 299, 385, 424, 432, 439n.5, 505

Irigaray, Luce 3,110, 112, 114-20, 135, 151-53, 162, 182, 186, 197, 253, 390, 446, 460n.10, 474-75, 490-91n.7, 529n.28

Kelly, Mary 51n.8, 158, 160-62, 268n.2, 350, 356

Kolodny, Annette 2, 89

Krauss, Rosiland 33-35, 170, 173, 176, 179, 212n.1, 467, 536

Kristeva, Julia 11, 51n.8, 106-07, 113-15, 120-26, 135, 136n.10,n.13, 160, 247, 336, 414n.3

Kroker, Arthur and Marilouise 414-15, 526n.3

Kruger, Barbara 51n.4, 159, 244, 268n.1, 484, 489

Lacan, Jacques 9, 13-27, 29, 34, 90, 116, 118-20, 145-46, 149-56, 161, 165-67, 169, 182-83, 186, 189-90, 192-94, 196, 198-99, 203, 210-12, 219-22, 224, 226, 236, 238, 243, 255, 258, 260, 263-68, 275, 360, 371, 400, 402, 406, 443, 446-48, 454, 470, 472-74, 479-80, 498-99, 533-34, 536-37, 539, 541, 543-44

Lovibond, Sabina 472

MacCannell, Juliet Flower 153, 237, 240n.3

Millot, Catherine 146, 155, 404, 414n.11, 425, 476, 512-13, 528-29n.20,n.22,n.24

Mulvey, Laura 182-84, 186-87, 198, 207, 214n.8, 219, 224-25, 227-28, 231, 234, 240n.1, 264, 360, 371, 497-98, 550

Neale, Steve 184, 186, 188, 215n.12, 497-98, 526n.9

Olalquiaga, Celeste 544-45

Pecheaux, Michel 282-83

Radway, Janice 233-34, 384, 529n.28

Rose, Jacqueline 55n.35, 116, 156, 214n.8, 227, 361, 434-35

Sedgwick, Kosofsky Eve 190, 378n.6, 396n.6, 403, 550-55

Showalter, Elaine 2, 11, 41, 60, 102, 291, 300n.2, 426, 440n.10, 443

Silverman, Kaja 10, 34, 61, 82, 125, 135n.5, 136n.10, 166, 178-79, 187, 189-99, 214n.8, 215n.16, 216n.24, 257, 259, 262-63, 360, 371, 397n.17, 404, 429-30, 437, 440, 449-50, 460n.8, 491n.11, 534, 546, 549-50, 552-53, 555n.10

Singer, Linda 396n.11, 411-13, 453, 459, 525n.2, 526n.3

Sobchack, Vivian iii, 259, 263, 524-25, 554n.1

Spivak, Gayatri Chakravorty 22, 41, 46, 51n.6, 55n.35, 143, 156, 281, 283-84, 294-95, 297, 336, 338n.12

Walkerdine, Valerie 214n.10, 231-34, 251, 481, 529n.29

Williams, Linda 226, 348, 357-58n.9,n.10, 360, 367, 369-73, 376, 385, 392, 491n.8, 553

Wittig, Monique 110, 113-15, 121-35, 138, 151, 186, 414, 442, 444, 446